T0210648

Lecture Notes in Computer Science 9751

Commenced Publication in 1973
Founding and Former Series Editors:
Gerhard Goos, Juris Hartmanis, and Jan van Leeuwen

More information about this series at http://www.springer.com/series/7409

Fiona Fui-Hoon Nah · Chuan-Hoo Tan (Eds.)

HCI in Business, Government, and Organizations: eCommerce and Innovation

Third International Conference, HCIBGO 2016
Held as Part of HCI International 2016
Toronto, Canada, July 17–22, 2016
Proceedings, Part I

 Springer

Editors
Fiona Fui-Hoon Nah
Missouri University of Science and
 Technology
Rolla, MO
USA

Chuan-Hoo Tan
National University of Singapore
Singapore
Singapore

ISSN 0302-9743   ISSN 1611-3349 (electronic)
Lecture Notes in Computer Science
ISBN 978-3-319-39395-7   ISBN 978-3-319-39396-4 (eBook)
DOI 10.1007/978-3-319-39396-4

Library of Congress Control Number: 2016939935

LNCS Sublibrary: SL3 – Information Systems and Applications, incl. Internet/Web, and HCI

Printed on acid-free paper

This Springer imprint is published by Springer Nature
The registered company is Springer International Publishing AG Switzerland

Foreword

The 18th International Conference on Human-Computer Interaction, HCI International 2016, was held in Toronto, Canada, during July 17–22, 2016. The event incorporated the 15 conferences/thematic areas listed on the following page.

A total of 4,354 individuals from academia, research institutes, industry, and governmental agencies from 74 countries submitted contributions, and 1,287 papers and 186 posters have been included in the proceedings. These papers address the latest research and development efforts and highlight the human aspects of the design and use of computing systems. The papers thoroughly cover the entire field of human-computer interaction, addressing major advances in knowledge and effective use of computers in a variety of application areas. The volumes constituting the full 27-volume set of the conference proceedings are listed on pages IX and X.

I would like to thank the program board chairs and the members of the program boards of all thematic areas and affiliated conferences for their contribution to the highest scientific quality and the overall success of the HCI International 2016 conference.

This conference would not have been possible without the continuous and unwavering support and advice of the founder, Conference General Chair Emeritus and Conference Scientific Advisor Prof. Gavriel Salvendy. For his outstanding efforts, I would like to express my appreciation to the communications chair and editor of *HCI International News*, Dr. Abbas Moallem.

April 2016   Constantine Stephanidis

HCI International 2016 Thematic Areas
and Affiliated Conferences

Thematic areas:

- Human-Computer Interaction (HCI 2016)
- Human Interface and the Management of Information (HIMI 2016)

Affiliated conferences:

- 13th International Conference on Engineering Psychology and Cognitive Ergonomics (EPCE 2016)
- 10th International Conference on Universal Access in Human-Computer Interaction (UAHCI 2016)
- 8th International Conference on Virtual, Augmented and Mixed Reality (VAMR 2016)
- 8th International Conference on Cross-Cultural Design (CCD 2016)
- 8th International Conference on Social Computing and Social Media (SCSM 2016)
- 10th International Conference on Augmented Cognition (AC 2016)
- 7th International Conference on Digital Human Modeling and Applications in Health, Safety, Ergonomics and Risk Management (DHM 2016)
- 5th International Conference on Design, User Experience and Usability (DUXU 2016)
- 4th International Conference on Distributed, Ambient and Pervasive Interactions (DAPI 2016)
- 4th International Conference on Human Aspects of Information Security, Privacy and Trust (HAS 2016)
- Third International Conference on HCI in Business, Government, and Organizations (HCIBGO 2016)
- Third International Conference on Learning and Collaboration Technologies (LCT 2016)
- Second International Conference on Human Aspects of IT for the Aged Population (ITAP 2016)

Conference Proceedings Volumes Full List

1. LNCS 9731, Human-Computer Interaction: Theory, Design, Development and Practice (Part I), edited by Masaaki Kurosu
2. LNCS 9732, Human-Computer Interaction: Interaction Platforms and Techniques (Part II), edited by Masaaki Kurosu
3. LNCS 9733, Human-Computer Interaction: Novel User Experiences (Part III), edited by Masaaki Kurosu
4. LNCS 9734, Human Interface and the Management of Information: Information, Design and Interaction (Part I), edited by Sakae Yamamoto
5. LNCS 9735, Human Interface and the Management of Information: Applications and Services (Part II), edited by Sakae Yamamoto
6. LNAI 9736, Engineering Psychology and Cognitive Ergonomics, edited by Don Harris
7. LNCS 9737, Universal Access in Human-Computer Interaction: Methods, Techniques, and Best Practices (Part I), edited by Margherita Antona and Constantine Stephanidis
8. LNCS 9738, Universal Access in Human-Computer Interaction: Interaction Techniques and Environments (Part II), edited by Margherita Antona and Constantine Stephanidis
9. LNCS 9739, Universal Access in Human-Computer Interaction: Users and Context Diversity (Part III), edited by Margherita Antona and Constantine Stephanidis
10. LNCS 9740, Virtual, Augmented and Mixed Reality, edited by Stephanie Lackey and Randall Shumaker
11. LNCS 9741, Cross-Cultural Design, edited by Pei-Luen Patrick Rau
12. LNCS 9742, Social Computing and Social Media, edited by Gabriele Meiselwitz
13. LNAI 9743, Foundations of Augmented Cognition: Neuroergonomics and Operational Neuroscience (Part I), edited by Dylan D. Schmorrow and Cali M. Fidopiastis
14. LNAI 9744, Foundations of Augmented Cognition: Neuroergonomics and Operational Neuroscience (Part II), edited by Dylan D. Schmorrow and Cali M. Fidopiastis
15. LNCS 9745, Digital Human Modeling and Applications in Health, Safety, Ergonomics and Risk Management, edited by Vincent G. Duffy
16. LNCS 9746, Design, User Experience, and Usability: Design Thinking and Methods (Part I), edited by Aaron Marcus
17. LNCS 9747, Design, User Experience, and Usability: Novel User Experiences (Part II), edited by Aaron Marcus
18. LNCS 9748, Design, User Experience, and Usability: Technological Contexts (Part III), edited by Aaron Marcus
19. LNCS 9749, Distributed, Ambient and Pervasive Interactions, edited by Norbert Streitz and Panos Markopoulos
20. LNCS 9750, Human Aspects of Information Security, Privacy and Trust, edited by Theo Tryfonas

21. LNCS 9751, HCI in Business, Government, and Organizations: eCommerce and Innovation (Part I), edited by Fiona Fui-Hoon Nah and Chuan-Hoo Tan
22. LNCS 9752, HCI in Business, Government, and Organizations: Information Systems (Part II), edited by Fiona Fui-Hoon Nah and Chuan-Hoo Tan
23. LNCS 9753, Learning and Collaboration Technologies, edited by Panayiotis Zaphiris and Andri Ioannou
24. LNCS 9754, Human Aspects of IT for the Aged Population: Design for Aging (Part I), edited by Jia Zhou and Gavriel Salvendy
25. LNCS 9755, Human Aspects of IT for the Aged Population: Healthy and Active Aging (Part II), edited by Jia Zhou and Gavriel Salvendy
26. CCIS 617, HCI International 2016 Posters Proceedings (Part I), edited by Constantine Stephanidis
27. CCIS 618, HCI International 2016 Posters Proceedings (Part II), edited by Constantine Stephanidis

HCI in Business, Government, and Organizations

Program Board Chairs: **Fiona Fui-Hoon Nah, USA, and Chuan-Hoo Tan, Singapore**

The full list with the program board chairs and the members of the program boards of all thematic areas and affiliated conferences is available online at:

http://www.hci.international/2016/

HCI International 2017

The 19th International Conference on Human-Computer Interaction, HCI International 2017, will be held jointly with the affiliated conferences in Vancouver, Canada, at the Vancouver Convention Centre, July 9–14, 2017. It will cover a broad spectrum of themes related to human-computer interaction, including theoretical issues, methods, tools, processes, and case studies in HCI design, as well as novel interaction techniques, interfaces, and applications. The proceedings will be published by Springer. More information will be available on the conference website: http://2017.hci.international/.

General Chair
Prof. Constantine Stephanidis
University of Crete and ICS-FORTH
Heraklion, Crete, Greece
E-mail: general_chair@hcii2017.org

http://2017.hci.international/

Contents – Part I

Social Media for Business

Technology Diffusion Through Social Networks: An Example
of Technology Integrated Instruction   3
   Tsai-Hsin Chu, Yen-Hsien Lee, and Shu-Fang Kuo

Exploring the Effects of Source Credibility on Information Adoption
on YouTube. 16
   Constantinos K. Coursaris and Wietske Van Osch

Phase 1 of 3: Will a LinkedIn™ Jr. Optimize Internships for High School
STEM Students?. 26
   Benjamin Fickes, Alexander Tam, Adithya Dattatri, Allen Tang,
   Alan Balu, and David Brown

Internet Use and Happiness 37
   Richard H. Hall

Bringing E-commerce to Social Networks 46
   Zhao Huang and Wang Yang Yu

Evaluating Academic Answer Quality: A Pilot Study on ResearchGate
Q&A. 61
   Lei Li, Daqing He, and Chengzhi Zhang

From Mumbai to Paris: Experiencing Disasters Across Social Media. 72
   Liza Potts and Kristen Mapes

Communicating Product User Reviews and Ratings in Interfaces for
e-Commerce: A Multimodal Approach. 82
   Dimitrios Rigas and Rajab Ghandour

Multimodal Impact on Consumer Purchase Decisions: Initial Results. 94
   Dimitrios Rigas and Nazish Riaz

Media Selection: A Method for Understanding User Choices Among
Popular Social Media Platforms 106
   Brian Traynor, Jaigris Hodson, and Gil Wilkes

Professional Personal Branding: Using a "Think-Aloud" Protocol
to Investigate How Recruiters Judge LinkedIN Profile Pictures 118
   Sarah F. van der Land, Lotte M. Willemsen, and Barbara G.E. Wilton

Social Media and Accessibility   129
   Gian Wild

The Effects of Social Structure Overlap and Profile Extensiveness
on Facebook Friend Requests   141
   Yi Wu, Ben C.F. Choi, and Jie Yu

Participation in Open Knowledge-Sharing Community: Expectancy
Value Perspective   153
   Manli Wu, Lele Kang, Xuan Li, and J. Leon Zhao

Electronic, Mobile and Ubiquitous Commerce

Credibility of Algorithm Based Decentralized Computer Networks
Governing Personal Finances: The Case of Cryptocurrency   165
   Sapumal Ahangama and Danny Chiang Choon Poo

Swiping vs. Scrolling in Mobile Shopping Applications   177
   Ben C.F. Choi, Samuel N. Kirshner, and Yi Wu

How Do Consumers Behave in Social Commerce? An Investigation
Through Clickstream Data   189
   Qican Gu, Qiqi Jiang, and Hongwei Wang

Semantic Support for Visual Data Analyses in Electronic
Commerce Settings   198
   Jens Gulden

Bridging the Gap Between the Stakeholders and the Users at Alibaba.com . . .   210
   Jonas Kong

The Role of a Retailer in Designing Our Connected Future   218
   Adam Laskowitz

Ontology-Based Adaptive and Customizable Navigation Method in Online
Retailing Websites   228
   Chi-Lun Liu and Hsieh-Hong Huang

Learning from Emerging and Mature Markets to Design Mobile P2P
Payment Experiences   238
   Masumi Matsumoto and Lucia Terrenghi

Knowledge Sharing-Based Value Co-creation Between E-Commerce
Enterprises and Logistics Service Providers   248
   Yumeng Miao and Rong Du

Website Location Strategies Review Under Hofstede's Cultural Dimensions . . .   258
   *Qian Wang, Chih-Hung Peng, Choon Ling Sia, Yu Tong,
   and Yi-Cheng Ku*

A Genetic Algorithm Based Model for Chinese Phishing E-commerce
Websites Detection 270
   Zhijun Yan, Su Liu, Tianmei Wang, Baowen Sun, Hansi Jiang,
   and Hangzhou Yang

Business Analytics and Visualization

Using Digital Infrastructures to Conceptualize Sensing and Responding
in Human-Computer Interaction 283
   Florian Allwein and Sue Hessey

Exploring a LOD-Based Application for Military Movie Retrieval. 294
   Liang-Chu Chen, Jen-Tsung Tseng, Yen-Hsuan Lien, Chia-Jung Hsieh,
   and I-Chiang Shih

High Availability of Big-Geo-Data as a Platform as a Service 306
   Tim Förster, Simon Thum, and Arjan Kuijper

Cognitive Benefits of a Simple Visual Metrics Architecture 319
   John King, Kathy Sonderer, and Kevin Lynch

Converting Opinion into Knowledge: Improving User Experience
and Analytics of Online Polls. 330
   Martin Stabauer, Christian Mayrhauser, and Michael Karlinger

Generating Competitive Intelligence Digests with a LDA-Based Method:
A Case of BT Intellact. 341
   Qiang Wei, Jiaqi Wang, Guoqing Chen, and Xunhua Guo

Visualizing Opportunities of Collaboration in Large Research
Organizations 350
   Mohammad Amin Yazdi, André Calero Valdez, Leonhard Lichtschlag,
   Martina Ziefle, and Jan Borchers

Branding, Marketing and Consumer Behaviour

The Influence of Trust Building User Interface Elements of Web Shops
on e-Trust 365
   Andreas Auinger, Werner Wetzlinger, and Liesmarie Schwarz

"Tell Me Who You Are, and I Will Show You What You Get" - the Use
of Individuals' Identity for Information Technology Customization 377
   Sonia Camacho and Andres Barrios

Social Influence and Emotional State While Shopping 386
   Jesus Garcia-Mancilla, Victor R. Martinez, Victor M. Gonzalez,
   and Angel F. Fajardo

Sensing Distress – Towards a Blended Method for Detecting and
Responding to Problematic Customer Experience Events   395
  Sue Hessey and Will Venters

The Multisensory Effects of Atmospheric Cues on Online Shopping
Satisfaction.   406
  So-Jeong Kim and Dong-Hee Shin

A Short-Term Twofold Impact on Banner Ads   417
  Harald Kindermann

Improving Online Customer Shopping Experience with Computer Vision
and Machine Learning Methods   427
  Zequn Li, Honglei Li, and Ling Shao

Why People Resist to Internet Finance: From the Perspective of Process
Virtualization Theory.   437
  Zhengzheng Lin, Yulin Fang, Liang Liang, and Jun Li

How Does the Device Change Your Choice: A Goal-Activation Perspective . . .   446
  Yang Liu and Deliang Wang

Interactive e-Branding in e-Commerce Interfaces: Survey Results
and Implications   457
  Dimitrios Rigas and Hammad Akhtar Hussain

The Social Dimension of Mobile Commerce – Engaging Customers
Through Group Purchase   468
  Wee-Kek Tan, Hock-Hai Teo, Chuan-Hoo Tan, and Yang Yang

Digital Innovation

Diffusion of Innovations: The Case Study of Oman's e-Payment Gateway . . .   483
  Badar H. Al-Lawati and Xiaowen Fang

Improving the Front End of Innovation: The Case of Mobile
Commerce Services.   491
  Karen Carey and Markus Helfert

Information Technology Adoption: Do Performance Objectives
and Incentive Structures Make a Difference?   502
  Brenda Eschenbrenner

The Outcome-Based Collaborative Brainstorming of Strategic
Service Design   511
  Rich C. Lee

The Role of HCI in Cross-Sector Research on Grand Challenges   519
  Roger Lew, Nathan Lau, Ronald L. Boring, and John Anderson

Building IT Capabilities to Deploy Large-Scale Synchronous Online
Technology in Teaching and Learning   531
  Stephen Low, Jenson Goh, Yeung Sze Kiu, and Ivy Chia

The Five Forces of Technology Adoption   545
  Dan McAran and Sharm Manwani

Digital Innovation and the Becoming of an Organizational Identity   556
  Nikolaus Obwegeser and Stefan Bauer

Leadership and Innovation Growth: A Strategic Planning and
Organizational Culture Perspective   565
  Dimitrios Rigas and Yehia Sabri Nawar

Comparative Study on China-Italy Design Driven Innovation Strategy
Furniture Firms.   576
  Zhang Zhang, Jianxin Cheng, Chaoxiang Yang, and Yongyan Guo

Erratum to: The Multisensory Effects of Atmospheric Cues on Online
Shopping Satisfaction E1
  So-Jeong Kim and Dong-Hee Shin

Author Index   585

Contents – Part II

Designing Information Systems

User-Centered Requirements Analysis and Design Solutions for Chronic
Disease Self-management.   3
   Maryam Ariaeinejad, Norm Archer, Michael Stacey, Ted Rapanos,
   Fadi Elias, and Faysal Naji

Defective Still Deflective – How Correctness of Decision Support Systems
Influences User's Performance in Production Environments 16
   Philipp Brauner, André Calero Valdez, Ralf Philipsen,
   and Martina Ziefle

Building a Classification Model for Physician Recommender Service
Based on Needs for Physician Information. 28
   Ming-Hsin Chiu and Wei-Chung Cheng

Flow and the Art of ERP Education 39
   Craig C. Claybaugh

Accessible Learning Experience Design and Implementation 47
   Phillip J. Deaton

Better Patient-Doctor Communication – A Survey and Focus Group Study. . . . 56
   Martin Maguire

The Contextual Complexity of Privacy in Smart Homes
and Smart Buildings 67
   Faith McCreary, Alexandra Zafiroglu, and Heather Patterson

Investigating HCI Challenges for Designing Smart Environments 79
   Zohreh Pourzolfaghar and Markus Helfert

The Influence of Personality on Users' Emotional Reactions 91
   Beverly Resseguier, Pierre-Majorique Léger, Sylvain Sénécal,
   Marie-Christine Bastarache-Roberge, and François Courtemanche

Colour Arousal Effect on Users' Decision-Making Processes
in the Warning Message Context. 99
   Mario Silic and Dianne Cyr

HCI Testing in Laboratory or Field Settings. 110
   Chuan-Hoo Tan, Austin Silva, Rich Lee, Kanliang Wang,
   and Fiona Fui-Hoon Nah

A Structure-Behavior Coalescence Method for Human-Computer
Interaction System Requirements Specification 117
    Yu-Chen Yang, Yi-Ling Lin, and William S. Chao

HCI in the Public Administration and Government

Collaboration Between Cognitive Science and Business Management
to Benefit the Government Sector 131
    Glory Emmanuel Aviña

Gamification Aspects in the Context of Electronic Government
and Education: A Case Study 140
    Fernando Timoteo Fernandes and Plinio Thomaz Aquino Junior

Aligning Public Administrators and Citizens on and Around Open Data:
An Activity Theory Approach 151
    Jonathan Groff, Michael Baker, and Françoise Détienne

Touchscreen Voting Interface Design for Persons with Dexterity
Impairments: Insights from Usability Evaluation of Mobile
Voting Prototype. 159
    Jennifer Ismirle, Ian O'Bara, James E. Jackson, and Sarah J. Swierenga

As Simple as Possible and as Complex as Necessary: A Communication
Kit for Geothermal Energy Projects. 171
    Johanna Kluge and Martina Ziefle

Planning Effective HCI Courseware Design to Enhance Online Education
and Training. 183
    Elspeth McKay and John Izard

"Core" Components in HCI Syllabi: Based on the Practice of CS
and LIS Schools in North America 196
    Lei Pei and Qiping Zhang

Identification of Future Human-Computer System Needs in Army Aviation . . . 209
    Kathryn A. Salomon and David Boudreaux

Bringing Service Design Thinking into the Public Sector to Create
Proactive and User-Friendly Public Services. 221
    Regina Sirendi and Kuldar Taveter

The City as an Interface Between Citizens and Public Administrations. 231
    Valentina Volpi, Antonio Opromolla, and Carlo Maria Medaglia

Exploring Human-Technology Interaction in Layered Security
Military Applications.   241
    Amanda Wachtel, Matthew Hoffman, Craig Lawton, Ann Speed,
    John Gauthier, and Robert Kittinger

An Agent-Based Study on the Relationship Between Tiao-kuai Structure
and Fragmentation Phenomenon of Crisis Governance.   251
    Yun-Feng Wang

A Toolkit for Prototype Implementation of E-Governance Service System
Readiness Assessment Framework.   259
    Ashraf Ali Waseem, Zubair Ahmed Shaikh, and Aqeel ur Rehman

HCI at Work

Prevalence of Mobile Phone Interaction in Workplace Meetings   273
    Robert Bajko and Deborah I. Fels

Data Glasses for Picking Workplaces: Impact on Physical Workloads   281
    Daniel Friemert, Rolf Ellegast, and Ulrich Hartmann

Degradations and Consequences of ICT in Occupational Prevention Terms
as Illustrated by the Transport and Logistics Sector.   290
    Virginie Govaere and Liên Wioland

Human-Robot Interaction Modelling for Recruitment and Retention
of Employees   302
    Rajiv Khosla, Mei-Tai Chu, and Khanh Nguyen

Operator Information Acquisition in Excavators – Insights from a Field
Study Using Eye-Tracking.   313
    Markus Koppenborg, Michael Huelke, Peter Nickel, Andy Lungfiel,
    and Birgit Naber

Extending the Effective Range of Prevention Through Design by OSH
Applications in Virtual Reality   325
    Peter Nickel

Scoping Review on Human-Machine Interaction and Health and Safety
at Work.   337
    Swantje Robelski and Sascha Wischniewski

A Model Based Approach to Web Application Design for Older Adults
Using MVC Design Pattern   348
    Christopher Romanyk, Ryan McCallum, and Pejman Salehi

Using Smart Glasses for the Inclusion of Hearing-Impaired Warehouse
Workers into Their Working Environment   358
   Antti Matthias vom Stein and Willibald A. Günthner

Biological, Biomimetic and Sociological Aspects of Human-Robot
Interaction in Work Environments.   369
   Alexandra Weidemann, Diego Compagna, Manuela Marquardt,
   Mirco Martens, and Ivo Boblan

Where Is Siri? The Accessibility Design Challenges for Enterprise
Touchscreen Interfaces.   380
   Shuang Xu, Chester Cornelio, and Marisa Gianfortune

Mobile Applications and Services

Evaluation Approaches for HCI Related Aspects of Occupational Safety
Regulations Exemplified by Mobile Hotel Booking Applications.   395
   Richard A. Bretschneider

Distracted Driving: Scientific Basis for Risk Assessments of Driver's
Workplaces   403
   Benno Gross, Sylwia Birska, Michael Bretschneider-Hagemes,
   and Endri Kerluku

Patient Engagement in the Medical Facility Waiting Room Using Gamified
Healthcare Information Delivery   412
   Raheel Hassan, Nathan W. Twyman, Fiona Fui-Hoon Nah,
   and Keng Siau

Understanding User Experience Journeys for a Smart Watch Device   424
   Jay Lundell and Corrie Bates

Designing and Evaluating Barrier-Free Travel Assistance Services   434
   Wolfgang Narzt, Stefan Mayerhofer, Otto Weichselbaum,
   Gustav Pomberger, Astrid Tarkus, and Martin Schumann

Wearable Technology in Hospitals: Overcoming Patient Concerns
About Privacy   446
   Ksenia Sergueeva and Norman Shaw

Adoption of Smartphone Apps by Hotel Guests: The Roles of Trust
and Word of Mouth   457
   Norman Shaw

Author Index   469

Social Media for Business

Technology Diffusion Through Social Networks: An Example of Technology Integrated Instruction

Tsai-Hsin Chu[1], Yen-Hsien Lee[2(✉)], and Shu-Fang Kuo[1]

[1] Department of E-Learning Design and Management, National Chiayi University,
Chiayi City, Taiwan
thchu@mail.ncyu.edu.tw
[2] Department of Management Information System, National Chiayi University,
Chiayi City, Taiwan
yhlee@mail.ncyu.edu.tw

Abstract. Many studies investigate IT integrated instruction adoption by discussing enablers and constraints. They suggest that school policies, infrastructures, and learning resources are critical for effectively implementing IT integrated instruction. However, few of the research explore the diffusion patterns of IT integrated instruction in educational organizations based on social network perspective. This study conducts a case study where an IT integrated instruction application is successfully diffused among teachers via social interactions. In this study, we seek answers of two research questions: (1) What kind of social networks are relevant to IT diffusion? And (2) How these social networks influence IT diffusion? Using social network analysis, this study examines the correlation between authority, consultation and affective networks and IT diffusion pattern. Our findings suggest that the authority, consultation, and affective networks are positively correlated to the IT diffusion. This study further illustrates and compares the characteristics of social networks and IT diffusion diagram. Our findings provide organizations a way to make good use of social networks for diffusing IT.

Keywords: Social network · IT diffusion pattern · IT integrated instruction

1 Introduction

With rapid development of information technology (IT), many educational organizations consider integrating IT into instructions with an expectation of improving education quality. IT integrated instruction refers to an instructional method that using IT to present learning materials and to design instructional activities [19]. The previous studies suggest that school policies, infrastructures, learning resources are critical for IT integrated instruction adoption [21]. In addition, peer support in organization and interpersonal interactions are also the important factors [20].

Most of previous studies investigate the adoption of IT integrated instruction by discussing enablers and constraints. Few of them explore the pattern that IT integrated instruction diffuses within educational organizations. In addition, IT integrated instruction, as an example of innovation, can be diffused through social interactions [16]. This study explores

© Springer International Publishing Switzerland 2016
F.F.-H. Nah and C.-H. Tan (Eds.): HCIBGO 2016, Part I, LNCS 9751, pp. 3–15, 2016.
DOI: 10.1007/978-3-319-39396-4_1

the relationship between IT diffusion and social network. We identify three kinds of social network in organization and examine their correlations to IT diffusion pattern. We seek the answers for two research questions: (1) Which social networks are relevant to IT diffusion? (2) How these social networks influence IT diffusion? Our research is anchored on a case study of IT integrated instruction in an elementary school. In that case, the IT integrated instruction was effectively diffused among teachers without formal manipulations. Most teachers in the school displayed interactive electronic books with computer and projector as the way of IT integrated instruction for delivering instructions. This case provides us a good observation target to explore how IT can be diffused by social networks. We applied a social network analysis to explore the factors of IT diffusion in an organization. Specifically, we analyzed the correlation between teacher's authority, consultation and affective networks and IT diffusion pattern.

2 Literatures

2.1 IT Integrated Instruction

IT integrated instruction is an instructional method that integrating information technologies into the design of instructional processes and activities [19]. This instructional method can enhance learning because it riches learning contents with multimedia and improves the interaction between students and learning materials [11]. The focus of IT integrated instruction is not only on using IT in classroom, but also on effectively applying IT features to design corresponding instructional activities, so as to enhance students' learning processes [11, 23]. This instructional method improves traditional instruction by providing richer learning material presentation, enhancing teacher-student interactions, and bringing much of creativity of instruction.

Although educational organizations promote IT integrated instruction with many advantages, it needs instructors accept and adopt such instructional method for realizing these advantages. The previous studies conclude the barriers of IT integrated instruction, including the lack of resources and support (i.e., funding, staff, and IT equipments), the unsupported norm, a lot of effort and stress on developing learning materials, and the insufficient computer literacy of using IT into instruction [13, 20, 27].

2.2 Theoretical Gap

Existing studies investigate IT integrated instruction by discussing the difficulties of implementation, including resources, IT infrastructure, instructor's IT literacy, and organizational norms. These studies contribute by proposing critical factors on facilitating the adoption of IT integrated instruction. However, they rarely discuss how IT is to be diffused within an organization, as well as by which channels it can be diffused. In the limited investigations, research suggests the importance of social interactions. For example, Wu and Wu [27] propose that IT integrated instruction diffuses through not only administrative policies, but also through the interpersonal exchanges and sharing among organization members. And Shih [20] suggests a significance of peer support.

These studies bring a implication that the interpersonal interactions embedded in working context can be important to the diffusion of IT.

The interpersonal connections are known as social networks which help individuals exchange information with group members [17, 18]. Interpersonal relationship in organizations is suggested to be a considerable influence on individual behaviors formation and change [7, 15]. Social network perspective provides a lens to understand IT adoption within organizations [22]. This perspective enables a creative solution of IT adoption by taking advantage of the existing interpersonal networks within an organization. Thus, this study applies the social network perspective to examine the relationships between the IT diffusion and social networks in an organization.

2.3 Social Network Perspective

Social network refers to the network of relationship that people connect with each other through a certain social interactions within an organization or group [18]. Social network perspective conceptualizes a social structure as a pattern of the embedded resources, opportunities, social supports and constraints that an actor can receive affording by her network position [22]. By analyzing social structures to study management and organizational behaviors, social network has been wildly applied by studies in various fields [4, 7, 15, 18, 22].

Social network perspective explains performance and outcomes by the actor's position in social network [2]. An actor's position in social networks indicates the embedded social interactions and exchanges for enhancing or constraining access to valued resources, such as work advice and strategic information, as well as social supports [6, 14, 22]. A social network is usually represented by a graph formed of numerous 'nodes' and 'ties', where a node refers to an individual actor and a tie indicates the relationship among two actors [6, 9, 10, 26]. As ties typically involved different kinds of resource exchanges [1, 22], we focus on three typical ties (i.e. social relationships) within an organization. Social relationships in an organization can include formal authority relationships (such as superiors and subordinates, peers, and colleagues), consultation relationships (such as obtaining help, and advising others), and affective networks formed by friendships and trust [25].

Many studies examine network centrality to capture social exchanges within a social network. Network centrality is defined as 'the extent of an actor's involvement in assistance exchanges with others' [22, p. 375]. Three types network centrality are identified, including degree centrality, closeness centrality, and betweenness centrality [8, 24]. Degree centrality measures the direct linkage of an individual for examining her control scope within networks. An individual with higher degree centrality connects to more actors and has greater influence within the social network. The closeness centrality determines the extent of closeness between an individual and others. An individual with higher closeness centrality is closer to others, and is able to acquire information quickly. Betweenness centrality presents the extent of mediation that the interactions among members must be introduced by an individual actor. An individual with higher betweenness centrality is more critical to disseminate information across groups within a social network [6].

3 Hypotheses Development

We develop a research framework for studying the relationship between three social networks and IT diffusion pattern (Fig. 1). Three typical social networks in organization were identified by previous studies, including authority, consultation and affective networks [1, 22, 25]. The complexity of integrating IT into instruction poses the need to support teachers in overcoming knowledge and emotional barriers of IT features and instructional design. In an organization, such a support can be brought by authority (i.e. the formal report system), informal information exchange (i.e. consultation), and friendship (i.e. affective support) among the organizational members.

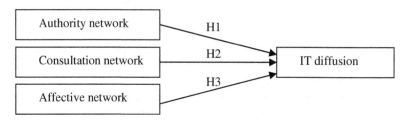

Fig. 1. Conceptual framework

Authority Network. Authority network refers to a social relationship formed by formal report system in an organization. In authority network, an actor interacts with her supervisor (or subordinates) and colleagues according to job position, rather than interpersonal relationship. When an actor interacts with others by authority, she can acquire the support of formal resources and information, and makes IT diffuse thereafter. Thus, we proposed the hypothesis H1.

H1: Authority network is positively influence IT diffusion.

Consultation Network. The deployment of an innovation (such as IT integrated instruction) usually create challenges as the organizational members have to learn technology features and interfaces, as well as to cope with new work processes [5]. Therefore, the individuals may pose substantial learning requirements [3, 22]. Learning how to integrate IT into instruction includes knowledge transfer across teachers with different levels of skills. It is easier for transferring knowledge among people with similar training, background and job characteristics. It implies that a teacher can benefit from consulting others for obtaining help or giving advices, and makes IT diffuse thereafter. Thus, we propose the hypothesis H2.

H2: Consultation network is positively influence IT diffusion.

Affective Network. When learning about a new innovation, an individual is also suffered from mentally fatigue and frustration [12, 22]. The affective network that build based on friendship and trust plays an important role for providing social support. An individual who highly involved in affective networks usually receives more emotional support and resources, with which they can cope with mentally fatigue and frustration of using IT into instructional activities. Thus, we propose the hypothesis H3.

H3: Affective network is positively influence IT diffusion.

4 Research Design

This study conducted a case study to examine the relationship between social networks and IT diffusion. Based on theoretical sampling, this study selected an IT diffusion case in a Taiwanese elementary school as the research site because of two reasons. Firstly, this case presented the corresponding phenomenon that this study wanted to discuss. In this case, the IT was diffused among most organizational members via social interactions, rather than formal administration. Secondly, the social interactions among elementary teachers school were very intensive. The teachers usually worked together for developing instructions of each subject-matter in grade fragments. Meetings, special interest groups, and workshops were formed for teaching works. The adjacency of both classroom locations and office seats would increase the potential social interactions among teachers in terms of observation, consultation, and friendship. Such the complexity of social interactions also increased the potential of research exploration.

4.1 Case Background

Alpha was an elementary school located at a small town in the middle Taiwan. Established for more than fifty years, at the research time, Alpha ran a G1–G6 program by forty-one classes with 1300 students. There were sixty-eight teachers, including forty-two main classroom teachers and twenty-six academic teachers. Among the teachers, 90 % of them were with IT literacy of using computer and applications.

In 2009, Alpha's teachers volunteering adopted a new way of IT integrated instruction by displaying electronic books with a projector for teaching students. In 2012, more than half of the teachers had adopted such an instructional method. In Alpha, this was the first time that teachers used IT into daily instructional activities without formal regulation. Before this success, Alpha experienced a failure on introducing interactive whiteboard (IWB) in 2007. Although the school administrated several tutorials for teaching teachers IWB features and set a reward system for encouraging IWB use, but that project was terminated in the sixth months after implementation. Most of the teachers kept distance from using IWB. When comparing the two IT implementations, two observations were found. First, the teachers adopted an IT that had simple technological features (i.e. e-book with projector) but they rejected an advanced one (i.e. IWB). Second, IT implementation failed when there were formal manipulations via policy, but it succeeded under informal social interactions. Those observations posted the question on how IT would be diffused via interpersonal social networks without formal administrations.

4.2   Data Collection

Data collection in this study was through questionnaires responded by individual teachers in Alpha. The questionnaires contained six questions for drawing the IT diffusion, authority, obtaining help, advising, friendship, and trust networks, respectively. For each of the six questions, the subjects noted three organizational members who were best fulfilled the description of the questions. For example, the question of 'authority' required the subjects to indicate three people who they formally interacted with frequently for completing task. For another example, the response of 'obtaining help' should be three people who the subject frequently consulted with for solving problems. To verify the content validity, the questions were reviewed by three instructors who served for elementary schools for clarifying the appropriateness of description and meaning. All teachers in Alpha were candidates of filling the questionnaire in order to construct social network models as real as possible. As eight teachers refused to respond, we acquired a total of 60 responses for the following analysis.

4.3   Data Analysis

For the data analysis, this study used UCINET to construct and to analyze the correlations among social networks. For each of six questions, researchers compiled the 60 responses into a 60×60 matrix and illustrated the correspondent social network diagram via UCINET illustrating tools. Then, as consultation and affective were second-order constructs, a CFA was used for versifying the reliability and validity. Next, principle component analysis was applied to generate the scores of consultation and affection matrices. Finally, a MRQAP (Multiple Regression Quadratic Assignment Procedure) regression was applied to estimate the correlations between authority, consultation, affective networks and IT diffusion network, respectively.

MRQAP was a regression analysis for matrices. MRQAP estimated the regression coefficients of a dependent matrix with several independent matrices with particular explanatory power. The calculation was in two steps. Firstly, a conventional regression analysis between the independent and the dependent matrices was carried out. Applying OLS (ordinary least squares) for calculating regression coefficient, MRQAP calculation procedure used N (N−1) observations in the matrices as the basis. After calculating the actual observation, secondly, a randomly permutation on the rows and columns in the matrices, then another OLS calculation was carry out to obtain another regression coefficients (i.e. β values). After repeated permutation and OLS calculations, a distribution of β values could be obtained. A comparison of the β values in the distribution with the β value obtained from actual observation was then carried out. If the possibility that β value after permutation was bigger or equal to the actual observed β value was lower than 5 %, it meant the actual observed β value has reached the 0.05 significance level.

5 Research Findings

5.1 Reliability and Validity

Since both of consultation and affective networks included two questions, we examined reliability and validity of these two constructs. The reliability was tested by Cronbach's α; and the greater value indicated the greater reliability. The Cronbach's α for the two constructs were all greater than 0.7, indicating a satisfied reliability (Table 1). The validity was tested by a CFA for checking whether the obtaining help and advising converged into a factor while friendship and trust converged into another. The results of Table 1 showed that obtaining help and advising converged to a factor (i.e. consultation network). And friendship and trust converged to another factor (i.e. affective network).

Table 1. Factor loadings and Cronbach's α

Items	Consultation network (Cronbach's α = .905)	Affective network (Cronbach's α = .856)
1. Obtaining help	.962	.116
2. Advising	.787	.507
3. Friendship	.237	.910
4. Trust	.207	.928

Since both of Consultation and Affective networks were composited by two variables, we calculated the values of two 60 × 60 matrices according to the factor loadings of Principle Component Analysis. The two 60 × 60 matrixes, each of which represented consultation network and affective network were used for following analysis.

5.2 Hypotheses Tests

This study used UCINET VI software with a MRQAP analysis for estimating the correlations between the authority, consultation, affective network, and IT diffusion, respectively. Each of the networks was represented by a 60 × 60 matrix according to the responses of the corresponding question. In MRQAP analysis, IT diffusion pattern was the dependent variable, whereas authority, consultation and affective networks were the independent variables. Table 2 showed the result of regression coefficients of MRQAP analysis.

Table 2. Regreesion coefficients

Independent matrix	β	Standardized β	p value
Authority network	0.407	0.393	0.001***
Consultation network	0.284	0.298	0.001***
Affective network	0.060	0.062	0.001***

Note: Dependent matrix: IT diffusion pattern, $*p < 0.1$ $**p < 0.01$ $***p < 0.001$, $R^2 = 0.446$; Adj $R^2 = 0.446$.

In Table 2, all the three constructs were significantly correlated to the IT diffusion pattern, indicating supports on the hypotheses H1, H2 and H3. Authority, consultation and affective networks explained the IT diffusion pattern well ($R^2 = 0.446$). These results indicated that the IT diffusion was significantly correlated to the teachers' authority, consultation and affective social networks. Among the three networks, the authority network was the most important predictor ($\beta = 0.393$), followed by the consultation network ($\beta = 0.298$), and then the affective network ($\beta = 0.062$). That was, in this case, the IT was diffused mainly through authority and consultation networks. Although affective network had significant influence, its importance was much less than the other two.

6   Discussions

This study examined the influences of authority, consultation and affective network on IT diffusion. Taking an example of IT diffusion in an elementary school, our findings showed the three social networks were significant on IT diffusion. The IT diffusion pattern was presented in Fig. 2. In Fig. 2, some clusters of IT diffusion, such as IT1 (11, 12, 13, 14, 16), IT2 (23, 24, 25, 26, 27), IT3 (31, 33, 34, 35, 38), IT4 (41, 42, 44, 45, 46), and IT5 (51, 52, 54, 57, L), could be identified. It also identified some key persons for the IT diffusion, such as G (standardized in-degree centrality = 38.806), L (26.866), F (11.940), M (11.940), and 42 (10.448). Among them, G and L were current and former IT chief. That showed that the IT specialists played an important role on IT diffusion. In addition, E (standardized betweenness centrality = 21.307), 16 (17.296), F (16.467), 13 (15.707), 32 (13.663) had higher betweenness centrality, indicating that they played as important hubs for bringing IT across subgroups.

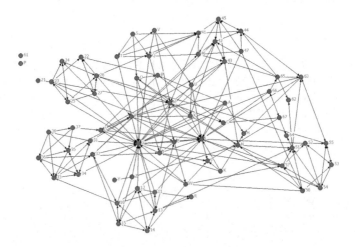

Fig. 2. IT diffusion pattern

Authority Network. Authority Network were proved by this study as the most important construct to IT diffusion. Figure 3 presented the authority network in Alpha. The authority network demonstrated the formal interaction based on job position and report system. In Fig. 3, the teachers who served in the same grade fragment had a lot of exchanges and formed several clusters in this diagram. A small group analyze identified six clusters in this network diagram, including A1 (11, 12, 13, 14, 15, 16), A2 (22, 23, 24, 25, 26, 27), A3 (31, 32, 33, 34, 35, 37), A4 (41, 42, 44, 45, 46), A5 (51, 52, 53, 54, 55, 57), and A6 (62, 63, 64, 65, 67). The members of these clusters were teachers in the same grade fragment (i.e. G1–G6). This phenomenon presented the way teachers work in an elementary school. In an elementary school, instructions and activities were usually run based on grade fragment level. For a semester, each grade fragment identified particular instructional themes and activities for each subject-matter. Teachers in grade fragments conducted extensive interactions for coordinating the instructional plan execution.

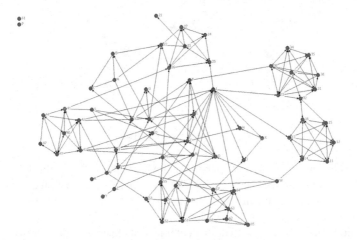

Fig. 3. Authority network

We found three overlaps when we compared the authority network with IT diffusion pattern. These overlaps were A1 (which overlapped IT1), A2 (which overlapped IT2), A3 (which overlapped IT3), A4 (which overlapped IT4), and A5 (which overlapped IT5). These evidences showed that the IT was diffused within grade fragments, especially in G1, G2, G3, G4, and G5.

The key actors with higher network centrality in authority network were 33 (standardized in-degree centrality = 10.448), E (8.955), F (8.955), 51 (8.955). Among them, E and F were also identified as key actors on IT diffusion network. Since E and F served for the Office of Academic Affairs, indicating that the staff in Office of Academic Affairs who had lots of interactions with teachers were also critical for such IT diffusion.

Consultation Network. The consultation network was also significant on IT diffusion. Excepting interactions based on authority, information exchange for problem solving was a critical path of IT diffusion. Such information exchanges could be obtaining help and advising others. Figure 4 presented the consultation network. In Fig. 4, six clusters could be identified, including C1 (11, 12, 13, 14, 15, 16), C2 (23, 24, 25, 26), C3 (31, 32, 33, 34, 37), C4 (42, 44, 45, 46, 47), C5 (51, 52, 53, 54, 56), and C6 (A, B, G, I, M, N). Most of the group members were teachers served in the same grade fragment, but C6 was a group formed by academic teachers.

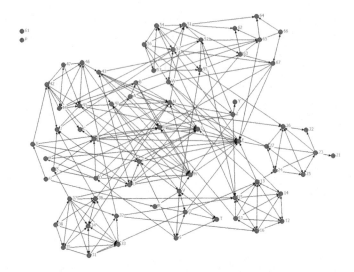

Fig. 4. Consultation network

The consultation network overlapped IT diffusion pattern on five clusters, they were C1, C2, C3 C4, and C5. This showed that IT was diffused along with the consultations (either obtaining help or advising) within grade fragments. It occurred especially in the grade fragments G1, G2, G3, G4, and G5.

In addition, the key actors with higher centrality in the consultation network were G (standardized in-degree centrality = 17.9100), E (14.925), D (13.433), 15 (11.940), and M (11.940). Among them, G had highest degree centrality in IT diffusion network as well. As G served as the IT chief in school, it was not surprised that he provided lots of consultation for IT use.

Furthermore, E presented the highest betweenness centrality in both consultation network (standardized betweenness centrality = 15.262) and IT diffusion network. These indicated that E not only assistant others but also an important referee. Acted as a hub, E helped the IT diffused across clusters when he provided consultations to teachers.

Affective Network. Figure 5 presented the affective network. The K-plex analysis indicated no significant clusters within this diagram. It meant that affective interaction among the teachers in Alpha didn't restrict to authority and work consultation. The actors with higher degree centrality was 32 (standardized in-degree centrality = 11.940), 36 (11.940), N (10.448), E (10.448), and I (10.448). Among them, only 32 had been identified as the hub (with higher betweenness centrality) in the IT diffusion diagram.

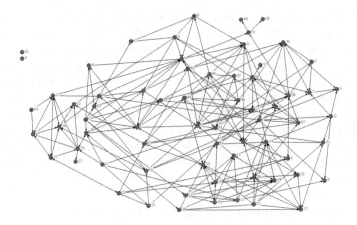

Fig. 5. Affective network

7   Conclusion

This study investigates the correlation between social networks and IT diffusion pattern. The results suggest that authority, consultation and affective network are significantly correlated with IT diffusion. These findings can bring three implications.

First, the authority network is effective for IT diffusion. For elementary teachers, the grade fragments formed based on authority is the critical channel for IT diffusion. Within grade fragment, the teachers need to interact with others closely for accomplishing the designed instruction plan and activities. Teachers hold meetings within grade fragment frequently, and these meetings increase the opportunities for teachers to share experiences on using IT into instruction. Besides meetings, the classrooms of the same grade fragment are usually located in the adjacent area. This arrangement makes it easy discuss, share and demonstrate how to use IT for instruction. As a result, teacher's authority network promotes close interactions, especially within grade fragment, and becomes an important enabler of IT diffusion.

Second, professional consultations in organization play a key role of IT diffusion. The diffusion of IT is also facilitated through the consultation network in organization. When teachers are confused with work problems, they usually seek advices within grade fragment. The consultants who are senior and experienced might introduce IT as the solutions for solving their colleagues' problems on instruction. These advices are often convincing and persuasive because the consultants are in the same situation of organizational environment, have similar work conditions and resources limitations. Consultants not only support teachers instantly but also act as the learning partner on using IT for instruction. Experience sharing and support providing from consultants reduce teachers' sense of uncertainty and anxiety of adopting IT, and therefore makes IT diffusion.

Third, the affective network provides hubs for IT diffusing across grade fragments. The friendship and trust network among teachers facilitated the transfer of IT relevant information to the colleagues in different grade fragments.

This study has academic and practical contributions. For the academy, this study illustrates and explains how social network may influence IT diffusion. Our findings remind organizations to make good use of social networks for diffusing IT. Authority, consultation and affective network in organization are effective and critical channels for diffusing IT. For practice, organizations can take three ways to facilitate IT diffusion through social networks: (1) Strengthen the interactions of authority network in order to increase the opportunities of information exchanging and sharing; (2) Pay attention to the members who are often consulted by others. They can be the consultants and supporters who make other individuals to adopt IT; (3) Use affective network to encourage teachers to share their experiences and reflections on using IT, and provide the information to the teachers who do not use IT for instruction.

Acknowledgements. This work was supported by the Ministry of Science and Technology of the Republic of China under the grant MOST 104-2410-H-415-014-MY2.

References

1. Adler, P.S., Kwon, S.W.: Social capital: prospects for a new concept. Acad. Manag. Rev. **27**(1), 17–40 (2002)
2. Ahuja, M.K., Galletta, D.F., Carley, K.M.: Individual centrality and performance in virtual R&D groups: an empirical study. Manag. Sci. **49**(1), 21–39 (2003)
3. Aiman-Smith, L., Green, S.: Implementing new manufacturing technology: the related effects of technology characteristics and user learning activities. Acad. Manag. J. **45**(2), 421–430 (2002)
4. Borgatti, S.P., Foster, P.C.: The network paradigm in organizational research: a review and typology. J. Manag. **29**(6), 991–1013 (2003)
5. Beaudry, A., Pinsonneault, A.: IT-induced adaptation and individual performance: a coping acts model. In: Storey, V., Sarkar, S., DeGross, J.I. (eds.) Proceedings of the 22nd International Conference on Information Systems, New Orleans, LA, pp. 475–480 (2001)
6. Degenne, A., Forse, M.: Introducing Social Networks. Sage Publications, London (1999)
7. Erickson, B.H.: The relational basis of attitudes. In: Wellman, B., Berknwitz, S.D. (eds.) Social Structures: A Network Approach, pp. 99–121. Cambridge University Press, Cambridge (1988)
8. Hanneman, R.A., Riddle, M.: Concepts and measures for basic network analysis. In: The Sage Handbook of Social Network Analysis. Sage (2011)
9. Kilduff, M., Krackhardt, D.: Bringing the individual back in: a structural analysis of the internal market for reputation in organizations. Acad. Manag. J. **37**(1), 87–108 (1994)
10. Kilduff, M., Tsai, W.: Social Networks and Organizations. Sage, London (2003)
11. Mills, S.C., Tincher, R.C.: Be the technology: a developmental model for evaluating technology integration. J. Res. Technol. Educ. **35**(3), 382–401 (2003)
12. Mumford, M., Weeks, J., Harding, F., Fleshman, E.: Measuring occupational difficulty: a construct validation against training criteria. J. Appl. Psychol. **72**(4), 578–587 (1987)
13. Mumtaz, S.: Factors affecting teachers' use of information and communications technology: a review of the literature. J. Inf. Technol. Teach. Educ. **9**(3), 319–342 (2000)
14. Podolny, J.M., Baron, J.N.: Resources and relationships: social networks and mobility in the workplace. Am. Sociol. Rev. **62**(5), 673–693 (1997)

15. Rice, R.E., Aydin, C.: Attitudes toward new organizational technology: network proximity as a mechanism for social information processing. Adm. Sci. Q. **9**(4), 219–244 (1991)
16. Rogers, E.M.: Diffusion of innovations, 4th edn. The Free Press, New York (1995)
17. Scott, J.: Social Network Analysis: A Handbook. Sage Publications, London (2000)
18. Scott, J.: Social Network: Critical Concepts in Sociology. Routledge, New York (2002)
19. Sheingold, K., Hadley, M.: Accomplished Teachers: Integrating Computers into Classroom Practice. Centre for Technology in Education, New York (1990)
20. Shih, W.: A theoretical model of introducing digital instruction. Living Technol. Educ. **39**(6), 30–36 (2006). (in Chinese)
21. Shyu, H., Wu, P.: The meaning and practice of technology integrated instruction. Instr. Technol. Media **59**, 63–73 (2002). (in Chinese)
22. Skes, T.A., Venkatesh, V., Gosain, S.: Model of acceptance with peer support: a social network perspective to understand employees' system use. MIS Q. **33**(2), 371–393 (2009)
23. Sprague, D., Dede, C.: If I teach this way, am I doing my job? Constructivism in the classroom. Learn. Lead. Technol. **27**(1), 6–9 (1999)
24. Tsvetovat, M., Kouznetsov, A.: Social Network Analysis for Startups: Finding Connections on the Social Web. O'Reilly, Sebastopol (2011)
25. Uhl-Bien, M., Graen, G., Scandura, T.: Implications of leader–member exchange (LMX) for strategic human resource management systems: relationships as social capital for competitive advantage. In: Ferris, G.R. (ed.) Research in Personnel and Human Resource Management, vol. 18, pp. 137–185. JAI Press, Greenwich (2000)
26. Wasserman, S., Faust, K.: Social Network Analysis. Cambridge University Press, New York (1994)
27. Wu, C., Wu, S.: A study of technology integrated instruction practices problems - an example of social studies teaching. In: Dai, W., He, R. (eds.) Curriculum Design for Information Education, pp. 163–178. National Taiwan Normal University Press, Taipei (2001). (in Chinese)

Exploring the Effects of Source Credibility on Information Adoption on YouTube

Constantinos K. Coursaris and Wietske Van Osch[✉]

Department of Media and Information,
Michigan State University, East Lansing, MI, USA
{coursari, vanosch}@msu.edu

Abstract. This research-in-progress paper explores the effects of information source credibility (brands versus vloggers), information type (how-to tutorial versus product demonstration), and viewer characteristics on perceptions of information quality, information usefulness, information satisfaction, and information adoption in the context of YouTube videos regarding a technology product, the Apple Watch. The primary goal of this study is to understand how users process information provided through YouTube videos by brands and vloggers, as well as extend existing models of information adoption that solely focus on information and source characteristics without considering characteristics of the user or viewer. Envisioned future steps in this project are discussed as well as implications for research and practice. Data collection will be completed prior to the HCII conference, where results will be presented.

Keywords: Source credibility · Information quality · Information usefulness · Information adoption · User characteristics · Youtube · Social media technology industry

1 Introduction

YouTube is the second largest search engine, making it a principal source of knowledge and information for consumers. Across the various product categories that may be showcased in YouTube videos, the Electronics industry is the most viewed industry, accounting not only for 16 % of all YouTube views but further accounting for 15 % of all video uploads making it the single largest industry, followed by beauty, auto, telecom, beverages, and other [26].

A large proportion of these videos are not created by brands themselves, but rather by electronics vloggers. Because of their popularity, brands are increasingly understanding and embracing the influence of these electronics vloggers. Although brands currently control a mere 3 % of YouTube's videos, recent marketing research reports show that brands are growing their investments for marketing through YouTube channels [26] to improve their presence on YouTube among the influence of electronics vloggers. However, do these massive amounts of views translate into brand or vlogger influence and do viewers act on the content or suggestions found in these videos?

Despite the growing popularity of Apple Watch videos on YouTube and the increasing use of this marketing channel by Apple Watch brands, no studies were

© Springer International Publishing Switzerland 2016
F.F.-H. Nah and C.-H. Tan (Eds.): HCIBGO 2016, Part I, LNCS 9751, pp. 16–25, 2016.
DOI: 10.1007/978-3-319-39396-4_2

identified that explore viewer behavior in the context of the electronics industry. Although various studies on online consumer behavior have studied social media such as Facebook [12] or Twitter, we identified only a single study regarding YouTube as a source of information on the H1N1 Influenza Pandemic. However, none of the above studies have focused on how viewers process information from videos, and how their information processing is either affected by source credibility or in turn influences the user's intention to act on the content or suggestions found in the video.

Therefore, this study aims to answer the following research question: What is the effect of the information's **source credibility** (brands vs. vloggers) on **information quality, information usefulness, information satisfaction, and information adoption** in the context of YouTube Apple Watch videos? In addition to analyzing perceived characteristics of the information embedded in the video, this study moves beyond existing Information Systems (IS) studies on information adoption in organizational settings (c.f., [33, 38]) by also incorporating viewer characteristics, such as prior knowledge and information relevance.

Therefore, this study offers two contributions to existing research on information adoption. First, by analyzing information adoption in the context of YouTube Apple Watch videos, we shift to an analysis of source credibility and information quality in a voluntary, online environment compared to studies focusing on organizational settings. Second, by incorporating viewer characteristics—prior knowledge and relevance—we extend existing models that have solely centered on characteristics of the source and the information itself thereby overlooking the interactions between the viewer and the source/information.

Beyond the abovementioned contributions to theory, this study is expected to generate practical implications by shedding light on the credibility of brands versus vloggers in the context of YouTube as well as reveal which types of product-related videos— how-to tutorials versus product demonstration—are most likely to result in information adoption.

The remainder of this research-in-progress paper is organized as follows. First, we review the prior literature on source credibility, information quality, and information adoption as well as literature pertaining to viewer characteristics. These theoretical foundations will be used to formulate a set of hypotheses regarding the interplay of these source/information and viewer characteristics. Subsequently, we present the hypothesized research model, envisioned research approach, experimental manipulations, and measurement scales. Finally, we discuss future steps of this study and expected contributions to research and practice.

2 Literature Review

In this section, we review the literature regarding the key constructs underpinning this study, namely: perceived source and information characteristics (source credibility and information quality), viewer characteristics (relevance and prior knowledge), and key dependent variables in this study (information usefulness, user satisfaction, information adoption).

2.1 Source and Information Characteristics

The two key characteristics of the source and information that will be explored in this study are source credibility and information quality.

The concept of credibility has previously been studied in psychology by [16], who studied how intrinsic attributes affect the credibility of a source. [16] analyzed intrinsic attributes such as, trustworthiness, expertise, and attractiveness and their effects on credibility and ultimately someone's attitude towards said source. It was found that high source credibility induces greater positive attitude toward the position advocated [10]. Specifically, these previous studies found that high source credibility leads to higher persuasion than low source credibility; hence source credibility plays a key role in the transmission of information and subsequent decisions to adopt content or suggestions provided by the source.

Although these original studies were conducted in offline environments, recent studies have extended source credibility into the online environment. For instance, [20] studied the differentiation of source, message, and media credibility in an online environment. [9] studied the perceived source credibility of websites regarding message features and structural features. However, these works have been largely exploratory in terms of developing measures of media credibility for online media rather than exploring impacts on information adoption.

For the present study, the following definition of source credibility is retained: *"the extent to which an information source is perceived to be believable, competent, and trustworthy by information recipients"* [3].

The other key characteristic in this study is information quality, a multi-dimensional concept. In what follows, we will discuss some of the various conceptualizations developed in different papers. For instance, [18] found that information quality has two sub-dimensions, which are information persuasiveness and information completeness. According to [34]'s definition of quality, information quality encompasses the dimensions of accuracy, comprehensiveness, currency, reliability, and validity. The latter is similar to [13] five-dimensional conceptualization of information quality as: accuracy, completeness, relevance, timeliness and amount of data. [21] discovered three main dimensions underpinning information quality including the perception of the user about the information, the information itself (completeness), and the process of accessing the information.

In the present study, we will analyze information quality as a subjective factor determined by the user's personal view, experience and his background in line with the suggestion of [32] who argue that information quality cannot be assessed independently of the people who use the information. Therefore, in line with this subjective approach to conceptualizing information quality as well as appreciating its multi-dimensional nature, we adopt the following definition of information quality by [33]: "the extent to which users think that information is relevant, timely, accurate, and complete".

2.2   Viewer Characteristics

In addition to the two characteristics of the source and information, this study also incorporates two characteristics of the viewer (or user), namely information relevance (or interest) and prior knowledge.

Information relevance or interest has long been studied to determine its effect on attention, engagement, and cognitive processing [6, 29, 30]. Given its direct link to engagement and attention, relevance or interest appears to be an important viewer characteristic in understanding information adoption.

Second, prior knowledge—a user characteristic that refers to a person's awareness of and information about a topic, product, or technology [28]—influences people's perception of the attributes of that product. Existing studies have found evidence for relationships between knowledge and perceived innovation attributes, including relative advantage [7], risk (i.e. uncertainty) [8], as well as observability and trialability [23] of a technology. Similarly, one can anticipate that a viewer's prior knowledge would interact with his or her perception of source credibility and information quality in the context of YouTube Apple Watch videos.

2.3   Dependent Variables: Information Usefulness, Information Satisfaction, and Information Adoption

In addition to the information- and viewer-centric independent variables, this study incorporates the following three dependent variables, namely information usefulness, information satisfaction, and information adoption.

Information usefulness has been studied across various settings including health [24] and organizational contexts [33]. Similar to the concept of usefulness in the technology acceptance model [5], research on information has identified information usefulness as an important driver of information adoption [31]. In this study, the following definition is retained: "information usefulness refers to the degree to which the information is perceived to be valuable, informative and helpful" [33].

Information satisfaction is the equivalent of user satisfaction in IS and consumer research, which is largely a function of the effectiveness of the interaction of a user with a technology or product [1, 4, 22]. Contemporary research links user satisfaction to attitude and attitude change (c.f., [17, 19]). In this study, we define information satisfaction as "a person's feelings or attitudes toward a particular informational message" (adapted from [38]).

Finally, information adoption—our ultimate dependent variable—has been previously studied in both offline [37] and online [36] settings. We will mostly leverage the literature on content and information adoption in computer-mediated communication contexts, such as [33]'s study about email information adoption and [36] study of information adoption in online communities. In line with [36], we define information adoption as "the extent to which people accept content that they are presented with as meaningful, after assessing its validity".

3 Research Model and Hypotheses

Given the limited space available, Table 1 summarizes the hypotheses underpinning our research model and provides references to supporting research. Figure 1 visualizes all hypothesized relationships in the overall research model.

Table 1. Hypotheses

Hyp.	Description	Supporting evidence
H1	Source credibility positively affects information quality	[33]
H2	Source credibility positively affects information usefulness	[36]
H3	Information quality positively affects information usefulness	[33]
H4	Information relevance will have a positive moderating effect on the relationship between source credibility and information usefulness	[6, 29, 30]
H5	Prior knowledge will have a negative moderating effect on the relationship between information quality and information usefulness	[11, 37]
H6	Source credibility positively affects information satisfaction	[18, 38]
H7	Information usefulness positively affects information satisfaction	[38]
H8	Information usefulness positively impacts information adoption	[5, 33]
H9	Information satisfaction positively impacts information adoption	[38]

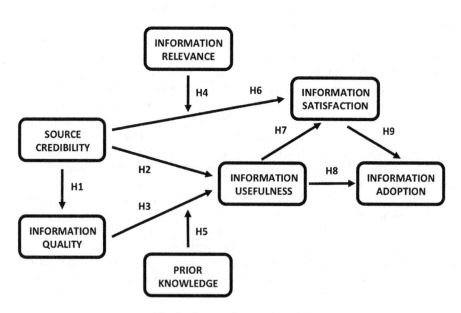

Fig. 1. Proposed research model

4   Methodology

For this study, we will adopt a 2 (Brands vs. Vloggers) * 2 (Product presentations vs. Tutorials) experimental design. Hence, participants will be randomly assigned to one of four videos prior to answering a research question.

4.1   Source and Video (Message) Selection

For the selection of vloggers, a selection will be made based on popularity as defined by total number of views and channel subscribers as well as experience as determined by the number of videos and date of joining YouTube. However, vloggers that have established official contracts with brands will be eliminated so as not to undermine the distinction between the information source—namely brand versus vloggers.

For the selection of official Apple Watch brands, we will use a ranking generated by [26] where they ranked electronics brands based on the total number of videos posted on YouTube.

For the content selection, we classify the videos into one of two main categories (see Table 1). Although two additional video types exist, hauls (showing off recently-purchased items) and vlogger's way of life (aimed at creating intimate relations with subscribers), these are not used by brands, hence, are inappropriate for comparing the two source types. For each cell, we will select a video from the selected vlogger or brand (Table 2).

Table 2. Video categories and descriptions

Category	Product presentations	Tutorials
Brand	Electronics brands are presenting their own products which are often adapted from existing commercials	"How to" videos published by brands which show how to use a particular electronics product
Vloggers	Vloggers create videos such as "50 + Apple Watch Tips and Tricks", or "Top Apps for the Apple Watch" which usually present multiple products	Similar "How To" videos that show how to use an electronic device (e.g., Apple Watch)

4.2   Measures

The constructs and items, as adapted from existing literature, are summarized in Table 3.

Table 3. Constructs and items

Construct	Definition (in this study)	Source	Sample items
Characteristics of the source			
Source credibility	The extent to which an information source (brand or vlogger) is perceived to be believable, competent, and trustworthy by viewers	[3]	"The person/brand who published the video was knowledgeable on this topic" "The person/brand who published the video was trustworthy"
Information quality (*adapted*)	A viewer's assessment of whether the information in the video is accurate, valid, and timely	[35]	"Information provided by this video is accurate" "Information provided by this video is reliable"
Viewer characteristics			
Relevance/topic interest (*adapted*)	The viewer's level of interest in electronics	[14, 15]	"Important- unimportant". "Irrelevant- relevant" "Means a lot to me- means nothing to me" "Unexciting- exciting"
Prior knowledge (*adapted*)	The viewer's familiarity, associations, and knowledge with/about electronics	[27]	"Please rate your knowledge of Apple Watch, as compared to the average person's knowledge of Apple Watch" "One of the least knowledgeable"-"one of the most knowledgeable"
Dependent variables			
Information usefulness (*adapted*)	The extent to which a viewer believes that a specific video would enhance his/her effectiveness in using the Apple Watch	[25]	"This video would be useful for getting valuable information about this product" "This video would enhance my effectiveness in getting useful information about Apple Watch product"
Information satisfaction (*adapted*)	The viewers feelings about the information provided in the video	[2]	"Very dissatisfied- very satisfied" "Very displeased- very pleased" "Absolutely terrible- absolutely delighted"
Information adoption (*adapted*)	The viewer's intentions towards adopting Apple Watch as advocated in the video	[33]	"How likely are you to act on the content of this video"? "To what extent does the content of the video motivate you to take action? Not at all motivated – Totally motivated"

5 Discussion and Concluding Remarks

Research on social media has proliferated in recent years; however, the majority of prior studies have focused on the message without regard for either the source or the recipient of that message. We attempt to overcome this gap in the literature through the study in progress. Hence, the foremost contribution to theory will be the provision of a unified view on the underlying mechanism of information adoption, one that incorporates characteristics of both the source/information as well as the user and explains their associated effects on information adoption.

Furthermore, results will highlight the extent to which mediation occurs between constructs that have previously been studied in isolation, such as the relationships between source credibility, information usefulness, and information adoption [33].

In regards to implications for practice, a clear contribution will be made in identifying which of the two prevalent, product-centered video types – product demonstrations and how-to tutorials – is more effective in leading to the viewer's adoption of the communicated information. Accordingly, a brand can invest in the creation of such digital assets, as they may ultimately lead to greater product sales.

Lastly, a two-fold analysis of source credibility will reveal whether (i) commercial brands are more or less credible than individuals when it comes to product information dissemination, and (ii) the relative effect of credibility on perceptions of information quality, information usefulness, and information satisfaction.

References

1. Bailey, J.E., Pearson, S.W.: Development of a tool for measuring and analyzing computer user satisfaction. Manag. Sci. **29**(5), 530–545 (1983)
2. Bhattacherjee, A.: Understanding information systems continuance: an expectation-confirmation model. MIS Q. **25**, 351–370 (2001)
3. Bhattacherjee, A., Sanford, C.: Influence processes for information technology acceptance: an elaboration likelihood model. MIS Q. **30**, 805–825 (2006)
4. Cameron, K.: A study of organizational effectiveness and its predictors. Manag. Sci. **32**(1), 87–112 (1986)
5. Davis, F.D.: Perceived usefulness, perceived ease of use, and user acceptance of information technology. MIS Q. **13**, 319–340 (1989)
6. Deci, E.L.: The relation of interest to the motivation of behavior: a self-determination theory perspective (1992)
7. Edmondson, A.C., Winslow, A.B., Bohmer, R.M.J., Pisano, G.P.: Learning how and learning what: effects of tacit and codified knowledge on performance improvement following technology adoption. Decis. Sci. **34**(2), 197–224 (2003)
8. Feder, G., O'Mara, G.T.: Farm size and the diffusion of green revolution technology. Econ. Dev. Cult. Change **30**(1), 59–76 (1981)
9. Hong, T.: The influence of structural and message features on web site credibility. J. Am. Soc. Inf. Sci. Technol. **57**(1), 114–127 (2006)
10. Hovland, C.I., Weiss, W.: The influence of source credibility on communication effectiveness. Public Opin. Q. **15**(4), 635–650 (1951)

11. Johnson, P.R., Yang, S.: Uses and gratifications of Twitter: an examination of user motives and satisfaction of Twitter use. In: Communication Technology Division of the Annual Convention of the Association for Education in Journalism and Mass Communication in Boston, MA August 2009
12. Kim, J.H., Kim, M.S., Nam, Y.: An analysis of self-construals, motivations, Facebook use, and user satisfaction. Intl. J. Hum.-Comput. Interact. **26**(11–12), 1077–1099 (2010)
13. Klein, B.: When do users detect information quality problems on the world wide web? In: Proceedings of AMCIS 2002, p. 152 (2002)
14. Koufaris, M.: Applying the technology acceptance model and flow theory to online consumer behavior. Inf. Syst. Res. **13**(2), 205–223 (2002)
15. McQuarrie, E.F., Munson, J.M.: A revised product involvement inventory: improved usability and validity. Adv. Consum. Res. **19**(1), 108–115 (1992)
16. McGuire, J.W.: The nature of attitude and attitude change. In: Hand Book of Social Psychology, vol. 3 (1968)
17. McGuire, W.J.: The nature of attitudes and attitude change. In: Lindzey, G., Aronson E. (eds.) The Handbook of Social Psychology, The Individual in a Social Context, 2e édn, vol. 3 (1969)
18. McKinney, V., Yoon, K., Zahedi, F.M.: The measurement of web-customer satisfaction: an expectation and disconfirmation approach. Inf. Syst. Res. **13**(3), 296–315 (2002)
19. Melone, N.P.: A theoretical assessment of the user-satisfaction construct in information systems research. Manag. Sci. **36**(1), 76–91 (1990)
20. Metzger, M.J., Flanagin, A.J., Eyal, K., Lemus, D.R., McCann, R.M.: Credibility for the 21st century: integrating perspectives on source, message, and media credibility in the contemporary media environment. Commun. Yearb. **27**, 293–336 (2003)
21. Naumann F., Rolker C.: Assessment methods for information quality criteria, In: Proceedings of 5th International Conference on Information Quality (2000)
22. Oliver, R.L., DeSarbo, W.S.: Response determinants in satisfaction judgments. J. Consum. Res. **14**, 495–507 (1988)
23. Pagani, M.: Determinants of adoption of third generation mobile multimedia services. J. Inf. Technol. **18**(3), 46–59 (2004)
24. Pandey, A., Patni, N., Singh, M., Sood, A., Singh, G.: YouTube as a source of information on the H1N1 influenza pandemic. Am. J. Prev. Med. **38**(3), e1–e3 (2010)
25. Pavlou, P.A., Fygenson, M.: Understanding and predicting electronic commerce adoption: an extension of the theory of planned behavior. MIS Q. **30**, 115–143 (2006)
26. YouTube statistics (2016). http://expandedramblings.com/index.php/downloads/youtube-statistic-report/
27. Roehm, M.L., Pullins, E.B., Roehm Jr., H.A.: Designing loyalty-building programs for packaged goods brands. J. Mark. Res. **39**(2), 202–213 (2002)
28. Rogers, E.M.: Diffusion of Innovations. Free Press, Glencoe (2003). 5(null)ed
29. Ryan, M.L.: Possible Worlds, Artificial Intelligence and Narrative Theory. University of Indiana Press, Bloomington (1991)
30. Sadoski, M.: Resolving the effects of concreteness on interest, comprehension, and learning important ideas from text. Educ. Psychol. Rev. **12**, 263–281 (2001)
31. Satzinger, J.W., Olfman, L.: Computer support for group work: perceptions of the usefulness of support scenarios and end-user tools. J. Manag. Inf. Syst. **11**, 115–148 (1995)
32. Strong, D.M., Lee, Y.W., Wang, R.Y.: Data quality in context. Commun. ACM **40**(5), 103–110 (1997)
33. Sussman, S.W., Siegal, W.S.: Informational influence in organizations: an integrated approach to knowledge adoption. Inf. Syst. Res. **14**(1), 47–65 (2003)

34. Taylor, R.S.: Value-Added Processes in Information Systems. Greenwood Publishing Group, Santa Barbara (1986)
35. Teo, T.S., Srivastava, S.C., Jiang, L.: Trust and electronic government success: an empirical study. J. Manag. Inf. Syst. **25**(3), 99–132 (2008)
36. Watts, S.A., Zhang, W.: Capitalizing on content: information adoption in two online communities. J. Assoc. Inf. Syst. **9**, 73 (2008)
37. Winter, F.W.: Laboratory measurement of response to consumer information. J. Mark. Res. **12**, 390–401 (1975)
38. Wixom, B.H., Todd, P.A.: A theoretical integration of user satisfaction and technology acceptance. Inf. Syst. Res. **16**(1), 85–102 (2005)

Phase 1 of 3: Will a LinkedIn™ Jr. Optimize Internships for High School STEM Students?

Benjamin Fickes[1], Alexander Tam[1], Adithya Dattatri[1], Allen Tang[1], Alan Balu[1], and David Brown[2(✉)]

[1] Computer Science Research Lab, The Charter School of Wilmington,
Wilmington, DE, USA
{fickes.benjamin,tam.alexander,dattatri.adithya,
tang.allen,balu.alan}@charterschool.org
[2] Chair of Computer Science Department, Computer Science Research Lab,
The Charter School of Wilmington, Wilmington, DE, USA
dbrown@charterschool.org

Abstract. Popular professional online networking sites, such as LinkedIn™, Monster™, CareerBuilder®, and others, focus on traditional jobs. Increasing demand for high school internships suggests an interest for an electronic networking database pertinent to high school opportunities [14]. In comparison to traditional methods of acquiring internships, such a database would provide increased accessibility and efficiency through an HCI conceptualized computer interface. Surveys were designed and distributed to stakeholders, an east coast, chartered high school (students grades 9–12, n = 132), businesses (n = 18), and parents (n = 143), to gather reactionary information. A Kruskal-Wallis, nonparametric algorithm found significant differences ($p < 0.05$) amongst the variables and eliminated errors due to a lack of homoscedasticity. The data found desirability, optimal implementation, and privacy concerns across independent variables. The degree that all stakeholders will feel comfortable in using a database to focus internship potential revolves about the efficacy, presentation, and portal attributes of the database.

Keywords: Internship · High school · Networking · HCI · Database · Survey · Privacy

1 Literature Review

An intern is "a student or trainee who works, sometimes without pay, at a trade or occupation in order to gain work experience" [9]. Internships distinguish themselves from other traditional jobs by focusing on work experience and learning. As a result, internships may not result in payment, since the pursuit of knowledge, instead of wealth, is the primary goal. High school students often seek internships as a means of furthering their knowledge and gaining recognition for their work. "Students who have participated in internships have reported better time management and communication skills, higher levels of self-discipline, increased initiative and improved self-image concepts" [13].

© Springer International Publishing Switzerland 2016
F.F.-H. Nah and C.-H. Tan (Eds.): HCIBGO 2016, Part I, LNCS 9751, pp. 26–36, 2016.
DOI: 10.1007/978-3-319-39396-4_3

Internships provide benefits for both the employer and the worker [2], and internships provide opportunities that can benefit all concerned. The demand for internships promises a steady increase, with a survey showing that 50 % of 326 surveyed companies were creating internship programs in 2014 [14]. High school and college students seek internships because they make the students' resume more attractive to potential employers. Employers may not give consideration to applicants without prior internships or work experience [16], which makes internships highly prized opportunities for students wishing to someday join the workforce. According to one study, 95 % of employers take work experience into account while recruiting [4]. Thus, internships are reliable sources of this crucial experience for those seeking employment but not yet directly involved in the workforce. Furthermore, internships help develop a skillset vital to a professional setting, including interpersonal relationship skills and confidence in one's work [4]. 92 % of high school interns said they interned in hopes of acquiring new skills, while 81 % said they sought internships for job experience [7].

LinkedIn™, a professional networking site, allows professionals and businesses to connect and network. However, LinkedIn™ is geared towards providing job opportunities, rather than internships. The LinkedIn™ user agreement states that profiles throughout the site specifically target job openings in clause 2.5 [15]. High school students lack diverse connections due to their lack of experience in the work force and the limitations of their age due to legal reasons; LinkedIn™'s concept of connections hinder a student's ability to be acquainted with professionals and thereby internship opportunities.

Social networking sites hold an infamous reputation for privacy concerns, as they, by design, appeal to a large body of people [6]. Barnes [1], sees difficulties stemming from the fact that users, especially those of high school age, may wish to keep their information private but still share it in a public area because they incorrectly assume that the information will be semi-private. A professional high school internship database may require more security than a traditional networking site, as its professional, as opposed to social, nature would require different types of information from the user [11], preventing the divulgence or misuse of information that commonly plagues similar networking sites. "Internships are the link between theoretical knowledge and concepts learned in the classroom setting, and real time industry applications. Internships have long been regarded as an important component in preparing undergraduate students for the entry-level job market" [13]. Knouse et al. [10], examined the relationships between students' academic performance, job offerings and internships and found that "students with internships had a significantly higher overall grade point average, were somewhat younger upon graduation, and were more likely to be employed upon graduation than students without internships" [10].

The main intentions of an internship are "personal real world insights and exposures to actual working life, an experiential, foundation to their career choices, and the chance to build valuable business networks" [12]. *The Atlantic* indicates internships only improve chances of obtaining a job by a "negligible 1.8 % points" in comparison to those who do not participate in internships [5]. The National Association of Colleges and Employers, on the other hand, states that over 63 % of interns are offered job opportunities through a survey in which over 38,000 students participated [3]. Gault et al. [9]

in "Undergraduate Business Internships and Career Success: Are They Related?" state that internship experiences result in "significantly higher levels of extrinsic success than their non-intern counterparts."

Gault et al. [9], in the Journal of Marketing Education, also found that interns reported receiving starting salaries that averaged $2,240 higher than their non-intern counterparts. In addition, the study found that higher salaries, later on in careers, were the result of earlier employment and that interns had obtained their positions approximately 2.36 months earlier than non-interns. The fact that interns started work earlier can be supported by the notion that the internships provided better preparation and "job acquisition skills" [9].

2   Methods

Using Google Forms, three distinct surveys were constructed for high school students, their parents, and local businesses and industries. Information was gathered from these groups. The following response choices were available: Yes or No, choose all that apply, and semantic differentials consisting of Strongly Agree, Agree, Moderately Agree, Moderately Disagree, Disagree, and Strongly Disagree. Student questions focused on the information a student wanted to make available to companies, privacy concerns regarding the database, vocational fields of interest, and a student's opinion on the usefulness. Parents received questions relative to their comfort levels concerning using the database, the opinions of the parents regarding information shared within the database, and any potential parental concerns. The company survey proffered questions on what information each company would require from a prospective intern, the discipline of each respective company, and their opinion on the usefulness of the database. All data was analyzed with the software Minitab®. Significant differences among variables were found by using the Kruskal-Wallis nonparametric statistical method at $p < .05$.

3   Findings

3.1   Student Survey

The student survey found that 97.0 % of students ($n = 132$) surveyed believed that a professional networking site focused on high school internships would assist them in acquiring internships (see Fig. 1). There was a significant difference pertaining to students who thought that this would be beneficial to college application and students who wanted to receive feedback with $p = 0.004$. The survey also revealed a significant difference between how strongly students thought the site would be useful for obtaining internships and how strongly they thought electronic networking would benefit their college application, suggesting that many students desired an internship as a means of obtaining college recognition. The data also showed that 90.9 % of students considered themselves 'comfortable' or 'strongly comfortable' with technology. Students also wanted to receive feedback from businesses through the site. All student respondents claimed to want business feedback on their internship performances, but not all students wished this feedback to be made public; 81.8 % of students stated that they would want feedback from businesses to be viewable by other businesses (see Fig. 2). 98.5 % of students reported that they wished to read peers' reviews of companies, and 96.2 % wished to write reviews (see Fig. 3). A significant difference with a p-value of .003 existed between the extent that students wanted feedback and the extent that they wished to review companies. Additionally, statistical significance existed between whether the feedback should be posted on the site and if they wanted to give companies feedback. Students, while positive about the prospects of obtaining internships, showed wariness concerning the potential privacy risks surrounding the site. 77.3 % of respondents stated that they would be concerned with having their personal information on a database. 84.8 % of students wanted their information to be viewable only by teachers and businesses, and not by their peers. 56.1 % of students said that they disagreed with including pictures of users on the website. Gender did not play a role with respect photo inclusion. Finally, there was a significant difference between believing an electronic network would be beneficial in the internship process and gaining feedback on one's performance as an intern.

I believe electronic networking would help me get an internship.

Strongly Agree	47	35.6%
Agree	61	46.2%
Moderately Agree	20	15.2%
Moderately Disagree	2	1.5%
Disagree	1	0.8%
Strongly Disagree	1	0.8%

Fig. 1. Breakdown of students' opinions on the potential benefits of electronic networking

I am comfortable with a company posting reviews about my work experience which other companies will be able to view.

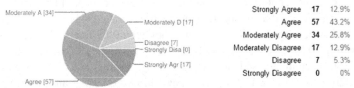

Strongly Agree	17	12.9%
Agree	57	43.2%
Moderately Agree	34	25.8%
Moderately Disagree	17	12.9%
Disagree	7	5.3%
Strongly Disagree	0	0%

Fig. 2. Breakdown of students' opinions on receiving review

I would like to be able to write reviews of companies that I work with.

Strongly Agree	47	35.6%
Agree	63	47.7%
Moderately Agree	17	12.9%
Moderately Disagree	4	3%
Disagree	1	0.8%
Strongly Disagree	0	0%

Fig. 3. Breakdown of students' opinions on reviewing companies

3.2   Parent Survey

Parents (n = 143) displayed similar enthusiasm for the creation of a database centered on internships for high school students. 91.6 % of surveyed parents believed that such a database would help their child find an internship (see Fig. 4). Parents supported the prospect of student and business reviews; 93.0 % supported receiving feedback from businesses concerning their child's performance as an intern, and 91.6 % supported their children reviewing companies. There was no significant difference between the support for giving or receiving reviews and the level of education of the surveyed parent. A strong significance existed between a parent's desire for receiving reviews and for students to be able to review companies, a response similar to that of the surveyed students. 85.4 % agreed that student-related/profile data posted on the site should only be accessible to approved business institutions (see Fig. 5). The parents shared a similar opinion concerning privacy and security, as only 57.3 % of parents were comfortable with their child's photo being displayed on the site. The age of the respondent had no significant effect on the response concerning this matter. A significant difference between the opinions of male, female, and 'did not wish to answer' parents who responded concerning the concept of a photo on the profile page existed. Furthermore, the majority of parents preferred that prospective interns be contacted via a school email, rather than a personal one, with 68.5 % stating that they would be fine with a child's school email being utilized for contact but only 16.1 % stating that they would be willing to have a child's personal email be used (see Fig. 6). Parents expressed a strong overall trust with their children concerning acquiring an internship, as 62.9 % stated that they would be comfortable with children using the site and applying for positions without parental approval, but many desired more involvement once the student acquired the internship, as 62.2 % stated that they would wish to be contacted before their children concerning an internship.

I think a database for my child to find internship opportunities would be beneficial.

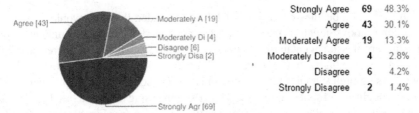

Strongly Agree	69	48.3%
Agree	43	30.1%
Moderately Agree	19	13.3%
Moderately Disagree	4	2.8%
Disagree	6	4.2%
Strongly Disagree	2	1.4%

Fig. 4. Breakdown of parents' opinions on the potential benefits of electronic networking

I would feel comfortable with my child's academic information on the site if it were secure and only accessible to approved businesses and institutions.

Strongly Agree	45	31.5%
Agree	52	36.4%
Moderately Agree	25	17.5%
Moderately Disagree	6	4.2%
Disagree	10	7%
Strongly Disagree	5	3.5%

Fig. 5. Breakdown of parent's opinion on displaying their child's academic information

I would feel comfortable with businesses contacting my child via (check all that apply):

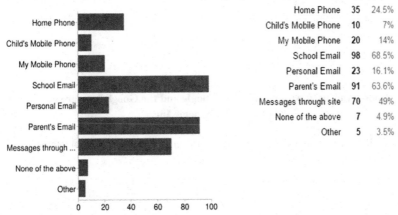

Home Phone	35	24.5%
Child's Mobile Phone	10	7%
My Mobile Phone	20	14%
School Email	98	68.5%
Personal Email	23	16.1%
Parent's Email	91	63.6%
Messages through site	70	49%
None of the above	7	4.9%
Other	5	3.5%

Fig. 6. Breakdown of parent's opinion on forms of contact between their child and a business

3.3 Business Survey

Of the surveyed businesses (n = 18), 61.1 % responded that they would be willing to hire high school students as interns and 61.1 % responded that they would be interested in using a professional database site to do so. Businesses were more interested in hiring junior and senior high school students; 66.7 % sought rising college freshmen and 72.2 % sought rising high school seniors, while only 38.9 % sought rising high school juniors, 16.7 % sought rising sophomores, and 11.1 % sought rising freshmen (see Fig. 7). 88.9 % of businesses were interested in knowing a student's GPA (see Fig. 8), but no significant difference existed between the type of business and its desire to know a student's GPA (see Figs. 8 and 9). There was no significant difference between how strongly a business valued standardized test scores and how strongly they valued GPA. Businesses also desired to retain security regarding a professional high school database; 66.7 % of businesses only wished to provide contact information to students they had selected for internships, and 33.3 % of businesses stated that they did not wish to make any contact information public to students at all. 94.4 % of businesses supported preventing students from putting inappropriate or vulgar content in their reviews, helping to prevent slander of companies. Businesses, regarding the style of review, shared a similar opinion with the parents and students. 66.7 % of companies surveyed desired the ability to leave comments apropos an intern's performance. 83.3 % of businesses said that they would only want students who had previously held an internship to be able to review the company.

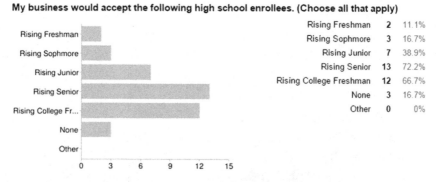

Fig. 7. Breakdown of business's opinion on the grade level for potential internships

My business would like to know prospective interns' GPAs.

Strongly Agree	5	27.8%
Agree	6	33.3%
Moderately Agree	5	27.8%
Moderately Disagree	0	0%
Disagree	1	5.6%
Strongly Disagree	1	5.6%

Fig. 8. Breakdown of business's opinion on the importance of GPA

My business would be interested in prospective interns' ACT, SAT, and/or other standardized testing scores.

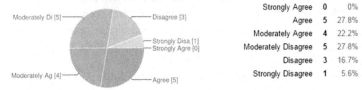

Strongly Agree	0	0%
Agree	5	27.8%
Moderately Agree	4	22.2%
Moderately Disagree	5	27.8%
Disagree	3	16.7%
Strongly Disagree	1	5.6%

Fig. 9. Breakdown of business's opinion on the importance of standardized test scores

4   Conclusion

Over 98.5 % of high school students want a way to connect to companies, and 91.7 % of parents encourage this relationship. High school students strongly desire internships and consider themselves comfortable with technology (98.5 %), which supports the plausibility of this platform. Literature and the study's data indicate student enthusiasm derives largely from the fact that they believe they will receive recognition from colleges (97.0 %) as a result of an internship, as well as work experience in their field of interest [12]. Businesses, overall, support the prospect, as 66.7 % of businesses agree with the idea of reviewing high school interns. Businesses are becoming more accepting of high school interns. The main concern for businesses is the students' young age (see Fig. 7). Student age also was a factor in the students' preference of company contact. A significant difference existed between the year of students and their desire to be contacted by businesses before their parents. Both the student and parent surveys revealed a relationship between a desire to write reviews and to receive them, showing the possibility for improvements to existing internship programs that companies offer. There was no significant difference relating education to giving or receiving reviews, showing that all want to contribute to making internships better; this, combined with the strong desire of students to read and write reviews, shows that all involved in this process want the opportunity to learn and grow. The fact that 66.7 % businesses who wish to review interns who have worked with them and that 83.3 % of business wish to receive comments from interns indicate that companies value both student feedback and security to help prevent students from posting inaccurate or fictitious reviews.

The combination of a more discriminatory selection process as well as dynamic responses allows for the active refinement of the intern through their experience. The fact that no significance exists between businesses wanting to know test scores and wanting to know GPA supports the null hypothesis that a business prefers GPA over standardized test scores, demonstrating that the two are interchangeable and either would be sufficient for the application process. The statistical significance between students believing electronic networking would be beneficial to obtaining an internship and receiving feedback shows that students wish to utilize a high school professional database to pursue internships and also highly value the maintenance of a completely professional and secure atmosphere on the proposed database. The fact that 28.0 % of student are willing to provide their personal email indicates a high concern for web safety and privacy. The lack of a significant difference between male and female opinion of their photo on the website highlights not only a universal concern for privacy, but also a related concern for professionalism.

Because the functionality of searching for interns, based on profile data, depends on students providing certain pieces of information, privacy concerns may arise due to the potential exploitation of this information. Concerns regarding security risks, expressed by parents and businesses, are inherent to any database containing personal information. Both students and parents displayed some reluctance in providing personal information, such as a child's photo, on the website. The surveys did find that students viewed as more mature by their parents were trusted to provide more of their personal information on the website, as a significant difference existed between how mature parents felt their students were and parents' willingness for students to display their photo. Both students and parents preferred divulging non-personal information to businesses, such as an official school email, over revealing information such as phone numbers and personal email addresses. The fact that 88.6 % of students are willing to provide a school email to companies, while only 28.0 % of students are willing to provide a personal email, supports this idea of dual concerns for privacy and professionalism.

Over 72.7 % of students, with no significant difference between males and females, wanted their parents, not just themselves, to be contacted by businesses. However, students valued importance of initial business contact; 79.5 % reported that they would be opposed to a business contacting a parent before the student, with significant differences existing between age and opinion; older students opposed the idea of parents being contacted first more strongly than younger students. The majority of each group desired to be the first contacted by a business, which suggests parents wish to ensure that their children are safe and students want to be independent in their search for work experience. This tension may derive in part from parental safety concerns, and a secure and professional site may relieve some of the concern of parents.

A significant difference existed between gender and willingness to display a child's photo, with parents who are reluctant to divulge their gender discouraging their child from divulging personal information through a photo. A significant difference existed between how mature a parent felt their child was and how willing the parent was to allow the child to display their photo; in other words, parents felt that more mature children could be trusted to reveal more personal information. Potential security fears could be ameliorated through careful measures taken by the coding team of such a website, as well as the private and professional nature of the site. By focusing this website with the sole intent of connecting employers to prospective interns, this database possesses the potential to circumvent many of the problems found in social media and social networking. A professional database, used by both students and businesses, would allow companies to identify prospective interns and students to identify prospective businesses to intern for, as well as increase the competition between interns by allowing companies to view a larger pool of prospective candidates. Analysis indicates that a database of this type would not only be feasible, but also desirable among both students, parents, and certain business types.

All participants in the survey desire to take part in the internship process; the major obstacle preventing a solid partnership between the prospective interns and companies is a lack of networking. Knouse et al. [10] substantiate the importance of connecting students with employers as soon as possible in order to provide students with the opportunities to excel. Gault et al. [9] indicate that graduates with direct industry experience had a higher tendency to receive a higher starting salary. These two goals drive students and parents to obtain internships. The addition of such a database would provide potential connections in a fast and efficient manner.

Acknowledgements. This research was conducted at the Computer Science Department of The Charter School Of Wilmington. Special thanks to all individuals and businesses that partook in the survey and the administration of The Charter School of Wilmington for distributing the survey.

References

1. Barnes, S.B.: A privacy paradox: social networking in the United States. First Monday **11**(9), 3 (2006)
2. Casella, D.A., Brougham, C.E.: What works: student jobs open front doors to careers. J. Career Plann. Employ. **55**, 4 (1995)
3. Class of 2013: Paid Interns Outpace Unpaid Peers in Job (2013). Accessed 6 May 2015
4. College Students: You Simply Must Do an Internship (2008). Accessed 6 May 2015
5. Do Unpaid Internships Lead to Jobs? Not for College Students (2013). Accessed 8 May 2015
6. Ellison, N.B.: Social network sites: definition, history, and scholarship. J. Comput. Med. Commun. **13**(1), 210–230 (2007)
7. Employers, Students Benefit from High School Internships (2014). Accessed 6 May 2015
8. Intern - Definition of Intern in English from the Oxford Dictionary (2013). Accessed 1 May 2015
9. Gault, J., Redington, J., Schlager, T.: Undergraduate business internships and career success: are they related? J. Mark. Educ. **22**(1), 45–53 (2010)
10. Knouse, S.B., Tanner, J.R., Harris, E.W.: The relation of college internships, college performance, and subsequent job opportunity. J. Employ. Couns. **36**(1), 35–43 (1999)
11. Breslin, J. G., Decker, S., O'Murchu, I.: Online Social and Business Networking Communities. DERI Technical Report 2004-08-11, pp. 8–10 (2004)
12. Purpose & Benefits of Internships, Singapore Management (2013). Accessed 2 June 2015

13. Radigan, J.: The role of internships in higher education. American Society for Engineering Education, 2 (2010)
14. The High School Careers Study, Millennial Branding – Gen (2014). Accessed 12 May 2015
15. User Agreement, LinkedIn (2013). Accessed 6 May 2015
16. Why Are Internships So Important? - CNN.com (2010). Accessed 6 May 2015

Internet Use and Happiness

Richard H. Hall[✉]

Department of Business and Information Technology,
Missouri University of Science and Technology, Rolla, MO, USA
rhall@mst.edu

Abstract. In order to explore the relationship between happiness and Internet use, an Internet Use Scale (IUS) was developed and administered to college students along with the Flourishing Scale [1] and the Satisfaction with Life Scale [2]. A factor analysis of the IUS revealed three components of Internet use (time spent on the Internet; use of the Internet for information gathering; and use of the Internet for affective expression). Time spent on the Internet was negatively related to both happiness measures; information gathering was positively related to Flourishing scores; and affective expression was unrelated to happiness.

Keywords: Happiness · Internet

1 What Is Happiness?

For the most part, researchers agree that happiness is inherently subjective. In fact, the term is often used interchangeably with "subjective well-being" (SWB) [3]. Myers [4], one of the leading researchers in the area, stated that happiness is "…whatever people mean when describing their lives as happy." (p. 57). Despite the potential for ambiguity with such a definition, there is considerable agreement, at least across Western culture as to what happiness means [5]. Most people equate happiness with experiences of joy, contentment, and positive well being; as well as a feeling that life is good, meaningful, and worthwhile [6].

As a consequence, self-report measures have served as the primary measure of happiness. Examples include the Satisfaction with Life Scale (SLS), the Subjective Happiness Scale (SHS), and the Steen Happiness Index (SHI). Psychometric studies of these self-report measures indicate that they are, by and large, reliable over time, despite changing circumstances; they correlate strongly with friends and family ratings of happiness; and they are statistically reliable. Lyubomirsky [6] sums this up, "A great deal of research has shown that the majority of these measures have adequate to excellent psychometric properties and that the association between happiness and other variables usually cannot be accounted for by transient mood" (p. 239). These psychometric studies illustrate the general agreement among people as to what constitutes happiness.

One other interesting point regarding the definition of happiness and its measurement is that mean happiness is consistently above a mid-line point in most populations sampled [3]. For example, three in ten Americans say they are "very happy", only 1 in

© Springer International Publishing Switzerland 2016
F.F.-H. Nah and C.-H. Tan (Eds.): HCIBGO 2016, Part I, LNCS 9751, pp. 37–45, 2016.
DOI: 10.1007/978-3-319-39396-4_4

ten report that they are "not too happy", and 6 in 10 say they are "pretty happy" [4]. Therefore, there appears to be a positive set-point, where most people appear to be moderately happy, and this is independent of age and gender [4].

2 Happiness and the Internet

Studies that have examined the relationship between the Internet and happiness have been conducted at least since the relatively early days of the World Wide Web. Most of these have focused on communication/collaborative activities and the Internet. As we mentioned, these types of activities have been found in non-internet studies to be strongly related to happiness.

2.1 The Internet Paradox

In 1998 Kraut and colleagues reported the results of a reasonably extensive study of early World Wide Web users where they followed the activity of mostly first time Internet users over a period of years. Researchers administered periodic questionnaires and server logs indicating participant activity on the web. (Participants were provided with free computers and internet connections) [7].

Over all, the results showed that the Internet had a largely negative impact on social activity in that those who used the Internet more communicated with family and friends less. They also reported higher levels of loneliness. Interestingly, they also found that email, a communication activity, constituted the participants main use of the Internet. The researchers coined the term "internet paradox" to describe this situation in which a social technology reduced social involvement.

These researchers speculated that this negative social effect was due to a type of displacement, in which their time spent online displaced face-to-face social involvement. Although they note that users spent a great deal of time using email, they suggest that this constitutes a low quality social activity and this is why they did not see positive effects on well being [7]. They find further support for this supposition in a study reported in 2002, where they found that business professionals who used email found it less effective than face-to-face communication or the telephone in sustaining close social relationships [8].

Since the time that this Internet paradox was identified, a number of studies over the next twelve years have found, fairly consistently, results that contradict the Kraut et al. results. More recent studies have indicated the potential positive social effects of the Internet and their relationship to well being. Further, the effect appears to be getting stronger as the Internet and the users mature.

In fact, one of the first challenges to this Internet paradox was provided by Kraut himself when he published follow up results for participants in the original Internet-paradox study, including data for additional participants. In this paper, "Internet Paradox Revisited," researchers report that the negative social impact on the original sample had dissipated over time and, for those in their new sample, the Internet had positive effects on communication, social involvement, and well being [5].

Therefore, it appears that the results of the original Kraut et al. study were largely due to the participants' inexperience with the Internet. Within just a few years, American society's experience with the Internet had increased exponentially. Further, the Kraut studies concentrated on email, whereas there are many other social communication tools available on the modern web.

2.2   Displacement Versus Stimulation Hypothesis

More recently, researchers have examined the relationship between on-line communication and users' over all social networks, explicitly addressing the question of whether or not on-line communication "displaces" higher quality communication, or "stimulates" it. Presumably, the former would negatively effect well being, while the latter would enhance it [9].

In this large scale study, over 1000 Dutch teenagers were surveyed regarding the nature of their on line communication activities, the number and quality of friendships, and their well being.

They found strong support for the stimulation hypothesis. More specifically, these researchers developed a causal model, which indicated that instant messaging lead to more contact with friends, which lead to more meaningful social relationships, which, in turn, predicted well being. Interestingly, they did not find this same effect for chat in a public chat room. They attributed this finding to the fact that participants reported that they interacted more with strangers in the chat room as compared to their interaction with friends with instant messaging [9].

2.3   The Internet and Social Connectedness

Despite studies, such as the one just mentioned, which have found a relationship between internet use and positive outcomes, there is still a great deal of press suggesting that the internet can effect users negatively, causing social isolation, and shrinking of social networks. This is purported to be especially true for adolescents [10].

Researchers with the Pew Internet and Daily Life Project set out to examine this concern directly in one of the most comprehensive studies of the effect of the Internet on social interaction, reported in 2009 [10]. Contrary to fears, they found that:

- A variety of Internet activities were associated with larger and more diverse core discussion networks.
- Those who participated most actively with social media were more likely to interact with those from diverse backgrounds, including race and political view.
- Internet users are just as likely as others to visit a neighbor in person, and they are more likely to belong to a local voluntary organization.
- Internet use is often associated with local activity in community spaces such as parks and restaurants, and Internet connections are more and more common in such venues.

Although these outcomes did not explicitly include happiness, they do support the contention that Internet activities can enhance the amount and quality of social relationships, which has been implicated in a number of studies as a strong and consistent predictor of happiness.

3   Research Overview

In this study we address the relationship between Internet use and happiness by re-examining the Internet paradox and the displacement-versus-stimulation hypothesis. We ask users about their overall amount of internet usage, and assess the relationship with happiness. We will also extend past research by exploring different types of internet usage through an Internet Usage Scale currently under development. In this way we can better explore the role of context in the relationship between Internet usage activities and happiness.

4   Questions

4.1   Internet Use Scale

How are the items of the Internet Use Scale related to one another and to what extent are these factors related to the five factors the scale was intended to measure?

4.2   Relationship Between Internet Use and Happiness

Are the Internet Use Scale factors related to happiness? If so, which factors and in what direction?

5   Research Method

5.1   Participants

Twenty-eight students enrolled in an undergraduate course in digital media at a small Midwestern technological research University served as the participants in this study.

5.2   Measures

Twenty-five statements were developed to represent five factors in Internet use, with five items representing each factor. The factors the items were intended to represent were: Time spent on the internet; Use of the Internet for Social Interaction; Use of the Internet for Affective Expression; Use of the Internet for Gaming; and Use of the Internet for Information Gathering.

In addition The Flourishing Scale (FS) [1], and the Satisfaction with Life Scale (SWLS) [2] were administered to represent happiness.

5.3 Procedure

Participants completed a survey on-line that consisted of the items from the IUS, FS, and SWLS. The items were presented in the form of a statements and participants responded with a number from 1–7 representing the degree of agreement.

6 Results

6.1 IUS Factor Analysis

In order to compare the relationship of the items of the IUS scale with the proposed/predicted factors a confirmatory factor analysis was carried out on all items. This was a Principal Components Analysis with a Varimax rotation with a five factor forced solution, to represent the five factors proposed. The items, proposed factors, computed factors, and primary loadings are presented in Table 1.

Table 1. Proposed and computed factors of the internet use scale

Proposed factor	Item	Computed factor				
		1	2	3	4	5
Affective Expression	I often post online "rants"				.74	
	Interacting socially online tends to make me angry					.62
	Interacting socially on the internet tends to calm me down	.57				
	I do not like people who vent their anger online in social forums				−.88	
	I feel better when I vent my anger online				.60	
Social interaction	I get a lot of social support from interacting with people online		.57			
	I tend to write positive and supportive comments when I interact online					.87
	I rarely use the internet to post everyday things like what I had for lunch, or pictures of my pets			.51		
	When I want to socialize, I'd rather interact face-to-face than online	−.73				
	I use the internet to connect with people			.73		
Gaming	I spend more time playing on-line games than I do on social media sites like Facebook		.84			
			−.51			

(Continued)

Table 1. (*Continued*)

Proposed factor	Item	Computed factor				
		1	2	3	4	5
	I participate in fantasy sports on the internet					
	I spend a lot of time playing on-line games		.91			
	I would rather play a game/sport that requires physical activity and skill than play an on-line game	−.74				
	I like to participate in off-line competitive games/sports	−.64				
Information Gathering	I often use the internet for finding facts				.53	
	I often use the internet for checking facts		.61			
	I'm skeptical of the accuracy of information I find on the internet			.57		
	When I don't know the answer to something, I immediately look it up online			.78		
	I check reviews online before I make any serious purchase			.59		
Time	I spend more time on line than off	.79				
	I spend a lot of my waking hours on the internet	.76				
	The internet often distracts me from healthy physical activity like exercise	.62				
	I believe it is rude for someone to check a mobile device (e.g. read a text message) when they are participating in a face-to-face conversation			.48		
	My on-line activity helps support my off-line activity		.68			

The scale was modified based on this factor analysis by reducing the factors to three (Time, Information Gathering, and Affective Expression). In addition some items were eliminated and some were expected to load on different factors than those initially predicted. A second Principal Components analysis with a Varimax rotation was computed with a forced three-factor solution based on the remaining three factors. The items, the remaining factors, and primary loadings are displayed in Table 2.

Table 2. Factor analysis of modified internet usage scale

Proposed factor	Item	Computed factor		
		AE	IG	T
Affective Expression (AE)	I often post online "rants"	−.83		
	I do not like people who vent their anger online in social forums	.80		
	I feel better when I vent my anger online	−.76		
Info Gathering (IG)	I check reviews online before I make any serious purchase		.71	
	I rarely use the internet to post everyday things like what I had for lunch, or pictures of my pets		.70	
	I'm skeptical of the accuracy of information I find on the internet		.62	
	When I don't know the answer to something, I immediately look it up online		.61	
Time (T)	I spend more time on line than off			.83
	I spend a lot of my waking hours on the internet			.80
	I would rather play a game/sport that requires physical activity and skill than play an on-line game			−.79
	When I want to socialize, I'd rather interact face-to-face than online			−.66
	The internet often distracts me from healthy physical activity like exercise			.62
	I like to participate in off-line competitive games/sports			−.60

6.2 Relationship Between Internet Usage and Happiness

In order to assess the relationship of the three internet usage factors and happiness, three factor scores were created by computing the mean of the items loading on a given factor (Table 2) with items subtracted or added depending on the direction of their loading (negative or positive). Scores for affective expression were reversed such that high scores represented more use of the Internet for affective expression. High scores on the time factor represented more time spent on the Internet and high scores on the Information Gathering factor represented more use of the Internet for Information Gathering Purposes. A zero-order Pearson correlation with two-tailed significance test was computed for each factor score with the happiness scale scores. These results are presented in Table 3.

Table 3. Correlation between factor scores and happiness

Happiness	Factor		
	Affective Expression	Info Gathering	Time
Flourishing	−.087	.469*	−.540**
SWLS	−.312	−.185	−.587**

*p < .05; **p < .01

7 Conclusions

Consistent with the original Internet paradox, and the displacement hypothesis, the total amount of time users reported spending on the Internet was strongly and negatively related to measures of happiness. The only specific Internet usage factor that was significantly related to happiness was the degree to which users reported carrying out information gathering activities, which was significantly related to Flourishing, but not the Satisfaction with Life Scale. Further, use of the Internet for affective expression was not significantly related to perceived happiness measures.

While these results are interesting as an exploratory study, including the development of an Internet Usage measure, the study has limitations, which can be addressed in future research. First, the sample size of 26 was quite small, resulting in weak statistical power. Second, the scale items will need to be further modified and categorized based on further psychometric analyses with larger sample sizes. Third, some important factors, such as social interaction on the Internet, could not be properly examined due to the lack of predicted relationship among scale items. More psychometrically sound items of important constructs, such as social interaction, will need to be developed for examination in future studies of the relationship between internet usage and happiness.

References

1. Diener, E., Wirtz, D., Tov, W., Kim-Prieto, C., Choi, D., Oishi, S., Biswas-Diener, R.: New measures of well-being: flourishing and positive and negative feelings. Soc. Indic. Res. **39**, 247–266 (2009)
2. Diener, E., Emmons, R.A., Larsen, R.J., Griffin, S.: The satisfaction with life scale. J. Pers. Assess. **49**, 71–75 (1985)
3. Diener, E.: Subjective well-being: the science of happiness and a proposal for a national index. Am. Psychol. **55**, 34–43 (2000)
4. Myers, D.G.: The funds, friends, and faith of happy people. Am. Psychol. **55**, 56–67 (2000)
5. Freedman, J.: Happy People: What Happiness IS, Who Has it, and Why?. Harcourt Brace Jovanovich, New York (1978)
6. Lyubomirsky, S.: Why are some people happier than others? The role of cognitive and motivational processes in well-being. Am. Psychol. **56**, 239–249 (2001)
7. Pavot, W., Diener, E., Fujita, F.: Extraversion and happiness. Personality Individ. Differ. **11**, 1299–1306 (1990)

8. Cummings, J., Butler, B., Kraut, R.: The quality of online social relationships. Commun. ACM **45**, 103–108 (2002)
9. Valkenburg, P.M., Peter, J.: Online communication and adolescent well-being: testing the stimulation versus the displacement hypothesis. J. Comput.-Mediated Commun. **12**, 1169–1182 (2007)
10. Hampton, K.N., Sessions-Goulet, L., Her E.J., Rainie, L.: Social isolation and new technology. Report of the Pew Internet and American Life Project (2009). pewinternet.org/2009/11/04/social-isolation-and-new-technology

Bringing E-commerce to Social Networks

Zhao Huang[(✉)] and Wang Yang Yu

Key Laboratory of Modern Teaching Technology,
Ministry of Education, Xi'an 710062, People's Republic of China
{zhaohuang,ywy191}@snnu.edu.cn

Abstract. Social commerce is where e-commerce meets social networks. Links between social network users are being leveraged to generate and propagate word-of mouth about a products, services and brands, creating new business opportunities, and more specifically, a new channel for online business. However, a close look at the academic and practitioner literature on e-commerce and social networks reveals a clear lack of consensus on social commerce concepts and implementation mechanisms. We argue that without such consensus, social commerce might not reach its full potential. Therefore this paper starts by providing an overview of social commerce research and practice in light of the wide attention it has drawn recently. We then propose a social commerce framework consisting of three key parts, namely implementors, enablers and activities. Using Facebook APIs and plugins, we design, develop and deploy a set of social commerce applications as proof-of-concept of our proposed framework.

Keywords: Social commerce · E-commerce · Social network · Viral marketing · Facebook API

1 Introduction

Nowadays people of all ages are using social media services including social networks such as Facebook, Twitter and LinkedIn to connect with their online communities and to generate and consume content. Businesses perceive this extensive and increasing use as an opportunity for new business applications [1] that fall within the realm of "social commerce". Generally speaking, social commerce is an Internet-based commercial application leveraging social media and Web 2.0 technologies which support social interaction and user generated content in order to assist consumers in their decision-making process for acquiring products and services within online marketplaces and communities [2]. In recent years, social commerce has proliferated not only because social media is popular, but because user participation, one of the core features of Web 2.0, has a significant impact on business [3]. Companies are moving beyond their corporate websites and taking an active part in social media because social media users participate in the marketing and promotion of their products and services.

Social commerce is an opportunity for businesses to leverage social media capabilities, specifically social ties (aka links) between users, in order to strengthen their strategies and achieve their goals. Rowan and Cheshire [4], for instance, adopted Facebook pages to implement social commerce for several of their brands, even though their

© Springer International Publishing Switzerland 2016
F.F.-H. Nah and C.-H. Tan (Eds.): HCIBGO 2016, Part I, LNCS 9751, pp. 46–60, 2016.
DOI: 10.1007/978-3-319-39396-4_5

products are mostly sold through online and offline retailers. They obviously have their corporate websites, various brands websites, and websites for individual product lines. Still, some Facebook pages dedicated to their products provide e-commerce functionalities for users to purchase those products, making Procter and Gamble one of the early adopters of social commerce.

Even though the aforementioned facts point to its rapid development, its nascent popularity, and the increasing attention dedicated to it, there is limited research that seriously examines the concept of social commerce, let alone its implementation [5]. As argued by Wang and Zhang [6], one of the distinct challenges of social commerce research is conceptualization, due to various points of view and positions and conceptual ambiguities including definitions and scopes. Existing academic research focuses on social shopping and regular e-commerce websites. Olbrich and Holsing [1] for example, analyze a social shopping community called Polyvore to study the effectiveness of social shopping features. Choi et al. [7] study e-commerce websites that offer rating, commenting and recommending functionalities in order to understand how people are influenced by social activities enabled by such functionalities.

Hence we believe it is important to clarify the concept of social commerce and identify mechanisms for its efficient and effective implementation. To this end, this paper explores social commerce by discussing and refining its various definitions, and by proposing a social commerce framework consisting of the following key elements: implementors, enablers, and activities. The paper also addresses social commerce implementation based on the proposed framework, using simple and freely available Web 2.0 technologies.

2   Social Commerce: Literature Review

The term "social commerce" refers to the delivery of e-commerce activities, services and transactions throughout social media environments [8], and according to Wigand and Benjamin [9] it consists of applying social media applications to shape business. Huang and Benyoucef [2], focusing on the user's perspective, give a more comprehensive definition where "social commerce" denotes a more social, creative and collaborative approach used in online marketplaces, supporting social interaction and user generated content in order to assist consumers in their decision-making process for acquiring products and services. Undoubtedly, social commerce involves multiple disciplines, including marketing, retailing, computer science, sociology and psychology, which contributed to the diversity of its definitions. Indeed, there are several conflicting characterizations of the concept in the literature. (1) Some researchers assert that social commerce is to sell products and services while others claim that it includes branding and marketing; (2) some regard social commerce as equivalent to social shopping whereas others differentiate between the two concepts; (3) some affirm that social commerce is to connect businesses to consumers (B2C) while others see social commerce as connecting consumers to consumers (C2C) or individuals to individuals, and (4) some claim social commerce to be a new phenomenon while others do not perceive it as new. We discuss these points of view below.

(1) **Social commerce for selling or marketing.** Social commerce is seen by Stephen and Toubia [10] as marketplaces where individual sellers can sell products by assorting them on personalized online shops, so they receive commissions on sold products. Leitner and Grechenig [11], who perceive social shopping and social commerce as the same thing, define social shopping as a unique e-commerce approach which offers a similar environment to social networks for consumers to collaborate and shop together. In contrast, Amblee and Bui [3] describe the characteristics of social commerce as facilitating the shopping experience and supporting social interactions by sharing the experience and aggregating consumer evaluations. In these two cases, social media and other technologies are devised to pursue marketing and communication rather than sales, although an increase in sales could be the ultimate goal. Such position is somewhat adopted by Constantinides and Fountain [5] who state that the basic differences between social media applications and previous internet applications is that the user, as an essential contributor, is a new marketing parameter instigating a migration of market power from products to consumers and from traditional mass media to new personalized ones. This highlights the importance of forming a relationship between the business and its customers. In other words, this is a way to build trust and relationships between organizations and customers in order to form loyalty. Based on the above discussion, it is clear that social commerce is not just limited to selling, but also includes marketing. Additionally, both selling and marketing are more affected by the power of users than the power of sellers, although sellers provide original content such as information, photos and videos of products, and set up events that users can participate in.

(2) **Social commerce and social shopping.** Some researchers see social shopping as equivalent to social commerce while others do not. But when social shopping is seen as equivalent to social commerce, the focus is usually on selling and buying rather than on marketing. For instance, as indicated by Kang and Park-Poaps [12], social shopping is a consumer behaviour involving consumers interacting with each other through online interpersonal communication in the process of shopping. Furthermore, Leitner and Grechenig [11] describe social shopping, which they also call social commerce, as a "conventional shopping platform with community driven functionalities", and the examples they provide are collaborative shopping networks such as ThisNext and Kaboodle as well as B2C social shopping websites such as Threadless and Zazzle. These websites are mostly known for shopping. On the other hand, characterizations that differentiate social commerce from social shopping include marketing and promotional activities undertaken by users who voluntarily share their shopping experiences. Well-known social shopping websites such as ThisNext and Kaboodle provide a bookmarking functionality, so users can share their bookmarks of items they discovered. Beisel [13] describes social commerce as creating places where people collaborate online, get advice from trusted individuals, find products/services and then purchase them, while describing social shopping as the act of sharing the experience of shopping with others. Although the main goal of social shopping is for users to gain shopping experiences for better purchasing decisions, merchants do use social shopping websites to

promote and sell their products. Providing shopping knowledge does not guarantee that users who saw the information will buy the items, but it increases product awareness. Furthermore, Wang and Zhang [6] state that social shopping is part of social commerce, and thus has a narrower scope than social commerce. In light of this, we argue that social commerce can include social shopping, whereas social shopping cannot include social commerce. In other words, social shopping is a subset of social commerce, and social commerce primarily signifies users' shopping and/or buying activities.

(3) **Social commerce connects business to consumers or consumers to consumers.** With regards to whether social commerce connects businesses to consumers or consumers to consumers, we believe that social commerce encompasses all aspects of both connections. But some researchers seem to make a distinction. For instance, in addition to differentiating social commerce from social shopping, Stephen and Toubia [10] claim that social shopping connects consumers invigorated by online word-of-mouth whereas social commerce connects sellers. Clearly, using social media for commercial purposes is not reserved for business organizations, but individuals can also use it - and they are in fact using it. Individual handicraftsmen sell their creations through websites like Etsy (http://www.etsy.com), known as a community based e-commerce website with a connection to social media. Wang and Zhang [6] argue that social commerce is a form of peer-to-peer communication, where users spread out a persuasive viral message by word-of-mouth through social networks to increase a company's brand recognition, product awareness and adoption. Gaulin [14] further support this view and indicate that that social commerce content is "crowdsourced" (a term referring to user-generated content) to the users; where the concept of "user" covers not only individuals, but also groups and communities. Finally, note that social commerce encompasses both online and offline business connections and does not necessarily mean that all business transactions must take place online. For example, Starbucks provided a coupon for a new coffee promotion event, which could be shared through social media, so anyone was able to print and bring it to an offline store to get the free coffee.

(4) **Social commerce is new or not.** With respect to whether social commerce is new or not, we note that the term "social commerce" itself is relatively new because it first appeared in 2005, but the concept is not [2]. When there was no fast transportation, markets were not just places for selling and buying but they were places for people to share information [15]. Even when there was no Internet, people still gathered information about products and services from testimonials and comments made by their family, friends or colleagues. Nowadays, a product catalogue on a social commerce website such as Kaboodle or ThisNext is filled up by individuals, and product information is delivered and propagated on social media through individuals' posting and sharing. Interestingly, as early as 1999, Amazon and Epinions had already adopted some of the basic social features, such as referral shopping, wish lists, email to friends, and sharing experiences and opinions [16]. Thus, even though social media is relatively new and is being used by consumers and businesses as a new communication channel, the fundamental notion that commerce gains power from individual users' sharing experiences is not new. It has just been

made faster, better, and broader through the use of social media. This is in line within a study by Wang and Zhang [6] who claim that social commerce reuses some of the traditional e-commerce strategies to bring social networks to the forefront to connect shoppers with one another or with products. Social commerce is not a new application or technology, but rather an evolution of e-commerce.

3   Social Commerce Framework

Based on the discussion in the previous section, we identified several characteristics of social commerce: e-commerce relying on social media and Web 2.0 technologies; not being limited to selling and buying but including management and operations, however mainly marketing; facilitating participative, contributive and collaborative activities by users through social media; and its activities can intensify the overall effects of specific business goals.

With this in mind, the concept of social commerce can be defined as e-commerce, in a broad sense, using the advantageous characteristics of Web 2.0 technologies such as participation, contribution and collaboration, which strengthen the effectiveness of commercial activities of users. We propose the following framework to highlight how we see this concept.

The framework (Fig. 1) illustrates social commerce's related entities and their inter-connections. First, there are two entities involved in social commerce: Enablers and Social Commerce Implementors. Enablers are social media users who are willing to participate in activities and contribute ideas, opinions and knowledge for use by other networked users. Enablers can also be customers who look for product information and possibly share their purchasing knowledge and experiences with others. Social Commerce Implementors, however, are operating bodies that implement social media or Web 2.0 technologies for the purpose of commercial activities such as advertising, promotion and selling. These Social Commerce Implementors are not limited to organ-izations, but also include individuals such as artists (e.g., musicians, photographers, movie stars, etc.), athletes and architects, who use social media to promote and/or sell their products and services.

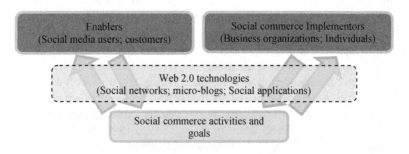

Fig. 1.   Social commerce framework

Social Commerce Implementors and Enablers are connected by social commerce activities and goals. Because Social Commerce Implementors leverage various Web 2.0

technologies which are well suited for their strategies or goals, these technologies allow Enablers to perform activities that support Implementors in achieving their strategies or goals. For example, a Social Commerce Implementor can utilize a blog to promote a product and to provide product information, then, through that blog, Enablers can propagate that information to their friends by sharing it within their social network. In other words, the original product information is provided by the Implementor through the blog and the Enablers who discover the product information participate in sharing that information (See Fig. 1). Most of all, in the participative activities of the Enablers, there should be a willingness or intention to take on roles that support certain business goals. Enablers can also be called "fans" in the Facebook terminology, since Facebook users become fans of certain brands once they click the "like" button on the brand pages. Although it is hard to regard users who click a "like" button as "real fans" of a brand, the action of clicking the "like" button signals the user's willingness to see postings by the brand. This is because by clicking the button, all shared postings from the brand will appear on that person's Facebook newsfeed.

Unlike traditional Web 1.0 ways of communication, in which organizations directly promoted or advertised their products and services through available media, such as corporate websites (where a user has to visit the corporate website to find product information), in a social commerce environment, Enablers discover product information anywhere and share it with their friends if they are interested in it. This means that product information is actually delivered by Enablers rather than by the organization itself, and that information can be exposed through the Enabler's newsfeed, where all people who are connected to him/her can see it.

Table 1 shows typical social commerce activities as identified from the literature. Liang and Turban [8] classify social commerce activities into four categories, namely "social media marketing", "enterprise management", "technology, support, integration" and "management and organization."

Table 1. Social commerce activities

Choi et al. [7]	Curty and Zhang [16]	Constantinides and Fountain [5]	Liang and Turban [8]

Awareness	Branding
	Content creation
		Informing new
		  opinion leaders
			Social ads/viral marketing:
			  recommendation/referral/
			  affiliate marketing/video
			  marketing

Consideration	Traffic generation
	Engagement
	Innovation/
	Ideation
	Lead generation
		Listening to customer's voice
		Personalized one-to-
		  one marketing
		Partnering with
		  talented amateurs
			Marketing research: ratings/
			  reviews
			Forum/
			discussion group/
			Social interaction

Conversion	Purchase decision	Providing personal- ized products	Direct selling

Loyalty	Loyalty/advocacy
	After sales service
		Interaction with
		  customers
			Social CRM, customer
			  service

This categorization broadly exemplifies activities related to commercial intentions and involvement through the use of social media. Choi et al. [7] list three purposes for using Web 2.0 technologies to achieve business goals: internal purposes, customer-related purposes and working with external partners/suppliers. These purposes are largely meant to increase speed, effectiveness, volume, and revenue; and to reduce cost and time. Constantinides and Fountain [5] list "reaching" and "informing" new online opinion leaders, "listening" to customers' voices, personalized one-to-one marketing and launching corporate blogs and podcasts as a channel of interaction with customers, partnering with talented amateurs and providing customers with personalized products. Curty and Zhang [16] list activities using social media, particularly for marketing; branding, content creation, traffic generation, engagement, innovation/ideation, lead generation, purchase decision, loyalty/advocacy, and after sales service.

Actually, the activities listed in Curty and Zhang [16] are categorized based on the so called Marketing Funnel which encompasses the following elements: Awareness, Consideration, Conversion and Loyalty. The Marketing Funnel was (and is still being) used to establish marketing strategies. In other words, the elements of the marketing funnel, namely awareness, consideration, conversion and loyalty can be seen as goals that Implementors strive to achieve. Hence, we classified the aforementioned social commerce activities based on the elements of the marketing funnel (see Table 1).

However, a new version of the marketing funnel dubbed the new customer lifecycle was proposed by Forrester research. It consists of the following four phases. Discover is the phase where a customer discovers brands, products or the need for products through positive word-of-mouth or other accessible media. Explore refers to a customer's journey of browsing, testing or trying a certain item to experience it until the purchasing decision is made. Buy includes not only purchasing but inventory look up, perceived actual value of the item, and the buying experience. Finally, Engage refers to the customer's activities after the purchase.

As Liang and Turban [8] points out, the traditional marketing funnel does not seem to reflect the customer's standpoint. In fact, it is written from an organization's point of view. In the new customer life cycle, customers discover, explore, buy and engage, whereas organizations endeavor to have customers discover in order to be aware of the brand and products, have them explore and be informed enough to consider the products, have them buy to be converted into actual buyers, and have them engage as loyal customers.

Consequently, with the new customer life cycle which stands for a customer's (i.e., Enabler's) perspective and the marketing funnel which represents an organization's (i.e., Implementor's) standpoints, achievable business goals from a social commerce implementation can be organized as shown in Fig. 2.

Enablers discover products or feel the need for them, and then explore to find detailed information about the products that satisfy their needs in order to make a good purchase decision. Then, Enablers buy the products and engage by sharing their shopping experiences with their community. Implementors utilize Web 2.0 technologies to have Enablers discover products and feel the need for products (to achieve the business goal of product awareness); have Enablers explore information provided by the Implementors (to achieve the business goal of consideration); have Enablers buy the products

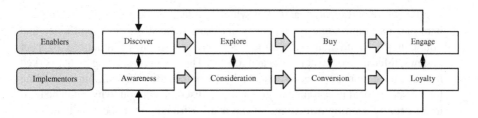

Fig. 2. Phases of business goal achievement from each entity's standpoint

(to achieve the business goal of conversion); and finally, have Enablers engage in contribution (to achieve the business goal of loyalty).

Note that from an Enabler's perspective, activities would directly reflect a key characteristic of Web 2.0 as described by O'Reilly [17], namely "Harnessing collective intelligence". This characteristic is leveraged for the sake of users' collaborative, participative and contributive activities which involve all phases of goal achievement from an enabler's standpoint (i.e., discover, explore, buy and engage) (see Fig. 2). For instance, a need for a product can be awakened by a contributive action such as a recommendation from a friend.

4   Using the Framework to Implement Social Commerce

In this section we show how the framework can be used to implement and deploy simple applications (apps) that realize a set of social commerce activities. We use Facebook APIs and plugins for they are easy to use and freely available, but we could have used those of Google plus, Twitter, or any other social network.

4.1   Implementation Process

We implemented four proof-of-concept social commerce apps, namely: a discount coupon sending app for viral marketing, a rating items app for market research, a limited time sales app for direct sales, and a photo contest event app for loyal customer contribution (see Table 2).

Table 2.   Apps to perform social commerce activities

Apps	Social commerce activities	Business goals
(1) Discount coupon sending	Viral marketing	Awareness
(2) Rating items	Market research	Consideration
(3) Limited time sales	Direct sales	Conversion
(4) Photo contest event	Loyal customer contribution	Loyalty

(1) **Discount coupon sending**: Social events held by Social Commerce Implementors are numerous, and decisions to select a certain type of event could depend on what Social Commerce Implementors want to pursue, yet the purpose is usually the same;

events require participative activities which will lead to the promotion of a certain item and its brand name by social media users themselves. Constantinides and Fountain [5] found that purchasing decisions are strongly influenced by peer reviews, referrals, social networks and forums. Thus, coupon sending by networked friends can be more persuasive than that by the brands themselves. Coupon sending for a discount deal is designed to give a user a discount coupon, which can be used in a store, by sending a message of the deal to friends on a social network and suggesting to them to purchase together, so that they can get a 50 per cent discount on any product in the store.

(2) **Rating items**: As discussed earlier, consumers no longer rely on traditional marketing media such as print or TV ads, but rather tend to believe their peers' opinions more. Consumer ratings and comments, for instance, represent one of the most important means for sellers to respond to consumers because they reflect what consumers really want and how they want it. Therefore, the insights gathered from ratings and comments can serve as input for product development and/or improvement. The rating app targets users who are regular visitors to a corporate social network page.

(3) **Limited time sale**: One classic marketing strategy to sell a product is to have customers feel that the product is somewhat special, by giving them limited access, limited offers, limited availability or time sensitive deals because when resources are scarce, people tend to put more value on them. In addition, the "Buy" stage in Forrester's new customer lifecycle considers the perceived actual value of items and the experience from the customer's standpoint. This app offers limited items for a limited time. When a user sees the limited offer through a newsfeed, he/she can reach to this app by linking from the newsfeed and purchasing items as long as the items are available by clicking the "Buy" button.

(4) **Photo contest event**: User generated photos of products are excellent marketing resources since users act as marketing personnel for the company. Besides, content created by users is more credible. As discussed earlier, such credibility strongly affects resources, rendering them more believable, persuasive and trustworthy to customers [3]. The photo contest event encourages users to post their photos and to allow people to vote on them, so that the photo with the highest vote will be rewarded. The activity requires users to draw more people such as friends, family members and colleagues who are willing to vote on their photos. Users discover the photo contest event information through a newsfeed or a message from their friends. Users can then visit the page through a link from the newsfeed or message and vote on the photo they like. They can also comment on and share any photo posted in the app.

We chose to develop the four social commerce apps using Facebook APIs and plugins (freely available and simple to use Web 2.0 technologies), which are known to connect to a large pool of potential audiences. For that we require a web server with SSL to store the apps and a database to store data. Since Facebook requires developers to provide an HTTPS web address of the app to protect user information, SSL is required on the client side. PHP SDK was installed within the client's web server. SDKs are available from Github (https://github.com), an external developers' community. The functionalities of each app are summarized in Table 3, each one divided into primary (i.e., core requirements for an app to fulfill its role) and supplementary (i.e., support an app but an app can fulfill its tasks without them) functions.

Table 3. Apps and their functionalities

Apps	Types of functionalities	Functionalities
Discount coupon sending	Primary functions	Sending a message/displaying the information/accepting an offer/ issuing a coupon
	Supplementary functions	Sharing, liking
Rating items	Primary functions	Listing, viewing, rating, commenting
	Supplementary functions	Sharing, liking
Limited time sales	Primary functions	Viewing of products, payment
	Supplementary functions	Sharing, liking
Photo contest	Primary functions	Listing, uploading, viewing, voting
	Supplementary functions	Sharing, commenting

Figure 3 shows the communication flow between a client, which contains the apps, and the server (in this case Facebook) where the apps live. When an app is displayed with data on Facebook, the app needs to call the corresponding Facebook APIs (e.g., when it accesses a user profile). Facebook then returns the data to the app, and using the data, it can show the complete results to the user.

Fig. 3. Social commerce app communication map

There are six steps in the development process of a social commerce app within the Facebook platform: (a) installing a SDK; (b) creating a Facebook Page; (c) creating an independent app on the client side; (d) registering the app on Facebook developer; (e) modification of the app if needed (some functions require a unique access token to perform, and in order to obtain it, the App ID and App Secret, which are created after the registration, are required); (f) adding the app on Facebook Page Tap. Once the app is completely settled as a Facebook app, in some cases, users' permission is required to access their profile when they first access the app.

The discount coupon sending app allows a user to send a message to a friend (or friends) by clicking the "Send a message to your friends" button as shown in Fig. 4(a). If the user is logged in (in most cases due to the fact that users would discover this while logged in to Facebook), by clicking the button "Send a message to your friends", a dialogue where a user can write a message and select recipients pops up. If it is the first time the user accesses the app, the user is asked to allow the app to obtain his/her data, particularly a list of friends. This allows the dialogue to suggest friends to the user, so that he/she can select them.

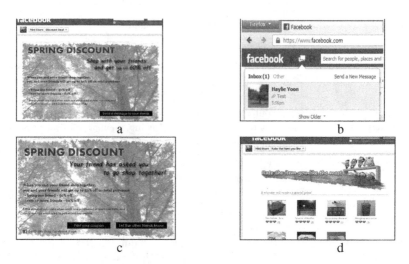

Fig. 4. (a) Discount coupon sending app, (b) Message on a recipient's side, (c) Recipient's view when the message is clicked, (d) Rating app

Checking the login status performs two tasks: verifying if the user is logged in and checking if the user already gave permission for the app to access a list of his/her friends. Once the message has been successfully sent, the discount coupon link becomes visible and the user can print the coupon.

At the same time, the recipient can see the arrival of the message (see Fig. 4(b)). The recipient is able to see the discount information shown in Fig. 4(c) by clicking the message in Fig. 4(b). The information in Fig. 4(c) includes two links: one to print out the coupon and one to send a message to other friends.

The rating app is shown in Fig. 4(d). A user can click items on the app and each item has its detailed view as in Fig. 5(a), which contains information on the item, rating, commenting, liking and sharing functions (see Fig. 5).

The Limited time sales app is shown in Fig. 5(b). As long as the app is accessible, anyone including non-Facebook users can purchase the items since the app shows product information and the payment method using PayPal. The use of the PayPal payment method is similar to that of Facebook plugins. By configuring a selected button with information regarding products (e.g., name, price, shipping cost, tax), the code of the payment button can be obtained, copied and pasted into any page (see Fig. 5(c)). The photo contest app is shown in Fig. 5(d). The functionalities used for this app are that users can upload photos with a simple message, and anyone can view and vote on the photos in each detailed view by clicking a photo.

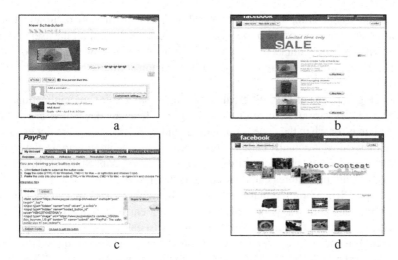

Fig. 5. (a) Rating view with rating, liking, sharing and commenting functions, (b) Limited time sales app, (c) PayPal Buy Now button setting, (d) Photo contest app

4.2 Discussion

In this subsection we briefly discuss our social commerce implementation process using Facebook's development platform (API and plugins). Our discussion is guided by the following attributes from the IEEE Standard for software quality [18]: resource economy, completeness, security, testability, software independence, and ease of learning.

In consideration of whether the implemented apps are capable of performing specific functions under stated conditions using appropriate amounts of resources, an app consists of two sections; client side where the actual app is stored and service provider's side where the app is embedded. This means that server side recourses are utilized and even if some functions are not available on the server side, they can be supported by developing them on the client side. Plugins can cause inefficiencies, for example, the photo contest app, created using the Like plugin, stores the Likes counts on the server side, so all count data has to be called from the server side, which makes the display very slow.

With regards to whether there are sufficient functions to satisfy developers, multiple SDKs including JavaScript, PHP, iOS and Android are supported by the Facebook platform, and various functions can be implemented with JavaScript alone. Additionally, there are different ways to call data. For instance, to fetch a user's name, one can query the data or use the Graph API with the GET function. But unlike Google based applications which are interoperable with various social networks, apps created for Facebook platform are not.

Regarding the question of whether the apps are secure enough to detect and prevent information leak, loss and illegal use, utilizing social networks is to tap into user demographic data which can be used for market research. To access demographic data, apps need to obtain permission to access user profiles. An access token, which stays valid for a couple of hours to allow certain activities on an app, is made available to developers. Once a user gives permission, the app can access user data such as list of friends, favourites, likes, education, work, and status. Although the permission request including information on what to access pops up when a user accesses the app, if the user does not pay attention and simply clicks to allow it, the user would not know what kind of information can be exposed to the app. It is the user's responsibility to be aware of what is being shared.

Debugging apps is not very different from that of other software applications, and Facebook provides various debugging tools. Problems faced by developers are that it is hard to find an error when the code is quite long, and sometimes, they are not even sure if the data they called is actually called or does exist. Using debugging tools, developers can test data availability and workability. In addition, JavaScript SDK which contains expanded checking procedures can be used for test purposes.

Do the apps depend on the platform they are being developed on? Is the platform stable? An app can perform without necessarily being embedded in a Facebook page, but to access the pool of information the app needs to call an API which requires an access token. But once it is registered as an app on the server side, it is required to contain an app ID and an app Secret to communicate with the Facebook platform. When a user is within Facebook, apps can be used seamlessly once the user gives the apps permission to access the user profile. Finally, the Facebook platform reflects one of the characteristics of Web 2.0: perpetual beta. Some functionalities, methods and objects have been changed, disappeared, or are being deprecated. Therefore, apps using those methods and objects have to be rewritten.

Is it easy to learn how to create apps? As for any other software project, the complexity of app development depends on the complexity of the required functionality. Apps that perform simple tasks, such as the photo contest and rating items created in this study are not as complicated as game software or e-commerce solutions. Therefore, programming expertise could be a less important factor. Thus, apps can be complicated depending on the required functionality to perform certain tasks. In contrast, the biggest hinder to develop apps using web APIs is how much time the developer has dealt with certain APIs and how well he/she knows about them. To create an app using what the service provider offers, the developer has to work in ways the provider allows him/her to do.

5 Conclusion

As a first step, this research sought to clearly establish the concept of social commerce. Hence various definitions from the literature and their different standpoints were analysed. We then proposed a social commerce framework consisting of Social Commerce Implementors, Enablers and their activities which rely on Web 2.0 technologies. Social commerce activities were categorized in the four stages of the marketing funnel, namely Awareness, Consideration, Conversion and Loyalty.

As a second step we addressed social commerce implementation and developed proof-of concept social commerce apps, each one performing specific social commerce activities. Four different social commerce apps were implemented, each one designed to achieve a goal that fits within a stage of the marketing funnel (a coupon sending app at the Awareness stage, a rating app at the Consideration stage, a limited time sale app at the Conversion stage, and a photo contest app at the Loyalty stage).

Overall, the contributions of this research consist of capturing the concept of social commerce in a framework aimed at supporting social commerce researchers and developers in understanding the core mechanisms of this concept. Further, social commerce implementation was investigated.

However, there are limitations to this research. First, although social media can be utilized in a B2B setting, this study has only dealt with B2C aspects. In addition, despite the fact that e-commerce includes not only selling and buying but also the whole spectrum of management of suppliers and customers, the proof-of-concept apps built for this study focused primarily on promotion and selling. Second, the apps were created using the Facebook platform and its APIs, even though there are other technologies available. Third, the apps were created as initially planned, but this research did not deal with how effectively they perform. The intended purpose was to understand what is available, how to utilize it, what the obstacles are, and how to overcome them through the app development process. Thus, social apps can be created with more sophistication and efficiency, and the evaluation of these apps to see how effectively they perform will be a next step, along with a thorough and formal evaluation of the development process itself.

Acknowledgments. This study was supported by a research grant funded by the "the Fundamental Research Funds for the Central Universities" (GK201503062) and "Support by Interdisciplinary Incubation Project of Learning Science of Shaanxi Normal University".

References

1. Olbrich, R., Holsing, C.: Modeling consumer purchasing behavior in social shopping communities with clickstream data. Int. J. Electron. Commer. **16**(2), 15–40 (2011)
2. Huang, Z., Benyoucef, M.: From e-commerce to social commerce: a close look at design features. Electron. Commer. Res. Appl. **12**(4), 246–259 (2013)
3. Amblee, N., Bui, T.: Harnessing the influence of social proof in online shopping: the effect of electronic word of mouth on sales of digital microproducts. Int. J. Electron. Commer. **16**(2), 91–144 (2011)
4. Rowan, D., Cheshire, T.: Commerce gets social: how social networks are driving what you buy. In: Wired, pp. 1–5 (2011)
5. Constantinides, E., Fountain, S.J.: Web 2.0: conceptual foundations and marketing issues. J. Direct Data Digital Mark. Pract. **9**(3), 231–244 (2008)
6. Wang, C., Zhang, P.: The evolution of social commerce: the people, management, technology, and information dimensions. Commun. Assoc. Inf. Syst. **31**, 1–23 (2012)
7. Choi, J., Lee, H.J., Kim, Y.C.: The influence of social presence on customer intention to reuse online recommender systems: the roles of personalization and product type. Int. J. Electron. Commer. **16**(1), 129–153 (2011)
8. Liang, T.P., Turban, E.: Introduction to the special issue social commerce: a research framework for social commerce. Int. J. Electron. Commer. **16**(2), 5–14 (2011)
9. Wigand, R. T., Benjamin, R. I.: Web 2.0 and beyound: implications for electronic commerce. In: The 10th International Conference on Electronic Commerce (2008)

10. Stephen, A.T., Toubia, O.: Driving value from social commerce networks. J. Mark. Res. **47**(2), 215–228 (2010)
11. Leitner, P., Grechenig, T.: Community driven commerce: design of an integrated framework for social shopping. In: Krishnamurthy S. (ed.), IADIS International Conference E-commerce, p. 4 (2007)
12. Kang, J., Park-Poaps, H.: Motivational antecedents of social shopping for fashion and its contribution to shopping satisfaction. Clothing Text. Res. J. **29**(4), 331–347 (2011)
13. Beisel, D.: The emerging field of social commerce and social shopping. In: Genuine VC (2006). Phil
14. Gaulin, P.: StoreAdore.com combines hyper localism, social shopping and crowd sourcing. In: Yahoo! Contributor Network (2008)
15. Locke, C.: Internet Apocalypso the Cluetrain Manifesto: The End of Business as Usual, pp. 1–38. Basic Books, A Memeber of the Perseus Books Group, Cambridge (2001)
16. Curty, R.G., Zhang, P.: Social commerce: looking back and forward. Proc. Am. Soc. Inf. Sci. Technol. **48**(1), 1–10 (2011)
17. Oreilly, T.: What is Web 2.0: design patterns and business models for the next generation of software. Commun. Strat. **1**, 17 (2007)
18. IEEE: IEEE Standard for a Software Quality Metrics Methodology (1993)

Evaluating Academic Answer Quality: A Pilot Study on ResearchGate Q&A

Lei Li[1,2(✉)], Daqing He[2], and Chengzhi Zhang[1]

[1] Department of Information Management, Nanjing University of Science and Technology, Nanjing, China
zhangcz@njust.edu.cn
[2] School of Information Sciences, University of Pittsburgh, Pittsburgh, USA
{lli,dah44}@pitt.edu

Abstract. Evaluating the quality of academic content on social media is a critical research topic for the further development of scholarly collaboration on the social web. This pilot study used the question/answer pairs of Library and Information Science (LIS) domain on ResearchGate to examine how scholars assess the quality of academic answers on the social web. This study aims to: (1) examine the aspects used by scholars in assessing the academic answer quality and identify the objective and subjective aspects; (2) future verify the existing of subjective aspects when judging the academic answers' quality by detecting the agreement of evaluation between different evaluators. Though concluding the evaluation criteria of the academic content quality from the related works, the authors identified nine aspects of the quality evaluation and mapped the participants' responds of the reasons for the answer quality judgment to the identified quality judgment framework. We found that aspects that related to the content of academic text and the users' beliefs and preferences are the two common used aspects to judge the academic answer quality, which indicated that not only the text itself, but also the evaluator's beliefs and preferences influence the quality judgment. Another finding is the agreement level between different evaluator's judgments is very low, compared with other non-academic text judgment agreement level.

Keywords: Academic answer quality · Academic social Q&A · Social media · ResearchGate

1 Introduction

As Web2.0 technology develops, user generated contents (UGCs) on social networking sites gradually become the main sources of internet information. How to quickly distinguish high quality UGCs to satisfied information consumers' needs becomes a critical research topic. Social Q&A platforms are one of the popular social networking sites to enable users to ask questions and provide plenty of answers. Over the past decade, we observed the growing popular of the social Q&A platforms. An increasing number of individuals are using social Q&A platforms to fulfil their information needs. Abundant available answers are obtained from different users with different quality. The information quality is greater reliance on the requirement of information consumers to make

© Springer International Publishing Switzerland 2016
F.F.-H. Nah and C.-H. Tan (Eds.): HCIBGO 2016, Part I, LNCS 9751, pp. 61–71, 2016.
DOI: 10.1007/978-3-319-39396-4_6

these quality judgments. Ferschke [1] clearly described "high quality information must be fit for use by information consumers in a particular context, meet a set of predefined specifications or requirements, and meet or exceed user expectations. Thus, high quality information provides a particular high value to the end user."

Meanwhile, academic social Q&A platforms, such as ResearchGate, change the traditional academic exchange channels and provide a new informal way that researchers interact and communicate with other researchers [2]. On social Q&A platforms, everyone can provide academic resources without any peer-reviewed. As a result, these are a mass of resources with diverse quality from high to low. This made it hard for scholars to find the high quality resources, which may result in decreasing the desire to join in the social Q&A platforms to acquire and share academic information [4]. So the information quality on the academic social networking sites is another necessary issue to be solved. We argue that the academic answers quality evaluation on academic social Q&A platforms is more critical than generic social Q&A platforms and different from the generic social Q&A evaluation [3]. Firstly, on the academic Q&A platforms, academic questions and answers are more professional and need much domain knowledge to understand. What's more, there may be no fixed high quality answers, especially for discussion seeking questions. Secondly, academic answers' quality maybe have multiple new facets which need other novel criteria to evaluate. Thirdly, for the academic social Q&A platforms, most information consumers are scholars with the different professional levels which are different from those information consumers who use generic Q&A sites [3].

In this study, we selected ResearchGate's Q&A platform as the academic social media platform for our study. ResearchGate[1] is one of the most well-known academic social networking sites (ASNSs) that support scholars' various activities, including asking and answering questions. We used the question/answer pairs of Library and Information Science (LIS) domain to examine how scholars assess the quality of academic answers on the social web. This study had two main motivations. One was to examine the aspects used by the evaluators to access the academic answer quality. Then based on the definition of each information quality evaluation aspects that acquired from the previous studies, we identified the objective and subjective aspects. The other was to detect the agreement of evaluation between different evaluators when judging the academic answers' quality, in order to further verify the exiting of the subjective aspects during the quality assessment. Moreover, by comparing the agreement level of the academic content assessment with the other kinds of content's evaluation agreement, this study can acquire the reliability of the evaluators' judgment on the academic content quality. The two research questions are:

- What aspects that evaluators use to access the quality of academic answers? What aspects are objective ones whose judgment are based on the information itself, and what aspects are subjective ones whose judgment are context sensitive?
- How about the agreement in evaluation the academic answers' quality between the evaluators?

---

[1] http://www.researchgate.net.

2   Related Works

Academic social media changed the way scholars obtain the academic resources [5]. There are rapidly growing existing works on academic social networking sites (ASNS), which include scholarly information exchange [6] and trustworthiness of scholarly information on ASNS [5, 7], motivation of joining in ASNS [8], and scholarship assessment through ASNS [9].

Although few existing work focused on the quality of academic answers, there are many related works on examining answer quality on generic social Q&A platforms. Some of the prior researches focused on finding the answers quality criteria, such as content, cognitive, utility, source, user relationship, socioemotional, to automatically evaluate the answer quality [10–12]. Some detected the relationship between the identified answer quality features and peer judgment quality [13–15]. Others were concentrated on comparing the quality of different Q&A platforms [16, 17].

For the assessment of academic content quality, judging research articles' quality was the earliest research topic. The previous works considered that "high quality journals are more likely to publish high quality research papers" [18]. So previous works focused on detecting the high quality journals, such as analyzing journals' citation, impact factor, and reputation [19, 20]. However, other researches argued that it is biased to judge an article's quality based on the journals' quality evaluation methods [21]. So the following studies were directly based on the papers' external features, such as using papers' authors reputation and citation [22, 23]. Then the following works researched into the papers' content and judgment context to explore the papers quality. Calvert and Zengzhi present the most accepted criteria given by the journal editors for evaluating research articles, including the new information or data, acceptable research design, level of scholarship, advancement of knowledge, theoretical soundness, appropriate methodology and analysis [24]. Clyde (2004) detected the influence of the evaluators' specialist knowledge on the research publications' quality judgment [43].

Until now there has few works about the quality of academic content on social media. Li et al. studied the effect of web-captured features and human-coded features on the peer-judged academic answers' quality in the ResearchGate Q&A platform [3]. There are some previous works undertook the relevance and credibility of academic information on the social media [27–33]. And some works had announced that "the relevance and credibility of information are aspects of the concept of information quality" [25, 26]. The studies about the relevance judgment of academic content focused on undertaking in detecting the criteria for evaluating the relevance of academic resources on the web [27–30]. For example, Park interviewed 11 graduate students to evaluate the bibliographic citations for the research proposal of masters' thesis. They identified three major categories, including internal context, external context, and problem context, of affecting relevance assessments [28]. The trustworthiness of the academic information on social media is another related topic. These studies concentrated on reporting what criteria influence users' judgment of the academic resources' trustworthiness [25, 31–33]. For instance, Watson examined the relevance and reliability criteria applied to information by 37 students for their research assignments or projects. The identified criteria was classified into two major categories, pre-access criteria and post-access criteria [25].

In summary, there are no clear evaluation frameworks for academic answer quality on ASNS. So this paper aims to review assessment criteria for answer quality among existing work and examine how users assessment of the academic answer quality.

3   Research Design

3.1   Study Platform: ResearchGate Q&A

ResearchGate (in short: RG) is one of the most well-known ASNS for scholars. RG has more than 5 million users by the end of 2014. Its mission is to connect scholars and make it easy for them to share and access scientific outputs, knowledge, and expertise. On RG, scholars can share their publications; connect with other scholars; view, download, and cite other scholars' publications; and ask academic questions and receive answers.

In this paper, we used RG's Q&A platform to investigate academic answer quality assessment. As Fig. 1 shown, scholar posts a question, and other researchers can view or follow this answer, provide answers to the question, or use "up vote" or "down vote" to rate the answers according to their criteria.

3.2   Dataset: Question/Answer Sets

In this study, we chose questions in the category of "Library Information Services[2]" on RG Q&A. This is because the authors are LIS researchers who knows the domain. These same question/answer pairs were used as dataset in other studies too [3, 6]. The dataset contains 38 questions with 413 corresponding answers. Following Choi, Kitzie and Shah classification [35], we focused on the discussion-seeking questions because they are relatively more complex than information seeking questions, and may require more quality assessment criteria. Therefore, we narrowed down to 17 discussion seeking questions with 188 answers.

We further cleaned the dataset by removing those answers that do not provide the information to answer the question. For example, some answers only contain askers' gratitude to the answerer, or some answerers declared that he had the same question or asking another related questions, answering another question that is put forward by other answerers. After we removed the above kinds of answers, we had 15 questions with 157 answers.

3.3   Research Method

Data Collecting. We recruited 15 LIS domain scholars, who have adequate domain knowledge to understand and assess the content of the answers. These participants are labeled as E_1–E_{15} in this paper. In order to obtain data for calculating the judgment agreement on the quality assessment, we divided the 15 questions with 157 answers into five groups by randomly assigning 157 question/answer pairs (QAPs) into the five

---

[2] https://www.researchgate.net/topic/library_information_services.

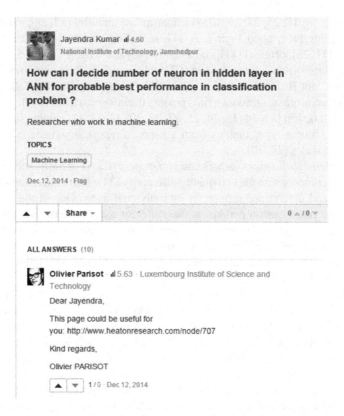

Fig. 1. A question/answering interface on RG (https://www.researchgate.net/post/ How_can_I_decide_number_of_neuron_in_hidden_layer_in_ANN_for_probable_best_perform ance_in_classification_problem)

groups. Through this way, we had three groups with 31 QAPs, and two groups with 32 QAPs. So, quality of each QAP in these five groups is judged by three participants. During our experiment, the participants used 11-point Likert scale (0 to 10) to judge the answer quality with 0 being the lowest quality and 10 as the highest. After finishing the judgments, the participants were asked to explain the criteria used for assessing the answer quality.

Data Analysis. Using the related work presented in Sect. 2 [11–41], we summarize the following nine groups of criteria for assessing academic answer quality:

- *Criteria related to the content of academic text (C1):* this group are the criteria that examine the characteristics of the text content and are objective. This group contains 23 criteria: recency [24, 27–32, 40], information type [25, 27, 28, 30, 32], theoretical soundness [24], appropriate methodology [24], appropriate analysis [24], readability [11, 14, 28–30, 32, 40, 41], balanced and objective point of view [25, 27, 30–32], the views of other scholars [32], scholarly [25, 27, 31, 32, 41], the scope [25, 28, 29, 31], depth [11, 14, 17, 25, 27–29, 40, 41], references [27, 30–32, 41], objective accuracy [2, 14, 17, 25, 27, 29, 40, 41], appropriate quantity [27, 28], examples [27, 30], discipline [30], good logic [32, 41], including contact information [32], no repetitive [11, 28], original [11], consistently [40] and writing style [15, 25, 27, 41].

- *Criteria related to the sources of text (C2):* this group are the criteria relating to the text source, not the information content. This group contains the following four criteria: clear information about who is posting the information and his/her goals [32], author's authorship [11, 14, 15, 24, 25, 27, 28, 30, 32, 33, 41], source status [25, 28, 29, 31–33], source type, such as from a paper, a report, a website, a forum, or a PowerPoint slides [28, 30].

- *Criteria related to the users' beliefs and preferences (C3):* For the quality evaluation, different users recognize the text quality differently [34]. There are criteria which are subjective and determined differently by individual users. One of the reasons that leads to this phenomenon perhaps is that different users have different beliefs and preferences. Several criteria related to users' beliefs and preferences were identified, which include topics satisfying the information needs [11, 27, 28, 30], subjective accuracy/validity/reasonableness/believable [14, 16, 29, 40, 41], interest/affectiveness [27–30, 41], and utility [11, 29, 41].

- *Criteria related to the users' previous experience and background (C4):* another reason is users' previous experience and background that results in the different quality judgment. In other words, users' domain knowledge influences the evaluation of some criteria, which are understandability [27, 29, 30, 40, 41], known source [29, 30, 32], language [30], content novelty [11, 29, 30, 40, 41], value of a citation [28], and source novelty [29].

- *Criteria related to the user's situation (C5):* different research situations maybe also affect users' quality judgment. This group contains the following five criteria: time constraints [29, 30], relationship with author [29], information consumers' purpose [28], stage of research [28, 30], and personal availability [28, 29].

- *Criteria related to the text as a physical entity (C6):* this group includes the criteria which are objective and external characteristics of the text, including obtainability [28–30], cost [16, 25, 29, 32], length [14, 15, 30, 41], and quickness [15, 41].

- *Criteria related to other information and sources (C7):* this group have the related criteria that associated with other information or sources to confirm the text quality. Consensus within the field [29, 32], external verification/tangibility/corroboration [17, 25, 29, 32, 41], cited by other authors in other documents [32] are the three identified criteria.

- *Criteria related to the texts' layouts and structure (C8):* this group criteria are proposed to how well the format of the text is organized. We recognized four criteria, which are having lists/diagrams/statistics/pictures [27, 32], fewer advertisements [32], working links [25, 32], structural clues (with topic sentences, first paragraph, and headings) [25].

- *Criteria related to the social environment (C9):* this group contains social and emotional value that express in the text, which include users' endorsement [14], polite [11], socioemotional value [40, 41], review [15], answerer's attitude/effort/experience [41], and humor [41] criteria.

Then, we classified the participants' responses according to the above mentioned nine groups of criteria using the directed content analysis method [36]. The classification results were discussed and confirmed among the authors to reach an agreement results.

We calculated the inter-rater agreement among the three sets of assessments on the QAPs using Fleiss' Kappa [39]. Fleiss' Kappa extended Cohen's kappa [38] by being able to handle more than two raters. Fleiss' kappa through a statistical measure assess the reliability of agreement between the raters when assigning categorical quality ratings to the answers [42]. Fleiss' kappa below 0 represent "poor agreement", 0.01 to 0.2 "slight agreement", 0.21 to 0.4 "fair agreement", 0.41 to 0.6 "moderate agreement", 0.61 to 0.8 "substantial agreement", 0.81 to 1.00 "almost perfect agreement" [37].

4   Results Analysis

4.1   Analysis of the Evaluation Criteria

The 15 participants who responded the reasons for answer quality judgment were mapped to the nine criteria groups. As shown in Table 1 of the results, the criteria related to the user's situation (C5), other information and sources (C7) were not supported by the participants. It is possible that the participants only gave the quality score to the answers under our requests rather than truly seeking such information. So they could not image the situation clearly and associated the quality of the answer with the other information or sources when judging the answer quality.

Table 1. Criteria of academic answer quality used by the participants

Criteria	Participants
C1	$E_1, E_2, E_3, E_4, E_5, E_6, E_7, E_9, E_{10}, E_{11}, E_{12}, E_{13}, E_{14}, E_{15}$
C2	E_1, E_6
C3	$E_2, E_3, E_4, E_5, E_6, E_7, E_{11}, E_{12}, E_{14}, E_{13}$
C4	E_2, E_{12}
C5	—
C6	E_5, E_6, E_8
C7	—
C8	E_{15}
C9	E_4, E_8

Table 1 also shows that the content of academic text (C1) is the most commonly used criterion to evaluate the quality. Fourteen of the 15 participants mentioned this group of criteria. Among the 14 participants, 6 participants used the objective accuracy criterion (E_4, E_6, E_9, E_{11}, E_{12} and E_{13}); for example, E_{12} mentioned that he needs objective evidences to support his quality evaluation. Meanwhile, completeness was also used by 6 among the 14 participants (E_2, E_3, E_7, E_9, E_{11} and E_{12}) to evaluate the quality. An example is E_7 said the answer should provide the enough arguments. Three of the 14 participants used the logic criterion (E_5, E_7 and E_{14}) to judge the quality; for example E_7 said the answer should express the idea logically. Readability and with references criteria are used by two participants, respectively (E_7 and E_{11} for readability and E_3 and E_9 for with references). There were one participant using having theoretical basis (E_2) and examples (E_3), respectively.

The second commonly selected group is related to the users' beliefs and preferences (C3). Ten of the 15 participants used this group criteria. Seven among the 10 participants used the relevance criterion (E_3, E_5, E_6, E_7, E_{12}, E_{13} and E_{14}), which means that the answer should provide relevant information to the question and meet the users' information need. An example mentioned by the E_{14} is that the answer should focus on the problem. E_2 and E_4 mentioned the criterion of reasonability, and E_{11} mentioned utility.

Criteria related to the text as a physical entity (C6) are used by three participants (E_5, E_6 and E_8). They mentioned such as accessibility, length and time constraint. The authorship was claimed by two participants (E_1 and E_6), which is the criterion related to the sources of text (C2). Two participants mentioned criteria related to the users' previous experience and background (C4) (E_2 and E_{12}), including creative and understandability. E_4 and E_8 claimed they value the socioemotional of the answer; for example, the answer should express with friendship, honest, and serious attitude. Criteria related to the texts' layouts and structure (C8) was selected by only one participant (E_{15}).

According to Table 1, we recognize that the criteria that are associated with the user, like users' preferences, background, and situation, were subjective quality evaluation criteria. Different user with different personality may perceive the quality differently. The other criteria are objective ones whose judgment are independent to different users' judgments and are based on the content of the information for evaluating the quality.

Table 2. Agreement results between three participants for each group

Question/answer sets	Fleiss' kappa
Group1	0.041
Group2	−0.049
Group3	−0.039
Group4	0.033
Group5	0.065

4.2 Agreements on Quality Judgments

As shown in Table 2, based on the Landis and Koch [37] interpreting, the agreement level on quality evaluation agreement among the three participants on each question/answer pair was low. The Fleiss' kappa of the five parts of data sets are all well below slight agreement (<0.2). The results gave us the indication that academic answer quality is a highly subjective concept. Based on results in Sect. 4.1, we known that different participants used different criteria to judge the quality, and 10 out of 15 participants used criteria that are related to their own preferences, background, and situations. This is the reason why the agreement of evaluating academic answer quality stay at very low agreement level. This result is somewhat consistent with a study of detecting the Wikipedia articles' quality evaluation, which reported their agreement value being between 0.06 and 0.16 [34]. This indicates that academic text quality judgment is probably more difficult than for that on Wikipedia articles.

5 Discussion and Conclusions

In this study, we used the LIS domain question/answer sets from ResearchGate to detect the criteria that evaluators use to evaluate the academic answer quality. Then, we mapped the participants' responds to the quality judgment framework. We found that the content of academic text and the users' beliefs and preferences are the two common used criteria to judge academic answer quality. Meanwhile, based on the previous works' definition, we identified the subjective criteria, which are dependent to different users, and objective criteria, which are only related to the content of the text. This investigation indicates that not only the text itself, but also the users' beliefs and preferences can influence the quality judgment. So it is hard to achieve high agreement on text quality based on different users' judgments. Especially for academic text, which are more complicated than generic text, it is even more difficult to get the high level agreement. This phenomena indicated that academic content quality evaluation cannot be simply based on a few users' judgments, because they cannot reach the acceptable agreement level.

The major contribution of this study is that we identified that the evaluation of the academic answer quality contains both objective and subjective criteria. The objective criteria include readability, depth, and recency, and automatic methods can be used to evaluate the quality from these criteria. Meanwhile, the subjective criteria should be judged based on different users' background and requirement. For example, the more expertise a user has on a particular domain, the higher chance that the user likes the professional content, whereas, the less knowledge a user has on a domain, the more likely the user would like to read some easy readable domain related text.

This is a pilot study regarding the evaluation of academic answer quality. A limitation of our study is that we just detected the one kind of academic text, ResearchGate academic answers on LIS domain. We plan to expand our study to other academic sources in different domains. More specifically, we hope to detect what criteria that belong to the nine criteria groups we identified are more important for scholars to judgment the academic content quality. This helps to set up a general quality evaluation framework for academic information on social media. Such framework would combine the subjective and objective criteria.

Acknowledgments. This work is supported by the Major Projects of National Social Science Fund (No. 13&ZD174), the National Social Science Fund Project (No. 14BTQ033).

References

1. Ferschke, O.: The quality of content in open online collaboration platforms. Dissertation (2014)
2. Thelwall, M., Kousha, K.: Academia.edu: social network or academic network? J. Assoc. Inf. Sci. Technol. **65**(4), 721–731 (2014)

3. Li, L., He, D., Jeng, W., Goodwin, S., Zhang, C.: Answer quality characteristics and prediction on an academic Q&A site: a case study on ResearchGate. In: Proceedings of the 24th International Conference on World Wide Web Companion, pp. 1453–1458. International World Wide Web Conferences Steering Committee, May 2015

4. Cheng, R., Vassileva, J.: Design and evaluation of an adaptive incentive mechanism for sustained educational online communities. User Model. User-Adap. Interact. **16**(3–4), 321–348 (2006)

5. Tenopir, C., Levine, K., Allard, S., Christian, L., Volentine, R., Boehm, R., Watkinson, A.: Trustworthiness and authority of scholarly information in a digital age: results of an international questionnaire. J. Assoc. Inf. Sci. Technol. (2015)

6. Jeng, W., DesAutels, S., He, D., Li, L.: Information exchange on an academic social networking site: a multi-discipline comparison on ResearchGate Q&A (2015). arXiv preprint arXiv:1511.03597

7. Watkinson, A., Nicholas, D., Thornley, C., Herman, E., Jamali, H.R., Volentine, R., Tenopir, C.: Changes in the digital scholarly environment and issues of trust: an exploratory, qualitative analysis. Inf. Process. Manag. **45**, 375–381 (2015)

8. Jeng, W., He, D., Jiang, J.: User participation in an academic social networking service: a survey of open group users on Mendeley. J. Assoc. Inf. Sci. Technol. **66**(5), 890–904 (2015)

9. Thelwall, M., Kousha, K.: ResearchGate: disseminating, communicating, and measuring scholarship? J. Assoc. Inf. Sci. Technol. **66**(5), 876–889 (2015)

10. Agichtein, E., Castillo, C., Donato, D., Gionis, A., Mishne, G.: Finding high-quality content in social media. In: Proceedings of the 2008 International Conference on Web Search and Data Mining, pp. 183–194. ACM, February 2008

11. Shah, C., Pomerantz, J.: Evaluating and predicting answer quality in community QA. In: Proceedings of the 33rd International ACM SIGIR Conference on Research and Development in Information Retrieval, pp. 411–418. ACM, July 2010

12. Liu, Y., Bian, J., Agichtein, E.: Predicting information seeker satisfaction in community question answering. In: Proceedings of the 31st Annual International ACM SIGIR Conference on Research and Development in Information Retrieval, pp. 483–490. ACM, July 2008

13. Blooma, M.J., Hoe-Lian Goh, D., Yeow-Kuan Chua, A.: Predictors of high-quality answers. Online Inf. Rev. **36**(3), 383–400 (2012)

14. John, B.M., Chua, A.Y.K., Goh, D.H.L.: What makes a high-quality user-generated answer? Internet Comput. IEEE **15**(1), 66–71 (2011)

15. Fu, H., Wu, S., Oh, S.: Evaluating answer quality across knowledge domains: using textual and non-textual features in social Q&A. In: Proceedings of the 78th ASIS&T Annual Meeting: Information Science with Impact: Research in and for the Community, p. 88. American Society for Information Science, November 2015

16. Harper, F.M., Raban, D., Rafaeli, S., Konstan, J.A.: Predictors of answer quality in online Q&A sites. In: Proceedings of the SIGCHI Conference on Human Factors in Computing Systems, pp. 865–874, April 2008

17. Fichman, P.: A comparative assessment of answer quality on four question answering sites. J. Inf. Sci. **37**(5), 476–486 (2011)

18. Lee, K.P., Schotland, M., Bacchetti, P., Bero, L.A.: Association of journal quality indicators with methodological quality of clinical research articles. J. Am. Med. Assoc. **287**(21), 2805–2808 (2002)

19. Blake, V.L.P.: The perceived prestige of professional journals, 1995: a replication of the Kohl-Davis study. Educ. Inf. **14**, 157–179 (1996)

20. Opthof, T.: Sense and nonsense about the impact factor. Cardiovasc. Res. **33**, 1–7 (1997)

21. Seglen, P.O.: Why the impact factor of journals should not be used for evaluating research. Br. Med. J. **314**, 498–502 (1997)
22. Ugolini, D., Parodi, S., Santi, L.: Analysis of publication quality in a cancer research institute. Scientometrics **38**(2), 265–274 (1997)
23. Mukherjee, B.: Evaluating e-contents beyond impact factor-a pilot study selected open access journals in library and information science. J. Electron. Publishing **10**(2) (2007)
24. Calvert, P.J., Zengzhi, S.: Quality versus quantity: contradictions in LIS journal publishing in China. Libr. Manag. **22**(4/5), 205–211 (2001)
25. Watson, C.: An exploratory study of secondary students' judgments of the relevance and reliability of information. J. Assoc. Inf. Sci. Technol. **65**(7), 1385–1408 (2014)
26. Rieh, S.Y., Danielson, D.R.: Credibility: a multidisciplinary framework. Annu. Rev. Inf. Sci. Technol. **41**(1), 307–364 (2007)
27. Cool, C., Belkin, N., Frieder, O., Kantor, P.: Characteristics of text affecting relevance judgments. In: National Online Meeting. Learned Information (EUROPE) LTD, vol. 14, p. 77, August 1993
28. Park, T.K.: The nature of relevance in information retrieval: an empirical study. Libr. Q. **63**, 318–351 (1993)
29. Barry, C.L.: User-defined relevance criteria: an exploratory study. JASIS **45**(3), 149–159 (1994)
30. Vakkari, P., Hakala, N.: Changes in relevance criteria and problem stages in task performance. J. Documentation **56**(5), 540–562 (2000)
31. Currie, L., Devlin, F., Emde, J., Graves, K.: Undergraduate search strategies and evaluation criteria: searching for credible sources. New Libr. World **111**(3/4), 113–124 (2010)
32. Liu, Z.: Perceptions of credibility of scholarly information on the web. Inf. Process. Manag. **40**(6), 1027–1038 (2004)
33. Rieh, S.Y.: Judgment of information quality and cognitive authority in the Web. J. Am. Soc. Inf. Sci. Technol. **53**(2), 145–161 (2002)
34. Arazy, O., Kopak, R.: On the measurability of information quality. J. Am. Soc. Inf. Sci. Technol. **62**(1), 89–99 (2011)
35. Choi, E., Kitzie, V., Shah, C.: Developing a typology of online Q&A models and recommending the right model for each question type. Proc. Am. Soc. Inf. Sci. Technol. **49**(1), 1–4 (2012)
36. Krippendorff, K.: Content Analysis: An Introduction to Its Methodology. Sage, Thousand Oaks (2012)
37. Landis, J.R., Koch, G.G.: The measurement of observer agreement for categorical data. Biometrics **33**, 159–174 (1977)
38. Cohen, J.: A coefficient for agreement for nominal scales. Educ. Psychol. Measur. **20**, 37–46 (1960)
39. Fleiss, J.L., Cohen, J.: The equivalence of weighted Kappa and the intraclass correlation coefficient as measures of reliability. Educ. Psychol. Measur. **33**, 613–619 (1973)
40. Chua, A.Y., Banerjee, S.: So fast so good: an analysis of answer quality and answer speed in community question-answering sites. J. Am. Soc. Inf. Sci. Technol. **64**(10), 2058–2068 (2013)
41. Kim, S., Oh, S.: Users' relevance criteria for evaluating answers in a social Q&A site. J. Am. Soc. Inf. Sci. Technol. **60**(4), 716–727 (2009)
42. Fleiss, J.L.: Measuring nominal scale agreement among many raters. Psychol. Bull. **76**(5), 378 (1971)
43. Clyde, L.A.: Evaluating the quality of research publications: a pilot study of school librarianship. J. Am. Soc. Inf. Sci. Technol. **55**(13), 1119–1130 (2004)

From Mumbai to Paris: Experiencing Disasters Across Social Media

Liza Potts[1]([X]) and Kristen Mapes[2]

[1] WIDE Research Center, Michigan State University, East Lansing, MI, USA
lpotts@msu.edu
[2] College of Arts and Letters, Michigan State University, East Lansing, MI, USA
kmapes@msu.edu

Abstract. This paper describes the use of social media during times of disaster. The Mumbai Attacks 2008 and the Paris Attacks of 2015 are used as examples of how data is validated into information and redistributed as community knowledge. Examining the tweets, Google tools, Vines, and postings of participants during these events, this paper argues for creating social web systems that can allow for participation and can help people locate relevant content.

Keywords: Social media · Disaster response · Terrorism · Twitter · Vine · Youtube · Paris attacks · Mumbai attacks · Actor-network theory · User experience

1 Introduction

During times of disasters, social media has become a dynamic center of activity. Across digital spaces, people work to connect each other with information about the event. Whether it is about missing persons, bombing locations, or memorials, people reach out to share and understand what they are experiencing across time and space. We are now awash in an array of social media systems, have increased access to technology, and are becoming a more digitally literate society.

Often, the experiences of trying to share, validate, and distribute information are disrupted by the systems we create. From locating the missing to validating content across sites such as reddit, YouTube, Twitter, Vine, and Facebook, people have an urgent need to connect and understand their situation and each other. In order to devise better solutions for these emergencies, we need to consider extreme use cases when designing user experiences within digital spaces.

This research builds upon findings from usability tests and ethnographic research from the past 10 years [1], including work examining the Indian Ocean earthquake and subsequent tsunamis [2], the London bombings [3], Hurricane Katrina [3], the Christchurch earthquake [4], and the Boston Marathon bombings [5]. In this paper specifically, we will compare the Mumbai attacks of 2008 to the Paris attacks of 2015, two terrorist events that share certain attributes across physical and digital spaces. Using a framework for understanding experience architectures based on actor-network theory and information studies, this paper examines these two events and presents research findings.

© Springer International Publishing Switzerland 2016
F.F.-H. Nah and C.-H. Tan (Eds.): HCIBGO 2016, Part I, LNCS 9751, pp. 72–81, 2016.
DOI: 10.1007/978-3-319-39396-4_7

2   Brief Literature on Understanding Data, Information, and Knowledge in Relation to Actor Network Theory

Across social media, people are able to upload images, update statuses, tag content, check-in to locations, and use other features to connect with others. In doing so, they are able to declare associations, identify with different social groups, and assign status to themselves and their communities. They – people, places, things – are all actors within various networks that work together across these systems.

For this study of social media use during times of disaster, our team has used actor-network theory to understand the communication networks and theory from information science to examine how people locate data, verify information, and distribute knowledge across these networks. Coupled together, this framework creates a method for understanding how participatory networks and technologies can help people cooperate during times of disaster.

A Brief Look at Actor-Network Theory. Actor-network theory (ANT) originated in the field of science and technologies studies as a way to talk about the interactions between and across people and technology. This theory began in the work of Latour [6], with later additions from Law [7], Callon [8], and Mol and Law [9]. ANT suggests that all participants, whether human or nonhuman, have equal agency to affect any given situation; my work here gives priority to human actors, while encouraging researchers and practitioners to look at how these moments are contextualized for people by space, time, and technology. Referred to as "actors," these participants can be people or technologies. During an event, these actors come together to form temporary, creating assemblages of relations and forming a collective, referred to as an "actant" [6]. An actant is a network comprising any actors — mobile devices, tweets, pins, people, and so on — that have the ability to act and do act within the network. Examining these actors and their networks provides a broader understanding of the people, groups, governments, organizations, technologies, and places, — the nouns — to researchers and practitioners [1].

For the purposes of this paper, an "actor" refers to any active participant in the network. Actors may include people, organizations, events, and technologies (e.g. devices, websites, apps) – an array of nouns. Actors join together in a network to accomplish certain tasks. This network of interconnected participants is a device for information coordination and flow. The Internet exemplifies flexibility in a distributed network: it is without hierarchy or predetermined routes between nodes, and it has solidly symmetrical nodes [10]. Networks of this nature therefore have the flexibility to come together and disband later. The social web provides such networks with systems for the coordination and dissemination of information.

Data → Information → Knowledge. Researchers and practitioners often hold strong opinions about what constitutes knowledge. In order to better understand knowledge creation, our team uses the concepts of data, information, and knowledge to see how people transform these ideas. These concepts are based in the work of industry practitioner Morville [11], systems analyst Kock [12], and internet studies scholar Weinberger

[13]. In our application, we take a more pragmatic approach. Our work is to pinpoint how content moves through these three stages, while also understanding the context in which this activity is taking place.

As addressed in our earlier research work, these three stages are described as follows:

1. The initial form of content is data. Data can appear in networks as words, phrases, images, symbols, and so on. A simple example of data is a Twitter stream. Without any context, a Twitter stream is just data: links, text, usernames, and hashtags.
2. Information is the second phase of content. Information is validated data, and validation can come in several forms. For instance, participants can connect two pieces of data, such as an image and a name, to pinpoint a person's identity. Participants validating data created richer, useful, and contextualized content.
3. Knowledge is the final stage of content. Knowledge is information that is shared within the network. It takes a form that allows for repurposing and distribution [1].

In considering these stages, it is important to see them as porous, rather than rigid. It is not always as simple as pinpointing each stage. In the case of international disasters, this inability to pinpoint these moments can be attributed to issues of translation and localization – in other words, understanding the cultures and contexts. In the examples below, we illustrate how participants push knowledge through these networks, moving through these three stages by leveraging their networks and deploying various social web tools.

3   Background on the Mumbai Attacks

From 26 to 29 November 2008, terrorist attacks in Mumbai, India resulted in 166 civilian deaths and at least 304 injuries [14]. At least 12 locations were affected by terrorism, including numerous transportation systems and tourism sites. Western journalists focused the majority of attention on the explosions and gunfire at the Taj Mahal Palace hotel and the Nariman House. Throughout this multiday event, many volunteers online and the mainstream media performed the challenging and daunting knowledge work of locating and validating information from eyewitnesses.

Countless social web participants worked to mobilize, locating data, verifying information, and distributing knowledge across the globe. From the use of Google Docs and Twitter to the numerous images uploaded to Flickr, Mumbai was a major tipping point for online participation in the wake of a disaster. This event began a new era for the social web, one where participation spanned multiple systems, where people were organized and knowledgeable in their own culture and systems of use.

Participants developed connections across systems in order to find and share information related to the attacks. At the same time, they encountered many obstacles and challenges as they attempted to exchange information about the attacks. They pushed information from blogs to spreadsheets, and tried to flush out misinformation on Twitter through hashtags. None of these systems were connected in ways that would have made their jobs of sharing information easier.

One major example of how this occurred is the use of Google tools. Specifically, Dina Mehta and others used Google Sheets to collect data, validate it as information, and share it as knowledge with their community. Gaining access to a faxed list of the injured and killed in hospital because of these attacks, they shared this data with their network through their blogs and on Twitter. They were able to recruit participants to hand type the content of the fax into a Google Sheet that was shared across the international network. People could then validate the content—who was killed, injured, or otherwise missing—and then repurpose this content as knowledge that they could share with the friends and relatives of those affected. In this way, the actors in this network—people, Google Sheets, Google Docs (now called Drive), Twitter, Blogs—were able to guide this content through these three stages of data, information, and knowledge through their participation in the network.

In describing this work and the group of participants who helped her, Mehta stated:

> [T]he "we" I speak of is not an organization but a loosely joined community. We are bonded, and I truly believe that in the face of utter horror, wherever it might occur, we have a strong pillar in this emotional connection we feel as equal human beings and not in our narrow identities prescribed by nationality or religion or race or gender. This is an evolving revolution sparked by how people are using social tools on the Web [15].

Mumbai was a pivotal moment for online participation during times of disaster. Text-based systems such as Twitter and Google Docs paired with Flickr's image uploading service to create a new era in the social web, one focused on linking and working across systems. Systems developers cannot ignore this new mode of use for the social web. In order to meet the needs of the new social knowledge workers, the industry and the field must think beyond their own single serving interfaces, systems, documents, and silos.

4 Background on the Paris Attacks

On the night of 13 November 2015, a series of terrorist attacks occurred across Paris, France. Resulting in 130 [16] deaths and hundreds of injuries, these planned attacks caused chaos throughout the city. From explosions outside the football stadium to gunfire at restaurants and bars, suicide bombers left the city in panic and caused major spikes in social media usage. The Bataclan concert hall was the site of shootings and explosions where many of the deaths and injuries occurred. Videos of these shootings were replayed across digital spaces, showing the band's reaction as the shootings began and showing the injured escaping through alleyways.

Within digital spaces such as Twitter, reddit, Vine, YouTube, and Facebook, participants raced to locate, validate, and share knowledge. Traversing among these systems, participants had an easier time of sharing what they found, but much of this information sharing was lost in a deluge of messages imparting sadness, prayer, and support. Finding and validating knowledge during such chaos is a key user aim for digital participants, yet we have not developed systems to improve these user experiences in times of disaster.

There are many compelling examples of compelling social media experiences from this disaster, from trying to locate the missing on Twitter to looping Vines showing scenes of horror outside the Bataclan, to the many instances of using Instagram to share photos and videos of scenes around the city. Characteristic of this new genre, great confusion at the scene of the attacks results from people's attempts to understand what (if anything) was happening, where it was happening, and who was affected.

Locating information across systems, participants began to piece together the event. From the original Vine that recorded explosions outside of the football stadium [17] that has more than 379,000,000 loops at this writing and was cross-posted to Twitter, to the eventual missing persons posts on Twitter [18], participants worked to understand what was happening. There were Vines and re-Vines of footage of both the start of the shootings as well as people escaping the Bataclan nightclub, where the majority of victims were killed. Finding the original Vine was difficult, as it was reposted relentlessly by other participants.

Across these systems, hashtag usage did not seem to normalize at first as is often the case in disasters [4], with #Paris #Parisattacks #Bataclan and others in use. During the early hours of the event, and among the chaos, the international participation across social media, the flood of reposted content, and the lack of stable hashtags, there was great difficulties in locating data and validating information.

5   Similar Issues Remain

In this section, we discuss the issues that remain over time. Social media participants have increased access to technology, along with increased literacy and skills for working across a multitude of apps and services. What this has led to is a lot of content – posts, tags, tweets, images, etc. Considering the growth of social media and the unrelenting constant that is terrorism and natural disasters, it is imperative that we create systems that allow data to flow, information to be validated, and knowledge to be shared.

Looking specifically at recent research from the Pew Research Center [19] in Fig. 1, it is obvious that social media is a growth area: Facebook reported 890 million active daily users in 2014, and Twitter reported 320 million monthly active users in 2015 [20, 21]. We need to consider these issues in the context of larger concerns for the future of digital technology and human computer interaction.

5.1   Problems Locating Relevant Data

Locating information may have been easier during the time of the Mumbai Attacks because the pool of users was smaller in 2008 than they were during the time of the Paris Attacks. In January 2009, there were an average of 2 million tweets per day, a number that grew to 200 million tweets per day by June 2011 [22]. The genre of how to respond to terrorist events has also evolved. We can expect to see a show of concern, in this instance using hashtags such as #prayforparis. There are also retweets, reposts, and a general recycling of content. These movements can clog the network, creating an echo chamber in which original content (data) cannot be located or verified (information) because the reposted content, and thus original, validated material cannot circulate the network as knowledge.

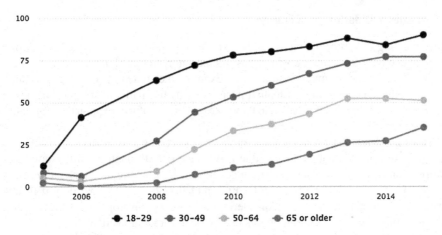

Fig. 1. Social networking site use as percentage among all American adults by age group, 2005–2015 (no data available for 2007) [19] (Color figure online)

An example of such use of Twitter during the Paris Attacks can be shown in Fig. 2. With millions of tweets being sent in the days after the attacks, locating relevant data can prove extremely problematic. How can we find useful, original content?

Language	Frequency
English	2,604,775
French	942,184
Spanish	257,522
Portuguese	135,366
Arabic	101,566
Japanese	85,548
Italian	73,973
Turkish	73,274
Indonesian	50,622
German	45,740

(Data: NYU Social Media and Political Participation (SMaPP) Lab; Figure: Alexandra Siegel)

Fig. 2. Top languages used in the 4 million tweets sent following the Paris attacks, using data from NYU Social Media and Political Participation (SMaPP) [23]

5.2   Issues Validating Information

After locating this information, it can be extremely difficult to validate it. Pinpointing original content often comes down to trusting the actors involved in the network. There are many questions we may consider as we examine the content. Is this account established? Is this content in line with other posts made by this participant? Does the poster make any claims to the data itself – do they take ownership of it or explain the originality of the content?

In an age where there term "Photoshopping" has become a verb, trusting content can become even more arduous. Being able to validate data through multiple sources of information is important. During extreme events such as natural disasters and terrorist attacks, we can use data such as geolocation metadata from posts, but only if people have turned on this information. Considering how often people opt out of these geolocation features, we cannot count on this data to be accurate or available.

5.3   Roadblocks for Circulating Knowledge

Major roadblocks for circulating knowledge are the systems themselves. Due to growth in social media use, increases in reposting original content, and posts in the #prayfor style, much of the original content can be lost. Recirculating validated content as knowledge, rather than simply reposting, can be a challenge.

From the Mumbai Attacks and the Christ Church earthquake, we have evidence showing that hashtags can be used advantageously to share information [4]. However, the participants during these events were in a much smaller community of people than those participating during the Paris Attacks, which drew a large, international set of users on Twitter [23].

One answer is in the ways that Twitter's new Moments feature operates, collecting and sharing posts that they deem relevant and useful. Their curated missing persons moment from the Paris Attacks is still posted as of this writing [24]. Such historical knowledge repository work is important to future generations of users of these systems and the histories, the stories, we leave behind.

And of course, as academic researchers—we need to be able to have archives for this knowledge. Many, many of the tweets, YouTube videos, Vines, and Instagram content are gone. They have been taken down by their content owners or by the systems themselves. How might we preserve this content for future generations, historians, and ourselves?

6   New Opportunities for Engagement and Knowledge Sharing

As we can tell from the issues discussed above, there are several opportunities available to us as researchers and practitioners. In this section, we discuss the ways in which we ought to improve the user experience of digital spaces and areas that need our research attention.

There has been a dramatic shift between "use" and "participation" in the popular use of social web tools, such as Twitter, Instagram, Facebook, Pinterest, Flickr, Snapchat,

Vine, and Wikipedia. "Use" is scaffolded by robust user-centered design theories and methods, while "participation" is pushing forward new ideas, theories, and techniques for best practices in researching, building, and supporting sociotechnical systems. In the past, experiences confined users to a set of interfaces contained within systems; now, social web participants consider a wide array of communication options across multiple networks. Researchers must explore these spaces as participants, open to re-evaluating preconceived notions of "social". We can learn how to build more flexible systems, methods, and policies through these activities.

6.1 Considerations for Practitioners

Above all else, it is important for practitioners to recognize that their content will be of the most benefit to all if they allow it to flow, unhindered, across other systems. Instagram's seamless posting to both Facebook and Twitter is a useful example, just as the difficulty in sharing search strings in these same digital spaces points to issues.

Considering the use cases in this paper, it can be argued that looking at such extreme examples can help in the testing of systems. How well can they scale to hundreds, thousands, or even hundreds of thousands of users? Are there spaces for participation? How do we let content move across systems?

More importantly, this kind of research can help us make important arguments about use, access, culture, and context. This research asks that we look at the networks in which our participants experience our systems – that we consider participating with them, that we use our own technologies to do this work, understanding the affordances and the limitations. How might we make more responsive, useful social media spaces? We can work within them and use them alongside our participants, engaging with them and experiencing it with them.

6.2 Areas of Future Research

We cannot ignore the possibilities and the participation of the social web. Each day, new systems are capturing our attention, our posts, and our pins. How these systems might be used during extreme cases of disaster point to the ways in which we can develop our networks and technologies.

While this longitudinal study has been an arduous undertaking given the severity of the topic and the reality of these situations, it has also been highly rewarding. Further areas of research should include eventual disasters, such that we can continue to understand these communication practices. Such contextualized data will help us create systems that make space for participation in times of stability as well. It is our responsibility to build systems that support human interaction and productive communication during times of disaster.

References

1. Potts, L.: Social Media in Disaster Response: How Experience Architects Can Build for Participation. Routledge, New York (2014)
2. Potts, L.: Peering into disaster: social software use from the Indian Ocean earthquake to the Mumbai bombings. In: Professional Communication Conference, pp. 1–8. IEEE Press, New York (2009a)
3. Potts, L.: Using actor network theory to trace and improve multimodal communication design. Tech. Commun. Q. **18**(3), 281–301 (2009)
4. Potts, L., Seitzinger, J., Jones, D., Harrison, A.: Tweeting disaster: hashtag constructions and collisions. In: Proceedings of the 29th ACM International Conference on Design of Communication, pp. 235–240. ACM, New York (2011)
5. Potts, L., Harrison, A.: Interfaces as rhetorical constructions: reddit and 4chan during the Boston marathon bombings. In: Proceedings of the 31st ACM International Conference on Design of Communication, pp. 143–150. ACM, New York (2013)
6. Latour, B.: Science in Action: How to Follow Scientists and Engineers through Society. Harvard University Press, Cambridge (1987, 2002)
7. Law, J.: Notes on the theory of the actor-network: ordering, strategy and heterogeneity. Syst. Pract. **5**, 379–393 (1992)
8. Callon, M.: Some elements of a sociology of translation: domestication of the scallops and the fishermen of St Brieuc Bay. In: Law, J. (ed.) Power, Action, and Belief: A New Sociology of Knowledge?, pp. 196–223. Routledge, London (1986)
9. Mol, A., Law, J.: Regions, networks, and fluids: Anaemia and social topology. Soc. Stud. Sci. **24**, 641–671 (1994)
10. Cantoni, L., Tardini, S.: Internet. Routledge, New York (2006)
11. Morville, P.: Ambient Findability: What We Find Changes Who We Become. O'Reilly Media, Sebastopol (2005)
12. Kock, N.: Systems Analysis and Design Fundamentals: A Business Process Redesign Approach. Sage, Thousand Oaks (2007)
13. Weinberger, D.: Too Big to Know: Rethinking Knowledge Now that the Facts Aren't the Facts, Experts are Everywhere, and the Smartest Person in the Room is the Room. Basic Books, New York (2012)
14. Chief Investigating Officer, Government of India. In the Court of Additional Chief Metropolitan Magistrate, 37th Court, Esplanade, Mumbai. "Final Form/Report" (underSection173Cr.P.C.) (2009). http://www.satp.org/satporgtp/countries/india/document/papers/kasab-chargesheet.pdf. Accessed 10 Feb 2016
15. Mehta, D.: Commentary: how social media shared pain and rage of Mumbai. CNN (2008). http://edition.cnn.com/2008/WORLD/asiapcf/12/02/mehta.mumbai/. Accessed 10 Feb 2016
16. BBC News: Paris attacks: what happened on the night. BBC News (2015). http://www.bbc.com/news/world-europe-34818994
17. ArsenalTerje, Vine (2015). https://vine.co/v/iBb2x00UVlv. Accessed 10 Feb 2016
18. Buckley, P.: Twitter (2015). https://twitter.com/polinabuckley/status/665538581600055301. Accessed 10 Feb 2016
19. Perrin, A.: Social media usage: 2005–2015, Pew Research Center (2015). http://www.pewinternet.org/2015/10/08/social-media-usage-2005-2015-methods/. Accessed 11 Feb 2016
20. Facebook: Annual Report 2014 (2014). https://materials.proxyvote.com/Approved/30303M/20150413/AR_245461/pubData/source/Facebook%20AR%204-27-15b%20BM.pdf. Accessed 21 Feb 2016

21. Twitter: Selected Company Metrics and Financials, Fourth Quarter 2015. Investor Relations (2015). http://files.shareholder.com/downloads/AMDA-2F526X/1572592617 x0x874451/6C751539-C3F1-459A-9811-4688A03BFE39/Q415_Selected_Company_ Metrics_and_Financials.pdf. Accessed 21 Feb 2016
22. Twitter: 200 Million Tweets Per Day. Blog (2011). https://blog.twitter.com/2011/200-million-tweets-per-day. Accessed 21 Feb 2016
23. Siegel, A.: Here's what we can learn from how Twitter responded to Paris. The Washington Post (2015). https://www.washingtonpost.com/news/monkey-cage/wp/2015/11/16/heres-what-we-can-learn-from-how-twitter-responded-to-paris/. Accessed 11 Feb 2016
24. Twitter: In search of those missing in Paris. Twitter Moments (2015). https://twitter.com/i/moments/665790688718532610?lang=en. Accessed 11 Feb 2016

Communicating Product User Reviews and Ratings in Interfaces for e-Commerce: A Multimodal Approach

Dimitrios Rigas[✉] and Rajab Ghandour

University of West London, London, W5 5RF, UK
{Dimitrios.Rigas,Rajab.ghandour}@uwl.ac.uk

Abstract. This paper describes a comparative empirical evaluation study that uses multimodal presentations to communicate review messages in an e-commerce platform. Previous studies demonstrate the effective use of multimodality in different problem domains (e.g. e-learning). In this paper, multimodality and expressive avatars are used to communicate information related to product reviews messages. The data of the reviews was opportunistically collected from Facebook and Twitter. Two independent groups of users were used to evaluate two different presentations of reviews and ratings using as a basis an experimental e-commerce platform. The control group used a text-based with emojis presentation and the experimental group used a multimodal approach based on expressive avatars. Three parameters of usability were measured. These were efficiency, effectiveness, user satisfaction, and user preference. The result showed that the two approaches performed similarly. These findings provide a basis for further experiments in which text, emojis and expressive avatars can be combine to communicate a larger volume of reviews and ratings.

Keywords: Multimodality · Expressive avatars · e-Commerce · Usability · Social media · Reviews · Effectiveness · Efficiency · User satisfaction

1 Introduction

The Web increases accessibility and removes geographical barriers [1]. As more people use the Internet for on-line transactions, the need for effective, efficient and user satisfying e-commerce interfaces becomes significant. Product reviews and ratings need to be easily understood by users. Therefore, issues such as usability of the presentation, accessibility and clarity contribute to the decision making of users. Good exemplars of good design would require fewer users 'clicks' and display transitions. The term "modality" refers to the use of human senses (e.g. vision, hearing, touch, smell and taste) [2]. Currently, commercial e-commerce interfaces predominantly use visual means to communicate information. This often results to a visual information overload. The introduction of the new web technologies (Web 2.0) facilitated additional capabilities for users. Users can easily publish opinions, beliefs and thoughts globally accessible by the social media. Ratings can be shared through social media in platforms such as Facebook and Twitter. This paper presents a brief overview of literature relating to e-commerce, social media, user reviews,

© Her Majesty the Queen in Right of the United Kingdom 2016
F.F.-H. Nah and C.-H. Tan (Eds.): HCIBGO 2016, Part I, LNCS 9751, pp. 82–93, 2016.
DOI: 10.1007/978-3-319-39396-4_8

emojis and multimodality. It also describes the experimental e-commerce platform developed, the experimental design, results and conclusions.

2   e-Commerce, Social Media and Multimodality

2.1   e-Commerce

e-commerce can be defined as *"the use of the Internet and other networking technologies for conducting business transactions"* [3]. An organisation is considered to be e-business functioning when most (or a significant proportion) of its business is delivered electronically. Exchanging information is often enabled through the use of information technology (IT) [4] and lowers the cost of exchanging information [5, 6]. Generally, e-commerce not just involving selling or buying products online but it extends the business process such as handling customer online queries, integrating payment from customers, promotion of product and services. e-commerce is an umbrella concept that integrates a wide range of existing and new applications [7]. The Web increases accessibility and defies geographical barriers [8]. This is the reason that firms across the world have implemented e-commerce. With the increasing number of companies available online, it is important to understand some of the utilisation drivers of one platform over another [9].

2.2   Social Media

Web 2.0 enables users to interact and freely share information online [10]. The Oxford English Dictionary [11] defines social media as *"websites and applications that enable users to create and share content or to participate in social networking"*. The ability to create content online creates an influence of one user over another in social media websites such as Facebook and Twitter.

   A key business component of social media is that it allows consumers to evaluate product, make recommendations, and link current purchases to future purchases through status updates and Twitter feeds [12]. Social media is rapidly becoming one of the main sources for product reviews. Previous research investigated the role of social media on business. Lucas [12] conducted a study on the influence of social media in consumer purchasing behaviour and found that most of the participants purchased online based on social media previews. This study had 249 participants, 59 % where using Facebook and 34 % using Twitter as social media tool in order to obtain peer reviews. Social media is generally regarded as a useful aid to customers who seek advice or peer reviews of products. For example, consider the Trip Advisor platform, people make purchases based on previous experience and recommendation from unknown people. Several studies have focused on the influence of social media on potential customers. Boomer [13] discussed the influence of social media and its role. This becomes even more relevant as increasingly people tend to share most of their online experience using social media networks (e.g. Facebook and Twitter). These sources are exemplars of frequently used platforms to extract or retrieve product reviews.

2.3   User Reviews

Social media appears to become the platform users rely on to get reviews. When users are sharing reviews regarding a product or service they are directly influencing the purchase decisions of other users. According to [33] consumers evaluate product information (e.g., product reviews) in order to achieve their consumption goals. Moreover, electronic word-of-mouth (eWOM) is created when users share information and their experiences online [34]. The eWOM is likely to be much more powerful than WOM as it could potentially reach unlimited number of users [35]. It is a powerful product information source [36]. User reviews are usually categorised as positive, neutral or negative. Positive product reviews provide information about satisfactory experiences with the product, and thus represent opportunities to attain positive outcomes [33].

A study focused on tripadvisor.com conducted by Vermeulen and Seegers [37] found that positive hotel reviews improve the perception of future customers. They concluded that exposure to any (positive or negative) hotel reviews increases hotel awareness, especially if the hotel is less known. A similar study conducted by Ye et al. [38] suggested that positive hotel reviews result to more bookings. Reviews being shared among other users or groups have different value to other users depending on the content of review and emotional context. For example, consumers that attribute negative emotions to the reviewer's personal dispositions rather than the product, those emotions are unlikely to influence other users [36].

2.4   Multimodality

Several user interfaces communicate reviews using text with some graphics to communicate product reviews. Although this is considered acceptable to users, it could result in overloading the users with textual information [14, 15]. When presenting consulting user reviews and ratings, other non-textual means can be used to aid efficiency, effectiveness and user satisfaction. For example, multimodal interaction for product reviews and ratings may help to browse large volumes of this data easier [16]. Multimodal applications may use non-speech sound, text and hypertext, animation and video, speech, handwriting, gestures and computer vision.

Combining visual and auditory metaphors enhances the user experience. The auditory metaphors consist of recorded speech, earcons and auditory icons. The more metaphors used, the greater the volume of information that can be communicated. Avatars often incorporate the use of speech and human-like animated facial expressions and body gestures [17]. For instance, in e-learning interfaces, multimodality has shown to be useful in enhancing the usability and users learning performance [18]. Previous studies suggest that the use of more metaphors, including graphics, often enables users to perform tasks faster. For instance, a study by Rigas and Memery [19] showed that multimedia helped users to learn more material than a typical text-and-graphics approach. Users also performed different tasks more successfully. Another study [20] showed that multimedia metaphors helped users to make fewer mistakes in intermediate and complex tasks. In some cases, the time taken to complete tasks was also reduced. This shows the importance of multimedia or multimodality in making tasks executions easier. Another study by Rigas and Memery [21] showed that multimedia helped users to learn more material than using text-and-graphics media and assisted them to perform tasks more successfully. This shows the importance of multimodality.

Multimodal systems have been developed to support functions such as increase system accessibility for diverse users [22]. Avatar is a computer-based character that has been utilised to virtually represent one party in an interactive context [23] using speech, facial expression or body gestures [32]. Avatars are often used as a tool to support e-learning environments [18]. As multimodality refers to the use of different communication channels, avatars are considered as an additional metaphor to improve the visibility and communication aspects of any system. Avatars can be classified into three groups. These are abstract, realistic and naturalistic [24].

3   Experimental Platform

An experimental e-commerce platform was developed to act as basis for this empirical investigation. Two interfaces were designed. These were a text-based with emojis and a multimodal with expressive avatars. Both interface versions communicated the same information relating to the reviews and ratings of products. All the reviews were sourced from Facebook and Twitter. The presentations were designed to deliver the same information about the products being displayed. This information included different type of reviews (positive or negative) along with ratings score (1 to 5). The products used in this platform were laptops with different specifications, prices and ratings. Figure 1 shows the conceptual model for this experiment.

The presented content included three sections the product, product specification and the reviews. The complexity of the reviews communicated increased in every task. Table 1 shows the mapping allocation of the multimodal metaphors to the information communicated. Customer review comments were communicated using text and the different ratings using text and multimodal metaphors. Guidelines for multimodal information presentation [22] were followed for the development of the interfaces. The expressive avatars used in the experiment had facial expressions correlating to the review

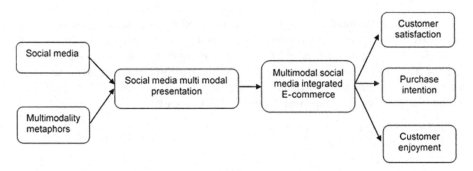

Fig. 1. Conceptual model showing the relationship between social media reviews messages and multimodal metaphors.

rating (positive, negative or neutral). These followed established guidelines in the literature [25]. Figure 2 shows the facial expressions used in the expressive avatars.

Table 1. The allocation of metaphors to the information communicated

Interaction Metaphor Content	Text	Graphics	Colours	Expressive Avatar
Product Description	✓			
Price	✓		✓	
Customer Reviews	✓			
Reviews Ratings	✓	✓		✓
Social Media Source	✓			

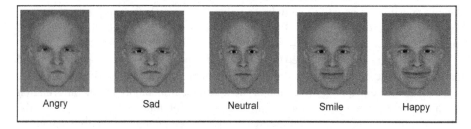

| Angry | Sad | Neutral | Smile | Happy |

Fig. 2. Facial expressions used in the expressive avatars

4   Experiment

The experiment measured efficiency, effectiveness and user satisfaction. Each user was presented with different presentations of reviews and ratings using four experimental tasks. The user sample consisted of 24 users that were opportunistically divided into two groups. The independent variable was the method used to communicate reviews and ratings. This variable has two versions. These were the text-based with emojis and an avatar-based design. The experiment consisted of four parts:

1. Pre-experimental questionnaire.
2. Perform tasks.
3. Post-task questions.
4. Post-experimental questions.

4.1   Procedure

For consistency throughout the experiment, the same procedure was applied for the two groups. The experiment started by requesting users to answer a pre-experimental questions that aimed to collect data relating to:

1. General user profile (e.g. age, gender and education).
2. Previous experience with computers, Internet and online shopping.
3. The frequency of use of social media networks.

During the pre-experimental questionnaire, users were presented with a video tutorial for five minutes. The tutorial presented an introduction to the experimental e-commerce platform. Two tutorial videos were used (one for each group of users). The control group was presented with a tutorial demonstrating the interface with the text-based reviews and emojis. The experimental group was presented with the facial expression avatar-based interface. The link between facial-expressions and the ratings of the reviews was also highlighted in the tutorials. Thereafter, the users in both groups performed the same tasks (i.e. four tasks) but using the different interface according to the group (i.e. control and experimental). On completion of the experimental tasks, users answered a user satisfaction questionnaire.

4.2   Experimental Proposition and Hypotheses

The experimental proposition is that multi-modal metaphors and facially expressive avatars will provide more effective, efficient and user satisfying presentations of social media based product reviews in an e-commerce platform compared to a textual based with emojis approach. This paper focuses on the effectiveness and efficiency parameters of the above proposition. The hypotheses are:

1. Presentations of reviews and ratings using facially expressive avatars will be more effective than text-based with emojis in terms of *tasks completed successfully.*
2. Presentations of ratings using facially expressive avatars will be more efficient than the text-based with emojis in terms of users' *products comparisons.*
3. Presentations of ratings using facially expressive avatars will have the same efficiency in *user-based comparisons for up to four products.*

4.3   Tasks

Each group performed the same four tasks but with the corresponding interface. Previous studies showed that the metaphor affect user performance depended on the level [20, 25] and the type of a task being examined [26, 27]. Hence, the tasks were designed to follow the same procedures as previous experiments. The level of difficulty in each task was gradually increased in a way that the first task was the simplest and the fourth task was the most complex. Therefore, the tasks were classified into easy, moderate and difficult. Each task had a set of requirements. Users had to choose the correct product based on criteria based on the reviews. The actual reviews varied from one task to another. For instance, for the Group 1 and task 1, the reviews were simply presented one-by-one (one product review presentation) but for task 2, reviews of products were presented together so as the user could compare products. In the multimodal presentation, as the user proceeded from one task to another, the complexity of the review rating also increased. Therefore, the more difficult the task, the more information was communicated. The complex tasks contained larger volumes of information compared to the easy and moderate tasks. On completion of each task, users answered questions based on that task. The aim of these questions was to evaluate the performance of the user based on the information and the review interface presented by the task.

4.4 Sample

The user sample consisted of 24 users who had no prior exposure to the experimental platform. All users had no prior knowledge on the multimodality metaphors as used in the experiment. They were requested to perform all tasks and answer all questionnaires. These 24 users were opportunistically assigned to two groups (n = 12) to evaluate the two conditions (i.e. text-based with emojis and facially expressive avatars). This volume of sample is considered to be sufficient for this usability evaluation [28].

5   Results and Discussion

The results were analysed in terms of the time taken by users to complete the tasks (efficiency), number of correct selections of products (effectiveness). Inferential statistics were used to examine the difference between variables [29]. When the data was not normally distributed, the Mann-Whitney t-test was used [30]. The mean, median and mode were used to perform the statistical analysis. Also, Kolmogorov-Smirnov test [31] was used in the statistical analysis to test, calculate and present the normal distribution of experimental results. The statistical analysis used $\alpha = .05$ and the significance using p-value = .05 (which refers to be less than 0.05).

5.1   Profile of the Sample

Pre-experimental questionnaires were used to collect the users' profile information (e.g. gender, age, education or prior experience). Figure 3 presents the profile of the sample. The control group (text-based with emojis) consisted of 58.33 % of users aged between 25 and 34, 36.11 % between 18 and 24 and 5.56 % between 35 and 44. The second group (multimodal) had an age range of 58.33 % between 25 and 34, 36.34 % between 18 and 24 and 5.33 % between 35 and 44. The gender distribution was 25 % females and 75 % males in the control group and 16.67 % females and 83.33 % males in the experimental group. The education level of the sample was predominantly undergraduates. Figure 4 shows the sample's prior experience relating to the use of computers and the Internet. The data suggests that the sample was knowledgeable and experienced. This was expected given that the sample was drawn from University students.

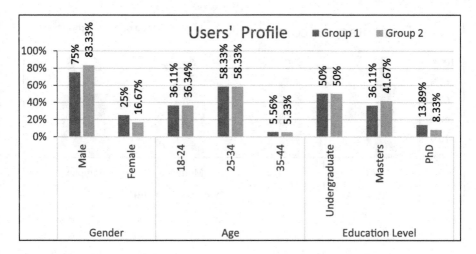

Fig. 3. Users' profile in terms of age, gender, and education level in the three groups

5.2 Effectiveness

The effectiveness was measured by the frequency of tasks completed successfully by users during the experiment. This measure was considered for all the tasks in total and for task complexity (easy, moderate, and difficult). Users in the experimental group performed marginally better than the users in the control group (Fig. 5).

The total number of correctly completed tasks in the experimental group (facially expressive avatars) was 43 compared to the 37 for the control group (text-based with emojis). The mean value of successfully completed tasks per user for the experimental and control groups was 3.58 and 3.08 respectively. This experimental group

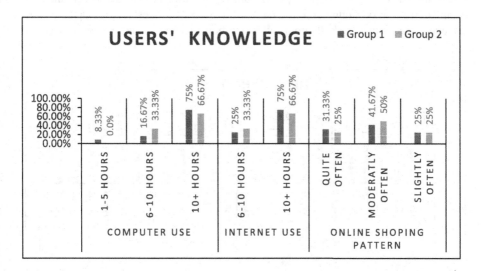

Fig. 4. Users' knowledge in terms of using computers, Internet and online shopping frequency

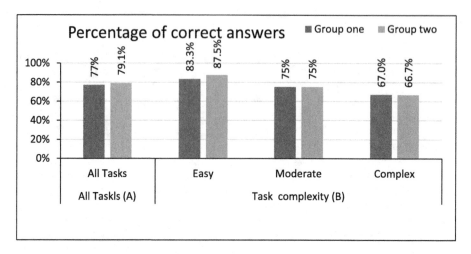

Fig. 5. Percentage of correctly completed tasks achieved by the users in the two groups for all tasks (A) and for task complexity (B).

demonstrates marginal improvement of successfully completed tasks compared to the control group. The ANOVA test results showed that that the variance was not significant (p at 0.05). The experimental group outperformed the control group in the easy tasks only. The experimental group had 87 %, 75 % and 66.7 % completion rate for easy, moderate and difficult tasks respectively. The control group had 83 %, 75 % and 67 %. Although these results do not show that one method is better than the other in terms of efficiency, there is a prima facie case that in principle the application of expressive avatars does not hinder the effectiveness of users. This results points to the fact that the two approaches can be collaboratively employed to communicate reviews and ratings. The emojis also helped users to quickly browse reviews that in turn accelerated the completion of tasks. Figure 6 shows the total number of successfully completed tasks achieved by each user for both groups. Results show that 4 users successfully completed

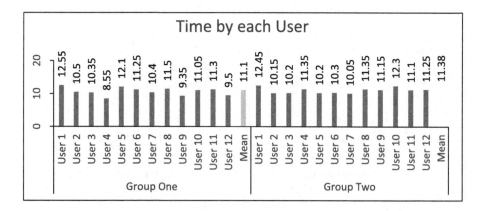

Fig. 6. Total number of successful completed tasks by each user

all tasks in the control group (users 1, 2, 3 and 6) while 3 users in experimental group (users 8, 9 and 12). The mean value of tasks completed successfully per user was 3.08 and 3.17 for the control and experimental groups respectively.

6   Conclusion and Future Work

The variance between the control and experimental groups was not significantly different in terms of tasks completed successfully. This indicates that both approaches taken to communicate reviews and ratings are valid. It is important to investigate further under different task circumstances. The use of emojis shown to be particular useful. Users obtained an overall viewpoint relating to the review and rating (positive, negative or somewhere in between) at a glance. This makes a strong prima facie case for the use of emojis as additional element of the review and rating entry. There is a need to understand the way in which emojis and expressive avatars can be combined to communicate larger volumes of data.

References

1. Nielson, M.J., Taher: Building Web Sites with Depth. Web Techniques (2001)
2. Meera, M.B., Ephraim, P.G.: Multimodal integration. IEEE Multimedia **3**, 14–24 (1996)
3. Turban, E., King, D., Lee, J., Viehland, D.: Electronic Commerce 2004: A Managerial Perspective. Prentice Hall, Upper Saddle River (2004)
4. Skipper, J.B., Craighead, C.W., Byrd, T.A., Rainer, R.K.: Towards a theoretical foundation of supply network interdependence and technology-enabled coordination strategies. Int. J. Phys. Distrib. Logistics Manag. **38**(1), 39–56 (2008)
5. Clemons, E.K., Row, M.C., Reddi, S.P.: The impact of information technology on the organization of economic activity: the move to the middle hypothesis. J. Manag. Inf. Syst. **2**, 9–36 (1993)
6. Chaffey, D.: E-Business and E-Commerce Management: Strategies. Pearson Education Limited, Harlow (2004)
7. Zwass, V.: Electronic commerce: structures and issues. Manag. Inf. Syst. **1**, 3–23 (1996)
8. Jakob, N., Marie, T.: Homepage Usability: 50 Websites Deconstructed, 1st edn. New Riders, Thousand Oaks (2001)
9. Deborah, E., Rosen, E.P.: Website design: viewing the web as a cognitive landscape. J. Bus. Res. **57**, 787–794 (2004)
10. Scott, S.V., Orlikowski, W.J.: Reconfiguring relations of accountability: materialization of the social media in the travel sector. J. Acc. Organ. Soc. **37**, 26–40 (2012)
11. Oxford, D.: Oxford English Dictionary - Multimedia (2014). http://www.oxforddictionaries.com/definition/english/social-media?q=social+media
12. Forbes, L.P.: Does social media influence consumer buying behaviour? An investigation of recommendations and purchases. J. Bus. Econ. Res. (JBER) **11**, 107–112 (2013)
13. Gary, B.L.: Social media: influence or control. Acc. Today **23**, 38 (2009)
14. Brewster, S.A., Crease, M.G.: Making menus musical. In: Howard, S., Hammond, J., Lindgaard, G. (eds.) Human-Computer Interaction: INTERACT 1997. JFJP, pp. 389–396. Springer, Heidelberg (1997)

15. Brewster, S., Grégory, L., Murray, C.: Using non-speech sounds in mobile computing devices. In: Proceedings of the First Workshop on Human Computer Interaction with Mobile Devices, pp. 26–29 (1998)
16. Zeljko, O., Dusan, S.: Modelling multimodal human-computer interaction. IEEE Comput. Mag. **37**, 65–72 (2004)
17. Alseid, M., Rigas, D.: Utilising multimodal interaction metaphors in e-learning applications: an experimental study. In: IEEE International Conference on Advanced Information Networking Applications, AINA 2009, pp. 945–950 (2009)
18. Annetta, A.L., Holmes, S.: Creating presence and community in a synchronous virtual learning environment using avatars. Int. J. Instr. Technol. Distance Learn. **3**, 27–43 (2006)
19. Rigas, D., Memery, D.: Multimedia e-mail data browsing: the synergistic use of various forms of auditory stimuli. In: Proceedings of the International Conference on Information Technology: Coding and Computing [Computers and Communications], ITCC 2003, pp. 582–586 (2003)
20. Rigas, D., Hopwood, D.: The Role of multimedia in interfaces for on-line learning. In: 9th Panhellenic Conference Informatics, PCI 2003 (2003)
21. Rigas D., Memery, D.: Utilising audio-visual stimuli in interactive information systems: a two domain investigation on auditory metaphors. In: Proceedings of the International Conference on Information Technology: Coding and Computing, pp. 190–195. IEEE (2002)
22. Sarter, N.B.: Multimodal information presentation: design guidance and research challenges. Int. J. Ind. Ergon. **36**(5), 439–445 (2006)
23. Bartneck, C., Takahashi, T., Katagiri, Y.: Cross cultural study of expressive avatars. In: International Workshop on Social Intelligence Design (2004)
24. Salem, B., Earle, N.: Designing a non-verbal language for expressive avatars. In: Proceedings of the Third International Conference on Collaborative Virtual Environments, San Francisco, California, United States, pp. 93–101. ACM (2000)
25. Fabri, M., Moore, J.D., Hobbs, J.D.: Expressive agents: non-verbal communication in collaborative virtual environments. In: Proceedings of Autonomous Agents and Multi-agent Systems (2002)
26. Rashid, S., Rigas, D.: A two-group evaluation to e-note. Int. J. Educ. Inf. Technol. NAUN **2**, 7–11 (2008)
27. Alotaibi, M., Rigas, D.: A usability evaluation of multimodal metaphors for customer knowledge management. Int. J. Comput. Commun. **2**, 59–68 (2008). University Press, UK
28. Nielsen, J.: Usability Engineering. Academic Press Inc., Cambridge (1993)
29. Aborokbah, M.: Multimodal ecommerce: usability and social presence. Ph.D. thesis, De Montfort University Faculty of Technology (2014)
30. Kranzler, J.H.: Frequency distributions. In: Statistics for the Terrified, 3rd edn. pp. 36–37. Prentice Hall (2003)
31. Field, A.P.: Exploring data. In: Discovering Statistics Using SPSS, 4th edn., pp. 65–109. SAGE Publications (2003)
32. Beskow, J.: Animation of talking agents. In: Proceedings of the ESCA Workshop on Audio-Visual Speech Processing, AVSP 1997, Rhodes, Greece (1997)
33. Duan, W., Gu, B., Whinston, A.B.: Do online reviews matter?—an empirical investigation of panel data. Decis. Support Syst. **45**(4), 1007–1016 (2008)
34. Cox, C., Burgess, S., Sellitto, C., Buultjens, J.: The role of user-generated-content in tourists' travel planning behaviour. J. Hospitality Mark. Manag. **18**, 743–764 (2009)
35. Ghandour, R., Bakalova, R.: Social media influence on the holiday decision-making process in the UK. J. Organ. Stud. Innov. **1**, 41–54 (2014)

36. Junyong, K., Pranjal, G.: Emotional expressions in online user reviews: how they influence consumers' product evaluations. J. Bus. Res. **65**, 985–992 (2012)
37. Vermeulen, I., Seegers, D.: Tried and tested: the impact of online hotel reviews on consumer consideration. J. Tourism Manag. **30**, 123–127 (2009)
38. Ye, Q., Law, R., Gu, B., Chen, W.: The influence of user-generated content on traveller behaviour: an empirical investigation of the effects of e-word of-mouth to hotel online bookings. Comput. Hum. Behav. J. **2**, 634–639 (2011)

Multimodal Impact on Consumer Purchase Decisions: Initial Results

Dimitrios Rigas[✉] and Nazish Riaz

University of West London, London W5 5RF, UK
{Dimitrios.Rigas,Nazish.Riaz}@uwl.ac.uk

Abstract. This paper aims to explore the ways in which multimodality can be integrated on social platforms and its impact on consumer purchase decision. It aims to investigate user views on the presence and absence of multimodal metaphors on social media platforms and its impact on consumer decision making. A questionnaire was conducted from 58 respondents. Results indicate multimodal metaphors not only aid user understanding but also positively affect consumer purchase decisions.

Keywords: Consumer behavior · Consumer purchase decision · Multimodality · Multimodal metaphors · Social media marketing

1   Introduction

People intrinsically interact with the world in a multimodal manner. In User Interface Design (UID), multimodal metaphors aim to influence and enhance natural human capabilities to communicate information using audio, visual, graphical 3-D, and other modalities. Changes in consumer behavior have forced businesses to rethink their marketing presentation strategies on the digital domain. The majority of the firms are now advertising using social media. Social Media marketing has caused a shift in consumer behavior. According to recent statistics [16], last year the annual average weekly spend online was £718.7 million.

It is generally accepted that social media marketing lacks "human warmth" as it is impersonal and automated compared to traditional marketing. In the online advertisement context, multimodality provides an additional bandwidth to communicate information. As the complexity of an online advertisement presentation increases, its clarity and effectiveness may decrease. In order to reduce complexity, the design and interactive features need to be balanced in a manner that the presented media impacts favourably on the purchase decision of a potential customer. However, the effect of multimodal metaphors to present and promote products on social platforms has still not been fully investigated. This paper aims to gather an overall viewpoint of user perception relating to the use or lack of multimodality.

© Her Majesty the Queen in Right of the United Kingdom 2016
F.F.-H. Nah and C.-H. Tan (Eds.): HCIBGO 2016, Part I, LNCS 9751, pp. 94–105, 2016.
DOI: 10.1007/978-3-319-39396-4_9

2   Social Media Marketing and Multimodality

Consumer behavior can be defined as "a study of the process involved when individuals or groups select, purchase, use or dispose of products, services, ideas, or experiences to satisfy needs and desires" [9]. Bagozzi et al. [18] defines consumer behaviour as a combination of social and psychological processes, which people endure through the possession, use and disposal of products or services. It is the understanding of the inter-personal and social reasons underpinning consumer decision-making and the transactions associated with it. Consumer behaviour is complex as it varies depending on individual characteristics and idiosyncrasies. Purchase can be either rational or emotional [17]. Consumers employ multiple senses in order to directly and indirectly explore their environment to improve belief and identify new information [10]. External stimuli contribute during information search and evaluation. When a product is presented on social media platform, multimodal metaphors provide additional bandwidth to communicate information and enable the better user understanding of the information communicated. Despite the existing knowledge of customers for a product, they will still require to enhance their knowledge with some form of external search. Some of this supplementary data is obtained through advertisement, friends and increasingly social media platforms [17].

Social media can be defined as a medium through which people interact in order to create, share and exchange information and ideas in virtual networks and communities. Social media is differentiated from traditional media by attributes such as permanence, immediacy, frequency, cost and reach [21]. The importance of social media has been widely accepted today and it is pervasive in both personal and professional environments. Over the last decade, the Internet and social media has grown in usage and acceptability. This has changed purchasing patterns and consumer behavior. Human interaction has fundamentally and profoundly changed by the extensive use of online social networks [15]. This change has been accompanied by a strong growth of web-based platforms that facilitate this interaction. Some of the in vivo social interactions and relationships have been replaced with an equivalent counterpart in virtual worlds using online communities. These online communities enable people to share their knowledge, experiences and engage and promote dialogues within different cultures [4]. Studies suggest that consumers show greater value to peer reviews and judgments rather than firm promotions, demonstrating a shift in the focus of persuasive power [5].

The growth of internet and online communities have significantly transformed consumers, cultures and organizations with easy access to vast information, enriched communications and improved social networking [19]. Social media has not only changed marketing and advertisement of products [11], but also altered the focus from product information search to post purchase behavior [8]. Social media allows organizations to communicate with customers in a way that increases intimacy and enables the growth of a relationship [12]. This could result to a positive or negative perception of a brand as the reviews cannot be controlled. Even a small amount of negative information or user feedback can have a significant impact on consumer attitudes [13]. Online groups exercise an evident influence on the behavior and consumer buying intent and indirectly on the purchase decision. Social media platforms provide individual consumers with a public forum which not only gives them own voice but access to product information which then aids their purchase decisions [14].

Multimodality is an integrated approach of different types of media. According to Bunt et al. [6], human interaction with the world is inherently multimodal. People use their senses sequentially and simultaneously to perceive their environment. Multimodal metaphors describe the interactive systems that aim to enhance computer communication using audio, visual, graphical and other modalities. Fortin and Dholakia [7] suggest that as the presentation complexity of an advertisement increases, the effectiveness of positive results decreases. This complexity is often alleviated through balancing design and interactive features in such way that they contribute to a positive consumer purchase decision.

Rigas and Alseid [1] demonstrated the successful use of multimodal metaphors to communicate information. Further Rigas and Alty [20] and Almutairi and Rigas [2] prescribed the use of multimodal interfaces and avatars to communicate with the target audience. Additionally, Rigas and Almutairi [3] identified the positive impact of multimodal metaphors on ease of use of learning materials. Interfaces that communicate information to users using several communication channels often provide a more engaging interaction [2]. The use of interactive multimodal features aids user understanding to complete online purchases. However existing literature lacks the understanding of the impact of specific metaphors (text, video, audio, graphical illustrations) used in online advertisement towards consumer purchase decision.

3   Methodology

A positivist approach was taken in this study. Structured questionnaire was designed to investigate the user comprehension on the use or lack of multimodality and explore whether its presence help users develop an understanding of a product advertisement. The questionnaire had questions of multiple format, including multiple choice, dichotomous questions, self-assessment Likert-scale questions and open ended question. This enabled the gathering of an overall user viewpoint relating to multimodal metaphors and their perceived impact on purchasing decisions. The opportunistic sample consisted of 58 participants, 29 male and 29 female aged between 18 and 35 years old. The age profile of respondents consisted of 18–21 years old (8.6 %), 21–25 (34.5 %), 26–30 (37.9 %) and 31–35 (19 %).

4   Data Analysis and Discussion

4.1   Sample Profile

A total number of 58 respondents took part in the survey, 29 (50 %) male and 29 (50 %) female and 58 valid responses were received as shown in Fig. 1. All the respondents fall in the age group between 18–35, with the largest group falling in the age group of 26–30, accounting for 37.9 %, out of which 20.70 % account for females and 17.20 % males.

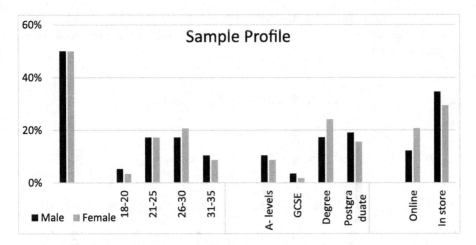

Fig. 1. Sample profile against gender

The second largest group falls in the age group of 21–25, making up 34.5 %, out of which 17.20 % account for females and 17.20 % for males. However, the smallest group of respondents fall in the age group of 18–20, accounting for only 8.6 %, of which 3.40 % are female and 5.20 % male. Out of the 29 female respondents, the educational profile consists of 14 (24.10 %), with Degree or Diploma, and 9 (15.5 %) with a Postgraduate degree. Whereas, out of the 29 male respondents, 10 (17.2 %) hold a degree and 11 (19 %) have acquired postgraduate degree. Out of the 58 respondents who took part in the survey 63.8 % prefer to shop in-store, out of which 34.50 % account for male and 29.30 % account for female. On contrary 32.8 % prefer to shop online, of which 20.70 % are female and 12.10 % male. This question had an invalid response of 3.4 %. Figure 2 highlights Internet proficiency, 25 respondents (43.1 % of which 22.40 % were female and 20.70 % male) indicated that they use internet most on their smart phone. The second largest group of 22 (37.9 % of which 15.50 % were female and 22.40 % male) indicated that they prefer using internet on their Laptop. This data suggests that females prefer to access the Internet on their smart phone and males on their laptop. However, from the results, smartphone seems to be the device on which majority of the respondents prefer using internet on as compared to laptop, tablet and desktop. This can be largely due to the convenience factor; as smart phones allow one to perform most tasks that one could do on a desktop or laptop.

A cross tabulation between gender and reasons for using internet most indicated that the largest group of females accounting for 13.8 % used internet most for work purposes. The second largest group (17.2 %) used internet for browsing, followed by 8.6 % who use internet for shopping. Whereas, 24.1 % of male respondents indicated that they use internet most for browsing, followed by 10.30 % who use for work purposes. However, the overall results indicate browsing to be the reason for which majority of total respondents (41.4 %) use internet for, followed by work (24.1 %), personal reasons (19.0 %) and shopping (10.3 %).

It is interesting to notice that the smallest group, consisting of 1.7 % male use internet for shopping purposes, which clearly indicates towards the difference in male and female shopping behavior.

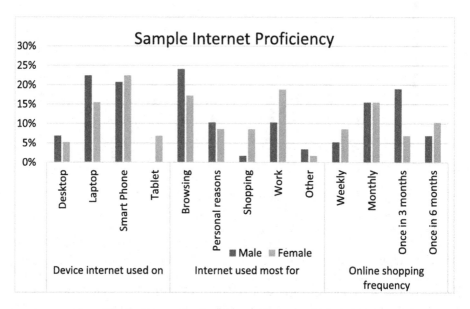

Fig. 2. Respondent internet proficiency against gender

The survey aimed to gather an understanding of the frequency of online shopping. Results indicated that a large number of respondents, (31.0 %) shop online on monthly basis, followed by 25.9 % who shop once in every 3 months. Only 13.8 % respondents shop on weekly basis. However, results indicate equal number of male and female (50 %) who shop online on monthly basis. These statistics indicate towards ever growing trend on shopping online on significantly regular basis, equally by both genders.

Figure 3 demonstrates user perception of different marketing modes. 41.40 % of the respondents strongly agreed that social media marketing is more 'influential' as compared to conventional marketing. 22.40 % agree, whereas only a small percentage of respondents (8.60 %) disagree that advertisements on social media are more influential than conventional marketing. On contrary, the largest group accounting for 34.50 % thought that advertisements through conventional marketing are more influential. However, 6.90 % disagree and 12.10 % strongly disagree to this claim. 69 % perceive social media marketing to be more information rich as compared to conventional marketing. Out of which 32.80 % strongly agreed and 36.20 % agreed. Only 17.2 % respondents did not consider social media to be more information rich. On the other hand, 34.50 % of respondents agreed and 13.80 % strongly agreed that conventional marketing is more information rich. These results highlight the importance of social media as a medium to transmit information. The ability of social media to allow organizations and individuals to upload and share information. The main aim of marketing along with product/service promotion and brand creation is to be able to aid user

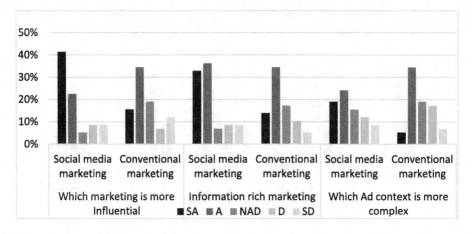

Fig. 3. User perception of different advertisement contexts

understanding of the product or service advertised. Hence it is vital to ensure that the users do not find the advertisement context and the information marketed too complex to digest. Results from the survey illustrated that a large group of respondents, accounting for 43.1 % found advertisements via social media marketing to be a lot more complex as compared to conventional marketing. However, 20.7 % respondents disagree that social media marketing is more complex. This indicates that out of the respondents who took part in the survey, most of them find advertisements on social to be more complex as compared to conventional marketing.

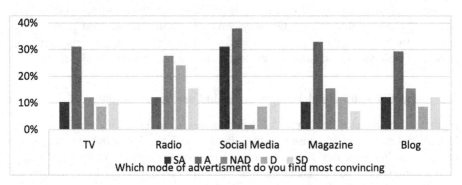

Fig. 4. Respondent viewpoint of different advertisement modes

4.2 User Perception of Advertisement Contexts and Modes

Figure 4 indicates the user perception of most convincing advertisement modes. 37.90 % strongly agreed and 31 % agreed that advertisements on social media are most convincing. The second most convincing advertisement mode form the results is magazine (32.80 % agreed), followed by TV (31 % respondents agreed). The least convincing mode was radio (12.10 % agreed and 24.10 % disagreed). In conclusion, the social media was found to be the most convincing mode of advertisement (Fig. 5).

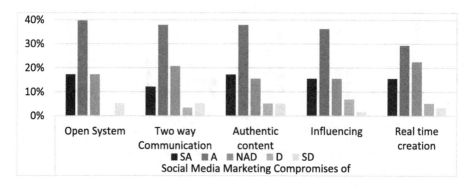

Fig. 5. User view point of social media marketing

4.3 User Understanding of Social Media Marketing

In order to develop an understanding of respondents view point of social media marketing, the social media marketing was tested against 5 variables including Open systems, Two-way communication, Authentic content, Influencing and Real time creation. The aim was to identify which variables are accepted amongst the most respondents as significant traits of social media marketing. 56.9 % (39.70 % agreed and 17.20 strongly agreed) believed social media marketing to be compromised of an open system. 55.1 % perceived social media marketing offers authentic content. 51 % claim it to be influencing and 50 % believed that offers a two-way communication. The smallest group which accounts for 44.8 % of the respondents found social media marketing offering real time creation. Open system and authentic content were considered as two major traits.

4.4 Impact of Multimodal Metaphors to Aid User Understanding

Figure 6 demonstrates the impact of different metaphors to aid user understanding. Multimodal metaphors are present on the digital domain to enhance user understanding of the product/service advertised. In order to identify the impact of individual multimodal metaphors to aid user understanding a series of Likert scale questions were posed to the respondents. Results illustrated that the largest group of respondents accounting for 81.1 %, where 28.30 agree and 52.80 strongly agree, find Video to be the most significant metaphor in developing a clear understanding of the product advertised. The next metaphor which aids user understanding most after video is Illustrations for which 38.30 % agree and 34.70 % strongly agree, making a total group of 73.5 %. 60 % of the respondents find Text to aid their product understanding and only 43.5 % find Audio to help them develop a clear understanding of the product advertised online.

The graph clearly illustrates that all 4 metaphors are significantly important to aid user understanding of the product advertised online. However, Video (which

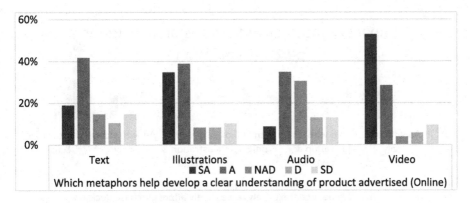

Fig. 6. Impact of multimodal metaphors to aid user understanding

compromises of all remaining metaphors) and Illustrations appear to be the most critical metaphors in enhancing user understanding (Fig. 7).

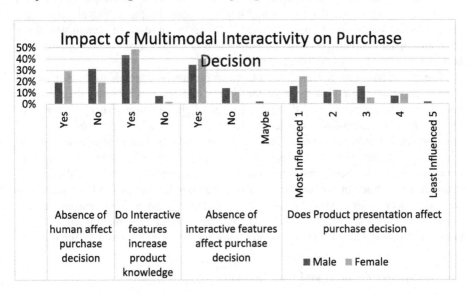

Fig. 7. Impact of multimodal interactivity on user purchase decision

4.5 Impact of Multimodal Interactivity on Purchase Decision

It is important to determine whether multimodal metaphors only act as informant tools to aid user understanding or if they have any impact on the consumer purchase decision. This has been addressed in the survey through dichotomous questions. 50 % of the respondents stated that absence of sales assistant (human) does not affect their purchase decision, whereas 48.30 % stated that it would affect their decision. However, a large percentage of females accounting for 29.30 % agree that absence of sales assistant would

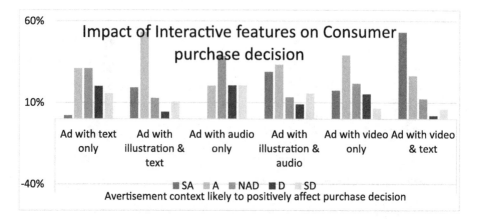

Fig. 8. Impact of interactive features on consumer purchase decision

affect their purchase decision, whereas a large proportion of the male respondents (31 %) stated that their purchase decision would not be affected by the human absence. This clearly shows that although majority users feel that the absence of human would not have an impact on their purchase decision there is clearly a difference of shopping behavior and preferences across genders.

The results have also revealed that a large proportion of respondents, both male and female, accounting for 91.4 % agree that interactive features increase their product knowledge. Only a mere 8.6 % disagree. This highlights the importance of interactive features to increase product knowledge. The respondents were further questioned to identify whether the absence of interactive features affects their purchase decision, to which 74.20 % answered yes. A small group of 24.1 % claim that interactive features have no influence on their purchase decision. 1.70 % were unsure. These results demonstrate the importance of interactive features in not only increasing product knowledge and aiding user understanding but also affecting the purchase decision. Further, a large number of respondents (39.6 %) stated that the product presentation affects their purchase decision. Only 1.70 % are barely influence by the presentation of the product.

4.6 Interactive Features and User Influence

Figure 8 shows 53.10 % strongly agreed and 26.50 % agreed that advertisements with a combination of video and text are most likely to positively affect purchase decision. For illustrations and text, 19.10 % strongly agreed and 53.20 % agreed. The advertisements via audio perceived to have a limited impact.

Figure 9 indicates that 49.10 % agreed that advertisements on social media are more efficient. 60.40 % wanted a more secure payment online procedure. 57.50 % strongly agreed that online shopping should have more clear refund and exchange policies. 29.30 % desired high human presence and 27.20 % strongly agreed that high human presence would improve their online purchase experience. The interactive multimodal features present on social media and integrated in online advertisements largely contributed to aid product understanding, influence and positively affecting consumer purchase decision.

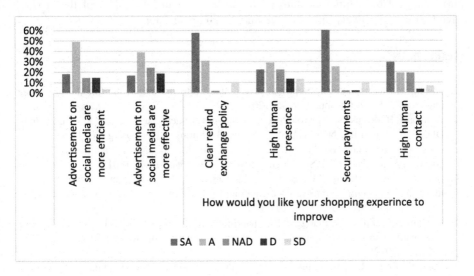

Fig. 9. Online buying effectiveness, efficiency and user satisfaction

5 Conclusion

Smartphone was the most common device on which majority of the respondents accessed Internet. The results indicate that the highest online shopping frequency of the respondents is on monthly basis, indicating equal number of male and female (50 %). A large number of respondents believed that social media marketing is more 'influential' and 'information rich' compared to conventional marketing. However most of the respondents find advertisements on social media to be more complex, but still find social media to be the most convincing mode of advertisement. Open system and authentic content are the two major traits of social media. The research also highlights that text, illustration, audio and video are perceived as significantly important to aid user understanding of the product advertised online. However, video and illustrations appear to be the most critical metaphors in enhancing the user understanding. Interactive features are perceived to increase product knowledge, aid user understanding and impact upon purchase decisions. The majority of users felt that the absence of human presence would not have an impact on their purchase decision. However, females felt that the absence of human presence might impact their purchase decision. It appears that there is a difference of shopping behavior and preferences across genders. The study also identified that combining metaphors in online advertisement is most likely to have a positive effect on the purchase decision (video with text and illustrations with text). Audio used on its own in advertisement context does not seem to have a significant impact to positively affect the purchase decision. Most of the respondents agreed that advertisements on social media are more efficient and effective, hence leading to a positive purchase decision. However, advertisements on social media are perceived as more complex. In conclusion, multimodal metaphors based on social media advertisement act as an informant tool by helping consumers to gain a better understanding of the product advertised and positively influence the final purchase decision.

References

1. Alseid, M., Rigas, D.: An empirical investigation into the use of multimodal e-learning interfaces. J. Hum.-Comput. Interact. (2011)
2. Almutairi, B., Rigas, D.: The role of avatars in e-government interfaces. In: Marcus, A. (ed.) DUXU 2014, Part II. LNCS, vol. 8518, pp. 28–37. Springer, Heidelberg (2014)
3. Rigas, D.I., Almutairi, B.: An empirical investigation into the role of avatars in multimodal e-government interfaces. J. Sociotechnol. Knowl. Dev. 5(1), 14–22 (2013)
4. Budden, C.B., Anthony, J.F., Budden, M.C., Jones, M.A.: Managing the evolution of a revolution: marketing implications of internet media usage among college students. Coll. Teach. Methods Styles J. 3(3), 5–10 (2011)
5. Berthon, P.R., Pitt, L.F., Plangger, K., Shapiro, D.: Marketing meets Web 2.0, social media, and creative consumers: implications for international marketing strategy. Bus. Horiz. 55(3), 261–271 (2012)
6. Bunt, H., Beun, R.-J., Borghuis, T.: Multimodal human–computer communication systems, techniques, and experiments. Lect. Notes Comput. Sci. 1374 (1998)
7. Fortin, D.R., Dholakia, R.R.: Interactivity and vividness effects on social presence and involvement with a web-based advertisement. J. Bus. Res. 58(3), 387–396 (2005)
8. Mangold, W.G., Faulds, D.J.: Social media: the new hybrid element of the promotion mix. Bus. Horiz. 52(4), 357–365 (2009)
9. Solomon, M.: Consumer Behaviour: A European Perspective, 3rd edn. Prentice Hall Financial Times, Harlow (2006)
10. Turk, M.: Multimodal interaction: a review. Pattern Recogn. Lett. 36, 189–195 (2014). Academic Search Elite, EBSCOhost
11. Hanna, R., Rohm, A., Crittenden, V.: We're all connected: the power of the social media ecosystem. Bus. Horiz. 54, 265–273 (2011)
12. Davis Mersey, R., Malthouse E, E., Calder, B.: Engagement with media. J. Media Bus. Stud. 7(2), 39–56 (2010)
13. Schlosser, A.E.: Posting versus lurking: communicating in a multiple audience context. J. Consum. Res. 32(2), 260–265 (2005)
14. Kozinets, R.V., Valck, K., Wojnicki, A.C., Wilner, S.J.S.: Networked narratives: understanding word-of-mouth marketing in online communities. J. Mark. 74(2), 71–89 (2010)
15. Tiago, M., Veríssimo, J.: Digital marketing and social media: why bother? Bus. Horiz. 57(6), 703–708 (2014)
16. Office for National Statistics. Consumer trends of United Kingdom for 2014. www.ons.gov.uk (2014). Accessed 24 Dec 2015
17. Solomon, M.R.: Marketing, Second European Edition. Pearson Education, Harlow, England (2013)
18. Bagozzi, R.P., Dholakia, U.M., Basuroy, S.: How effortful decisions get enacted: the motivating role of decision processes, desires and anticipated emotions. J. Behav. Decis. Making 16, 273–295 (2003)
19. Kucuk, S.U., Krishnamurthy, S.: An analysis of consumer power on the internet. Technovation 27(1/2), 47–56 (2007)

20. Rigas, D.I., Alty, J.L.: Using sound to communicate program execution. In: Proceedings of the 24th EUROMICRO Conference, vol. 2, pp. 625–632 (1998)
21. Katona, Z., Sarvary, M.: Maersk line, B2B social media, "Its communication not marketing". Univ. Calif. Berkeley Spring **56**(3), 142 (2014)

Media Selection: A Method for Understanding User Choices Among Popular Social Media Platforms

Brian Traynor[1], Jaigris Hodson[2($\boxtimes$)], and Gil Wilkes[1]

[1] Mount Royal University, Calgary, Canada
{btraynor,gwilkes}@mtroyal.ca
[2] Royal Roads University, Victoria, Canada
jaigris.hodson@royalroads.ca

Abstract. How a person perceives social media platforms should provide insight on the platforms they choose to use or not. Literature reviews highlight studies focused on demographic, familiarity, social influence, application, and usefulness as a means to differentiate choice/use. This study combines quantitative and qualitative techniques to examine Social Media Platform (SMP) preferences.

Using a web-based card sorting application, 59 participants completed an open sort activity on 19 SMPs. Information was also collected on SMP usage, age and gender. The strength of the paired-relationships between SMPs is presented in the form of a similarity matrix and a dendogram (hierarchical cluster analysis). A set of decision rules were developed in order to arrive at 44 standardized categories. A matrix of categories and SMPs provides means to explore associations. These relationships are examined for overlap and absence. This allows researchers to discuss findings in terms of current theory and practice.

Keywords: Pile sort · Media richness theory · Media synchronicity theory · Social media platforms

1 Introduction

Scholars have engaged in many different lines of inquiry in an effort to understand why users adopt certain social media platforms over others. For example, different work has investigated social media with respect to user intentions [1], demographics, and kinds of interactions afforded by different sites [2, 3]. This work, however, seeks to extend and deepen our understanding of user engagement, by getting users to categorize the platforms they use in an effort to understand more about how users think about their interactions with these tools. When combined with simple demographic data on the users and a series of survey questions about social media use, it is hoped that this method can shed light on connections that may or may not be immediately apparent through survey/ questionnaire and demographic data alone.

Demographic categories have been considered in the existing literature as predictors of trends in use. For example, Saul discusses an "exodus" of younger users from Facebook [4]. Related work by Chan *et al.* show how gender influences Facebook engagement, with women more likely to (a) have an account and (b) participate more often than

© Springer International Publishing Switzerland 2016
F.F.-H. Nah and C.-H. Tan (Eds.): HCIBGO 2016, Part I, LNCS 9751, pp. 106–117, 2016.
DOI: 10.1007/978-3-319-39396-4_10

their male counterparts [5]. Studies by Malone and Kinnear [6] as well as Hagag *et al.* [7] discuss how shared culture or cultural values can influence preferences for a specific website or web platform. Related to the question of demographics are studies of affordances which highlight the motivation for certain segments to use specific online platforms. For example, Bell *et al.* [8] showed how Facebook can help older adults feel less lonely. And Chen showed that women bloggers tend to use social media for the purposes of recreation and information sharing [1]. This is supported by market research showing that new moms tend to be frequent and engaged users of Facebook, since they are able to form a community which helps with information sharing, recreation, and social stimulation [9]. Despite this research, demographics alone does not tell the story of why people engage (or ignore) different social networks, and thus the question tends to be much more complex than which gender, age segment or cultural group a person belongs to, especially when these categories so often intersect.

Moving beyond the demographic question, other factors have been considered in the literature as possible explanations for why certain people use different social media platforms. For example, Correa *et al.*'s work showed that certain traits, namely, openness and extraversion show a positive correlation with social media use (in contrast to traits like emotional stability, which exhibit a negative correlation) [10]. Other studies have shown a relationship between familiarity with a social network (or perceived familiarity) and the likelihood that users would continue to engage with it [11]. Similar research has revealed that convenience and cognitive effort has a simple and direct impact on social network adoption [12]. Other studies have honed in on the relationships between people and corresponding social network influence as a predictor of social network use. Cataldi and Aufaure showed how influence can spread the adoption of a network (or a message along that network) [13]. Palazon *et al.* showed that the willingness of individuals to join brand related pages on sites like Facebook depends on their social network and the influential individuals within that network [14], and Herrerro *et al.* demonstrated how online search behaviour is directly influenced by the social network of the individual doing the searching [15]. This type of behaviour would seem on the surface to confirm an affordances thesis. That is to say, since social media affords a certain type of networked social interaction, social interactions should therefore drive a person's choice of platform and the way they interact on it [16].

Following the extensive body of research on social media use and affordances [2, 17], studies have shown that people often use specific platforms because they offer a certain type of interaction with others. For example, Gomes and Pimentel developed a series of "if-then" rules that describe user behaviors using "data mining procedures." Their results showed that users engaging with each other on Facebook for Blackberry tended to demonstrate reciprocity to the exclusion of other mechanisms of social or collective influence [18]. This is reasonable from an affordances perspective as Facebook.com itself—as well as all other social media—affords posts that demonstrate reciprocity through likes, clicks and shares. But while this work highlights an important user motivation related to social media engagement, the reduction of user behaviors to simple if-then formulas may not take into account all the ways that people choose to interact using these platforms. Rather than simply data mining, it is advisable to understand social media use, or really any human social behaviour with respect to a complex spectrum of deeply contextual and sometimes contradictory human understandings, and motivations [19].

The question of context—who chooses what and why—has thus far received little investigation outside of high-level market or demographic categories. To achieve a contextual and rich analysis of individual motivations for social media use, we recommend that demographics and affordances be considered alongside other cues. For this, it is useful to draw from and expand earlier models of media choice. Building on Media Richness Theory [20], which showed that interlocutors seek out and choose richer media in order to better understand and communicate issues with others, Dennis and Valacich's Media Synchronicity theory tries to build a model that takes into account multiple processes, in this case five: immediacy, symbol variety, parallelism, rehearsability and reprocessability to explain how people choose to engage with a particular medium of communication [21]. This understanding is useful because it supports different user motivations for adopting a particular communication medium and thus can be very useful for understanding motivations for social media use. For example, Chan showed how asynchronicity can motivate shy people to engage with social media platforms like Facebook as a way to experience social interaction in a less threatening context [22]. Similarly, Taipale showed a relationship between demographic social media choices and the synchronicity of the chosen medium or platform of communication–making a link here between demographics, affordances, and media richness that is a step forward in understanding the varied complexity of human motivation [23]. However, media synchronicity theory is still limited as it assumes that media choice is directly related to a conscious goal of communication between two or more individuals, and as such it may not account for some of the less conscious or un-inferred categories of experience. Examples could include social influence, felt but seldom reflected upon group or collective or social-network hierarchies that impact personal preference, personal or group experience or history related to different platforms or assumptions or attitudes about services that defy rational explanation.

Free pile sort has been used in anthropology and sociology in such diverse fields as health care, organizational communication, cultural anthropology, and food studies [24–28]. It is generally used in combination with the collection of demographic data and survey research as a way to reveal taken for granted assumptions or demographic and network relationships not immediately apparent through survey data alone. While it is quite common outside of communication studies, it has not yet been employed extensively to understand computer mediated communication. Its great strength is that it allows for both quantitative data collection, in the sorting and categorization of elements, and qualitative data collection [29] these are then combined to form a detailed explanation of why participants sorted different elements in a specific way. When combined with the demographic details of the participants, it thus has the power to extend an analysis offered through a media synchronicity lens by offering (1) demographics, (2) professed motivation (3) relationships between different media as uncovered through categorization (4) social cues and other less-conscious influences (5) the discovery of other motivations not anticipated by the researcher or research team (in contrast to a survey instrument with pre-determined lines of questioning or scales of answers). The pilot study detailed here, thus employs free pile sort in a new way, that is in the understanding of social media preferences in order to address several hypotheses related to user motivations.

2   Methodology

2.1   Participant Recruitment

Active social media users were recruited through open calls on Reddit and personal connections (LinkedIn, individual emails, etc.). Participants had the option of passing along contact information (snowball effect) but most did not do this. The engagement protocol can be broken down into three parts. We used the Optimal Workshop *OptimalSort* web-based application to collect questionnaire and card sort data.

Pre-Activity Questionnaire – Usage. Participants responded to the questions below. These questions not only allowed the collection of participant data, but also primed participants for the subsequent card sort (equivalent of pile sort) activity.

(a)   What social media applications/services are you a registered user of?
(b)   What social media applications/services did you use yesterday?
(c)   Think about the last three things you posted on any social media service/application. What were they?

Card Sorting Activity. Participants were presented with 19 cards to sort by moving individual cards from a list to an area where cards can be grouped together in clusters (categories). Participants had freedom regarding the arrangement of the cards and the naming of the clusters. This is known as an open card sort and is most commonly used by Information Architects [30].

With 19 cards for our participants to sort, there is a potential for 18 pairs for each card. The higher the frequency that two cards are paired together, the stronger the association. The resulting similarity matrix (Fig. 1) shows the grouping of cards together (%) by the 59 participants.

Post-Activity Questionnaire - Category Grouping, Frequency of Use, Demographics.
We asked participants to describe why they ordered the list the way they did, and had them provide answers to some standard demographic and use-pattern questions, including frequency of use, gender, age, and the habits of their offline social or family networks. Importantly, this allowed us to understand the contextual information that helped make sense of the patterns we observed in the free pile sort data.

Grouping Categories – Meta Analysis. Participants in the exercise of sorting and categorizing 19 social media platforms generated 390 categories. The OptimalSort application allows researchers to standardize categories so it is possible to examine individual cluster labels and group them together. We developed the following decision rules in order to get to a reasonable number of standardized categories.

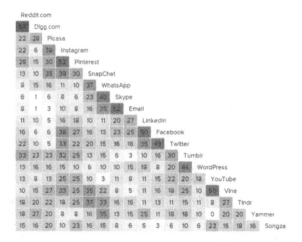

Fig. 1. Similarity matrix for 19 social media platforms (59 participants)

Decision Rule 1 Basic Synonymy: Category labels that researchers agreed were synonymous on their face were standardized.

Decision Rule 2 Temporal Character: Categories that suggest time, periodicity, or routine were grouped together.

Decision Rule 3 s Pass Limit: After first standardization pass, researchers could only combine 2 categories at a time.

Decision Rule 4 Qualifying Language: Qualifying terms or phrases in category labels were decisive in determining synonymy. See Rule 1: Basic Synonymy.

Decision Rule 5 Noise Categories: Groups that were unclassifiable (researchers termed these as 'noise categories'), groups with no conceptual link among services in the category that the researchers could identify with confidence or consensus. Examples include category labels like 'Lookout!,' 'Meh,' etc., group labels where the group label terms themselves provide too little guidance to make a clear determination.

Decision Rule 6 Standardization Naming: Standardized categories were named using the term most commonly used among the category labels of the participants. Different terms were grouped under common descriptors or terms when the common term or descriptor represented a concept or activity shared by the terms (e.g. to curate content requires the browsing of content, hence a label that suggested or used the term 'curate' was standardized to 'Browsing').

Using Decision Rules 1–6 above the researchers reduced the participant categories to 44 standardized categories. The researchers ceased standardization when their consensus formation reached its limit; when they could reduce no further. Table 1 shows the standardized category labels.

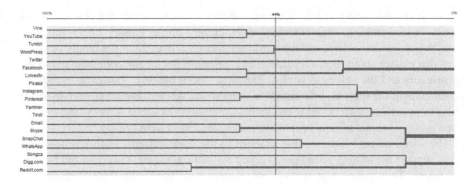

Fig. 2. Dendogram indicating pair relationships based on % agreement by participants

Table 1. Standardized categories identified by researchers

Aggregator	Content	Frequency	Network	Sharing
Blogging	Core	Fun	News	Social
Broadcasting	Dating	Hosting	Noise	Social ranking
Browsing	Don't use	Images	Occasional	Time killers
Business	Downtime	Information	old	Tools: images editing
Chat:text	Email	misc	Personal	Video
Communications	Entertainment	Multimedia	Photo	Visual
Communities	Favourites	Music	Private	watch
connecting	Forums	Necessary	Professional	

Using the strength of the association between paired cards, OptimalSort can execute a hierarchical cluster analysis to generate dendograms showing these relationships. The Actual Agreement Method generates a dendogram that shows the % of participants in agreement with actual groupings. These groupings are quite easy to pick out in Fig. 2. Information architects typically use these types of charts to identify how participants group content in comparison to proposed or current designs.

The dendogram helps to show how the social media platforms cluster together even though participants used different strategies for developing their categories. Table 2 shows the % Agreement for the top 7 pairs. Two sub-pairings are also presented in Table 2 to show the level at which a subsequent pairing occurs.

3   Discussion

Our study assumes a systems ecology of possibilities in the form of social platforms, situated in a common medium, and equally available to all the users who participated in our study. We maintain that as social media platforms consolidate or converge, the technical affordances of the platforms become less useful for explaining patterns of use. For example, Twitter.com can host lean, rich or richer media, as can Facebook.com, or nearly any other platform in our sample [31].

Based on the meta analysis described above, we determined that the categories 'social,' 'social ranking,' and 'communities' warranted further inquiry. Importantly, the term "social," as in society, and the term "community," overlap in the family of synonyms that cluster about them on paradigmatic grounds. Social and community connote the structure and the values of groups. The term 'social ranking,' however, introduces a distinction in the form of differentiation along strata, where some elements rise above others in priority, status, or perceived value. Community or social activity tend to indicate a group; systems of rank or ranking tend to indicate a tiered group.

The social media platforms that attached to the standardized categories, however, fail to support the affinity group-tiered group distinction. Figure 3 is organized by type and token. This means that tokens, are examples of platforms (like Digg.com or Pinterest.com) that attach to the larger category or type terms (like community or social ranking). Digg.com, for example, a social news site and tagging engine that filters content on grounds of participant response–a community-based ranking engine–appears in all three categories. Reddit.com, another social news site, also appears in all three categories. See Fig. 1, the Similarity Matrix, for how Digg.com and Reddit.com relate to other services. 64 % of the participants grouped Reddit.com and Digg.com together. Both are popular news and content aggregation sites that allow users of the service to post content that can be voted up or down by other users. This means a different form of analysis is needed to understand patterns between user categories, and platforms are too alike to support an affordances analysis alone.

As with natural language itself the types in the form of standardized categories and their tokens in the form of concrete social media platforms seem to relate to one another along lines of family resemblance [32]. This is not what one would consider to be a logical way of making sense of social media, is not a symbolic way of making sense of social media and does not conform to popular theories of social media use. To identify

Table 2. Relationship strengths indicating paired relationships

Pairing	% Agreement	Subpairing	% Agreement
Digg.com			
Reddit.com	65		
Instagram			
Pinterest	52	Picassa	24
Email			
Skype	52		
Facebook			
LinkedIn	51	Twitter	27
Vine			
YouTube	51		
Tumblr			
WordPress	45		
SnapChat			
WhatsApp	37		

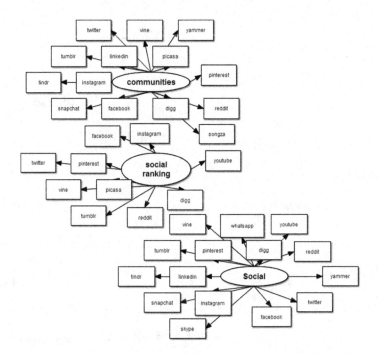

Fig. 3. Standardized categories 'social,' 'social ranking,' and 'communities' as logic trees. The child categories are the services the participants sorted into like groups at various levels of frequency.

by means of statistical inferencing across broad samples the denser clusters of semantic pattern–where terms or like terms appear in the company of other terms with higher frequencies–is the principle that guides that both corpus linguistics and the study of semantic graphs, therefore it is reasonable to use a network analysis to understand the social media platforms. When we treated the social media platforms as three semantic meta-networks, we were able to produce the following network diagram, Fig. 4.

The resulting merged meta-network yielded 17 unique nodes for a network density– or measure of actual as opposed to potential connections–of 46 %. Betweeness centrality —a network metric—registers the percentage of paths that pass through a node. Nodes with high betweenness centrality indicate mediating elements. Skype, and Songza, though they each appear in only one of the merged meta networks as seen in Fig. 3, register at the highest level of betweenness centrality in Fig. 4 at 0.091 and 0.047 respectively. Digg.com, by way of contrast, though it appears at a frequency of 3 in the merged meta-networks, falls below the top 10 in betweenness centrality. Importantly, this reveals user preferences that an affordances framework and standard survey instruments would probably fail to detect.

Skype and Songza are less generalized platforms of communication or content delivery; one specializes in social playlists and music delivery, the other in voice and video calls. They are easier to differentiate among platforms in a rich environment of platforms. Whereas other platforms blend and merge into a generalized field of services

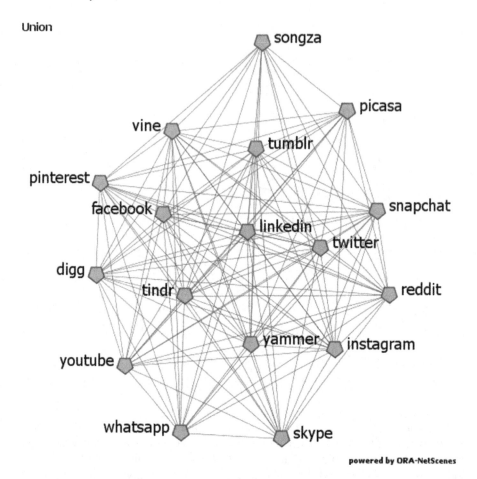

Fig. 4. Social media platforms that attach to the categories social, social ranking, and communities expressed as the union of three meta-networks (adapted from [33]).

where choice may be less clear, Skype and Songza assume a more specific character. This expresses itself in a semantic network as betweenness centrality. This finding would predict that similarity strength, or a platform's similarity or relations of similarity with other platforms defeats a sense of a clear choice among services. In other words, the only time affordances can predict user choice is when the platform in question is sufficiently different in features from every other platform. Otherwise, it may be social connections, trendiness or other contextual factors that are driving trends in use.

4 Conclusion

The ecology of social media platforms may be described by

(a) the services they offer,
(b) the technical affordances they support

(c) the opportunities they offer to develop, circulate, and curate content
(d) the opportunities they offer to discover or to develop contacts and relationships, and to connect with or to develop affinity groups

It is the primary assumption of this research that (a)–(d) underdetermine patterns of user selection among platforms or services within platforms because of the redundancy of services or opportunities among platforms, because of the tendency of users to use only the most immediate means to meet the most immediate need without respect to the richness of any platform's feature set, and because the experience of users with any objective process tends to develop independently of the process itself [31]. We hypothesized that users would sort the social media platforms that they use or that they know about based on criteria that include services, technical affordances, and so forth, what we referred to as "platform sorts" or "content sorts" But we also hypothesized other criteria consistent with categories of work, leisure, or social influence, sorts like liking, compliance-conformity, or reciprocity [31].

On its face our pilot study findings support our hypotheses. The Similarity Matrix derived from user responses is consistent with prior literature on the relative degree of use and familiarity of social media platforms, with Facebook.com, Twitter.com, and other familiar services, dominating user consciousness of what opportunities for social media activity exist. Where our methodology as evidenced by our findings may offer a unique contribution is at the level of user perception. User perception, we would argue, when conditioned by choices among rich feature sets, tends to blur platforms into a generalized field of activity that can be freely sorted any number of ways. The generalized platform such as Facebook.com, Twitter.com, or Wordpress.com, seems to follow a Walmart generalist strategy of non-differentiation by design, where Skype or Songza, by way of contrast, seem to follow a boutique strategy of differentiation by means of content or medium specialization.

If the generalized field hypothesis holds we would expect to find folds or concentrations that obtain between or among services as users would select among services or opportunities not based on platform but on combinations of services that may obtain across platforms, such as using Tumblr to park images from Instragram.com or Imagur.com, of Facebook.com to circulate memes from Tumblr or WordPress.

References

1. Chen, G.M.: Why do women bloggers use social media? Recreation and information motivations outweigh engagement motivations. New Media Soc. **17**(1), 24–40 (2015)
2. Wellman, B., Quan-Haase, A., Boase, J.: The social affordances of the Internet for networked individualism. J. Comput. Mediat. Commun. **8**(3) (2003)
3. Steinfield, C., Ellison, N.B., Lampe, C.: Social capital, self-esteem, and use of online social network sites: a longitudinal analysis. J. Appl. Dev. Psychol. **29**(6), 434–445 (2008)
4. Saul, D.J: 3 Million Teens Leave Facebook In 3 Years: The 2014 Facebook Demographic Report – ISL (2014). https://isl.co/2014/01/3-million-teens-leave-facebook-in-3-years-the-2014-facebook-demographic-report/. Accessed 10 Feb 2016
5. Chan, T.K.H., Cheung, C.M.K., Shi, N., Lee, M.K.O.: Gender differences in satisfaction with Facebook users. Ind. Manag. Data Syst. **115**(1), 182–205 (2015)

6. Malone, E.L., Kinnear, S.: How and why: complementary analyses of social network structures and cultural values: improving flood response networks in Queensland, Australia. Qual. Quant. **49**(1), 203–220 (2015). Springer, Netherlands
7. Hagag, W., Clark, L., Wheeler, C.: A framework for understanding the website preferences of Egyptian online travel consumers. Int. J. Cult. Tour. Hosp. Res. **9**(1), 68–82 (2015)
8. Bell, C., Fausset, C., Farmer, S., Nguyen, J., Harley, L., Fain, W.B.: Examining social media use among older adults. In: Proceedings of the 24th ACM Conference on Hypertext and Social Media - HT 2013, pp. 158–163 (2013)
9. eMarketer: Why are moms so social? http://www.emarketer.com/Article/Why-Moms-Social/1009855. Accessed 10 Feb 2016
10. Correa, T., Hinsley, A.W., de Zúñiga, H.G.: Who interacts on the Web?: The intersection of users' personality and social media use. Comput. Hum. Behav. **26**(2), 247–253 (2010)
11. Sánchez-Franco, M.J., Buitrago-Esquinas, E.M., Yñiguez-Ovando, R.: What drives social integration in the domain of social network sites?: Examining the influences of relationship quality and stable and dynamic individual differences. Online Inf. Rev. **39**(1), 5–25 (2015)
12. Lin, K.-Y., Lu, H.-P.: Predicting mobile social network acceptance based on mobile value and social influence. Internet Res. **25**(1), 107–130 (2015)
13. Cataldi, M., Aufaure, M.-A.: The 10 million follower fallacy: audience size does not prove domain-influence on Twitter. Knowl. Inf. Syst. **44**(3), 559–580 (2015)
14. Palazon, M., Sicilia, M., Lopez, M.: The influence of 'Facebook friends' on the intention to join brand pages. J. Prod. Brand Manag. **24**(6), 580–595 (2015)
15. Herrero, Á., Martín, H.S., Hernández, J.M.: How online search behavior is influenced by user-generated content on review websites and hotel interactive websites. Int. J. Contemp. Hosp. Manag. **27**(7), 1573–1597 (2015)
16. Boyd, D.M., Ellison, N.B.: Social network sites definition history and scholarship. J. Comput.-Mediated Commun. **13**(1), 210–230 (2007)
17. Obar, J.A.: Canadian advocacy 2.0: an analysis of social media adoption and perceived affordances by advocacy groups looking to advance activism in Canada. Can. J. Commun. **39**(2), 211–233 (2014)
18. Gomes, A.K., da Pimentel, M.G.C.: Measuring media-based social interactions provided by smartphone applications in social networks. In: Proceedings of the 2011 ACM Workshop on Social and Behavioural Networked Media Access - SBNMA 2011, pp. 59–64 (2011)
19. Lin, K.-Y., Lu, H.-P.: Why people use social networking sites: an empirical study integrating network externalities and motivation theory. Comput. Hum. Behav. **27**(3), 1152–1161 (2011)
20. Dennis, A.R., Kinney, S.T.: Testing media richness theory in the new media: the effects of cues, feedback, and task equivocality. Inf. Syst. Res. **9**(3), 256–274 (1998)
21. Dennis, A.R., Valacich, J.S.: Rethinking media richness: towards a theory of media synchronicity. Proc. MIS Q. **32**(3), 575–600 (2008)
22. Chan, M.: Shyness, sociability, and the role of media synchronicity in the use of computer-mediated communication for interpersonal communication. Asian J. Soc. Psychol. **14**(1), 84–90 (2011)
23. Taipale, S.: Synchronicity matters: defining the characteristics of digital generations. Inf. Commun. Soc. **19**(1), 80–94 (2016)
24. Maiolo, J.R., Young, M.M., Glazier, E.W., Downs, M.A., Petterson, J.S.: Pile sorts by phone. Field Methods **6**(1), 1–2 (1944)
25. Dongre, A.R., Deshmukh, P.R., Garg, B.S.: Perceptions and health care seeking about newborn danger signs among mothers in rural Wardha. Indian J. Pediatr. **75**(4), 325–329 (2008)

26. Siar, S.V.: Knowledge, gender, and resources in small-scale fishing: the case of Honda Bay, Palawan, Philippines. Environ. Manag. **31**(5), 569–580 (2003)
27. Yeh, H.-W., Gajewski, B.J., Perdue, D.G., Cully, A., Cully, L., Greiner, K.A., Choi, W.S., Daley, C.M.: Sorting it out: pile sorting as a mixed methodology for exploring barriers to cancer screening. Qual. Quant. **48**(5), 2569–2587 (2015)
28. Neufeld, A., Harrison, M.J., Rempel, G.R., Larocque, S., Dublin, S., Stewart, M., Hughes, K.: Practical issues in using a card sort in a study of nonsupport and family caregiving. Qual. Health Res. **14**(10), 1418–1428 (2004)
29. Boster, J.: The successive pile sort. Field Methods **6**(2), 11–12 (1994)
30. Tullis, T., Albert, W.: Measuring the User Experience: Collecting, Analyzing, and Presenting Usability Metrics, 2nd edn. Elsevier/Morgan Kaufmann, Boston/Amsterdam (2013)
31. Wilkes, G., Traynor, B., Hodson, J.: Folk classification of social media services as grounds for explaining or predicting trends in use. In: 2014 IEEE International Professional Communication Conference (IPCC), pp. 1–5 (2014)
32. Bloor, D.: Wittgenstein: A Social Theory of Knowledge. Columbia University Press, New York (1983)
33. Carley, K.M., Pfeffer J., Reminga, J., Storrick, J., Columbus, D.: ORA User's Guide 2012. No. CMU-ISR-12-105. Carnegie-Mellon Univ. Pittsburgh, PA, Inst. of Software Research Internat (2012)

Professional Personal Branding:

Using a "Think-Aloud" Protocol to Investigate How Recruiters Judge LinkedIN Profile Pictures

Sarah F. van der Land[1(✉)], Lotte M. Willemsen[2], and Barbara G.E. Wilton[1]

[1] Erasmus University Rotterdam, Rotterdam, The Netherlands
vanderland@eshcc.eur.nl, barbarawilton@hotmail.com
[2] University of Applied Sciences Utrecht, Utrecht, The Netherlands
lotte.willemsen@hu.nl

Abstract. This study builds on previous work on personal branding [1, 2] and is one of the first to qualitatively explore how and why *actual recruiters* make certain decisions in selecting a candidate on LinkedIN. In this study, recruiters reviewed seven different Linkedin pictures of a job candidate applying for a ficticious entry-level Marketing Consultant Job, while using a think-aloud method. Each picture displayed the candidate in a different way, making certain cues more salient (e.g. smiling, casual holiday shot, avoiding eye gaze). The results of this study indicated that especially the cues of smiling and eye-contact (looking in the camera) appear to have a positive influence on the perception of perceived credibility. Theoretical and practical implications of these findings are discussed.

Keywords: Personal branding · Strategic social media · Impression management · Recruitment · Think-aloud method · Credibility · Job interview success · LinkedIN

1 Introduction

Recruiters are increasingly screening potential applicants via Social Network Sites (SNSs) such as Facebook and LinkedIn, before deciding to invite them to a job interview [3]. In an "ideal" world, recruiters should base their selection decisions on objective assessment of information provided by the candidate (e.g. cv, cover letter). However, in practice, identically skilled candidates may not be invited to an interview due to stereotyped interpretation of information available on their physical appearance [4]. Although recruiters ought to look beyond these cues and base their hiring decisions on all work-related information available, in reality, these practices do take place. When screening SNSs, particularly profile pictures receive the most attention [5]. Moreover, the few visual cues displayed in these pictures (e.g. attire) are often magnified and stereotyped [6].

So how can job applicants combat these perceptions and make the most of their online self-presentation? Compared to face-to-face communication, an online setting offers individuals more control over their self-presentation allowing them to strategically

© Springer International Publishing Switzerland 2016
F.F.-H. Nah and C.-H. Tan (Eds.): HCIBGO 2016, Part I, LNCS 9751, pp. 118–128, 2016.
DOI: 10.1007/978-3-319-39396-4_11

"plan" impressions [7]. This act of "personal branding" is increasingly emerging among individuals and is defined as "the process by which individuals attempt to control the impressions others form of them" [8, p. 34]. In our previous work, we manipulated LinkedIN pictures with glasses and beards and investigated how this influenced the generation of "positive" stereotypes related to Ohanian's perceived credibility [1, 2].

This study is one of the first to qualitatively explore how actual *recruiters* make decisions in selecting candidates. Hereby this study goes beyond previous, more quantitative approaches (e.g. experiments) that predominately relied on student and the general public samples to investigate perceived credibility of job candidates [1, 2, 9]. The aim of this study is to gain more insight into how certain visual cues in pictures of potential candidates influence the decision-making process of recruiters. Therefore, the following research question is formulated: *"How does a LinkedIn profile picture contribute to the perceived credibility of a job applicant on the likelihood to obtain a job interview?"*

2   Theoretical Framework

2.1   LinkedIn as a Tool for Screening and Selection

Since its introduction in 2003, Linkedin has grown into the world's largest professional network with more than 345 million users as of 2015 [10]. Linkedin strives to connect professionals worldwide to increase the success of both job seekers and recruiters [10]. This is facilitated by the setup of the platform. As a social networking site, Linkedin allows job seekers to create a public profile, present themselves as professionals, share personal information, work experiences, and relevant skills, and link up with other professionals, recruiters or organizations. Similarly, Linkedin allows organizations, or recruiters working on behalf of these organizations, to create a public profile, to present themselves to job seekers, share employment opportunities, and link up with potential candidates [10, 11]. Thus, Linkedin simultaneously functions as an online resume, professional network, and as a tool for screening and selection. Indeed, as much as 81 % of Inc. 500 companies use LinkedIn for talent acquisition [12].

When judging the credibility of an individual through a LinkedIn profile there is an inherent level of bias and subjectivity involved because it is completely user-generated [13]. Job applicants are increasingly becoming aware of the opportunities of Linkedin as a screening and selection tool by future employers [3]. As personal profiles shape first impressions, applicants may spend time and energy in creating a profile that is likely to leave a positive impression. In doing so, individuals engage in impression management [14] also known as self-presentation: "the process by which individuals attempt to control the impressions others form of them" [8]. Candidates have control over their self-presentation given the allowance of user-generated content in SNSs such as Linkedin. Thus, impressions can be strategically manipulated to present oneself as more competent, likeable, and trustworthy [7].

Research shows that a profile picture is one of the most important tools that people use for visual impression management in CMC contexts [15, 16]. The value of a profile picture lies not only in its ability to display physical appearance, but also in its ability to (rightly or wrongly) display a person's personality. Appearance, facial expression, and attire may signal qualities that are supportive of an individual's proclaimed set of skills and on his/her profile [5, 15]. Considering that a job applicant intends to 'sell' his or her qualities to a future employer in order to successfully obtain a job interview, a profile picture may be manipulated in various ways. For example, wearing spectacles in order to look more intelligent [2].

Despite their potential for manipulation, recruiters are relying on Linkedin for screening and selection, as user profiles are believed to be a valid and truthful source of information [17], even more so than a résumé, application form or cover letter. Unlike the latter forms of communication, a Linkedin profile is accessible to anyone with whom the profile owner is connected. These connections (e.g., current or former colleagues and employers) can verify or contradict provided information [18]. Recruiters infer that, due to the risk of being contradicted by others, job applications are more likely to share truthful information.

2.2 Visual Cues as Input for Credibility Assessments

The primary concern of recruitment professionals is to assess whether a candidate is qualified for the job. Thus when evaluating person's profile for job fit, recruiters should base their selection decisions on a careful and rational analysis of all job-related information available. However, research on the selection process of recruiters in face-to-face settings, shows that impressions are not only based on job-related information but also on the simple cues, such as those captured by non-verbal communication (e.g., facial expressions, voice intonation), that are unrelated to qualifications of the candidate [19]. Constraints in time and cognitive capacity may induce recruiters to rely no more cues than necessary to form an impression. These cues provide mental shortcuts that ease the cognitive load of making a decision, as described by the Elaboration Likelihood Model [20] and the Heuristic-Systematic Model [21].

Thus, recruiters may base first impressions on very minimal cues of information [22–24]. This is not different in CMC settings. According to Social Information Process theory (SIP) [25] individuals form impressions of each other, regardless of the medium being used. As CMC contexts are devoid of non-verbal cues that accompany face-to-face communication, people tend to look for other cues to shape impressions [6]. Given the absence of non-verbal communication, people rely more heavily on whatever cues remain available, such as those captured by a person's profile photo.

LinkedIn allows candidates to upload a photo, which is typically not present in traditional means of initial employee evaluations, such as the résumé. Research shows that people rely on the visual appearance of a person's face to form impressions. For example, one's facial expressions and attire reveal information about a person's qualities, such as attractiveness, trustworthiness and competence that can be less quickly obtained from textual information. Perceptions based on facial information are shaped as quickly as 39 ms [26]. This is facilitated by a specific area of the brain that is involved in the processing of visual information, in particular faces [27].

Thus, facial signals play a crucial role in how people infer meaning to personality traits [28], especially in a context that is devoid of other visual cues such a non-verbal communication. This is confirmed by the study of Chiang and Suen [19], who showed that recruitment professionals use visual cues (heuristics) from the online profiles of job applicants and that these cues are likely to evoke positive responses amongst the recruitment professionals if the source is believed to be credible. Additionally they add that these cues may be more important than job related information such as prior work experience or education.

According to a recent study by Edwards et al., [29] the presence of picture/no picture) affect credibility perceptions, i.e., a set of perceptions that a receiver holds of a source, including its perceived competence, trustworthiness and attractiveness. Results indicated that users who post a profile picture along with their LinkedIn profile are perceived as more attractive and more competent than users who do not post a picture. Although these studies confirm that visual cues of Linkedin profiles shape impressions, there is a dearth of research on the question whether visual cues directly affect perceptions of credibility, and if so in what way [30]. This is surprising, as credible subjects are more persuasive than non-credible subjects [31]. In the context of recruitment selection it is therefore likely that perceived credibility results in a higher likelihood of obtaining a job interview. Therefore, this study aims to examine whether visual cues have any influence on the decision-making *process* of recruitment professionals. A more detailed discussion will follow in the methodology section.

3 Method

3.1 Sample

In total, 11 recruitment professionals were interviewed with an average age of 29.2 (ranging from 22 to 41 years old), of which 73 % were female. Only recruitment professional were selected that spend at least 20 h a week in recruiting potential job candidates, over a period of at least 1 year, working at an organisation that has a 1000 employees or more. All recruitment professionals were familiar with using LinkedIn as a recruitment tool. Recruitment professionals were chosen as the sample of this study, to increase the external validity of this study since a major part of recruitment professionals' daily job consists of "selecting online job candidate selection" within a limited time frame. Although the sample size of this study was relatively small [32], it was sufficient as information saturation was achieved in these interviews.

3.2 Research Design

This study took on a qualitative approach and used a think-aloud protocol in combination with photo-elicitation. The think-aloud method is a technique where the respondent is asked to vocalize thoughts and reactions while evaluating information (e.g. photos) in real-time [33]. Think-aloud was previously predominately used in usability testing of products and websites [e.g. 34], as it is a relatively cheap and fast way to gather feedback from users [35]. Advantages of this approach are that it enables the researcher to ask follow-up questions to specify and clarify certain motivations [36]. This way, a more rich and in-depth contextual understanding of recruiters' decision-making process is obtained, which is particularly important as the exploration of decision-processes is rather complex. To a certain extent, the think-aloud method minimizes the possibility of socially desirable answers, since the respondent is requested to express all thoughts verbally in real-time [33].

Photo-Elicitation Material. Seven different pictures of a potential job candidate applying for a ficticious entry-level Marketing Consultant Job were shown to recruiters. Each picture displayed the potential candidate in a different way, making certain cues more salient, namely: (1) smiling, (2) formal attire (3) black and white picture (4) causal holiday shot (5) avoiding eye gaze (6) neutral face and (7) avoiding eye contact, but smiling. The rationale for these selection of these specific cues, is as follows:

First, the smiling picture was chosen because previous research has demonstrated that a smile is a positive emotion that may enhance a person's attractiveness and approachability [37]. Second, formal attire was chosen because several studies demonstrated that a more masculine outfit such as business suit leads to job interview success [38]. However, blogs state that to dress for success, you should match the industry's culture, as in a more creative industry such as advertising, more casual attire may be more effective than formal attire [39]. Third, the black and white pictures were chosen because they are associated with aesthetic photography, and set an intellectual, scientific tone [40]. However, other studies have demonstrated that black-and-white photography creates a distance between the depicted individual and the perceiver, and displays the individual less realistic due to the lack of colour [41]. Four, the casual holiday shot was chosen because this is considered as a faux pas for the professional SNS LinkedIN according to popular press [e.g. 42], but has not yet been empirically tested. Five, avoiding eye gaze was chosen as a picture because many LinkedIN profiles use this composition assuming it may be a "dreamy", aesthetical appealing picture. However, eye gaze is an important indicator of trust [43]. Therefore, it's important to further investigate the impact of this cue. Six, a neutral face was chosen because some people believe that on LinkedIN this signifies "seriousness". However, research has demonstrated that people perceive a non-smiling person (neutral expression) as someone who is in the possession of less positive traits in comparison to a smiling person [44]. Finally, avoiding eye contact but smiling was chosen because the results on this combination have been mixed [cf. 45]. Together, all of these visual cues can be used to explore perceived credibility by looking at the elements of attractiveness, trustworthiness and expertise.

In order to create a realistic setting, the manipulated photos were presented to the recruitment professionals as a profile picture placed in a real screenshot of a LinkedIn profile page. Any additional information that may contain cues (e.g. number of contacts) was blurred. The model in this study was 27-year old male. This age indicates that the job candidate is a recent graduate or starter with little to no working experience [46]. The same model was used in every profile picture, to avoid unwanted interaction effects (Fig. 1).

Moreover, it requires a certain level of grooming, yet it is not fully dependant on the physical appearance of the model. The job vacancy was based on several existing descriptions of starter positions for marketing consultant, and resonated the three

Fig. 1. Pictures for photo-elicitation (NB: All pictures were of identical size. The numbers displayed on the pictures here are for clarity purposes; they were not present on the actual photos).

different sub dimensions of Ohanian's perceived credibility [47]. First, the attractiveness aspect is conveyed by mentioning that the ideal candidate is a team player that possesses excellent communication skills and dynamic, strong presentation skills. Second, expertise aspect corresponds to the requirement for a Master's degree, excellent project management, presentation and analytical skills. Third, although trust is not explicitly stated in the job description, it is implicitly required in order to form mutually beneficial relationships, such as those encountered in a typical working environment. In terms of format, the job-description showed similarities with our previous work [see 1, 2].

3.3 Procedure

All interviews were recorded and transcribed in order to assure replication of the data-analysis process. The interview started by stressing confidentially and that information was only to be used for research purposes. As the researcher was the "measurement-instrument", she took care to remain an open, non-judgemental, objective approach, and to stimulate the respondent to talk freely and comfortably.

First, the recruiter was offered the fictitious job vacancy. After allowing sufficient time (2–3 min) the researcher determined if the job vacancy was clearly understood to ensure full understanding and to prevent any language barriers. Hereafter, an introduction was given stating that the recruitment professional was looking to hire a new marketing consultant and had the access to online profiles of job applicants. The recruiters were asked to 'think-aloud' on their cognitive processes when judging the pictures of the shown candidates. To prevent any bias, the visualisations were shown in a set order as demonstrated in this article. After the last visualisation had been shown the respondent was asked to turn around all the visualisations and to rank them from high (1) to low (7) in respectively attractiveness, trust, expertise and likelihood to invite the job applicant. The reason for this ranking was to explore whether the recruiters had a specific preference for one visualisation over the other. In order to guarantee a systematic analysis of the data, the six steps of thematic data analysis from Braun and Clarke [48] were used. After the interviews were transcribed and familiarized, interesting passages or quotes were highlighted to identify data segments. However it is important to note here that during this process there was no selection yet of importance or relevance, as this does not correspond with an open approach [49]. In phase 3 and 4 [48], the data segments were organized in thematic maps and sorted per visual cue. Each visual cue was analysed thoroughly on how the recruiters perceived the job applicant, conforming to the three components of Ohanian's [47] perceived credibility: attractiveness, trustworthiness and expertise. Additionally, the results of the rankings of the visualisations altogether, on the three components of Ohanian [47], were taken into account and analysed. Eventually in phase 5 and phase 6, a final analysis of the visual cues was conducted and repeated patterns of meaning were uncovered.

3.4   Operationalization

To enhance validity and reliability during the interview process [49], a set script of interview questions was followed.

Questions for the interview on perceived credibility were adapted to a qualitative open approach based on the theory of Ohanian [48]. If, how and why the subject was perceived as credible was examined by questioning the respondent on three areas: attractiveness, trustworthiness and expertise. Example questions were:

- What is your first impression of this person?
- What are the qualities of this person?
- Does this person fit the job description?

4   Results

For the first picture (the smile), the data demonstrates that there is a clear tendency to be perceived as a socially skilled, ambitious, trustworthy and professional candidate. This is for instance displayed in the following remark by a recruiter: *"He looks open, very positive and has a smile. I also think his communication skills are very good and those are the most important requirements for this function."* Another recruiter mentioned: *"He looks confident due to his posture and open appearance."* For the second picture, for formal attire, the results were somewhat mixed. Some recruiters were positive and indicated the candidate looked more experienced. However, three recruiters expressed that the formal attire could also be used by the applicant as a tool for a more fortunate presentation in order to hide his insecurity or lack of work experience. This was indicated by a 26 year old recruiter: *"He looks very serious and arrogant and that gives me the feeling that he is maybe trying too hard, so he is pretending he is someone he's not and is actually very insecure."* For the third picture (black and white) the data demonstrates that a black and white picture does not hinder, nor help a person's appearance on LinkedIn. This is illustrated by the following comment: *"Well my preference would go to a photo with colour because that looks more natural and attracts more attention than a black & white photo. However overall, I think this is a good profile shot and it looks professional"*. For the fourth picture (the holiday picture), the data obtained from the interviews demonstrates that a slight majority of the recruiters was still likely to invite the candidate. However, they would have preferred a more representative photo. For the fifth picture (avoiding eye gaze), the results demonstrate that the visual cue of eye-contact has a noticeable influence on the perception of recruiters. A majority of recruiters said that they couldn't gauge this person's personality because they don't feel a connection. Moreover, they perceive this person is less trustworthy due to the avoidance of eye contact, which is illustrated by the following remark of an recruiter: *"I always want to look someone in the eye. For me that's an important indicator if someone is trustworthy or not."* For the sixth picture (neutral face) recruiters are not very positive, but also certainly not negative. Some recruiters noted that it was so difficult to "read" this job applicant, and others found him a bit boring. Finally, for the seventh picture (avoiding eye contact, but smiling) the smile had a positive influence on the overall perception, however, the avoidance of eye-contact remained a disturbing factor for trust perceptions. Recruiters perceived this job applicant as more distant and to himself. However, as for expertise, all the recruiters perceived this applicant as an expert as they perceived the "staring in infinity"-expression as someone who is an intellectual thinker that clearly sets his goals.

5 Discussion

The results indicated that especially the cues of smiling and eye-contact (looking in the camera) appear to have a positive influence on the perception of perceived credibility. For the other cues the results were rather mixed. For example, the recruiters that indicated that formal attire was preferred also worked in more "formal" organisations, while other recruiters worked in more informal settings.

The contribution of this study is that it demonstrates that even recruitment professionals process information in a similar vein as other "human beings", and they may also be led by heuristics. This finding adds to the discussion on the validity of studies on perceived credibility of which the sample were not recruitment professionals. However, further research on the investigated cues is necessary in a more controlled, experimental setting and with larger samples in order to draw more definite conclusion.

This study also has practical implications. Based on the insights obtained in this study, job applicants (particularly in the field of marketing) are advised to smile and make eye-contact on their profile picture, as these seem to be universal cues that positively influence perception of credibility. Regarding wearing formal or informal attire, the job applicant is advised to adapt their dress code to the specific type of organisational culture. As in today's world one is the CEO of ones own brand, the likelihood to successfully obtain a job interview is just a few visual cues away.

References

1. van der Land, S., Muntinga, D.G.: To shave or not to shave? In: Nah, F.F.-H. (ed.) HCIB 2014. LNCS, vol. 8527, pp. 257–265. Springer, Heidelberg (2014)
2. van der Land, S.F., Willemsen, L.M., Unkel, S.A.: Are spectacles the female equivalent of beards for men? How wearing spectacles in a LinkedIn profile picture influences impressions of perceived credibility and job interview likelihood. In: Fui-Hoon Nah, F., Tan, C.-H. (eds.) HCIB 2015. LNCS, vol. 9191, pp. 175–184. Springer, Heidelberg (2015)
3. Kluemper, D.H., Rosen, P.A.: Future employment selection methods: evaluating social networking web sites. J. Manag. Psychol. 24(6), 567–580 (2009)
4. Hatfield, E.: Mirror, Mirror: The Importance of Looks in Everyday Life. Suny Press, New York (1986)
5. Hum, N.J., Chamberlin, P.E., Hambright, B.L., Portwood, A.C., Schat, A.C., Bevan, J.L.: A picture is worth a thousand words: a content analysis of Facebook profile photographs. Comput. Hum. Behav. 27(5), 1828–1833 (2011)
6. Walther, J.B.: Computer-mediated communication impersonal, interpersonal, and hyperpersonal interaction. Commun. Res. 23(1), 3–43 (1996)
7. Krämer, N.C., Winter, S.: Impression management 2.0: the relationship of self-esteem, extraversion, self-efficacy, and self-presentation within social networking sites. J. Media Psychol. Theor. Meth. Appl. 20(3), 106 (2008)
8. Leary, M.R., Kowalski, R.M.: Impression management: a literature review and two-component model. Psychol. Bull. 107(1), 34–47 (1990)
9. Caers, R., Castelyns, V.: LinkedIn and Facebook in Belgium: the influences and biases of social network sites in recruitment and selection procedures. Soc. Sci. Comput. Rev. 29, 437–448 (2010)
10. LinkedIn (n.d.). About Us. http://www.linkedin.com/about.us. Accessed 8 Jan 2015
11. Thew, D.: LinkedIn—a user's perspective using new channels for effective business networking. Bus. Inf. Rev. 25(2), 87–90 (2008)
12. Barnes, N.G., Lescault, A.M.: The 2012 Inc. 500 social media update: blogging declines as newer tools rule (2012). www.umassd.edu/cmr/studiesandresearch/2012inc500socialmedia update/. Accessed 10 Oct 2015
13. Fawley, N.E.: LinkedIn as an information source for human resources, competitive intelligence. Online Searcher, 31–50 (2013)
14. Gosling, S.D., Gaddis, S., Vazire, S.: Personality impressions based on facebook profiles. In: ICWSM 2007, pp. 1–4 (2007)
15. Ellison, N., Heino, R., Gibbs, J.: Managing impressions online: self-presentation processes in the online dating environment. J. Comput. Mediated Commun. 11(2), 415–441 (2006)
16. Siibak, A.: Constructing the self through the photo selection-visual impression management on social networking websites. Cyberpsychol. J. Psychosoc. Res. Cyberspace 3(1), 1 (2009)
17. Clark, L., Roberts, S.: Employer's use of social networking sites: a socially irresponsible practice. J. Bus. Ethics 95, 507–525 (2010)

18. Narisi, S.: Social networking profiles more accurate than resumes? (2009). http://www.hrtechnews.com/social-networking-profiles-more-accurate-than-resumes/. Accessed 12 Dec 2015

19. Chiang, J.K.H., Suen, H.Y.: Self-presentation and hiring recommendations in online communities: lessons from LinkedIn. Comput. Hum. Behav. **48**, 516–524 (2015)

20. Chaiken, S.: Heuristic versus systematic information processing and the use of source versus message cues in persuasion. J. Pers. Soc. Psychol. **39**(5), 752–766 (1980)

21. Petty, R.E., Cacioppo, J.T., Schumann, D.: Central and peripheral routes to advertising effectiveness: the moderating role of involvement. J. Consum. Res. **10**(2), 135–146 (1983)

22. Labrecque, L.I., Markos, E., Milne, G.R.: Online personal branding: processes, challenges, and implications. J. Interact. Mark. **25**(1), 37–50 (2011)

23. Duck, S.W.: Interpersonal communication in developing acquaintance. In: Miller, G.R. (ed.) Explorations in Interpersonal Communication, pp. 127–148. Sage, Beverly Hills (1982)

24. Wang, S.S., Moon, S.I., Kwon, K.H., Evans, C.A., Stefanone, M.A.: Face off: implications of visual cues on initiating friendship on Facebook. Comput. Hum. Behav. **26**(2), 226–234 (2010)

25. Walther, J.B., Parks, M.R.: Cues filtered out, cues filtered in. In: Handbook of Interpersonal Communication, pp. 529–563 (2002)

26. Bar, M., Neta, M., Linz, H.: Very first impressions. Emotion **6**(2), 269–278 (2006)

27. Kanwisher, N., McDermott, J., Chun, M.M.: The fusiform face area: a module in human extrastriate cortex specialized for face perception. J. Neurosci. **17**(11), 4302–4311 (1997)

28. Frith, C.D., Frith, U.: Interacting minds: a biological basis. Science **286**(5445), 1692–1695 (1999)

29. Edwards, C., Stoll, B., Faculak, N., Karman, S.: Social presence on LinkedIn: perceived credibility and interpersonal attractiveness based on user profile picture. Online J. Commun. Media Technol. **5**(4), 102–115 (2015)

30. Pornpitakpan, C.: The persuasiveness of source credibility: a critical review of five decades' evidence. J. Appl. Soc. Psychol. **34**(2), 243–281 (2004)

31. Woodside, A.G., Davenport, J.W.: The effect of salesman similarity and expertise on consumer purchasing behavior. J. Mark. Res. **11**(2), 198–202 (1974)

32. Baarda, B.: Basisboek kwalitatief onderzoek. Noordhof Uitgevers, Groningen (2013)

33. Kucan, L., Beck, I.L.: Thinking aloud and reading comprehension research: inquiry, instruction, and social interaction. Rev. Educ. Res. **67**(3), 271–299 (1997)

34. Lewis, C.: Using the "thinking-aloud" method in cognitive interface design. IBM TJ Watson Research Center Human Services, Cengage Learning (1982)

35. Nielsen, J.: Thinking Aloud: The #1 usability tool (2012). http://www.nngroup.com/articles/thinking-aloud-the-1-usability-tool/. Accessed 27 Jan 2015

36. Monette, D., Sullivan, T., de Jong, C.: Applied Social Research: A Tool for the Human Services. Cengage Learning, Belmont (2013)

37. Miles, L.K.: Who is approachable? J. Exp. Soc. Psychol. **45**(1), 262–266 (2009)

38. Forsythe, S.M.: Effect of applicant's clothing on interviewer's decision to hire. J. Appl. Soc. Psychol. **20**(19), 1579–1595 (1990)

39. Hoeller, S.C.: What to Wear to a Job Interview: Expert Tips for Every Industry (2014). http://stylecaster.com/what-to-wear-to-a-job-interview/. Accessed 10 Jan 2016

40. Noyima, Y.: Black and White Photography (Unpublished dissertation). The University of Utah, Utah (2003)

41. Sassen, S.: Black and white photography as theorizing: seeing what the eye cannot see. Sociol. Forum **26**(2), 438–443 (2011). Blackwell Publishing Ltd.

42. Vermeiren, J.: How to REALLY use LinkedIn. Step by Step Publishing, Ghent (2009)

43. Sundaram, D.S., Webster, C.: The role of nonverbal communication in service encounters. J. Serv. Mark. **14**(5), 378–391 (2000)
44. Reis, H.T., Wilson, I.M., Monestere, C., Bernstein, S., Clark, K., Seidl, E., Franco, M., Gioioso, E., Freeman, L., Radoane, K.: What is smiling is beautiful and good. Eur. J. Soc. Psychol. **20**(3), 259–267 (1990)
45. Jones, B.C., DeBruine, L.M., Little, A.C., Conway, C.A., Feinberg, D.R.: Integrating gaze direction and expression in preferences for attractive faces. Psychol. Sci. **17**(7), 588–591 (2006)
46. Bendick Jr., M., Brown, L.E., Wall, K.: No foot in the door: an experimental study of employment discrimination against older workers. J. Aging Soc. Policy, **10**(4), 5–23 (1999)
47. Ohanian, R.: Construction and validation of a scale to measure celebrity endorsers' perceived expertise, trustworthiness, and attractiveness. J. Advertising **19**, 39–52 (1990)
48. Braun, V., Clarke, V.: Using thematic analysis in psychology. Qual. Res. Psychol. **3**(2), 77–101 (2006)
49. Boeije, H.: Analysis in Qualitative Research, pp. 93–121. Sage, London (2010)

Social Media and Accessibility

Gian Wild[✉]

AccessibilityOz, Melbourne, VIC, Australia
gian@accessibilityoz.com

Abstract. Social media is an integral part of the web, and it is becoming even more important when it comes to employment prospects. People with disabilities already find it difficult to access employment and any web sites that are inaccessible to them makes the issue that much harder. LinkedIn is one social network that is becoming essential for employees in the twenty-first century. A subset of requirements from the W3C Web Content Accessibility Guidelines were used to test how accessible LinkedIn is to people with disabilities. A large number of issues were found, indicating that LinkedIn is not an accessible social network and is unlikely to provide the same functionality to people with disabilities using the system as those provided to the general public.

Keyword: Accessibility

1 Introduction

Social media is an incredibly important tool in modern society. There are five main reasons people access social media: personal (such as sharing photos on Instagram), work (such as finding jobs on LinkedIn), entertainment (such as following celebrities on Twitter), provision of goods and services (such as responding to user complaints on Facebook) and education (such as watching instructional videos on YouTube) [1]. It is not just the young who access social media, with close to 30 % of people over the age of 65 interacting on social networking sites, and 50 % of people aged 50–64 [2].

1.1 Social Media and Employment

Social media is becoming an essential part of negotiating the current working environment. Of all US adults who use social media, 35 % have used social media to look for or research a job, 34 % have used social media to inform friends of a job in their current company and 21 % have applied for a job found through social media contacts [3]. Thirteen percent of social media users state that their existing social media profile has helped with finding a job [3].

As the percentage of recruiters who use LinkedIn to review job candidates is now 95 % [4], this social network is integral to one's employment prospects. With over 414 million users [5] (including over 120 million registered members in the US [6]), two new users every second [5] and 3 million active job listings at any one time [7], it is a formidable network.

© Springer International Publishing Switzerland 2016
F.F.-H. Nah and C.-H. Tan (Eds.): HCIBGO 2016, Part I, LNCS 9751, pp. 129–140, 2016.
DOI: 10.1007/978-3-319-39396-4_12

Thus the accessibility compliance of these social networks is of paramount importance to people with disabilities. People with disabilities are already discriminated against in the workforce, as the many instances of litigation under the Americans with Disabilities Act attests to [8]. Although the employment rate of people without disabilities has increased slightly over the last 25 years – from 76 % to 78 %, the employment rate of people with disabilities has almost halved – from 29 % to 16 %, despite no significant change in the percentage of people with disabilities over the twenty-five years [9]. With the employment participation rate of people without disabilities close to three times that of people with disabilities [10], any barrier to employment must be rectified.

When it comes to LinkedIn, one's success is greatly improved by interacting with the network. For example, adding a professional photo to one's profile means that one is fourteen times more likely to be found in LinkedIn [11]. Adding skills to one's profile increases one's views thirteen times [12]. The number of comments on a LinkedIn post doubles if that post contains an image [13]. Therefore, LinkedIn is not just about creating a profile, but updating it as required. It is therefore essential that these features are fully accessible.

1.2   About Web Accessibility

Web accessibility is about making sure web sites, web applications and mobile apps (including social media networks) are accessible to people with disabilities. There are four groups of people assisted by an accessible site: people with cognitive disabilities; people with vision impairments; people with physical disabilities; and people with hearing impairments. The estimate of people with disabilities in the US varies between 40 million [14] and 57 million Americans [15]. This is a conservative estimate.

W3C Web Content Accessibility Guidelines, Version 2.0. Web accessibility of web sites is best achieved by following the Web Content Accessibility Guidelines, Version 2.0. The World Wide Web Consortium (W3C) has worked in the area of web accessibility since 1998 and they have developed a set of recommendations called the W3C Web Content Accessibility Guidelines, which have been endorsed around the world. The W3C states that "following these guidelines will make content accessible to a wider range of people with disabilities, including blindness and low vision, deafness and hearing loss, learning disabilities, cognitive limitations, limited movement, speech disabilities, photosensitivity and combinations of these" [16].

The W3C Web Content Accessibility Guidelines, Version 2.0 consists of four principles (Perceivable, Operable, Understandable and Robust) with 12 guidelines and 61 success criteria. There are three conformance levels: Level A (minimum), Level AA (medium) and Level AAA (high). Most countries require conformance to Level AA.

2 Methodology for Testing the Accessibility Compliance of Social Networks

The LinkedIn web site and mobile app was tested against the W3C Web Content Accessibility Guidelines on a desktop computer, an iPhone and an Android phone.

The following pages were tested:

- Homepage
- Create an account
- Login
- Profile page
- Add a post

2.1 Testing Against the W3C Web Content Accessibility Guidelines

A selection of success criteria from the W3C Web Content Accessibility Guidelines were used to assess the accessibility compliance of LinkedIn. These success criteria are representative of the most serious accessibility issues that people with disabilities encounter when accessing a web site.

Success Criterion 1.1.1: Non-text Content (Level A). This success criterion requires that text alternatives are provided for all non-text content, such as images, for assistive technologies to interpret. Without text alternatives ("ALT attributes") all images would be unavailable to screen reader users. Missing text alternatives to form features, such as image submit buttons, means that assistive technology users, such as screen reader users and speech recognition users (for people with vision impairments and physical disabilities respectively), will be unable to use a form at all.

This success criterion was tested using Chris Pederick's FireFox Web Developer Toolbar [17] using the following features:

- Outline all images without ALT attributes
- Outline images with empty ALT attributes
- Display ALT attributes

Images and other non-text content in LinkedIn were tested for the presence and accuracy of text alternatives. LinkedIn was also tested for the ability for a user to add text alternatives to user-generated content.

Success Criterion 1.3.1: Info and Relationships (Level A). This success criterion requires that important information about the content be coded so that it can be interpreted by assistive technologies. For example, headings can be coded in a particular way so that screen reader users can access a list of headings in the page, and therefore access an overview of the content of the page.

This success criterion was tested manually by reviewing the code of a social media site and with Chris Pederick's FireFox Web Developer Toolbar [17] using the following features:

- Outline headings

LinkedIn was tested for the presence and accuracy of headings and for the presence of appropriately coded form elements.

Success Criterion 1.4.3: Contrast (Minimum) (Level AA). This success criterion requires that the colour contrast between foreground text and the background meets certain requirements. People with failing eyesight and people who are colorblind have difficulty reading content with low colour contrast. Approximately 8 % of men are colorblind [18], therefore it is a common ailment (although it is not defined as a disability). Due to the high prevalence of colorblindness amongst the general population this success criterion was deemed integral to the accessibility compliance of the LinkedIn web sites, despite the fact that it is in the Level AA (medium) category, not the minimum category.

This success criterion was tested using the Paciello Group's Colour Contrast Analyser [19]. Items that were deemed mandatory to understanding and interacting with the social media site were tested for adequate colour contrast.

Success Criterion 2.1.1: Keyboard (Level A). This success criterion requires that all content and functionality in a web site be accessible via the keyboard. A number of different physical disabilities restrict a user's ability to use a mouse, and these people often rely on a keyboard to access a site. Keyboards can also be implemented with mobile devices, for people who have difficulty using the touchscreen feature.

This success criterion was tested manually on a FireFox browser (Version 44) on Windows 10.

Success Criterion 2.1.2: No Keyboard Trap (Level A). This success criterion requires that any component that can be entered via a keyboard can also be exited via a keyboard. There are some instances where features, such as video players, trap the keyboard focus and the user cannot escape the feature. In order to continue using the site the user must close the browser and begin again. Success Criterion 2.1.2 is one of the four "non-interference" success criteria in WCAG2 [20]. These four success criteria must be met across an entire site, even if part of the site is deemed to be inaccessible. Failing one of these four success criteria interferes so significantly with some user's interaction with the site that it is deemed a critical failure.

This success criterion was tested manually on a FireFox browser (Version 44) on Windows 10.

Success Criterion 2.4.1: Bypass Blocks (Level A). This success criterion requires that users that can only access content sequentially can jump over repeated content such as navigation straight to the body of the page. One of the most common methods of achieving this is to provide "skip links" which provide an anchor link to the content of the page. According to WCAG2, skip links must be the first focusable link on a page [21]. For example, this allows screen reader users to jump past the navigation, which, if there were no skip links, would be repeated on every page that they visit.

This success criterion was tested manually on a FireFox browser (Version 44) on Windows 10.

Success Criterion 2.4.3: Focus Order (Level A). This success criterion requires that the order of content is meaningful to the user. There are three different content orders:

- Visual order of content on the page
- Source order of the code
- Order in which items receive keyboard focus

It is important that these three orders are the same. Often people with disabilities will have access to more than one content order, and if there are differences between these content orders it can cause serious confusion to users. For example, a keyboard-only user of a site will have access to the visual order of the content of the page, as well as the order in which items receive keyboard focus. As another example, people with cognitive disabilities who use screen readers to assist in reading content will have access to the visual order of the content in the page and the source order of the code (which is used by the screen reader).

This success criterion was tested in conjunction with Success Criterion 2.1.1: Keyboard, by manually reviewing the visual order of the content on the page and by displaying the content with style sheets disabled using an internal AccessibilityOz FireFox bookmarklet.

Success Criterion 2.4.7: Focus Visible (Level AA). This success criterion requires that an element that has keyboard focus is visually indicated to the user ("keyboard focus indicator"). If this is the case, the user can easily follow keyboard movement through the page, and activate appropriate items. Where items do not have a highly visible keyboard focus indicator the user will not know where on the page their focus is located. This makes a site incredibly difficult, if not impossible to use. As this is a feature that is essential to keyboard-only users in interacting with a site it was deemed integral to the accessibility compliance of the LinkedIn web site, despite the fact that it is in the Level AA (medium) category, not the minimum category.

This success criterion was tested manually on a FireFox browser (Version 44) on Windows 10.

3   The Accessibility Compliance of Social Media

3.1   Results of Testing Against the W3C Web Content Accessibility Guidelines

Success Criterion 1.1.1: Non-text content (Level A). Surprisingly the LinkedIn site does not have many images, however they all include accurate ALT attributes. Unfortunately, there is no way for a user, when posting a status with an image, to add an ALT attribute to that image. As a result, all images added to a status or a post have empty ALT attributes.

Success Criterion 1.3.1: Info and Relationships (Level A). The forms in LinkedIn have been coded appropriately as specific form elements. This should make it straightforward for screen reader users to access the site.

Headings have been coded in the site, however the hierarchy of the headings are incorrect. In the example below the text 'Platinum Asset Management Limited shared:' is a heading 3. The article title 'Sugar addiction – breaking the cycle' is a heading 4. However, the names of the commenters on the article ('Alan Wallace', 'Brett Elliott') are also coded as heading 4 (see Fig. 1). These commenter names are sub-headings to the article name and should be coded as a heading 5.

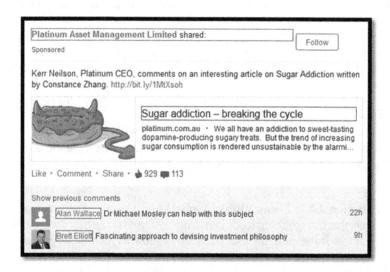

Fig. 1. Heading structure (headings outlined) in the main profile page of LinkedIn

Success Criterion 1.4.3: Contrast (Minimum) (Level AA). Colour contrast is problematic, with some information presented as medium-grey text on a light-grey background on a mobile device. Whether a person is a first degree contact or a second-degree contact is provided as medium-grey text on a light-grey background and fails WCAG2 colour contrast requirements (see Fig. 2).

When entering an incorrect password into the login box, the error text is red on a grey background (see Fig. 3) and this also fails WCAG2 colour contrast requirements.

Fig. 2. Colour contrast failures in the login feature (Color figure online)

Fig. 3. Colour contrast failures in the iPhone LinkedIn mobile app (Color figure online)

Success Criterion 2.1.1: Keyboard (Level A). When creating an account some important features are not keyboard accessible, including the ability to skip importing contacts (see Fig. 4), and sending another email if the original email was not received (see Fig. 5).

Fig. 4. The 'Skip' importing contacts link can only be accessed via a mouse

Fig. 5. The 'Send me another email' option can only be accessed by the mouse

Fig. 6. Many options in the add post feature can only be accessed by the mouse

Some features are not keyboard accessible, such as saving, publishing or formatting functions when adding a post (Fig. 6).

Success Criterion 2.1.2: No Keyboard Trap (Level A). When first accessing the site as a new user a popup appears over the top-left navigation with information about messaging (see Fig. 7). This popup cannot be closed by the keyboard. In addition, a user tabbing through the navigation will not be able to see the items currently in focus as they are overlapped by the popup. This is referred to as a 'reverse keyboard trap' [22] – where content cannot be closed with the keyboard and this content overlaps important information. This can only be closed by leaving LinkedIn and logging in again – on subsequent logins this popup does not appear.

Fig. 7. The messaging popup overlaps important navigation items in the top-left and can only be closed using the mouse

Success Criterion 2.4.1: Bypass Blocks. LinkedIn contains quite detailed skip links. There is a popup available on keyboard focus that allows users to jump to sections such as profile activity, update status, network updates and search (see Fig. 8).

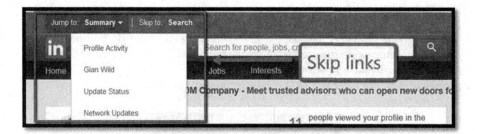

Fig. 8. LinkedIn includes comprehensive skip links that appear on keyboard focus

Success Criterion 2.4.3: Focus Order (Level A). In the sign up process the source and keyboard focus order do not match the visual order of content (see Fig. 9). The first item is the field, however the second item that receives keyboard focus is a 'Learn more' link which appears below the 'Continue' button. The 'Continue' button subsequently receives keyboard focus.

Fig. 9. The source order of content does not match the visual order in the sign up process

Success Criterion 2.4.7: Focus Visible (Level AA). LinkedIn often has a highly visible keyboard focus indicator so keyboard-only users know where they are positioned on the page. When looking at pending invitations in the menu the focus indicator is a bright blue outline (see Fig. 10).

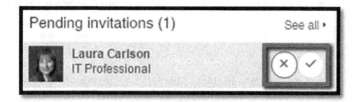

Fig. 10. Some items, such as rejecting an invitation have a highly visible keyboard focus indicator (Color figure online)

Unfortunately, some items that have a keyboard focus indicator do not meet colour contrast requirements. In the dropdown for the menu, when an item receives keyboard focus it changes to a deep-blue colour (see Fig. 11). This colour, against the dark-grey background does not meet WCAG2 colour contrast requirements.

Fig. 11. The keyboard focus indicator is a deep-blue against a dark-grey background and does not meet colour contrast requirements (Color figure online)

4   Conclusions

In conclusion LinkedIn still has many accessibility problems that are likely to cause problems to different groups of people with disabilities. As a result, these groups are less likely to be able to find relevant employment, contributing to the under-employment of people with disabilities.

4.1   Why Is Social Media Inaccessible?

The main reason why social media is not accessible is that social networking sites and apps are almost continually refreshed. Facebook sometimes changes twice a day [23]. This, coupled with a lack of a formal testing process, means that what may be accessible today may be literally gone tomorrow. Although there have been some improvements in the accessibility of social networks over the last year; namely the removal of a CAPTCHA in the signup process for LinkedIn, any accessibility features can be instantaneously lost as the site or mobile app is updated.

References

1. Kietzmann, J.H., Hermkens, K., McCarthy, I.P., Silvestre, B.S.: Social media? Get serious! Understanding the functional building blocks of social media. Bus. Horiz. **54**(3), 241–251 (2011)
2. Perrin, A.: Social Media Usage: 2005–2015 (2015). http://www.pewinternet.org/2015/10/08/social-networking-usage-2005-2015/
3. Smith, A.: Searching for Work in the Digital Era (2015). http://www.pewinternet.org/2015/11/19/searching-for-work-in-the-digital-era/
4. Pratt, S.: How Recruiters and Job Seekers Use Social Media in 2015 (Infographic) (2015). http://www.socialtalent.co/blog/how-recruiters-and-job-seekers-use-social-media-in-2015
5. Sordello, S.: LinkedIn's Q4 2015 Earnings (2016). http://blog.linkedin.com/2016/02/04/linkedins-q4-2015-earnings/
6. LinkedIn. https://press.linkedin.com/about-linkedin
7. LinkedIn Corporate Communications Team: LinkedIn Announces Second Quarter 2015 Results (2015). https://press.linkedin.com/site-resources/news-releases/2015/linkedin-announces-second-quarter-2015-results
8. United States Department of Justice Civil Rights Division: Information and Technical Assistance on the Americans with Disabilities Act (2016). http://www.ada.gov/enforce_current.htm#TitleI
9. Brucker, D.L., Houtenville, A.J.: People with disabilities in the United States. Arch. Phys. Med. Rehabil. **96**(5), 771–774 (2015)
10. Bureau of Labor Statistics: Employment Situation Summary: Employment Status of the Civilian Population by Sex, Age, and Disability Status, not Seasonally Adjusted (2016). http://www.bls.gov/news.release/empsit.t06.htm
11. Rao, N.: Celebrating Leadership & LinkedIn Power Profiles 2015 in India (2015). http://blog.linkedin.com/2015/08/13/celebrating-leadership-linkedin-power-profiles-2015-in-india/
12. Bastian, M.: Your Skills Are Your Competitive Edge on LinkedIn [INFOGRAPHIC] (2014). http://blog.linkedin.com/2014/10/16/your-skills-are-your-competitive-edge-on-linkedin/

13. Seiter, C.: Master The LinkedIn Company Page: 12 New Data-Backed Tips To Max Out Yours (2015). https://blog.bufferapp.com/linkedin-company-pages
14. Houtenville, A.J., Brucker, D., Lauer, E.: Annual Compendium of Disability Statistics: 2014. University of New Hampshire, Institute on Disability, Durham, NH (2014)
15. Brault, M.W.: Americans with Disabilities: 2010. Current Population Reports, P70–131 (2012)
16. World Wide Web Consortium: Web Content Accessibility Guidelines (WCAG) 2.0 (2008). https://www.w3.org/TR/WCAG20/
17. Pederick, C.: FireFox Web Developer Toolbar (2013). http://chrispederick.com/work/web-developer/history/firefox/
18. Color Blind Awareness. http://www.colourblindawareness.org/
19. The Paciello Group: Contrast Analyser (2016). https://www.paciellogroup.com/resources/contrastanalyser/
20. World Wide Web Consortium: Understanding WCAG 2.0: Understanding Conformance (2008). https://www.w3.org/TR/UNDERSTANDING-WCAG20/conformance.html
21. World Wide Web Consortium Understanding WCAG 2.0: Bypass Blocks: Understanding SC 2.4.1   (2008).   https://www.w3.org/TR/UNDERSTANDING-WCAG20/navigation-mechanisms-skip.html
22. Wild, G.: Mobile Accessibility Issues - Part One: Hover (2015). https://www.linkedin.com/pulse/mobile-accessibility-issues-part-one-hover-gian-wild
23. Rossi, C.: Ship Early and Ship Twice as Often (2012). https://www.facebook.com/notes/facebook-engineering/ship-early-and-ship-twice-as-often/10150985860363920

The Effects of Social Structure Overlap
and Profile Extensiveness
on Facebook Friend Requests

Yi Wu[1], Ben C.F. Choi[2], and Jie Yu[3(✉)]

[1] College of Management and Economics, Tianjin University, Tianjin, China
yiwu@tju.edu.cn
[2] School of Information Systems, Technology and Management,
UNSW Australia Business School, Kensington, Australia
chun.choi@unsw.edu.au
[3] Nottingham University Business School, Nottingham, China
jie.yu@nottingham.edu.cn

Abstract. In online social networks, new social connectivity is established when a respondent accepts a friend request from an unfamiliar requestor. While users are generally willing to establish online social connectivity, they are at times reluctant in constructing profile connections with unfamiliar others. Drawing on the privacy calculus perspective, this study examines the effects of social structure overlap and profile extensiveness on privacy risks as well as social capital gains and how the respondent responds to a friend request (i.e., intention to accept). The results provide strong evidence that social structure overlap and profile extensiveness influence privacy risks and social capital gains. In addition, while privacy risks reduce intention to accept, social capital gains increase intention to accept online social connectivity.

Keywords: Online social networks · Online social connectivity · Impression formation · Privacy calculus · Intention to accept

1 Introduction

Online social connectivity is highly important to online service providers. A new online social connectivity is initiated when an unfamiliar requestor sends a friend request to a request respondent [1]. The respondent's response to the friend request is often influenced by his or her impression of the requestor, and the impression is formed based on the requestor's personal profile on online social networks. Personal profiles typically contain a variety of information about the requestor, such as photographs, personal interests, and social circles.

Past studies reveal that developing online social connectivity with an unfamiliar requestor can be beneficial to the respondent. Furthermore, the establishment of online social connectivity enables the respondent to develop additional relationships based on the social networks of the requestor. As a key function of online social networks is to facilitate the development and maintenance of online social connectivity, we contend

© Springer International Publishing Switzerland 2016
F.F.-H. Nah and C.-H. Tan (Eds.): HCIBGO 2016, Part I, LNCS 9751, pp. 141–152, 2016.
DOI: 10.1007/978-3-319-39396-4_13

that gains in social resources are an important benefit in developing new online social connectivity.

It has, however, been observed that while online social connectivity enables increasing in social resources, its establishment might subject the respondent to risks. Research in the interpersonal communication domain provides insights into this phenomenon. For example, Stern and Taylor [2] examined students' Facebook usage behavior and reported that while students did accept friend requests from unfamiliar others, those who were concerned about their privacy information denied friend requests. In essence, the respondent might deny profile connections in response to privacy risks on online social networks.

In this paper, we propose and empirically test a research model that integrates the interpersonal cognition literature and the privacy calculus perspective. In sum, the model maintains that the effects of category-based information and attribute-based information are summarized into privacy risks and social capital gains, which in turn, drive the respondent's response to online social connectivity (i.e., intention to accept).

2 Literature Review

2.1 Impression Formation

The literature on interpersonal cognition suggests that individuals form impression of others by considering two types of social information, namely category-based information and attribute-based information. Category-based information triggers social categorization, which invokes relational frames stored in memory [3]. Researchers suggest that category-based information facilitates sense-making by providing mechanisms for comprehending relational communications [4]. Attribute-based information activates individualization in social information processing. By considering others' specific attributes systematically, individuals are likely to develop deep understanding of others.

2.2 Privacy Calculus

The privacy calculus perspective posits that individuals' decision in allowing boundary accessibility is the outcome of a tradeoff, in which individuals consider the risks associated with boundary accessibility against certain social gains [5]. While past research has considered a variety of risks and gains, privacy risks and social capital gains are suggested to be particularly relevant to individuals' behavior when their personal information is concerned. This study defines privacy risks as the threats to personal information associated with the establishment of profile connections. This type of privacy risks is particularly important in online social networks because establishment of online social connectivity exposes individuals' privacy space to unforeseen danger. Social capital gains are defined as the estimated increase in resources accumulated through relationship development [6]. Past research has regarded gains in social capital as the main enticement for individuals to engage in social interactions.

While privacy risks are known to be a prime inhibitor to online social networking, the respondent's social capital gains are found to be a major driver of online social connection development. Overall, privacy risks and social capital gains, which represent the two components in the respondent's privacy calculus, are particularly important in influencing his or her response to online social connectivity.

3   Research Model and Hypotheses

The research model is presented in Fig. 1.

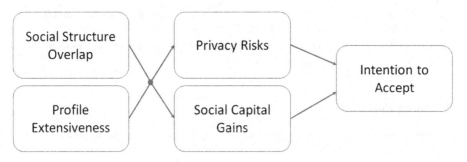

Fig. 1. Research model

3.1   Determinants of Privacy Risks

Social structure overlap refers to the degree to which the respondent and the requestor share common interpersonal contacts. The respondent who shares similar social networks with the requestor tends to share a common perspective with regards to relationship development, and this commonality reduces risks in developing connections. The resulting social cohesion engendered by social structure overlap lessens the likelihood that the requestor will engage in exploitive behavior, hence reducing risks to the respondent's privacy. Thus, we predict that:

H1: Compared to low social structure overlap, high social structure overlap leads to lower privacy risks.

In addition to social structure overlap, we expect privacy risks to be influenced by requestor's profile extensiveness, which refers to the extent to which the personal profile contains detailed personal information. Researchers have noted the importance of personal profiles in the initial stage of relationship development. When requestor's profile extensiveness is high, the respondent may develop rich understanding of the requestor, hence reducing privacy risks with regards to establishing online social connectivity. Therefore, we posit that:

H2: Compared to low profile extensiveness, high profile extensiveness leads to lower privacy risks.

High social structure overlap helps the respondent converge his or her focus on social similarity with the requestor, that is, the respondent is likely to perceive the requestor as someone who shares common social circles and interpersonal connections [7]. Hence, the effect of profile extensiveness is likely diminished when social structure overlap is high.

In contrast, low social structure overlap suggests less commonality in interpersonal relationships. As a result, the respondent is likely to become more prudent in forming impression of the requestor. Low social structure overlap would not be sufficient in finalizing the respondent's impression of the requestor. Compared to low profile extensiveness, high profile extensiveness connotes more informative profile content and hence reduces privacy risks with regards to establishing online social connectivity. Thus, we hypothesize that:

H3: There is an interaction effect between social structure overlap and profile extensiveness on privacy risks, i.e., in the high social structure overlap condition, the effect of profile extensiveness in terms of reducing privacy risks is less prominent than that in the low social structure overlap condition.

3.2   Social Capital Gains

In online social networks, social structure overlap is a concise representation of similarity in social networks as well as commonality in interpersonal connections. Research on interpersonal relationship has consistently uncovered strong links between social structure overlap and liking, which is also termed as the similarity effect. Typically, individuals believe others, who shared common social connections, would also believe what individuals believe [8]. Past research suggests that a positive relationship between social structure overlap and individuals' expectation of social capital gains in relationship development. Therefore, we hypothesize that:

H4: Higher social structure overlap leads to higher social capital gains.

From a social penetration perspective, when an unfamiliar requestor reveals himself or herself through self-disclosure, the respondent is better able to understand the requestor and predict his or her future behavior. In online social networks, the lack of physical presence limits attribute-based information to the requestor's self-disclosure in personal profiles. As a result, the respondent has to rely heavily on the requestor's personal profile in assessing his or her social capital gains. Accordingly, high profile extensiveness is likely to induce large social capital gains in establishing online social connectivity. Thus, we predict that:

H5: Higher profile extensiveness leads to higher social capital gains.

When social structure overlap is high, the respondent feels assured that the requestor would have common interests and share mutual understanding in developing relationships, thereby reducing the respondent's reliance on profile information in assessing social capital gains. However, when social structure overlap is low, mutual understanding and common interests cannot be guaranteed; hence, the respondent would pay more attention to information available in the requestor's personal profiles. Thus, we propose that:

H6: There is an interaction effect between social structure overlap and profile extensiveness on social capital gains, i.e., in the high social structure overlap condition, the effect of profile extensiveness in terms of increasing social capital gains is less prominent than that in the low social structure overlap condition.

3.3   Privacy Tradeoff and Request Acceptance

Accepting a friend request can be risky because it represents the respondent's willingness in exposing himself or herself to the requestor in online social networks. Much research suggests that in online social networks, relationship acceptance can be impeded by the respondent's privacy risks perceptions in establishing online social connectivity [9]. Therefore, we posit that:

H7: Higher privacy risks lead to lower intention to accept.

A number of studies suggest that social capital gains significantly influence intention to accept a friend request. For example, in a study on Facebook, Lampe et al. [10] reported that individuals who had favorable impression of others were more willing to establish online profile connections. These findings imply that the respondent's gains in social capital may induce acceptance to a friend request. Therefore, we hypothesize that:

H8: Higher social capital gains lead to higher intention to accept.

4   Research Methodology

This research employed a quasi-experimental design (i.e., 2×2 factorial design) that integrates the characteristics of field surveys and lab experiments. Facebook was chosen as the online social network platform for this study. Respondents were university students who had online social networking experience. In the experiment, respondents were presented with one of the four scenarios (i.e., varied across the two categories of social structure overlap and profile extensiveness) in which they received a friend request from an unfamiliar requestor.

Social structure overlap was manipulated by the number of mutual friends the respondent has in common with the requestor. In this study, low social structure overlap was represented by 5 % of the respondent's total Facebook friends, whereas high social structure overlap was represented by 50 % of the respondent's total Facebook friends. Profile extensiveness was facilitated by manipulating the amount of content items in the mock-up personal profile of the requestor that mimicked actual Facebook layout and technology features (e.g., sponsored advertisements, profile pictures, and timeline elements).

Low profile extensiveness was represented by 5 timeline items, while high profile extensiveness was represented by 20 timeline items. The timelines items were developed based on a pool of actual timeline items contributed by students from the same university. Respondents were told to imagine that the scenario was real and read through it carefully. Afterwards, they were instructed to complete a questionnaire that contained manipulation checks and measurements of the research variables, as well as the relevance and realism of the friend request scenario.

The survey ran for one week, and collected 76 responses, who were not friends of the contributors.

5   Data Analysis and Results

5.1   Respondent Demographics and Background Analysis

Among the 76 respondents participating in the study, 37 were females. The age of the respondents ranged from 19 to 22, with average Internet experience and average Facebook experience being 6.28 years and 4.2 years, respectively.

5.2   Results on Privacy Risks

ANOVA with privacy risks as dependent variable reveals that higher social structure overlap significantly leads to lower privacy risks ($F (1, 72) = 75.04$, $p < 0.01$) (see Table 1).

Table 1. ANOVA results

Source	Sum of squares	Df	Mean square	F	Sig.
Overall sample					
SSO	68.89	1	75.04	75.04	.000
PE	18.81	1	18.81	20.49	.000
SSO * PE	8.73	1	8.73	9.50	.003
Error	89.06	72	.92		
Total	1786.72	76			
SSO = Low					
PE	26.89	1	26.89	22.67	.000
Error	58.11	37	1.19		
Total	1254.28	38			
SSO = High					
PE	.95	1	.95	1.47	.232
Error	30.95	36	.65		
Total	532.44	39			

Notes:
Dependent Variable: Privacy Risks.
SSO = Social Structure Overlap, PE = Profile Extensiveness.
R Squared = .52 (Adjusted R Squared = .50)

Further, profile extensiveness is found to have a significant main effect on privacy risks ($F (1, 72) = 20.49$, $p < 0.01$), meaning that compared to low profile extensiveness, high profile extensiveness reduces privacy risks. Hence, H1 and H2 are supported. Simple main effect analysis (Table 2 and Fig. 2) reveals that (1) high profile extensiveness is associated with significantly higher social capital gains than low profile extensiveness under the low social structure overlap condition (F (1, 37) = 22.67, p < 0.01), and (2) low profile extensiveness and high profile extensiveness are not different from each other in affecting social capital gains under the high social structure overlap condition (F(1, 36) = 1.47, p = 0.23). Therefore, H3 is supported.

Table 2. Mean values of privacy risks

	Low PE	High PE	Mean
Low SSO	5.56	4.10	4.79
High SSO	3.31	3.04	3.16
Mean	4.46	3.57	

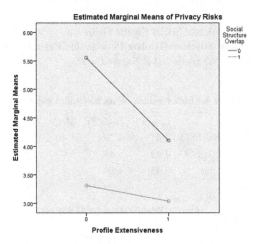

Fig. 2. Mean plot of privacy risks

5.3 Results on Social Capital Gains

ANOVA with social capital gains as dependent variable reveals that higher social structure overlap significantly leads to higher social capital gains (F (1, 72) = 90.11, p < 0.01) (see Tables 5 and 6). Further, profile extensiveness is found to have a significant main effect on social capital gains (F (1, 72) = 69.26, p < 0.01) (see Table 3). Hence, H4 and H5 are supported.

In line with our prediction, the effect of profile extensiveness is more prominent in the low social structure overlap condition than in the high social structure overlap condition (Table 4 and Fig. 3). Therefore, H6 is supported.

Table 3. ANOVA results

Source	Sum of squares	Df	Mean square	F	Sig.
Overall sample					
SSO	67.46	1	67.46	90.11	.000
PE	51.85	1	51.85	69.26	.000
SSO * PE	4.96	1	4.96	6.62	.012
Error	72.62	72	.75		
Total	1982.56	76			
SSO = Low					
PE	44.95	1	44.95	37.21	.000
Error	59.19	37	1.21		
Total	694.38	38			
SSO = High					
PE	12.23	1	12.23	43.73	.000
Error	13.43	36	.28		
Total	1288.19	39			

Notes:
Dependent Variable: Social Capital Gains
SSO = Social Structure Overlap; PE = Profile Extensiveness.
R Squared = .63 (Adjusted R Squared = .62)

Table 4. Mean values of social capital gains

	Low PE	High PE	Mean
Low SSO	2.41	4.29	3.40
High SSO	4.49	5.48	5.03
Mean	3.43	4.88	

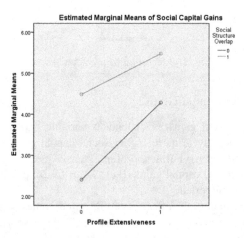

Fig. 3. Mean plot of social capital gains

5.4   Results on Request Acceptance

Partial Least Square (PLS) was used to test remaining hypotheses. The measurements generally load heavily on their respective constructs, with loadings above 0.8, thus demonstrating adequate reliability (Table 5).

Table 5. Loadings and cross-loadings of measures

	PR	SCG	IA
PR1	*0.84*	−0.42	−0.57
PR2	*0.84*	−0.38	−0.51
PR3	*0.84*	−0.35	−0.48
PR4	*0.85*	−0.35	−0.46
PR5	*0.81*	−0.46	−0.48
SCG1	−0.37	*0.86*	0.53
SCG2	−0.36	*0.84*	0.56
SCG3	−0.49	*0.85*	0.64
SCG4	−0.38	*0.87*	0.61
IA1	−0.53	0.58	*0.89*
IA2	−0.54	0.66	*0.88*
IA3	−0.51	0.58	*0.88*

Notes:
PR = Privacy Risks;
SCG = Social Capital Gains;
IA = Intention to Accept.

Subjects' intention to accept was captured using three items. The high composite reliability and Cronbach's alpha scores shown in Table 6 lend support to satisfactory internal consistency.

Table 6. Internal Consistency and Discriminant Validity of Constructs

	CR	CA	PR	SCG	IA
PR	0.89	0.92	**0.70**		
SCG	0.88	0.91	−0.47	**0.73**	
IA	0.86	0.91	−0.60	0.69	**0.78**

Notes: CR = Composite Reliability;
CA = Cronbach's Alpha.

The diagonal elements in Table 6 represent the square roots of average variance extracted (AVE) of latent variables, while off-diagonal elements are the correlations between latent variables. For adequate discriminant validity, the square root of the AVE of any latent variable should be greater than correlation between this particular latent variable and other latent variables. Data shown in Table 6 therefore satisfies this requirement. Moreover, in Table 5, the loadings of indicators on their respective latent variables are higher than loadings of other indictors on these latent variables and the loadings of these indicators on other latent variables, thus lending further evidence to discriminant validity.

Results shown in Fig. 4 indicate that privacy risks has a significant and negative effect on intention to accept ($\beta = -0.352$, $p < 0.01$). Hence, H7 is supported. Furthermore, the results demonstrate that social capital gains have a significant and positive effect on intention to accept ($\beta = 0.525$, $p < 0.01$). Therefore, H8 is supported.

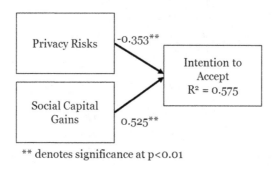

** denotes significance at $p<0.01$

Fig. 4. Nomological network model testing

6   Theoretical Implication

This study makes important theoretical contributions. Past IS research examining privacy issues in online social networks has paid little attention to social connectivity regulation. This lack of attention to the establishment of social connections is somewhat surprising since a prime reason for individuals to adopt online social networks is to establish, develop, as well as maintain social connections. On the basis of the privacy calculus perspective, we identify privacy risks and social capital gains, as the cost and benefit elements of a privacy tradeoff, whereby individuals consider the privacy threats and social benefits in establishing social connectivity. Our findings show that privacy risks and social capital gains are indeed important determinants of individuals' response to a request for profile connections. To the best of our knowledge, this study is the first to employ the notion of privacy boundary regulation to understand the establishment of social connectivity.

Further, we contribute to the IS literature by providing evidence on the importance of impression formation in regulating social connectivity. While past studies have identified a myriad of factors pertinent to privacy perceptions, rarely have researchers examined the effects of social information processing on individuals' assessment of privacy threats and social benefits. Based on the interpersonal cognition literature, this study identifies two important antecedents of privacy calculus, namely social structure overlap and profile extensiveness. Specifically, social structure overlap is a type of social category-based information, which invokes relational frames to facilitate social categorization. Profile extensiveness concerns the details of requestor's specific information (i.e., social attribute-based information), which is essential for individualization in social information processing. Taken as a whole, we combine literature on impression formation and privacy calculus and then show the efficacy of this integrative approach in the context of online social networks.

7 Practical Implication

Our findings have important implications to application designers as well as online social networks providers. Application designers of online social networks often provide mechanisms that address users' perception of privacy risks. While mechanisms that address privacy risks are somewhat common, little design efforts have been made on enhancing the appreciation of social capital gains. To this end, we advocate a design strategy which improves recognition of social capital gains. As predicted by the proposed model, social capital gains are found to be enhanced by greater social structure overlap and profile extensiveness. While this result is largely consistent with conventional wisdom, a more interesting finding of this study is probably that the joint effect of social structure overlap and profile extensiveness on social capital gains is more pronounced in the low social structure overlap condition than that in the high social structure overlap condition. This finding suggests that the extensiveness of profile details is crucial for relationship development between users who do not share a high degree of social commonality. This is because an extensive profile provides comprehensive information about the requestor, thereby reducing uncertainty and enhancing interpersonal understanding. Thus, it is important that application designers consider enriching profile extensiveness, such as photo album previews and timeline abstracts on online social networks.

8 Limitations and Future Directions

Our contributions can be limited by friend request scenario. Evidence suggests that the effects of social structure overlap and profile extensiveness may depend on the friend request scenario. For example, Pagani [11] revealed that individuals were generally reluctant to reject connectivity with those they had actual social relationships. In our experiment, respondents were presented with a friend request scenario in which an imaginary friend had sent them a Facebook friend request. Result has shown that respondents perceived the friend request scenario as relevant (mean = 6.02) and realistic (mean = 5.54), thus lending confidence that our scenario selection is appropriate.

This study opens up a number of exciting avenues for further research. We see the value in investigating "objective" measures of social connectivity acceptance, as opposed to our current behavioral intention measurements. It is possible that individuals' actual behavior may not completely reflect their behavioral intentions. To this end, a further investigation of actual acceptance using a field experiment could be a future research avenue.

Furthermore, it is likely that some individuals' responses to a friend request might manifest in behavior beyond acceptance. For example, they might report the requestor as a spammer or block the requestor from future relational approaches. We encourage researchers to explore other behavioral responses which might be important in online social networks.

9   Conclusion

Despite various measures taken by online social networks providers, privacy issues continue to be a major impediment to the development of social connectivity. Given the importance of profile connections, practitioners have expressed substantial concerns on individuals' disinterests in accepting social connectivity. To that end, we offer a theory-driven approach to evaluating the two key types of social information in helping practitioners to promote the development of social connectivity. Our findings clearly indicate that an integration of the interpersonal cognition literature and the privacy calculus perspective is essential for a better understanding of individuals' intentional to accept. We believe that the model proposed in this study can serve as a solid foundation for future work in this important area.

References

1. Boyd, D., Heer, J.: Profiles as conversation: networked identity performance on friendster. In: Hawaii International Conference on System Sciences, vol. 3, p. 59c (2006)
2. Stern, L.A., Taylor, K.: Social networking on facebook. J. Commun. Speech Theatre Assoc. North Dakota **20**, 9–20 (2007)
3. Hayes, S.C., Barnes-Holmes, D.: Relational operants: processes and implications: a response to Palmer's review of relational frame theory. J. Exp. Anal. Behav. **82**(2), 213–224 (2004)
4. Solomon, D.H., Dillard, J.P., Andersen, J.W.: Episode type, attachment orientation, and frame salience: evidence for a theory of relational framing. Hum. Commun. Res. **28**(1), 136–152 (2002)
5. Laufer, R.S., Wolfe, M.: Privacy as a concept and a social issue: a multidimensional development theory. J. Soc. Issues **33**(3), 22–42 (1977)
6. Coleman, J.S.: Social capital in the creation of human capital. Am. J. Sociol. **94**, 95–120 (1988)
7. Chen, Y.-R., Chen, X.-P., Portnoy, R.: To whom do positive norm and negative norm of reciprocity apply? effects of inequitable offer, relationship, and relational-self orientation. J. Exp. Soc. Psychol. **45**(1), 24–34 (2009)
8. Ross, L., Greene, D., House, P.: The "false consensus effect": an egocentric bias in social perception and attribution processes. J. Exp. Soc. Psychol. **13**(3), 279–301 (1977)
9. Ellison, N.B., Steinfield, C., Lampe, C.: The benefits of facebook "friends:" social capital and college students' use of online social network sites. J. Comput. Mediated Commun. **12**(4), 1143–1168 (2007)
10. Lampe, C., Ellison, N., Steinfield, C.: A familiar face(book): profile elements as signals in an online social network. In: CHI 2007, San Jose, CA, USA (2007)
11. Pagani, M.: The influence of personality on active and passive use of social networking sites. Psychol. Mark. **28**(5), 441–456 (2011)

Participation in Open Knowledge-Sharing Community: Expectancy Value Perspective

Manli Wu[1], Lele Kang[2(✉)], Xuan Li[3], and J. Leon Zhao[1]

[1] Department of Information Systems, City University of Hong Kong,
Kowloon Tong, Hong Kong
manli@mail.ustc.edu.cn, jlzhao@cityu.edu.hk
[2] School of Information Management, Nanjing University, Nanjing, China
lelekang@nju.edu.cn
[3] School of Management, Zhejiang University, Hangzhou, China
lixuannju@163.com

Abstract. The success of open knowledge sharing community requires individuals to involve in and make continuous commitment to it. The aim of this study is to develop an integrated understanding of the factors that influence individuals' open knowledge sharing community involvement and continuous commitment. We employed the expectancy-value theory as our theoretical basis, and proposed that knowledge sharing expectancy, knowledge sharing value, and knowledge sharing affect characterized by six motivational constructs influence individuals' community involvement and continuous commitment. We conduct a survey to collect data and validate the research model. Our findings contribute to the understanding of knowledge-sharing community success and augment the research on digital services for knowledge sharing in the open communities.

Keywords: Expectancy value theory · Open knowledge sharing community · Expectancy · Value · Affect

1 Introduction

Open knowledge-sharing communities (OKSCs) as a typical type of virtual communities are developed to facilitate open discussion and promote knowledge sharing. OKSC is a group of people who share knowledge, develop relationships, and attain certain goals individually or collectively in an information technology-supported context (Ma and Agarwal 2007). One famous example here is the stackoverflow.com, which has attracted millions of programmers to share their knowledge by asking questions and posting answers. To attract participants, various mechanisms are designed to encourage OKSC participation and knowledge sharing (Kang 2011). For instance, badge system in stackoverflow.com is developed to reward the active participants. However, it is no guarantee that the community will be successful. Despite the proliferation of OKSCs, the factors leading to their success are still unclear.

Prior studies on knowledge sharing communities took the perspective of knowledge contributors and were mainly focused on knowledge contribution and its antecedents (Kim et al. 2011; Ma and Agarwal 2007; Wasko and Faraj 2005). However, OKSCs

© Springer International Publishing Switzerland 2016
F.F.-H. Nah and C.-H. Tan (Eds.): HCIBGO 2016, Part I, LNCS 9751, pp. 153–162, 2016.
DOI: 10.1007/978-3-319-39396-4_14

involve not only knowledge contributors, but also knowledge seekers and other participants (Chen and Hung 2010). All roles are critical to fostering OKSC success. Rather than only focusing on knowledge contributors, this study investigates individuals' knowledge sharing behaviors - OKSC involvement and OKSC continuous commitment - which involve both knowledge contributors and knowledge seerks. As indicated in prior studies, there is a belief that involvement and commitment are important issues for virtual community success (Chang and Chuang 2011) by fostering better membership relationships and improving community development, growth and survival (Ma and Agarwal 2007).

To design effective strategies to enhance OKSC involvement and continuous commitment, it is first necessary to find out the factors relating to involvement and continuous commitment. Some theoretical perspectives have been taken to explain individuals' behaviors in knowledge sharing communities, including cost-benefit framework (Bock et al. 2005; Kankanhalli et al. 2005; Wasko and Faraj 2005), social capital perspective (Chiu et al. 2006; Wasko and Faraj 2005), social network perspective (Chow and Chan 2008; Wasko and Faraj 2005), organizational climate (Bock et al. 2005), incentive systems (Bock et al. 2005; Kankanhalli et al. 2005). These perspectives were more rationality-driven in explaining individuals' behaviors. Although knowledge sharing researchers emphasized rational motivations, the importance of irrational factors, such as emotions, should not be ignored. However, scant research, of which we are aware, have investigated emotional factors in the study of knowledge sharing.

Both rational and irrational motivational factors are examined in this study. We adopt the expectancy-value theory (EVT) to identify six motivational constructs that belong to knowledge sharing expectancy, knowledge sharing value and knowledge sharing affect and examine their relationships with OKSC involvement and continuous commitment. The research model is tested using the data collected by survey.

2   Theoretical Foundation

Expectancy-value theory (EVT) is a basic paradigm for understanding individuals' motivations and behaviors (Liu and Liu 2011). It describes the cognitive-motivational process in attaining a goal (Liu and Liu 2011). Adopting EVT to explain individuals' behavior, three motivational components were identified – expectancy, value, and affective components (Pintrich and De Groot 1990). The three motivational components identified by EVT include both rational and irrational factors. EVT provides a good theoretical perspective to explain why individuals are motiveted to involve in and continuously commit to OKSC.

EVT supports that expectancy component is a good predictor of behavior (Liu and Liu 2011). Expectancy has been conceptualized in two forms: efficacy expectancy and outcome expectancy (Chiu et al. 2006). Efficacy expectancy is the belief about one's competence to perform the behavior successfully, while outcome expectancy is the belief that one's behavior will lead to certain outcomes (Chiu et al. 2006). The expectancy of a good outcome does not mean that an individual has the ability to perform the behavior, and vice versus (Eccles and Wigfield 2002). Efficacy expectancy and outcome expectancy are regarded as major determinants of one's willingness to expend effort and be engaged in a behavior (Liu and Liu 2011). In this study, we conceptualize knowledge sharing expectancy as an efficacy expectancy to perform knowledge sharing behavior and an outcome expectancy to produce good outcomes. As an efficacy expectancy, knowledge sharing self-efficacy is defined as an individual's confidence in one's competence to share valuable knowledge with others in the same virtual community (Chen and Hung 2010). Perceived compatibility is defined as an individual's cognition of likely value, need and experience that one's behavior in knowledge sharing community is similar to the original value system (Chen and Hung 2010). Individuals in online community want to build reputations, and develop social relationships (Ma and Agarwal 2007). Compatibility with the community value system is the outcome being pursued. As such, we regard perceived compatibility as one type of outcome expectancy. Thus, knowledge sharing expectancy includes two constructs: knowledge sharing self-efficacy and perceived compatibility.

Value component in EVT refers to an individual's perception of the value and interest of performing a behavior (Miltiadou and Savenye 2003). It deals with individuals' reasons for doing a task (Eccles and Wigfield 2002). Knowledge sharing value is conceptualized as that individuals perform knowledge-sharing behavior for the sake of the values and interests they can derive from knowledge sharing. It explains individuals' reasons for conducting knowledge sharing. Two reasons are highlighted: desire for self-presentation, and perceived relative advantage. Desire for self-presentation is defined as the extent to which individuals want to present their images in OKSC (Kim et al. 2012). Drawing on identity theories, individuals are more likely to conduct tasks that allow them to present their self-images. Perceived relative advantage refers to individuals' cognitions about the advantages and benefits brought by knowledge sharing behavior (Chen and Hung 2010). Pursuing benefits and advantages is also an important reason for individuals' participation in OKSC.

Affective component in EVT concerns individuals' affective or emotional reactions to perform certain behaviors (Pintrich and De Groot 1990). It deals with "How do I feel about the behavior?" Knowledge sharing affect is conceptualized as forward-looking affective reactions where individuals imagine the emotional consequences of conducting or not conducting knowledge sharing behavior (Tsai and Bagozzi 2014). Model of goal-directed behavior suggests that anticipated emotions as an important affective component are significant determinants of individuals' behavior (Perugini and Bagozzi 2001). Anticipated emotions are reflected by positive and negative anticipated emotion (Tsai and Bagozzi 2014).

3   Research Model and Hypotheses Development

The research model is developed based on the expectancy-value theory and knowledge sharing literature. As shown in Fig. 1, we specify that individuals' knowledge sharing expectancy, knowledge sharing value and knowledge sharing affect are reflective second-order factors and they influence individuals' OKSC involvement and continuous commitment.

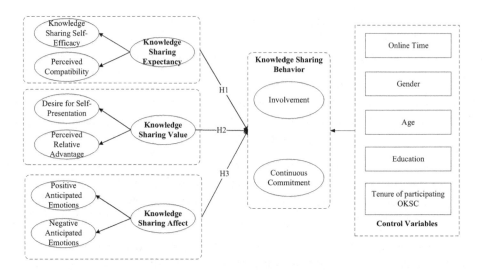

Fig. 1. The Proposed Research Model

3.1   Knowledge Sharing Expectancy

Knowledge sharing self-efficacy reflects how well individuals believe that they can perform knowledge sharing successfully (Ray et al. 2014). It is suggested as a key motivational factor that drives individuals' knowledge sharing decisions and behaviors (Chen and Hung 2010; Kankanhalli et al. 2005; Ray et al. 2014). The willingness to involve in the community is largely dependent on one's confidence in performing it well (Rich et al. 2010). High self-efficacious members tend to be more self-motivated (Bock et al. 2005), and they are more willing to involve in community activities and be responsive to others' inquiry (Ray et al. 2014). In contrast, low self-efficacious members are fearful of acting wrongly (Ardichvili et al. 2003), so they are likely to withdraw from the community activities when difficulties are encountered (Kankanhalli et al. 2005). Thus, we suppose a positive relationship between knowledge sharing self-efficacy and OKSC involvement.

Knowledge sharing self-efficacy is also an important factor that influences individuals' continuous community commitment. First, besides an ability evaluation, self-efficacy also reflects an inherent desire for mastery (Bandura 1993). Individuals invest time and effort to foster their efficacy in the online community, and the time and effort become sunk cost if they leave the community. They are likely to stay in the community when sunk cost is high (Polites and Karahanna 2012). Second, as high self-efficacious members own much knowledge about the community, they have the desire to maintain cognitive consistency (Polites and Karahanna 2012). Thus, they tend to main their status quo through continuously commit to the present online community. Third, by virtue of self-efficacy, individuals gain positive experience from successful knowledge sharing, which may enhance their continuous commitment.

The second expectancy factor – perceived compatibility is also expected to be associated with OKSC involvement and continuous commitment. Compatibility is the congruency between one's behavior and the value system (Chen and Hung 2010). Individuals are motivated to participate by the expectation to be in congruity with their value systems (Lin et al. 2009). Once the compatibility is perceived to be high, individuals become comfortable with the OKSC, and they increase their involvement and commitment (Lin et al. 2009). In OKSC, individuals depend on the platform to share knowledge and derive value (Ray et al. 2014). And the amount of value they expect to obtain is partly determined by the perceived compatibility. Perceived compatibility is also considered as a psychological barrier (Budman 2003). Once individuals' cognitions and behavior are incompatible with the community value, they may face the risk of being criticized which undermines their involvement and psychological attachment.

H-1a: Knowledge sharing Expectancy in OKSC, reflecting by knowledge sharing self-efficacy and perceived compatibility, is positively related to individuals' OKSC involvement.

H-1b: Knowledge sharing Expectancy in OKSC, reflecting by knowledge sharing self-efficacy and perceived compatibility, is positively related to individuals' OKSC continuous commitment.

3.2   Knowledge Sharing Value

Knowledge sharing value includes desire for self-presentation and perceived relative advantage. The two factors explain why individuals engage in knowledge sharing. The development of internet technology offers opportunities for individuals to present themselves through digital channels (Kim et al. 2011). Individuals are willing to participate in the OKSC when they can express and present themselves (Ma and Agarwal 2007). We anticipate that desire for self-presentation influences individuals' OKSC involvement and continuous commitment. First, it is important that members achieve a shared understanding in OKSC. By presenting one's self-identity, individuals can be understood and accepted by other members. The acceptance and acknowledgement from other members can increase one's intention to get involved and stay in the community. Second, the revelation of similar interests and experiences resulting from self-presentation facilitates relationship building. Individuals are more willing to participate in relationships and continue the relationships when their identities can be presented, and social relationships built in OKSC can promote community persistence (Ma and Agarwal 2007). Third, Individuals can present a desired self through how they behave (Kim et al. 2012). The involvement and commitment in OKSC is seen as an act of self-presentation that can express one's preferred identity to others (Ray et al. 2014). Individuals involve in and commit to OKSC not only because of altruism, but also for reputation (Wasko and Faraj 2005) and self-esteem (Bock et al. 2005). Efficient identity presentation is encouraged by reputation system. When community members want to build good reputation, they involve in helping behavior, and make commitment to OKSC.

Perceived relative advantage is a multidimensional construct and it is mainly manifested as increased efficiency and effectiveness, economic benefits, and enhanced status (Lin et al. 2009). Prior studies suggested that individuals participate in virtual community in hope of enriching their knowledge, seeking support, making friends, or being seen as skilled, knowledgeable and respected (Lin et al. 2009). When potential benefits are expected to generate as a result of community participation, individuals are more willing to invest effort and time to the community. Furthermore, the lack of formal obligations in OKSC means that community participation is voluntary (Ray et al. 2014). As OKSC members are anonymous and distant from each other, the normative pressure is less than that in offline communities (Ray et al. 2014). The knowledge acquisition and relationship building are of significance in motivating OKSC involvement. Continuous commitment occurs as one weighs the benefits associated with staying in a community against the costs of leaving (Teunissen et al. 2009). When the perceived relative advantage is high, the cost of leaving is high. In contrast, if individuals see no advantages, they won't get involved and make commitment to it. In this sense, perceived relative advantage is a necessary condition for OKSC involvement and continuous commitment.

H-2a: Knowledge sharing Value in OKSC, reflecting by desire for self-presentation, perceived relative advantage, is positively related to individuals' OKSC involvement.
H-2b: Knowledge sharing Value in OKSC, reflecting by desire for self-presentation, perceived relative advantage, is positively related to individuals' OKSC continuous commitment.

3.3 Knowledge Sharing Affect

In addition to expectancy and value component of motivation, knowledge sharing affect is also an important motivational factor in driving OKSC involvement and continuous commitment. Knowledge sharing affect is reflected by anticipated emotions, which are expected emotional consequences of participating or not participating in OKSC (Perugini and Bagozzi 2001). An individual usually expects a good or bad result before making a decision, and positive and negative anticipated emotions are invoked as a result of the expectations (Tsai and Bagozzi 2014). Positive anticipated emotions are evoked when individuals imagine desired outcomes if they participate in the community, while negative anticipated emotions are evoked when individuals expect undesired outcomes if they fail to participate in the community (Baumgartner et al. 2008). As Taylor and Pham put it, the emotions one anticipates provide the fuel for taking further actions (Taylor 1991). Perugini and Bagozzi (2001) added anticipated emotions to the theory of planned behavior and found that both positive and negative anticipated emotions are significant antecedents of individuals desires and behaviors (Perugini and Bagozzi 2001).

Individuals have the tendency to pursue positive emotions and avoid negative emotions, which is believed to be significant sources of decision making (Zeelenberg 1999). If individuals are aware that participating in OKSC can lead to positive emotions afterward, they will be more likely to participate. Positive anticipated emotions transmits the signal that the environment is unproblematic and safe, which enables individuals to freely participate in community activities, share their knowledge, and seek for knowledge without being criticized (George and Zhou 2007). Moreover, when the community is believed to be safe, individuals are comfortable to get involve and willing to stay in it in the future (Loi et al. 2006).

Negative anticipated emotions are also powerful in predicting individuals' behaviors (Baumgartner et al. 2008). When individuals experience failure in OKSC participation, the negative anticipated emotions related to psychological effects of worry may arise (Zeelenberg 1999). The worry drives individuals to taken relevant actions (Baumgartner et al. 2008). As a result, individuals involve in OKSC to release the worry. Since negative emotions are usually intense, more effort is needed to committed to the community (Taylor 1991). For example, an individual who plans to pass an exam imagines having been unsuccessful in passing it. The anticipated negative emotions resulting from the likely failure may stimulate a hard-working behavior to pass the exam as people have the tendency to avoid failure (Zeelenberg 1999). In addition, negative anticipated emotions are associated with affective cost of not being community members (Astrachan and Jaskiewicz 2008). The affective cost thus plays as a barrier for members to get out of the community.

H-3a: Knowledge sharing Affect in OKSC, reflecting by positive anticipated emotions and negative anticipated emotions, is positively related to individuals' OKSC involvement.

H-3b: Knowledge sharing Affect in OKSC, reflecting by positive anticipated emotions and negative anticipated emotions, is positively related to individuals' OKSC continuous commitment.

4   Research Methodology

Our sample was obtained from several major OKSCs in Mainland China, including zhidao.baidu.com, zhihu.com, csdn.com, and others. These OKSCs enable users to ask questions and post answers in the form of discussion thread. Because of page limitation, we cannot comprehensively explain all details here. The PLS results for the structural model are illustrated in Fig. 2, in which knowledge sharing expectancy, knowledge sharing value, and knowledge sharing affect generally significantly improve participants' knowledge sharing behavior in OKSC.

5   Discussion

Despite the rapid development of knowledge sharing communities beyond organizational boundary, a theory relating both rational and irrational factors to knowledge sharing behaviors is lacking. To fill this gap, we proposed a second-order-factor research model by extending the expectancy-value theory to the OKSC context. Six constructs belonging to knowledge sharing expectancy, knowledge sharing value, and knowledge sharing affect were identified as first-order factors. Using a survey to collect data, we found that knowledge sharing expectancy, knowledge sharing value and knowledge sharing affect are good predictors of individuals' knowledge sharing behaviors.

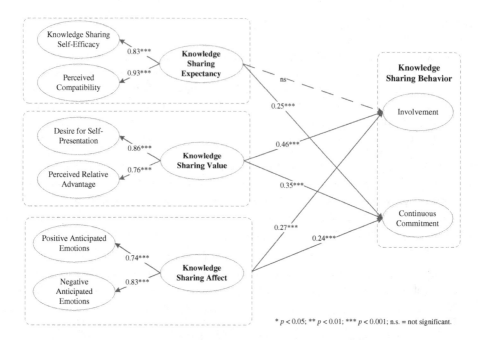

Fig. 2. Results of PLS analysis

This study has both theoretical and practical implications. From a theoretical perspective, this study empirically supports that both rational and irrational factors should be considered when studying online knowledge sharing. From a practical perspective, this study offers insights to the success of virtual communities. To enhance the development of virtual communities, participants' knowledge sharing expectancy, knowledge sharing value, and knowledge sharing affect should be well fostered.

Acknowledgement. The work was partially supported by a grant from NSFC (Project No. 71471157) and a grant from NSFC (Project No. 71110107027).

References

Ardichvili, A., Page, V., Wentling, T.: Motivation and barriers to participation in virtual knowledge-sharing communities of practice. J. knowl. Manag. **7**(1), 64–77 (2003)

Astrachan, J.H., Jaskiewicz, P.: Emotional returns and emotional costs in privately held family businesses: advancing traditional business valuation. Fam. Bus. Rev. **21**(2), 139–149 (2008)

Bandura, A.: Perceived self-efficacy in cognitive development and functioning. Educ. Psychol. **28**(2), 117–148 (1993)

Baumgartner, H., Pieters, R., Bagozzi, R.P.: Future-oriented emotions: conceptualization and behavioral effects. Eur. J. Soc. Psychol. **38**(4), 685–696 (2008)

Bock, G.-W., Zmud, R.W., Kim, Y.-G., Lee, J.-N.: Behavioral intention formation in knowledge sharing: examining the roles of extrinsic motivators, social-psychological forces, and organizational climate. MIS Q., 87–111 (2005)

Budman, M.: Internet life: what your customers are doing online. Across Board **40**(1), 59–60 (2003)

Chang, H.H., Chuang, S.S.: Social capital and individual motivations on knowledge sharing: participant involvement as a moderator. Inf. Manag. **48**(1), 9–18 (2011)

Chen, C.J., Hung, S.W.: To give or to receive? Factors influencing members' knowledge sharing and community promotion in professional virtual communities. Inf. Manag. **47**(4), 226–236 (2010)

Chiu, C.M., Hsu, M.H., Wang, E.T.G.: Understanding knowledge sharing in virtual communities: an integration of social capital and social cognitive theories. Decis. Support Syst. **42**(3), 1872–1888 (2006)

Chow, W.S., Chan, L.S.: Social network, social trust and shared goals in organizational knowledge sharing. Inf. Manag. **45**(7), 458–465 (2008)

Eccles, J.S., Wigfield, A.: Motivational beliefs, values, and goals. Ann. Rev. Psychol. **53**(1), 109–132 (2002)

George, J.M., Zhou, J.: Dual tuning in a supportive context: joint contributions of positive mood, negative mood, and supervisory behaviors to employee creativity. Acad. Manag. J. **50**(3), 605–622 (2007)

Kang, J.: Social media marketing in the hospitality industry: the role of benefits in increasing brand community participation and the impact of participation on consumer trust and commitment toward hotel and restaurant brands (2011)

Kankanhalli, A., Tan, B.C.Y., Wei, K.K.: Contributing knowledge to electronic knowledge repositories: an empirical investigation. MIS Q., 113–143 (2005)

Kim, H.-W., Chan, H.C., Kankanhalli, A.: What motivates people to purchase digital items on virtual community websites? The desire for online self-presentation. Inf. Syst. Res. **23**(4), 1232–1245 (2012)

Kim, H.-W., Zheng, J.R., Gupta, S.: Examining knowledge contribution from the perspective of an online identity in blogging communities. Comput. Hum. Behav. **27**(5), 1760–1770 (2011)

Lin, M.-J.J., Hung, S.-W., Chen, C.-J.: Fostering the determinants of knowledge sharing in professional virtual communities. Comput. Hum. Behav. **25**(4), 929–939 (2009)

Liu, N.-C., Liu, M.-S.: Human resource practices and individual knowledge-sharing behavior–an empirical study for Taiwanese R&D professionals. Int. J. Hum. Resource Manag. **22**(04), 981–997 (2011)

Loi, R., Hang-Yue, N., Foley, S.: Linking employees' justice perceptions to organizational commitment and intention to leave: the mediating role of perceived organizational support. J. Occup. Organ. Psychol. **79**(1), 101–120 (2006)

Ma, M., Agarwal, R.: Through a glass darkly: information technology design, identity verification, and knowledge contribution in online communities. Inf. Syst. Res. **18**(1), 42–67 (2007)

Miltiadou, M., Savenye, W.C.: Applying social cognitive constructs of motivation to enhance student success in online distance education. AACE J. **11**(1), 78–95 (2003)

Perugini, M., Bagozzi, R.P.: The role of desires and anticipated emotions in goal-directed behaviours: broadening and deepening the theory of planned behaviour. Brit. J. Soc. Psychol. **40**, 79 (2001)

Pintrich, P.R., De Groot, E.V.: Motivational and self-regulated learning components of classroom academic performance. J. Educ. Psychol. **82**, 33 (1990)

Polites, G.L., Karahanna, E.: Shackled to the status quo: the inhibiting effects of incumbent system habit, switching costs, and inertia on new system acceptance. MIS Q. **36**(1), 21–42 (2012)

Ray, S., Kim, S.S., Morris, J.G.: The central role of engagement in online communities. Inf. Syst. Res. **25**(3), 528–546 (2014)

Rich, B.L., Lepine, J.A., Crawford, E.R.: Job engagement: antecedents and effects on job performance. Acad. Manag. J. **53**(3), 617–635 (2010)

Taylor, S.E.: Asymmetrical effects of positive and negative events: the mobilization-minimization hypothesis. Psychol. Bull. **110**(1), 67–85 (1991)

Teunissen, P.W., Stapel, D.A., van der Vleuten, C., Scherpbier, A., Boor, K., Scheele, F.: Who wants feedback? An investigation of the variables influencing residents' feedback-seeking behavior in relation to night shifts. Acad. Med. **84**(7), 910–917 (2009)

Tsai, H.-T., Bagozzi, R.P.: Contribution behavior in virtual communities: cognitive, emotional and social influences. MIS Q. **38**(1), 143–163 (2014)

Wasko, M.M.L., Faraj, S.: Why should I share? Examining social capital and knowledge contribution in electronic networks of practice. MIS Q. **29**, 35–57 (2005)

Zeelenberg, M.: Anticipated regret, expected feedback and behavioral decision making. J. Behav. Decis. Making **12**(2), 93 (1999)

Electronic, Mobile and Ubiquitous Commerce

Credibility of Algorithm Based Decentralized Computer Networks Governing Personal Finances: The Case of Cryptocurrency

Sapumal Ahangama[✉] and Danny Chiang Choon Poo

Department of Information Systems, School of Computing,
National University of Singapore, 13 Computing Drive, Singapore 117417, Singapore
{sapumal,dannypoo}@nus.edu.sg

Abstract. In spite of the virtual nature and the system operating purely based on pre-formulated computer algorithms, cryptocurrency networks have reached greater popularity with a significant follower base with people placing trust on the system operation. As credibility is an important factor for systems facilitating financial transactions, in this study we will be presenting a simple model facilitating identification of relevant important factors to be considered by users and a methodology for assessing the credibility of cryptocurrency networks. We identify two routes, systems and the psychological perspective in the credibility assessment process which varies with the user expertise.

Keywords: Credibility · Cryptocurrency · Information systems in finance · Bitcoins

1 Introduction

Cryptocurrency is simply a mode of exchange of goods and services similar to cash but with virtual existence as a digital currency where cryptography is used to secure the transactions. More specifically, the virtual founder of this currency, Satoshi Nakamoto proposed it as a decentralized peer-to-peer electronic currency system relying on digital signatures to prove the ownership and public transaction history known as a "block chain" to record transactions [1]. In Bitcoins; a version of cryptocurrency, the transactions are handled peer-to-peer without the intervention of a central authority such as a bank or a financial institution. Further there is no central authority such as a central bank to govern the currency. It could be considered as a network of currency with no reference to a nation, owner or transaction parties in a transaction and hence anonymous. The Bitcoins owned by a person are stored in a digital wallet for future use or exchanged and cleared to conventional cash in a Bitcoin exchange. In addition, the Bitcoin generation is governed by a protocol adopted by the currency network.

Although cryptocurrency is a very recent and an unconventional Information Systems (IS) phenomenon, the concept has achieved immense popularity with an increased number of individual enthusiasts, media attention and many real world stores as well as popular online stores recently starting to accept Bitcoins as a currency [2].

© Springer International Publishing Switzerland 2016
F.F.-H. Nah and C.-H. Tan (Eds.): HCIBGO 2016, Part I, LNCS 9751, pp. 165–176, 2016.
DOI: 10.1007/978-3-319-39396-4_15

It should be noted that the Bitcoins currency network achieved this success with general public and organizations placing their trust and value on a concept with a merely virtual existence. It is purely based on an IS phenomena with no recognized regulatory body such as a government or a central bank governing the system.

Under such circumstances, it raises an interesting question on how users would assess the credibility of a virtual currency and what factors are important in the credibility assessment when they are presented with information on the network. Specifically, credibility would be an essential factor as cryptocurrency networks facilitate financial transactions that by nature are required to be secure, reliable and accurate. The problem is further complicated with the virtual nature without a liable entity where all the decisions on the control of the network are being made solely by pre-formulated computer algorithms. Further, the cryptocurrency networks have in recent times been criticized for being utilized to facilitate illegal transactions such as narcotics trade and it has faced setbacks with key entities of the network such as Bitcoin exchanges closing down with bankruptcy [3].

Hence in this study, we will develop a simple theoretical model on how users would evaluate the credibility of the cryptocurrency networks when users are presented with background information of a network.

2   Theoretical Background and Research Model

In this section we will go through the theoretical background related to the research model proposed and the hypotheses proposed.

2.1   Credibility

The definition, dimensions and antecedents of credibility has been interpreted in different but related ways in prior information systems research. For example, the term credibility has been referred to as believability, trust, reliability, accuracy, fairness, objectivity and many other combinations [4]. However it should be noted that there are many conflicts on these conceptualizations [4, 5]. In another view, credibility along with benevolence have been modelled as sub-dimensions of trust [6]. In the case of buyer-seller relationships, it is noted that the most accepted form of credibility is as one sub-dimension of trust with the other sub-dimension being benevolence [7]. In such a relationship credibility is with regard to the competence, honesty and reliability of the seller (trustee) [8]. Benevolence is identified as the willingness of the seller (trustee) to behave with a genuine concern for the buyer even at a cost [9]. However as mentioned previously in the context of cryptocurrency networks, as the logics of operations are predefined based on algorithms and there is no identified central party to govern the system, benevolence may not be applicable to the context. Hence we would explore the dimension of credibility as it would be involved in the cognitive process of assessing the trust of the network.

Credibility of information in communication has been researched in-depth and one of the main goals in such research is identifying the factors and paths that lead humans in judging whether a particular piece of information and its source could be considered as credible for various information seeking goals and tasks [4].

Due to the importance and high dependence of computer products Fogg and Tseng. [5] have conceptualized the credibility of such computer products. Here, credibility is simply defined by them as "believability" of a system and that it is a perceived quality. Credibility is also conceptualized as a multidimensional construct where the key components contributing to credibility evaluations are trustworthiness and expertise. In the case where a computer product is assessed for credibility, a person would base the assessment on these concepts. In further discussion on credibility, we would consider the conceptualizations presented by Fogg and Tseng [5] as a base of our research study.

However it has been noted that credibility is not an important aspect in case of all computer products as explained below [5]. For example the authors state that in the case of the computer product that is not visible or there is no doubt on the incompetence, credibility will not be an important factor in human computer interaction. Yet if the computer product is used for purposes such as providing knowledge, instructing users, involving in decision making, reporting measurements, running simulations, rendering virtual environments, reporting on work performance and reporting on current state, credibility will be an important factor influencing the human computer interaction. In the case of cryptocurrency networks, the users would highly weigh on credibility as a decisive factor as the network will be handling personal financial transactions by a virtual network without the guarantee by a central agency. Financial transactions would be obviously conducted in a secure system that is found to be credible to be trusted upon.

Further in the discussion on credibility on computer products [5], two routes are presented where users will be focusing on in evaluating the credibility. The two perspectives are (1) the systems perspective and (2) the psychological perspective. Here the systems perspective directly evaluates the different aspects of the computer product such as the device, the interface, the functionality, and the information.

Due to architecture of cryptocurrency networks, the key devices such as miners or the network architecture are not visible to the end user to carry out a credibility assessment. Further the interfaces would include a basic payment gateway which cannot be considered as a unique aspect when utilizing the network. In our case we are evaluating the credibility assessment on the basis that the cryptocurrency network will be utilized in the process of general transactions. As a result the informational aspect would not be a differentiating factor with general information such as past transactions, account balance etc. which are common to any payment system. However the functional processes of cryptocurrency networks which support state of the art transaction recording, validation, anonymity of users among many other benefits are considered as the core of the system which has grabbed much of the attention. Hence it could be concluded that, the most important aspect in the systems perspective assessment would be the evaluation of functional credibility. In order to evaluate functional credibility, we have utilized the popular information system evaluation criteria of task and technology fit [10, 11]. This will be explained in Sect. 2.3.

As mentioned previously, [5] proposes the role of psychological perspective in the overall evaluation of credibility by users. In the context of computer products, for example the brand or the popularity of the creator behind the product is proposed by the authors as possible targets to consider in conceptualization. Further "reputed credibility" is defined as one of the four types of credibility [12]. Reputed credibility is defined as the extent to which a user would believe on an entity based on what third parties have reported. We can conclude that psychological perspective would have a link in creating reputed credibility. In the context of cryptocurrency the evaluation of psychological properties would not be straightforward as in the case of a general computer product. For example, there are no strong and direct psychological properties such as brand or a clear initiator of the project. However the reputation among the general public as well as the structural assurance placed by authoritative entities can be considered as possible candidates. These will be explored in Sect. 2.4 below.

2.2 Elaboration Likelihood Model

According to Elaboration Likelihood Model (ELM), the attitude change process of a user is a result of central or peripheral route of processing [13, 14]. ELM has been used extensively in prior research to characterize the credibility assessment process [5, 15–17]. ELM states that while users would process in the central route when they are able to use adequate cognitive resources they would opt for peripheral route when they lack the ability and motivation to process the information. The ability and motivation to elaborate is captured by the elaboration likelihood in the model. In prior research, for example argument quality was proposed as the central cue which source credibility as the peripheral cue in the context of decision management systems while job relevance and user expertise were proposed as the moderators [18]. In the context of trusting online vendors, information quality was proposed as the central cue and third party seals on websites as the peripheral cue [19]. In the current context we conclude that the systems perspective would be in the central route as it requires and involves higher cognitive capability to understand the concepts behind the cryptocurrency networks and to make a task and technology fit assessment. In contrast, the psychological perspective would take the peripheral route due to the nature of assessment involved. In addition, in order to capture the ability of the user to elaborate, we use user expertise as the elaboration likelihood.

2.3 Task Technology Fit Assessment

As mentioned previously, the central route requires a user to assess arguments critically in an informational message and then decide based on the relative merits of the arguments prior to the judgment on the decision. For example in the IT acceptance context, potential benefits of system acceptance, comparison of alternative systems, availability and quality of system support etc. have been considered [18]. Similarly for the systems perspective we utilize Task Technology Fit (TTF) as the assessment criteria.

TTF in brief refers to the correspondence between the technology characteristics and task characteristics where a proper "fit" would be the case in which technology provides sufficient features and support that is required by the user of the technology to carry out the intended tasks [10, 11]. TTF model argues that individuals will assess the fit between the task requirements and the characteristics of the technology supporting the task, which will strongly influence user beliefs about consequences of utilization. Therefore TTF assessment is a good indicator of functionality assessment by an individual of the system. Hence in the research model, we will be using TTF as the representation of the systems perspective assessment.

Since the task requirements of a financial system would be highly diverse and complex, we are considering the task requirements that are relevant only to the general users who use cryptocurrency network as a payment medium. The TTF model and its extensions along with other theories have also been extensively utilized in many finance related contexts similar to our scenario such as E-Commerce [20], mobile commerce [21] and banking [22] to name a few. In addition, the TTF model has been utilized to investigate emergent phenomena in the past such as blogging [23]. Thus we hypothesize,

- H1: TTF assessment indicating a proper fit will affect the credibility assessment of cryptocurrency networks positively.

2.4   Reputation and Structural Assurance

As proposed previously, the peripheral route will be involving the psychological perspective in the evaluation of credibility by users. Due to the nature of cryptocurrency networks where the visibility of the system is at a minimum to the general users, the peripheral routes would be heavily evaluated on what the third parties have reported. The third parties could include other users as well as various organizations that comment on the issue. Under such conditions, we identify reputation and structural assurance as two key contributors in the peripheral route, which has been used in prior research as well [24].

In prior research, reputation has been identified as a significant determinant of trust building [24, 25]. The importance of reputation has also been identified as an important driver in credibility [5]. Hence in the case of a user who lacks the ability to assess cryptocurrency networks in a functional perspective, they will rely on the information made available by various third parties. Therefore reputation would play a key role in the attitude change process. Thus we hypothesize,

- H2: Reputation will affect the credibility assessment of cryptocurrency networks positively.

Since personal financial transactions are handled by cryptocurrency networks and due to the nature of sensitivity of such transactions, another important peripheral cue that could be identified relevant to the context is the structural assurance. Structural assurance reflects that there exists a legal structure to ensure security when using the system [24]. Although the governance of the cryptocurrency networks by a central authority is against the principles of founding the network, increased legal pressure could be observed worldwide with new regulations adopted over time by various countries. For example Monetary Authority of Singapore has set anti-money-laundering compliance requirements for business institutions utilizing cryptocurrency [2]. Further, in recent research on cryptocurrency domain, it has argued on the importance of regulation based assurance to keep the users safe and to build confidence in the system [26]. Thus, similar to trust transference [27], having a structural assurance may affect the credibility building process of users on the cryptocurrency networks.

– H3: Structural assurance will affect the credibility assessment of cryptocurrency networks positively.

2.5 User Expertise

ELM states that an attitude change of a user through the central or peripheral route is determined by the elaboration likelihood. User expertise has been used in prior research in ELM based studies as a measure of ability [18]. In their context, the authors state that expert IT users will scrutinize new facts on IT more carefully in making a judgment on IT acceptance, thus relying less on peripheral routes. However least expert users would rely heavily on peripheral cues. In the context of cryptocurrency, as it could be considered as a novel and disruptive information systems innovation, we observe that the understanding the operations of the network would require knowledge on information technology to a greater extent. Hence we hypothesize that a user with higher expertise in the information technology domain would be more reliant on the systems perspective. Thus we propose,

– H4: User Expertise moderates the effect of TTF assessment on credibility of cryptocurrency networks positively.
– H5: User Expertise moderates the effect of reputation on credibility of cryptocurrency networks negatively.
– H6: User Expertise moderates the effect of structural assurance on credibility of cryptocurrency networks negatively.

Figure 1 indicates our hypotheses built to test the factors affecting the credibility.

3   Research Methodology

This study was carried out through a survey[1]. The survey questionnaires were distributed among a class of students undergoing a technological course in a university. The questionnaires were distributed at the end of a 2 h seminar on cryptocurrency. The goal was to identify which paths will be influencing the credibility assessment based on the information on cryptocurrency networks given.

3.1   Operationalization of Constructs

Previously validated scales were used in the process of developing the survey instruments. The scales were updated to suit the cryptocurrency context. To measure the credibility, items were adapted from Newell and Goldsmith [28]. The scales for task technology fit were adapted from Lin and Huang [29]. Items for reputation and structural

---

[1] The survey questionnaire is not attached to this paper due to the page limitations. Please contact authors should it be required.

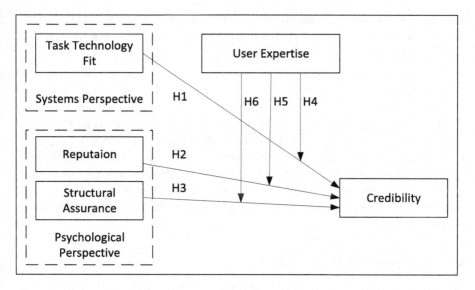

Fig. 1. Research Model

assurance were adapted from Zhou [24]. User expertise for information systems domain was adapted from Bhattacherjee and Sanford [18].

A seven-point Likert scale ranging from 1 (strongly-disagree) to 7 (strongly-agree) was used in the questionnaire. Review of the survey questions were carried out with IS researchers as well as with a person knowledgeable on cryptocurrency networks prior to the actual survey, in order to validate the appropriateness of the questions. Further, a separate pilot study was carried out among a sample of 30 suitable individuals in order to improve the validity and reliability of the instruments.

3.2 Data Collection

As mentioned previously the sampling frame included students. In order to collect responses, paper based survey forms were used. The participation of the survey was on a voluntary basis.

A total of 136 valid responses were collected. 10 responses were incomplete and were not used in the analysis. As a consequence of the student sample, the range of age distribution of the sample was within the range of 21 and 25 years of age (mean 23.0, standard deviation 0.886). Further the sample consisted of 55.9 % female and 44.1 % male participants. As a general rule of thumb, in order to carry out a reliable survey the minimum number of responses has to be 10 times the largest number of predictors for any dependent variable in the model [30]. On this assumption the sample size of 136 is adequate.

Since the data is sourced from a single source, there is a high probability of common method bias. As a result, in the design of the survey, we took several measures such as neutral wording of the items and use of multiple items for each construct [31]. In addition, the anonymity of the respondents was guaranteed requesting the students to participate in the survey as honestly as possible [31].

4   Analysis

The data analysis was carried out using partial least squares (PLS), using the SmartPLS software package. PLS was selected to carry out the analysis as it enables to access the measurement model (relationship between items and constructs) within the context of the structural model (relationship among constructs) and also as it does not require large sample sizes of data or strict multivariate normal distribution of data [31]. Validity assessment of the measurement instruments and results from hypothesis testing are presented below.

4.1   Measurement Model Evaluation

All constructs in the research model were measured using reflective constructs. For reflective constructs, the measurement model could be evaluated by assessing the convergent validity and discriminant validity statistical tests.

The convergent validity of the constructs was assessed using item reliability, composite reliability (CR) and average variance extracted (AVE). The generally accepted rule of thumb for thresholds for item loading for constructs, CR and AVE are 0.5, 0.7 and 0.5 respectively [31]. One item of the user expertise construct had to be dropped due to poor item loading. Upon dropping of the items, the minimum item loading reported was 0.766. The minimum item loading was also above the rule of thumb threshold value. The values of CR and AVE can be found in Table 1. The CR and AVE values reported are also above the accepted threshold value. Thus we concluded that the convergent validity is satisfactory.

Table 1. Factor correlation coefficients, composite reliability and average variance extracted

	CRD	EXP	REP	STA	TTF	CR	AVE
CRD	**0.8298**					0.8983	0.6885
EXP	0.1657	**0.8316**				0.8162	0.6915
REP	0.4134	0.1758	**0.8525**			0.8883	0.7268
STA	0.5159	0.0859	0.5264	**0.8280**		0.8969	0.6856
TTF	0.3674	0.2172	0.5141	0.4688	**0.8221**	0.8618	0.6759

Notes. Leading diagonal shows the squared root of AVE of each construct. CRD – Credibility, EXP – User Expertise, REP – Reputation, STA – Structural Assurance, TTF – Task Technology Fit, CR – Composite Reliability, AVE – Average Variance Extracted

The discriminant validity of constructs is satisfied if square root of AVE for each construct is greater than its correlation with other constructs. The square root of AVE is presented on the diagonal of Table 1. Based on the results, discriminant validity is also supported.

4.2 Hypotheses Testing

Since the measurement model could be considered satisfactory, the structural model was evaluated to test the hypotheses. The explanatory power of the model was assessed based on the amount of variance the endogenous construct could account [31]. The endogenous construct credibility had 37.80 % of the variance accounted, which is an indication of substantive explanatory power. In order to assess the significance of the paths, boot-strapping resampling method was used in PLS.

The strength of the paths and the t values of the paths are shown on Fig. 2. Although each of the hypothesized paths is showing the expected sign, the interaction effect of user expertise on reputation was not found to be significant. Therefore, while H1, H2, H3, H4 and H6 are supported H5 is not supported.

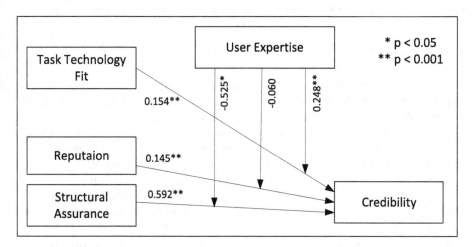

Fig. 2. Hypotheses testing

5 Discussion

Based on the above results, it is evident that both the central and peripheral routes are collectively and significantly important in the credibility assessment of cryptocurrency networks. As expected, the task technology fit is found to be a significant factor. Under this construct we evaluated the systems perspective where the users will be evaluating functional requirements specific to a financial system, such as reliability, accuracy, security etc. which can be supported by the proposed technologies of the system. Further, as hypothesized, user expertise positively moderates this relationship. Thus information technology experts would rely heavily on this path due to their cognitive capabilities.

Considering the factors on the peripheral route, both reputation and structural assurance are significant influencers on the credibility. Due to the sensitive nature of finance, these psychological assurances will play an important role. Any bad signs of reputation would negatively impact on the credibility. However, user expertise was not found to be a significant influencer on reputation. Similar results have been found in prior research as well [24]. It would be the case where, due to the sensitive nature of finance related technologies or organizations; both experts as well as non-experts look towards reputation alike as an important factor. In another probable scenario, it could be the case that average experts do also look into reputation due to the complexity and novelty of technologies behind cryptocurrencies such that a complete task technology fit assessment cannot be done.

However, it was found that the structural assurance has the strongest effect on credibility. Although cryptocurrencies were designed to operate without such assurances from third parties, this is a quantitative confirmation that regulation based assurance is required to keep the users safe and to build confidence in the system which was mentioned in prior research as well [26]. Further it was found that user expertise has a significant negative moderating effect on credibility as expected. Thus expert users would be relatively less reliant on structural assurances compared to non-experts.

6 Conclusion

The research was carried out with the intention of determining how information on cryptocurrency networks would be utilized by different users in the credibility assessment process. The uniqueness of cryptocurrency networks due to its virtual and complexity nature presents an interesting scenario to test the elaboration likelihood research model. As theoretical implications, we could confirm the dual routes of credibility assessment which is moderated by user expertise in the current context as well.

As practical contribution, we proved the stronger relationship of structural assurance with regard to building credibility. Although this is against the initial concept of cryptocurrency, incorporation of such assurance will be important in reaching a far more user base. For example, if a regulatory entity launches a cryptocurrency network using similar technology, users would weigh on the credibility of the system positively.

Several limitations were encountered in carrying out this study. Firstly the limited sample size of 136 individuals should be pointed out as if a larger sample size was obtained, the results would have been more robust. In addition, the sample included only university students leading to issues related with student samples. In addition the research model we adopted was a simple model considering only a few relevant factors identified in prior research. Thus in future research, further exploration should be done to identify other cues that will be applicable to central and peripheral routes.

References

1. Nakamoto, S., Bitcoin: A peer-to-peer electronic cash system (2008)
2. Vigna, P., Casey, M.J.: The Age of Cryptocurrency: How Bitcoin and Digital Money are Challenging the Global Economic Order. St. Martin's Press, New York (2015)
3. Yermack, D., Is Bitcoin a real currency? An economic appraisal. National Bureau of Economic Research (2013)
4. Hilligoss, B., Rieh, S.Y.: Developing a unifying framework of credibility assessment: construct, heuristics, and interaction in context. Inf. Process. Manage. 44(4), 1467–1484 (2008)

5. Fogg, B.J. and H. Tseng. The elements of computer credibility. ACM (1999)
6. Ba, S., Pavlou, P.A.: Evidence of the effect of trust building technology in electronic markets: price premiums and buyer behavior. MIS Q. **26**(3), 243–268 (2002)
7. Dimoka, A.: What does the brain tell us about trust and distrust? evidence from a functional neuroimaging study. MIS Q. **34**(2), 373–396 (2010)
8. Sirdeshmukh, D., Singh, J., Sabol, B.: Consumer trust, value, and loyalty in relational exchanges. J. Mark. **66**(1), 15–37 (2002)
9. Garbarino, E., Lee, O.F.: Dynamic pricing in internet retail: effects on consumer trust. Psychol. Mark. **20**(6), 495–513 (2003)
10. Goodhue, D.L.: Understanding user evaluations of information systems. Manage. Sci. **41**(12), 1827–1844 (1995)
11. Goodhue, D.L., Thompson, R.L.: Task-technology fit and individual performance. MIS Q. **19**(2), 213–236 (1995)
12. Tseng, S., Fogg, B.J.: Credibility and computing technology. Commun. ACM **42**(5), 39–44 (1999)
13. Petty, R.E., Cacioppo, J.T.: The elaboration likelihood model of persuasion. Springer, New York (1986)
14. Petty, R.E., Cacioppo, J.T.X.: Attitudes and persuasion: Classic and contemporary approaches. Westview Press, Boulder (1996)
15. Wathen, C.N., Burkell, J.: Believe it or not: factors influencing credibility on the web. J. Am. soc. Inf. Sci. Technol. **53**(2), 134–144 (2002)
16. Sundar, S.S.: Technology and credibility: cognitive heuristics cued by modality, agency, interactivity and navigability. In: Metzge, M.J., Flanagin, A.J. (eds.) Digital Media, Youth, and Credibility. MacArthur Foundation Series on Digital Media and Learning, pp. 73–100. MIT Press, Cambridge (2007)
17. Eastin, M.S., Yang, M.-S., Nathanson, A.I.: Children of the net: an empirical exploration into the evaluation of Internet content. J. Broadcast. Electron. Media **50**(2), 211–230 (2006)
18. Bhattacherjee, A., Sanford, C.: Influence processes for information technology acceptance: an elaboration likelihood model. MIS Q. **30**(4), 805–825 (2006)
19. Yang, S.C., et al.: Investigating initial trust toward e-tailers from the elaboration likelihood model perspective. Psychol. Mark. **23**(5), 429–445 (2006)
20. Klopping, I.M., McKinney, E.: Extending the technology acceptance model and the task-technology fit model to consumer e-commerce. Inf. Technol. Learn. Perform. J. **22**, 35–48 (2004)
21. Lee, C.-C., Cheng, H.K., Cheng, H.-H.: An empirical study of mobile commerce in insurance industry: task–technology fit and individual differences. Decis. Support Syst. **43**(1), 95–110 (2007)
22. Zhou, T., Lu, Y., Wang, B.: Integrating TTF and UTAUT to explain mobile banking user adoption. Comput. Hum. Behav. **26**(4), 760–767 (2010)
23. Shang, R.-A., Y.-C. Chen, and C.-M. Chen, Why people blog? An empirical investigations of the task technology fit model. In: Proceedings of PACIS, p. 5 (2007)
24. Zhou, T.: Understanding users' initial trust in mobile banking: An elaboration likelihood perspective. Comput. Hum. Behav. **28**(4), 1518–1525 (2012)
25. Beldad, A., De Jong, M., Steehouder, M.: How shall I trust the faceless and the intangible? A literature review on the antecedents of online trust. Comput. Hum. Behav. **26**(5), 857–869 (2010)
26. Ingram, C., M. Morisse, and R. Teigland. 'A Bad Apple Went Away': Exploring Resilience Among Bitcoin Entrepreneurs. In: Twenty-Third European Conference on Information Systems (ECIS), Münster, Germany (2015)

27. Pavlou, P.A., Gefen, D.: Building effective online marketplaces with institution-based trust. Inf. Syst. Res. **15**(1), 37–59 (2004)
28. Newell, S.J., Goldsmith, R.E.: The development of a scale to measure perceived corporate credibility. J. Bus. Res. **52**(3), 235–247 (2001). ISSN: 0148-2963
29. Lin, T.-C., Huang, C.-C.: Understanding knowledge management system usage antecedents: an integration of social cognitive theory and task technology fit. Inf. Manage. **45**(6), 410–417 (2008)
30. Gefen, D., Straub, D.W., Rigdon, E.E.: An update and extension to SEM guidelines for admnistrative and social science research. Manage. Inf. Syst. Q. **35**(2), iii–xiv (2011)
31. Kankanhalli, A., Lee, O.-K.D., Lim, K.H.: Knowledge reuse through electronic repositories: a study in the context of customer service support. Inf. Manage. **48**(2), 106–113 (2011)

Swiping vs. Scrolling in Mobile Shopping Applications

Ben C.F. Choi[1], Samuel N. Kirshner[1(✉)], and Yi Wu[2]

[1] UNSW Business School, University of New South Wales, Sydney, Australia
{chun.choi,s.kirshner}@unsw.edu.au
[2] College of Management and Economics, Tianjn University, Tianjin, China
yiwu@tju.edu.cn

Abstract. Smartphone gestures are an essential feature of app design that influence both behavioral attitudes and user performance. Due to the popularity of Tinder, a number of high profile shopping applications have adopted interfaces utilizing the swiping gesture to navigate and make sequential evaluation decisions. To understand the impacts of adopting a swipe-based interface over a traditional scroll-based interface, we construct an experiment to study the two types of haptic interactions. The results suggest that the swiping interface leads to greater cognitive absorption and playfulness in shopping applications. We find convincing support that cognitive absorption and not playfulness is significant in increasing reuse intentions and task performance.

Keywords: Gestures · Cognitive absorption · Playfulness · Mobile shopping apps

1 Introduction

Recently, there has been a plethora of mobile shopping apps on Android and iOS platforms enabling users to discover and purchase products on their smartphones. These apps are virtual marketplaces featuring thousands of products from international chains and independent retailers. To lighten the cognitive burden associated with choice overload, apps encourage users to save products that they may be interested in purchasing to a consideration list. At any point in time, the user can review the list of saved items to make actual purchases.

There are two prevailing haptic interfaces for saving products to consideration set lists. The first is a scroll-based interface where the user views items on a product discovery screen and uses the scrolling gesture to navigate through the set of products. To save an item, the user taps on the image and is directed to an individual product page. The user has the option of saving the product by tapping a soft button on the screen or tapping on a soft back button to return to the product discovery page. The second method is a swipe-based interface where the app presents the user with an image of a product, and the user swipes right (left) to save (dismiss) the item. After swiping, the next item appears on the

© Springer International Publishing Switzerland 2016
F.F.-H. Nah and C.-H. Tan (Eds.): HCIBGO 2016, Part I, LNCS 9751, pp. 177–188, 2016.
DOI: 10.1007/978-3-319-39396-4_16

screen. Typically, tapping on the item will also lead the user to the individual product page.

There is an emergent literature demonstrating that differences in haptic interfaces can impact user experience with respect to enjoyment and level of engagement [17]. As a result, small differences in haptic navigation can potentially impact task performance and behavioral attitudes towards the application. In the case of mobile shopping apps where the user is required to identify a manageable list of products that they like and may consider purchasing (from the thousands of available items), we theorize that haptic navigation utilizing swiping will foster greater cognitive absorption and playfulness than those relying on scrolling.

Cognitive absorption and playfulness are two important constructs within the IS literature that can impact task performance (the user's ability to save products that they like) and reuse intention. If the user experiences a greater level of cognitive absorption, then there will be greater levels of engagement and enjoyment while using the app. This will potentially lead to more accurate assessments of the streamed products as well as a greater intention to reuse the app. Although playfulness is associated with higher reuse intention, the influence on task performance in many cases is less clear. Within the context of mobile shopping apps, playfulness may reduce task performance, because the user may spontaneously save products that they are not actually interested in. Saving products that are not of sufficient interest can cause the user to forgo purchases due to the phenomenon of choice overload. Therefore, understanding the influences of cognitive absorption and playfulness is critical for designing a successful shopping app.

We designed an experiment to test the impact of haptic navigation on cognitive absorption and playfulness and the resulting consequences on task performance and reuse intention by manipulating the haptic interface of a shopping application. The study suggests that the swiping interface is more playful and facilitates greater cognitive absorption, compared to the scrolling interface. Cognitive absorption is found to improve task performance and increase reuse intention. Although we find some support that playfulness reduces task performance and increases reuse intentions, the results are not statistically significant. These findings are particularly relevant given the popularity of the dating app Tinder, which has inspired a large number of high profile shopping apps to adopt a swiping interface.

2   Theoretical Background

Cognitive absorption is a multi-dimensional construct describing "a state of deep involvement with software" [1]. The five dimensions are temporal dissociation (TD), focused immersion (FI), heightened enjoyment (HE), control (CON), and curiosity (CUR). TD is a user's failure to register the passage of time while using the software. FI is a level of concentration where the user ignores anything outside of the software. HE is the intrinsic interest and pleasure related to using the software. CON is the user's perception of being in charge of the interaction with the software. CUR is the arousal of sensory and cognitive interest from the interaction with the software. Playfulness is a related construct to cognitive absorption and represents the degree of cognitive spontaneity in interactions with software [19].

Both cognitive absorption and playfulness are intrinsic motivations. Consequently, both constructs are connected to the technology acceptance model (TAM), which demonstrates that perceived ease of use (PEoU) and perceived usefulness (PU) influence attitude and the behavioral intentions to use IT. Agarwal and Karahanna [1] demonstrate that cognitive absorption positively influences PEoU and PU, which in turn positively impact intention to use. Moon and Kim [11] formally integrate playfulness into TAM and finds that playfulness positively relates to PEoU and behavioral attitudes towards IT. The potential antecedents to cognitive absorption and playfulness stem from the inter-related literatures on flow and engagement and can be classified into cognitive aspects (such as control, challenge, and involvement) and IT characteristics (such as feedback, variety, and speed) [1,5].

Although the influence of both cognitive absorption and playfulness are often seen as antecedents to factors that influence behavioral intentions and IT usage, Burton-Jones and Straub [4] argue that in many cases these two-step processes should be recast into a single richer measure of outcomes. To support this idea, Burton-Jones and Straub empirically study the relationship between system usage and task performance in cognitively engaging tasks and find that cognitive absorption directly increases performance. While the impact of cognitive absorption on task performance is typically positive, playfulness can have both positive and negative impacts on performance [20].

3   Research Model and Hypothesis Development

This study examines two modes of haptic navigation, i.e., scrolling navigation and swiping navigation. The effects of haptic navigation on individuals' usage experience are investigated in terms of cognitive absorption and playfulness. Furthermore, we assess the effects of these two perceptions on individuals' behavioral responses, namely reuse intention and decision uncertainty. The research model analyzed is presented in Fig. 1.

3.1   Effects of Haptic Navigation

Swiping is seen as an intuitive and more natural action (closely related to flipping through a book or magazine) compared to scrolling, which was specifically developed for mouse-based navigation on a computer screen [17]. The natural mapping ability and intuitiveness of an interface positively influences the engagement process and cognitive absorption [12], which implies that the haptic gesture of swiping may lead to increased cognitive absorption.

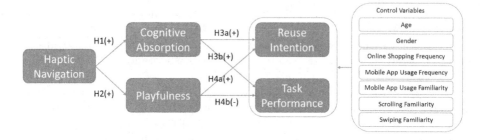

Fig. 1. Research model

Users are likely to experience heightened enjoyment when positively evaluating and subsequently saving a product compared to rejecting (swipe navigation) or passing over (scroll navigation) a product. This implies that it is also important to consider the differences between swiping and tapping. [7] examine the impact of adding swiping to a tap-only mobile website on engagement and usage intention. The analysis suggests that swiping leads to a greater sense of control, enjoyment, user engagement, and increases re-use intentions. Furthermore, the discussion proposes that swiping creates curiosity within the user because swiping "resembles turning the pages of a book, which appears to promote exploration of content" [7]. Thus, we postulate that users are likely to experience greater enjoyment when saving items in a shopping app with the swipe gesture rather than a two stage process based on scrolling and tapping.

In the swipe interface, users cannot revisit rejected items, making each decision final. Although users rarely scroll upwards, users are aware that they can view previous items in the scrolling interface. This implies that products are never completely dismissed from consideration. The knowledge of being able to revisit items implies that items that the user was close to saving may remain in memory. This creates a greater cognitive load, which can diminish the experience of flow, and hence lessen cognitive absorption and playfulness [14,21]. The finality of the swiping interface promotes greater engagement, while also potentially creating greater satisfaction from making a decision.

The differences in haptic navigation can lead to varying levels of stimuli created by the product images. In the swiping interface, the user is focused on a single task of saving or rejecting the image on the screen by swiping right or left. In the scrolling interface, user attention is divided between the dual tasks of searching and evaluation, resulting in weaker stimuli from images. Since scrolling is almost always unidirectional, the haptic motion of scrolling is more repetitive and predictable. Conversely, the swiping motion is used to make decisions, which implies that the directional movement is less predictable compared to scrolling, and provides the user with a greater sense of haptic variety.

Predictability demands less attention from the user and stimulates less curiosity and interest [2]. The repetitiveness and predictability of scrolling enables the user to disengage with the application. Scrolling may become habitual, resulting in a lack of engagement and mind-wandering, which impairs task-relevant stimuli [15]. This suggests that products displayed in the swiping interface will produce a stronger visual signal and have higher cognitive absorption compared to the scrolling interface. In addition, the swiping interface is likely to be more playful, since users perceive playfulness when they experience curiosity, interest, and their attention is focused while interacting with software [11].

Consumer evaluation and choices are influenced by consumer imagery-based responses [13]. Mental imagery and fantasies involving the ownership of the product are stimulated by product images and influence consumer attitudes towards the product [16]. Within the context of mobile shopping for clothing and accessories, user imagery such as the fit of the item, events where the user can wear the item, and how the item coordinates with the user's existing wardrobe, will likely influence the user's evaluation of the product. Thus, the weaker stimuli in the scrolling interface may impact the user's level of creativity, imagination, and fantasy, which are important elements of playfulness when using software.

Scrolling navigation epitomizes the traditional method of online shopping, whereas swiping is a comparatively novel approach to shopping navigation and evaluation. Interestingness, which is associated with the emotion dimension of positive activation, can be triggered by novelty [8]. In addition, interactions with novel features promote greater cognitive thought and engagement relative to familiar features, where users may have transitioned from controlled information processing towards automatic behavior [18]. Novelty in a product or service can result in emotions such as delight, which contributes to the level of playfulness [10].

Given the haptic nature of the gesture, lower cognitive load, the greater level of engagement, visualization strength, and novelty associated with the swiping navigation, we propose the following:

H1. Compared with scrolling navigation, swiping navigation will lead to a higher level of cognitive absorption.
H2. Compared with scrolling navigation, swiping navigation will lead to a higher level of playfulness.

3.2 Effects of Cognitive Absorption

Cognitive absorption implies that the user is immersed and experiencing enjoyment while using the mobile device to find products. Consistent with the literature that has demonstrated behavioral intention to use software is positively impacted by cognitive absorption, we posit that cognitive absorption will lead to higher reuse intention of mobile shopping apps. Moreover, the engagement from cognitive absorption implies that users will be more focused on evaluating items, which will lead to greater performance in saving choice items. Thus, we posit the following:

H3a. Stronger cognitive absorption will increase reuse intention.
H3b. Stronger cognitive absorption will increase task performance.

3.3   Effects of Playfulness

There is strong evidence in the literature that playfulness also increases re-use intention, and we expect that to hold in the context of mobile shopping applications. A key element of playfulness is spontaneity. Within the context of mobile shopping, spontaneity may lead users to positively evaluate items on impulse and without deliberation of whether the user truly likes the item. As a result, unlike cognitive absorption, playfulness may have a negative effect on task performance. Therefore, we posit the following:

> *H4a. Stronger playfulness will increase reuse intention.*
> *H4b. Stronger playfulness will decrease task performance.*

4   Experimental Design

An experiment was conducted to test the proposed hypotheses. The two modes of haptic navigation, namely scrolling navigation and swiping navigation, were manipulated by presenting subjects with a scrolling (swiping) mobile app inter-action interface.

We recruited 57 subjects from a large public university to participate in the experiment. Subjects were randomly assigned to one of the two experimental conditions in which they were presented with a mobile shopping app with a scrolling (swiping) interface. To ensure adequate familiarity with the shopping app, a simple demonstration session was first performed to familiarize subjects with the shopping app. Afterwards they were instructed to spend 15 min to use the app and "save" as many items as they liked.

At the end of the 15-min period, subjects were asked to complete a ques-tionnaire assessing measurement items of the research variables (i.e., cognitive absorption and playfulness). Subsequently, they were given the opportunity to revisit the list of saved items to discard any merchandise from the list as they deemed necessary. Subjects were then instructed to complete a final survey cap-turing their behavioral intentions. Finally, subjects were debriefed and thanked.

5   Data Analysis

5.1   Subject Demographics and Measurement

Of the 57 subjects, 23 were female. The age of the subjects ranged from 18 to 25. No significant differences were found among subjects with regards to age, gender, online shopping frequency, and mobile app usage familiarity, indicating that the subjects' demographics were fairly homogeneous across different conditions.

The measurement items are presented in Table 5 (found in the Appen-dix). The measurement scale proposed by Agarwal and Karahanna [1] was adapted to measure cognitive absorption (Cronbach's alpha = 0.91). Seven items measuring playfulness were adapted from Webster and Martocchio [19]

Table 1. Results of factor analysis.

	1	2	3
Temporal Dissociation	**0.98**	0.2	-0.07
Focused Immersion	**0.98**	0.19	-0.08
Heightened Enjoyment	**0.97**	0.22	-0.08
Control	**0.98**	0.2	-0.07
Curiosity	**0.98**	0.2	-0.07
Playfulness 1	0.23	**0.93**	0.21
Playfulness 2	0.22	**0.91**	0.24
Playfulness 3	0.2	**0.92**	0.23
Playfulness 4	0.19	**0.91**	0.29
Playfulness 5	0.19	**0.93**	0.14
Playfulness 6	0.2	**0.92**	0.26
Playfulness 7	0.16	**0.91**	0.27
Reuse Intention 1	-0.13	0.33	**0.93**
Reuse Intention 2	-0.13	0.33	**0.93**
Reuse Intention 3	-0.13	0.35	**0.93**

(Cronbach's alpha = 0.98). Three items measuring reuse intention were adapted from Jarvenpaa [9] (Cronbach's alpha = 0.95). Task performance was captured by computing the ratio between the final number of saved items and the initial number of saved items. A high (low) value denotes a small change in the number of saved items and better (poor) task performance. Exploratory factor analysis shows that, in general, items load well on their intended factors and lightly on the other factor, indicating adequate construct validity (see Table 1).

5.2 Results on Cognitive Absorption and Playfulness

This study investigates two modes of haptic navigation mechanisms, namely scrolling navigation and swiping navigation. First, to investigate the impact of haptic navigation on cognitive absorption and playfulness, an independent sample t-test was conducted. As shown in Table 2, the results indicate that the difference in terms of cognitive absorption between the two modes of haptic

Table 2. Comparing cognitive absorption and playfulness across two navigation mechanisms.

	Average	Scrolling Navigation	Swiping Navigation	
Cognitive Absorption	4.09	3.1	4.92	$t = 41.04***$
Playfulness	4.18	2	6.01	$t = 48.18***$

Note: *** $p < .001$

navigation mechanisms were significantly different (t = 41.04, ρ < .001). The respective means suggest that compared to the scrolling navigation condition (mean = 3.10), swiping navigation (mean = 4.92) led to significantly stronger cognitive absorption. Therefore, H1 is supported.

Furthermore, results of the independent sample t-test revealed that the difference in terms of playfulness between the two modes of haptic navigation mechanisms were significantly different. (t = 48.18, ρ < .001). The respective means suggest that compared to the scrolling navigation condition (mean = 2.00), swiping navigation (mean = 6.01) led to significantly stronger cognitive absorption. Therefore, H2 is supported.

5.3   Results on Reuse Intention and Task Performance

Linear regressions were performed to investigate the effects of cognitive absorption and playfulness on reuse intention and task performance respectively. To control for the potential confounding effects, the regression analysis was performed with the consideration of gender, age, online shopping frequency, mobile app usage frequency, mobile app usage familiarity, scrolling familiarity, swiping familiarity, perceived usefulness, and perceived ease of use as the control variables.

As shown in Table 3, cognitive absorption had a significant positive effect on reuse intention (β=1.4, ρ < .05). Hence, H3a is supported. However, contrary to expectation, playfulness was found to have no significant effect on reuse intention (β=0.29, ρ=.35), and hence H4a is not supported.

As shown in Table 4, cognitive absorption had a significant positive effect (β=0.19, ρ < .01). The positive coefficient suggests that higher absorption reduces the number of discarded items, indicating higher task performance. Hence, H3b is supported. Contrary to expectation, playfulness is not found to

Table 3. Linear regression results for reuse intention.

	Unstandardized Coefficients		Standardized Coefficients	t-stat	Sig
	B	Std. Err	β		
Constant	-5.54	5.27		-1.05	0.3
Cognitive Absorption	1.4	0.66	0.64	2.11	< .05
Playfulness	0.29	0.31	0.29	0.94	0.35
Age	-0.12	0.07	-0.14	-1.83	0.07
Gender	-0.45	0.28	0.11	-1.63	0.11
Mobile App Usage Frequency	0.22	0.26	0.1	0.84	0.4
Mobile App Usage Familiarity	0.17	0.24	0.05	0.7	0.49
Scrolling Familiarity	0.59	0.48	0.09	1.23	0.23
Swiping Familiarity	-0.06	0.27	-0.02	-0.21	0.84
Online Shopping Frequency	0.11	0.09	0.09	1.24	0.22
Perceived Usefulness	-0.17	0.36	-0.04	-0.47	0.64
Perceived Ease of Use	0.03	0.35	0.01	0.08	0.93

Note:
Dependent Variable: Reuse Intention
R Squared = .81 (Adjusted R Squared = .75)

Table 4. Linear regression results for task performance.

	Unstandardized Coefficients		Standardized Coefficients	t	Sig
	B	Std. Err	β		
Constant	0.37	0.54		0.69	0.5
Cognitive Absorption	0.19	0.07	1.08	2.85	< .01
Playfulness	-0.03	0.03	-0.36	-0.91	0.37
Age	0.01	0.01	0.12	1.33	0.19
Gender	-0.03	0.03	-0.1	-1.13	0.26
Mobile App Usage Frequency	-0.02	0.01	-0.22	-2.34	0.02
Mobile App Usage Familiarity	-0.01	0.03	-0.02	-0.13	0.9
Scrolling Familiarity	-0.06	0.05	-0.11	-1.15	0.26
Swiping Familiarity	0.01	0.03	0.04	0.38	0.71
Online Shopping Frequency	-0.02	0.09	-0.23	-2.43	0.05
Perceived Usefulness	-0.03	0.04	-0.08	-0.84	0.4
Perceived Ease of Use	0.01	0.04	0.04	0.37	0.71

Note:
Dependent Variable: Task Performance
R Squared = .82 (Adjusted R Squared = .60)

have a significant effect on task performance (β=-0.03, ρ =.37), and hence H4b is not supported.

6   Discussion and Conclusion

6.1   Discussion of Results and Implications

As technology advances and user-interfaces offer greater interactivity, physical interactions with the technology are becoming increasingly important aspects of behavioral attitudes, intentions, and outcomes. User engagement is particularly important for smartphone, since the devices are often used in conjunction with other activities or in distracting environments [3,7]. Given the recent popularity of utilizing swiping gestures in mobile shopping apps, we investigated the impact of this interface on cognitive absorption and playfulness over traditional interfaces using scroll based navigation.

Our results support the hypothesis that a swiping interface leads to greater levels of cognitive absorption and playfulness compared to a scrolling interface. Furthermore, we find support that cognitive absorption positively influences task performance and reuse intentions, even when accounting for perceived ease of use and usefulness of the technology. These results have important implications for app design by providing empirical support for swiping as a more engaging and playful method of navigation. Although our results pertain to shopping, they may be applicable to other mobile apps involving navigation and sequential evaluation.

Contrary to expectation, playfulness did not exhibit a significant impact on task performance. The literature on playfulness has produced contradictory results in terms of its impact on task performance. Thus, playfulness within shopping applications may have both positive and negative aspects that influence performance, which resulted in an insignificant effect. Although the overall effect of playfulness on performance was not significant, it was inversely related to improvements in task performance. The insignificant effect of playfulness on intention to reuse suggests that continued use of the app is based more on its utilitarian value as a tool for shopping rather than the hedonic experience it provides.

6.2 Limitations and Future Research

An important limitation of the study is that we only considered task performance in one direction, i.e. users were able to review the merchandise that they saved and decide which items to remove. A more complete measure of task performance would be to allow the users to revisit a sample of non-saved items to assess whether they rejected items that they were actually interested in. Another important limitation of the results is the impact of time. The subjects were instructed to use the app for a duration of 15 min. However, measures of absorption and playfulness while using the app for shopping may depend on time. Understanding the interaction between interface design and usage duration is an interesting avenue for future research.

Appendix

Table 5. Measurement items.

Cognitive Absorption (CA)	Adapted from Agarwal and Karahanna [1]
TD1	Time appears to go by very quickly when I am using the mobile shopping app
TD2	I lose track of time when I am using the mobile shopping app
TD3	Time flies when I am using the mobile shopping app
TD4	I believe I have spent more time on the mobile shopping app than I had intended
FI1	While using the mobile shopping app, I am able to block out most other distractions
FI2	While using the mobile shopping app, I am absorbed in what I am doing
FI3	While using the mobile shopping app, I am immersed in the shopping task I am performing
FI4	When using the mobile shopping app, my attention does not get diverted very easily (R)
HE1	I have fun using the mobile shopping app
HE2	Using the mobile shopping app provides me with a lot of enjoyment
HE3	I enjoy using the mobile shopping app
HE4	Using the mobile shopping app bores me (R)

(continued)

Table 5. (*continued*)

Cognitive Absorption (CA)	Adapted from Agarwal and Karahanna [1]
CTL1	When using the mobile shopping app, I feel in control
CTL2	I feel that I have no control over my interaction with the app
CTL3	The mobile shopping app allows me to control my interaction with the app
CUR1	Using the mobile shopping app excites my curiosity
CUR2	Interacting with the mobile shopping app makes me curious
CUR3	Using the mobile shopping app arouses my imagination
Playfulness (PLY)	Adapted from Webster and Martocchio [19]
PLY1	When using the mobile shopping app I am Spontaneous
PLY2	When using the mobile shopping app I am Imaginative
PLY3	When using the mobile shopping app I am Flexible
PLY4	When using the mobile shopping app I am Creative
PLY5	When using the mobile shopping app I am Playful
PLY6	When using the mobile shopping app I am Original
PLY7	When using the mobile shopping app I am Inventive
Perceived Ease of Use (PEoU)	Adapted from Davis [6]
PEoU1	Learning to operate the mobile shopping app is easy for me
PEoU2	I find it easy to get the mobile shopping app to do what I want it to do
PEoU3	It is easy for me to become skillful at using the mobile shopping app
PEoU4	I find the mobile shopping app easy to use
Perceived Usefulness (PU)	Adapted from Davis [6]
PU1	Using the mobile shopping app enhances my effectiveness in shopping
PU2	I find the mobile shopping app useful in my shopping activities
PU3	Using the mobile shopping app improves my sense of fashion
Reuse Intention (RI)	Adapted from Jarvenpaa et al. [9]
RI1	In the medium term, it's likely that I will use the app again
RI2	In the long term, it's likely that I will use the app again
RI3	All things considered, it's likely that I will use the app again

Note:
All items are measured using 7-point Likert scale.
(R)indicates reversed items.

References

1. Agarwal, R., Karahanna, E.: Time flies when you're having fun: cognitive absorption and beliefs about information technology usage. MIS Q. **24**, 665–694 (2000)
2. Berlyne, D.: Uncertainty and epistemic curiosity. Br. J. Psychol. **53**(1), 27–34 (1962)
3. Bragdon, A., Nelson, E., Li, Y., Hinckley, K.: Experimental analysis of touch-screen gesture designs in mobile environments. In: Proceedings of the SIGCHI Conference on Human Factors in Computing Systems, pp. 403–412. ACM (2011)
4. Burton-Jones, A., Straub Jr., D.W.: Reconceptualizing system usage: an approach and empirical test. Inf. Syst. Res. **17**(3), 228–246 (2006)

5. Chung, J., Tan, F.B.: Antecedents of perceived playfulness: an exploratory study on user acceptance of general information-searching websites. Inf. Manag. **41**(7), 869–881 (2004)
6. Davis, F.D.: Perceived usefulness, perceived ease of use, and user acceptance of information technology. MIS Q. **13**(3), 319–340 (1989)
7. Dou, X., Sundar, S.S.: Power of the swipe: why mobile websites should add horizontal swiping to tapping, clicking and scrolling interaction techniques. Int. J. Hum. Comput. Interact. **32**(4), 352–362 (2016)
8. Frijda, N.H.: Emotion, cognitive structure, and action tendency. Cogn. Emot. **1**(2), 115–143 (1987)
9. Jarvenpaa, S.L., Tractinsky, N., Vitalec, M.: Consumer trust in an Internet store. Inf. Technol. Mgmt. **1**(1), 45–71 (2000)
10. Lucero, A., Holopainen, J., Ollila, E., Suomela, R., Karapanos, E.: The playful experiences (plex) framework as a guide for expert evaluation. In: Proceedings of the 6th International Conference on Designing Pleasurable Products and Interfaces, pp. 221–230. ACM (2013)
11. Moon, J.W., Kim, Y.G.: Extending the tam for a world-wide-web context. Inf. Manage. **38**(4), 217–230 (2001)
12. Oh, J., Bellur, S., Sundar, S.S.: Clicking, assessing, immersing, and sharing an empirical model of user engagement with interactive media. Commun. Res. 1–27 (2015). Advance online publication
13. Oliver, R.L., Robertson, T.S., Mitchell, D.J.: Imaging and analyzing in response to new product advertising. J. Advertising **22**(4), 35–50 (1993)
14. Pilke, E.M.: Flow experiences in information technology use. Int. J. Hum. Comput. Stud. **61**(3), 347–357 (2004)
15. Smallwood, J., Schooler, J.W.: The restless mind. Psychol. Bull. **132**(6), 946 (2006)
16. Song, K., Fiore, A.M., Park, J.: Telepresence and fantasy in online apparel shopping experience. J. Fashion Mark. Manage. Int. J. **11**(4), 553–570 (2007)
17. Sundar, S.S., Bellur, S., Oh, J., Xu, Q., Jia, H.: User experience of on-screen interaction techniques: an experimental investigation of clicking, sliding, zooming, hovering, dragging, and flipping. Hum. Comput. Interact. **29**(2), 109–152 (2014)
18. Underwood, G., Everatt, J.: Automatic and controlled information processing: the role of attention in the processing of novelty. Handb. Percept. Action **3**, 185–227 (1996)
19. Webster, J., Martocchio, J.J.: Microcomputer playfulness: development of a measure with workplace implications. MIS Q. **16**(2), 201–226 (1992)
20. Webster, J., Trevino, L.K., Ryan, L.: The dimensionality and correlates of flow in human-computer interactions. Comput. Hum. Behav. **9**(4), 411–426 (1993)
21. Woszczynski, A.B., Roth, P.L., Segars, A.H.: Exploring the theoretical foundations of playfulness in computer interactions. Comput. Hum. Behav. **18**(4), 369–388 (2002)

How Do Consumers Behave in Social Commerce? An Investigation Through Clickstream Data

Qican Gu, Qiqi Jiang$^{(\boxtimes)}$, and Hongwei Wang

School of Economics and Management, Tongji University, Shanghai, China
{1531066_guqican, jiangqq, hwwang}@tongji.edu.cn

Abstract. The social commerce has received considerable attentions in both academia and practitioners in last decade. However, most of current studies investigated such topic from consumers' psychological impetus, but lack of the objective evidence. In this work, we employed the clickstream data analysis to depict online consumers' cross-site browsing behaviors in the context of social commerce. Four prominent clusters depicting distinctive consumers' online browsing behaviors are found. Additionally, the consumers' online behaviors characterized by the browsing patterns are also unveiled and discussed.

Keywords: Social commerce · Clickstream data · Cluster analysis · Chinese consumers

1 Introduction

Social commerce, as an emerging business model that combines social network and e-commerce [1], has received considerable attentions in recent years. Comparing with the conventional e-commerce, social commerce facilitates buying and selling products by using social interaction and user contributions on social media. Various topics related to social commerce have been discussed in previous studies [2, 3]. Such findings make us spontaneously raise the research question: How will consumers behave in social commerce context?

To answer the question above, we collaborated with a leading marketing research agency in Mainland China and attempted to apply the clickstream data to investigate the consumers' online behaviors in social commerce. In particular, the clickstream data included the browsing histories (in the URL form) generated by 2000 randomly selected consumers from December 2014 to January 2015. Besides the individual's online browsing trajectories (the URL records), the demographics of the focal 2000 consumers including gender, age, education and area were also collected. After a series of sophisticated data analysis, several key findings are obtained. First, four groups were highlighted from the cluster analysis after several attempts, which were named as width browsing, depth browsing, goal-oriented browsing, and hedonic browsing. Second, a series of regression models were employed to understand the consequence on purchase commitment in each group. We first unveiled that higher likelihood of being guided into e-commerce websites from social media in the depth browsing, goal-oriented

© Springer International Publishing Switzerland 2016
F.F.-H. Nah and C.-H. Tan (Eds.): HCIBGO 2016, Part I, LNCS 9751, pp. 189–197, 2016.
DOI: 10.1007/978-3-319-39396-4_17

browsing, and hedonic browsing clusters. Besides, we also unveiled that the goal-oriented group had the highest propensity to the purchase commitment, which was consistent with the findings in prior literatures [4].

For the remainder of this work, an introduction and a succinct literature reviews on social commerce research are presented in Sect. 2. The research proposition and data analysis are given in Sect. 3. We concluded the study in Sect. 4.

2   Social Commerce

The term "social commerce" was first created by Yahoo! on 2005 with the introduction of Shoposphere and Pick Lists, i.e. the two social tools assisting consumers for online shopping [5]. After that, social commerce evolved rapidly from traditional e-commerce with the support of emerging technologies associated with Web 2.0. In line with Liang and Turban [6], we considered social commerce as an environment in which social interaction and user-generated content assist the acquisition of products and services.

The social commerce was composed of two fundamental elements, i.e. social media and commercial activities [6]. From Social perspective, consumers in social commerce can interact with others in shopping activities. For example, they can search product information and share with friends, or aggregate products and make collaborative decision [7]. These social features such as wish lists, chat rooms, tagging, ranking tools and blogs carry unique and interesting capabilities for online shopping [8]. Curty and Zhang [9] analyzed 42 social features found in the top 5 e-commerce websites and categorized them into 4 groups, all of them are found to have the goal of promoting social interactions and exchanges among consumers thus improving their shopping experience. From Commercial perspective, social commerce websites are expected to have ecommerce functions to help consumers accomplishing shopping activities after selecting products. However, for current social commerce websites, few of them provide consumers with tools such as shopping cart, payment zone and confirmation to finish the whole shopping process. Others provide users with product descriptions, price comparison and the link to a third party to accomplish the rest shopping transaction [10].

In the past decade, social commerce has been studied from different angles with diverse methods. Some academic studies were found to investigate the design features and their impacts on perceived usefulness and enjoyment of consumers [8]. Some marketing scholars observed the factors like loyalty [11], social influence [12] and network ties [13] and examined their influence on marketing strategy. For examples, Curty and Zhang [10] studied the framework of social commerce and categorized social commerce websites into two groups: direct sales and referrals. Direct sales refer to websites that contains a full-transaction platform such as Amazon, while referrals provide users with an external site to complete their transactions, which refer to a social commerce process.

Differing from prior studies employing the self-reported data for studying social commerce, we collaborated with a leading marketing agency in China for collecting the clickstream data from 2,000 real users. After a series of sophisticated data analysis, several key findings are obtained. The details of the analysis are given below.

3   Proposition and Data Analysis

3.1   Data Description

With the help with a leading marketing research agency in Mainland China, we randomly collected the clickstream data (browsing histories in the URL form) generated by 2000 consumers, including 1120 males and 880 females, which is consistent with the gender ratio in CNNIC's report of China's netizens [14], from December 2014 to January 2015. For these clickstream data, we firstly removed the extreme observations such as the top one percentage of users who viewed the most pages and we finally got 7,560,000 records.

Afterwards, the cleaned dataset was aggregated into sessions. The session denotes a sequential series of queries submitted by a user when he/she is seeking for certain information during a period of time [15], which was mainly employed to study online consumer behaviors in prior literatures [16]. In this study, we set 30 min as the interval threshold of the visiting times in order to segment the clickstream data (the URL form) into the respective sessions of each user. Finally, 240,000 sessions were obtained. Next, two actions were made to enable these sessions to characterize the social commerce. First, only the sessions containing the browsing histories of both e-commerce websites and social network websites were kept. Second, we removed the sessions in which e-commerce sites were viewed prior to visiting social media websites. The description and descriptive analysis[1] of the variables (with 13412 observations) of each session are given in Table 1.

Table 1. Description of key variables in sessions

Variable	Mean	Min	Max	Description
TOTAL_PAGES	$-2.46\text{e-}17$	-1.012	10.587	Total number of pages viewed in each session
TOTAL_AVG_DURATION	$8.82\text{e-}15$	-1.052	22.062	Average time spent per page
EC_PAGES	$1.06\text{e-}17$	-0.004	0.007	% of pages that were e-ecommerce pages
EC_AVG_DURATION	$4.95\text{e-}15$	-0.379	45.712	Average time spent per e-commerce page

(Continued)

---

[1] The standard deviation is not listed due to the same value after standardizing the variables.

Table 1. (*Continued*)

Variable	Mean	Min	Max	Description
EC_DIFFSITE	1.21e-17	−0.894	9.617	Number of unique e-commerce sites in this session
C_SEARCHPAGE	3.06e-15	−0.461	10.122	% of pages that were e-ecommerce search pages
EC_PRODUCTPAGE	3.12e-15	−0.723	6.948	% of pages that were e-ecommerce product pages
EC_CHANNELPAGE	−5.97e-16	−0.343	17.062	% of pages that were e-ecommerce channel pages
EC_ACTIVITYPAGE	−5.46e-16	−0.247	21.885	% of pages that were e-ecommerce activity pages
EC_CARTPAGE	−8.28e-16	−0.287	16.464	% of pages that were e-ecommerce cart pages
SNS_PAGES	1.17e-17	−0.444	29.317	% of pages that were social media pages
SNS_AVG_DURATION	3.03e-15	−0.422	35.170	Average time spent per social media page
SNS_DIFFSITE	−1.08e-16	−.5134445	10.20456	Number of unique social media sites in this session

3.2 Cluster Analysis

After cleaning and preprocessing the raw session data, we applied cluster analysis with K-means algorithm to segment consumers' trajectories in social commerce context. K-means algorithm aims to segment the observations into k clusters in which each observation belongs to the cluster with the nearest mean [17], i.e. the center of the cluster, and the center serves as the average level of the cluster.

Notably, in K-means clustering process, we did not know the exact number of clusters beforehand, so we tried each time with different number of groups with the use of "distance", denoting the sum of distance between each point and its center, to measure the satisfaction of the result. The "distance" decreased when the number of groups increased because the points were closer to their center. However, less distance means more clusters but too many clusters cannot reflect the real pattern in consumer behavior. In this way, we consider both the number of cluster and their distance and finally got a solution with 5 clusters, the centers of dimensions in each cluster were presented in Table 2.

Table 2. Description of distinguished clusters

Cluster	Width browsing (Cluster 1)	Depth browsing (Cluster 2)	Goal-oriented browsing (Cluster 3)	Hedonic browsing (Cluster 4)	Shallow
N	2025	244	2151	1028	7962
TOTAL_PAGES	216.943	28.450	89.635	70.743	65.722
TOTAL_AVG_DURATION	36.030	234.144	48.850	37.500	47.610
EC_PAGES	0.322	0.322	0.323	0.322	0.322
EC_AVG_DURATION	31.322	394.010	44.710	28.084	38.340
EC_DIFFSITE	4.144	1.401	2.604	3.141	1.914
EC_SEARCHPAGE	0.021	0.016	0.123	0.010	0.011
EC_PRODUCTPAGE	0.062	0.058	0.230	0.055	0.035
EC_CHANNELPAGE	0.005	0.002	0.004	0.064	0.002
EC_ACTIVITYPAGE	0.004	0.003	0.004	0.024	0.002
EC_CARTPAGE	0.003	0.001	0.022	0.003	0.002
SNS_PAGES	24.850	3.662	4.770	3.823	5.477
SNS_AVG_DURATION	48.580	536.287	62.960	42.888	60.264
SNS_DIFFSITE	2.350	1.106	1.183	1.188	1.225

Cluster 1 consists of the sessions containing massive viewed pages with great variety, with a cluster average of 216.943 pages viewed (TOTAL_PAGES) and 4.144 unique e-commerce websites (or 2.350 unique social media websites). The consumers in this cluster are found to spend little time on each page (36.030 TOTAL_AVG_DURATION), which depicted a width-browsing pattern.

In Cluster 2, consumers were found to spend a significant amount of time on viewing each page with high level of TOTAL_AVG_DURATION, EC_AVG_DURATION and SNS_AVG_DURATION, which depicted a deep involvement of users. Furthermore, the number of unique websites consumers viewed (low EC_DIFFSITE and SNS_DIFFSITE value) indicates that users in this cluster visited websites with specific destinations like men's online stores or baby products websites to obtain target information. Thus, Cluster 2 was named as "Depth Browsing".

The sessions in Cluster 3 are distinctive in the large amount of searching pages (EC_SEARCHPAGE = 0.123), product pages (EC_PRODUCTPAGE = 0.230) and cart pages (EC_CARTPAGE = 0.022), exhibiting a focused goal-driven behavior. In this cluster, consumers were found to purposively retrieve the information for subsequently purchase. Thus, Cluster 3 was named as "Goal-oriented Browsing".

Cluster 4 was denoted as hedonic browsing, in which high ratio of activity pages and channel pages with relatively low duration of visiting time were found. An alternative explanation of such patterns depicted in this group is that the consumers were driven by the stimulus like the activities listed on the homepage, the products recommended by system or the advertisements encountered during the visits.

Moreover, the fifth cluster contained sessions that had few pages and less visiting time, and these sessions are named "Shallow" to represent a type of visitors who may visit the site just to see what the site is. This kind of behavior is common in web environment because the Internet inflows users who are exploring different and new features of websites [18].

3.3   Investigation of Post-hoc Behaviors

To investigate the Post-hoc behaviors in each cluster, two additional analyses were made. We first investigate whether the browsing behaviors in the different clusters will lead to different extent of subsequent click-out, denoting clicking a link to e-commerce website after visiting a social media site. Next, we delve into how the probability of purchase commitment in different clustered groups.

For investigating the click-out, a logistic regression model was employed. In particular, a binary dependent variable was set to denote the action of whether the click-out was made (INTRODUCE = 1) or not (INTRODUCE = 0). In the regression model, the predictor is the categorical variable of each cluster, and the click-out is the dependent variable. In addition, the demographics of the focal 2000 consumers including gender, age, education and area were also collected and included. The descriptive statistics of such control variables are given in Table 3 below.

Table 3. Description of demographic variables

Variable	Observations	Mean	Std. Dev.	Min	Max
INTRODUCE	13412	0.323	0.468	0	1
GENDER	13412	0.407	0.491	0	1
AGE	13412	32.788	8.232	5	73
AREA	13412	2.795	1.724	1	7
EDUCATION	13412	3.536	1.108	0	5

Table 4 showed the results of the logistic regression with the reference group of "Width Browsing". A significant likelihood ratio test (Log likelihood = −7839.347) was yielded from the model, which implies that our model fits better than an empty model as a whole. According to the coefficient, cluster 2, 3 and 4 performed better than cluster 1 in clicking-out to e-commerce websites (coefficient > 0) and the results were statistically significant at 0.05 and 0.001 level. Therefore, we can conclude that the online consumers behaving the browsing patters in the groups of depth browsing, goal-oriented browsing and hedonic browsing have higher probability to be redirected to e-commerce website.

Table 4. Results of Click-out behaviors

Independent variables	Coefficient	Z	p-value
Depth browsing (Cluster 2)	0.309	2.200	0.028[*]
Goal-oriented browsing (Cluster 3)	0.576	4.510	0.000[***]
Hedonic Browsing (Cluster 4)	0.361	8.901	0.000[***]
GENDER	0.309	8.080	0.000[***]
AGE	−0.126	−5.300	0.000[***]
AREA	−0.045	−4.061	0.000[***]
EDUCATION	0.420	2.450	0.014[*]

N = 13412, Log likelihood = −7839.347, *p < 0.05;** p < 0.01; ***p < 0.001

Following the result, we also tested the difference among cluster 2, 3 and 4 in clicking-out performance. In this regard, we attempt to unveil how these three clusters differentiate in the purchase commitment. Similarly, a binary variable PURCHASE is set to present whether consumers commit purchase (PURCHASE = 1) or not (PURCHASE = 0), then the logistic regression was adopted and the result was showed in Table 5 below.

Table 5. Results of purchase commitment

Independent variables	Coefficient	Z	p-value
Depth browsing (Cluster 2)	−1.832	−5.310	0.000***
Hedonic Browsing (Cluster 4)	−1.231	−8.790	0.000***
GENDER	−0.295	−2.860	0.004**
AGE	−0.001	0.250	0.840
AREA	0.079	2.670	0.007**
EDUCATION	0.070	1.520	0.127

N = 13412, Log likelihood = −7839.347, *p < 0.05; ** p < 0.01;***p < 0.001

According to the results presented in Table 5, we could conclude that consumers behaving goal-oriented browsing patterns (Cluster 3) showed higher purchase commitment than those who behaved in depth browsing (Cluster 2) and hedonic browsing (Cluster 4). Such finding is consistent with the prior literatures in e-commerce research [4, 18].

4 Conclusion

Although the social commerce has been aroused plenty of attentions in the past decade, the multifaceted research on social commerce is still limited. In this work, we employed the clickstream data analysis to depict online consumers' cross-site browsing behaviors in the context of social commerce. In particular, we first applied the cluster analysis with K-means algorithm to segment consumers' behaviors and obtained 4 clusters, i.e. width browsing, depth browsing, goal-oriented browsing, and hedonic browsing. Second, we unveiled how various browsing behaviors depicted in each cluster influence consumers' post-hoc behaviors, i.e. visiting e-commerce site and making the purchase commitment. This study affords several key contributions to both theoretical and practical implications. For researchers, our study provides a better explanation of variation in consumers' behaviors in social commerce context. For practitioners, the segmentation in our findings conduces to a more accurate personalized recommendation, which is expected to bring a higher conversion rate.

Acknowledgement. This work was partially supported by Program for Young Excellent Talents in Tongji University (2014KJ002), the Fundamental Research Funds for the Central Universities (2850219028), and the National Natural Science Foundation of China (NSFC 71532015).

References

1. Zhou, L., Zhang, P., Zimmermann, H.D.: Social commerce research: an integrated view. Electron. Commer. Res. Appl. **12**(2), 61–68 (2013)
2. Kim, S., Park, H.: Effects of various characteristics of social commerce (s-commerce) on consumers' trust and trust performance. Int. J. Inf. Manage. **33**(2), 318–332 (2013)
3. Liang, T.P., Ho, Y.T., Li, Y.W., et al.: What drives social commerce: the role of social support and relationship quality. Int. J. Electron. Commer. **16**(2), 69–90 (2011)
4. Phang, C.W., Kankanhalli, A., Ramakrishnan, K., et al.: Customers' preference of online store visit strategies: an investigation of demographic variables. Eur. J. Inf. Syst. **19**(3), 344–358 (2010)
5. Rubel, S.: Trends to watch part II: social commerce. Micro Persuasion Vom **2006**, 23 (2005)
6. Liang, T.P., Turban, E.: Introduction to the special issue social commerce: a research framework for social commerce. Int. J. Electron. Commer. **16**(2), 5–14 (2011)
7. Shen, J., Eder, L.B.: An examination of factors associated with user acceptance of social shopping websites. In: Mesquita, A. (ed.) User Perception and Influencing Factors of Technology in Everyday Life 28–45. Information Science Reference, Hershey (2012)
8. Grange, C., Benbasat, I.: Online social shopping: the functions and symbols of design artifacts. In: 2010 43rd Hawaii International Conference on System Sciences (HICSS), pp. 1–10. IEEE (2010)
9. Curty, R.G., Zhang, P.: Website features that gave rise to social commerce: a historical analysis. Electron. Commer. Res. Appl. **12**(4), 260–279 (2013)
10. Curty, R.G., Zhang, P.: Social commerce: looking back and forward. Proc. Am. Soc. Inf. Sci. Technol. **48**(1), 1–10 (2011)
11. Huang, Z., Benyoucef, M.: From e-commerce to social commerce: a close look at design features. Electron. Commer. Res. Appl. **12**(4), 246–259 (2013)

12. Amblee, N., Bui, T.: Harnessing the influence of social proof in online shopping: the effect of electronic word of mouth on sales of digital microproducts. Int. J. Electron. Commer. **16**(2), 91–114 (2011)
13. Stephen, A.T., Toubia, O.: Deriving value from social commerce networks. J. Mark. Res. **47**(2), 215–228 (2010)
14. CNNIC. Statistical Report on Internet Development in China (2015)
15. Huntington, P., Nicholas, D., Jamali, H.R.: Website usage metrics: a re-assessment of session data. Inf. Process. Manage. **44**(1), 358–372 (2008)
16. Elbaum, S., Karre, S., Rothermel, G.: Improving web application testing with user session data. In: Proceedings of the 25th International Conference on Software Engineering, pp. 49–59. IEEE Computer Society (2003)
17. Ghosh, S., Dubey, S.K.: Comparative analysis of k-means and fuzzy c-means algorithms. Int. J. Adv. Comput. Sci. Appl. **4**(4), 34–39 (2013)
18. Moe, W.W.: Buying, searching, or browsing: differentiating between online shoppers using in-store navigational clickstream. J. Consum. Psychol. **13**(1), 29–39 (2003)

Semantic Support for Visual Data Analyses in Electronic Commerce Settings

Jens Gulden[(✉)]

University of Duisburg-Essen, Universitätsstr. 9, 45141 Essen, Germany
jens.gulden@uni-due.de

Abstract. While the value of visualizations for understanding and exploring knowledge is considered high in diverse fields of application, the efforts for creating effective and efficient data visualizations often outweigh the capacities of individuals and organizations to create their own data visualizations from scratch. Hence, software tool support is demanded to allow users who are not experts in creating visualizations to have access to these visual means of expression as well.

The question whether a data visualization is "good" in the sense of whether it can fulfill the information needs of involved stakeholders, however, highly relies on an understanding of the way domain stakeholders view the available information and ask questions about it. This semantic aspect of data visualization is not explicated by existing approaches for data visualization development. The following article proposes a methodical approach which explicates knowledge about the meaning of data in the form of conceptual models, and interweaves the creation process of visualizations with an analysis of the information needs of involved domain stakeholders. An exemplary application of the method in the e-commerce domain is included.

1 Methodical Support for the Creation of Data Visualizations

The use of data visualizations in information systems increasingly attracts interest in science and practice [6,11,15]. Especially in the area of electronic commerce (EC), which inherently combines business scenarios with underlying automation facilities [17,19,20], rich sets of data are generated during every-day operation. They cover a broad range of semantics, are available at large volumes, and reach a comparably high data quality due to the high degree of automation in their creation. In order to retrieve knowledge from such amounts of data, visual analyses tools are regarded as efficient means for humans to aggregate, combine, and navigate data interactively [8,18].

The human mind generally performs multiple cognitive actions in parallel, on diverse levels of detail and granularity. Presenting data visually, and preparing the visualization in a way that relevant relationships and facts become perceivable as simultaneous elements of a rich information environment [9], is one next consequent step in increasing the quality of existing EC systems. It is thus

© Springer International Publishing Switzerland 2016
F.F.-H. Nah and C.-H. Tan (Eds.): HCIBGO 2016, Part I, LNCS 9751, pp. 198–209, 2016.
DOI: 10.1007/978-3-319-39396-4_18

desirable to support involved groups of user, e.g., analysts, managers, and data scientists, with methodical support to perform these analyses efficiently in terms of invested efforts for creating visual representations, and effectively with respect to the goal of understanding and / or discovering business relevant knowledge in the data.

The examination presented in this paper proposes a method for suggesting data visualizations based on the domain-specific information needs of stakeholders specifically in EC analysis settings. To achieve this, semantics of the specific domain of electronic commerce is incorporated with the help of enterprise models [12,16].

2   Related Work

A few approaches have been proposed that offer basic support to generate visual representations from business data [5,10], and diverse software products offer visualization wizards which allow for automatic visualization generation [1–4].

These approaches make use of syntactic features of the available data, and typically propose a set of possible visual representations and navigation options that can validly be constructed from the syntactic features. The drawback of such approaches is that depending on the complexity of the underlying data, there may be many syntactically possible forms of visualizations and navigation options, which from a semantic point of view make no sense or are even counter-productive to be offered in an analysis environment. This is because the visualization mechanisms are agnostic towards domain-specific semantics associated with the available data.

It would instead be desirable that the creation of visualizations for data analysis could exploit knowledge about the semantic domain from which the data originates, so it would be better able to propose which combinations of data to visualize, and which visual expression means are best suitable to fulfill information needs relevant to the given domain.

A central deficiency of visualization methods that follow state-of-the-art approaches, is that they typically offer direct mappings from available data to visual means of expression only [15]. The major software products for data visualization [1–4] seem to compete in providing growingly complex mapping types and extensive libraries of presets and templates, but the fundamental problem remains that for each visualization type to be created, the mappings have to be decided ad-hoc over and over again. Means for expressing design decisions about *why* mappings have been chosen, are not systematically integrated into the applied visualization method. As a consequence, it is typically not possible to reuse design rationales, since they are not recorded nor reproducable in a systematic way.

3   A Method for Visual Data Analyses with Semantic Support in Electronic Commerce Settings

Using information systems in electronic commerce is a special case of using information systems in general, with the EC domain determining a special contextual realm. This domain comprises of specific stakeholders (e.g. *seller, buyer*), objects (e.g. *product, catalog, sale, invoice*), and processes (e.g. *order, delivery, return*). Especially with regard to the processes and structures behind EC interactions, specific information needs of the involved stakeholders can be identified for this domain, which make it possible to perform an in-depth analysis of requirements towards the analysis demands in EC that wouldn't be possible to perform on a general domain-independent level of reflection.

It is central to the suggested approach, that instead of mapping available data directly onto input variables for visualizations, it gets associated with conceptual models that describe selected EC scenarios and corresponding information needs. The conceptual models in turn are associated with visualizations that are suitable for fulfilling these information needs. Conceptual models that describe business-scenarios in such a domain-specific way are called enterprise models [12]. The involvement of enterprise models shifts the expressiveness of the suggested approach onto a level of economic meaning of data, rather than operating on a purely syntactic level of matching combinations of available values to input types of visualizations.

For the end-user, the application of the approach follows this procedure: Available data sources of EC systems are described using a standard data model, as it can be exported, e.g., by a relational database management system. With this model as input, a configuration wizard can iterate over all elements of the previously developed conceptual enterprise models and ask the user, which elements of the input data should serve as instances of the domain-specific types described in the conceptual models. Interactively, the user associates the available data with elements of the conceptual models, thus defines their domain-specific semantics.

3.1 Requirements Towards an Approach for Domain-Specific Data Visualization

This section shortly discusses 5 main requirements towards an improved methodical approach for visualization specifications in e-commerce.

Req. 1: Explicate the meaning of data as part of the method. As argued, assuming a purely syntactic relationship between data and possible visualizations thereof does not offer a distinctive enough basis for making automatic suggestions for visualizations types. The larger the number of input variables, and the more complex the relationship structures among data sources get, the less effective automatic suggestions can be made which fulfill information needs of domain stakeholders. As a consequence, a higher degree of expertise and experience is required for choosing meaningful visualizations among automatically provided suggestions, which in turn limits the amount of users who can create visualizations on their own, and the range of applications where visualizations can be used in an economically reasonable way.

A method for creating data visualizations should thus incorporate means for explicating domain-specific semantics, i.e., describe the meaning of data with the help of conceptual models, as a basis for more focused automatic means for suggesting meaningful visualizations.

Req. 2: Support identification of information needs. To identify information needs of involved stakeholders, an understanding of the domain from which data to be visualized originates is required, both independent from any actually available data, as well as from possible visualization options.

The use of conceptual models, e.g., enterprise models for business related domains, allows to point out relevant objects of interest for visual analyses as elements of conceptual models, which themselves can have a visual notation which connects to visual metaphors known in the modeled domain. This way, as an initial part of the method, domain experts can consciously negotiate on which information elements to put in focus of an analysis.

Req. 3: Justify meaningful visual means of expression. It is a consequent next step after having identified the stakeholders' information needs, to choose visual means of expression that can fulfill these needs effectively and in a cognitive efficient way. This requires a high level of design expertise, and is thus a task that should be performed by specially trained experts as part of the preparation phase of the method. It is possible to shift this into the preparation phase, because specific domain knowledge is already available at this point, and the method allows to explicate the meaning of data constructs (see Req. 1).

Req. 4: Enable reuse of domain-specific visualization types. The responsibility for justifying choices of visualization types should lie in the initial preparation phase of the method, where domain experts and visualization designers consciously reflect on the use of visualization types for the purpose of fulfilling information needs.

A visualization method should thus support the specification of visualization types in relation to semantic domain concepts in the preparation phase, and later allow to reuse these specifications by an end-user in concrete application contexts.

Req. 5: Provide automatic guidance in creating visualizations. Finally, the target requirement is the demand for efficient and effective automatic guidance in creating visualization that answer stakeholders' information needs and allow to explore existing data from the relevant perspectives of domain experts. The fulfillment of this requirement is achieved when all previous ones are fulfilled; in this sense, this last requirement subsumes the previous ones and represents the overall goal to develop an effective and efficient visualization method based on semantic characteristics of a domain.

3.2   Method Architecture

The method elaborated in the following suggests the use of enterprise models as a semantic intermediate layer when defining connections between data and meaningful visualizations. This way, enterprise models take in the role of a semantic repository, which allows to systematically express how meaning of data is reflected through visual representation means in the range of a given domain. The building blocks of this methodological architecture, in contrast to direct mapping approaches, are depicted in Fig. 1.

3.3   Procedural Steps and Involved Roles

The method consists of 5 steps, which are shown in List 1 for an overview, and are described in depth in the following sub-sections. The procedure is divided into an

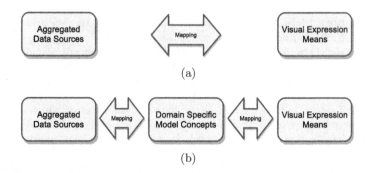

Fig. 1. Overview on the (a) traditional direct mapping architecture for visualizations, compared to the (b) approach suggested in this paper

initial sequence of steps which are performed once to configure the method for a specific domain. This is done by expert method engineers, together with domain experts from the domain in focus and visualization designers. When applying the configured method, a role change can take place, which allows any involved domain stakeholder to define concrete visualizations for particular instances of the domain, based on re-usable definition previously defined in the configuration steps. The different responsibilities throughout the process and a possible point for division of labor is symbolized by a horizontal line between steps 3 and 4.

Step 1: Explicate relevant semantic concepts of the examined domain
Step 2: Derive domain-specific information needs from the modeled scenarios
Step 3: Design visual expression means to fulfill the identified information needs in an effective and efficient way

Step 4: Associate available data from operative systems based on the semantic models
Step 5: Select visualization types and navigate data to achieve concrete data visualizations

List 1: Steps of the suggested method

This general conceptualization of a semantics-based visualization method is applied to the e-commerce domain in the following section.

4 Application to the E-Commerce Domain

To further describe a concrete application scenario of the method, this section puts its focus on exemplifying the adaptation phase of the method to the e-commerce domain, which is performed in the methodical steps 1 to 3 (Sect. 3.3). This is done by first introducing fundamental concepts of the e-commerce domain with models of a prototypical e-commerce setting (step 1), then deriving domain-specific information needs from the modeled setting (step 2), and finally designing justified effective and efficient visualizations (step 3). The end-user application steps 4 and 5 complete the method description.

4.1 Step 1: Model Typical Business Scenarios of the Examined Domain

The method preparation starts by capturing domain-specific processes and structures with multiple interconnected enterprise models [12,16]. As an example, the core business process model of a general e-commerce shop is shown in Fig. 2. The business process starts with a customer placing an order via the internet, which is shown on the left-hand-side of the business process model. Subsequent tasks for processing the order are shown in left-to-right order, with black lines between them indicating the control flow of the process. The model also contains references to involved actors, as well as to resources of diverse kinds [13].

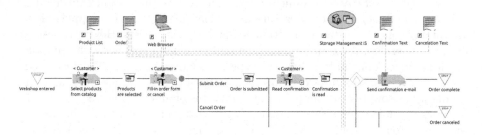

Fig. 2. Excerpt of the business process model of an online order process

Figure 3 shows an exemplary model of the organizational structure of actors and a model of resources.

These domain-specific models carry a high degree of semantics in their conceptual elements. Unlike with models in general purpose modeling languages, which intentionally provide highly general concepts such as *Object* or *Relationship*, each single model element in domain-specific models can be interpreted deeply on the basis of domain knowledge about it. This is, e.g., the case with the modeled concept of a *customer* actor, and resources such as *products* and *product-lists*. With the domain-specific knowledge attached to these concepts, and their contextual settings explicated in the conceptual models, specific information needs and justified domain-specific analytical questions towards the available data can be formulated in the following step.

4.2 Step 2: Derive Domain-Specific Information Needs from the Modeled Scenarios

Because the domain of the analysis setting is described on an abstract level by domain-specific models, classes of analysis questions can now be identified

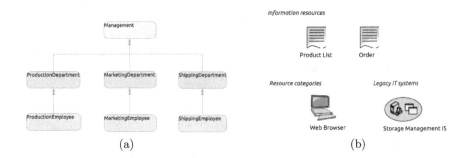

Fig. 3. Organization model (a) and resources model (b) according to the example process

which characterize information needs of the involved stakeholders. In e-commerce settings, it can generally be spoken of *products* that are offered through an automatic *catalog* mechanism to *customers*, with whom *sales* are performed, and sometimes *returns* of products occur. This conceptualization captures the domain of an e-commerce business on a general level, which makes it applicable to almost any concrete instance of actual e-commerce enterprises. However, despite its wide generality, the conceptualization still provides a rich body of semantics about the given domain for which meaningful visualizations are to be developed.

This degree of semantics can now be harnessed to anticipate general analytical questions towards the development and status of an e-commerce business. It becomes possible to explicate the information needs of involved stakeholders in the domain on the general level of questions that are induced by the semantic specifics of the domain.

In case of the e-commerce domain, the semantically rich basic concepts *products*, *catalog*, *customers*, *sales*, and *returns* can be brought in relation prior to creating any visualization by formulating domain-related analytical questions. These can operate with the specific semantics of the basic concepts, e.g., the assumptions that relationships between customers and products they buy are of specific interest for some stakeholders, and that both products and customers can be categorized to customer-groups and products-groups. This allows to formulate detailed, yet re-usable, analytical questions towards the status and development of an e-commerce business. The validity of these questions can be evaluated through professional discourse among domain experts without the need for expertise in information visualization.

An initial set of questions for the e-commerce domain is suggested in List 2, which take in the perspective of owning and operating stakeholders of e-commerce businesses. Naturally, this list is not finite and can be extended whenever additional information needs are identified by domain experts.

- Are there any products, which are particularly attractive / unattractive for specific customers or customer groups?
- How have sales or returns of particular products and / or product groups developed over a given period of time?

– How frequent and at which volumes do selected customers and / or customer groups place orders?
– Are there products and product groups which cause unexpected amounts of product returns?
– Are there periods of time in which particular customers or customer groups show different order / return behavior than usual?
– How is the relationship between views of products in the product catalog compared to actual sales of these products?
– ...

List 2: Analytical questions derived from the domain models

The analytical questions derived on an abstract level can now be examined by experts for visual information representation, and default visualization types can be developed specific for the information needs in the examined domain. This is done in the following step for a sub-set of the above listed analytical questions.

4.3 Step 3: Design Visual Expression Means to Fulfill the Identified Information Needs

Based on the previously elaborated analytical questions, classes of meaningful visualizations are now suggested which serve the purpose to give cognitive efficient and effective insight into answers on analytical questions. It cannot be the aim of this paper to summarize the body of knowledge in the entire discipline of information and data visualization. Therefore, the actual process of deciding in detail which visual means of expression are suited best to serve the identified analytical purposes, relies on the expertise of visualization designers and literature from the data and information visualization domain, e.g. [6,7,11,18]. Examples of principles and best practices applied during this step are, e.g., that relations among values can be expressed well by projecting them onto a 2D plane (e.g. using scatter-plots of values), or that quantitative values are best represented by one-dimensional visual constructs. Based on these principles, for each previously identified analytical question (Sect. 4.2) one or more visualization types are now to be designed.

Visualization types for two of the identified analytical questions are sketched in Fig. 4 to demonstrate the applicability of the method. Figure 4 (a) depicts a scatter-plot diagram, which is suitable to provide insight into relationships between customers, products and sales figures, either for individual instances of the customer and product concepts, or for categorized groups formed out of individuals. This visualization type thus is suitable to fulfill information needs imposed by the analytical question "Are there any products, which are particularly attractive / unattractive for specific customer groups?" (Sect. 4.2). It provides a rich set of navigation options by selecting the entities to display, which makes it a powerful visual tool both for data explanation, as well as for exploration. Terms written in angle brackets "<" and ">" indicate placeholders for

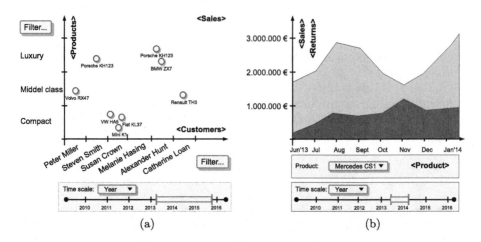

Fig. 4. Two example visualization types derived from analysed information needs

concepts from the domain model, which will need to be associated to concrete data sources, before a concrete visualization will be available.

Figure 4 (b) shows the sketch of a timeline diagram, which displays the development of sales versus returns in a configurable range of time, filtered by products, or their respective categories. This type of visualization is suitable to answer analytical questions such as "How have sales or returns of particular products and / or product groups developed over a given period of time?" (Sect. 4.2).

The actual values to render in instances of these diagram types are not known at this stage of visualization design yet. It will be up to the end-user to determine appropriate data sources which match the semantics of the modeled domain concepts (see the following Sect. 4.5). To give an impression of the utility of the visualization types, the sketches in Fig. 4 are displayed with example values that represent possible appearances of the visualizations.

4.4 Step 4: Associate Available Data from Operative Systems Based on the Semantic Models

At this point in applying the method, the user role potentially changes to be fulfilled by any domain expert and involved stakeholder with domain-specific information needs. This means, no specific competencies in designing visualizations, especially in justifying effectiveness and efficiency of data visualizations, is required for this and the next task. Expert knowledge can be reused that has been explicated in the earlier adaptation steps of the method.

In order to define actual data sources of e-commerce systems as sources for domain-specific data visualization, the user now associates data elements to concepts specified in the domain models. This can, e.g., be carried out by providing a mapping between domain model concepts to results of queries or views on a relational database. In such a setting, each row in a query result table represents an instance of the associated domain model concept, table columns can subsequently be mapped onto attributes of the respective concepts.

Figure 5 exemplifies the integration of SQL query definitions to map between data sources and conceptual models elements into the graphical user interface (GUI) of the MEMOCENTERNG enterprise modeling tool [14]. The process of associating database queries can be supported by a semi-automatic wizard, which iterates through all available conceptual model elements and guides the user to fill in the appropriate settings.

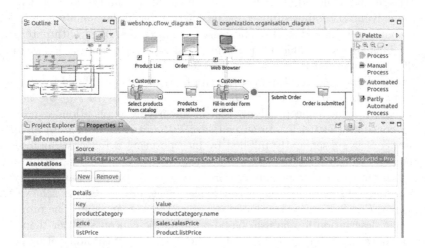

Fig. 5. Integration of SQL query definitions into MEMOCENTERNG

As a difference to existing approaches, it is important to note that at this point the user does not have to think in terms of axes, intercepts, coordinates, colors, or any visual property of the visualizations to be created, as it is the case with existing approaches. Instead, data is mapped to concepts of the analysis domain, which have previously been adapted to justified visualization types. Via this intermediate semantic layer, the method increases effectiveness and efficiency of the proposed visualizations and becomes reusable for multiple cases of concrete applications.

4.5 Step 5: Select Visualization Types and Navigate Data to Achieve Concrete Data Visualizations

With a growing number of specified associations between data and conceptual models, gradually more analysis scenarios become accessible. A selection wizard can dynamically display the list of visualization types that are possible to be rendered on the basis of the currently available associations between data sources and model concepts. Interactivity features, such as navigation options and aggregation possibilities, can be derived from the semantic information about temporal, spatial, and categorial relationships specified in the conceptual enterprise models.

The result are data visualizations for concrete analysis scenarios specified by the end-user, derived from visualization types with underlying justified design decisions, that ensure effective and efficient analyses in the specified domain.

5   Conclusion

With the results achieved, a software-implementable method is described which provides advanced tooling support for interactive visual data analyses for electronic commerce (EC), based on business semantics described with enterprise models. This allows to efficiently perform visual analyses of data in EC settings, and effectively gain business-relevant knowledge for this particular domain.

The requirements stated in Sect. 3.1 can be regarded as fulfilled by the proposed approach. *Req. 1: Explicate the meaning of data as part of the method* is fulfilled by using conceptual models as underlying explication of relevant domain concepts (Sect. 4.1). As argued, *Req. 2: Support identification of information needs* is subsequently fulfilled by incorporating a reflective analysis of stakeholders' views on the domain into the sequence of domain adaptation steps (Sect. 4.2). Shifting the responsibility for developing justified visualization types into the method's domain adaptation phase (Sect. 4.3), serves to achieve the purposes of *Req. 3: Justify meaningful visual means of expression*. The proposed interfacing description mechanism based on semantic concepts rather than only syntactic data characteristics (Sect. 4.4) makes the result of the adaptation phase applicable for later concretizations in practical settings as demanded by *Req. 4: Enable reuse of domain-specific visualization types*. By fulfilling these four key requirements, the subsuming *Req. 5: Provide automatic guidance in creating visualizations* gets fulfilled in total as well.

Future work will consist of elaborating a richer set of analytical visualization types and performing user studies based on prototypical tooling.

References

1. IBM Watson Analytics. http://www.ibm.com/analytics/watson-analytics/
2. Lyra Visualization Design Environment (VDE). http://idl.cs.washington.edu/projects/lyra/
3. SAP Lumira. http://saplumira.com/
4. Tableau Visual Analytics Software. http://www.tableau.com/
5. Al-Kassab, J., Ouertani, Z.M., Schiuma, G., Neely, A.: Information visualization to support management decisions. Int. J. Inf. Technol. Decis. Making **2**, 407–428 (2014)
6. Borner, K., Polley, D.E.: Visual Insights: A Practical Guide to Making Sense of Data. MIT Press, Cambridge (2014)
7. Cairo, A.: The Functional Art. Voices That Matter. Pearson Education, New York (2010)
8. Chen, C.: Information visualization. Springer, London (2010)

9. Cooper, A.: About Face: The Essentials of Interaction Design, 4th edn. Wiley, Hoboken (2014)
10. de Sousa, T.A.F., Barbosa, S.D.J.: Recommender system to support chart constructions with statistical data. In: Kurosu, M. (ed.) HCI 2014, Part I. LNCS, vol. 8510, pp. 631–642. Springer, Heidelberg (2014)
11. Few, S.: Information Dashboard Design: The Effective Visual Communication of Data. O'Reilly, Sebastopol (2006)
12. Frank, U.: Multi-perspective enterprise modeling (MEMO) - conceptual framework and modeling languages. In: Proceedings of the Hawaii International Conference on System Sciences (HICSS-35), Honolulu (2002)
13. Frank, U.: Multi-perspective enterprise modelling: background and terminological foundation. Technical report 46, ICB Institute for Computer Science and Business Information Systems, University of Duisburg-Essen, Essen, December 2011
14. Gulden, J., Frank, U.: MEMOCenterNG - a full-featured modeling environment for organization-modeling and model-driven software development. In: Soffer, P., Proper, E. (eds.) Proceedings of the CAiSE Forum Hammamet. CEUR Workshop Proceedings, Tunisia, 9–11 June, vol. 592, pp. 76–83. CEUR (2010). ISSN 1613–0073
15. Gulden, J., Reijers, H.A.: Toward advanced visualization techniques for conceptual modeling. In: Grabis, J., Sandkuhl, K. (eds.) Proceedings of the CAiSE Forum Stockholm, CEUR Workshop Proceedings, Sweden, 8–12 June. CEUR (2015)
16. Sandkuhl, K., Stirna, J., Persson, A., Wißotzki, M.: Enterprise Modeling - Tackling Business Challenges with the 4EM Method. Springer, Heidelberg (2014)
17. Shaw, M., Blanning, R., Strader, T., Whinston, A.: Handbook on Electronic Commerce. Springer, Heidelberg (2000)
18. Whitney, H.: Data Insights: New Ways to Visualize and Make Sense of Data. Morgan Kaufman, Waltham (2013)
19. Yokoo, M., Ito, T., Zhang, M.: Electronic Commerce: Theory and Practice. Springer, Heidelberg (2008)
20. Zhang, F.: The application of visualization technology on e-commerce data mining. In: Second International Symposium on Intelligent Information Technology Application, IITA 2008, vol. 2, pp. 563–566. IEEE (2008)

Bridging the Gap Between the Stakeholders and the Users at Alibaba.com

Jonas Kong[✉]

Alibaba.com Inc., 400 S El Camino Real, Suite 400, San Mateo, 94402, USA
jonas.kong@alibaba-inc.com

Abstract. At Alibaba.com, the product, design and engineering teams are located in China, while a large proportion of the site's users are in the United States. It was not easy for these stakeholders to interact with the US users for research due to geographical and language barrier. Consequently, the stakeholders initially did not have a reliable way to understand the users' needs. This paper will discuss the methods and approach utilized by the author, who is a user experience researcher based in an Alibaba.com satellite office, to help bridge the gap between the stakeholders and the users.

Keywords: Influencing stakeholders · Focus group · Contextual inquiry · Customer journey map · Distributed teams · User experience research · Qualitative research

1 Introduction

Alibaba.com is the world's largest online business to business (B2B) trading platform, allowing global suppliers to wholesale their products to buyers all over the world. The Alibaba.com office is headquartered in China, where almost everyone involved in creating the platform including business development, product management, user experience and engineering teams are located. However, a significant portion of the Alibaba.com users, particularly those who use the site to purchase goods, are located in the United States. This poses a challenge for the stakeholders when trying to understand their users, due to geographical separation, communication barriers and knowledge gap between the stakeholders and the users.

1.1 Time Zone Differences

Stakeholders have difficulty finding a convenient time to talk with users. Because of 12 to 15 h in time difference between the stakeholders in China and the users in the US, they can only communicate in real time during one another's after business hours. This reduces the number of users available and willing to participate in studies or interviews. Certainly the stakeholders can travel to meet the users in person, but it would become cost prohibitive from a budget and time resource standpoint to require overseas travelling for every project.

© Springer International Publishing Switzerland 2016
F.F.-H. Nah and C.-H. Tan (Eds.): HCIBGO 2016, Part I, LNCS 9751, pp. 210–217, 2016.
DOI: 10.1007/978-3-319-39396-4_19

1.2 Communication Barrier

Language differences pose a barrier for the stakeholders when trying to communicate with the English speaking users located in the US. Even though generally most of the stakeholders have competency in written English, their verbal capacity varies. As such, it is difficult for them to carry on an in-depth conversation with the users to discuss their experience in using Alibaba.com or wholesale trading in general.

1.3 Knowledge Gap in User Needs

Unable to easily access the core users for insights, most of the stakeholders initially did not have an easy way to identify user needs, understand their pain points and implement solutions to address them. As a result, many of the stakeholders had to rely on their own assumptions when developing products and creating feature designs. However, the problem is that the process of B2B global trading is highly complex with specific import and export laws and regulations unique to each country. It is complicated to understand how users navigate these laws. The stakeholders' assumptions often do not correctly match the users' actual needs, resulting in products and features that did not support the users.

2 Approach

The author is a user experience researcher at Alibaba.com based in a satellite office in the United States, and therefore had better access to the majority of the Alibaba.com users for research. Being closer to the users allowed for more flexibility when conducting research with them and larger available pool of users to participate in research. Because of this, the author was able to utilize different methods to help the Alibaba.com stakeholders to better understand how the users normally use the platform and be able to discover their true needs. This paper is a case study describing the approach and methods used by the author to help bridge the gap between the stakeholders and its product users.

2.1 Using Focus Groups to Gather User Feedback on Key Product Concept

Initially the business and product management leaders at Alibaba.com did not have a clear understanding of the capability of user experience research. Due to limited exposure to research methods in the past, they misconceived user experience research as solely usability testing and nothing else. Therefore, when there was an opportunity that these top business and product management team leaders were travelling to the US for a business meeting, a focus group study was organized specifically for them to attend in person. The focus group served multiple purposes:

- Expose the top decision makers to additional methods to break the misconception that user research only involves user testing
- Provide influence and impact on product strategy early on during the concept development stage

- Allow these top decision makers to receive first hand user feedback on key product initiatives
- Gather feedback from a group of targeted users in a shorter amount of time
- Provide opportunity for stakeholders to ask users questions and discuss product experience issues face to face with users

Two focus group sessions were conducted over two days with eight participants in each session. The participants were composed of one group of B2B buyers who were existing Alibaba.com buyers and another group of B2B buyers who were not. Other employees from the US office attended the session to provide interpretation to the stakeholders during focus group discussions.

Topics discussed in the focus group were specifically chosen to help the stakeholders, who rarely have the opportunity to come face to face with their users, to build a general profile of them based on actual user feedback rather than assumptions. Participants were asked about their motivations for and barriers from using Alibaba.com, as well as key benefits and top concerns of using the platform, just to name a few examples.

From the focus group, the stakeholders were able to hear the users' explanations of the commonly heard issues on the platform. For instance, the stakeholders had previously learnt from customer support that it was difficult for users to find products on the platform, but did not receive a concrete example of how and clear explanation of why. The participants during the focus group, with proper moderation by the researcher, were able to provide more details to bring clarity to the stakeholders.

The key objective of the focus group was to gather feedback on a new product concept. This portion of the research was particularly impactful as user's reaction and feedback revealed aspects in the new product concept that required significant refinement for it to be considered useful by the users. Without these insights, the product would have launched and likely resulted in negative impact to the business.

The focus group sessions were recorded and a summary report was created to present the insights with the product development teams in China. Overall, the focus groups enabled the stakeholders to better understand the user experience issues on the platform and the contributing factors. But most importantly, after they attended the focus groups, the stakeholders realized that the user experience research is more than just design testing as they previously believed. They now realized that user research could provide significant impact to the product direction in the very early stage of the process.

2.2 Contextual Inquiry to Understand the User Process

After the product concept was refined based on user feedback from the focus groups, the product entered the next stage of the development cycle. A prototype version of the product was created and an initial round of remote user testing commenced with Alibaba.com users in the US to assess the interactions and designs of the product. However the results gathered from the remote user testing were mostly negative because the page design did not match what the users would normally do. Apparently, important steps within the trading process were missing in the product which led to user confusion. After discussing with the product managers and the designers, it was realized that additional information was needed to fully understand the specific details in the complex process of B2B trading on and off the Alibaba platform.

To gain better understanding of the trading process conducted by the targeted users, a contextual inquiry study was planned with 10 online B2B buyers. As a semi-structured interview method, contextual inquiry can be used to gather information about the context of use, where users are first asked a set of standard questions and then observed and questioned while they work in their own environments [1]. The results from contextual inquiry can be used to define requirements, learn what is important to users, and discover information about a domain to inform future projects [1].

Typically, contextual inquiry takes place at the users' home or work environment for realistic and direct observation. However, time constraints as well as the lack of available qualified participants in the vicinity limited the possibility of visiting all the participants at their locations. Instead, half of the contextual inquiry sessions took place remotely with the users across different regions in the United States. Those remote sessions occurred with the users sharing their computer screen to show online steps and any important documents created during the B2B trading process.

The buyers were asked to complete the steps of the most recent business purchase they made with a supplier found online, while the team members observed with minimal interruption. The researcher observed the users explaining the steps and asked questions along the way to better understand the details.

The results provided clarity on certain details in the B2B trading process, which helped to refine the missing flow in the new product. In addition, it provided a more complete picture of the typical user work flow, as well as identified aspects in the process where new features on the Alibaba.com platform could further support the users when conducting B2B trading.

2.3   Using Customer Journey Map to Document the Process

One of the goals of the contextual inquiry was to identify the user process to help the product managers and designers to create site features and page flow. It was important to present it in a visual medium to illustrate the steps. Therefore the customer journey map was utilized as a tool to show the steps the users go through when on and off the Alibaba website when conducting B2B trading. As shown in Fig. 1, a customer journey map illustrates a visual representation of a user's needs, the step-by-step flow of interactions required to fulfill those needs, and the resulting emotional states a user experiences throughout the process [2].

By showing how customers feel throughout their journey, customer journey maps invite stakeholders to enter the world of customers and share in their experience. In turn, stakeholders are better able to convey their story to management, fellow colleagues, and the teams who are responsible for improving the service and product experience [2].

As shown in Fig. 2, the map organized the B2B process into several phases to represent the different goals of the users. It illustrated the key pain points in each phase of the process to highlight areas of opportunity for improvement during product design. The map was presented to various product teams. It was used as a reference tool for product managers during new product planning and a guide for designers during website

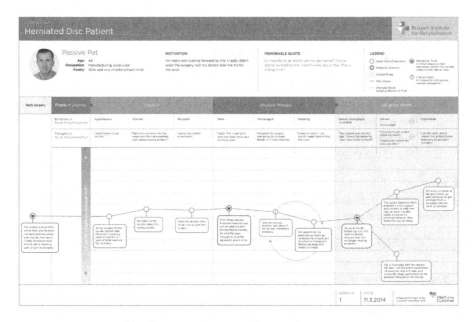

Fig. 1. Example of a customer journey map [3]

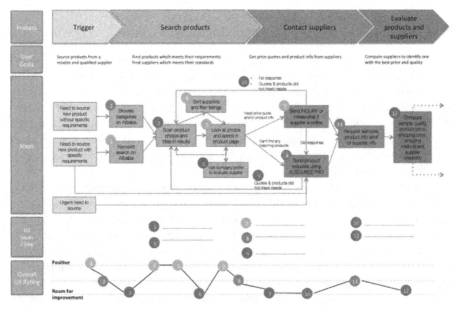

Fig. 2. An early version of the customer journey map

design. It served as a living document that the product development teams in China could use to understand the complex B2B trading process and identify issues in the user experience. Once new significant changes in the user process are found, the map will be updated and continue to serve as a living document.

2.4 Collecting Quantitative Data to Identify the Users

Results gathered from the focus groups and contextual inquiry provided qualitative insights on the product and the users' work process. But one missing facet of data for the stakeholders was quantitative information on the users, both on those who currently use the Alibaba.com platform and those who do not. Such data helps the stakeholders to identify who the users are, their purchase activities, their motivations for using Alibaba.com, and barriers to using the platform.

A survey was designed and launched to gather data from general B2B buyers in the United States regarding their demographics, company information, buying needs, buying frequency, reasons for current users to use the platform for B2B trading and concerns that non-Alibaba.com B2B buyers have for the platform. Because this data was previously not available to the stakeholders, many of them made assumptions regarding these aspects based on user feedback from qualitative research, external research report or educated guess. The availability of these quantitative data helped to validate their assumptions and was used as a reference for planning business, product and marketing strategies.

3   Discussion

The use of these previously described methods are standard practice within the user experience industry. However, the combination of these four methods and the sequence in which they were used provided timely and appropriate insights to help the stakeholders to understand the users.

For instance, the focus groups impacted the product strategic direction during the early stage of the product development cycle. It also established credibility of user experience research and broadened the scope of influence research was capable of in the perspective of the stakeholders. It helped to open up their trust and their understanding of the capability of user experience research. The successful outcome of this first phase of research led to assigning additional resources to support the next research initiative, the contextual inquiry.

The contextual inquiry was instrumental in identifying the details of the core user experience - a complete picture of the user process. The information gathered from the contextual inquiry was valuable in helping the stakeholders to understand the typical online and offline processes of trading with suppliers, their points of interaction within the Alibaba.com website, and the problems they encountered when using the website. They were fundamental to the product development and user experience teams in creating useful and usable features.

The customer journey map was a visual way to present information on the user experience process by illustrating the process step by step and highlighting barriers that were presented along the way. The product and design teams were able to use this to properly plan product designs. After all, information that is not usable to the audience is the same as the absence of information.

4   Building up the Research Participant Database

As mentioned before, the stakeholders in China faced the problem of insufficient number of users in the US willing to participate in paid research studies during afterhours. One strategy that the research team has been using to help quickly find and schedule qualifying participants is to retain the names of those who have previously participated in research. Even though limited in numbers, they tend to be willing to participate in research again if the previous experience was worthwhile to them. Also, in every project there are a handful of users who expressed interest in participating in research but did not meet the required screening criteria. These users are another source of participant leads available to quickly contact for future research.

To store their contact information, an internal spreadsheet accessible only to the user research team was created. Their contact information, along with the project name, last research participation date and last contacted date were recorded. It is important to not contact someone who has attended a research study in the past 3 months or in similar projects in order to avoid sampling bias.

5   Guiding Principles

The methods and approaches described here were effective in providing user insights and data to the stakeholders. Every organization is structured differently and has different needs so they might not be applicable to all. However, based on this experience, the author has come up with some guidelines to help those researchers based in the satellite office to work effectively and provide more impact in their research work.

1. Identify the needs of the stakeholders: The stakeholders are internal customers to the research team. Understand what projects or initiatives they are working on is imperative to creating meaningful impact in your research. The stakeholders will not always know what they need. Be proactive in determining what information they could use to help answer the questions that they have in those projects.
2. Discover your strengths and play to your advantages: Working in satellite offices has many challenges, such as delayed or lack of updates in business critical information, as well as difficulty in providing impact in an isolated environment. However, there are advantages to being in a satellite office such as ability to work independently and access to different external resources not available elsewhere. Identify the unique advantages of being in remote office and use it to support the team.

3. Show the value of research: Not everyone understands what user experience research is about and what it can do. Demonstrate what research is capable of by inviting stakeholders to participate or observe. Provide insights that they did not expect but can fulfill their needs.
4. Create data artifacts to show the results: A picture is worth a thousand words. PowerPoint is a great presentation tool, but is not as effective for reporting. Often times it is more meaningful to document insights by illustrating it in a visual medium. It helps the teams to remember the findings that you have discovered and help them to create products because it can be displayed in front of them during product planning or discussions.

References

1. Usability Body of Knowledge. Contextual Inquiry. http://www.usabilitybok.org/contextual-inquiry. Accessed 31 Jan 2016
2. UX Matters. The value of customer journey maps (2011). http://www.uxmatters.com/mt/archives/2011/09/the-value-of-customer-journey-maps-a-ux-designers-personal-journey.php#sthash.XkRGDeZh.dpuf. Accessed 19 Feb 2016
3. Heart of the Customer. Customer journey map, the top 10 requirements (2015, revisited). http://www.heartofthecustomer.com/customer-journey-maps-the-top-10-requirements-revisited/. Accessed 11 Feb 2016

The Role of a Retailer in Designing Our Connected Future

Adam Laskowitz[✉]

Consumer IoT, Target Corporation, San Francisco, CA, USA
adam.laskowitz@target.com

Abstract. Even though it was coined nearly two decades ago, the Internet of Things (IoT) didn't really break into the market until around 2013 when it became evident the most popular topic at CES was smart, connected living with an endless showcase of consumer products embedded with sensing and communication technologies. As fundamental mediating bodies between manufacturers and consumers, it is up to retailers to adopt this concept and sell valuable solutions in order for the category to truly penetrate the market. In this paper we will explore trends in the public's awareness of IoT as well as how different retailers have marketed this category over time - and the different angles to storytelling they are each taking.

Keywords: Internet of Things · Smart home · Retail · Consumer electronics · Market strategy

1 Introduction

The nascence of the IoT market is extremely important because the ability for a retailer to make a statement and mediate - at a large scale - which products consumers are exposed to will shape the future of our connected lives. Whether this is direct-to-consumer commerce or big box, like Target, Lowes, or Walmart, the impact of different approaches to exposing the IoT concept to consumers will undoubtedly have lasting effects, with positive or negative consequences. Due to its nascence, this becomes even more complex and uncharted as manufacturers strive to provide unique value to consumers during the same time retailers follow the first-mover advantage paradigm; differing retailer and manufacturer strategies may not always align. One common negative consequence is the confusion and lack of compatibility experienced by the consumer where one product might not interact or communicate properly with another product.

As Rob Tedeschi points out, "if you buy a set of smartbulbs and you'd like them to flash if your smoke alarm is triggered at night or your webcam detects an intruder, for instance, you may be out of luck" [1]. With that in mind, if we briefly look at Lowe's IoT strategy of building a proprietary branded ecosystem, called Iris, we'll notice immediately that Philips Hue smart bulbs are not offered in their assortment. This is problematic for the consumer since Philips was one of the first of its kind to market and produces the most well known and compatible smart bulb in the category. Therefore, the likelihood a consumer would be experiencing these interoperability issues between devices due to proprietary ecosystems is quite high. Unfortunately, these examples are

© Springer International Publishing Switzerland 2016
F.F.-H. Nah and C.-H. Tan (Eds.): HCIBGO 2016, Part I, LNCS 9751, pp. 218–227, 2016.
DOI: 10.1007/978-3-319-39396-4_20

seemingly endless and become more compounded as consumers naturally purchase different products from different retailers.

The working definition of IoT in this paper will focus on consumer applications and use cases. Although, a clear context of understanding is needed in order to avoid semantic debates and maintain a scope for this analysis. For example, this paper will not focus on such IoT applications for retailers related to supply chain, employee tools, or shelf stocking technologies. Since we are focused on consumers, a working definition will be established by reviewing how IoT terms and concepts have trended in popular culture.

After this analysis we will survey the ways in which retailers are communicating the concepts and value of IoT to consumers. This will be done largely through online marketing, but also through an analysis of the products they offer and how those products are categorized. Retailer's product categorizations will be reviewed in their current states as well as how they have changed over time, looking at milestone dates and marketing or branding changes.

2   The Rise and Awareness of *Consumer* Internet of Things

A Google Trends[1] analysis of the search terms "smart home," "internet of things," "home automation," and "Nest thermostat"[2] reveals a number of interesting observations as we can see from Fig. 1. First, "Nest thermostat" immediately grew to over 25 % of search volume relative to the four terms when introduced to the market in Q4 of 201. Second, the search term "internet of things" which is the widely used industry term for this domain really only grew to 25 % of search volume around Q1 of 2014. A third observation is that the term "home automation" has gone from nearly 100 % of search volume in early 2004 to roughly flatlining around 25 % by 2008. Interestingly, "home automation" has the least search volume of the four terms as of 2015. To further emphasize this observation is *Fortune* and Gigaom writer Stacey Higginbotham's comment during an interview with Jason Johnson, CEO of August Smart Lock, at Target Open House[3], "[…] maybe I need to step back and rethink how I've been thinking about the smart home. Maybe it's not home automation which is where we've been very focused" [2] but rather focus on highly valuable single-product solutions. This is a trend that we will also see evident in retailer's category messaging.

One might argue that as consumers and industries are introduced to new terms there would be heavy initial search interest, eventually declining as familiarity and awareness grows over time. But if we look at the same Google Trends graphic with the addition of the term "smartphone," shown in Fig. 2, this claim of interest versus familiarity is quickly debunked.

---

[1] Data are represented in relative percentages, not absolute volume numbers. 100 % represents the highest frequency a given term was searched for relative to every other search term possible. This value is then remapped to all other terms to enable search volume comparisons.

[2] Nest Thermostat is included in this initial analysis because of its common recognition of being the first smart home consumer product to hit some level of mass adoption or awareness.

[3] Target's flagship experience store for smart home technology in San Francisco.

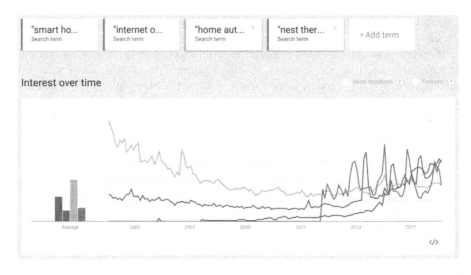

Fig. 1. Google Trends search volume data. (Data Source: Google Trends (www.google.com/trends)). Color figure online

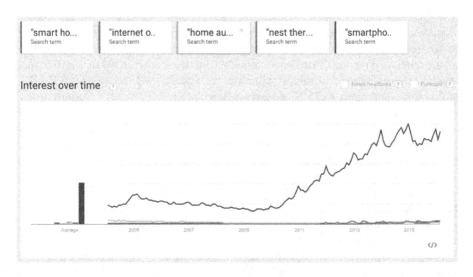

Fig. 2. Google Trends graph with the addition of "smartphone" term in purple. (Data Source: Google Trends (www.google.com/trends)). Color figure online

While Google Trends data only goes as far back as 2004, the origins of IoT dates five years prior. MIT's Auto-ID Center co-founder Kevin Ashton coined the term Internet of Things in 1999 with the definition, "computers that knew everything there was to know about things—using data they gathered without any help from us—we would be able to track and count everything, and greatly reduce waste, loss and cost. We would know when things needed replacing, repairing or recalling, and whether they were fresh or past their best" [3]. This definition comes from a very specific context of

RFID and small sensor technologies that can be embedded in physical objects - not dissimilar to Bruce Sterling's concept of GIZMOS and SPIMES[4] in 2005 [4]. The applications of this concept at the time, and to Sterling, revolved around information management of physical goods in the world; literally taking the idea of the internet and attaching physical objects to it. This is why the technologies being focused on and developed at the time were primarily for identification tracking. The benefits for industry, supply chain, and inventory management are obvious; but Sterling instantly positions this concept towards the consumer. In the third chapter of his book "Shaping Things" when discussing the importance of the "Product-Consumer technosociety" he says, "[a]s an End-User today, even a wine bottle will deliberately lure and reward me for becoming a stakeholder" [4].

Interestingly, the same year the Internet of Things was coined, the made-for-TV movie "Smart House" aired on the Disney Channel[5]. IMDb describes the plot of this movie, "A teenager wins a fully automated dream house in a competition, but soon the computer controlling it begins to take over and everything gets out of control" [5]. The movie addresses two aspects of a smart home: home automation and artificial intelligence - hence the term, "smart." The house can control temperature and lighting, take blood samples and match it to historical medical data, manage calendars, make phone calls, and even cook meals specifically for each household member's preferences. Both Disney's "Smart House" and the origination of the Internet of Things point to some shared technological qualities: embedding computers and sensors into physical elements in the world, information analysis and sharing, control or automation, efficiency, and the management of goods.

There is a difference though that is important to this paper's topic: Disney's movie and Ashton's term have little to do with brands for consumers. Ashton is focused on tracking technologies in industry and Disney's story is purely about the emotional interactions with an extremely personified smart home. Brands are producers of goods that consumers purchase which is much more in line with Sterling's book, having references to the words "consumer(s)(ism)" collectively 33 times over 77 pages. His first example of an object that participates in this technosocial world, the wine bottle, is from a specific brand within a specific context of purchasing goods - from a supermarket - and then advertises more goods through a user's interactions [4]. The brand observation is particularly important to note because it signals the bold effect a retailer has on influencing consumer purchasing, and ultimately post-purchasing, behaviors in the new world that Sterling describes.

The goal of this overview has been to look at how IoT-related concepts have trended in popular culture. With this we can now establish a working definition of *consumer* IoT. This takes into consideration insights from Google Trends, early definitions and concepts for IoT, and a reference from the one of the world's most popular consumer brand, Disney. Consumer IoT relates to products for consumers to purchase and interact

---

[4] "'SPIMES' are manufactured objects whose informational support is so overwhelmingly extensive and rich that they are regarded as material instantiations of an immaterial system" [4].

[5] We consider Disney to be a telling source towards understanding consumer awareness and interest in IoT due to its market reach and brand awareness.

with that have elements of wireless control, analytics, and communication to devices and services. Those interactions open opportunities for consumers to become stakeholders in the technology itself, as Bruce Sterling discusses, that both affect consumer's lives and interrogate and improve the efficacy of the product through real time feedback mechanisms; as feedback is received, the ability for a product to positively affect a user's life increases. Consumer IoT encompasses products embedded with sensors and actuators like a Nest thermostat, wearable trackers like Fitbit, and the number of internet services - both paid and free - that consumers connect to these physical products such as IFTTT (If This Then That) or MyFitnessPal.

3 Retailer's Marketing and Product Categories

The above working definition for consumer IoT is purposely abstract. There are many aspects to a smart home, and retailers take different approaches to introducing the concept. Since retailers are attempting to sell, more or less, the same products - or at least value - it is important to have a singularly abstract view of consumer IoT that is encompassing of these differing approaches.

We will now review a number of major retailers to understand the landscape of marketing messages to consumers and product assortment and categorizations. But first, it must be acknowledged that retailers have unsuccessfully attempted to sell "home automation" for much over a decade now. In 2002 Sears launched its Connected Home initiative partnering with Home Director to provide a complete home automation installation solution. And in 2006 Best Buy launched its own automation package called ConnectedLife.Home, which was a $15,000 equipment and installation solution to help automate your home centered around a media hub [6]. There are a number of other examples like Sears and Best Buy from both current and defunct retailers. Not surprisingly, these solutions are nearly identical in technical integration to the appearance of the smart home in Disney's "Smart House."

The fundamental differences between this wave a decade ago and the current IoT boom can be attributed to two major points, one experiential and the other technical. First, smartphones and tablets did not exist in the early noughties. The significant change that this brought was to the overall user experience of a smart home system. Previous to the interface of a smartphone, interactions with a smart home were through a website or a proprietary display with buttons installed in a wall similar to that of a light switch, as seen in Fig. 3. The second major difference is that consumers were not purchasing products to place in their homes, they were buying a complete service as an infrastructure installation. As Mashable points out, the standalone elements of a home automation service a decade ago were not available to consumers directly, "[...] because many of the components are sold and marketed within the realm of the professional installers, who buy this gear wholesale from suppliers and then mark it up to a price this well-heeled market will bear" [6]. Fortunately, this model has changed significantly ever since the hardware and maker movements exploded. Once startups and larger companies were able to hack their own products together (from improvements to technology miniaturization), with easily available hardware and wireless communication capabilities, the home automation market truly turned into a consumer electronics market where consumers could purchase individual products instead of solely installation services.

Fig. 3. Intelligent building control panel ca. 2009 [7]

Now that we are in the second wave of retailers selling the concept of a smart home to consumers, the focus is currently on products with strong brand affinity as opposed to installation services from a professional installer partnering with a retailer. Therefore, there are more products to sell and more stories to be told by retailers and their vendors. A common theme we will see is how retailers are building out distinct landing pages for their smart home category of products in order to sell the concept. In the following analysis we will emphasize the main marketing text that titles the IoT category on each retailer's website so we can quickly look at the similarities or differences across companies.

Lowe's has its own IoT platform called Iris, but it does have a minimal landing page on its main commerce site; these products are categorized as "**Home Automation & Security.**" They define this category as, "Home automation marries devices, utilities and home features with your smartphone, tablet or web browser." On the more specific IrisByLowes.com website the tagline is, "Life, Made Easier." Lowe's is clearly marketing consumer IoT through the lens of automation and convenience, or simplifying your life. Interestingly, the Iris platform is built exclusively around home automation. They are one of the only remaining retailers to focus heavily on automation.

Walmart has their IoT section under the Electronics category. They market to their customer as, "**Your Life. Connected.** More living your life, less figuring out how to manage it." Walmart then has the following subcategories: routers, entertainment, health, home automation, and monitoring. From the marketing copy it would seem that Walmart is similar to Lowe's Iris in pushing a message of convenience and life simplification, even more overtly than Lowe's and without the sole focus on automation. But when we look at the categories of products, Walmart appears to be adopting a broader categorization of IoT by including entertainment and health along with smart home products.

This broad approach is similar to Target's marketing and product categorization. Target.com has a landing page found through the Electronics & Office category. Although, interestingly, if you follow the breadcrumb trail after navigating to the IoT category you'll notice it doesn't sit within electronics, but actually Home Improvement. The landing page talks about IoT as "**smart home & connected living**" with the description of, "building [sic] a smart home is a smart idea. from [sic] conserving energy to increasing safety to simply reminding, connected living is as easy as a few connections." Providing a contextual experience for the consumer, Target provides an interactive room selector showing different smart products placed around the rendering. These rooms consist of a home's entryway, living room, kitchen, nursery, and home gym. Target sub-categorizes this section with energy & lighting, security & monitoring, entertainment, smart hubs & routers, and lastly wearable tech. Similar to Walmart, but with much more clarity, Target brings health and fitness to the category. This is completely in line with its "connected living" messaging rather than home automation like other retailers.

Sears also uses the Electronics category to guide users into what they call "**Connected Solutions**." They describe this category as, "From wireless, streaming entertainment, media and devices; to smart thermostats, home security and wifi [sic] baby monitors; to fitness trackers, smart watches [sic] and wearables, Sears Connected Solutions has the cutting-edge home automation products and services to streamline your routine, save you money and put control in the palm of your hand. Smart Made Simple." The experience reads as very deliberately using the word "solutions" and offering the word "simple" not as an effect of smart technology, but as the value Sears offers to the customer through simple solutions for integrating this technology into your life. In contrast to Lowe's "Life, Made Easier" Sears is instead saying "Smart Made Simple." It's about the solution being simple, not your life becoming simpler. This is evidenced by the amount of educational content available to consumers from its website, such as buying guides and shopping by compatibility.

Amazon, like Sears, has a much greater lens on educational content that most other retailers. Amazon's IoT section is navigated to via Home, Garden & Tools where the high level categorization is "SmartHome." Amazon's tagline messaging is, "**Smart Home. Smart Life.**" with an immediate reference to Amazon Echo. Products within this category are under the following subcategories: thermostats, lighting, cameras, entertainment, kits & bundles, and Echo smart home. As we navigate Amazon's various pages and navigations around its smart home category (unfortunately the information hierarchy is not very evident), we are peppered with Amazon Echo throughout the page. The immediate reference to Amazon Echo on the main smart home landing page brings us to yet another landing page dedicated to Echo. This page states, "Echo Smart Home, explore compatible devices and solution." Amazon's overall marketing and product approach doesn't have a singular lens like some other retailers, like automation or security, but it's much more broad trying to educate the consumer about the multiple aspects to a smart home. Because Amazon is also pushing its own proprietary platform some of the messaging and content focus is quite similar to that of Lowe's with its Iris platform. Interestingly there is no mention of Amazon Dash[6] anywhere on their smart home pages.

Lastly we have Best Buy. Similar to Lowe's, Bestbuy.com doesn't route customers to its IoT category through another existing category. Rather, it created a dedicated top-level category called "Connected Home & Housewares." Unlike every other retailer, Best Buy doesn't have any introduction messaging to explain to consumers what the category is. Instead of marketing a high level story for consumers, Best Buy chooses to explain each subcategory as the value proposition. And there are many subcategories: smart & Wi-Fi- thermostats, security cameras & systems, networking & wireless, appliance & outlet control, home alarms & sensors, remote home monitoring systems, smart lighting, smart door locks, streaming media players, wireless & multi-room audio, and finally TV & internet service providers. Importantly, the word "smartphone" is referenced in nearly all of these solution descriptions. This is a strategy that is also found on Apple's website where all of their smart home products are categorized under iPhone accessories, where phone covers and cables are also listed.

In summary, there are only a few marketing strategies being applied across a number of retailers. These loosely fall under (1) automation and simplifying life's routines, (2) connectivity and the ability to track and control from a smartphone), and then (3) an educational focus (buying guides and compatibility lists). In terms of product assortment, retailers who rely on the automation message are less likely to include products like health and fitness trackers in this category as opposed to retailers focusing on the broader connected or smart story. These strategies are even more interesting when taking into consideration the Google Trends data showing "home automation" significantly declining in search term volume. As noted before, "smart home" along with "internet of things" are exploding terms as of 2014, surpassing home automation. This is aligned with the timelines in which retailers have changed their messaging to consumers.

By digging through the Internet Archive's Wayback Machine for each retailer's websites we can see that the Home Automation category has largely existed on site maps since around mid-2013. These categories remained stagnant for nearly two years as these retailers adopted a new language and site structure by adding their new landing pages for smart, connected, and still automation categories. For example, Best Buy first introduced "home automation" to its website in August 2013 [9], as did Amazon in September 2013 [8]. Then in October 2015 [10] Best Buy eventually removed the 2nd-level category of home automation from under its higher-level Home section by evolving "connected home" branding to a top-level category. Not much later, in February 2016 [11], Amazon introduced its "smart home" branding replacing the home automation

---

[6] Amazon Dash is a replenishment service for consumer brands to integrate as a fulfillment option for quickly reordering consumable products, like laundry detergent or coffee. The product is a backend service for device makers as well as a consumer product in the form of a physical "order now" button.

category entirely. Each retailer has followed this trend within similar timelines. Based on Wayback Machine data and Google Trends data, it isn't unreasonable to assert that retailers will likely grow their marketing in the IoT category more specifically around education and "smart" or "connected" rather than "automation." This trend will likely be followed with product offerings focusing less on automation and more on single product solutions by a multitude of consumer brands from both established companies and the startup world.

4 Conclusion

We have shown through analyzing mainstream sources that IoT as a realistic consumer market has really only broken into the public eye within the past four to five years. As Mashable wrote, "[2013] was the first year that home automation and tangible smart home products truly dominated the forefront of CES" [12]. Home automation seemed to be fairly popular in years past, but the market was largely controlled by professional installation companies. These installations required wholesaler technologies not available to consumers and complete installations of control systems in a home. The smartphone as an interface and the maker movement catalyzed the push of this paradigm into a consumer-manufacturer relationship with electronics rather than the previous wholesaler-professional installer-consumer relationship. The major consequence of this shift is the explosion of consumer electronics brands building smart home products rather than complete home automation solutions. It is with this shift that the role of a retailer in the smart home market has really taken a stronghold.

While the interfacing role of retailers is critical to the success of a brand in all markets, it is even more significant in emerging markets such as the Internet of Things (IoT). More so than devices like cellphones or tablets, selling IoT products becomes more politically charged as brands try to take over the consumer's home with both products and platforms. For example, Apple's recently removed the Nest Thermostat (widely recognized as the "gateway drug" for consumer IoT) from its retail stores in July 2015 as it shifted its focus to its HomeKit platform [13].

Indeed, IoT is still an early-adopter market, with most retailers only adopting a strategy within the last year, but as more brands and retailers make big moves into the ecosystem it will quickly grow into a mass market category where relationships and curation will be impactful to the shaping of our connected future. This is evidenced by Home Depot teaming up with Wink home automation hub to offer its customers a curated solution with what it felt was a good, affordable hardware and software integration [14]. Although, a quick look at the app's reviews reveal that consumers don't feel the same towards Wink, with an average rating of 3 out of 5 and many complaints about the hardware. Equally, with a recent Chapter 11 filing by Wink (and Quirky, its parent company) [15] it appears Home Depot may have bet on the wrong horse.

As Sterling discussed in Shaping Things, IoT will (and arguably has) enable a new form of interaction between consumers, data, and brands. This interaction will fundamentally change the historical relationship consumers have had with retailers, potentially causing an effect of disintermediation. Therefore, it will be imperative that retailers explore new business opportunities that become exposed through this relationship change or they run the risk of being shut out and potentially becoming defunct. As seen with Wink and Home Depot, large strategic decisions may not always pan out, but these efforts must be made. Strategic approaches to the IoT ecosystem by retailers, while unfortunately out of scope for this paper, should be considered next. Retailers have many choices in forming IoT strategies; what they decide will have lasting ramifications on consumers and the future of consumer IoT at large. With the exhaustingly multi-faceted considerations needed for successfully developing IoT products and selling the value to consumers, often a cohesive approach cannot be taken due to technical and political roadblocks - even when it is the best approach for the consumer.

References

1. The Rise of the Smartbulb - The New York Times. http://www.nytimes.com/2015/01/22/garden/the-rise-of-the-smartbulb.html?_r=1
2. Smart Home Show Live - Technology.fm. http://www.technology.fm/thesmarthomeshow/live
3. That 'Internet of Things' Thing - RFID Journal. http://www.rfidjournal.com/articles/view?4986
4. Sterling, B.: Shaping Things. The MIT Press, Cambridge (2005)
5. Smart House (TV Movie 1999) – IMDb. http://www.imdb.com/title/tt0192618/
6. Best Buy's ConnectedLife.Home Automates the Life of Luddites for $15,000. http://gizmodo.com/224440/best-buys-connectedlifehome-automates-the-life-of-luddites-for-15000
7. File:AMX-8400.JPG - Wikimedia Commons. https://commons.wikimedia.org/wiki/File:AMX-8400.JPG
8. Amazon.com–Earth's Biggest Selection. http://web.archive.org/web/20130901150256/, http://www.amazon.com/gp/site-directory
9. Best Buy: Making Technology Work For You. http://web.archive.org/web/20130814034511/, http://www.bestbuy.com/
10. Best Buy: Expert Service. Unbeatable Price. http://web.archive.org/web/20151030142607/, http://www.bestbuy.com/
11. Amazon.com - Earth's Biggest Selection. http://web.archive.org/web/20160217165701/, http://www.amazon.com/gp/site-directory
12. Home smart home: A history of connected household tech. http://mashable.com/2015/01/08/smart-home-tech-ces/#DmFNf5TDukqh
13. Apple pulls Nest Thermostat from online stores and some retailers - Silicon Valley Business Journal. http://www.bizjournals.com/sanjose/news/2015/07/24/apple-stops-selling-nest-thermostat-as-its-home.html
14. Gigaom Home Depot wants every connected gadget it sells to be Wink compatible. https://gigaom.com/2014/08/15/home-depot-wants-every-connected-gadget-it-sells-to-be-wink-compatible/
15. Wink Corporate Update – Wink Blog. http://blog.wink.com/wink-blog/2015/9/22/wink-corporate-update

Ontology-Based Adaptive and Customizable Navigation Method in Online Retailing Websites

Chi-Lun Liu[1]([✉]) and Hsieh-Hong Huang[2]

[1] Department of Multimedia and Mobile Commerce,
Kainan University, 1, Kainan Road, Taoyuan, Luzhu 33857, Taiwan
tonyliu@mail.knu.edu.tw
[2] Department of Information Science and Management Systems,
National Taitung University, 684, Sec. 1, Chunghua Road,
Taitung 95002, Taiwan
kory@nttu.edu.tw

Abstract. Different users need different navigation designs to facilitate effective communication. Simplifying the navigation interfaces and help consumers find and purchase products with ease is a big challenge. This work proposes a novel navigation method integrating adaptive and customizable approaches. The proposed method comprises the metadata and a set of conflict detection rules. The metadata defines the structure of adaptation and customization rules. The conflict detection rules analyze inconsistencies between adaptation and customization rules. Ontology is the theoretical foundation in the proposed navigation method. Navigation module ontology, webpage area ontology, priority ontology, role ontology, and personal characteristics ontology are used in this method to provide semantic information for conflict detection rule execution. A scenario of checkout process in an online store is also provided in this paper. In the expectation, this method can provide a convenient way for online retailing websites to simplify navigation interfaces according to evolving organizational and personal knowledge.

Keywords: Adaptive interface · Customizable interface · Navigation system · Personal characteristics · Ontology

1 Introduction

Online retailing is a channel for consumers to buy products. Navigation interfaces are important to help consumers to arrive somewhere to find and purchase products (Dailey 2004). Simplifying user interfaces and avoiding complexity are essential for a good user interface (Ramachandran 2009). However, such simplification is a challenge considering diversity of users.

Two approaches are common in providing an appropriate interface to different users: adaptive and customizable user interfaces. Adaptive user interfaces controlled by administrators consider the diversity of users to simplify the user interfaces and help users complete their tasks with ease (Ramachandran 2009). Adaptive user interfaces

© Springer International Publishing Switzerland 2016
F.F.-H. Nah and C.-H. Tan (Eds.): HCIBGO 2016, Part I, LNCS 9751, pp. 228–237, 2016.
DOI: 10.1007/978-3-319-39396-4_21

provide flexibility to administrators in dealing with such issue. Customizable user interfaces controlled by users involve various layout setting and configuration, such as changing color and content on web pages (Levene 2010). Customization means that the user deliberately tailors user interfaces by choosing options (Sundar and Marathe 2010). Rules are used in configure adaptive and customizable user interfaces.

Role is an essential element to classify users in online retailing websites. Using role-based approach to control information access is common in business. For example, Role-Based Access Control (RBAC) is very popular for information security in companies. Role is also applied in adaptive web interfaces, such as a health care application (Ramachandran 2009). In practice, role-based approach are widespreadly used in online retailing websites.

Personal characteristics are another important element to classify users in constructing adaptive user interfaces. There is a lot of literature discussing the relationships between personal characteristics and user interfaces. For example, old and young users have different preferences to operate user interfaces in mobile devices (Hölzl and Schaffer 2013). Wholistic users prefer one webpage comprising all steps and analytical users prefer step-by-step approach in checkout processes in online retailing websites (Belk et al. 2014). The literature of Elaboration Likelihood Model (Wang et al. 2009) implies that high and low involvement consumers needs different navigational information in online retailing. Therefore personal characteristics of users should be considered in providing an appropriate navigation interface to different users.

This work proposes an adaptive and customizable navigation method based on role and personal characteristics in online retailing websites. The proposed navigation method provides interface flexibility to administrator by means of adaptive navigation mechanism and to users by customizable navigation mechanism. The proposed navigation method comprises the metadata and conflict detection rules. The proposed the metadata reveals what information should be considered in adaptation and customization rules for navigation interfaces. For example, an adaptation rule metadata comprises six elements: navigation module, webpage area, online retailing website, priority, personal characteristics, and role. Therefore an adaptation rule can be: Step-by-step checkout process (navigation module) in checkout area (webpage area) of online music store (online retailing website) has 1st priority (priority) to support analytical (personal characteristics) customer (role). The proposed conflict detection rules are used to detect inconsistencies in adaptation and customization rules.

Ontology is the theoretical foundation of the proposed navigation method. Ontology is an explicit and shared conceptual model to represent a domain knowledge (Gruninger and Lee 2002). Ontology can provide semantic information to execute rules automatically (Liu 2012).

The reminder of this paper is structured as follows. Section 2 discusses related works about navigation mechanisms. Section 3 proposes the navigation method comprised of method overview, metadata, and rules. Section 4 provides a scenario about checkout process in an online retailing store. The final conclusion section includes research contribution and further works.

2   Related Work

Several related works in the literature are summarized in Table 1. All these navigation mechanisms provide several navigation interfaces to different users. Most of these works do not provide the configuration function for flexibly specifying adaptive navigation rules. Only two works (Ramachandran 2009; Martin and Ivan 2013) provide configurable adaptive navigation rules in their mechanisms. One work (Martin and Ivan 2013) uses ontology. None of these works provide a conflict handing function including rule conflict detection and resolution. And none of these works focus on the

Table 1. Related navigation mechanisms

	Navigation approach description	Configurable navigation rules	Ontology and conflict handling	Applied context
Brusilovsky (2003)	Providing different adaptation techniques for different knowledge level students	Not revealed	Not revealed	Educational hypermedia
Ramachandran (2009)	Using XML to provide adaptive navigation and presentation techniques for different roles	Yes	Not revealed	Health Care applications
Hölzl and Schaffer (2013)	Providing adaptive helping system and book-oriented application design for novice elderly users	Not revealed	Not revealed	Smart phones
Deshpande et al. (2013)	Providing and evaluating various web interfaces for different learning task's complexities	Not revealed	Not revealed	e-Learning
Martin and Ivan (2013)	Providing adaptive web environment according to user, domain, goal, and context models	Yes	Ontology is applied The conflict handling issue is not revealed	Adaptive hypermedia
This work	Using adaptive and customizable rules to present navigation interfaces	Yes	Yes	Online retailing websites

electronic commerce context. Hence this work proposes an ontological navigation method based on role and personal characteristics which are concern about the above issues.

3 Proposed Adaptive and Customized Navigation Method

This work proposes a novel adaptive and customizable navigation method including five step in Fig. 1. The five steps in the proposed navigation method are introduced as follows. In step 1, the administrator models the organizational knowledge comprising adaptation rules and ontologies. The organizational knowledge stores adaptation rules. All concepts used in adaptation rules are also stored in ontologies. Then step 1 uses ontologies to detect conflicts between adaptation rules. The administrator uses priorities to resolve conflicts between adaptation rules.

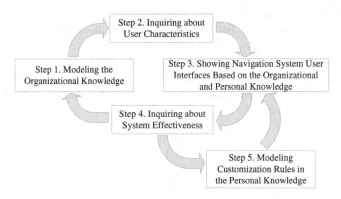

Fig. 1. Adaptive and customizable navigation method overview

In step 2, each user fill in the questionnaire to descript personal characteristics in personal knowledge. This questionnaire is developed to describe user characteristics according to the personal characteristics ontology in organizational knowledge, such as wholistic and analytic cognitive styles. Step 3 shows navigation system user interfaces according to both organizational and personal knowledge. In step 4, users are asked to fill in the questionnaire to measure the navigation system's effectiveness. In other words, the system effectiveness questionnaire is developed to inquire user satisfaction about the navigation system. If a user does not satisfy the navigation system, step 5 will be executed. In step 5, a user model his or her own customization rules in the personal knowledge to configure his or her own navigation system user interfaces. For conflicts handling, step 5 detects and resolves conflicts between customization rules in the personal knowledge. Step 5 also detects and resolves conflicts between an adaptation rule in the organizational ontology and a customization rule in the personal ontology. Then step 3 is executed according to the organizational and personal knowledge.

The core elements in the proposed adaptation rule metadata are six-folds: navigation module, webpage area, online retailing website, priority, personal characteristics, and role. These elements are depicted in Fig. 2. The adaptation rule metadata offers the administrator to specify adaptation rules in the organizational knowledge. For example, adaptation rule A is "One page checkout process (NM_{AR1}) in checkout area (WA_{AR1}) of online games store (ORW_{AR1}) has 1st priority (P_{AR1}) to support analytical (PC_{AR1-1}) customer (R_{AR1})".

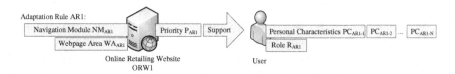

Fig. 2. Adaptation rule metadata

The proposed customization rule metadata has five elements: navigation module, webpage area, online retailing website, priority, and user. The customization rule metadata offers general users to specify customization rules in the personal knowledge to configure user interfaces. For example, customization rule B is "Top-down step-by-step checkout process (NM_{CR1}) in checkout area (WA_{CR1}) of online games store (ORW_{CR1}) has 1st priority (P_{CR1}) to support John (U_{CR1})".

This work proposes three rules for detecting conflicts in adaptation and customization rules. These conflict detection rules are developed based on the metadata in Figs. 2 and 3. These rules are introduced as follows.

Fig. 3. Customization rule metadata

Rule$_{IAR}$:

IF an inequality relationship is between navigation module NM_{AR1} and NM_{AR2}, an equality relationship exists between webpage area WA_{AR1} and WA_{AR2}, an equality or kind relationship is between online retailing website ORW_{AR1} and ORW_{AR2}, an equality relationship is between priority P_{AR1} and P_{AR2}, an equality or kind relationship is between role R_{AR1} and R_{AR2}, an equality or kind relationship is between personal characteristics PC_{AR1-1} and PC_{AR2-1}, an equality or kind relationship is between personal characteristics PC_{AR1-2} and PC_{AR2-2}, ... and an equality or kind relationship is between personal characteristics PC_{AR1-n} and PC_{AR2-n}, THEN a conflict occurs between adaptation rule AR1 and AR2.

Rule$_{IAR}$ is a conflict detection rule for finding inconsistencies between adaptation rule AR1 and AR2. Rule$_{IAR}$ is defined as above in the if-condition-then-statement structure. The semantic relationships between adaptation rule AR1 and AR2 in the condition are depicted in Fig. 4. The ontologies in organizational knowledge provide semantic information between concepts for executing Rule$_{IAR}$. The administrator should prioritize adaptation rule AR1 and AR2 to resolve the conflict.

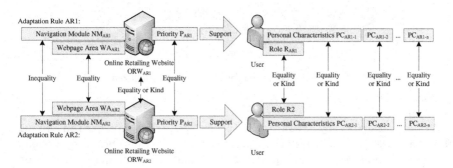

Fig. 4. Conflict detection rule for inconsistent adaptation rules

Rule$_{ICR}$:

IF an inequality relationship is between navigation module NM$_{CR1}$ and NM$_{CR2}$, an equality relationship exists between webpage area WA$_{CR1}$ and WA$_{CR2}$, an equality or kind relationship is between online retailing website ORW$_{CR1}$ and ORW$_{CR2}$, an equality relationship is between priority P$_{CR1}$ and P$_{CR2}$, and an equality relationship is between user U$_{CR1}$ and U$_{CR2}$, THEN a conflict occurs between customization rule CR1 and CR2.

Rule$_{ICR}$ is a conflict detection rule for finding inconsistencies between customization rule CR1 and CR2. Rule$_{ICR}$ is defined as above in the if-condition-then-statement structure. The semantic relationships between customization rule CR1 and CR2 are depicted in Fig. 5. The ontologies in organizational knowledge provide semantic information between concepts for executing Rule$_{ICR}$. The users should prioritize customization rule CR1 and CR2 to resolve the conflict. Moreover, users can suggest which concepts and semantic relationship should be added in the ontologies which are managed by administrators.

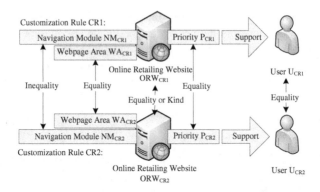

Fig. 5. Conflict detection rule for inconsistent customization rules

Rule$_{ICAR}$:

IF an inequality relationship is between navigation module NM$_{CR1}$ and NM$_{AR1}$, an equality relationship exists between webpage area WA$_{CR1}$ and WA$_{AR1}$, an equality or kind relationship is between online retailing website ORW$_{CR1}$ and ORW$_{AR1}$, an equality or kind relationship is between role R$_{CR1}$ and R$_{AR1}$, an equality or kind relationship is between personal characteristics PC$_{CR1-1}$ and PC$_{AR1-1}$, an equality or kind relationship is between personal characteristics PC$_{CR1-2}$ and PC$_{AR1-2}$, ... and an equality or kind relationship is between personal characteristics PC$_{CR1-n}$ and PC$_{AR1-n}$, THEN a conflict occurs between customization rule CR1 and adaptation rule AR1.

Rule$_{ICAR}$ is a conflict detection rule for finding inconsistencies between customization rule CR1 and adaptation rule AR1. Rule$_{ICAR}$ is defined as above in the if-condition-then-statement structure. The semantic relationships between customization rule CR1 and adaptation rule AR1 are depicted in Fig. 6. The ontologies in organizational knowledge provide semantic information between concepts for executing Rule$_{ICAR}$. Personal characteristics PC$_{CR-1}$, PC$_{CR-2}$,... and PC$_{CR-n}$ and role R$_{CR1}$ are identified when customization rule CR1 is executed for user U$_{CR1}$. Priority P$_{CR1}$ should be set as first priority to resolve the conflict because customization rule CR1 specified by user U$_{CR1}$ must take precedence over adaptation rule AR1 specified by an administrator.

4   Scenario of Checkout Process

This section provides a scenario of checkout process in an online retailing website. This scenario comprises five ontologies and three examples for Rule$_{IAR}$, Rule$_{ICR}$, and Rule$_{ICAR}$. These ontologies are navigation module ontology, webpage area ontology, priority ontology, role ontology, and personal characteristics ontology. Some ontologies which are important for demonstrating the examples are depicted in the following figures.

The following adaptive and configurable navigation system examples use the above ontologies (in Figs. 7, 8 and 9) and the metadata (in Figs. 2 and 3) to demonstrate and validate the proposed conflict detection rules (in Figs. 4, 5 and 6). The $Rule_{IAR}$ example describes the situation of two inconsistent adaptation rules. In the $Rule_{IAR}$ example, adaptation rule AR1 is: "One page checkout process (NM_{AR1}) in checkout area (WA_{AR1}) of online game store (ORW_{AR1}) has 1st priority (P_{AR1}) to support analytical (PC_{AR1-1}) customer (R_{AR1})". Adaptation rule AR2 is: "Top-down step-by-step checkout process (NM_{AR2}) in checkout area (WA_{AR2}) of online game store (ORW_{AR2}) has 1st priority (P_{AR2}) to support any cognitive style (PC_{AR2-1}) customer (R_{AR2})". In this example, Fig. 7 indicates that one page checkout process (NM_{AR1}) is unequal to top-down step-by-step checkout process (NM_{AR2}). Checkout area (WA_{AR1}) which is placed on a checkout navigation module equals checkout area (WA_{AR2}). Online game store (ORW_{AR1}) equals online game store (ORW_{AR2}). The concept of 1st priority (P_{AR1}) equals the concept of 1st priority (P_{AR2}). Figure 9 shows that the concept of analytical (PC_{AR1-1}) is a kind of the concept of any cognitive style (PC_{AR2-1}). And customer (R_{AR1}) equals customer (R_{AR2}). According to $Rule_{IAR}$, a conflict exists between adaptation rule AR1 and AR2.

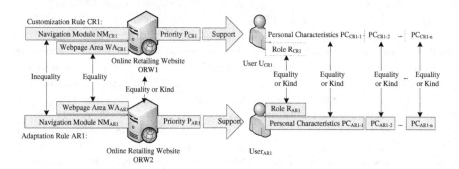

Fig. 6. Conflict detection rule for inconsistent customization and adaptation rules

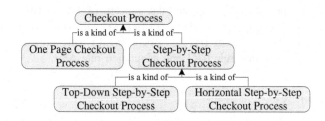

Fig. 7. Navigation module ontology

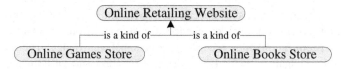

Fig. 8. Online retailing websites ontology

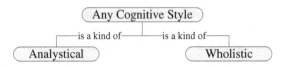

Fig. 9. Personal characteristics ontology

The Rule$_{ICR}$ example describes the situation of two inconsistent customization rules. In the Rule$_{ICR}$ example, customization rule CR1 is: "Horizontal step-by-Step checkout process (NM$_{CR1}$) in checkout area (WA$_{CR1}$) of online store (ORW$_{CR1}$) has 1st priority (P$_{CR1}$) to support Cynthia (U$_{CR1}$)". Customization rule CR2 is: "Top-down step-by-step checkout process (NM$_{CR2}$) in checkout area (WA$_{CR2}$) of online books store (ORW$_{CR2}$) has 1st priority (P$_{CR2}$) to support Cynthia (U$_{CR2}$)". In this example, the parent of both horizontal and top-down step-by-step checkout process is step-by-step checkout process. Therefore horizontal step-by-Step checkout process (NM$_{CR1}$) is unequal to top-down step-by-step checkout process (NM$_{CR2}$). Checkout area (WA$_{CR1}$) equals checkout area (WA$_{CR2}$). Figure 8 reveals that online books store (ORW$_{CR2}$) is a kind of online store (ORW$_{CR1}$). The concept of 1st priority (P$_{CR1}$) equals the concept of 1st priority (P$_{CR2}$). And Cynthia (U$_{CR1}$) equals Cynthia (U$_{CR2}$). According to Rule$_{ICR}$, there is a conflict between customization rule CR1 and CR2.

The Rule$_{ICAR}$ example describes the inconsistency between customization and adaptation rules. In the Rule$_{ICAR}$ example, customization rule CR1 is: "Top-down step-by-step checkout process (NM$_{CR1}$) in checkout area (WA$_{CR1}$) of online books store (ORW$_{CR1}$) has 1st priority (P$_{CR1}$) to support Anne (U$_{CR1}$)". Adaptation rule AR1 is: "Horizontal step-by-step checkout process (NM$_{AR1}$) in checkout area (WA$_{AR1}$) of online store (ORW$_{AR1}$) has 1st priority (P$_{AR1}$) to support Wholistic (PC$_{AR1-1}$) customer (R$_{AR1}$)". The user data collected from a personal characteristics questionnaire show that Anne is a wholistic (PC$_{CR1-1}$) customer (R$_{CR1}$). In this example, Fig. 7 indicates that top-down step-by-step checkout process (NM$_{CR1}$) is unequal to horizontal step-by-step checkout process (NM$_{AR1}$). Checkout area (WA$_{CR1}$) equals checkout area (WA$_{AR1}$). Figure 8 shows that online books store (ORW$_{CR1}$) is a kind of online store (ORW$_{AR1}$). The concept of 1st priority (P$_{CR1}$) equals the concept of 1st priority (P$_{AR1}$). Anne (Role$_{CR1}$) equals Anne (Role$_{AR1}$). Wholistic (PC$_{CR1-1}$) equals wholistic (PC$_{AR1-1}$). And customer (R$_{CR1}$) equals customer (R$_{AR1}$). According to Rule$_{ICAR}$, a inconsistency occurs between customization rule CR1 and adaptation rule AR2.

5   Conclusion

Simplification of navigation interfaces to facilitate effective communications is necessary for designing good online retailing websites. Adaptation and customization are two common approaches to simplify navigation interfaces. In this context, administrators of online retailing websites specify new adaptation rules for navigation interfaces according to organizational knowledge. Consumers of online retailing websites specify new customization rules according to personal knowledge. Therefore developing a flexible navigation method integrating adaptation and customization is necessary to quickly fit administrators' and consumers' requirements.

This work proposes an ontology-based method to provide adaptive and customizable navigation interfaces according to role and personal characteristics. The proposed method open a new direction based on ontology theory from the individual differences perspective. This work has two theoretical contributions. The first theoretical contribution of the proposed method is applying ontology in the new phenomenon about flexible website navigation. The second theoretical contribution of this work is proposing a set of innovative rules for inconsistent rules detection. Besides, the practical contribution of this method facilitate online retailers integrating organizational and personal knowledge to simplify navigation interfaces in their websites.

Developing system architecture to support the proposed method is under way. System implementation and evaluation are also valuable directions for further works.

References

Brusilovsky, P.: Adaptive navigation support in educational hypermedia: the role of student knowledge level and the case for meta-adaptation. Br. J. Educ. Technol. 34(4), 487–497 (2003)

Ramachandran, K.: Adaptive user interfaces for health care applications. IBM (2009). http://www.ibm.com/developerworks/library/wa-uihealth/

Hölzl, M., Schaffer, C.: An adaptive and book-oriented mobile touch screen user interface concept for novice senior users. In: Proceedings of The 11th International Conference on Advances in Mobile Computing and Multimedia, Vienna, Austria (2013)

Deshpande, Y., Bhattacharya, S., Yammiyavar, P.: A study of the impact of task complexity and interface design on e-Learning task adaptations. In: Proceedings of the 11th Asia Pacific Conference on Computer Human Interaction, Bangalore, India, pp. 19–27 (2013)

Martin, B., Ivan, J.: Generic ontology-based model for adaptive web environments: a revised formal description explained within the context of its implementation. In: Proceedings of IEEE 16th International Conference on Computational Science and Engineering, Sydney, Australia, pp. 495–500 (2013)

Levene, M.: An Introduction to Search Engines and Web Navigation, 2nd edn. Wiley, Hoboken (2010)

Sundar, S.S., Marathe, S.S.: Personalization versus customization: the importance of agency, privacy and power usage. Hum. Commun. Res. 36, 298–322 (2010)

Belk, M., Germanakos, P., Asimakopoulos, S., Andreou, P., Mourlas, C., Spanoudis, G., Samaras, G.: An individual differences approach in adaptive waving of user checkout process in retail eCommerce. In: Nah, F.F.-H. (ed.) HCIB 2014. LNCS, vol. 8527, pp. 451–460. Springer, Heidelberg (2014)

Wang, K., Wang, E.T.G., Farn, C.K.: Influence of web advertising strategies, consumer goal-directedness, and consumer involvement on web advertising effectiveness. Int. J. Electron. Commer. 13(4), 67–95 (2009)

Gruninger, M., Lee, J.: Ontology: applications and design. Commun. ACM 45(2), 39–56 (2002)

Liu, C.L.: Payment status and service level agreement based access control method in cloud service business. In: Proceedings of the Sixth International Conference on Genetic and Evolutionary Computing, Kitakyushu, Japan, pp. 67–70 (2012)

Dailey, L.: Navigational web atmospherics - explaining the influence of restrictive navigation cues. J. Bus. Res. 57(7), 795–803 (2004)

Learning from Emerging and Mature Markets to Design Mobile P2P Payment Experiences

Masumi Matsumoto[✉] and Lucia Terrenghi

Google Inc., Zurich, Switzerland
masumim@google.com, luciat@google.com

Abstract. Since 2011 the authors have researched and designed mobile payments applications for mature and emerging markets. Building on our extended research in the mobile payments domain across different markets, and drawing upon the identification of global trends in social and payments mobile services, we derive design implications and recommendations for mobile P2P payment experiences.

Keywords: Mobile · Payments · Social · Emerging markets · Kenya

1 Introduction

The social meaning of money has been discussed in the literature [1], addressing how monetary value goes well beyond its utilitarian nature and is deeply rooted in the culture and social patterns in which money is embedded and exchanged.

As technology mediates money exchange, it affects people's mental models and social relationships around money. In this paper we reflect on how mobile technology is affecting the way in which person-to-person (P2P) money transfers are becoming increasingly embedded in social communication and discuss implications for design. Building on our extended research on mobile payments in both emerging and mature markets, we argue that there are several learnings we can take from both markets that can inform the design of mobile P2P experiences that better support people's social communication globally.

2 Background and Related Work

P2P money transactions have been very common across geographies for decades – be it through bank transfers, remittances, or cash. In so called emerging, cash-based economies, the use of mobile technologies for such a purpose has been one of the main drivers towards the shift from cash to digital payments [2]. These economies have embraced mobile payments much earlier than developed economies, since the service enabled users to effectively cope with the risks and costs of physically traveling upcountry to deliver cash to their loved ones. Since 2007 [3] people in Kenya, often unbanked [4], have been able to send money to family and friends through mobile money by simply using their feature phones and USSD applications, through services enabled by the

© Springer International Publishing Switzerland 2016
F.F.-H. Nah and C.-H. Tan (Eds.): HCIBGO 2016, Part I, LNCS 9751, pp. 238–247, 2016.
DOI: 10.1007/978-3-319-39396-4_22

mobile operators. Moving from cash to electronic payments has shown to have a deep socio-economic impact on emerging markets [5, 6], tackling issues around security, cost of money production and transportation, hygiene and transparency [7], just to name a few. Such a shift is not trivial in terms of mental models and related financial behaviors. As discussed by Ignacio Mas [8], a leap from cash to digital economies deeply affects the way in which people think about and store money, plan their expenses, save and manage liquidity. In this sense the design of technology enabling money transfer can have a major influence on people's interaction with finance and with other people. As shown by Kusimba et al. [9], mobile money has been co-shaping the way in which people nurture their social relationships and communication. For example, male users in Kenya send air-time bundles to women as a form of courtship and gifting [9].

To better understand and analyze day-to-day use of mobile payments in emerging markets, specifically urban areas, the authors conducted qualitative field research in Kenya, Philippines, Brasil and India from 2013 to 2015. We conducted individual and group interviews with over 260 urban, middle-income participants across these countries. In particular, we focused on Kenyan mobile payments, conducting 7 field research trips in 2014 and 2015, interviewing over 120 people. The analysis on emerging markets in this paper is informed by this original research and existing literature.

In addition, for mature markets, the authors of this paper have been researching and designing mobile payments apps for the US and UK market since 2012. This paper's analysis on mature markets uses findings from research conducted in this capacity. Studies were conducted in London, San Francisco, Los Angeles and New York focusing on mobile payments, with the bulk carried out in San Francisco. Monthly interviews with 4–6 mobile payments users, over 120 participants total, were interviewed during the product development process.

In mature markets the shift from cash to digital transactions, i.e. using "plastic" or "intangible" money, has happened much earlier [10], largely driven by the emergence of debit and credit cards, followed by e-banking and e-commerce services. The adoption of mobile phones for P2P transfers, on the other hand, has only emerged in recent years, through the introduction of smartphone apps like Google Wallet, Venmo, Square, the Paypal app [11], and mobile banking services. Those services have mainly been adopted by so-called millennials [12], i.e. people reaching young adulthood around the year 2000.

The recent uptake of smartphones across mature and emerging markets [24] sets the stage for a new era in which both types of markets will increasingly use mobile phones to exchange money. Given how smartphones have been shaping social communication, we reflect on how this trend is shaping P2P money transfers globally, and argue that it is a time of behavioral convergence between mature and developing economies. Analyzing that convergence and building on our research in mature and emerging markets, particularly in Kenya, we then draw design implications for mobile P2P payment experiences.

In the section below we call out the differences and similarities of how mobile wallets work in the different geographies and discuss how those differences affect people's mental models and shape social behaviors.

3   How Mobile Wallets Work

3.1   In Emerging Markets

In emerging markets mobile money services provide a way for people to store value with the mobile service provider. In those markets the relationship between consumers and providers has been traditionally based on a pre-paid format: i.e., users top up their air-time accounts by paying cash at a mobile carrier agent. Differently from traditional financial institutions, mobile carriers have built extended agent networks reaching rural areas: relying on the same network and cash-in model, in 2007 Safaricom in Kenya started offering mobile wallets [3], i.e. the possibility for people to store value with the operator similarly to a bank account and transfer money from a person to another one through that network using their phone.

This works in the following way: people open a mobile wallet account, linked to their phone number, with their mobile operator and top it up in cash at physical location run by an agent. When opening the account they get a PIN. When they want to send money to one of their contacts (e.g. family and friends living in a rural area), they: (1) enter a USSD application available on feature phones and linked to the phone SIM card; (2) enter the phone number of the recipient; (3) enter the amount; (4) enter the PIN. After that, they receive a confirmation over SMS, and the recipient gets an SMS notification that money has been transferred to their mobile number/account. At that stage recipients can: (1) visit an agent in their area to cash out the money; (2) store money in their mobile balance; or (3) convert it to air-time value.

As the model in Fig. 1 shows, mobile wallets in emerging markets build on the concept of a stored value that can be transferred from person to person through a provider. Although mobile money enables and drives the shift from cash to digital, the mental model of mobile money is rather close to how people handle physical, cash-based value.

Mobile wallets in Mature Markets, on the other hand, normally build on a different model, as discussed below.

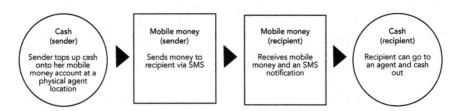

Fig. 1. The diagram shows the typical conversion flow of money from cash to digital value stored by the operator and further converted into cash. Mobile money is often used as conduit for cash to cash transfers. In some markets this kind of transactions have so frequent that users now increasingly transfer mobile money balances without withdrawing cash immediately [8].

3.2 In Mature Markets

Mobile wallets in mature markets, e.g. Google Wallet, Apple Pay, Venmo, Square cash, normally rely on a proxy model, where the P2P app serves as a proxy for money transfers between the sender and receiver's bank accounts.

This works in the following way (see Fig. 2): Users download an app onto their smartphones and link that to their email account and banking credentials in the sign up flow. In most cases the banking credentials are entered via debit or credit card details. The app syncs to their email and social contacts. When a user is sending money to a recipient s/he selects a contact from the ones available or enters a phone number (e.g. in Venmo), enters an amount, and sends. For the recipient to receive the money, she may need to sign up for the app, or receive the money as an in-app stored value before transferring on his/her bank account.

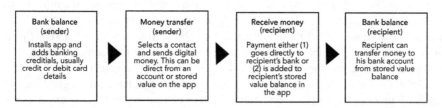

Bank balance (sender)	Money transfer (sender)	Receive money (recipient)	Bank balance (recipient)
Installs app and adds banking creditials, usually credit or debit card details	Selects a contact and sends digital money. This can be direct from an account or stored value on the app	Payment either (1) goes directly to recipient's bank or (2) is added to recipient's stored value balance in the app	Recipient can transfer money to his bank account from stored value balance

Fig. 2. The diagram shows the typical flow for P2P mobile transfers in mature markets. Differently from emerging markets, the value remains digital throughout the transaction and the mobile app serves as proxy to people's bank accounts.

There are three key differences between the mental models of P2P money transfers when comparing emerging and mature markets. First, in emerging markets the conceptual starting point is cash being transferred from one person to another. Whereas in mature markets, digital values stored in formal financial tools like banks and credit cards is the starting point.

Second, in emerging markets, cash must be converted to a digital stored value before it is sent. In contrast, stored values are optional in mature market apps and not required to complete a transfer. But in the mature markets, users must have a formal financial instrument, such as a bank account. Lastly, in emerging markets the ability to quickly convert stored value into physical cash is a necessary feature, whereas in developed markets it is not. People in emerging markets often do not have enough funds [25] and financial stability to be able to open a bank account, which often require minimum balances.

Building on these considerations we analyze other global trends that indicate opportunities for convergence in the landscape of mobile wallets.

4 Converging Trends

One of the evident trends seen at a global scale is the growth of mobile natives [13, 14], i.e. people who experience computing and the Internet on mobile first. Not only the majority of people in emerging markets are more likely to afford a phone than a laptop or a desktop computer, but due to falling smartphone prices in recent years, those have become key entry points for people's access to communication and information services. 67 % Of phones sold by Safaricom in 2013 were smartphones, far outpacing feature phone sales [15]. In addition, Safaricom has already pledged to phase out the sale of feature phones in Kenya [16]. Furthermore, populations in emerging economies have the fastest growth rates [17], meaning they have a very young population which is increasingly developing social communication behaviors that are similar to young people in mature markets [18].

At the same time, young people in mature markets are learning to interact with computing and the Internet on mobile touch-screen devices from an early age. Across the two type of markets, it is clear [13, 18] how messaging (e.g. Whatsapp, Line), social networks (e.g. Facebook, Instagram) and entertainment (e.g. YouTube) are the main drivers of mobile services usage. Recent research has also shown how the millennials in mature markets are less likely to use credit cards and other services from formal financial institutions [19]. Similar to what can be observed in emerging markets, this is due to either lack of financial stability and fixed income, or to a sense of mistrust in traditional financial institutions that is growing in some mature markets [4].

Lastly, messaging apps like Whatsapp, Line and WeChat have seen a great growth especially in some emerging economies [20], and obviously amongst younger users. Some of these apps already offer the opportunity to purchase digital stickers and games that users can exchange as gifts in their social communication. Many of these apps are planning to support P2P payments [21].

5   Design Implications

Based on the considerations above we claim there are learnings we can derive from the way smartphones are supporting people's payment and social behaviors in both markets to design P2P payment experiences that are globally relevant.

5.1   Learnings and Implications from Emerging Markets

Physical Storage and Attachment Metaphors. As discussed above, people in cash-based economies tend to have a mental model of mobile wallets similar to the physical storage of money, e.g. like the jars in which they would store cash to save for a specific goal [8]. At the same time, millennials in mature markets have less access to and familiarity with the proxy model of bank cards, and are more likely to deal with cash and bank transfers for P2P payments.

In terms of user interface design, this suggests that using the metaphor of an attachment to a message could leverage that same mental model around stored value, resembling the experience of sending money to a friend in an envelope, or attaching a stored file to a text message. The same metaphor has been used by Google, where users "attach" money to emails in Gmail [22], but we believe there are even greater opportunities to embed that behavior and related ones in real time communication.

Already today people are using messaging apps to enhance their communication by combining multiple media, e.g. sending each other stickers-enhanced photos (e.g. Line Camera), videos, and audio files. From a design perspective this seems like a good opportunity for design to enhance people's P2P behaviors by allowing them to "wrap up" the value they want to send to each other in visually engaging forms. For example, WeChat changes its visual design for Chinese New Years to resemble traditional red money envelopes, which recipients "open up" in the user interface to claim their money, carrying the feeling of receiving and opening a physical gift, into the mobile app environment [23].

The Notion of a Visible Stored Balance. For people with inconsistent funding and financial instability, being aware of the balance they have available at a specific point in time is particularly relevant. While the notion and perception of available balance is rather clear in the physical and stored-value models, it is less so in the proxy model. Apps like Square Cash, for example, make debit transfers directly from the sender's bank account to the recipient's account, but does not display bank account balances for either. One of our investigations through Google Consumer Survey, polling 2000 young adults from the US who used mobile financial apps, indicated that checking bank account balances was the most frequent activity, and heavy users sometimes checked their balances multiple times a day to make sure they could afford purchases.

This observation suggests that for users of mobile P2P payments it is valuable to have an immediate access to their available balance in the user interface. In mobile money services in emerging markets today, users need to look up their SMS history and go through the service notifications, or initiate a query in the USSD app to check their balance. Only recently some smartphone apps like M-ledger (see Fig. 4a) have become available in those markets and provide a simpler access to the users' balance in the mobile money account. Similarly, Venmo in mature markets displays the user's mobile wallet stored value (i.e. the Venmo balance), however, it does not display the user's bank account balance and most of mobile payments apps don't either (see Fig. 4b).

Our recommendation is that considering the type of users who are adopting these services across markets - i.e. people with fluctuating income - it makes sense to consistently show in the interface the balance that is most relevant to users, to support people's awareness of the amount they have at disposal and are able to share. In emerging markets, that might be the balance in their the mobile money account, whereas in developed markets showing the bank account balance may be more useful.

5.2   Learnings and Implications from Mature Markets

Visual Cues for Real Time Communication. As shown in the diagram in Fig. 3, people in mature markets are evolving their usage of mobile devices for real time social communication into mobile wallets. In emerging markets the use of mobile money has traditionally been based on SMS protocols, i.e. on asynchronous communication. When a person sends money to another one via mobile money, she needs to receive an SMS confirmation to be reassured that the payment has gone thorough. In our field research in Kenya and the Philippines we have also observed how people often switch to voice, calling the recipient, to make sure that s/he has actually received the money and there were no mistakes in the number that was typed to indicate the recipient.

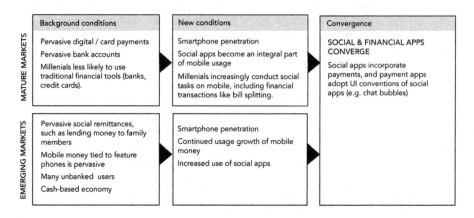

Fig. 3. This diagram illustrates how social interactions and mobile payments have evolved in mature markets and emerging markets. The two developmental paths differ, but are converging – social apps are incorporating payments, and payments apps have increasingly begun to incorporate UI patterns from social apps, such as chat bubbles (see Fig. 4d).

Based on these considerations we believe there are design opportunities for making the mobile P2P payment experience feel more immediate and familiar to the way people already use social apps. Examples for that are visual cues that provide a notion of presence, sending and receipt status similar to the cues used by apps like Whatsapp or Hangout. Additionally, a conversational UI similar to messaging apps builds on existing mental models around P2P and group communication that can be easily enhanced by enabling the sharing of money in the same fashion.

Square Cash and SnapCash are already moving in that direction (e.g. see Fig. 4d) and, as mentioned above, social apps are planning to include payments in their services [21]. Based on our research (see next section) while a conversational UI is promising, it is also important that it doesn't simply consist of speech bubbles sending money to each other. For payments to be embedded in the social communication they need to maintain the richness of the social context in which the money exchange is embedded: e.g., enabling thank you messages in the same thread, or connecting the payment to a group event people have contributed pictures and videos to.

Paying a Contact vs. Paying a Business. In order to better understand how a conversational UI similar to the Square Cash one (Fig. 4d) would be perceived in comparison to a list-based one more conventionally associated with financial tracking, similar to the Google Wallet (Fig. 4c) one, we ran a qualitative study with 7 college students from the US who had no or limited experience with mobile wallet apps. In the study we asked them to send money to someone with both interfaces and we collected their feedback around usability and overall experience. For all participants a conversational UI felt natural in a conversational context, i.e. in a messaging app, but would feel less secure

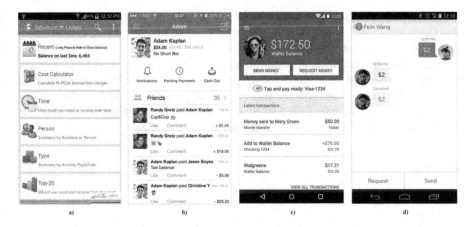

Fig. 4. User interfaces of different mobile payment applications. (a) M-Ledger, available in Kenya; (b) Venmo app; (c) Google Wallet app; (d) Square Cash app

and too casual in a payment app. Additionally, they felt like they could imagine using the conversational UI for sending money to their contacts, but they couldn't' imagine using it for paying a business.

This insight is consistent with our field research in Kenya, where people talk about paying a business as a "transaction" vs. paying a person as a "social experience". In 3 of the focus groups we ran in Kenya, we found that participants distinguished between: (1) sharing money with friends and family; and (2) paying a merchant at a store and went as far as to use different verbs: "sharing" described P2P payments, and "paying" described merchant-customer payments.

Overall, people across markets seem more inclined to use a social payment experience to send money to family and friends, but they wouldn't necessarily want the same interface to send money to a business. These observation suggest that while embedding payments into social conversations is promising, further research into a classification of payment types would be helpful to understand design implications around users' perception of security and privacy.

6   Conclusion

By highlighting global trends around social and payment mobile services, and building on our research in the field across mature and emerging markets, in this paper we argue that the convergence of users' behaviors calls for converging design solutions. To that end we have identified design opportunities for creating mobile P2P payment experiences that build on the learnings from both markets and strive for more engaging and globally relevant interfaces.

We believe there is scope for further embedding payments in mobile communication by gathering a deeper understanding of how P2P payments networks map to social communication ones. Research has been done on M-PESA, especially in Kenya, [9], but more comparative research is needed across regions of varying market levels. Along the same line, it is important to understand how cultural differences related to gifting, allowances and bills sharing might influence people's behaviors and expectation with regard to the interaction with the mobile service.

To that end, we aim at conducting further investigation across markets to identify and compare what type of connections people send money to, the frequency, amounts and reasons for sending, and how the communication patterns around that may vary. In doing so, we believe we can drive further insights to inform the design of mobile P2P payment services that are globally relevant, useful and engaging.

References

1. Zelizer, V.: The social meaning of money: "Special Monies". Am. J. Sociol. **95**(2), 342–377 (1989)
2. Medhi, I., Ratan, A., Toyama, K.: Mobile-banking adoption and usage by low-literate, low-income users in the developing world. In: Aykin, N. (ed.) IDGD 2009. LNCS, vol. 5623, pp. 485–494. Springer, Heidelberg (2009)
3. Celebrating 7 years of changing lives (2015). http://www.safaricom.co.ke/mpesa_timeline/timeline.html. Accessed 30 Jan 2015
4. Demirguc-Kunt, A., Klapper, L.: Measuring financial inclusion: the global findex database, WPS6025 (2012)
5. Plyler, M., Haas, S., Nagarajan, G.: Community-level economic effects of M-PESA in kenya: initial findings. IRIS Center University of Maryland (2010)
6. Suri, T., et al.: Documenting the birth of a financial economy. Proc. Nat. Acad. Sci. **109**(26), 10257–10262 (2012)
7. Terrenghi, L., Davies, B., Eismann, E.: Simplifying payments in emerging markets. Interactions **21**(2), 48–52 (2014)
8. Mas, I.: Financial inclusion challenge: the big picture (2013). https://www.youtube.com/watch?v=dfFMgPzinok. Accessed 29 Jan 2015
9. Kusimba, S., Chaggar, H., Gross, E., Kunyu, G.: Social networks of mobile money in Kenya. IMTFI Working Paper 2013-1, Irvine, CA (2013)
10. Sienkiewicz, S.: Credit cards and payment efficiency. Payment Cards Center Working Paper, Federal Reserve Bank of Philedelphia, Philedelphia, PA (2001)
11. History - PayPal (1998). https://www.paypal-media.com/history. Accessed 29 Jan 2015
12. Cao, J.: Millennials Say 'Venmo Me' to Fuel Mobile-Payment Surge (2014). http://www.bloomberg.com/news/2014-08-18/millennials-say-venmo-me-to-fuel-mobile-payment-surge-tech.html. Accessed 29 Jan 2015
13. Madden, M., Lenhart, A., Duggan, M., Cortesi, S., Gasser, U.: Teens and Technology 2013. Pew Research Center (2013)
14. International Telecommunication Union (2013). Measuring Information Society (2014). http://www.itu.int/en/ITU-D/Statistics/Documents/publications/mis2014/MIS2014_without_Annex_4.pdf. Accessed 29 Jan 2015
15. 67 % of phones sold smartphones – Safaricom (2013). http://www.humanipo.com/news/42985/kenyas-smartphone-penetration-at-67-safaricom/. Accessed 29 Jan 2015
16. Kenya: Safaricom to phase out feature phones | IT News Africa- Africa's Technology News Leader (2015). http://www.itnewsafrica.com/2013/02/kenya-safaricom-to-phase-out-feature-phones/. Accessed 29 Jan 2015
17. World Bank Data: Population growth (annual %) | Data | Map (2015). http://data.worldbank.org/indicator/SP.POP.GROW/countries?display=map. Accessed 29 Jan 2015

18. Wike, R., Oates, R.: Emerging Nations Embrace Internet, Mobile Technology. Pew Research Center (2014)
19. FICO. Millennial Banking Insights and Opportunities (2014)
20. Asian Messaging Apps Challenge Silicon Valley (2013). http://www.wsj.com/articles/ SB10001424052702303643304579108924275071910. Accessed 30 Jan 2015
21. Line Pay, The Messaging App's Mobile Payments Service, Will Make Its Global Debut Soon (2015). http://techcrunch.com/2014/12/04/line-pay-the-messaging-apps-mobile-payments-service-makes-its-debut/. Accessed 29 Jan 2015
22. Google Wallet now lets you send money as an attachment in Gmail (2013). http:// www.theverge.com/2013/5/15/4334348/send-money-email-attachment-in-gmail-with-google-wallet. Accessed 29 Jan 2015
23. WeChat's little red envelopes are brilliant marketing for mobile payments (2014). http:// qz.com/171948/wechats-little-red-envelopes-are-brilliant-marketing-for-mobile-payments/. Accessed 29 Jan 2015
24. Worldwide Smartphone Usage to Grow 25 % in 2014 (2014). http://www.emarketer.com/ Article/Worldwide-Smartphone-Usage-Grow-25-2014/1010920. Accessed 29 Jan 2015
25. Zollman, J., et al.: Kenya financial diaries. Report of the Financial Sector Deepening Kenya (2015). http://www.fsdkenya.org/news/186-news-new-list-34.html. Accessed 29 Jan 2015

Knowledge Sharing-Based Value Co-creation Between E-Commerce Enterprises and Logistics Service Providers

Yumeng Miao[✉] and Rong Du

School of Economics and Management,
Xidian University, Xi'an 710071, Shaanxi, China
ymmiao@stu.xidian.edu.cn, durong@mail.xidian.edu.cn

Abstract. Under the new economic forms of China's "Internet +" strategy, the Internet technologies spill over into different areas in a variety of traditional industries. As a result, electronic commerce develops rapidly. With the sustainable increase of consumers shopping online, the logistics problems have become the biggest obstacle of the development of electronic commerce. We argue that one can solve the current problems in logistics and improve consumers' satisfaction by establishing a long-term relationship of value co-creation between electronic commerce enterprises and logistics service providers. In this paper, we build a game model of electronic commerce enterprises and logistics service providers based on knowledge-sharing. We analyze the cases of one-shot game and repeated game. According to model analysis, we propose strategies for electronic commerce enterprises and logistics service providers to co-create value on the basis of knowledge-sharing from two different angles, i.e., the whole supply chain's and its members' perspective. These strategies may have implications to practice.

Keywords: Knowledge sharing · Value co-creation · E-commerce enterprises · Logistics service providers · Game theory

1 Introduction

With the development of Internet technology, the convenience of e-commerce emerges gradually, and different kinds of e-commerce enterprises appear, especially those with online shopping grow rapidly, such as Jingdong Mall, Alibaba and Taobao in China. Data show that by the end of 2014, netizens in China reached 649 million, and the number of online shopping users reached 361 million, with an increase of 55.7 % [8].

In March 5th, 2015, "Internet+" was first proposed in the Chinese governmental work report. "Internet+" emphasizes the advantages of Internet and making innovations by integrating Internet technologies, such as big data, cloud computing and so on, with traditional industries [2]. For example, in electronic commerce and its logistics service, the traditional logistics distribution is focused on the transporting route, and cost, and thereby optimization of logistics is concerned with cost saving and time saving. But modern logistics distribution is more focused on service quality that is related to other aspects of customer satisfaction, such as customer preference, etc. The Internet as a tool

© Springer International Publishing Switzerland 2016
F.F.-H. Nah and C.-H. Tan (Eds.): HCIBGO 2016, Part I, LNCS 9751, pp. 248–257, 2016.
DOI: 10.1007/978-3-319-39396-4_23

has multiple influences on the e-commerce and logistics, including impacts on online transactions, offline transactions and online-offline interactions. For e-commerce and logistics service providers, therefore, "Internet +" may help them solve the current problems such as high delivery cost, delayed delivery and wrong delivery in e-commerce and its logistics.

With the sustainable increase of consumers shopping online, the insufficient logistics service have become the biggest obstacle in the development of electronic commerce. For electronic commerce enterprises and logistics service providers, the biggest challenge is how to collaborate to solve the current problems in logistics and to improve consumers' satisfaction by establishing a long-term relationship between them. Nowadays, more and more enterprises tend to be value-co-created enterprises, as a result, the electronic commerce enterprises can concentrate on solving the problem of logistics to co-create value together with the related logistics service providers. If so, they can also improve their competitiveness. However, in fact, the development of logistics lags behind that of e-commerce. Consequently, consumers are forced to accept logistics service of low level which they are not very satisfied with. The purpose of this study is to work out some solution.

This paper is organized as follows. The next section reviews the pertinent literature. Subsequently, we analyze the one-shot model and the repeated model in Sect. 3. In Sect. 4, we propose some strategies for value co-creation, while results and discussions are presented in Sect. 5.

2 Literature Review

In this section, we briefly review literature about knowledge sharing and value co-creation.

2.1 Knowledge Sharing

Knowledge sharing is a way of exchanging knowledge to increase value and effects of knowledge. Researchers have different views about knowledge sharing, and they do research from different angles. Previous research on knowledge sharing focuses on the issues of effective factors, technology realizing, and specific practice.

Some researchers attribute the difficulties of knowledge sharing to transferring implicit knowledge, trust issues of in knowledge sharing, intentions and potential threat of knowledge sharing. They summarize the factors to facilitate knowledge sharing, 16 properties in four aspects including enterprise culture, employee motivation, leadership and information technology. On this basis, they propose a fuzzy evolutionary model to determine the weights of the related property [19]. A network model is proposed based on the analysis of literature about knowledge codification and knowledge-sharing networks. The findings show that the growth of knowledge codification may lead to the damage of knowledge-sharing ties [6]. Some studies investigate the effects of two types of trust, i.e. organization-institution-based trust and interpersonal trust, on knowledge sharing by building a conceptual model. The model is tested by an empirical study of

294 Chinese IT firms [20]. Some researchers argue that conflicting incentives among managers may affect knowledge sharing which can bring potential benefits through an analysis of leasing data [11].

Trust plays an important role in knowledge sharing in a supply chain, so there are several studies on it. A multi-period model is constructed to examine trust in a supply chain in terms of salespersons. It shows that salespersons who share demand forecast information with retailers are always trusted in a long-term relationship [5]. An investigation of capacity decision of suppliers reveals that the cooperation of suppliers and manufacturers depends on trust. Thus, an analytical model is developed to observe behavioral regularities [10]. A study on Group Buying indicates that social interactions between sellers and consumers can bring benefits through knowledge sharing, accordingly some new strategies are developed, such as Referral Rewards programs, which are different from traditional individual-selling strategies [3].

As for the practical applications of knowledge sharing, many researchers study the issues in different areas including healthcare, education and supply chain in business. The factors influencing the improvement of supply chain are investigated by using structural equation modeling. As a result, adaptability and, openness and innovation orientation are found to be very important factors [18]. A method with two steps is proposed to solve the problem of capturing implicit knowledge and develop a semantic web platform for knowledge sharing [9]. Some researchers have explored the relationship among trust, perceived risk workplace spirituality and knowledge sharing behavior by applying confirmatory factor analysis and structural equation modelling. Their findings show that there is a strong tie between workplace spirituality and knowledge sharing, and the perceived risk is a moderator variable between trust and knowledge sharing [13].

Researchers also have studied the issue of knowledge sharing in the context of supply chain using game theory. Some propose to build knowledge sharing networks to achieve optimal investment [1], and to reduced cost.

2.2   Value Co-creation

Value co-creation is a new concept in recent years. The generalized value co-creation means that the interactions of consumers' participating in the links of products design, manufacturing and sales circulation can create value. Doorn et al. argue that consumers and enterprises can create value in the cooperation of collecting ideas and realizing design and this is called value co-creation [4]. Thus, value co-creation covers two kinds of situations. One is value co-creation driven by enterprises who occupy resources, and the other is driven by consumers who occupy resources. At present, most researchers study value co-creation from the aspect of empirical thought.

In past years, most studies about value co-creation are based on the collaboration between enterprises and individual consumers. But now more and more studies focus on the value co-creation among enterprises.

Current two views are value co-creation theory based on consumers' experience [12] and value co-creation theory based on service-dominant logic [17]. The former believes that value co-creation is demonstrated in the aspect of consumers' experience.

Enterprises provide consumers with a context to experience consumption. It is inter-actions that create value including interactions among consumers, and interactions between consumers and enterprises. While value co-creation theory based on service-dominant logic states that value co-creation is realization of consumers' use value. In the process of value co-creation, consumers need to use their own knowledge and enterprises need to create good circumstances to facilitate value co-creation. When consumers use the products, value is co-created.

Researchers have studied the issues of value co-creation in different areas. The following are some examples. In one study, ideas are developed by linking service logic to an ecosystem perspective and the results show the challenges of the base of the pyramid environment [7]. In another study, it is proposed that the antecedents for value co-creation in health care include flexibility, responsiveness and co-innovation, and they are analyzed by using structural equation modeling. And it is tested by a survey of 225 health care professionals [15]. Some researchers verify the relationship between firms' degree of involvement in co-creation activities and the degree of articulation of their service value attributes via principal component analysis and artificial neural networks based on online textual data [16]. Above all, there are many studies on value co-creation in different fields, but very few on value co-creation between e-commerce enterprises and logistics service providers. To fill in this gap, in the presented research we build a game model and study knowledge sharing-based value co-creation between e-commerce enterprises and logistics service providers.

3   The Model

There is an important link between e-commerce enterprises and logistics providers, which are key nodes in supply chain in the context of Internet economics. Knowledge sharing between them helps to prompt their value co-creation. Two situations will be discussed in the framework of game theory. Figure 1 shows the conceptual supply chain model we study.

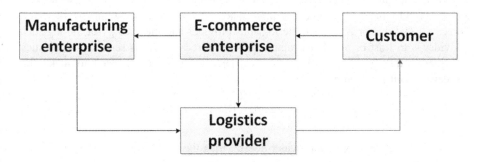

Fig. 1. The conceptual model

Before customers' ordering, e-commerce enterprises offer forecast about customers' ordering, then logistics providers will allocate the logistics capacity for customers.

When customers finish their ordering, logistics providers offer distribution service to customers. We assume that there is one e-commerce enterprise and one logistics provider. And the e-commerce enterprise wants to know about the logistics capacity of the logistics provider before signaling forecast.

3.1   One-Shot Game

Inspired by the model proposed in reference [14], we consider a different context with knowledge sharing between e-commerce enterprise and logistics provider. In this paper, knowledge sharing represents the exchange of information, such as forecast of consumers' orders and consumers' preference, and preference of logistics providers and preference of packaging. We assume that X is nonnegative normal random variable, $X \sim N(\mu, \sigma^2)$, and the market demand of customers is a scaled random variable $\omega \cdot X$. Here ω is the demand-size parameter, $\omega \in R^+$, it has two possible situations "high" and "low", thus we have ω_i, with $i = \{h, l\}$, with the probabilities of "high" and "low" respectively as $P(\omega_l) = \alpha$, $P(\omega_h) = 1 - \alpha$, $\alpha \in (0, 1)$.

We denote c as the unit service capacity cost of logistics provider. With knowledge sharing, the logistics provider can get the forecast of consumers' orders offered by the e-commerce enterprise to allocate service capacity. The logistics provider charges the e-commerce enterprise a price of a for each unit allocated and the e-commerce enterprise earns b for each unit. If the service capacity can't satisfy consumers' real demands, the e-commerce enterprise will pay for a unit service capacity of d. If the service capacity exceed consumers' real demands, there will be an extra cost of e. Define Q as the service capacity that logistics provider allocated. For notational convenience, define $f(x) = \max(x, 0)$, and

$$\pi_1(\omega_i, Q) = a \min(Q, D_i) - e.f(Q - D_i) - cQ \tag{1}$$

$$\pi_2(\omega_i, Q) = (b - a) \min(Q, D_i) - d.f(D_i - Q) \tag{2}$$

When the game begins, there is a random demand state of $\omega(\omega_h$ or $\omega_l)$, which can be observed by the e-commerce enterprise. Then the e-commerce enterprise will send a forecast $K(K = H$ or $K = L)$ to the logistics provider and the strategy of the logistics provider is to trust or not. For example, when a forecast of H is sent, and if logistics provider's strategy is to trust, service capacity Q_h will be allocated to make the expected profit maximum:

$$Q_h = \arg \max_Q E[\pi_1(\omega_h, Q)] \tag{3}$$

Of course, if the logistics provider doesn't trust the e-commerce enterprise, service capacity Q_0 will be allocated:

$$Q_0 = \arg \max_Q \{(1 - \alpha)E[\pi_1(\omega_h, Q)] + \alpha E[\pi_1(\omega_l, Q)]\} \tag{4}$$

Denote d_r as the realized demand of consumers, and o as the orders that the e-commerce enterprise tells the logistics provider to distribute. In the cooperative and truthful knowledge-sharing situation, the expected profit of the logistics provider and that of the e-commerce enterprise respectively are:

$$\begin{aligned} \pi_1^* &= (1-\alpha)\mathrm{E}[\pi_1(\omega_h, Q_h)] + \alpha\mathrm{E}[\pi_1(\omega_l, Q_l)] \\ \pi_2^* &= (1-\alpha)\mathrm{E}[\pi_2(\omega_h, Q_h)] + \alpha\mathrm{E}[\pi_2(\omega_h, Q_h)] \end{aligned} \qquad (5)$$

However, in the noncooperative situation, the expected profit of them respectively is:

$$\begin{aligned} \pi_1^0 &= (1-\alpha)\mathrm{E}[\pi_1(\omega_h, Q_0)] + \alpha\mathrm{E}[\pi_1(\omega_l, Q_0)] \\ \pi_2^0 &= (1-\alpha)\mathrm{E}[\pi_2(\omega_h, Q_0)] + \alpha\mathrm{E}[\pi_2(\omega_h, Q_0)] \end{aligned} \qquad (6)$$

We can imagine that when the e-commerce enterprise's forecast of consumer's demand is low, he or she is likely to send H to the logistics provider to assure sufficient service capacity can be allocated to him. If this happens, it may cause that the logistics provider can't distinguish the real incentive, and his/her best strategy is to ignore e-commerce enterprise's forecast information. So there is an equilibrium of non-truthful knowledge-sharing.

PROPOSITION 1. It occurs as a noncooperative case in the equilibrium of the one-shot game. The logistics provider allocates service capacity Q_0 with ignoring the forecast of the e-commerce enterprise.

Above all, it is necessary to study the case of repeated game to seek a best strategy for both the logistics provider and the e-commerce enterprise when having truthful knowledge-sharing.

3.2   Repeated Game

In fact, there is always a long-term supply chain relationship between the logistics provider and the e-commerce enterprise. The repeated game is composed of several stage games. At each time t $(t = 1, 2, \cdots, \infty)$, a stage game is played which is same to the one-shot game. As the time goes to $t+1$, the game renews. We denote $K^t = (K_1, \cdots, K_{t-1})$ as the forecast, $o^t = (o_1, \cdots, o_{t-1})$ as the distributed orders, $Q^t = \{Q_1, \cdots, Q_{t-1}\}$ as the service capacity allocated, and $h^t = K^t \times o^t \times Q^t$ as the public knowledge at time t. And the private knowledge $h^t_{private} = (\omega_1, \cdots, \omega_{t-1}) \times (d_1, \cdots, d_{t-1})$ can be only observed by the e-commerce enterprise.

In the repeated game, a Pareto-efficient outcome can emerge as an equilibrium by using a review strategy. The process of the review strategy is as follows:

(1) Divide time into several review phases. In every phase, the logistics provider marks G_t as the e-commerce enterprise's score and sets a credibility threshold for the e-commerce enterprise. After finishing the distributed orders o_t, the logistics provider checks the reliability of the e-commerce enterprise.

(2) If the e-commerce enterprise passes the check, his score updates: $G_t = G_{t-1} + 1$. If he cheats repeatedly, it is necessary to check low-forecast. It is likely that the e-commerce enterprise is at the risk of suspect forges low-forecast information.

(3) At the end of each period, the logistics provider checks the incentive of the e-commerce enterprise for truthful knowledge sharing. If the e-commerce enterprise has truthful knowledge sharing, the review phase continues and the game renews. If not, it stops and it comes to the punished phase.

(4) The logistics provider always trusts the e-commerce during the review phase. Once he/she doesn't allocate the system-optimal service capacity, the e-commerce enterprise can publish him by stopping the truthful knowledge sharing until he allocates the system-optimal service capacity.

PROPOSITION 2. A Pareto-dominant outcome can emerge as an equilibrium in the repeated game and the logistics provider and the e-commerce enterprise will realize the truthful knowledge sharing between them.

In the long run, the review strategy can help with the truthful knowledge sharing.

4 Strategies for Value Co-creation

4.1 The Whole Supply Chain Perspective

Based on the above game model analysis, three strategies could be used to improve value co-creation from the perspective of the whole supply chain.

Firstly, to build an effective knowledge sharing mechanism between the e-commerce enterprise and the logistics provider, the whole supply chain should take some incentive measures to promote the truthful knowledge sharing, such as decreasing logistics fees for the e-commerce enterprises. If so, in the long cooperation, the review phase will be shorten. And then value will be co-created in various aspects, including reputation, efficiency and precise grasp of consumers' demand and so on.

Secondly, to facilitate value co-creation, an integrated information system platform should be built for the whole supply chain. In the real world, parties of supply chain have difficulties to coordinate information. For example, the e-commerce enterprises may not know the accurate logistics information while the logistics providers may not provide in time delivery to consumers. This may cause consumers' complaints and brings bad effects on the performance of both the e-commerce enterprise and the logistics provider. To solve this problem, the supply chain members can cooperate to build an integrated information system to increase the information transparency. For example, GPS can be used for package positioning to help the consumer know the package's state and update information in the system in time. Moreover, one can make surveys with consumers about logistics service through the system to find out problems and to improve the logistics service. Consumers can get good experience through the integrated system, and the enterprises can gain good word of mouth from consumers. So value could be co-created in different aspects, including explicit profits, implicit reputation, and consumers' experience.

Thirdly, build the proper competition mechanism. In fact, one e-commerce enterprise always cooperates with several logistics providers and one logistics provider also cooperates with several e-commerce enterprises. Our model in this paper ignores the competition between them. Parties of supply chain will try to improve their competition through the competition mechanism which can help to realize supply chain optimization and create value including branding and good competition.

4.2 The Supply Chain Members' Perspective

Firstly, e-commerce enterprises need to offer knowledge about consumers such as forecast of orders and individual preference. It is important for e-commerce enterprises to know consumers' information to provide personalized service. In terms of logistics, the consumers who are in badly need of specific products, may have a high demand against logistics speed; the consumers who prefer box-packed than bag-packed delivery may choose to purchase some bulky goods. Moreover, if consumers purchase birthday presents to their friends, they may need cards and beautiful packaging. If the e-commerce enterprises know these consumer information well and make improvements in their service, they will gain consumers' intention of repeated visits to the website and their repeated purchases.

Secondly, logistics providers need to maintain good cooperation with e-commerce enterprises to realize value co-creation. A motivation mechanism for e-commerce enterprises' truthful knowledge sharing may help a lot. Then a specialized knowledge base can be built to enhance the management of consumers' relationship. The knowledge base should cover individual preference, feedback information, demands of logistics or packaging from consumers. When the knowledge accumulates to a certain degree, one can use big data technology to analyze it.

5 Discussion and Conclusion

In this paper, we have built and studied the game model of one logistics provider and one e-commerce enterprise with knowledge-sharing between them. The findings show that a review strategy can help to realize the optimal equilibrium of the system and improve the truthful knowledge sharing between the two parties. Accordingly, we have proposed strategies for electronic commerce enterprises and logistics service providers to co-create value. This study contributes to the understanding of knowledge sharing and its impacts in supply chains.

This research provides the following managerial implications. First, our results demonstrate that a review strategy can be effective in knowledge sharing and value co-creation between e-commerce enterprises and logistics service providers. Therefore, review strategy can be applied in practice to solve the logistics problems. Second, the idea of co-creating value through knowledge sharing in the field of e-commerce has managerial insights to practitioners. Finally, the strategies for value co-creation provide managerial guidelines for both e-commerce enterprises and logistics service providers.

Throughout our work, there are some limitations in this study. First, we just consider one logistics provider and one e-commerce enterprise in our model. Obviously it is not what it is in real world. Second, no case study is addressed to test the model and strategies. Finally, as for value co-creation, we have just proposed some general strategies but no survey-based quantitative analysis.

In future research, one may consider to do the case study and experimental study on a specific e-commerce platform, such as Jingdong Mall. Also one can extend the game model by taking multiple enterprises into account.

Acknowledgements. This research is supported by the National Natural Science Foundation of China through grant 71271164, and Humanities and Social Science Talent Plan in Shaanxi through grant ER42015060002, and partially supported by the Soft Science Research Program in Xi'an through grant BD33015060002.

References

1. Bernstein, F., Kök, A.G., et al.: Cooperation in assembly systems: the role of knowledge sharing networks. Eur. J. Oper. Res. **240**, 160–171 (2015)
2. Haosoubaike. http://baike.haosou.com/doc/7869991-8144086.html
3. Jing, X., Xie, J.: Group buying: a new mechanism for selling through social interactions. Manag. Sci. **57**, 1354–1372 (2011)
4. van Doorn, J., Lemon, K.N., et al.: Customer engagement behavior: theoretical foundations and research directions. J. Serv. Res. **13**, 253–266 (2010)
5. Ebrahim Khanjari, N., Hopp, W., et al.: Trust and information sharing in supply chains. Prod. Oper. Manag. **21**, 444–464 (2011)
6. Liu, D., Ray, G., Whinston, A.B.: The interaction between knowledge codification and knowledge-sharing networks. Inf. Syst. Res. **21**, 892–906 (2010)
7. Ben Letaifa, S., Reynoso, J.: Toward a service ecosystem perspective at the base of the pyramid. J. Serv. Manag. **26**, 684–705 (2015)
8. My Drivers. http://news.mydrivers.com/1/381/381898.htm
9. Mezghania, E., Ernesto, E., et al.: A collaborative methodology for tacit knowledge management: application to scientific research. Future Gener. Comput. Syst. **54**, 450–455 (2016)
10. Özer, Ö., Zheng, Y., et al.: Trust in forecast information sharing. Manag. Sci. **57**, 1111–1137 (2011)
11. Pierce, L.: Organizational structure and the limits of knowledge sharing: incentive conflict and agency in car leasing. Manag. Sci. **58**, 1106–1121 (2012)
12. Prahalad, C.K., Ramaswamy, V.: Co-creation experiences: the next practice in value creation. J. Interact. Mark. **3**, 5–14 (2004)
13. Rahman, M.S., Osmangani, A.M., et al.: Trust and work place spirituality on knowledge sharing behaviour. Learn. Organ. **22**, 317–332 (2015)
14. Ren, Z.J., Cohen, M.A., et al.: Information sharing in a long-term supply chain relationship-the role of customer review strategy. Oper. Res. **58**, 81–93 (2010)
15. da Silva, A.S., Farina, M.C., et al.: A model of antecedents for the co-creation of value in health care an application of structural equation modeling. Braz. Bus. Rev. (Engl. Ed.) **12**, 121–149 (2015)
16. di Tollo, G., Tanev, S., et al.: Using online textual data, principal component analysis and artificial neural networks to study business and innovation practices in technology-driven firms. Comput. Ind. **74**, 16–28 (2015)

17. Vargo, S.L., et al.: On value and value co-creation: a service systems and service logic perspective. Eur. Manag. J. **26**, 145–152 (2008)
18. Yang, J., Yu, G., et al.: Improving LearningAlliance performance for manufacturers: does knowledge sharing matter? Int. J. Prod. Econ. **171**, 301–308 (2016)
19. Yang, T.M., Wu, Y.J.: Exploring the determinants of cross-bboundary information sharing in the public sector: an e-government case study in Taiwan. J. Inf. Sci. **40**, 649–668 (2014)
20. Yuan, X., Olfman, L., et al.: How do institution-based trust and interpersonal trust affect interdepartmental knowledge sharing? Inf. Resour. Manag. J. **29**, 15–38 (2016)

Website Location Strategies Review Under Hofstede's Cultural Dimensions

Qian Wang[1(✉)], Chih-Hung Peng[1], Choon Ling Sia[1],
Yu Tong[1], and Yi-Cheng Ku[2]

[1] City University of Hong Kong,
83 Tat Chee Avenue, Kowloon, Hong Kong, China
{qwang45,chpeng,iscl,yutong}@cityu.edu.hk
[2] Department of Business Administration,
Fu Jen Catholic University, New Taipei, Taiwan
023089@mail.fju.edu.tw

Abstract. With the rapidly development of Internet and e-commerce in recent years, broaden business into multicultural marketplaces is easier and more profitable, and an important step for a firm to exploit its new markets is to launch proper websites to communicate with customers in different areas. Culture is so diversified that the design strategies of website for different countries should be localized according to each culture. As a result, in this study, we will conduct a review based on the pervious scattered website localization design strategies and classify them into different cultural dimensions. Such classification can be a summary of the current studies on website localization, an indication for detecting future studies in this area, as well as a guideline for designing website in different cultures.

Keywords: Website localization · Hofstede's cultural dimension theory

1 Introduction

In recent years, geographical considerations have no longer been a major impediment to conduct business around the world, and marketers have new opportunities to extend their business globally and pursue larger profits in multicultural markets. According to eMarketer (2014) and Miglani (2012), the sales of global B2C e-commerce market have reached $1.5 trillion in 2014, and more than 66 % of the world's online population have purchased online in 2014. The surge of the Internet users and the popularity of online shopping mode motivates marketers to consider corporate websites as a valuable media to communicate with their customers. It has been proved that any delay in launching international websites might be a fatal mistake for a corporation (Alvarez et al. 1998).

An attractive, easy to use and user-friendly interface of website is vital to keep consumers on the site long enough to make decision without switching to another site (Nassar and Abdou 2013). As a result, the design of firm's international websites is

© Springer International Publishing Switzerland 2016
F.F.-H. Nah and C.-H. Tan (Eds.): HCIBGO 2016, Part I, LNCS 9751, pp. 258–269, 2016.
DOI: 10.1007/978-3-319-39396-4_24

quite vital and various questions are coming along: should the designs of web sites in different cultures be distinct or should they follow similar trends? How do different cultures represent themselves on the Web? If cultural differences are found, what role do they play and how to adapt them to such differences? and so on. The origin of these problems is that different culture-background consumers have different product/brand knowledge structures, as well as different perceptions of and preferences for the products (Keller et al. 2011). Thus, only language translation in international websites is doomed to impede brand building process and a successful international website needs more respect to local culture.

In previous research, such operation by using international website strategies to adapt and respect to local culture is called "website localization" (Jain 1989), and ample studies have already demonstrated that proper website localization can improve customers' impression of websites (Badre 2001), increase their willingness to visit the websites (Badre 2001), enable the websites to increase their hit rate by almost 2000 % (Tixier 2005), simplify the navigation and promote favorable attitudes toward the website (Luna et al. 2002), as well as enhance the trust of online shopping customers (Singh and Boughton 2005). Another research by Tixier (2005) also shows that, through effective website localization, a firm could increase its online sales by 200 %.

However, practically, current operations on cultural adaptation in website localization areas are far from enough. A survey of the top 900 companies websites listed by Forbes reveals that only 225 of these companies have built localized websites (Singh and Boughton 2005). Similar research by Forrester finds that 67 % of the Fortune 100 companies' use standardized but not localized websites, in which English is the only language. Besides, although some international firms' websites have already adapted to local language and contents, the adaptation is still very limited with simply uniform website designs and features (Card et al. 1996).

Insufficient and inadequate website localization guidance may be part of reasons for the operation deficiency. Besides, improper website localization strategies are not only ineffective but also wasting money. Thus, firms can benefit a lot if some criterions can be developed to direct their international website designs. However, previous research which investigate the effect of website localization strategies are often too scattered to be used as the guideline by firms. Inspired by this vacancy, we conduct a review to all the website localization strategies, as well as classify each strategy into different dimensions of Hofstede's cultural theory.

The paper proceeds as follows. Section 2 introduces Hofstede's cultural theory, which is used as the framework for summarizing website localization strategies in this research; Sect. 3 reviews previous studied website localization strategies and classify them into different cultural dimensions accordingly; Sect. 4 is used to analyze and detect the insufficient of current research on website localization strategies and concludes the research with the theoretical and practical contributions.

2   Literature Review

The flourishing of the Internet and e-commerce has introduced a new research area, website localization, in marketing and information system areas, and increasing studies are conducted to investigate the effectiveness and importance of website localization. For example, Singh et al. (2006) use a technology acceptance model to study the B2C international websites of several countries, and empirically prove that cultural adaptation of Web content can increase purchase intentions significantly and lead to favorable attitudes towards a website. Besides, Sia et al. (2009) compare the application of two website strategies across Australia and Hong Kong, proving that web strategies can affect customers' trust online. Additionally, Badre (2001) surveys people with two different genres, e-shopping and news sites on the World Wide Web, and investigates their preferences and performance as a function of Web cultural experience.

Admittedly, as the service channels and mediums to serve their customers, firms' websites should not be culturally neutral, but be full of cultural markers (Singh and Boughton 2005). As a result, previous analysis and investigation for website localization strategies are always based on various kinds of cultural topology. The first category is the single-dimension national culture classification model. This model includes high versus low context (Hall and Hall 1987), monochromic versus polychromic (Lewis 1992), and high versus low trust (Fukuyama 1995). Another stream of national culture classification models is the multiple-dimension models, such as two-dimension categorizations (Lessem and Neubauer 1994), Newman five-dimensional classification, and (Trompenaars and Hampden-Turner 1994) seven-dimension models.

Among these studies, Hofstede's cultural theory is one of the most extensively applied and validated theories in cultural context and management research (Singh et al. 2005). Hofstede's cultural theory is developed by Geert Hofstede (Singh et al. 2005), and it describes the effects of a society's culture on the values of its members and how these values relate to their behaviors. Initially, Hofstede's cultural theory provides four categories to understand how national culture relates to social psychological phenomena, and the four categories are Power Distance Index (PDI), Individualism verse Collectivism (IDV), Uncertainty Avoidance Index (UAI), and Masculinity verse Femininity (MAS). The conclusion IS based on a survey research conducted between 1967 and 1978 at foreign subsidiaries of IBM. In 1991, Long-Term Orientation (LTO) is added as a new dimension to upgrade Hofstede's cultural theory.

Despite some critiques of Hofstede's cultural dimensions regarding the methodology and context (Fernandez et al. 1997; Huo and Randall 1991), significant more empirical evidence has verified that Hofstede's cultural typology is a valid differentiator to detect cultural differences and an effective basis for the analysis of regional differences (Bochner 1994; Dorfman and Howell 1988; Søndergaard 1994; Simon 2000). In addition, in 1987, the Chinese Culture Connection conduct a 40-item cultural value survey which is based on the themes identified by Chinese social scientists and philosophers, and results show that three out of four dimensions are highly correlated with Hofstede's cultural dimension index. As a result, in this study we use Hofstede's cultural dimension theory as a framework to conduct the website strategies review, and each strategy is categorized into one cultural dimension depending on its effect is mainly impacted by the differences across culture in which cultural dimension.

3 Website Strategies Review

We focus on the review of the studies investigating website localization strategies during the latest 15 years (2000–2015) in both marketing and information system areas.

3.1 PDI-Classified Web Strategies

The first dimension in Hofstede's cultural dimension theory is PDI which is defined as "the extent to which the less powerful members of organizations and institutions (like the family) accept and expect that power is distributed unequally" (Hofstede 1980). A country (e.g., China or Japan) with high PDI indicates that hierarchy in this country is clearly established in society without doubt. Conversely, in country (e.g., Canada, the US or Germany) with low PDI, people tend to question authority and attempt to distribute power.

Firstly, Power Distance would be more involved with the presence of authority (Robbins and Stylianou 2002) and status (Mueller 1987), that is because the character of admiring power in such countries. Correspondingly, pride of ownership appeal and quality assurance gain more favor in such countries. In the research, web strategies will be classified into high-PDI category if they are more preferred by people value society hierarchy, and reversely be sorted into low power Distance category if they are more appreciated by people who tend to question authority. Web-specific cultural traits in previous research on PDI categories are summarized in Table 1.

3.2 IDV-Classified Web Strategies

The second category is IDV, which explores the "degree to which people in a society are integrated into groups (Hofstede 1980a)", and this category focuses on the individual's relationships with others (Hofstede 1991). In a collectivist society (e.g., Brazil, China, Egypt, India, Japan, and Mexico), individuals are presumed to value the interest of their group more than that of themselves. As a results, collectivists will display greater group loyalty and are ready to protect the interests of group members. On the other hand, people in a individualism society (e.g., Australia, Canada, Denmark, France, Ireland or the US) are expected to care primarily for themselves and their immediate families. Individualists will be relatively less pressured from others and tend to be more self-centered.

Table 1. PDI-classified web strategies

High-PDI	Low- PDI	Studies
Symmetrical home page	Asymmetrical home page	Callahan (2005), Marcus and Gould (2000)
Frequency of logos		Callahan (2005)
Frequency of images of faculty		Callahan (2005)
	Frequency of images of students	Callahan (2005), Marcus and Gould (2000)
Tall hierarchies	Shallow hierarchies	Marcus and Gould (2000)
Official seal, national emblems		Marcus and Gould (2000)
Photographs of leaders	Images of both gender	Marcus and Gould (2000)
Monumental buildings	Images of people	Callahan (2005), Ackerman (2002)
Company hierarchy information		Singh et al. (2003)
Pictures of awards		Singh et al. (2003)
Pictures and information of CEOs		Singh et al. (2003)
Group identity symbols in newsletter		Singh et al. (2003)
Theme of family		Mueller (1987)
Links to local websites		Mueller (1987)

Website strategies are classified into IDV category if they affect very differently between individualistic persons and collectivistic ones. Specially, in one hand, website strategies are categorized into collectivistic items when they are more preferred by people who value group interests as well as the endorsement from others. In another hand, ones classified into individualistic category appreciate more on personal interests (Table 2).

3.3 UAI-Classified Web Strategies

UAI, the third dimension in Hofstede's cultural theory, is defined as "a society's tolerance for ambiguity (Hofstede 1980b)", and it is mainly used to deal with how societies accommodate high levels of uncertainty and ambiguity in the environment (Hofstede 1984; Tricker 1988). Specifically, society (e.g., Japan) with a high UAI has stiff codes of behavior, guidelines, and laws, and people in such country tend to absolute rely on widely accepted truth or belief. In addition, such people also seek to avoid ambiguity and therefore develop rituals and rules for virtually every possible situation. On the contrary, persons from a low UAI culture (e.g., Canada, Denmark,

Table 2. IDV-Classified web strategies

Individualistic	Collectivistic	Studies
Images of groups	Images of individuals	Callahan (2005), Marcus and Gould (2000)
Young individuals	Older individuals	Callahan (2005)
Number of links	Figurative images	Callahan (2005)
High modality pictures	Low modality pictures	Callahan (2005)
	Pictures of women	Callahan (2005)
	Animated pictures	Callahan (2005)
Country specific news		Singh et al. (2003)
Newsletter		Singh et al. (2003)
Symbols of national identity		Singh et al. (2003)
Pictures of family		Singh et al. (2003)
Links to local websites		Singh et al. (2003)
Customer endorsement		Singh et al. (2003)
Portal affiliation		Singh et al. (2003)
Clubs/Chat rooms		Singh et al. (2003)

England, Hong Kong, Sweden, or the US) might be more reflective and relatively broad-minded, resulting in the reduction of the need in them for social approval.

In our study, web-special traits belonging to the UAI dimension when their effects are vary significantly in different UAI countries. In particular, the application of the high-UAI strategies will work on alleviating customers' uncertainty level when using the websites, and vice-versa. The detailed website strategies on UAI-classified category are reviewed in Table 3.

Table 3. UAI-classified web strategies

High-UAI	Low-UAI	Studies
Guided navigation		Singh et al. (2003)
Tradition theme		Singh et al. (2003)
Free trials or downloads		Singh et al. (2003)
Limited choices	Variety of choices	Marcus and Gould (2000)
Restricted amounts of data	Long pages with scrolling	Marcus and Gould (2000)
Limited scrolling	Abstract images	Marcus and Gould (2000)
References to daily life		Ackerman (2002)
Redundancy		Ackerman (2002)
	Frequency of abstract images	Callahan (2005)
	Number of links	Callahan (2005)
Frequency of horizontal pages		Callahan (2005)

3.4   MAS-Classified Web Strategies

The fourth dimension is MAS, which is grounded in the ways sex roles are allocated in the culture (Hofstede 1991). In this dimension, masculinity is defined as "a preference in society for achievement, heroism, assertiveness, and material rewards for success", and its counterpart, femininity, represents a preference for cooperation, modesty, caring for the weak, and quality of life (Hofstede 1980b). Country (e.g., Denmark, Finland Netherlands, Norway, or Sweden) is categorized to the dimension of "femininity" when it minimizes the distinctions between sex roles, or emphasize the quality of life. Instead, other countries (e.g., Austria, Italy, Japan, Mexico, and Brazil) which maximize the distinctions between the sex roles and highlight the quantity of life, are labeled "masculinity". Individuals from masculine cultures will value material success and assertiveness, and they may seek to respond in a manner that compliments their own ambitions.

Masculinity and Femininity society persons generally have different preferences towards website designs. For example, Tsikriktis (2002) finds that masculinity is associated with higher expectations on a website interactivity, and Pollay (1983) proposes that ads in masculine cultures emphasize on the level of enjoyment. More studies on this category are summaries in Table 4.

Table 4. MAS-classified web strategies

Masculinity	Femininity	Studies
Quizzes and games		Singh et al. (2003)
Realism theme		Singh et al. (2003)
Interactivity		Pollay (1983)
Limited choices	Multiple choices	Ackerman (2002)
Orientation towards goals	Orientation toward relationships	Dormann and Chisalita (2002)
Emphasis on tradition and authority		Dormann and Chisalita (2002)
Frequent images of buildings	Frequent images of people, especially showing them laughing, talking or studying together	Dormann and Chisalita (2002)
Utilitarian-purposed graphics		Dormann and Chisalita (2002)
Number of links		Callahan (2005)
	Frequency of figurative images	Callahan (2005)
High modality pictures	Low modality pictures	Callahan (2005)
Number of pictures of women		Callahan (2005)
Frequency of animated pictures		Callahan (2005)
Website interactivity		

3.5 LTO-Classified Web Strategies

The last category in Hofstede's cultural theory is LTO, which acknowledges the connection of the past with current and future connection/challenges (Hofstede 1991). Strategic and financial caution are highly prized by persons who exhibit a long-term orientation (Hofstede 1991). Individuals from the societies (e.g., Pakistan and Mexico) with a short-term orientation may be more forthright and explicit in their interactions with others. Conversely, those in the societies (e.g., China and Japan) with a high degree of LTO view adaptation, circumstantial behaviors, and pragmatic problem solving as a necessity. Such people will be posited to place great significance on the values of thrift, persistence, and long-term alliances.

However, few research are based on long/short-term orientation to analyze web-special traits, and previous research only simply mentioned that long-term orientation would be indicated by the presence or lack of a search engine, site map, FAQ, corporate history, etc.

4 Review Analysis

According to the cultural dimension index listed in Item International (http://geert-hofstede.com/about-us.html) which is endorsement of Professor Geert Hofstede, we calculate the average of the five dimension indexes (Table 5) in different locations

Table 5. Cultural dimension index in different locations

Nation	Average PDI	Average IDV	Average MAS	Average UAI	Average LTO
Africa	66.6	33.6	48.7	66.8	41.8
Australia	32.8	84.5	49.8	47.0	43.0
Central America	70.2	25.6	46.4	64.2	43.3
Middle East	69.1	31.3	47.8	66.5	41.7
Japan & Korea	72.7	28.7	50.9	65.0	37.4
Middle Euro	38.0	64.3	74.7	75.3	62.7
South America	71.1	25.8	50.8	67.5	37.9
North America	62.5	40.1	49.8	65.8	43.4
North Euro	63.7	37.8	48.3	65.9	43.9
Southeast Asia	69.3	30.5	47.6	65.7	41.0
Volkswagen China	70.0	20.6	45.7	58.1	51.3
West Euro	62.0	39.8	48.6	65.3	44.7

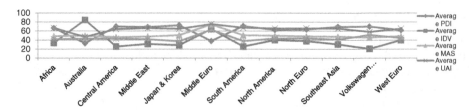

Fig. 1. Cultural dimension fluctuation across different locations

Table 6. Statistics analysis in cultural dimension index in different locations

STAT	N	MIN	MAX	MEAN	STD	Q1	MEDIAN	Q3
Average PDI	12	32.8	72.7	62.33333	13.08659	62.25	67.85	70.1
Average IDV	12	20.6	84.5	38.55	18.26659	27.25	32.45	39.95
Average MAS	12	45.7	74.7	50.75833	7.706603	47.7	48.65	50.3
Average UAI	12	47	75.3	64.425	6.661576	64.6	65.75	66.65
Average LTO	12	37.4	62.7	44.34167	6.767765	41.35	43.15	44.3

around the world, and the statistical analysis in Table 6 shows its fluctuated trend. IDV and PDI are the two most significantly fluctuated dimensions across locations around the world. As a result, when designing international website strategies, if companies pay more attention on the IDV- and PID-classified website strategies, the effect of their operation can be more obvious. In addition, Fig. 1 tends to give a more visualized description for the fluctuation of different cultural dimensions across different locations in the world.

5 Conclusion

In this research, we conduct a review on previous investigated website localization strategies, and this review is encouraged by the low level of comprehensiveness in studies in this area. The review is aimed at providing a general guideline for website designers and marketers when they want to build international websites in multi-countries.

Practically, if a country has specially characters in a certain dimension (with a relative high/low index value) and firms want to locate their website into such country, they can refer to the corresponding website localization strategies in this study and try to build more outstanding designs on them. Particularly, among all the Hofstede's cultural dimensions, IDV is the one which varies most across countries around the world, and the next fluctuated one is PDI. As a result, in practical international website design process, if marketers pay more attention on the cultural traits in these two dimensions, and the designs will be more effectual.

6 Future Research

This study relied exclusively on Hofstede's typology of culture, which is one of the most widely accepted and frequently cited cultural theories. However, the use of Hofstede's clusters, did not allow us to classify some web-special traits in content parts (e.g., hard sell approach and explicit comparisons). Future research may benefit from the use of some new typology. In addition, few research analyze web-special traits based on LTO dimension, so in the further this category could be further investigated.

References

Ackerman, S.: Mapping user interface design to culture dimensions. Paper presented at the International Workshop on Internationalization of Products and Systems, Austin, TX, July 2002

Alvarez, S.E.: Latin American feminisms "go global": trends of the 1990s and challenges for the new millennium. In: Alvarez, S., Dagnino, E., Escobar, A. (eds.) Cultures of Politics, Politics of Cultures: Re-visioning Latin American Social Movements, pp. 293–324. Westview Press, Boulder (1998)

Badre, A.: The effects of cross cultural interface design orientation on World Wide Web user performance (2001)

Bochner, S.: Cross-cultural differences in the self concept a test of Hofstede's individualism/collectivism distinction. J. Cross Cult. Psychol. 25(2), 273–283 (1994)

Callahan, E.: Cultural similarities and differences in the design of university web sites. J. Comput. Mediated Commun. 11(1), 239–273 (2005)

Card, S.K., Robertson, G.G., York, W.: The WebBook and the Web Forager: an information workspace for the World-Wide Web. Paper presented at the Proceedings of the SIGCHI Conference on Human Factors in Computing Systems (1996)

Dorfman, P.W., Howell, J.P.: Dimensions of national culture and effective leadership patterns: Hofstede revisited. Adv. Int. Comp. Manag. Res. Annu. 3, 127–149 (1988)

Dormann, C., Chisalita, C.: Cultural values in web site design. Paper presented at the Proceedings of the 11th European Conference on Cognitive Ergonomics, ECCE11 (2002)

Fernandez, D.R., Carlson, D.S., Stepina, L.P., Nicholson, J.D.: Hofstede's country classification 25 years later. J. Soc. Psychol. 137(1), 43–54 (1997)

Fukuyama, F.: Social capital and the global economy: a redrawn map of the world. Foreign Aff. 74(5), 89–103 (1995)

Hall, E.T., Hall, MR.: Hidden Differences: Doing Business with the Japanese. Doubleday, New York (1987)

Hofstede, G.: Culture and organizations. Int. Stud. Manag. Organ. 10(4), 15–41 (1980a)

Hofstede, G.: Motivation, leadership, and organization: do American theories apply abroad? Organ. Dyn. 9(1), 42–63 (1980b)

Hofstede, G.: Culture's Consequences: International Differences in Work-Related Values, vol. 5. Sage, Newbury Park (1984)

Hofstede, G.: Cultures and Organisations-Software of the Mind: Intercultural Cooperation and Its Importance for Survival. McGraw-Hill, London (1991)

Huo, Y.P., Randall, D.M.: Exploring subcultural differences in Hofstede's value survey: the case of the Chinese. Asia Pac. J. Manag. **8**(2), 159–173 (1991)

Jain, S.C.: Standardization of international marketing strategy: some research hypotheses. J. Mark. **53**, 70–79 (1989)

Keller, K.L., Parameswaran, M., Jacob, I.: Strategic Brand Management: Building, Measuring, and Managing Brand Equity. Pearson Education India, Delhi (2011)

Lessem, R., Neubauer, F.-F.: European Management Systems: Towards Unity out of Cultural Diversity. McGraw-Hill, London (1994)

Lewis, R.D.: Finland: Cultural Lone Wolf: Consequences in International Business. Transcreen Publications, Winchester (1992)

Luna, D., Peracchio, L.A., de Juan, M.D.: Cross-cultural and cognitive aspects of web site navigation. J. Acad. Mark. Sci. **30**(4), 397–410 (2002)

Marcus, A., Gould, E.W.: Crosscurrents: cultural dimensions and global Web user-interface design. Interactions **7**(4), 32–46 (2000)

Miglani, J.: Forrester Research World Online Population Forecast, 2012 to 2017 (Global). Forrester Research, Cambridge (2012)

Mueller, B.: Reflections of culture-an analysis of Japanese and American advertising appeals. J. Advertising Res. **27**(3), 51–59 (1987)

Nassar, M., Abdou, S.H.: Brand-building website design for independent hotels: a replicated model (2013)

Pollay, R.W.: Measuring the cultural values manifest in advertising. Curr. Issues Res. Advertising **6**(1), 71–92 (1983)

Robbins, S.S., Stylianou, A.C.: A study of cultural differences in global corporate web sites. J. Comput. Inf. Syst. **42**(2), 3–9 (2002)

Søndergaard, M.: Research note: Hofstede's consequences: a study of reviews, citations and replications. Organ. Stud. **15**(3), 447–456 (1994)

Sia, C.L., Lim, K.H., Leung, K., Lee, M.K., Huang, W.W., Benbasat, I.: Web strategies to promote internet shopping: is cultural-customization needed? MIS Q. **33**, 491–512 (2009)

Simon, S.J.: The impact of culture and gender on web sites: an empirical study. ACM SIGMIS Database **32**(1), 18–37 (2000)

Singh, N., Boughton, P.D.: Measuring website globalization: a cross-sectional country and industry level analysis. J. Website Promot. **1**(3), 3–20 (2005)

Singh, N., Fassott, G., Chao, M.C., Hoffmann, J.A.: Understanding international web site usage: a cross-national study of German, Brazilian, and Taiwanese online consumers. Int. Mark. Rev. **23**(1), 83–97 (2006)

Singh, N., Kumar, V., Baack, D.: Adaptation of cultural content: evidence from B2C e-commerce firms. Eur. J. Mark. **39**(1/2), 71–86 (2005)

Singh, N., Zhao, H., Hu, X.: Cultural adaptation on the web: a study of American companies' domestic and Chinese websites. J. Glob. Inf. Manag. (JGIM) **11**(3), 63–80 (2003)

Tixier, M.: Globalization and localization of contents: evolution of major internet sites across sectors of industry. Thunderbird Int. Bus. Rev. **47**(1), 15–48 (2005)

Tricker, R.I.: Information resource management—a cross-cultural perspective. Inf. Manag. **15**(1), 37–46 (1988)

Trompenaars, F., Hampden-Turner, C.: L'entreprise multiculturelle. Maxima-L. du Mesnil, Paris (1994)

Tsikriktsis, N.: Does culture influence web site quality expectations? an empirical study. J. Serv. Res. **5**(2), 101–112 (2002)

A Genetic Algorithm Based Model for Chinese Phishing E-commerce Websites Detection

Zhijun Yan[1(✉)], Su Liu[1], Tianmei Wang[2], Baowen Sun[2],
Hansi Jiang[1], and Hangzhou Yang[1]

[1] School of Management and Economics, Beijing Institute of Technology, Beijing, China
{yanzhijun,2120141523,2120111706,hangzhou}@bit.edu.cn
[2] School of Information, Central University of Finance and Economics, Beijing, China
{wangtianmei,sunbaowen}@cufe.edu.cn

Abstract. We propose a new Chinese phishing e-commerce websites detection model which integrates the URL features and web features of websites. Some unique features of Chinese e-Commerce websites are included and Sequential Minimal Optimization (SMO) algorithm is applied to identify the phishing e-commerce websites. At the same time, we adopt the genetic algorithm (GA) to optimize the detection model. The evaluation results show that the performance of SMO algorithm is better than the baseline model and GA improves the detection accuracy significantly.

Keywords: Chinese phishing website detection · E-commerce · Sequential minimal optimization · Genetic algorithm

1 Introduction

With the rapid development of Internet, e-commerce has gradually become an essential part of people's life. In 2013, the market transactions of China's online shopping exceeded 1.8 trillion RMB and annual growth rate was 39.4 % [1]. However, online shopping also results in a series of security problems, such as phishing attack. Phishing websites are usually spread by emails that look like coming from legitimate sources, and lure users to visit fraudulent websites through disguised URL. When the users disclose password and other account information in these phishing websites, their money will be transferred or stolen [2]. Between July 2011 and June 2012, 60 million Chinese online users became victims of phishing sites, and the cumulative loss was more than 30 billion RMB [3]. Therefore, it is important to develop an effective method to detect phishing websites and minimize consumers' financial loss.

Detecting phishing e-commerce websites is a challenging task. Phishing websites usually present professional webpages and provide similar sophisticated shopping process with real counterparts, making users difficult to distinguish real websites from fake ones [4]. Aiming to improve the accuracy of Chinese e-Commerce phishing websites detection, this paper proposes a new integrative approach by incorporating the unique features in Chinese e-commerce websites and applying the SMO and genetic algorithm to classify e-commerce phishing websites. Specifically, the proposed method defines the classification

© Springer International Publishing Switzerland 2016
F.F.-H. Nah and C.-H. Tan (Eds.): HCIBGO 2016, Part I, LNCS 9751, pp. 270–279, 2016.
DOI: 10.1007/978-3-319-39396-4_25

features from the view of URL features and web features, then the websites can be classified by the SMO algorithm, which is enhanced by the genetic algorithm. The proposed model neither needs expertise knowledge nor whitelist or blacklist, avoiding the maintenance work and increasing the reliability of classification system.

The rest of this paper is organized as follows. In Sect. 2, related works on the detection of phishing websites are introduced. Then, we propose a new Chinese e-commerce phishing websites detection model based on SMO and genetic algorithm. In Sect. 4, the experiment results are presented. Finally, we conclude our work.

2 Related Research

Existing phishing detection method can be roughly divided into four categories: URL blacklist based method, the visual similarity based method, the URL and text feature based method and the third-party search engine based method. We discuss the main result of these four types of research in the rest of this section.

URL blacklist based method is mainly based on a list of known phishing sites to identify phishing sites [5]. Some agencies or websites (such as PhishTank.com, Escrow-Fraud.com) maintains a blacklist, a collection of phishing sites that reported by Internet users around the world. If the URL of a target website is in the blacklist, it will be identified as a phishing site and blocked by application software. However, it is only used to prevent users from identified phishing sites and cannot detect new phishing sites. And you need to update the list constantly, which greatly increases the maintenance workload [6].

The visual similarity based method converts the detection of phishing sites to an image matching problem [7–9]. This kind of method assesses different website parts' similarity between the target website and the authentic website. If the similarity is higher the threshold value, the target website will be identified as phishing website. The visual similarity based method should divide the target website into different images, its detection performance lies in the development of web segmentation and image comparison algorithm.

URL and text feature based method identifies phishing sites according to the characteristics of URL and content characteristics of the target website [10–12]. By analyzing the sensitive characteristics of URL and text feature, it can distinguish the phishing website from the real website. The URL and text feature based method is the most common detection methods, but most of the existing detection models are generic method and do not include any context-related characteristics, which cannot have the best performance in specific domains.

The last kind of detection method is to search target URL information in third-party search engine, and then uses the collected information to make judgments [13, 14]. By comparing the search results with top and second level domain name of the target URL, it can identify the phishing websites. The big challenge faced by this method is that phishing site designer can optimize the search result of phishing sites, which makes this method invalid.

In summary, the current phishing website detection methods make great effort to detect phishing e-commerce websites using generic classification model, but they have various weakness. At the same time, as the fast growth of e-commerce, lots of small and medium e-commerce companies emerge in China. Some of them vanish soon because of the highly competitive e-commerce environment. That also makes it infeasible to apply the previous methods to recognize and block phishing websites.

3 A Detection Model of Chinese Phishing E-commerce Websites

The proposed model incorporates the unique features of Chinese e-commerce websites, which are defined from the view of URL features and web features. Based on the defined feature vector, the SMO algorithm and genetic algorithm are applied to detect the phishing websites effectively. Different with the existing method, the proposed method does not rely on prior knowledge of real authentic websites, fits the e-commerce context of China, and has better classification accuracy.

3.1 The Phishing Website Feature Vector

By combining the prior website features used in literatures and new unique features of Chinese e-commerce websites, this study defines a feature vector for Chinese phishing e-commerce websites detection, which is divided into two parts: URL features and web features [15].

URL Features. URL features refer to a number of basic information extracted from the URL of a target website, which include the following sections:

IP-based URL: A phishing website URL usually uses IP address rather than a domain name, which can hide their real identification. For example, a phishing website may use http://121.73.1.108 to replace the URL of the official homepage of Jingdong.com, one of the largest B2C websites in China.
Presence of symbol '@': In the URL, the contents before the symbol '@' are the username and password for identity validation, and the content behind this symbol is the real address.
Presence of UNICODE characters: Phishing websites usually use UNICODE in their URL.
Number of dots ('.'): We can determine phishing sites by detecting whether the URL contains many '.' symbol.
Number of domain suffixes: The URL of a phishing website may contain many domain suffixes, such as.com,.cn,.org or other common Chinese domain name suffixes. For example, http://www.z.cn.1z.com.cn is a typical phishing site URL.
Age of domain name: The closer the date that a domain name was registered, the higher the possibility that it is a phishing website.
Expiration time of domain name: If the remaining valid date of a domain name is very short, it is likely to be a phishing website.

Consistence between DNS (Domain Name System) server address of domain name and URL: If the DNS server addresses of the domain name and URL are inconsistent, there may be a phishing site.

Registration status: By searching the MIIT website, we can find out whether the domain name of the target website is registered.

Registration subject: The website can be registered in MIIT by an individual or an enterprise. Considering the strict regulations on enterprise in China, the website registered by an individual has the higher probability to be a phishing one.

Registration site name: We can check whether the registered site name and actual site pointed by the URL are consistent.

WEB Features. Web features are obtained from website's source code through a web crawler. It includes the following sections:

Valid ICP (Internet Content Provider) certificate number: Real e-commerce websites will present ICP number at the bottom of the webpage, which is a unique identification issued by MIIT.

Number of void (null) links: Normally, the phishing website is likely to have more void links compared with authentic websites.

Number of out links: A phishing website tends to have more out links.

Valid e-commerce certificate information: In china, many authentic e-commerce websites receive certificates from industrial associations. They may post images of e-commerce certificates at the bottom of its website. Consumers can browse the detailed certificate information in industrial associations through these images.

3.2 Detection Algorithm

This study uses the machine learning algorithm SMO to detect Chinese phishing websites. SMO method is a simple algorithm [16]. It can quickly solve the Support Vector Machine (SVM) quadratic programming problems [17, 18]. For a binary classification problem with a dataset $(x_1, y_1), ..., (x_n, y_n)$, where x_i is an input vector and y_i is a binary class label, a soft-margin support vector machine can be trained by solving a quadratic programming problem described as follows:

$$\max_{\alpha} \sum_{i=1}^{n} \alpha_i - \frac{1}{2} \sum_{i=1}^{n} \sum_{j=1}^{n} y_i y_j K(x_i, x_j) \alpha_i \alpha_j$$

$$\text{subject to:} 0 \leq \alpha_i \leq C, \text{for } i = 1, 2, ..., n, \sum_{i=1}^{n} y_i \alpha_i = 0$$

(1)

where C is an SVM hyperparameter (called penalty parameter) and $K(x_i, x_j)$ is the kernel function, both provided by the user; variables α_i and α_j are Lagrange multipliers. This optimization problem will be decomposed by SMO into a series of smallest possible sub-problems, and then solves them successively. Compared with other algorithms, the SMO method selects and solves a minimum optimization problem in each step. The major advantage of SMO approach is that the entire quadratic programming problem is broken into many small problems which completely avoided using the iterative algorithm. At the same time, its implementation doesn't require huge storage.

3.3 Model Parameter Optimization

Different kernel functions of SMO algorithm have a large impact on the classification accuracy [19]. The kernel function parameter r mainly affects the complexity degree of the sample's distribution in high-dimensional feature space, and the penalty parameter C is used to determine the level of confidence interval and experimental risk in a given feature space, and affect the SMO generalization capability.

In order to get the best algorithm performance, it is of vital importance to determine the appropriate combination of parameters for SMO algorithm. Genetic algorithm provides a general framework for solving complex system optimization problems. Based on the fitness function and genetic operators, the algorithm has the ability to reach the global optimization [20]. Prior literature showed that genetic algorithm has a good performance in parameters optimization [21]. However, it is rarely applied in phishing website detection. In this study, we used it to optimize the SMO parameters and identify phishing website more efficiently.

Chromosome Design. The first step of genetic algorithm is to design individual gene and its coding scheme. SMO algorithm is mainly related to three parameters: kernel function, kernel parameter r and penalty parameter C. In order to simplify the optimization and computation process, the chromosome is designed to be 31 genes. The first gene a1 represents the kernel function. Two widely adopted kernel functions are considered: the value 0 is for polynomial kernel function, the value 1 is for Gaussian kernel function. The penalty parameter C is represented by 15 genes, from a2 to a16, which describes that the range of penalty parameter C is from 0 to 327.68. Moreover, the kernel parameter r is described by 15 genes, from a17 to a31.

Fitness Function. The fitness function is objective function of the parameter optimization process. It is used to evaluate individuals' performance (fitness) in the search space. In this study, genetic algorithm is adopted to optimize the SMO parameters and provide a high degree of overall classification accuracy. Thus the overall accuracy of the classification model is defined as the fitness function.

Genetic Operators Design. The genetic algorithm has three basic operations: selection, crossover and mutation [22]. Selection makes sure that only some chromosomes of the population will be included in next generation. As the most common method, roulette wheel selection is used in this study. In roulette wheel method, the probability of an individual is included in the next generation is equal to the ratio of the fitness value of the individual and the entire population.

The crossover operation is conducted on the new population to improve the fitness of new population. It exchanges the gene at the same position on two different individuals (chromosomes), resulting in two new individuals. The single-point crossover method is applied, i.e., choosing an intersection point randomly and interchange the genes before and after the intersection. The default crossover rate is set as 0.75.

The mutation operator is helpful for finding the global optimal solution. It modifies the value of a random bit in the chromosome and improves the performance of the population resulting from crossover operation. In this study, the random selected relevant bits should be mutated through change of every 0 bits to 1, and every 1 bits to 0. The default mutation rate is set as 0.2.

Parameter Optimization Process. At first, the initial population is randomly generated, which has 10 individuals. Then the SMO classification model is invoked and the fitness value of each individual is calculated. If the fitness value is low than 99 % and the iteration number doesn't reach 10,000 times, the selection, crossover and mutation operators will be applied in sequence. Thus the next generation is derived and SMO classification model will be called again. Iterate the above steps until the optimal parameters are gotten or the upper iteration time is reached.

4 Evaluation

4.1 Data Set

We have conducted an empirical evaluation of the proposed method by using the authentic and phishing e-commerce websites registered in third-party service platforms. Phishing e-commerce sites are from the online transaction security center (http://www.315online.com.cn) and Security Alliance (http://www.anquan.org), which validated and registered the phishing e-commerce websites complained by online consumers. Authentic e-commerce sites are collected from the online transaction security center. In order to optimize the training effect, the number of authentic and phishing websites are nearly same. Specifically, there are 1462 authentic e-commerce sites and 1416 phishing e-commerce sites.

A popular tool, called WebZIP, is used to download the source code of the collected e-commerce websites. Then the feature vector is extracted from the source code of online websites. We also used Weka (Waikato Environment for Knowledge Analysis), a widely adopted data mining tool, to train the proposed models.

4.2 Evaluation Metric

We use precision (P), recall (R), F-measure (F) and overall accuracy (O) as metrics to assess the effectiveness of the proposed detection model [23]. Specifically, precision is the percentage of correct detections. Recall measures the proportion of actual positives in the population being tested. The F-measure is a harmonic average of precision and recall, which represents the overall performance of precision and recall. The overall accuracy evaluates the overall detection precision of authentic sites and phishing sites. Higher values of P, R, F and O indicate better performance.

We use N_{pp}, N_{ap}, N_{pa}, and N_{aa} to denote the number of phishing sites detected as phishing sites, the number of authentic site detected as phishing sites, the number of phishing sites detected as authentic sites and the number of authentic sites detected as authentic sites respectively.

The detection accuracy of the authentic sites P_1 and phishing sites P_2 are given as follows:

$$P_1 = \frac{N_{aa}}{N_{pa} + N_{aa}}, \quad P_2 = \frac{N_{pp}}{N_{pp} + N_{ap}} \qquad (2)$$

The detection recall of the authentic sites R_1 and phishing sites R_2 are given as follows:

$$R_1 = \frac{N_{aa}}{N_{ap} + N_{aa}}, \quad R_2 = \frac{N_{pp}}{N_{pp} + N_{pa}} \qquad (3)$$

The F-measure of authentic sites F_r and phishing sites F_p are given as follows:

$$F_r = \frac{2 * P_1 * R_1}{P_1 + R_1}, \quad F_p = \frac{2 * P_2 * R_2}{P_2 + R_2} \qquad (4)$$

Meanwhile, the overall detection accuracy O is defined as follows:

$$O = \frac{N_{pp} + N_{aa}}{N_{pp} + N_{ap} + N_{pa} + N_{aa}} \qquad (5)$$

4.3 Experiment Design

To evaluate the effectiveness of the proposed method, the Abbasi et al.'s [6] phishing website detection model is chosen as the baseline method. It also consists of many URL and web content features for phishing website detection. Based on these features, the method has a very high accuracy for phishing website detection. However, it doesn't include any domain-specific features, and we can examine whether the incorporation of domain-specific features improves the detection performance. At the same time, we also want to assess the detection performance of the inclusion of genetic algorithm. Thus the experiment consists of two parts. The first experiment is performance comparison between the SMO classification model and Abbasi model, and the second experiment explores the optimization effect of genetic algorithm.

In the first experiment, the collected websites is randomly divided into a training data set and a testing data set. 1023 authentic websites and 991 phishing websites are included in the training data set, while the testing data set consists of 439 authentic websites and 425 phishing websites. The detection precision, recall and F-measure can be calculated for the baseline model and the proposed model without parameter optimization (SMO model).

In the second experiment, we first generated the 10 initial individual genes. Then the individual chromosome was decoded as the value of classification model parameters. Using K cross-validation method, the fitness value of each chromosome is calculated. Iterate the above steps until the best parameters are derived. Based on the derived optimal SMO parameters, the proposed model with parameter optimization (SMO-GA model) and baseline model are trained by a training data set. Then the detection precision, recall and F-measure are calculated for the test data set.

4.4 Data Analysis and Results

At first, we conducted a pair-wise T-test to compare the precision, recall, and F-measures of the SMO model against the baseline model (Table 1). The results indicate that the SMO model significantly outperforms the baseline model across all three performance metrics. These results also illustrate that the proposed context-related feature set results in the higher overall precision in detecting Chinese phishing e-commerce websites than the generic feature sets adopted in the baseline model.

Table 1. The precision (%) comparison of SMO model and Abbasi model

Metrics		SMO model		Abbasi model		MD (M1-M2)
		Mean (M1)	SD	Mean (M2)	SD	
Phishing site	Precision	93.7	0.9	92.0	0.9	1.7**
	Recall	94.5	0.9	91.0	1.1	3.5**
	F1	94.1	0.4	91.5	0.5	2.6**
Authentic site	Precision	94.6	0.8	91.4	0.9	3.2**
	Recall	93.8	0.1	92.3	0.9	1.5**
	F1	94.2	0.5	91.8	0.5	2.4**
The overall accuracy (O)		94.1	0.4	91.7	0.5	2.4**

SD: Standard Deviation, MD: Mean Difference.
* $p < 0.05$.
** $p < 0.01$.

In order to check whether the genetic algorithm significantly improves the classification accuracy, we conducted a pair-wise T-test to compare the detection performance with and without parameters optimization based on the genetic algorithm. The results shown in Table 2 indicate that the genetic algorithm based parameters optimization significantly improve the performance of authentic websites and phishing websites classification across all three metrics.

Table 2. The precision (%) comparison of SMO model and SMO-GA model

Metrics		SMO model		SMO-GA model		MD (M1-M2)
		Mean (M1)	SD	Mean (M2)	SD	
Phishing site	Precision	93.7	0.9	96.6	0.9	−2.9**
	Recall	94.5	0.9	96.5	0.1	−2.0**
	F1	94.1	0.4	96.5	0.5	−2.4**
Authentic site	Precision	94.6	0.8	96.6	0.1	−2.0**
	Recall	93.8	0.1	96.7	0.9	−2.9**
	F1	94.2	0.5	96.6	0.4	−2.4**
The overall accuracy(O)		94.1	0.4	96.6	0.4	−2.5**

SD: Standard Deviation, MD: Mean Difference.
* $p < 0.05$.
** $p < 0.01$.

5   Conclusion

Developing effective methods for Chinese phishing e-Commerce websites detection has become an urgent task for e-commerce development. However, existing models mainly focus on generic websites classification, which may not be a wonderful solution to detect Chinese phishing e-Commerce websites because they do not consider the specific context-related features in China and face the performance problem. Targeting at detecting Chinese phishing e-commerce websites efficiently, this research incorporates context-related features into the phishing website detection model and adopts the genetic algorithm to determine the optimal classification model parameters. The experiment results show that the context-related features and the parameters optimization method significantly improve the accuracy of Chinese phishing e-commerce websites detection.

There are several limitations of this study. First, we only focus on Chinese phishing e-commerce websites detection. The proposed method needs to be validated in other domains in the future. Second, this study only adopts the genetic algorithm as the parameters optimization method. Considering there are many other artificial intelligence algorithms, it might be interesting to explore the impact of other main artificial intelligence algorithms on parameters optimization.

Acknowledgments. This research is supported by the National Natural Science Foundation of China (Grant No. 71272057, 71572013) and the National Social Science Fund of China (Grant No. 14AZD045).

References

1. iResearch. Annual report of China's E-Commerce (2014). http://report.iresearch.cn/2153.html. Accessed 2014
2. Herzberg, A., Jbara, A.: Security and identification indicators for browsers against spoofing and phishing attacks. ACM Trans. Internet Technol. **8**(4), 36 (2008)
3. APAC. Annual report of Anti-Phishing Alliance of China (2012). http://www.apac.org.cn/gzdt/qwfb/201408/P020140826493067614020.pdf. Accessed 2012
4. Wu, M., Miller, R.C., Garfinkel, S.L.: Do security toolbars actually prevent phishing attacks? In: Proceedings of the 2006 Conference on Human Factors in Computing Systems (CHI 2006), Montréal, Québec, Canada (2006)
5. Ma, J., et al.: Learning to detect malicious URLs. ACM Trans. Intell. Syst. Technol. **2**(3), 24 (2011)
6. Abbasi, A., et al.: Detecting fake websites: the contribution of statistical learning theory. MIS Q. **34**(3), 435–461 (2010)
7. Fu, A.Y., Wenyin, L., Deng, X.T.: Detecting phishing web pages with visual similarity assessment based on Earth Mover's Distance (EMD). IEEE Trans. Dependable Secure Comput. **3**(4), 301–311 (2006)
8. Zhang, H.J., et al.: Textual and visual content-based anti-phishing: a Bayesian approach. IEEE Trans. Neural Netw. **22**(10), 1532–1546 (2011)
9. Mao, J., et al.: BaitAlarm: detecting phishing sites using similarity in fundamental visual features. In: 2013 5th International Conference on Intelligent Networking and Collaborative Systems (INCoS). IEEE (2013)

10. Huang, H., Qian, L., Wang, Y.: A SVM-based technique to detect phishing URLs. Inf. Technol. J. **11**(7), 921–925 (2012)
11. Gowtham, R., Krishnamurthi, I.: A comprehensive and efficacious architecture for detecting phishing webpages. Comput. Secur. **40**, 23–37 (2014)
12. Bartoli, A., Davanzo, G., Medvet, E.: A framework for large-scale detection of web site defacements. ACM Trans. Internet Technol. **10**(3), 37 (2010)
13. Akiyama, M., Yagi, T., Hariu, T.: Improved blacklisting: inspecting the structural neighborhood of malicious URLs. IT Prof. **15**(4), 50–56 (2013)
14. Xiang, G., et al.: CANTINA+: a feature-rich machine learning framework for detecting phishing web sites. ACM Trans. Inf. Syst. Secur. **14**(2), 21 (2011)
15. Zhang, D., et al.: A domain-feature enhanced classification model for the detection of Chinese phishing e-Business websites. Inf. Manag. **51**(7), 845–853 (2014)
16. Platt, J.: Sequential minimal optimization: a fast algorithm for training support vector machines. IEEE Trans. Neural Netw. **17**(4), 1039–1049 (1998)
17. Chang, C.-C., Lin, C.-J.: LIBSVM: a library for support vector machines. ACM Trans. Intell. Syst. Technol. **2**(3), 27–38 (2011)
18. Zanni, L., Serafini, T., Zanghirati, G.: Parallel software for training large scale support vector machines on multiprocessor systems. J. Mach. Learn. Res. **7**(3), 1467–1492 (2006)
19. Wang, M., Wang, W.: Approach for kernel selection from SVM ensemble. Comput. Eng. Appl. **45**(27), 31–33 (2009)
20. Kucukkoc, I., Karaoglan, A.D., Yaman, R.: Using response surface design to determine the optimal parameters of genetic algorithm and a case study. Int. J. Prod. Res. **51**(17), 5039–5054 (2013)
21. Rahman, M.A., Islam, M.Z.: A hybrid clustering technique combining a novel genetic algorithm with K-Means. Knowl.-Based Syst. **71**, 345–365 (2014)
22. Ilhan, I., Tezel, G.: A genetic algorithm-support vector machine method with parameter optimization for selecting the tag SNPs. J. Biomed. Inform. **46**(2), 328–340 (2013)
23. Khonji, M., Iraqi, Y., Jones, A.: Phishing detection: a literature survey. IEEE Commun. Surv. Tutor. **15**(4), 2091–2121 (2013)

Business Analytics and Visualization

Using Digital Infrastructures to Conceptualize Sensing and Responding in Human-Computer Interaction

Florian Allwein[1(✉)] and Sue Hessey[2]

[1] London School of Economics and Political Science, London, UK
f.o.allwein@lse.ac.uk
[2] BT Plc, Ipswich, UK
sue.hessey@bt.com

Abstract. This paper extends existing Information Systems perspectives towards Human-Computer Interaction (HCI) to consider HCI within Digital Infrastructures (DI) – heterogeneous and evolving systems comprising both IT and its design and user communities. Using the example of a new interface that has significantly decreased call handling times for sales and support agents (knowledge workers within a contact center), the paper finds that DI create an amount of flexibility that enables employees to shape tools over time. It argues that DI are a useful concept for HCI, as they stress the socio-technical and evolving nature of IT artefacts.

Keywords: Digital infrastructures · Information Systems · Call centers

1 Introduction

The field of Information Systems (IS) research is focused on "questions regarding the development, use and implications of information and communication technologies in organizations" [1]. It has strong roots in the social sciences and thus looks at how IT, people and organizations interact with and shape each other [e.g. 2–4]. Thus, there is a significant tradition of Human-Computer Interaction (HCI) research in the field [5–8]. Such research, however, faces the challenge to differentiate itself within the broader field of HCI research. This paper supports this effort as it takes up Benbasat's [5] suggestion "to treat technology as more than a static, objective, tool-like entity" (p. 19).

IS researchers are increasingly conceptualizing their objects of research as digital infrastructures (DI). Tilson et al. [9] define these as "shared, unbounded, heterogeneous, open, and evolving sociotechnical systems comprising an installed base of diverse information technology capabilities and their user, operations, and design communities" (p. 748 f.), arguing that they will play a "pivotal role (…) in shaping the future uses of IT" (p. 749). Such research, however, is often constrained to the areas where the concept originated. Thus, it may be beneficial to apply the concept of DI to research on HCI.

From a practical point of view, well designed interfaces and a good support of the existing workflow are key features for Information Systems (IS) in organizations. This paper reports on a wider research project with BT plc that is focused on how the company uses DI to increase its organizational agility – its "ability to sense relevant change and

F.F.-H. Nah and C.-H. Tan (Eds.): HCIBGO 2016, Part I, LNCS 9751, pp. 283–293, 2016.
DOI: 10.1007/978-3-319-39396-4_26

respond readily" [10]. It takes up the view of IS in organizations as DI as it looks at the way developers and users interact with a tool to better support sales agents in its call centers. The research question is: How do DI support sensing and responding for employees and customers? The paper finds that DI create an amount of flexibility that enables employees to shape tools over time. Furthermore, it argues that DI are a useful concept for HCI, as they stress the socio-technical and evolving nature of IT artefacts. Such a view extends existing IS perspectives towards HCI [5] to consider human-computer interaction within digital infrastructures. This contribution is necessary as today's knowledge workers increasingly rely upon complex arrays of different evolving technology within their work tasks [11], drawing upon these portfolios in sensing and responding to tasks.

2   Conceptualizing DI for HCI

This paper follows the tradition of socio-technical Information Systems (IS) research. This section will discuss relevant prior research from the field of HCI as well as HCI based research in the field of IS, before outlining new conceptualizations of IS deemed relevant for HCI research in IS.

2.1   HCI Literature Review

HCI literature often refers to the *experience* of enterprise users of IT systems, and how they are often fragmented across multiple devices, platforms, legacy systems and vendors, with humans themselves acting as the "glue" connecting these disjoint infor-mation systems [12]. As a result, it is observed that within large service organizations, IT support functions are increasingly turning to user-centered approaches as a means of improving user productivity, increasing business velocity and in general making enter-prise solutions more appealing to users [12]. In McCreary et al.'s previous paper [13], the opportunities of utilizing big data collected within the normal every-day practices within organizations is outlined as an input to user-centered approaches to developing enterprise IT, however it needs to be augmented by traditional UX methods (observa-tions, participatory design sessions, surveys etc.) to be meaningful. The term "Thick Data", meaning "ethnographic approaches that uncover the meaning behind Big Data visualization and analysis" [14] has been coined to attempt to discover the "stories" the big data is telling us. This is a difficult procedure, but the paper states that sociotechnical systems theory and macro ergonomics offer a way of connecting this disparate data and provide a theoretical model for understanding the holistic user experience, and to enable IT developers to understand how their "technology" impacts other elements of the users' world [13]. Its importance is again underlined by Wang [14] in her comment: "Thick Data is the best method for mapping unknown territory. When organizations want to know what they do not already know, they need Thick Data because it gives something that Big Data explicitly does not—inspiration. The act of collecting and analyzing stories produces insights."

Culen and Kriger [15] outline a rationale for using Design Thinking and HCI Design to shape conditions for long-term "health" of IT intensive organizations. They also underline the point that there is a necessity for organizational culture to be receptive to innovation and change, arguing that "HCID will not be lasting without the presence of supportive, and larger, top-down changes". This theme is reinforced by Aldarbesti et al. [16] commenting: "For a successful implementation, IS projects always require power realignments; understanding the impact of organizational culture, and a conducive environment within the organization."

Li [17] observes that the interfaces of large IT systems are hard to change due to the scale and legacy of the software, which can be traceable many years back. The implementation of such systems involves huge investment and takes a very long period of time – and it may be hard to enforce user adoption of new developments when old habits are ingrained in the users. To assist this, understanding of user emotions and hedonics play an important role in adopting and optimizing IT usage in workplace, and as such constitute an important consideration of the human agent's needs and motivations within the DI. Therefore improvement of the social and emotional perspective of the enterprise systems should improve employees' adoption rate of the information technology, leading to improved productivity [17]. Our case study demonstrates how user motivation, users' willingness to affect change and business objectives combined to create a new interface which is satisfying and effective to use, allowing more effective sensing of customer issues and appropriate and timely responses.

2.2   IS Research on HCI

Benbasat [5] discusses how IS researchers can make a significant contribution to the wider field of HCI. He argues that discussions at a low level of detail (response times, colors etc.) are best left to other HCI researchers, who are better prepared to contribute to these. IS research, on the other hand, "should be focusing on topics that reflect 'higher level' designs such as those that impact decision making, virtual groups, company-customer relationships and other matters that are in line with a management focus in MIS" (p. 17). Specifically with regards to interfaces, he argues researchers should "treat technology as more than a static, objective, tool-like entity" (p. 19), namely "as a social actor in communication" (ibid.). One example for such an approach in HCI is the paper by Al-Natour and Benbasat [18], who see IT artifacts as social actors whose characteristics are manifested within the context of interactions. Bloomfield and Vurdubakis [6] reflect on the way technology is recognized as such as users construct a boundary between the social and the technical. This boundary is by no means universal, but subject to sense-making practices among the users.

The question of how to conceptualize IS in organizations has also been discussed in the broader field of IS research [e.g. 19, 20]. This is partly due to the fact that employees tend to build portfolios of services they use, rather than relying on a few monolithic systems [11]. Consequently, the view of the monolithic system itself has been questioned. This paper argues that, as digitization has separated information from a fixed medium for storage and transfer, more flexible, modular IS are possible [20]. This increases generativity, "a system's capacity to produce unanticipated change through unfiltered contributions from broad and varied audiences" [21], as e.g. systems can communicate with each other via APIs.

Specifically, the concept of DI is increasingly used in IS research (e.g. Tilson et al.'s [9] paper has been quoted 113 times according to a recent database search). Yet such research is often constrained to the areas where the concept originated, e.g. mobile communication [22] or the iOS ecosystem [23] – despite Tilson et al.'s broad call for IS research that aims at a "better understanding of the ways in which infrastructural change shapes IT governance, IS development, and promotes new effects across all levels of analysis" (p. 758 ff.). As Yoo [24] points out, IS research in general needs "a more precise and nuanced understanding of the nature of digital technology that enables and constrains activities that produce generative innovations." (p. 231). This paper hopes to drive such an understanding by applying the concept of DI to the area of HCI. Thus, the IS at the center of the study will be seen as part of a heterogeneous, evolving sociotechnical system as per Tilson et al.'s definition of DI. The research question is: How do DI support sensing and responding for employees and customers?

Following the research question, the conceptual framework looks first at the DI involved in this case. As we have seen, Mathiassen and Sorensen [11] argue that IT in organizations should be seen through a service rather than a systems lens as users increasingly rely on "configurations of heterogeneous information processing capabilities" (p. 313). In order to conceptualize these portfolios of services from an IS perspective, this paper applies the concept of digital infrastructures. These are heterogeneous and evolving, i.e. they can be made up of a variety of different systems that are added and adapted over time and are often adapted according to ad-hoc needs. Consequently, it may not be possible to develop them according to a central plan. DI are also seen as sociotechnical systems. The systems consist of technology as well as the "user, operations, and design communities" who are a crucial part of the system, as they change it by engaging with it and adapting it over time.

3   Research Design

This paper reports on a case study conducted within BT, a telecommunications company in the UK, between 2014 and 2015 as part of a larger research project on organizational agility. Overall, 40 interviews and 10 observation sessions of BT employees were conducted. A small number of documents deemed relevant by interviewees was also considered – these included screenshots of relevant tools as well as some emails. The case study focused on some specific projects that seem to show successful changes to BT's agility. This paper looks at one of these projects, the development and use of SalesTool (a pseudonym) in call centers. Interviews were typically 45 min to 1 h in length. Besides this, 10 employees in the call centers were observed at their workplaces, using a variety of tools. All interviews and notes from observation sessions were transcribed and analyzed using ATLAS.ti. Data was then analyzed using thematic analysis [25], following a hybrid approach of theory-driven and data-driven codes.

3.1   Case Study

The case study concentrates on the development of DI as an evolution of user needs, business needs and IS developments, concentrating on the development of a CRM tool to enhance its usability and effectiveness. Previously, agents working in the company's call centers were using a CRM system for all the information processing related to their job. The need for a better solution became apparent as the operation of the previous CRM system used to manage orders caused a number of issues, for example:

"The trouble is that all of the data is locked into the [system] database, which is unwieldy and difficult [to access]" (CIO team – Product consultant).

"So once you've done with that, you then go into orders and start building the order. But with [this system], you almost manually have to [do] all of these little bits, you have to put [them] on. You have to go into this catalogue[1] first and then you would search for the broadband packages…. It's not very user friendly" (Sales Advisor).

At the same time, it was found that customers were able to submit orders through the company's web portal faster than agents did through the CRM system:

"We were finding an order journey [online] was taking 4 min, and on [the CRM system] it was taking double – 8, 9 min. We were like "why are we doing this?" It does not make sense that we've got one journey for customers and one for agents." (Online capability specialist)

A new tool (here called SalesTool) was therefore developed for agents working in the call centers. The idea came from one of the sales agents:

"I think it was the Chief Executive …. So, not small fry, really big fry… He used to do these roadshows and get feedback from agents, and one of the feedbacks in one of his sessions was "if bt.com is easy enough for our customers, why don't we just use that for agents?" So I think that's where the idea came from… I think it came from the agent feedback." (Online capability specialist)

This was planned as an additional layer on top of the existing tool, but with a simpler, more intuitive interface:

"Effectively, it's a layer or platform that sits before [CRM system]. [SalesTool] and [the public web portal] are based on the same off-the-shelf framework, and we tailor [SalesTool] slightly more to suit some of the agent activities and things that they do, so the agent can do a little bit more in [SalesTool] than the customer can do with [the web portal]." (Online capability specialist)

Thus, SalesTool was created as an added layer on top of the existing system. While it accesses the same database, it uses the interface from the company's public web portal, modified and extended to match agents' needs.

Specifically, agents are supported with a linear workflow following the order journey customers go through during a typical call. Throughout the process, SalesTool gives them exactly the information they need, e.g. relevant customer data, or reminders of

---

[1] There are categories to choose from (e.g. broadband), and then lists of items within these categories. As commented by the agent observed, there were more than 11 pages of results in the "broadband" category (each with a number of items on it), although only a handful of items are actually used. Agents also commented that it was unclear how the results are sorted.

what they have to tell customers. This includes legal disclaimers that agents must include. This is illustrated in the screenshot of the system (Fig. 1).

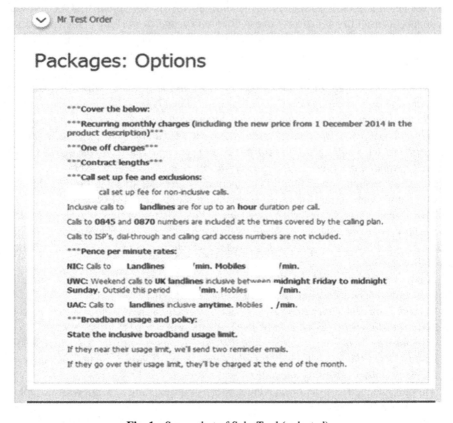

Fig. 1. Screenshot of SalesTool (redacted)

The Benefits of SalesTool. SalesTool led to a number of expected and unexpected improvements, which were observed post-implementation, for example:

- Agent Training time was reduced from 3 months to 10 days.
- Call Handling time was reduced by 20 % (target was 50 %).
- Sales conversion rate increased 6 % (not anticipated).
- Sales attachment rate increased 6 % (not anticipated) (source, BT Manager via email).

Interviewees also commented on significant increases in speed when working with the new tool:

Q: *Would you say the experiences with [SalesTool] are good in general?*

A: *Yeah, they're very good. Good system, but it's a good way of making a terrible system acceptable.*

Q: *I heard it saves dramatic amounts of time.*

A: Yeah. I would suggest it saves an average maybe 400 s CHT [call handling time] per call. An old order to place line, broadband, TV would take about 45 min. "

These days, you're talking 20, half an hour tops. Half the time for those ones. " (Sales center manager)

The main difference that was commented on by agents is that the tool made their work a lot easier:

"I've gone through training with new entrants quite a few times now, and they just find it so much simpler, they're used to placing online orders in general, to shopping, things like that." (Sales center team leader)

In particular, the tool follows the script of a normal sales call and shows the exact information needed at each stage:

"If you look at [SalesTool], everything is exactly where it should be said. You're talking about purchases for TV, it will tell them when you actually order that product, whereas on [previous system] it was just – you told them (according to what you thought best). " (Technical sales specialist)

Because of this simplicity, training time has also gone down significantly:

Q: So how long is the training now vs. in the old days?

A: Now, it's 3 weeks in classroom and 6 weeks of support on the phone. Previously, the training varied, so some advisors would come in just with a two day, really quick burst. Some advisors, it would take a year for them to be fully up to speed with [previous system]. (Sales manager)

Another consequence of the simplified work flow was that agents have more time to focus on the customer rather than on their tools:

"I remember having a conversation with some of the advisors when we first trained on [previous CRM system] – say hello to the customer, have the conversation, but then turn away from the computer, because it was that much information that you had to remember you had to do, you would forget about the conversation, whereas now, they can do both at once". (Sales center team leader)

As the system is an extension of the existing CRM system, there are still some conflicts over which tool to use at what time. This is especially true in teams that are working on more complex cases:

"So the amount of time that we still have to use [previous system] – when it first came out, we had a [previous system] "naughty list" – anyone who was using [previous system] was slapped on their hands. But now we realize that we do need to use it, so everyone is on the list! For Retentions [SalesTool] is fantastic, but [previous system] is still key. I don't know what the percentage is, but I would suggest it is probably 70:30 – if you're skilled in [previous system]. Problem is, not everyone is, so for them it's pretty much 100 % [SalesTool] or we transfer someone else. (Sales center manager).

4 Analysis

This section will apply the conceptual framework outlined above to the data of the case study in order to answer the research question, "How do DI support sensing and responding for employees and customers?" It evaluates the new system before looking at the role of DI.

Evaluation of the New System. The main difference between SalesTool and the previous CRM system it complements is the interface. While the old tool has a traditional database interface (see the description of the catalogue given above), SalesTool is based on the UI of the company's customer-facing web portal and thus has a much simpler interface with fewer options and a clear order in which interaction takes place.

Consequently, SalesTool is also much better at supporting the workflow of sales agents ("*everything is exactly where it should be said*", as one interviewee put it). It achieves the observed improvements in call handing time by building upon the existing workflow and supporting agents by giving them exactly the information they need, when they need it. In contrast, the previous CRM system did not support the workflow, but showed data the way it was stored in the system, so that agents had to jump between different tabs while entering data. They also had to keep track of what they did, e.g. remembering which of the legal disclaimers they had already read.

As we have seen, SalesTool led to a number of improvements, especially around reducing training and call handling times, as mentioned in the email quoted above and confirmed by interviewees. An additional bonus was that sales agents felt they had more time to focus on the customer rather than on their tools. Agents observed for the case study generally liked the tools, e.g. because it is simpler to use.

While SalesTool has improved work, there are still issues, especially around the question of how SalesTool should coexist with the previous CRM tool and when agents should use one over the other. Due to the modular nature of the tool (since it is an added interface over the existing CRM), there is also the question how the tool should be further developed in the future, i.e. whether an entirely new system would be desirable or feasible at some point (Technical sales specialist).

Digital Infrastuctures. Looking at this case from a Digital Infrastructures perspective, we can identify an infrastructure that consists of:

- The previous CRM system. This has evolved to be the main tool used for processing orders, even though this was not the intended purpose of the tool.
- SalesTool as a later modification of the DI to facilitate the agents' workflow.
- Sales agents in the call centers using the tools and e.g. negotiating which tool to use for which purpose.
- Data (e.g. from real time analytics) supporting agents in their work, e.g. by displaying a customer's history when they call.

This infrastructure clearly shows the qualities of being heterogeneous and evolving as described by Tilson et al. [9]: Tilson et al. mention "an installed base" (p. 748) of IT capabilities that DI build upon. This is evident in this case, as SalesTool was built as an extension to the existing CRM system. The development of SalesTool started because one user had the idea to create it as a simplified interface. Thus, we see how users in a DI can affect its design. Furthermore, the interface of the *old* DI was the foundation for the design of the new, as the system had to process the same data as in the previous system. Lastly, the new interface also drew on the DI of the company web portal. In this case, the company website can be seen as a kind of installed base for the design of the new interface. This change was achievable because of new technology – website systems using technologies like HTML and browsers – which the previous CRM application preceded. These systems were able to take the existing data out of its context and present it in a context that is more familiar to the users in the call centers, but that also made it possible to support their workflow more directly, by displaying the right information at the right time.

Thus we see how the users have played a key role in the design of this system. It makes sense to see it as a DI, which, as we have seen consists of technology as well as the "user, operations, and design communities" [9]. Such a development as SalesTool may not have occurred if it had been planned as a centralized, monolithic system according to a design plan. As BT allowed for an element of adaptability (by encouraging employees to submit ideas), and as they used flexible technology to implement it (the existing database along with a new web interface), SalesTool could be developed on top of the extant CRM system and has led to the improvements described above.

Thus the answer to the question of how DI support sensing and responding for employees and customers is that they create an amount of flexibility that enables employees to shape tools over time. Moreover, conceptualizing IS as DI enables us to focus on such socio-technical processes, rather than seeing IT as static tools.

5 Discussion

This part of the paper summarizes the findings from the case study and relates them to the literature, as discussed above. With regards to the specific case discussed here, we have seen that the DI creates an amount of flexibility that enables employees to shape tools over time. The design of SalesTool is working well because of some good decisions that have been made, namely using the metaphor of the company's web portal, supporting the agents' workflow and allowing for the adaptation and evolution of an existing system.

This paper has limitations in that it only looks at one system in one organization. While it is hoped that the findings will be applicable beyond this case, further research using this concept would be beneficial for developing an understanding of the socio-technical, evolving nature of IT artefacts in organizations.

Applying the concept of DI to HCI research in IS has shown to be useful in this case, for two reasons: Firstly, it helps extend the use of the concept of DI into new areas not traditionally associated with it. As we have seen, areas like HCI in the context of a large company can be described as evolving DI. This paper hopes to encourage future research along similar lines. In addition, it strengthens the theoretical position of IS researchers on HCI, as the theory of DI is a powerful concept to be applied in future research.

References

1. Avgerou, C.: Information systems: what sort of science is it? Omega **28**, 567–579 (2000). doi:10.1016/S0305-0483(99)00072-9
2. Avgerou, C., Cornford, T.: Developing Information Systems: Concepts, Issues and Practice. Macmillan, London (1993)
3. Mumford, E.: The story of socio-technical design: reflections on its successes, failures and potential. Inf. Syst. J. **16**, 317–342 (2006). doi:10.1111/j.1365-2575.2006.00221.x
4. Walsham, G.: Interpreting Information Systems in Organizations. Wiley, Chichester (1993)
5. Benbasat, I.: HCI research: future challenges and directions. AIS Trans. Hum.-Comput. Interact. **2**, 16–21 (2010)
6. Bloomfield, B.P., Vurdubakis, T.: Boundary disputes: negotiating the boundary between the technical and the social in the development of IT systems. Inf. Technol. People **7**, 9–24 (1994). doi:10.1108/09593849410074007
7. Hasan, H.: Integrating IS and HCI using activity theory as a philosophical and theoretical basis. Australas J. Inf. Syst. **6**, 44–55 (1999)
8. Lyytinen, K.: HCI research Future directions that matter. AIS Trans. Hum.-Comput. Interact. **2**, 10–22 (2010)
9. Tilson, D., Lyytinen, K., Sorensen, C.: Digital infrastructures: the missing IS research agenda. Inf. Syst. Res. **21**, 748–759 (2010). doi:10.1287/isre.1100.0318
10. Overby, E., Bharadwaj, A., Sambamurthy, V.: Enterprise agility and the enabling role of information technology. Eur. J. Inf. Syst. **15**, 120–131 (2006). doi:10.1057/palgrave.ejis. 3000600
11. Mathiassen, L., Sorensen, C.: Towards a theory of organizational information services. J. Inf. Technol. **23**, 313–329 (2008). doi:10.1057/jit.2008.10
12. McCreary, F., Gomez, M., Schloss, D.: Infusing user experience into the organizational DNA of an enterprise IT shop. In: Fui-Hoon Nah, F., Tan, C.-H. (eds.) HCIB 2015. LNCS, vol. 9191, pp. 513–524. Springer, Heidelberg (2015)
13. McCreary, F., Gómez, M., Schloss, D., Ali, D.: Charting a new course for the workplace with an experience framework. In: Nah, F.F.-H. (ed.) HCIB 2014. LNCS, vol. 8527, pp. 68–79. Springer, Heidelberg (2014)
14. Wang, T.: Big data needs thick data. Ethnogr. Matters (2013). http://ethnographymatters.net/blog/2013/05/13/big-data-needs-thick-data/
15. Culén, A.L., Kriger, M.: Creating competitive advantage in IT-intensive organizations: a design thinking perspective. In: Nah, F.F.-H. (ed.) HCIB 2014. LNCS, vol. 8527, pp. 492–503. Springer, Heidelberg (2014)
16. Aldarbesti, H., Goutas, L., Sutanto, J.: A critical examination of the causes of failed IS implementation: a review of the literature on power and culture. In: Fui-Hoon Nah, F., Tan, C.-H. (eds.) HCIB 2015. LNCS, vol. 9191, pp. 667–678. Springer, Heidelberg (2015)
17. Li, H.: Enhancing User experience of enterprise systems for improved employee productivity: a frist stage of case study. In: Fui-Hoon Nah, F., Tan, C.-H. (eds.) HCIB 2015. LNCS, vol. 9191, pp. 493–500. Springer, Heidelberg (2015)
18. Al-Natour, S., Benbasat, I.: The Adoption and use of IT artifacts: a new interaction-centric model for the study of user-artifact relationships. J. Assoc. Inf. Syst. **10**, 661–685 (2009)
19. Grover, V., Lyytinen, K.: New state of play in information systems research: the push to the edges. MIS Q. **39**, 271–296 (2015)
20. Yoo, Y., Henfridsson, O., Lyytinen, K.: The new organizing logic of digital innovation: an agenda for information systems research. Inf. Syst. Res. **21**, 724–735 (2010). doi:10.1287/isre.1100.0322

21. Zittrain, J.: The Future of the Internet-And How to Stop It. Yale University Press, New Haven (2008)

22. Sørensen, C., de Reuver, M., Basole, R.C.: Mobile platforms and ecosystems. J Inf Technol **30**, 195–197 (2015). doi:10.1057/jit.2015.22

23. Eaton, B., Elaluf-Calderwood, S., Sørensen, C., Yoo, Y.: Distributed tuning of boundary resources: the case of Apple's iOS service system. MIS Q. **39**, 217–243 (2015)

24. Yoo, Y.: The tables have turned: how can the information systems field contribute to technology and innovation management research? J. Assoc. Inf. Syst. **14**, 227 (2013)

25. Boyatzis, R.E.: Transforming Qualitative Information. Sage Publications, Thousand Oak (1998)

Exploring a LOD-Based Application for Military Movie Retrieval

Liang-Chu Chen[✉], Jen-Tsung Tseng, Yen-Hsuan Lien,
Chia-Jung Hsieh, and I-Chiang Shih

Department of Information Management, National Defense University,
No. 70, Sec. 2, Zhongyang North Road, Beitou, Taipei 112, Taiwan
nctuhorse@gmail.com

Abstract. In recent years, the number of video film has been in the constant expansion dramatically due to the rapid development of digital devices and network/communication technologies. The increasing diversity and complexity of video contents make a challenge toward file management and fast retrieval. This study considered military movies as research targets and used ELAN (a video annotation tool) to increase the descriptive data of the movie, which provides more detail metadata for improving video retrieval. The objective of this study is to develop a military movie knowledge retrieval service based on the Linked Open Data, which not only provides basic metadata and annotated words that include the timeline characteristic, but also links specified concepts with the related and extensive knowledge. Results represent that the service system is helpful for enhancing the effectiveness of military movie retrieval.

Keywords: Linked Open Data · Annotation · Metadata · Military movie retrieval

1 Introduction

The concept of Web 2.0 proposed by O'Reilly and Battelle [10] describes the interactive share and collaborative involvement among users in the cyber world. The Internet and digital product complement each other nowadays. Widespread digital camera and smart phone bring people the convenience, hence instant share of photo and video has become entertainment in our life. In turn, the easy access to the Internet shortens users' distance, further facilitating the trend of multimedia-content uploading and sharing. After video work is digitalized in computer information system; however, people still cannot search or even know its digital information without textual descriptions. The number of video film nowadays has been in the constant growth dramatically, which makes a challenge towards file management and fast retrieval [13]. Thus it is necessary to establish retrieval system for better file management, alone with the users' efficiency in search and browsing mode. Although video web portal (e.g. YouTube, DailyMotion, Metacafe, and Vimeo) allows users manually annotate the title of video file and content description, video retrieval is still ineffective since annotation function could only present summary of whole video film. Therefore, the issues like "How to deal with semantic description in more precise manner" and "How to extend the application of metadata from video

© Springer International Publishing Switzerland 2016
F.F.-H. Nah and C.-H. Tan (Eds.): HCIBGO 2016, Part I, LNCS 9751, pp. 294–305, 2016.
DOI: 10.1007/978-3-319-39396-4_27

film" will be more obvious and difficult [1]. For most of current video film with general description, Yu et al. [13] suggested increasing detailed description on single frame or scene fragment through timeline-based annotation can be the solution.

Web of Documents in Web 2.0 era is built for people's easy reading and browsing information while Linked Data aims to establish a structured-data network where a machine can understand and interpret its semantic content [3]. Linked Data has collected many data sets from diverse fields: General encyclopedia knowledge (e.g. DBpedia, YAGO), movie (e.g. LinkedMDB), academic publication (e.g. DBLP, RKB Explorer) and so on. After Linked Data is added with the concept "Open Data" and satisfy both standards, it called Linked Open Data (LOD). Through other data sets online, LOD is to strengthen the exchange and connection of knowledge among multimedia metadata, and eventually increase the value of data on the Internet [1]. The utilization of LOD on development system or application has been growing. Many relevant researches on video film have been published. The project "Euscreen[1]" funded by the European Union, for instance, is to convert earlier analog TV data into RDF (Resource Description Framework) format and link to the other LOD data set, preserving and extending its knowledge implication of culture and history. Yu et al. [13] proposed using Linked Data technology to reinforce distance learning-supported education video files; Mirizzi et al. [9] focused on the link between the core data set of LOD (i.e. DBpedia) and semantic technology. Thus it can be seen that linking the existing video film resources to derivative knowledge via linked data technology is still in a sustainable developing way.

Taiwan's video files for military-information delivery, by contrast, are only available for independent program or movie without further description on content. If a fast and effective video retrieval environment could be provided for certain military video contents, it will be significantly helpful for users to get not only preferred video file but also knowledge supplement.

Based on the property of LOD, this research reinforced the semantic model of military video resources. Then, it further conducted the meta-analysis of knowledge extension by structured (i.e. Metadata) and unstructured (i.e. Annotation data) information contents. The aims of this research are as follows:

- Propose a video retrieval service architecture with the integration of metadata, annotation data and LOD. Meanwhile, it can further increase clues for film search by increasing detailed description on film. According to annotation-based knowledge extension mode, it also extends knowledge scope covered by video resource.
- Present the diversity of military issues by retrieval service system with military movie examples, as well as the concept of mashup. Furthermore, verify the feasibility and utility of the proposed architecture.

---

[1] http://lod.euscreen.eu.

2   The Development and Application of LOD

The internet content nowadays is mostly presented in HTML webpage. For computer, HTML format represents the expression syntax of web file, but computer cannot understand the meaning inside the format content. To make computer read semantic meaning behind the words, Berners-Lee et al. proposed Semantic Web in 2001. Computer could comprehend webpage content by interlinked data on the web, and then convert it to semantic documents and data. This enables the linking of knowledge network increases the efficiency and accuracy of web search.

Regarding the issue "How to embody the concept of full-function and meaningful semantic web", Berners-Lee proposed "Linked Data" in 2006. It is the technology to publish, share and interlink the structured data on the web. As the best practice of semantic web, Linked Data enables machine find and link web data from each field [7]. In short, Linked Data publish structured data in RDF format on the web via HTTP URI method. This lowers the data providers and users' thresholds to access data; meanwhile, it is expected to form a rich and available data space [6].

The World Wide Web Consortium (W3C) promoted the LOD program in 2007, so the existing data can be interlinked by Linked Data technology and released on the web for people's utilization. LOD connects numerous data sets; it could be regarded as an Internet-scale data space which unites multiple fields [6]. To prevent its application-level development from copyright concerns, all Linked Data should announce authorization for use during their release on the web.

As the main core of Linked Data, DBpedia locates in the hub location of LOD. It is a special application example of semantic web: it extracts structured data from Wikipedia webpage by semantic technology; meanwhile, it also uses RDF property to link and integrate data sets from other fields. In consequence, DBpedia with a wide range of topics and contents has become the largest interdisciplinary Ontology in the world. Besides, DBpedia provides all potential concepts a chance to be a concrete URI, which links different data sets through the share and reference of URI form.

Once data sets are published in the LOD cloud and interlinked with others, all published data will be equipped with LOD property. When an organization owns abundant information document, they can be changed into specific LOD data sets by data conversion, or further connection with internal database system to provide solutions for organization and enterprise's resource decision, disaster management, knowledge management or market intelligence & research report [2]. With the wide use in many ways, the development of LOD application has reached considerable achievements thus far.

Public sector publishes data on the LOD web, increasing its transparency in government; The Linked Data application has brought people convenient life information, and the links of music or movie optimize users' reference integrity [4, 7]. Among few Linked Data researches in video films nowadays, the early-stage of them proposed solutions for different multimedia formats and annotation system [12]. Although scholars later conducted applied researches based on LOD technology such as education video resource and academic conference video (Table 1), researches on military movies are still in the blank so far.

Table 1. The studies of Linked Data on video and movie.

Author	Service category	Research findings and conclusion
Haslhofer et al. [5]	Video annotation	1. Proposed a unified annotation model for multimedia content and different types of annotation systems
		2. Adopted Linked Data principle for video documents on the web, increased interoperability and deference among annotation data. Besides, made it be open and used on the web
Li et al. [8]	Video annotation	1. Use multimedia annotation application (Synote) to show video data fragment, then publish annotation made by users on the web through Linked Data principle
		2. Reused the existing word bank, and embedded RDFa standard on annotation data in order to consolidate its mutual connection with other data sets
Mirizzi et al. [9]	Movie recommender	1. MORE, an application program of Facebook serves as a movie recommender system
		2. The background knowledge of MORE utilizes the external semantic data sets; collected the data of movie director, actor and producer though DBpedia and LinkedMDB
		3. The algorithm of recommender system uses the semantic version of Vector Space Model
Sack and Waitelonis [11]	Video data retrieval	1. Developed professional video search engine "Yovisto" for academic lecture recordings and conference talks
		2. According to Linked data principle, they mapped/projected Yovisto video data to DBpedia data sets
Yu et al. [13]	Video annotation	1. Through the semantic video tool, Annomation, users can annotate and publish education video resource on the basis of video annotation ontology. Annotation also allows annotators use particular LOD term to describe video resource, and these annotations can link to video resource of other websites
		2. As a semantic-based video retrieval browser, SugarTube provides video research function, and further links to web video education resources inside LOD

3 Research Framework

"The knowledge retrieval service of linked movie annotation data" developed by this study presented the basic metadata of military movies where the specific movie scenes are annotated by timeline. The extensible data of annotation word inside were thus linked to LOD data sets through Linked Data technology, further expanding its knowledge inside the content. The research framework is shown as Fig. 1.

The Source of Movie Data. Considering the efficiency of system operation, the research narrowed down the scope of video films, from all military films to movies with the World War II issues for study. Among military movie titles associated with the World War II in military-movie blogs worldwide and Wikipedia entries, the known films released in Taiwan were thus selected as candidate list (e.g. Saving Private Ryan and Pearl Harbor, etc.). Each experimental video mainly extracted video resources from the multimedia data from the library of National Defense University, other sources were Chinese Taipei Film Archive, National Digital Archives Program and other open sources on the web (e.g. YouTube).

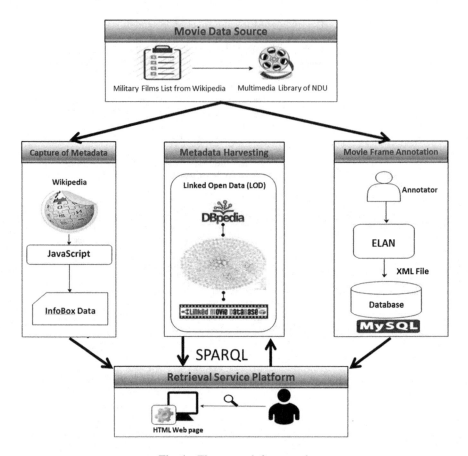

Fig. 1. The research framework

The Capture of Metadata. The related attributes of movies' metadata were explained in words, including films' credits (e.g. performer, filmmaker) and information (e.g. running time, publisher, and language). They are all the basic data of movie, without any changes. Through JavaScirpt program, InfoBox data captured from Wikipedia movie webpage were directly presented in retrieval service area, which not only provides movies with the existing attribute data but also conceptual basis for extended data.

The Frame Annotation of Movie. For people who do not have expertise on military background or historical battle, they might not understand meaning behind the scenes such as the certain historical people, military facilities or equipment shown in the movies. Therefore, the frame annotation formed by timeline could strengthen users' understandings besides the existing metadata. It also can benefit annotators' frame and scene annotation based on timeline. Moreover, annotation words were stratified and categorized themselves by classes. To link each data set from LOD's fields, the research conducted annotation description on film fragment or people, place and military aircraft.

Afterwards, exported annotated data as XML file, and transferred to local MySQL database.

The Extraction of Linked Data. After movie frames were annotated and saved, the research then utilized the built-in RDF library of ARC2 and SPARQL to do syntax-module query. When keywords were sent, the data mapped to corresponding attributes and attribute values by triples from the RDF file of LOD data sets like DBpedia, GeoNames and LinkedMDB. The data structure of triples mapped to corresponding RDF pattern inside the specific LOD data sets, and then SPARQL endpoint retransmitted the extracted triples as JSON files to local server. After JSON files were received as array form, they were read by loop of PHP's for each function. Then, their corresponding attributes and attribute values were saved. Eventually, three variable data (people, places and military aircrafts) were shown in PHP syntax on the webpage.

The SPARQL syntax and target data of the three-type annotation word are further explained below.

- Person annotation

Because retrieval results of keyword query conducted by people's nicknames usually show poor efficiency, the research utilized UNION syntax to link two RDF predicates "rdfs:label[2]" and "dbpo:wikiPageRedirects[3]". In this way, SPARQL query firstly checked whether the linked URI of "rdfs:label" match, then compared "dbpo:wikiPageRedirects". To eliminate ambiguity problems caused by people's nicknames and aliases, it followed the attribute value of "wikiPageRedirects" to provide two RDF patterns with replaceable URI names inside the DBpedia.

- Place annotation

In general, most place annotations for movie scenes normally focus on the names of geographical locations, administrative regions and famous buildings. However, these annotation words cannot deliver further data description. In this study, we linked to the RDF data of DBpedia and GeoNames's endpoints by SPARQL syntax and extracted the extended data of place names which include the longitude, latitude, profile of site, names and pictures of local cities. Through Google visualization tools, these data were presented as tables and map markers, which helped users' easy understandings and comparisons. Besides, the additional use of Sgvizler (i.e. a RDF query tool developed by JavaScript) can be further combined with Google Chat Tools, in order to visualize the collected data; that is, it is much easier for users to understand the geographical locations occurred in the movie, through the map method.

- Military aircraft annotation

With the diverse categories, military aircrafts also differ in their performances and specifications. As a result, the extended information of military aircraft annotation took

---

[2] http://www.w3.org/2000/01/rdf-schema#lable.
[3] http://dbpedia.org/ontology/wikiPageRedirects.

the "Template: Aircraft Specifications" from Wikipedia InfoBox as the basis of data extraction. It extracted the required attribute value, then selected the more common aircraft (e.g. Crew, Wingspan, Max. takeoff weight), performance data (e.g. Cruise speed, Rate of climb, Service ceiling) and weapon (e.g. Bombs). During the information query, every aircraft showed different attribute data because the RDF linked description data of DBpedia entity URI still shows no unified attribute specification nowadays.

Retrieval Query Interface. The research designed web retrieval interface by combing PHP, JavaScript and CSS (Cascading Style Sheets) syntax. The interface was divided into query function area and data presentation area. The former provided the retrieval service of military movies; the latter displayed the query results like basic data of movies and annotation word.

4 Implementation and Evaluation

This retrieval service is a Mashup web application, which combines LOD technology, HTML5 video tag, JavaScript webpage capture, Sgvizler and Google tools. As shown in Fig. 2, the process starts from query category. There are three types: movie title, the name of actor and director as well as extensible query of annotation word. During selection of movie title, users can obtain the basic data of movie and annotation word list. Regarding the query on the name of actor or director, results show their information from LinkedMDB, following with the titles of their past movies. As for the place annotation, people and military aircraft inside the type "Annotation word query", it facilitates users' selections and retrievals based on their own demands. The system first filters out keyword type from Freebase, then conducts the query in order to improve search accuracy. During the process, the metadata and the same annotation word list shown in other movies are transmitted in SPARQL syntax.

4.1 Functions of the Retrieval Service

The retrieval service system consists of three main functions.

1. The retrieval of movie's information
   Through the retrieval by inputting movie title "Pearl Harbor", the system was divided into two categories displaying related data (Fig. 3): one as "The retrieval section of movie's basic information" provided the retrieval results of basic data, including movie's content and its metadata. Another one as "The retrieval section of movie's annotation data" shows movie's annotation type, time and frame screenshot.
   - The movie's play: Embedded with HTML5 video tag, film's play function provides dynamic fragment and frame review. Besides, the time-display button combining with annotation word enables users to directly browse the scene fragment of word shown in the film. This not only dramatically shortens retrieval time, but also strengthens users' concepts towards annotation word.
   - *The movie's metadata*: After selecting movie (e.g. movie "Pearl Harbor") for query by capturing Wikipedia webpage by PHP and JavaScirpt, system

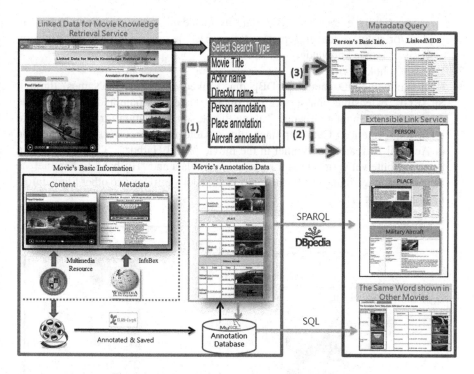

Fig. 2. The function and process of retrieval service.

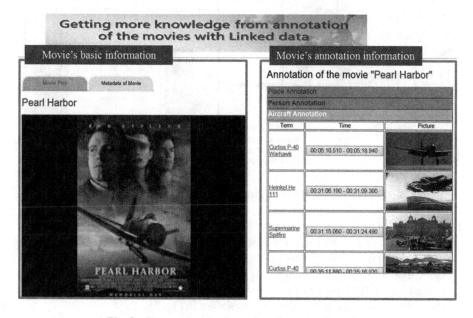

Fig. 3. The system interface of movie retrieval service.

automatically extracts InfoBox data as metadata, namely attribute data (e.g. director, actor, producer, screenwriter, etc.) as the same as the concept extension basis of movie knowledge.

2. Extensible link service

By linking to LOD data sets (DBpedia, LinkedMDB and GeoNames) through SPARQL, extensible link service can obtain related attribute and attribute value extended from annotation word. Taking the person annotation for example, Colm Feore is an American-Canadian stage, film and television actor who plays as the role of Admiral Husband E. Kimmel in the movie "Pearl Harbor." "Colm Feore" is a basic attribute value (actor) in the movie's metadata and "Husband E. Kimmel" is an annotation word that can be linked to Wikipedia's infobox and other films' information (see Fig. 4).

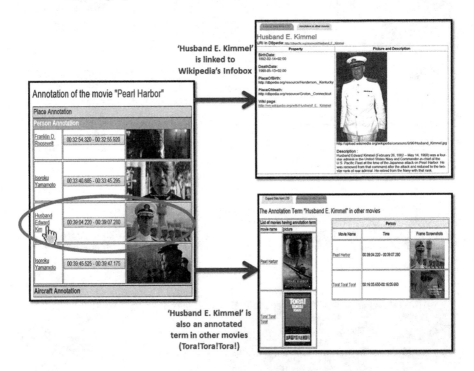

Fig. 4. The link service of person annotation - the case of Husband E. Kimmel.

3. The Linked Data query of actor and director

Actor and director are basic metadata in the movie which are acquirable in the retrieval of movie title. If users request more related information in the movie, they can conduct the query through this retrieval service. In addition, the research also treats LinkedMDB as one of the movie sources, which provides the query for the past movies list of actor and director (as shown in Fig. 5).

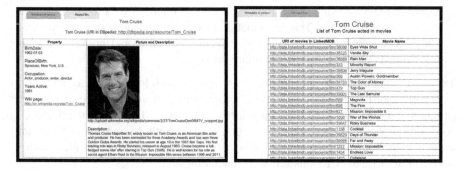

Fig. 5. The retrieval service of actor's film list - the case of Tom Cruise.

4.2 System Evaluation

Based on the reference of software product quality requirement and evaluation criteria (ISO25010), the research conducted an evaluation for item "User's satisfaction" involved by Quality in Use. The five-point Likert scale was applied into online questionnaire in the research. As a result, the importance of each indicator was firstly divided into five responses: "Strongly disagree", "Disagree", "General", "Agree" and "strongly agree". Then, the five responses were converted into 1 (lower importance) to 5 (higher importance) points for the statistical analysis of questionnaire. The questionnaire was designed from two aspects: literature review and the reference of measurement variable proposed by foreign researchers. A total of 30 users were evaluated in system satisfaction by online questionnaire after they operated the system.

The statistics of evaluation showed that the average value among questions from five dimensions (system effectiveness, reliability, operating comfort, enjoyment, and overall satisfaction) is greater than 3 while standard deviation shows insignificant/tiny difference. This can indicate users are generally satisfied with the retrieval content and result of system.

5   Conclusion

The research focused on the application of abundant LOD resources, and studied the related data of military movies by Linked Data technology. With the establishment of a retrieval-service platform ultimately, it can provide users with the query of basic data and the extensible knowledge and concept of annotation word link. The main contributions of the research are summarized as follows:

- Establish LOD-based retrieval service to get the data sets from different fields by SPARQL syntax. The direct acquirement of available open data indeed decreases redundant databases with overlapping contents, the consumption of storage resources and data maintenance costs. Furthermore, this retrieval service can integrate different videos or movie data, achieving advanced application.

- Combine LOD with video annotation to provide the reference for knowledge learning and teaching assistance. This combination mode also provides a new orientation to add pilot concept for military information media application and innovative thinking for national defense system in the future internet era.

The video annotation software adopted by the research still focuses on text mode as the main annotation description. During the extensible query of annotation word, it first uses strings to get URI, and then links outwards to other data. To achieve the purpose of semantic annotation, the research thus suggests that the further development of semantic annotation tool can reinforce semantic description by URI, which reduces the ambiguity word and increase the URI-link scope of annotation word.

Besides, Linked Data along with the data are converted and published to the phases like data integration and inter-correlation. The research merely used application programs to acquire data link by adding annotation word through SPARQL syntax. For this reason, the user-built annotation word bank can be used to publish. Furthermore, SILK (Link Discovery Framework) can also help it conduct the RDF link of triples from different data sets. This eventually makes annotation data and each LOD data set inter-linked, maximizing knowledge exploration ability of Linked Data.

Acknowledgements. This research was partially sponsored by the Ministry of Science and Technology, Taiwan (MOST 103-2410-H-606-005-MY2).

References

1. Arias Gallego, M., Corcho, O., Fernández, J.D., Martínez-Prieto, M.A., Suárez-Figueroa, M.C.: Compressing semantic metadata for efficient multimedia retrieval. In: Bielza, C., Salmerón, A., Alonso-Betanzos, A., Hidalgo, J., Martínez, L., Troncoso, A., Corchado, E., Corchado, J.M. (eds.) CAEPIA 2013. LNCS, vol. 8109, pp. 12–21. Springer, Heidelberg (2013)
2. Bauer, F., Kaltenböck, M.: Linked Open Data: The Essentials. Edition mono/monochrom, Vienna (2011)
3. Berners-Lee, T.: Linked Data-Design Issues. https://www.w3.org/DesignIssues/LinkedData.html
4. Bizer, C., Heath, T., Berners-Lee, T.: Linked data - the story so far. Int. J. Semant. Web Inf. Syst. **5**(3), 1–22 (2009)
5. Haslhofer, B., Jochum, W., King, R., Sadilek, C., Schellner, K.: The LEMO annotation framework: weaving multimedia annotations with the web. Int. J. Digit. Libr. **10**(1), 15–32 (2009)
6. Hausenblas, M., Karnstedt, M.: Understanding linked open data as a web-scale database. In: 2010 Second International Conference on Advances in Databases Knowledge and Data Applications (DBKDA), Menuires, pp. 56–61 (2010)
7. Heath, T., Bizer, C.: Linked data: evolving the web into a global data space. Synth. Lect. Semant. Web Theor. Technol. **1**(1), 1–136 (2011)
8. Li, Y., Wald, M., Omitola, T., Shadbolt, N., Wills, G.: Synote: Weaving media fragments and linked data. In: 5th International Workshop on Linked Data on the Web (LDOW 2012), Lyon, France (2012)

9. Mirizzi, R., DiNoia, T., Ragone, A., Ostuni, V., DiSciascio, E.: Movie recommendation with DBpedia. In: 3rd Italian Information Retrieval Workshop (IIR 2012), Bari, Italy (2012)
10. O'Reilly, T., Battelle, J.: Opening Welcome: State of the Internet Industry, San Francisco, California (2004)
11. Sack, H., Waitelonis, J.: Towards exploratory video search using linked data. Multimedia Tools Appl. **59**(2), 645–672 (2012)
12. W3C Interest Group Note: Cool URIs for the Semantic Web. http://www.w3.org/TR/cooluris/
13. Yu, H., Pedrinaci, C., Dietze, S., Domingue, J.: Using Linked Data to Annotate and Search Educational Video Resources for Supporting Distance Learning. IEEE Trans. Learn. Technol. **5**(2), 130–142 (2012)

High Availability of Big-Geo-Data as a Platform as a Service

Tim Förster[1], Simon Thum[2], and Arjan Kuijper[1,2(✉)]

[1] Technische Universität Darmstadt, Darmstadt, Germany
[2] Fraunhofer IGD, Darmstadt, Germany
arjan.kuijper@igd.fraunhofer.de

Abstract. There are ever-increasing challenges in the development of spatial data. The data increase rises continuously. The sharp rise in these information collections more and more data storage is required. Furthermore, should the systems have high availability and provide acceptable response time under load. The fulfillment of such requirement can be limited realized with a simple client / server system, since these do not scale well and act slowly in poor conditions. Therefore, more and more applications are deployed in the cloud as a service. This brings many benefits; inter alia, improving the availability and scalability of services. In this work the design decisions is demonstrated using an existing server system that are necessary for the realization of the product in the cloud. This product is then provided as a "Platform as a Service". Here points are as discussed persistence in distributed systems and cloud API design. This is then tested in a distributed system and compared against a simple client / server system. Also, a model is presented, thus the availability of the system is calculated.

1 Introduction and Motivation

The number of services that are provided on the Internet increases continuously. Concepts like "Big Data" and "cloud computing" play an increasingly important role. With Cloud computing, resources can be used more effectively. This allows more services to be operated with the same number of servers. This reduces the costs of procuring the servers that are necessary for the operation of new services. Furthermore, cloud computing offers the advantage that it is possible that resources can be added dynamically to the current task. Thus applications can be scaled-up better. Consequently, cloud computing is one of the most effective ways to provide scalable and robust services.

Availability plays an increasingly important role in the provision of services. This can only limited be realized in a simple client-server system. This is because that in such a case, there is always a "single point of failure". Furthermore, the data is constantly growing. This increases the need for a dynamic "growing" system. Cloud computing offers a good alternative to a standard client-server system. It provides the ability to scale applications and to achieve a higher availability. The problem is to make an existing system scalable. Still, the system

© Springer International Publishing Switzerland 2016
F.F.-H. Nah and C.-H. Tan (Eds.): HCIBGO 2016, Part I, LNCS 9751, pp. 306–318, 2016.
DOI: 10.1007/978-3-319-39396-4_28

should have a high availability. In addition, various client applications should use this system. It is therefore necessary to define a "clean" system API is. At the same time the system should be easily expandable.

The aim of this work is the extension of an existing implementation of a geo-server system. The system should be scalable and additionally have high availability. These are the first steps on the way to a cloud system. For this purpose an API must be developed, which individual client applications can access. To meet the scalability other ways of data persistence must be taken into consideration. We present different scenarios for the system. Full results can be found in [6].

2   Cloud Computing

In cloud computing (CC) IT resources and services on the Internet are provided. So far is meant by cloud computing outsourcing of IT services. Meanwhile, many companies, such as Amazon, IBM, Google has established itself as a platform provider in the cloud computing market. There are also many companies that rely on their own applications and consulting services.

Generally, cloud computing is an IT development, deployment and distribution model, which makes it possible to provide services, products and solutions over the Internet in real time [1,9]. The term cloud is defined as a large collection of easily usable and accessible resources (such as hardware, platforms or services). In order to allow optimal utilization of resources, these can be adapted dynamically to variable loads and configured accordingly. These models are based on consumption-based billing models. The assurance in the form of service level agreements (SLAs) will be covered within the infrastructure. Cloud Camputing ultimately forms the technical platform to offer cloud services with a consumption-based billing. This includes, for example, infrastructure, system and application software [10,15]. The NIST definition [12] of cloud computing in this case provides the following five characteristics: On-demand Self-Service, Broad Network Access, Resource Pooling, Rapid Elasticity, and Measured Service.

These services can be provided through a variety as a Service models. Here, three models have been developed [4,12]: Infrastructure as a Service (IaaS), Platform as a Service (PaaS), and Software as a Service (SaaS). Providing cloud application provides the seller several advantages for compliance / achievement of specific service-level agreement (SLA) or service agreement (DLV) [2,18]: availability, scalability, redundancy, and a fault-tolerant and robust behavior of the system.

Despite the high popularity of cloud computing still exist challenges for developing cloud applications. For the persistence of data, there is no uniform APIs to address the database systems. Thus, each developer is forced to provide their own database management system. The same problem exists for the APIs of the services (PaaS) [2].

3   Distributed Database

Usually there are applications that access a database on a computer. These requests are started from there. Unlike old known relational database systems, the approach of distributed databases going in a different direction. Here, the database is distributed to several computers in a system. Many software applications require access to data stored. The distributed database systems provide application programs and users to access interface, as on a central database. In order to achieve transparency of the distribution, however, from the side of the database software, to manage a number of technical problems. The use of distributed database systems has some advantages. They allow an adjustment of the system structure of an organizational structure, without affecting the database property. Through the interaction of database systems to application programs and users all the factors of the distribution remain hidden. There is no change in the access interface for them. This distribution transparency is the great advantage of distributed database systems. Furthermore, the distribution of data from the database system of distributed database is removed. In distributed database systems increases performance because multiple servers for processing the data are available. Thus, the response times are shortened. A further advantage is that in a computer failure can continue to access the database.

3.1   CAP Theorem

The CAP Theorem or also called Brewer theorem states that may be satisfied simultaneously only two of the following three characteristics: Consistency (all nodes have the same data at the same time), Availability (all requests that are sent to the system get, always an answer), and Partition tolerance (when a part of the system has a malfunction, the system must not collapse). A proof of this theorem is provided in the work of Gilbert and Lynch [7].

3.2   ACID vs BASE

For the persistence of data, there are several concepts. ACID The concept, which is mainly used for relational databases is defined as follows: 1. Atomic: A transaction is completed when all the operations are completed, otherwise a rollback is performed. By conducted rollback the database is to achieve a consistent state. 2. Consistent: A transaction may not lead to the collapse of the database. However, should this be the case, so the operation is not permitted and it is carried out a rollback. 3. Isolated: All transactions are independent of each other and can not influence each other. 4. Durable: If a transaction has been executed successfully, should it be guaranteed that the data is permanently stored in the database. This must also be the case when a system error occurs.

Compared to the ACID concept BASE concept for scalable, distributed database used by abandoning the consistency of the data. BASE is in this case composed of the following terms: *Basically availiable*: All data are available, even if an error exists in the system. *Soft State*: The states of the system may change over time, even if no transaction is executed on the system. *Eventually consistent*: The system guarantees, when data is not consistent, that they will after a time. Thus, BASE relies on a highly available system, the abandonment of the consistency of the data, after each transaction. This concept is used by many distributed databases used, including in NoSQL databases.

3.3   NoSQL

called "Not only SQL" or "noseequel" [11], is a database approach, which relies on the distribution of databases instead of keeping everything on a central database server. In 1998, an open-source database was introduced that did not provide SQL access options. Due to the lack of interfaces it did the name "NoSQL". The special thing about it was not the lack of interface, but approaches that have broken the relational database concepts. After a short time the term was forgotten. 2009 the term NoSQL came when Eric Evans was looking for a name for a distributed open source DBMS. Since the beginning of 2010, the name "Not only SQL" established in the Community. Database management systems (DBMS) are now regarded as a NoSQL system, if they have the property of a horizontal scaling. Here, no-SQL databases differ in types [8,16]: Key-Value, Document, Column-family/BigTable, and Graph.

3.4   MongoDB

MongoDB is developed in C ++ as an open source project and was published in the year of 2009. MongoDB is a NoSQL database that falls under the type of document persistence. The documents are in so-called "Collections" grouped. In the document the data as BSON (Binary - JSON) are stored. Whereas indexation MongoDB uses the "_id" field and in addition also generates a unique index (the unique id). These indexes are then held by MongoDB as B-tree structure.

MongoDB supports using replica sets, only the load distribution for the reading of data. The master alone is responsible for writing. This offers the advantage that the master alone on the persistence of data is responsible. Likewise awards the master is the only new ID's when writing new records. Thus, in this process does not occur in collisions Replica Set. Reading on the other hand, there are several strategies to make a load distribution. These are: **Primary-Only:** In this strategy, the Primary for the reading and writing of all data is responsible. Thus, it acts as a normal client / server system. The slaves in the replica set to work only as a backup in case the primary fails. **Primary and Secondary:** This allows all the users that has permission to read, in the Replica Set read the data. Thus, a uniform distribution of the read accesses are achieved. **Secondary-Only:** In the Secondary-only strategy all read accesses are distributed to the secondaries. Thus, the Primary is relieved and is purely responsible for writing the data.

Sharding is a method for distributing data across multiple servers. This provides the possibility to persist a large number of data (Big Data) in the system effectively. Sharding can also be used in combination with Replicas. In this case, both a data distribution as well as a data replication can be achieved. However, this requires a high number of servers (> 6) to operate this application useful.

4   Service API

The Internet and its data is steadily increasing. Distributed systems reach more and more popularity among the service providers. In the growing process of distributed systems some interfaces have been developed. These were designed to part for specific problems and are therefore difficult reusable. Others can be expanded only part. Thus standardization measures have formed in time. The interfaces can be divided into two architectures. Both architectures have the aim to decouple the client from the server. Thus, the two systems can be developed independently.

1. Service Oriented Architecture (SOA). In SOA, the focus is on performing actions on the server as a function. Here messages are sent with the desired call to a service endpoint. This message is then interpreted and routed to the appropriate instance. This approach has been around longer outside of the Web. Due to the long existence of SOA already several standards have been established. These can be highly optimized, but are relatively cumbersome expandable.

2. Resource Oriented Architecture (ROA). Unlike SOA are the resources in the front point in ROA. Here no services are addressed, but directly addressed any requests to the resources. On this resource base operations can be defined. The operations may be extended to the addressed resource. This involves a simple expansion of the interface, since the functions can be implemented separately from other resources. The most famous ROA technology is Representational State Transfer (REST), on which we will discuss in Subsect. 4.2.

To explain the choice of API architecture, briefly the pros and cons of SOAP and REST are attached explained. SOAP and REST interfaces are the most used.

4.1   SOAP

SOAP defines a messaging architecture that is based on XML. The XML schema is used to interpret SOAP messages to the endpoints (unmarshall) and to create queries (marshall). The Web Services Description Language (WSDL) is an interface description language. Its purpose is to define Web service interfaces. It indicates, for example, which operations the client can perform. Given this description SOAP requests can be created and sent to the server.

Advantages. SOAP and WSDL have a good use in heterogeneous middleware systems because of their complexity. The advantage is the transparency and independence of systems to one another. Interfaces can be defined, and must not follow appropriate standard. Furthermore, both synchronous and asynchronous connections are supported.

Disadvantages. Due to the high freedom and thickness often occur interoperability problems with different systems. Also has SOAP XML due to performance problems that are discussed in Sect. 4.2 detail. Furthermore, the creation of Web Services with stable marshalling not trivial and takes a lot of time [13].

4.2 REST

Representational State Transfer (REST) was originally developed to create large scalable distributed hypermedia systems [5]. REST case has four basic characteristics: Addressability of resources by URI, Uniform interface, Statelessness, and Support for multiple representations

Advantages. REST is a combination of several existing standards (HTTP, XML, JSON, URI, MIME), which can be used easily and quickly. Thus, the cost of implementation of RESTful Web services will be lower than what the SOAP. Furthermore REST supports the building of dynamic websites. Due to the unique identification of resources and the stateless access RESTful web services using scalable caching and load balancing.

Disadvantages. A problem that may occur by the strict separation of POST and GET is that certain requests may be for the URL is too long. Another challenge is to meet the client authentication.

4.3 HATEOAS

"Hypermedia as the Engine of Application State" [5] is a design principle for REST APIs. Here, the idea is as follows: "The client thus moves through a set of pages; what this may be, is set by the server and thus limits; which are requested specifically, the client (or its user) decides. At any time the resources of the server have a defined status " [17]. The URIs to resources is passed as "href" attribute. The relation to this resource will be supplied as "rel". Other attributes of the resources are dealt with separately in different description languages.

For HATEOAS there are already some description languages. Basically, individual markup languages can be divided into two categories:

XML (Extensible Markup Language[1]) results from the Standard Generalized Markup lanaguage (SGML) language. Here were some of the design decisions, such as "XML shall be straightforwardly usable over the Internet." And "XML shall support a wide variety of applications.". Because of the extensibility of XML, it is used today in many areas. One is the presenting of resources. In the source code 1, an example is shown that a resource layer is in XML form. **JSON** (JavaScript Object Notation) is a simple data exchange format that is easily readable for humans and machines. JSON uses key-value pairs and provides a simple display of objects. Parsing of objects is up to a hundred times faster than XML (http://json.org/). To the detriment belongs the poor extensibility of JSON. Furthermore, JSON provides no validation options. There are other markup languages that define multiple attributes and build on JSON.

---

[1] https://www.w3.org/TR/1998/REC-xml-19980210.

HAL (Hypertext Application Language) is a by Mike Kelley developed standard, which is used for web APIs. He himself describes[2] it as "HAL is a generic media type with Which Web APIs can be developed and exposed as series of links. Clients of thesis APIs can select left by Their link relation type and traverse them in order to progress through the application."

Siren, "a hypermedia specification for representing entities" provides the same functionality as HAL. Siren also offers the possibilities to define entities sent as classes. Additionally, the links are broken. A distinction is made between actions and links to other resources. In the Actions is additionally defined, assumes what types of data the server. These are the standard HTML5 - specify input types.

Collection + JSON is a JSON-based read / write hypermedia-type designed to support management and querying of simple collections. Just as HAL and Siren supports Collection + JSON hypermedia types. Unlike the other two supports Collection + JSON queries. In this case, in addition in addition to the "href" and "rel" attribute, also indicated with data that can be sent to the server. It answers the Collection + JSON serve as templates for new requests to the server.

Comparison. Compared between JSON and XML JSON offers several advantages for using REST interfaces over XML. XML is used primarily for SOA interface description. JSON, however, is already used in many REST interfaces. Furthermore JSON due to the origin provides a JavaScript support, which many web applications are developed. Due to the ease of implementation, the faster processing time by JSON [14] and better support in Spring Framework3 a JSON representation is supported first. Because of HATEOAS approach can fetch additional forms of presentation, such as HAL or XML, are added.

5   Existing System: CityServer3D

"Our world is becoming increasingly recognized in three dimensions. 3D computer models play an increasingly important role in urban planning, tourism and knowledge transfer. By CityServer3D it is first possible to use 3D city models alive. The software can manage two and three dimensional geographic data and link together. The CityServer3D automatically creates three-dimensional models and so performs simulations in the 3D world." Here, describing the product itself as follows: "The technology of CityServer3D consists of a geo-database, a server with numerous interfaces for import and export of data and applications for the development of the landscape models. A management software allows to process the data and the web viewer brings these internet users to the screen Fig. 1."

Due to the prolonged existence of the product, relational databases were used at the beginning. Over time, the distributed databases began to play a greater role. Thus, already first basic elements for the use of MongoDB were laid. This

---

[2] https://tools.ietf.org/html/draft-kelly-json-hal-06.

Clients   API's   CityServer3D   Datenbank

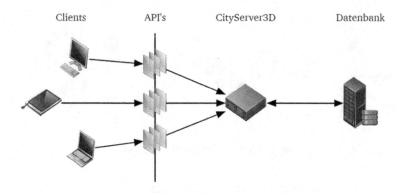

Fig. 1. The existing CityServer3D - System.

created a MongoDB driver MVCC (Multi Version concurrency control) supports. Thus, already a first step towards data distribution was done. Currently a total of 5 databases are supported, including MongoDB and MySQL.

At the moment a number of API's are used to CityServer3D. This was due to the development of the Web. It always more technologies have been developed to have accumulated at the end of a set of APIs with different technologies. Among them are, for example, JSF calls or REST interfaces.

A number of data are necessary for the pure operation of the server. The individual display levels are called "Layer" shown. This may be certain neighborhoods or different heights, as above-ground structures or underground structures. Each layer consists of so-called "features". This is a group of models and metadata. This can for example be building complexes, which consist of several blocks, which in turn are a feature. Furthermore, the information is stored on the features as "metadata". It can be stored a few details, such as "Year" or "style". The individual city models are then persists as a "model". This finally have a set of images (Image) that represent the model eventually.

6   System Availability

The availability is a measure, by increasing the availability of the system is measured in percent. The availability is a quality criterion and is therefore defined as a property in "Service Level Agreement" (SLA). Experiments [6] show that two MongoDB servers have a negative impact on the availability. This is because at least half of the MongoDB server must be accessible in order to elect a new Primary server. If in two servers, an unreachable (for example, when a network error), so you can edit both of no requests. A high availability of MongoDB component can already be achieved by three servers, as long as the availability of the server is not under 99 % (normal availability) lies. It would also be sufficient to operate a MongoDB server that is itself highly available (99.999 %). High availability is achieved when at least two CityServer3D and three MongoDB servers are used in the system.

Clients   CityServer3D   MongoDB

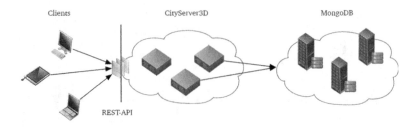

REST-API

Fig. 2. The CityServer3D - System.

7   Extension of City Server Systems

To make the system capable cloud that had properties: robustness, scalability, and availability are achieved. The following should model was being considered, such as found in Fig. 2. To achieve this, the following points were addressed:

The first objective was to obtain the persistence of data robust and scalable. So I put a MongoDB because it is one of the most common distributed databases and the properties are thus achieve robustness, scalability and availability of well [3]. In order to achieve the robustness of the persistence, the MongoDB Replica Set were used. The data in the replica set to replicate to every MongoDB server. Thus was achieved a high availability of data, which was shown in the Sect. 6 In addition MongoDB provides the ability to allow a load distribution when reading the data. This has the advantage that in data reading under load takes place a faster response time (see Sect. 3). If no more resources to be free to handle the load, more MongoDB servers can be added in replica set. Thus scaled the persistence of CityServer3D system. Thus, the persistence of CityServer3D system meets the requirement to a cloud system.

The MongoDB accessed through the MongoMVCC plugin from the IGD. This in turn used the official MongoDB Java driver. The driver provides the advantage that in the future, old / overwritten data could be read. But this is not yet implemented and will be discussed further in subsect. 10.6. Furthermore, they offer MongoDB driver an iterative learning about MongoDB system. For access to the distributed database only a single arbitrary server is necessary. The MongoDB client automatically learns about the MongoDB server know the network and can access on the other in case of failure of a MongoDB server, due to the iterative learning over the network.

Another step towards the realization of cloud services is defining the API. In order to enable a distributed access to the system, a uniform service API is defined. This service API is used to access the PaaS interface. Since there are no uniform standards for cloud APIs [2], different approaches have been presented and compared in the Sect. 4 The aim is to develop a stateless API in order to better isolate the requests between client and server. The Service API to be easily expanded to later develop client applications can use this API. Thus, the PaaS product in combination with client applications can be offered as a SaaS product.

8   Evaluation of the System

For the experiment, the VMware cluster at the Fraunhofer IGD is used. This five Virtual Machines (VM), each with 2 CPU cores, 4 GB RAM and 15 GB of disk space used. On a VM both CityServer3D, as well as a MonogDB (v2.6.4) instance can be operated. The operating system used is "Ubuntu" in the version of "4.14 LTS (GNU / Linux 3.13.0-37-generic x86_64)". Therefore for each scenario different constellations of instances on the VM to operate. Read more in the following chapter. The tests are run on a VM, the computer-operation Group (RBG) of the computer science area of the Technical University of Darmstadt. To determine the bandwidth between the two servers, a 1 GB file was sent to ten times the respective servers. Here, an average transfer rate of 44.8 MB/s between the test system and the VMware cluster revealed. Here, a maximum data transfer rate of 65.3 MB/s and a minimum speed of 27.4 MB/s was achieved. In the other direction, an average speed of 43.6 MB/s was achieved. In this case, the minimum value was 38 B/s and a maximum at 57.2 MB/s. The latency of 9.8 ms in both directions.

Scenarios: To check the behavior of the system, four scenarios were tested: S1: A simple server system with a database and a CityServer3D (1:1), S2: A server system with a CityServer3D and multiple databases (1:4), S3: Several CityServer3D with a database (4:1), and S4: Several CityServer3D with multiple databases (5:5).

Tests: Three different tests were carried out on each scenario. Here, the tests differed in the visits to the data. In the first test (Complete) the information has been retrieved from the server. The second test (Metadata) the metadata of all available data sets were queried. This represents the display of buildings and objects information. In the third test (model) all textures and models have been downloaded from the server. The model test represents loading the data to display a city. Here all information has been loaded, which were necessary for the display. The metadata of the buildings were not also loaded. To get confirmed, the results of each test was repeated three times (trials). Here, the first attempt was always compared.

User Number: In a normal operating environment, a number of 10 users are usually achieved. In weddings, it can also be the 20th To test the scaling of the system better, a maximum of 50 users have been simulated. Here each test started with a simulated users. Every 36 s was the User number increased by one. This was done as long until the number of users 50 min. Subsequently, the number of simulated users held for a further 120 s. Thus, a test was run a total of 32 min. After the test was terminated.

Utilized Program: The tests were performed using one of JMeter7. If the users were simulated. Each simulated users running as a separate thread on the RBG-VM. Each of these threads held exactly one active request to the server open. Once the thread was told that the message has been parsed later and it opened up the next requests.

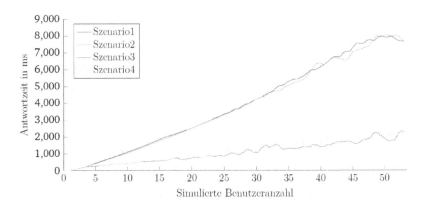

Fig. 3. All scenarios.

Inquire: First, all the layers were always requested. Then, the client received a list of available layers, which he queried afterwards. In response, the query to the models- and feature metadata addresses that were requested directly afterwards were. The same thing happened for the Models. Plus provided the models for the address of pictures from the model, which were eventually charged. Standen in the test several CityServer3D available so random (uniform distribution) was chosen a CityServer3D for each request.

Assumptions: To perform the test, the following assumptions were used: Acceptance: All addresses of the available CityServer3D are known to all clients. Adoption: For each request is selected a random available (under the uniform distribution) CityServer3D.

Scenarios: At first glance, the big difference between scenarios 1 and 2 versus 3 and 4 can be clearly seen in Fig. 3. Due to the high capacity utilization in the first two scenarios of CityServer3D these scenarios could not keep up with the results of the last two scenarios. The fourth scenario scored a slower results in terms of response time, but is compared to the most robust. The availability of the scenarios can be found in Table 1. Compared to the first and third scenario, the scalability of the CityServer3D can be seen. Three additional servers improved the system to an average response time to 336 %, or more than three times.

Hypotheses: Based on the number of tests that were carried out in the different scenarios, we created a number of hypotheses in advance. (H1) In the first and second scenario CityServer3D will achieve a CPU utilization of 100 %. Thus, the response time will increase: We found that the CityServer3D already achieved a 75 % occupancy with a single user. In the following tests was simulated with up to 50 users. So a 100 % CityServer3D component were achieved in scenario 1 and 2 as early as two users. In the third and fourth scenario was achieved due to the distribution of these amounts only from a number of ten simulated users. Despite the high utilization, the system did not collapse. (H2) Due to the high utilization of CityServer3D in the second scenario, no improvement over the

Table 1. Availability in %

Scenario	CS3D	MongoDB	Total
1st	99.000 00	98.999 01	98.009 02
2nd	99.000 00	99.999 00	98.999 01
3rd	99.999 99	98.999 01	98.999 01
4th	99.999 99	99.999 00	99.999 00

first scenario is achieved: This is what the test results showed. This is mainly due to the CPU utilization of CityServer3D component. In order to achieve a power ramp, the implementation of the CityServer3D system would have to be checked. (H3) The third and fourth scenario will provide a better response time than the first two scenarios: Due to the distribution of CityServer3D significant improvements compared to the first and second scenario were obtained.

9 Conclusion

By analyzing the system it becomes clear which benefits distributed applications in the cloud can have. This requires a distribution of every component, but rewards the operator with a highly available service. In this work, a model for determining the availability of a distributed system was introduced. This model has been evaluated for CityServer3D, with the use of a distributed database (MongoDB). A high availability ($>99.999\,\%$) can be achieved with less about 5 servers, assuming a normal availability of each server. In addition, both components can scale: increasing number of users as well as growing volumes of data. This allows the entire system to be provided as "Platform as a Service" in the cloud. Furthermore, different ways of cloud API designs were presented. These mainly provide the opportunity to develop more cloud applications for the end user. Thus, the entire system can be implemented as a "Software as a Service" in the cloud.

References

1. Aderhold, A., Wilkosinska, K., Corsini, M., Jung, Y., Graf, H., Kuijper, A.: The common implementation framework as service – towards novel applications for streamlined presentation of 3D content on the web. In: Marcus, A. (ed.) DUXU 2014, Part II. LNCS, vol. 8518, pp. 3–14. Springer, Heidelberg (2014)
2. Armbrust, M., Fox, A., Griffith, R., Joseph, A.D., Katz, R., Konwinski, A., Lee, G., Patterson, D., Rabkin, A., Stoica, I., Zaharia, M.: A view of cloud computing. Commun. ACM **53**(4), 50–58 (2010)
3. Cattell, R.: Scalable SQL and NOSQL data stores. SIGMOD Rec. **39**(4), 12–27 (2011)
4. Dillon, T., Wu, C., Chang, E.: Cloud computing: issues and challenges. In: 24th IEEE International Conference on Advanced Information Networking and Applications (AINA), pp. 27–33 (2010)

5. Fielding, R.T.: Architectural styles and the design of network-based software architectures. Ph.D. thesis, University of California, Irvine (2000)
6. Förster, T.: Hochverfügbarkeit (analytisch) von big-geo-data als platform as a service. Technical report, TU Darmstadt (2014)
7. Gilbert, S., Lynch, N.: Brewer's conjecture and the feasibility of consistent, available, partition-tolerant web services. SIGACT News **33**(2), 51–59 (2002)
8. Indrawan-Santiago, M.: Database research: are we at a crossroad? reflection on NOSQL. In: 2012 15th International Conference on Network-Based Information Systems (NBIS), pp. 45–51 (2012)
9. Kahn, S., Bockholt, U., Kuijper, A., Fellner, D.W.: Towards precise real-time 3D difference detection for industrial applications. Comput. Ind. **64**(9), 1115–1128 (2013)
10. Limper, M., Jung, Y., Behr, J., Sturm, T., Franke, T.A., Schwenk, K., Kuijper, A.: Fast, progressive loading of binary-encoded declarative-3D web content. IEEE Comput. Graph. Appl. **33**(5), 26–36 (2013)
11. Lith, A., Mattsson, J.: Investigating storage solutions for large data - a comparison of well performing and scalable data storage solutions for real time extraction and batch insertion of data. Master's thesis, Chalmers University of Technology (2010)
12. Mell, P., Grance, T.: The nist definition of cloud computing. Technical report, pp. 800–145. National Institute of Standards and Technology (NIST), Gaithersburg, MD (2011)
13. Monson-Haefel, R.: J2EE Web Services. Addison-Wesley Professional, Upper Saddle River (2004)
14. Nurseitov, N., Paulson, M., Reynolds, R., Izurieta, C.: Comparison of JSON and XML data interchange formats: a case study. In: Proceedings of the ISCA 22nd International Conference on Computer Applications in Industry and Engineering, CAINE 2009, pp. 157–162 (2009)
15. Stein, C., Limper, M., Kuijper, A.: Spatial data structures for accelerated 3D visibility computation to enable large model visualization on the web. In: The 19th International Conference on Web3D Technology, Web3D 2014, Vancouver, BC, Canada, 8–10 August 2014, pp. 53–61 (2014)
16. Stonebraker, M.: SQL databases v. NOSQL databases. Commun. ACM **53**(4), 10–11 (2010)
17. Tilkov, S.: REST und HTTP: Einsatz der Architektur des Webs für Integrationsszenarien. dpunkt, verlag (2009)
18. Undheim, A., Chilwan, A., Heegaard, P.: Differentiated availability in cloud computing slas. In: Proceedings of the 2011 IEEE/ACM 12th International Conference on Grid Computing, GRID 2011, pp. 129–136 (2011)

Cognitive Benefits of a Simple Visual Metrics Architecture

John King[(✉)], Kathy Sonderer, and Kevin Lynch

Raytheon Missile Systems, Tucson, AZ, USA
{john.king,Kathy_M_Sonderer,Kevin_J_Lynch}@raytheon.com

Abstract. Many organizations produce metrics dashboards that take a long time to develop, are visually inconsistent, require specialized staff and skills, and (of most concern) don't clearly and rapidly identify actions or draw focus for further analysis. We addressed these issues, and realized unanticipated benefits as well, by creating a strong design and development architecture. Our results include: a templated set of metric visualizations, a radical decrease in cycle time, and realizing "self-service" business intelligence capabilities, empowering business users with expert domain knowledge to own and develop metrics. In this presentation, we discuss the visual architecture and design, the small set of templates, and the cognitive benefits of the visualizations now in use. The approach has garnered success at the company, program, directorate, and department levels, in large part due to the low cognitive burden for visualization understanding and development.

Keywords: Cognition · Visual architecture · Metrics

1 Introduction and Motivation

It is increasingly popular to display sets of disparate metric information as individual tiles laid out in grid fashion on the screen [1]. Our approach utilizes a library of standard templates in two categories, key performance indicators (KPI) and dashboards [2, 3]. Our metric development instructions are themselves visual, allowing them to be constructed easily by novices [4]. Our most utilized template, and the core visual element of our design, is our "metric display tile." Each tile delivers a discrete and easily discernible quantum of status. We designed a tile that visually encodes a substantial amount of status and trend data while boldly highlighting the primary messages, providing an economy of information interaction [5]. The library contains additional templates that provide more detailed charting capability for further analysis. The system works together so that tiles can link to other metrics displays, comment threads, and metric documentation, in snap-together fashion [6]. Finally, the templates are built to receive data from any source as long as the data are structured compatibly. Business analysts, data developers, and dashboard builders have a clear target for their data-related work; they simply get the template, set parameters and produce a functional, highly usable visualization. Constructed templates are simple to modify, highly reusable, and quick to deploy.

Cost and elapsed time are significant considerations for metrics development inside the enterprise. Different representations for metrics pose a challenge for consistent

© Springer International Publishing Switzerland 2016
F.F.-H. Nah and C.-H. Tan (Eds.): HCIBGO 2016, Part I, LNCS 9751, pp. 319–329, 2016.
DOI: 10.1007/978-3-319-39396-4_29

interpretation and intuitive action across departments, directorates and programs. A framework was needed in which metrics could be developed and maintained at low cost, to produce metrics that were readily understood. The framework needed to scale to a large number of metrics, and produce metrics that required little or no customization, with an extremely low cognitive burden. To accomplish this, a small set of reusable templates with strong user experience principles needed to be developed and supported. The templates had to accommodate a wide range of data sources, and be deployable by subject matter experts, not requiring technical experts. The framework had to support reusable templates that produced consistent, high-quality metrics visualizations, both to facilitate standardization and to keep cost low and elapsed development time short.

This paper is organized as follows. Section 2 presents the metrics architecture. Section 3 describes the composition of the visual metrics. Section 4 outlines business value. Section 5 describes the cognitive benefits of this approach. The conclusion is provided in Sect. 6.

2   Metrics Architecture

Layered software architecture is a very common design for client-server configurations [7]. A multi-layered metrics architecture facilitates the creation of the visualizations by encapsulating and segregating functionality. Each layer has a well-defined interface to communicate with the connecting layer (Fig. 1). The architecture has several advantages; (1) it enables the ability to make changes in any layer without affecting the other layers, as long as the communication interface remains unchanged, (2) each layer can be independently worked, (3) work can be completed in parallel or asynchronously and (4) different teams can work on different layers.

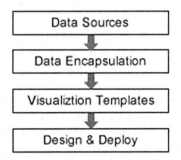

Fig. 1. Overview of the metrics architecture

2.1   Data Sources

The foundational data layer can be traditional data warehouse tables, Excel or text files (Fig. 2). Connectivity to Excel or text files provides the option for metric development prior to data automation or when automation is not an option.

Data Sources

Spreadsheet   Database   Text File

Fig. 2. Data can be consumed from most common sources

2.2 Data Encapsulation

The data source is connected to a pre-defined template which generates the required number of data points to render a visualization (Fig. 3). A single web service for each metric visualization is produced. Any data calculations or transformations can be encapsulated within the pre-defined template or performed prior to connecting to the data source.

Data Encapsulation

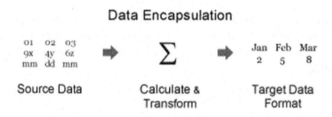

Source Data   Calculate &   Target Data
                     Transform   Format

Fig. 3. Data are manipulated for delivery to visualization templates

2.3 Visualization Templates

The single web service is connected to the template via an external interface connector which provides the data to the template in the correct format with the correct number of data points. The template contains a map that aligns each data point to the appropriate visual component (Fig. 4).

Visualization Templates

Fig. 4. Visualization templates

2.4 Design & Deploy

The completed metrics are deployed in a highly configurable web-based framework. Supplied parameters drive individual page configurations. Pages can be configured by role (executive level, mid-level management, program lead), and by product lines or locations (plant, warehouse, factory). The standard visualizations plug into the framework via a parametrized URL. The visualization can be arranged in any order and integrated with other types of objects such as PowerPoint presentations. The plug and play components make it easy to create, customize and change pages (Fig. 5).

Design & Deploy

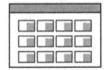 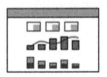 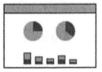

Fig. 5. Standardized visualizations are arranged for final delivery

3   Visual Metrics

Metric information is presented as a grid or series of tiles. Each tile delivers a discrete, digestible, quantum of status information "at-a-glance," while more focused attention reveals further detail and additional features. At-a-glance, each tile highlights 3 performance parameters:

- *Current Metric Health Status* - performance relative to established expectations, e.g., exceeds, meets, or fails.
- *Latest Performance Delta* - performance improved or degraded over the latest measurement period.
- *Performance Trending*. The changes in performance over a series of measurement periods.

Additional details on the tile include the *Current Numeric Metric Value* and the *Maximum and Minimum Values* recorded over the entire measurement period. Moreover, users can interact with tiles by clicking or tapping to reveal additional features, including a *Link to Further Analysis*, a *Link to Threaded Notes* so that users can contribute comments regarding performance, and a *Link to Metric Definition Documentation* for additional information about how the metric is calculated.

We can present a great deal of information without confusing users because each performance parameter is communicated via a distinct visual display parameter. These include hue, intensity, and form (Fig. 6).

- Hue: *Current Metric Health Status* is indicated by one of three contrasting background-colors.
- Intensity: *Latest Performance Delta* is indicated by the background-color intensity and saturation.
- Form: *Performance Trending* is shown as a sparkline that is colored to indicate the health of the overall trend.

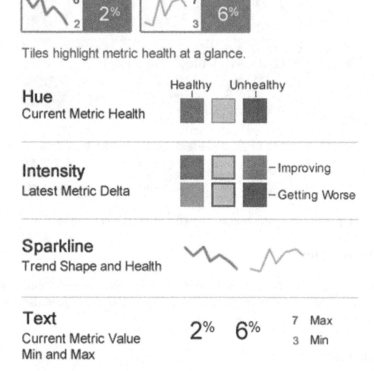

Fig. 6. Each tile communicates hight-level status information through visual properties: color (hue and intensity) and form. Further detail is available by reading text values and by interacting with the tile. (Color figure online)

While form and color are powerful properties for preattentive detection, conjunction objects are not perceived preattentively [8]. In our implementation, we separate these properties. When viewing a set of tiles, any red background-color indicates an unhealthy status, while light- or dark-red indicates that the performance over that last measurement period improved or got worse respectively. Meanwhile, a green sparkline would indicate improvement over time, even in a metric that is currently unhealthy.

Because each mode is free of noise, critical information can be identified among a large set of tiles (see e.g., Fig. 7), exploiting cognitive expectation and attention [9]. Background colors are prominent and "chart junk" is minimized. Additional information (e.g., min and max values) contextualizes the metric without diluting the signal.

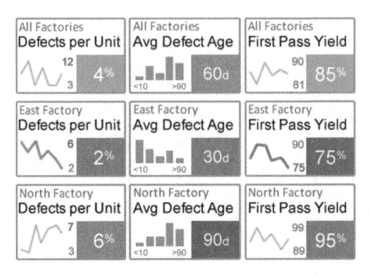

Fig. 7. A set of tiles grouped into a dashboard (Color figure online)

4   Business Value

During a 12-month period, we implemented our metric display architecture on three major projects. We compared these projects to equivalent work done using the old development process. Our results are as follows.

4.1   Cycle Time

Cycle times were reduced by 50–70 % for the equivalent work as compared to our previous development process. The overall architectural approach of having more atomized visualizations saves time as well since we are making files that are more simple and straightforward rather than building more complex displays into a single file.

4.2   Productivity

- The "fill out the form" nature of the development expands the number and types of staff that can produce metrics. File development can be accomplished by non-Developers, e.g., Business Analysts can set parameters and create a production ready visualization. This can also be extended to represent a Self Service BI capability [9].
- Rework involved in the development process was reduced for the equivalent work as compared to our previous development process.
- The templates are built to receive data from any source as long as the data are structured compatibly. This means that Business Analysts and Data Developers and Dashboard builders have a clear target for their data-related work.

- Having a standard set of visualizations streamlines the process of defining and refining customer requirements by allowing us to rapidly recycle through mockups and prototypes with customer input.

4.3 Quality

- The common visual vocabulary can be used by every organizational unit and functional area from Finance to Quality whether the intent is strategic or operational.
- Overall quality and consistency are improved.

4.4 Sustainability

- The visualizations are easier to maintain because they are simpler and the standardization makes the changes easier to locate. The changes that have been experienced so far have been in the data encapsulation layer.

5 Cognitive Benefits

The cognitive benefits of information visualizations are well-known [11, 12]. Visual imagery can have an important role in cognitive tasks [13, 14]. In this section we identify specific benefits for metrics display using the tile format based on our current work.

5.1 Scanning Dashboards or Scorecards Is Cognitively Costly

Tiles that are arranged into dashboards are useful for identifying metrics that may require intervention. A typical dashboard would lay out a set of tiles in positions specified during development, or possibly positioned by an end-user at run-time. The metrics consumer is required to scan the dashboard for metrics that may require further attention. Alternatively the user may formulate an a priori condition for which to scan, e.g., metrics that are out of control, or perhaps metrics that are performing exceptionally well.

These activities incur a cognitive burden for the user. Activities like formulating an *a priori* query or scanning the display for conditions that meet the query, or scanning the display for exceptions requires cognition and is subject to a host of external contextual demands and preexisting biases. There has been directed interest in identifying visualization techniques that reduce this cognitive burden [15, 16].

5.2 Sorting and Ordering the Display Structures and Prioritizes Attention

If a display is populated by tiles that are arranged dynamically at run-time, tiles can be arranged to highlight a higher-order level of insight. For example, in Fig. 10 the dashboard is split in half. Tiles representing Healthy metrics are one side while tiles for Unhealthy metrics are on the other (see Fig. 8 for details of how categories are assigned).

Evaluating Metrics into Healthy and Unhealthy Categories

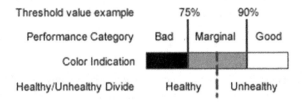

Midpoint of the middle range divides Healthy and Unhealthy

Fig. 8. Assuming three performance categories, *healthy* metrics are those with values on the desirable side of the midpoint of the middle range.

Healthy and *Unhealthy* metrics are further divided into those that improved over the latest measurement period and those that did not improve. This produces four cases. Each case is presented as a column in a grid layout.

- Unhealthy metrics that got even worse.
- Unhealthy metrics that improved.
- Healthy metrics that got worse.
- Healthy metrics that improved.

Within each column, metric tiles are sorted in decreasing order of the *Latest Performance Delta* (i.e., the normalized magnitude of change over the latest measurement period). See Fig. 9 for an illustration.

5.3 Performance Signals Parsed into Distinct Channels

One implication of arranging tiles in this way (Figs. 9 and 10) is that four distinct performance signals are resolved with greater clarity as compared to statically positioned tiles. These performance signals are: (1) failing performance, (2) poor performance that may be turning around, (3) good performance that may be slipping, and (4) good performance that is getting even better, a.k.a., superstars.

5.4 Dynamically Sorted Dashboard Example

Figure 10 is an example of how metrics might be arranged to focus on metric improvement.

- The metric at position (a) is unhealthy and has gotten worse by the largest margin among all the unhealthy metrics that have gotten worse over the last reporting period. In this case, Alpha Factory has experienced an alarming spike in injuries.
- The metric at position (b) is unhealthy, but has improved by the largest margin among all the unhealthy metrics that have improved. In this case, Echo Factory has improved their ability to meet their schedule and they have made it into the middle (grey) range.

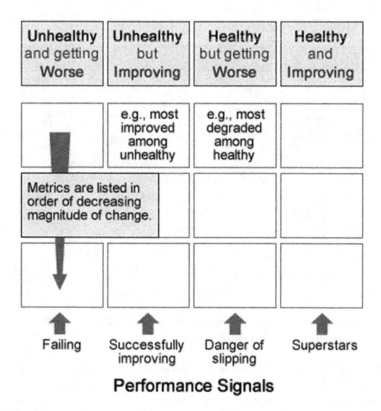

Fig. 9. Tiles are arranged dynamically within a structure that focuses on metric improvement. Tiles are divided into healthy and unhealthy metrics that have either improved or declined (i.e., gotten worse). Within each column, metrics are sorted in decreasing order of the *Latest Performance Delta* (i.e., the normalized magnitude of change over the latest measurement period).

- The metric at position (c) is healthy. But over the latest reporting period it has gotten worse by the largest margin among all the healthy metrics that have gotten worse over the same period. In this case, Alpha Factory has experienced a substantial slip in their ability to meet their schedule.

6   Conclusion

We present a simple visual metrics architecture composed of reducible, reusable, and serializable elements. These elements represent an inclusive approach that is concerned with source data at one end, and extends to user perception at the other end. Our data visualization architecture is Data are provided to the visualization templates in a platform agnostic way. These processed data are then provided to the visualization part of the architecture. Visualization elements are arranged in a purposeful way to facilitate orthogonal exploration of data by directing attention. That is, a viewer can scan among elements on the surface for high-level information but can also drill into further detail

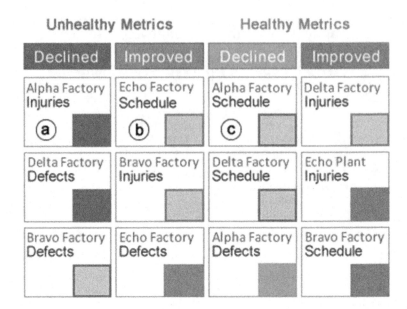

Fig. 10. Example of a dashboard with dynamically sorted tiles. We have omitted some details (sparklines and text) in order to illustrate this dashboard.

by focusing attention on a single element. These two levels of attention may be referred to as "orientation" and "engagement" [8]. Our visualization architecture is effective because any part of the visualization can "get out of the way" to allow the user to efficiently transition between orientation and engagement, and to transition among elements (e.g. among tiles or among elements within a tile).

References

1. Lamantia, J.: Enhancing the portal experience. Enhancing Enterp. Serv.-Oriented Archit. Adv. Web Portal Technol. 245 (2012)
2. Parmenter, D.: Key Performance Indicators: Developing, Implementing, and Using Winning KPIs. Wiley, Hoboken (2015)
3. Palpanas, T., Chowdhary, P., Mihaila, G., Pinel, F.: Integrated model-driven dashboard development. Inf. Syst. Front. 9(2–3), 195–208 (2007)
4. Grammel, L., Tory, M., Storey, M.A.: How information visualization novices construct visualizations. IEEE Trans. Vis. Comput. Graph. 16(6), 943–952 (2010)
5. Tudoreanu, M.E.: Designing effective program visualization tools for reducing user's cognitive effort. In: Proceedings of the 2003 ACM Symposium on Software Visualization, June 2003, pp. 105–ff. ACM (2003)
6. North, C., Shneiderman, B.: Snap-together visualization: can users construct and operate coordinated visualizations? Int. J. Hum.-Comput. Stud. 53(5), 715–739 (2000)
7. Sharma, V.S., Jalote, P., Trivedi, K.S.: Evaluating performance attributes of layered software architecture. In: Heineman, G.T., Crnković, I., Schmidt, H.W., Stafford, J.A., Ren, X.-M., Wallnau, K. (eds.) CBSE 2005. LNCS, vol. 3489, pp. 66–81. Springer, Heidelberg (2005)

8. Healey, C.G., Enns, J.T.: Attention and visual memory in visualization and computer graphics. IEEE Trans. Vis. Comput. Graph. **18**(7), 1170–1188 (2012)
9. Sonderer, K., Lynch, K.: Metrics visualization templates case study in aerospace product development. In: International Symposium on Electronic Imaging Visualization and Data Analysis Conference, 16–18 February 2016, San Francisco, California (2016)
10. Summerfield, C., Egner, T.: Expectation (and attention) in visual cognition. Trends Cogn. Sci. **13**(9), 403–409 (2009)
11. Fekete, J.-D., van Wijk, J.J., Stasko, J.T., North, C.: The value of information visualization. In: Kerren, A., Stasko, J.T., Fekete, J.-D., North, C. (eds.) Information Visualization. LNCS, vol. 4950, pp. 1–18. Springer, Heidelberg (2008)
12. Ware, C.: Information Visualization: Perception for Design. Elsevier, Amsterdam (2012)
13. Kosslyn, S.M., Thompson, W.L., Ganis, G.: The Case for Mental Imagery. Oxford University Press, New York (2006)
14. Chen, C.: Top 10 unsolved information visualization problems. IEEE Comput. Graph. Appl. **25**(4), 12–16 (2006)
15. Melcher, J., Seese, D.: Visualization and clustering of business process collections based on process metric values. In: 10th International Symposium on Symbolic and Numeric Algorithms for Scientific Computing, SYNASC 2008, pp. 572–575 (2008)
16. Peng, W., Ward, M.O., Rundensteiner, E.: Clutter reduction in multi-dimensional data visualization using dimension reordering. In: IEEE Symposium on Information Visualization, INFOVIS 2004, pp. 89–96 (2004)

Converting Opinion into Knowledge
Improving User Experience and Analytics of Online Polls

Martin Stabauer[✉], Christian Mayrhauser, and Michael Karlinger

Johannes Kepler University, Linz, Austria
martin.stabauer@jku.at

Abstract. A vast majority of internet users has adopted new ways and possibilities of interaction and information exchange on the social web. Individuals are becoming accustomed to contribute and express their opinion on various platforms and websites. Commercial online polls allow operators of online newspapers, blogs and other forms of media sites to provide such services to their users. Consequently, their popularity is rapidly increasing and more and more potential areas of application emerge. However, in most cases the expressed opinions are stored and displayed without any further actions and the knowledge that lies in the answers is discarded.

This research paper explores the possibilities, advantages and limits of applying semantic technologies to these online polls. For this purpose, a list of requirements was assembled and possible system architectures for semantic knowledgebases were investigated with the focus on providing consistent and extensive data for further processing. In a next step, the current state of the art of relevant visualization technologies was analyzed and further research challenges were identified.

Our results discuss possible applications within the scope of a challenging case study. A comprehensive data pool provided by our industry partner allows for testing various improvements to user experience and traction of the polling system.

Keywords: Online polls · Named entity recognition · Information extraction · Semantic technologies · Ontology engineering · Dashboards · Graphical user interfaces

1 Introduction

1.1 Online Polls

Online polls are becoming more and more popular on a large variety of websites, e.g., online newspapers, blogs and other forms of media sites. These single-question polls allow users of the respective sites to express their opinion and contribute to the outcome of a question drafted by the operator of the website. This opportunity is appreciated very much by large numbers of internet users. Figure 1 shows such an online poll.

© Springer International Publishing Switzerland 2016
F.F.-H. Nah and C.-H. Tan (Eds.): HCIBGO 2016, Part I, LNCS 9751, pp. 330–340, 2016.
DOI: 10.1007/978-3-319-39396-4_30

Fig. 1. Online Poll

Many of today's single-question online polling systems are operated by the website owners themselves. Giving their users the possibility to contribute to parts of the site's content is first priority for most systems; it seems that great usability or analytical features are only insufficiently considered. However, gaining knowledge from the answers to polls – in contrast of simply displaying the results and then discarding the information contained therein – could bring enormous benefits:

- Polls can be clustered and categorized by their respective topic. This makes various applications possible like automatically showing a poll that fits the content of the article that it will be complementing, or showing users a related poll after they have answered a first one.
- The website visitors who answer one or more polls can be analyzed in regard to their specific attitudes and preferences. By learning about their users, publishers can verify current assumptions about their target groups and get to know entirely new groups.
- These target groups can then be displayed graphically, e.g., via Venn or Euler diagrams. This gives the website operators a better overview of their users and allows them to select specific groups of persons for further actions.
- One of these further actions is using the target groups as input for retargeting advertisements across platforms. This type of advertising has emerged as one of the most widely used across the internet and facilitates custom-tailored ads for segmented user groups.
- A semantic knowledgebase of relevant information can be generated and consequently connected to other linked data available online. This database is intended to show interconnections and dependencies in a more detailed and precise way than classic relational data structures. New knowledge can be discovered by techniques of the semantic web like reasoning.
- Combining the answers of several independent polls for creating more detailed user profiles becomes feasible. The website content can be adapted to better match the discovered user profiles.
- Extracting and aggregating private information about claims that can not be verified turn out to be of great value and online polls can contribute in doing that. [11]

1.2   Methodology and Contribution

Natural Language Processing (NLP), the languages of the semantic web and other technologies relevant to this study's field of research have achieved immense progress in the last years. This paper explores the possibilities of tools and techniques for improving user experience for both common internet users and website operators. While the former can profit from a better quality of suggestions for further articles and polls as well as from better categorized question/answer pairs, the latter can benefit from a greatly improved admin dashboard that provides whole new possibilities for analyzing and illustrating the outcomes of their polls and use them as basis for further applications.

To achieve these advances, current state-of-the-art technologies in the field of knowledge extraction (KE) from natural language question/answer pairs are analyzed. Consequently, the implementation of a semantic knowledgebase designed specifically to the requirements of online polling systems is demonstrated within the scope of an extensive case study based on a real-world data pool of more than 10,000 questions with approx. 36,000 answers and 653,000 user votes given worldwide in the years 2014 and 2015. This is followed by discussing UI elements for the administrator's dashboard like displaying suggestions for future target groups by employing Euler diagrams as well as prototypical advertising capabilities.

1.3   Related Work

Great advances in NLP and the Semantic Web have led to various fields of research related to our task. Recent examples are NLP for question/answer pairs as described in [14] or [5], and paraphrasing (e.g., [2]). Knowledge representation has been in the center of attention of research for decades (e.g., [4,13]) and still great progress is being achieved (e.g., [1,3,8]).

Applications of the Semantic Web like DBpedia [15] and other knowledgebases are making it possible to link shared knowledge and build new solutions on top of existing ones. While early research was mainly done for texts in English, globalization of Linked Data brought the necessity to deal with different languages. Significant progress has been made in multilingual entity extraction [6]. This is exemplified by research on German language (e.g., [12,17]).

Modern approaches suggest recursive self-learning methods when it comes to entity detection and extraction [9] and various methods for semi-automatic ontology development [16].

2   Semantic Technologies

2.1   Knowledge Extraction

To be helpful for extracting knowledge from single-question online polls, a semantic system needs to fulfil a number of requirements. Some of these are:

- While most ontologies and NLP technologies specialize on a certain domain, online polls can relate to pretty much everything. In most cases, the topic of a poll is not even known in advance. This means that if there are external knowledgebases for specific domains involved, they need to be made compatible and get interconnected. Finding out the scope of a poll is also very important to determine the relevance for specific user groups. The scope of some questions is limited to a certain time or region, e.g. *Who will win the football world cup?* or *Who have you voted for in South Africa's General Elections?*.
- The knowledge to be extracted in many cases lies within the question combined with the chosen answer. The question *How often do you play video games?* by itself does not contain any knowledge about the user who answers the question, the chosen answer *Daily* needs to be taken into consideration as well. This means that there is the need to combine question and answer and/or to paraphrase the question. Even relatively simple Yes/No polls like *Hillary Clinton: First female U.S. President?* need to be converted to a positive and a negative version for further processing.
- The focus in NLP research traditionally lies on English language. However, the online polls in our case study are being created in many different languages. The findings of NLP for texts in English can not be transferred to other languages, but there is an increasing number of research projects on multilingual entity extraction.
- Another special requirement for a KE system for online polls is that it needs to have the capability to sort out inappropriate, manipulative or suggestive polls. These can occur, because most of the polls in the data pool are created and published by media websites or blog owners who can pose all the questions they like. These "bad" polls should not be taken into consideration for further analysis.

A comprehensive set of requirements for a system coping with knowledge extraction from online polls can be found in the work of Stabauer, Grossmann and Stumptner [20]. For a comparison of knowledge extraction tools, see [7]. At the time of writing there is no known system able to deal with all the aforementioned special requirements. Therefore, there is the need for an alternative way of annotating polls manually. Figure 2 shows a mockup. For each possible answer to a question the administrator can choose from predefined relations and semantic concepts, thus creating new object properties in the knowledgebase.

2.2 Knowledgebase

The semantic knowledgebase in our case study is embedded in a complex system architecture, Fig. 3 gives an overview. The analytical subsystem is responsible for storing and analyzing the knowledge that is extracted from the polls and the users' answers, respectively. Some information in the analytical subsystem (e.g., meta information of polls and votes) is stored in an auxiliary database. This divide is due to size limitations in the semantic knowledgebase and to the structure of the data to be stored. All databases and systems work together seamlessly

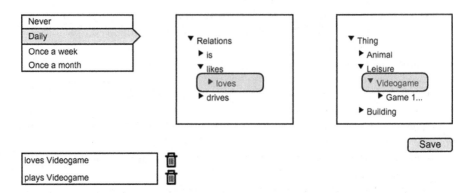

Fig. 2. Semantic Annotation

and enable the administrator to gradually build up a consistent, accurate and extensive knowledgebase.

Following the approach of semantic annotation as depicted in Fig. 2, knowledge about a specific user is stored in RDFS/OWL triples as follows:

<http://polling.com/pollees#Pollee123>
    <http://polling.com/ontology#loves>
        <http://polling.com/ontology#Videogame>.

To comply with the ideas of Linked Data, the concepts in the knowledgebase (*#Videogame* in the example above) are linked to external knowledgebases. In this case there might be a link to DBpedia as follows:

<http://polling.com/ontology#Videogame>
    rdfs:subClassOf
        <http://dbpedia.org/ontology/VideoGame>.

2.3 Reasoning and Analysis

The knowledge about users and concepts that is stored in the analytical subsystem, is consequently being analyzed by a series of algorithms, beginning with standard RDFS and OWL reasoners. This enables clustering users by their preferences and characteristics and so very advanced retargeting applications become feasible. Additionally, users can profit as they are given suggestions for further articles and polls that meet their specific interests without breaking the simplicity and anonymity of the polling process. Immediate results of the reasoning process are sets of persons with specific properties, their intersections and the respective set sizes. These will be used for visualization in the administrator dashboard and for further applications in retargeting advertising.

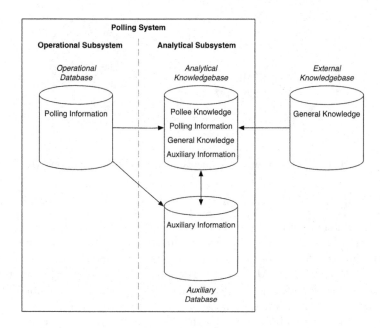

Fig. 3. Polling System Architecture

3 Knowledge Visualization

The consequent step after building up a consistent and extensive knowledge base is to use that data to improve certain aspects of the polling process. In this case we try to enhance the administrator's user experience and provide additional functionality by visualizing the findings of the analysis within the framework of the existing dashboard. This chapter gives an overview of existing means of visualizing bigger data sets and their issues.

Common representation techniques can be used to gain new knowledge about given data. Both Euler and Venn diagrams show the size of data sets that are built from a data pool as well as the correlations between these sets. Euler and Venn diagrams use geometrical shapes to represent data sets and intersecting sets, which contain named data sets. To build an Euler or Venn diagram two sets of data are needed: A set to store all data sets M and a set of intersections U, where every set $e \in M$ is at least part of one intersection set in U.

Following the definition of Venn diagrams, all possible intersections have to be shown, and intersections that are not contained in U must be marked as empty. Figure 4 shows common Euler and Venn diagrams of the sets $M = \{A, B, C\}$ and $U = \{A, B, C, AB, AC\}$ and reveals the problem of Venn diagrams in regard to empty intersection sets. If the amount of sets in M increases, Venn Diagrams get more and more complex and harder to understand. This problem makes it clear that Venn diagrams can not be efficiently used for the visualization of bigger sets such as the ones in our case study.

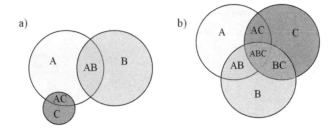

Fig. 4. Examples of an Euler diagram (a) and a Venn diagram (b)

3.1 Visualization Technologies

Calculating Euler diagrams gets more complicated and difficult when the complexity of the diagram grows [19]. The complexity is defined by the amount of sets in the intersection sets in U, which can be as high as 2^n, whereby n equals the amount of sets in M. More issues become apparent when the complexity increases. To verify if an Euler or Euler-like diagram (such as described in e.g., [19]) is correctly drawn, an agreement about the visualization is needed. The following points need to be fulfilled by the diagram in order to be recognized as correctly drawn:

- Every set $e \in M$ needs to be visualized by at least one marked geometrical form and e has to be at least part of one set in U.
- The area of the used geometrical form representing $e \in M$ has to be sized in reference to the amount of elements in the set e.
- For every set $e \in M$ that is part of an intersection set $i \in U$, which contains more than one set, there needs to be an area where every set $s \in i$ intersects with every other set in i.
- If two or more geometrical forms are intersecting, there has to be at least one intersection set in U that contains the sets of the intersecting forms. Furthermore, the intersecting area has to be sized according to the amount of elements in the geometrical form.
- Only sets that are part of M and intersection sets that are part of U are allowed to be visualized.

Stapleton et al. describe 3 base methods to generate Euler diagrams: Dual graphs, inductive and using particular shapes [21]. The first method calculates a dual graph based on the intersection sets in U and draws the geometrical forms in a way, so that every geometrical form representing a set $e \in M$ contains every node that is included in the set e. The inductive method uses a step by step procedure to calculate the position of the geometrical forms. The last method changes the shapes of the geometrical forms to create drawable Euler diagrams.

3.2 Issues and Solutions

On the basis of the afore-mentioned generation methods and the used geometrical forms, several issues become apparent. Euler diagrams using circles as geometrical indicator of sets, such as shown in Fig. 4, can not always be drawn in a way that every requirement defined in Chap. 3.1 is fulfilled. As an example, a diagram containing the set $M = \{A, B, C\}$ and the set $U = \{A, B, AC, BC\}$ is not drawable with one circle per set $e \in M$ and without creating a fictional intersection set with C and $\{\}$ in U.

In order to avoid creating fictional intersection sets, a simple method is to remove intersection sets that violate the requirements defined in Chap. 3.1. Another method is to remove certain sets $e \in M$ and the intersection sets that contains e. As an example: Fig. 4 shows the desired facts by removing the conflict set C or the conflict sets A and B. This creates two potential, rough approximations of the given example. The conflict sets could be calculated through variants of the MinRelax or the QuickXPlain algorithms [10]. For every visualization problem, there are 1 to n conflict sets linked with the problem, which could be removed to solve the problem.

Another way to create drawable Euler diagrams is to split or clone sets [19]. The newly created or cloned sets can then be drawn as several geometrical forms that are not intersecting each other. All sets have to be marked as either the starting set or be linked together to improve the readability of the diagram. The total amount of intersections, which the newly created sets are part of, should equal the amount of sets in U containing the starting set. According to the defined requirements for Euler diagrams in Chap. 3.1, the size of the forms represents the amount of objects in one set. If a set is cloned, the sum of the areas of the cloned sets will represent the wrong amount of objects in the starting set. Figure 5 shows the issues and the solutions of the afore-mentioned example.

Since geometrical forms in our study represent a set of persons with specific properties, generalizing these properties to create drawable forms is another option. With the assumption that a property is composed of a type and a noun, both could be generalized individually. As an example, the property "loves Dog" could be generalized to "likes Dog", "likes Animal", "loves Animal", "loves Thing", and so on. Every set of properties with the option to be generalized will form a combined new set in M, which contains the generalized properties. The starting set of properties has to be removed from M. Properties in U that do not exist any longer in M need to be replaced with the new generalized set. With reference to the shown approach to split or clone sets [19], it is possible

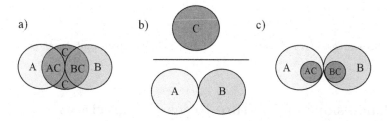

Fig. 5. (a) shows the sets $M = \{A, B, C\}$ and $U = \{A, B, AC, BC\}$, (b) shows rough approximations of the starting diagram and (c) shows a solution for the problem.

to generalize only one part or clone of a set. The generalization is supposed to reduce the amount of intersections between sets in M, and the generalized set has to be one of the sets that were identified with the described method before, creating rough approximations.

Sets in Euler diagrams can also be visualized by using abstract forms [18]. The diagrams can be created and calculated with the use of planar graphs and triangles. Used planar graphs represent the set U and extend the set with a null set for every set in U which only contains one set. The nodes in the planar graph are represented by sets in U, while the edges are represented as lines between two nodes. A line is drawn between two nodes a and b, if the set of a is fully contained in b. The line between a and b is omitted, if there exists a node c that fully contains the set of a and its set is fully contained in b. The drawing area is divided into several triangular sectors that can be used to calculate the area of several abstract forms for the different sets in M [18]. Figure 6 shows an example.

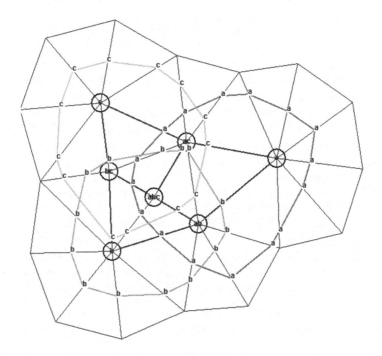

Fig. 6. A diagram for the sets $M = \{a, b, c\}$ and $U = \{a, b, c, ab, bc, abc, ac\}$ [18]

4   Conclusions and Future Research Directions

We have presented the findings of a conducted case study that turned the results of simple textual single question online polls into extensive knowledge about polls, answers and above all, the users. We have shown the structure and functioning of an analytical subsystem that complements the existing operational polling system responsible for the basic functions of displaying polls and collecting votes. It does so without breaking the main strengths of simplicity and anonymity and with maintaining full independency from third-party APIs.

We also have presented possibilities and challenges of visualizing the obtained knowledge in an administration dashboard. The created diagrams not only serve as a source of information but also let the administrator select groups of users for further usage in retargeting advertising. There are still some issues in visualizing semantic models using common Euler diagrams that need to be solved.

The interaction of semantic technologies with visualization strategies turned out to be quite challenging. However, there were promising advances in basic visualization of a limited number of sets, which proved to be very useful and intuitive for administrators of polling systems and could create a fair quantity of new useful knowledge. While not being explicitly designed for further refining of the knowledgebase, the visualizations do contribute to a better understanding of the collected knowledge. This is of particular importance when building extensively large ontologies like the one in our case study, where it is hard to stay on top of things.

Future research will include improvements in analysis of the knowledgebase. Building on standard RDFS and OWL reasoning many useful extensions need to be considered, e.g., calculation of probabilities (*has been to Russia* could have a probability of 80 % for *likes travelling*) in order to extend target groups in case they have been conceived too narrowly. Another research direction shall be alternative visualization techniques for different applications within the administrator dashboard like conveniently navigating the knowledgebase or displaying explanations of inferences being made. As the relevance for polls being elements of the social web keeps growing, investing more efforts in them will certainly be worthwhile.

References

1. Amir, S., Ait-Kaci, H.: Cedar: efficient reasoning for the semantic web. In: Proceedings of the 10th International Conference on Signal-Image Technology and Internet-Based Systems, pp. 157–163. IEEE (2014)
2. Androutsopoulos, I., Malakasiotis, P.: A survey of paraphrasing and textual entailment methods. J. Artif. Intell. Res. **38**, 135–187 (2010)
3. Bekkerman, R., Gavish, M.: High-precision phrase-based document classification on a modern scale. In: Proceedings of the KDD. ACM (2011)
4. Bench-Capon, T.J.M.: Knowledge Representation: An Approach to Artificial Intelligence. Academic Press Ltd, London (1990)
5. Berant, J., Liang, P.: Semantic parsing via paraphrasing. In: Proceedings of the 52nd Annual Meeting of the Association for Computational Linguistics, pp. 1415–1425 (2014)
6. Daiber, J., Jakob, M., Hokamp, C., Mendes, P.N.: Improving efficiency and accuracy in multilingual entity extraction. In: Proceedings of the 9th International Conference on Semantic Systems (2013)

7. Gangemi, A.: A comparison of knowledge extraction tools for the semantic web. In: Cimiano, P., Corcho, O., Presutti, V., Hollink, L., Rudolph, S. (eds.) ESWC 2013. LNCS, vol. 7882, pp. 351–366. Springer, Heidelberg (2013)

8. Hellmann, S., Lehmann, J., Auer, S., Brümmer, M.: Integrating NLP using linked data. In: Alani, H., Kagal, L., Fokoue, A., Groth, P., Biemann, C., Parreira, J.X., Aroyo, L., Noy, N., Welty, C., Janowicz, K. (eds.) ISWC 2013, Part II. LNCS, vol. 8219, pp. 98–113. Springer, Heidelberg (2013)

9. Huang, E.H., Socher, R., Manning, C.D., Ng, A.Y.: Improving word representations via global context and multiple word prototypes. In: Proceedings of the 50th Annual Meeting of the Association for Computational Linguistics, pp. 873–882 (2012)

10. Jannach, D., Zanker, M., Felfernig, A., Friedrich, G.: Recommender Systems - An Introduction, Chapter Knowledge-Based Recommendation, pp. 81–123. Cambridge University Press, New York (2010)

11. Jurca, R., Faltings, B.: Incentives for expressing opinions in online polls. In: Proceedings of the 9th ACM Conference on Electronic Commerce, pp. 119–128. ACM (2008)

12. Kallmeyer, L., Maier, W.: Data-driven parsing using probabilistic linear context-free rewriting systems. Comput. Linguist. $39(1)$, 87–119 (2013)

13. Kamp, H.: A theory of truth and semantic representation. In: Groenendijk, J., Janssen, T., Stokhof, M. (eds.) Formal Methods in the Study of Language, pp. 277–322. Mathematisch Centrum, University of Amsterdam (1981)

14. Kumar, A., Irsoy, O., Su, J., Bradbury, J., English, R., Pierce, B., Ondruska, P., Iyyer, M., Gulrajani, I., Socher, R.: Ask me anything: dynamic memory netorks for natural language processing. CoRR, abs/1506.07285 (2015)

15. Lehmann, J., Isele, R., Jakob, M., Jentzsch, A., Kontokostas, D., Mendes, P.N., Hellmann, S., Morsey, M., van Kleef, P., Auer, S., Bizer, C.: DBpedia - a large-scale, multilingual knowledge base extracted from wikipedia. Semant. Web J. $6(2)$, 167–195 (2015)

16. Pazienza, M.T., Stellato, A. (eds.): Semi-Automatic Ontology Development - Processes and Resources. IGI Global, Hershey (2012)

17. Rafferty, A., Manning, C.D.: Parsing three german treebanks: lexicalized and unlexicalized baselines. In: Proceedings of the Workshop on Parsing German at ACL, pp. 40–46 (2008)

18. Rodgers, P., Zhang, L., Stapleton, G., Fish, A.: Embedding wellformed euler diagrams. In: Proceedings of the 12th International Conference on Information Visualisation, pp. 585–593. IEEE (2008)

19. Simonetto, P., Auber, D.: Visualise undrawable euler diagrams. In: Proceedings of the 12th International Conference on Information Visualisation, pp. 594–599 (2008)

20. Stabauer, M., Grossmann, G., Stumptner, M.: State of the art in knowledge extraction from online polls: a survey of current technologies. In: Proceedings of the Australasian Computer Science Week Multiconference, vol. 58, pp. 1–8. ACM (2016)

21. Stapleton, G., Zhang, L., Howse, J., Rodgers, P.: Drawing euler diagrams with circles. In: Goel, A.K., Jamnik, M., Narayanan, N.H. (eds.) Diagrams 2010. LNCS, vol. 6170, pp. 23–38. Springer, Heidelberg (2010)

Generating Competitive Intelligence Digests with a LDA-Based Method: A Case of BT Intellact

Qiang Wei[✉], Jiaqi Wang, Guoqing Chen, and Xunhua Guo

School of Economics and Management, Tsinghua University, Beijing 100084, China
{weiq,wangjq3.10,chengq,guoxh}@sem.tsinghua.edu.cn

Abstract. Internet has transformed the ways that organizations gather, produce and transmit competitive intelligence (CI), especially in the age of big data. This paper introduces a competitive intelligence digest generation method based on LDA topic modelling and representative text extraction. With the incorporated metric of perplexity, the proposed method is capable of automatic grouping of the texts and generating CI digests in an appropriate number of topics. Moreover, the method is applied to the context of BT Plc in the form of a case study, demonstrating its effectiveness in practical use.

Keywords: Competitive intelligence · LDA-based · Topic generation · Representative documents extraction

1 Introduction

Competitive intelligence (CI) such as market environmental dynamics, rivals' updates, techniques' hot spots, etc., plays a critical role in supporting executives and managers to make strategic decisions for an organization [1]. Nowadays, the Internet, as an information-rich open-source platform and an inter-organizational communications tool, has transformed the ways that organizations gather, produce and transmit competitive intelligence.

In the age of big data, competitive intelligence is generally hidden and should be discovered from various information sources online including news, business reports, surveys, financial reviews, etc., whereas traditional search tools and information retrieval methods can hardly provide satisfactory outcomes for competitive intelligence in an automatic and effective fashion. For instance, every day, a market researcher could easily collect/crawl a huge amount of rivals' data and market surveys, but is usually facing a problem of information overload due to the fact that the data/information is often sparse, conflicting, diverse or redundant, which makes CI difficult to generate and comprehend. In this regard, providing insightful digests (small and manageable sets of extracted important results/entries) of competitive intelligence (hereafter also referred to as CI digests) is considered meaningful and important for market researchers and then managers. Unlike traditional techniques such as information retrieval/summarization with manual manipulation and hand crafting, our work focuses on a LDA-based method for generating CI digests with an application in the context of British Telecommunications Plc (BT).

© Springer International Publishing Switzerland 2016
F.F.-H. Nah and C.-H. Tan (Eds.): HCIBGO 2016, Part I, LNCS 9751, pp. 341–349, 2016.
DOI: 10.1007/978-3-319-39396-4_31

BT is Britain's largest telecommunication company, whose business covers more than 170 countries and extensive entities. In meeting rapid market changes where new technologies and competitors are emerging, BT created an internal business intelligence unit called BT Intellact Department (BTID), aimed to collate and refine industry-related text information on the Internet for all employees in BT Group, and to continue daily updates of the information. The original sources of information BTID handles include online business news, trade journals/magazines, non-public information BT purchases from press operators and industry institutes, as well as internal research reports. Finally, CI digests are summarized under various topics and provided to end-users every week after users subscribe their preferred channels (i.e., labelled with topic tags). Though BTID has brought BT a solid competitive advantage through CI digests, handcrafting of human experts was heavily involved in the text analysis. The workflow for the service is illustrated in Fig. 1.

Apparently, BTID's service was practically valuable but encountered two challenges: (1) low efficiency of hand-crafting in the timely updating big-data environment; and (2) high hand-crafting burden for the BTID experts on not only clustering the huge amount of texts, but also extracting diverse and representative texts. This motivated us to develop a data-driven intelligent method.

In consideration of large-scaled and unlabeled data sources as well as their rapid updates, unsupervised clustering is deemed methodologically appropriate in processing and generating CI digests. Concretely, the Latent Dirichlet Allocation based (i.e., LDA-based) method is adopted in forms of text topic modelling, so as to effectively extract the valuable latent topics intelligently and group similar texts automatically, thus largely reducing the manual involvement [2].

The paper is organized as follows. Section 2 briefly overviews the related literature on competitive intelligence analysis and the LDA methods. Section 3 presents a LDA-based CI digest generation method. Section 4 analyzes a case on BT Intellact with the proposed CI digest generation. Finally, Sect. 5 provides concluding remarks and future work.

2   Literature Overview

Competitive Intelligence (CI) digests can be applied to various business areas. CI digests in marketing are to understand the latest market needs and users' feedbacks. Production

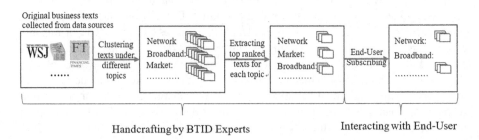

Fig. 1. Current workflow in BTID

departments can pick better suppliers and be informed of newest technologies of competitors with help of CI digests. Strategic CI digests can help top managers capture business insights to support their strategic decisions. Through concise and valuable information brought by CI digests, the overall efficiency of organizations could be greatly enhanced [1].

In CI digest generation, prior research efforts have resulted in a series of findings and techniques with regard to semantic modelling with natural language, representative information extraction and evaluation, competitive keyword suggestion and marketing method, semantic transitivity analysis as well as the corresponding information retrieval methods, text mining methods, etc.

Formally, given a set C of online collected n business texts, CI digest generation is to extract a small set of m texts, denoted as D, where $m << n$. Since the collected business texts are generally without explicit and structural labels, thus unsupervised clustering could be conducted, which can divide texts based on their similarities into several categories [3–6]. Furthermore, considering the semantic nature in CI digest generation, the texts can be grouped more effectively based upon their topic similarities rather than word similarities. Thus, in this spirit, the well-known LDA methodology is regarded suitable [4]. LDA is a three-level Bayesian clustering for latent topic modeling [7–11].

For grouping unstructured and latent text topics, LDA possesses the following merits [12–17]. First, LDA's effectiveness for large-scale text clustering is very desirable, and its efficiency performance is also acceptable. Second, its probability model is solid, showing strong adaptability and scalability in many applications. Third, it is conscious of the influence of the text structure on text meaning in addition to word frequency, which could dig out the hidden semantics of texts. Fourth, it allows for characteristics of multi-topics of texts, which conforms to practical cases.

3   A LDA-Based Intelligent CI Digest Generation Method

Generally, given a set C of n texts (business news, reports, blogs, surveys, etc.) collected from open sources, a LDA-based semantic text mining method is used to extract a small set D of m texts, where $D \subseteq C$, and the text in D is the most representative text with respect to its corresponding category in C.

Concretely, the CI digest generation process is composed of two stages, i.e., LDA-based clustering with topic tag assignment and representative texts extraction for each clustered category.

In the LDA-based clustering stage, first, each text in C is preprocessed and parsed, represented by a vector of extracted keywords along with their frequencies, based on which the corresponding LDA semantic model can be built. Second, all keywords represented by a vector of keywords with latent semantic relevance will be clustered into different categories based on the LDA model, i.e., m clusters/categories are generated. Third, for each cluster with multiple keywords along with latent semantic relevance, an appropriate topic ID or tag will be assigned to each category. Thereafter, the texts are automatically clustered into m categories. Obviously, its efficiency outperforms manual labelling operation.

Next, in the representative texts extraction stage, the text with highest LDA relevance in each category (e.g., containing usually tens or hundreds of texts) could be extracted as the most representative text. Thus, the whole set of a CI digest is generated with m texts with respect to the original set of n texts.

The general framework of the proposed method is shown in Fig. 2.

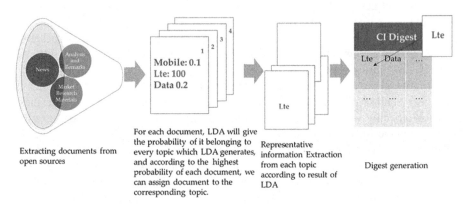

Fig. 2. General framework of the LDA-based CI digest generation

During the process of the proposed method, the number of topics, i.e., m, is to be predetermined. If m is set too small, i.e., too few topics, the derived CI digest will be less informative; on the contrary, too big m means that too much tedious information will be retained in the derived CI digest. Therefore, to determine an appropriate m value significantly affects the final results. However, due to the users'/experts' cognitive difficulty in getting a whole picture for totally n texts, it is hard for them to configure an appropriate value of m. Therefore, according to Blei et al. [4], a metric, i.e., *Perplexity*, could be used here for helping determine the m value by assessing the quality of topic model through its prediction effect. *Perplexity* is as defined in Eq. (1). The lower *Perplexity* is, the more representative this topic model is.

$$Perplexity(D) = \exp\left\{\frac{-\left(\sum_{d=1}^{m}\log(p(w_d))\right)}{\sum_{d=1}^{m}N_d}\right\}, \tag{1}$$

where d is a derived topic, N_d is the number of words in d, and $p(w_d)$ is the probability of every word in d, m is the number of topics. Thus, by minimizing the *Perplexity* of the original set of D, the appropriate number of topics, i.e., m, can be derived.

By integrating the *Perplexity* optimization process into stage 1, the method is finally devised. With this proposed method, a CI digest could be automatically and intelligently extracted from a large amount of original texts. For the example of BTID workflow in Fig. 1, if the proposed method could be integrated, the workflow could be improved as shown in Fig. 3.

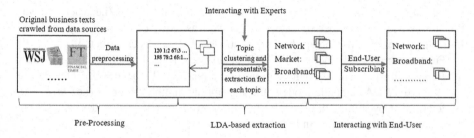

Fig. 3. Improved workflow in BTID

Figure 3 shows that, first, the crawled texts could be pre-processed into structured data, which can be used in the LDA-based extraction. Then, with the LDA-based extraction, the number of topics, and all the topics as well as representative texts for corresponding categories could be derived. Theoretically, this step can be conducted automatically without human intervention. Nevertheless, in our method, an interface is designed to interact with experts (e.g., BTID experts) for investigating the results and necessarily adjusting, e.g., tag names, text assignments, according to their domain knowledge, which provides more flexibility and robustness of the workflow.

It should be emphasized that human intervention integrated in the method does not weaken the contribution of the method. First, exogenous knowledge is only used to name the tags, which does not affect the automation of the method. Second, as a typical decision support process, the LDA-based extraction does not substitute experts' knowledge, but significantly augment experts' insights on the crawled texts, essentially leading to better CI digest generation.

Finally, with the experts-improved results, the end-users can browse related CI digest by subscribing preferred topics. To further demonstrate the effectiveness of the proposed method and the improved workflow, one analytic case of BT is discussed in the next section.

4   A Case of BTID CI Digest Generation

BTID produced weekly Competitive Intelligence digests to push to the employees within the corporation according to their subscription since BTID was established, but the whole process including topic generation, text clustering and representative text extraction were all processed by hand or simple tools. Therefore, it was then considered meaningful to improve the workflow with the proposed method that is of business analytics nature. This section introduces the analysis on the real data from BTID.

In a joint research project with BT, more than 1,300 full business texts were provided by BTID, covering the topics such as the analysis of competitors, telecom & IT industry, new techs, market environment, government policies, sales, etc., handcrafted by BTID experts. On average, there are 560 words per text. After filtering with explicitly noisy texts, 1,277 full texts were used for analysis.

Subsequently, data preprocessing was firstly conducted, i.e., stop words deletion, case changing, title weighting (i.e., 3 times weighting on title was used, which is a typical configuration for related text mining [18]), input format preparation (i.e., each text was transformed as the number of keywords as well as a list of pairs of keyword and frequency), finally a vocabulary for corpus about the texts was constructed.

Furthermore, the widely-used JibbsLDA package was used for conducting the LDA modeling, with the typical configuration, i.e., alpha = 0.01, beta = 0.1, etc. Before retrieving the LDA semantic models, the appropriate number of topics (i.e., m) had to be determined by minimizing *Perplexity*. Different m ($m = 1, 2, ..., 20$) values were tested, with results as shown in Fig. 4.

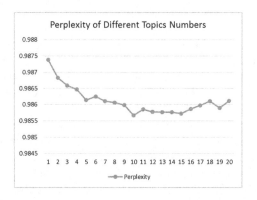

Fig. 4. Perplexity of different topic numbers

Figure 4 exhibits that the best topic number of the case was around 10. Since the *Perplexity* value decreased continuously before $m = 10$ and was stable and higher after $m = 10$, in the following discussion of the case, $m = 10$ was used.

Moreover, based on the 10 topic configuration, to be more understandable, the number of top keywords for each topic was set as 5 for LDA modeling and topic generation. The topics and corresponding keywords from LDA modeling are represented in Table 1. It should be noted that, LDA modeling itself can only present the topic IDs not topic names. In this case, experts were involved to help generalize an appropriate topic tag for each category. In addition, experts were also asked to help check whether obtained topics, extracted keywords, and categorized texts below each topic were reasonable based on their industry knowledge, and they were authorized to make necessary adjustments accordingly. Here, with LDA topic modeling, the experts only endowed topic tags without other intervention in particular, saving the vast amounts of efforts in otherwise human-involved text preparation, reading, and grouping, which nowadays becomes more and more impossible when huge volume of data pertains in practice.

Table 1. Generated topics from BT corpus

	Topic 1	Topic 2	Topic 3	Topic 4	Topic 5
Topic category with 5 keywords	Airline	India	Data	Ford	Bank
	United	Crore	Services	Fraud	Capital
	Airport	Patients	Business	Blackberry	Tests
	Flight	Health	Cloud	Aluminum	Financial
	Aircraft	Delhi	Technology	Vodafone	Lloyds
Topic tag	Airline	Indian Health	Data Service	Partner	Finance
	Topic 6	Topic 7	Topic 8	Topic 9	Topic 10
Topic category with 5 keywords	Company	Mobile	Government	People	Car
	Market	Broadband	Public	Social	Vehicles
	Year	BT	People	Online	BMW
	Billion	UK	Law	Media	Engine
	Sales	EE	Police	Facebook	Power
Topic tag	Market	Mobile	Government Policy	Social Media	Vehicles

Compared with previous hand-crafted topics, the LDA-based method could generate most of the topics listed by experts in BT, such as Market, Government Policy and Social Media, Mobiles, Data Services, Vehicles, etc. In addition to these existing ones, some new topics appeared such as Airline, Finance, Indian Health and so on. After discussions with telecom experts, these new topics (though they were not listed by experts with handcrafting) were also acknowledged as BT's focuses at that time, reflecting the power of the proposed method for finding more novel and useful topics.

Table 2. Representative texts' index for every topic in BT corpus

Topic	1	2	3	4	5	6	7	8	9	10
Index of text	1247	851	6	876	689	417	1276	802	242	391

With Table 1, the representative texts for the 10 topics were further extracted respectively. Due to the limitation of space, Table 2 only lists the index of the 10 texts, which form the final derived CI digest for this case. Moreover, for illustrative purposes, the texts, i.e., No. 802 and No. 391, for topics "Government Policy" and "Vehicle", are listed in Table 3.

Finally, to justify the quality of the final derived results, a TREC test was conducted, where each derived text was investigated by 3 human experts to assess whether the content was consistent with its assigned topic tag. As a result, an over 90 % accuracy was reported in the test, further showing the effectiveness of the proposed CI digest generation method.

Table 3. Partial CI digest of BT

CI digest of BT	
Government Policy	Vehicles
Warning Over Planning Policy: The Government's flagship planning policy is leading to "inappropriate and unwanted housing development", MPs have warned. The cross-party Communities and Local Government Committee also raised concerns that town centres were not being given proper protection against the threat from large out-of-town retail developments. They called for the Government to scrap rules allowing small shops and offices to be converted to housing without the need for planning permission, arguing that the changes could lead to town centres becoming "an unattractive place to visit or, indeed, live"…	Germany: BMW 2 Series Coupe to feature new entry-level engines from March 2015. From March 2015, new entry-level engines, a further four-wheel drive model and additional equipment options will increase the diversity of features available for the BMW 2 Series Coupe. With the market launch of the new BMW 218i Coupe, a three-cylinder petrol engine from the BMW Group's latest engine family will be featured for the first time in the brand's sporty and elegant compact model…

5   Concluding Remarks

In this paper, a Competitive Intelligence (CI) digest generation method has been introduced to help organizations effectively and intelligently generate CI digests, significantly alleviating the burden of human work in text analytics and semantic modeling with huge volume of data. The proposed method is composed of two parts, namely, LDA-based topic modeling and representative texts extraction, where the metric of perplexity has been incorporated into the determination of the topic modeling quality. Moreover, a case of BTID CI digest generation has been illustrated and analyzed with the proposed method, showing the effectiveness of the proposed method.

Future work will be carried out in two respects. One is to apply the method to other large-scaled business environments; the other is to develop an incremental strategy for timely updating environments.

Acknowledgements. The work was partly supported by the National Natural Science Foundation of China (71490724/71110107027/71372044) and the Tsinghua-BT Advanced ICT Lab at Tsinghua University. The authors highly appreciate the support and cooperation of BT and Dr. Quan Li at BT China Research Centre for the work.

References

1. Teo, T.S., Choo, W.Y.: Assessing the impact of using the Internet for competitive intelligence. Inf. Manag. **39**(1), 67–83 (2001)
2. Zhe, G., Dong, L., Qi, L., et al.: An online hot topics detection approach using the improved ant colony text clustering algorithm. J. JCIT **2**, 243–252 (2012)

3. Sathiyakumari, K., Manimekalai, G., Preamsudha, V., et al.: A survey on various approaches in document clustering. Int. J. Comput. Technol. Appl. (IJCTA) **2**(5), 1534–1539 (2011)
4. Blei, D.M., Ng, A.Y., Jordan, M.I.: Latent Dirichlet Allocation. J. Mach. Learn. Res. **3**, 993–1022 (2003)
5. Sahoo, N., Callan, J., Krishnan, R., et al.: Incremental hierarchical clustering of text documents. In: Proceedings of the 15th ACM International Conference on Information and Knowledge Management, pp. 357–366. ACM (2006)
6. Young, S., Arel, I., Karnowski, T.P., et al.: A fast and stable incremental clustering algorithm. In: 2010 Seventh International Conference on Information Technology: New Generations (ITNG), pp. 204–209. IEEE (2010)
7. Bradley, P.S., Fayyad, U.M., Reina, C.: Scaling clustering algorithms to large databases. In: KDD, pp. 9–15 (1998)
8. Farnstrom, F., Lewis, J., Elkan, C.: Scalability for clustering algorithms revisited. ACM SIGKDD Explor. Newsl. **2**(1), 51–57 (2000)
9. O'callaghan, L., Meyerson, A., Motwani, R., et al.: Streaming-data algorithms for high-quality clustering. In: ICDE, p. 0685. IEEE (2002)
10. Hulten, G., Spencer, L., Domingos, P.: Mining time-changing data streams. In: Proceedings of the Seventh ACM SIGKDD International Conference on Knowledge Discovery and Data Mining, pp. 97–106. ACM (2001)
11. Kifer, D., Ben-David, S., Gehrke, J.: Detecting change in data streams. In: Proceedings of the Thirtieth International Conference on Very Large Data Bases, VLDB Endowment, vol. 30, pp. 180–191 (2004)
12. Zhong, S.: Efficient streaming text clustering. Neural Netw. **18**(5), 790–798 (2005)
13. Banerjee, A., Basu, S.: Topic models over text streams: a study of batch and online unsupervised learning. In: SDM 7, pp. 437–442 (2007)
14. Maskeri, G., Sarkar, S., Heafield, K.: Mining business topics in source code using Latent Dirichlet Allocation. In: Proceedings of the 1st India Software Engineering Conference, pp. 113–120. ACM (2008)
15. Canini, K.R., Shi, L., Griffiths, T.L.: Online inference of topics with Latent Dirichlet Allocation. In: International Conference on Artificial Intelligence and Statistics, pp. 65–72 (2009)
16. Bíró, I., Siklósi, D., Szabó, J., et al.: Linked Latent Dirichlet Allocation in web spam filtering. In: Proceedings of the 5th International Workshop on Adversarial Information Retrieval on the Web, pp. 37–40. ACM (2009)
17. Blei, D., Hoffman, M.: Online learning for Latent Dirichlet Allocation. In: Neural Information Processing Systems (2010)
18. Banerjee, S., Ramanathan, K., Gupta, A.: Clustering short texts using wikipedia. In: Proceedings of the 30th Annual International ACM SIGIR Conference on Research and Development in Information Retrieval, pp. 787–788. ACM (2007)

Visualizing Opportunities of Collaboration in Large Research Organizations

Mohammad Amin Yazdi[1], André Calero Valdez[2(✉)], Leonhard Lichtschlag[3],
Martina Ziefle[2], and Jan Borchers[3]

[1] RWTH Aachen University, Aachen, Germany
amin.yazdi@rwth-aachen.de
[2] Human-Computer Interaction Center, RWTH Aachen University, Aachen, Germany
{calero-valdez,ziefle}@comm.rwth-aachen.de
[3] Media Computing Group, RWTH Aachen University, Aachen, Germany
{lichtschlag,borchers}@cs.rwth-aachen.de

Abstract. In order to support interdisciplinary collaboration in a large
organization, providing opportunities to meet new collaborators is essential. Besides offline approaches (e.g., conferences, colloquia, etc.) data
driven and online approaches can be considered. Using the publication
data and the additional profile information of researchers on a scientific
portal, we try to support the process of uncovering opportunities for
collaboration. For this purpose we develop a visualization that focuses
on revealing potential co-authors that are a good fit according to track-
record and profile information. In a design study we present the result of
an iterative user-centered design process – a novel prototype and its evaluation. Overall, our visualization was able to inform researchers about
valid collaboration opportunities while at the same time effectively con-
veying organizational information. Our prototype showed a high usability
and loyalty score (SUS=82.5, NPS=40).

Keywords: Design study · Interdisciplinarity · Visualization collaboration · Recommender system

1 Introduction

Interdisciplinary collaboration is considered both boon and bane of scientific
advancement in recent years. Funding organizations like the NSF have shifted
capacities to interdisciplinary research efforts [1]. Interdisciplinary research is
considered to be an effective solution for large scale complex problems overarching the limits of disciplinary boundaries. In spite of its promises, interdisciplinary
teams face several challenges in their collaboration [2]. Differences between disciplinary cultures (e.g., language, methodology, scientific performance evaluation)
and individuals, in combination with shorter project run-times, inhibit effective
collaboration, which requires a mutual understanding of the topics and the team
itself [3]. The more experienced researchers are in interdisciplinary research, the
more successfully they collaborate [4].

© Springer International Publishing Switzerland 2016
F.F.-H. Nah and C.-H. Tan (Eds.): HCIBGO 2016, Part I, LNCS 9751, pp. 350–361, 2016.
DOI: 10.1007/978-3-319-39396-4_32

Larger research clusters (over 100 researchers) are part of the German strategy for scientific excellence (forty funded research clusters in Germany. Whether these clusters surpass simple smaller research projects heavily depends on the effort to interlink researchers within such a cluster. In order to address the staff volatility and sheer size of such a research cluster, as one measure we devised the "Scientific Cooperation Portal" (SCP). [5]. The SCP is a web-based social portal that serves as a means to centralize communication, file-exchange, member profiles, and offers interdisciplinary collaboration support and output tracking of the individual researchers. One part of the SCP is track-keeping of publications generated in the cluster to enable steering. The publications of the researchers are visualized to assist both the researchers themselves as well as the cluster administration to assess the interdisciplinary collaboration [6]. In this paper we use this data to construct visualizations that help facilitate collaboration.

2 Related Work

In order to understand how effort (i.e., money) is spent effectively some form of performance evaluation is necessary. For this purpose bibliometric methods are used (often with a smattering of knowledge) to evaluate performance of individual researchers. Certain criteria can be measured relatively directly from publication data. Citation data is often used to evaluate institutions but is badly suited for automated researcher evaluation due to problems like insufficient database coverage, citation lag, disciplinary differences and bad interpretability [7].

Co-authorship analysis [8] reveals who has published with whom, and thus collaborated successfully (in the widest sense of the word). It is also used to identify who could collaborate on what topics [9] and when analyzing the content of communally published documents. Using text-mining approaches like document clustering enables identifying topics and relevant keywords [10]. Both co-authorship analyses [11] and document clustering approaches have been used to visualize the status quo, but not in the scope of recommending possible collaborators. Wu et al. [12] even visualized the change in research topic per individual researcher over the path of their careers.

Yu et al. [13] have developed a system to find collaborators in the PubMed database using a controlled vocabulary for the medical sciences (UMLS) and evaluated its usability with 26 experts. However, suggestions of collaborators were not based on prior collaboration but only on shared research interests. Chaiwanarom et al. [14] proposed a method for finding collaborators within the author's co-author networks and based on keyword similarity. Using a prediction test their method could find approx. 89 % of all actual collaborators. Suggestions were then shown as a list.

Visualizing suggestions for collaborators has not been attempted to our knowledge. Ehrlich et al. [15] propose such a solution, but (also) rely on analyzing email content to find collaborators. This approach is quite unthinkable in a research cluster of independent research groups in a German cultural background that values data privacy highly. Loep et al. [16] presented a recommendation system for movies based on previous choices and showed its superiority over manual search in lists. Visualizing recommendations increased trust in them and revealed sufficiently novel information. Suggesting collaborators goes beyond a simple expert search [17] attempted by using social network analysis methods such as HITS. It requires finding a person willing to collaborate, thus sharing similar work ethics, procedures and methods.

When analyzing co-author relationships for reasons of their successful collaboration two types of relationships are dominant. Successful researchers are either similar ("birds of a feather flock together") in their co-authorship network and publication output or complementary ("opposites attract") [18,19]. In general inferring interests from social relationships can be very successful when done adequately [20].

Scientific social networks and analytic sites like ResearchGate, Academia.edu, ArnetMiner, ResearcherId, etc. address understanding researcher profiles. ResearchGate and Academia.edu are Social Networking Sites for scientists that incorporate research interests, discussion boards but among others also present citation and activity based metrics. Nonetheless, they do not address the task of finding or even suggesting collaborators with a specialized visualization. Arnet-Miner does provide various visualization in order to understand research foci's of scientists (mostly from computer science). From our experience data coverage is highly insufficient in order to suggest collaborators effectively.

In a research cluster with over 200 researchers from different disciplines, making interdisciplinary collaboration in the cluster [3] is hard work.

Initially we visualized existing collaboration by visualizing publication behavior. This visualization was seen to be beneficial in the cluster [21] and can be used for analyzing the degree of interdisciplinarity [6]. Still the requirement to actively suggest collaborators was considered necessary. An approach to do this was to model the suggestions on more than one variable – keyword similarity and a common social network.

3   Research Questions

In our design study, we try to apply the findings from related work to visualize opportunities of possible collaboration. Regarding this visualization we investigate the following research questions:

RQ1 What are user's expectations of a visualization tool to enhance collaboration and organizational knowledge?

RQ2 How can a visualization approach be used to suggest collaborators?

RQ3 Does the visualization at the same time inform members how the organization is structured?

4   Method

Using a user-centered approach, we established *user requirements* first addressing RQ1. For this purpose, we conducted semi-structured interviews, which generated a list of requirements. These requirements were then used to develop

Table 1. Selection of participants from different experience levels for both studies

Category	Sample	Interviews	User study
Beginner	4	2	3
Intermediate	5	1	4
Expert	4	2	3
Total	13	5	10

several paper prototypes. The design elements of the prototypes were selected in accordance with criteria of visual ergonomics.

Two of these prototypes were selected for data-driven evaluation. This evaluation was based on a speak-aloud scenario-based user test addressing both RQ2 and RQ3. Prototypes were improved in each iteration by immediate feedback evaluation from the researchers.

4.1 Participants

At a local university an integrative interdisciplinary research cluster addresses research in production technology. Currently there are 209 researchers in the cluster in 21 institutes with over 30 faculty. Interdisciplinary collaboration (ranging from material sciences to logistics) is highly important for the given topic and strongly encouraged.

We identified three different user categories, which we refer to as beginners (2 or less publications), intermediates (3-9 publications) and experts (10 or more publications). From this population we selected 40 participants for our studies by randomly selecting researchers from the three experience levels. Thirteen participants from seven different institutes agreed to take part in the study (see Table 1).

5   Requirements Analysis – Interview Method

For requirement analysis we conducted five semi-structured interviews (see Table 1). The interviews were divided in three sections. First, questions regarding the participants' background knowledge were asked (i.e. role within the research organization, level of expertise as in published scientific articles, self-evaluation in regard to scientific impact, interdisciplinary experience, software usage, interdisciplinary motivation).

The second part dealt with the process of publishing scientific articles (i.e. track record, publishing frequency, interdisciplinary publications, favorite publications, literature study process, collaboration and publication practice, joys and frustrations of publishing). This particularly included questions that directly addressed the process of writing and finding co-authors that possibly have required knowledge. It also included the perceived importance of choosing good and relevant keywords.

The last part of the interview related to publishing in the cluster specifically, in particular whether finding co-authors from within the cluster is necessary and whether other members of the cluster show a willingness to collaborate. Interviews took less then one hour and audio was recorded.

5.1 Results from the Interviews

From the transcription of these semi-structured interviews we derived a total of six requirements by categorization (given in italics). For this purpose interviews were transcribed and evaluated according to Mayring [22]. We determined that researchers would like to *form a mental model* (i.e. a structural representation $R1$) of the cluster, the institutes, and the connections between researchers to improve the understanding of the main organizational research interests and orientation of the cluster as a whole ($R2$). Members are willing to *present their own research interests* to others through keywords in order to identify each researcher's expertise and skills. Here they referred to *similarities of keywords* between two researchers as a satisfying indication of relatedness between two researchers ($R3$). We found that members of the cluster often face the challenge of *discovering new co-authors or experts* in a specific field from another discipline that also match their research interests. Some authors have left the cluster but are still considered for consultation, but they should be identifiable clearly ($R4$). Interviewees referred to *willingness to collaborate and motivation* as key factors for identifying possible candidates that want to get involved in interdisciplinary collaboration ($R5$). However, they also struggle to determine a common research method prior to initiating research. It is necessary to *acknowledge current and preceding research interests* to evaluate a possible collaboration ($R6$).

The results from this requirement analysis adequately address RQ1 and were used to generate the visualizations described in the next section.

6 Visualization Prototypes

We observed that our participants were struggling to comprehend the functionality of our prototype using medium fidelity prototypes with imaginary data, hence we decided to take our prototype into high fidelity using real data. For this purpose, we acquired a database of publications from the research cluster from 2012 to early 2014. Furthermore, we extracted authors and keywords from the titles of the papers. Additionally, we identified authors that were no longer in the cluster. Slight improvements were integrated between trials to incorporate user feedback.

The interactive visualization is a bubble graph. Authors are represented as bubbles. Institutes are represented as bubble bags, containing all authors from the respective institute. Bubble size is determined by publication output and increases linearly with increasing publications (see Fig. 1, addressing $R5$). The position of the each author is fixed to a relative location by using the name as a hash for its positioning within its institute. Institute bubbles contain the

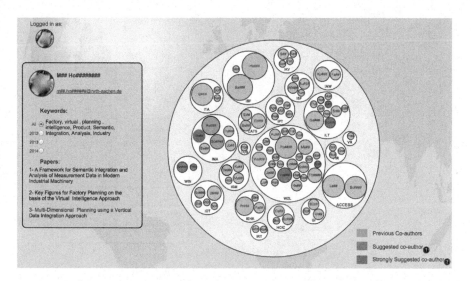

Fig. 1. Prototype 1 showing all members of the cluster. Orange bubbles are used for previous co-authors, green bubbles indicate having at least two similar keywords, and blue bubbles imply two common co-authors that also have at least two similar keywords. The user itself is highlighted in red. By clicking on a bubble the respective colors are overlaid on the suggested collaborators. Names are blurred for reasons of privacy. (Color figure online)

acronym of the institute. These design choices were made to allow users to visually explore and interrogate the structure of the cluster by visualizing the relevant dimensions of data (addressing $R1 - 2$). Interactive bubble-bag visualizations allow encoding of multiple dimensions (e.g. numbers of papers, keywords, institute, previous/possible connections, etc.), which were indicated as relevant by the users. Bubbles are furthermore spatially efficient and their shape naturally encodes the behavior of transient grouping [23]. Additionally and most importantly participants stated, that their mental image of the cluster was indeed bubble shaped (instead of hierarchically as a triangle for instance).

We used two types of parameters to find new collaborators. We used heuristics to determine possible co-authors according to the "birds of a feather flock together" rationale [19]. Similarity according to keywords and a shared co-authorship network were used to find suggestions for new collaborators (addressing $R3, 5-6$). In our initial stage of our prototype we found that having only one similar keyword is not a sufficient indication of similarities in research interests according to the users. Validity of extracted keywords was assessed by asking the respective interviewees. Recommendations are given by hovering of author nodes. Relevant recommendations are shown by highlighting recommended co-authors. By color-coding the degree of recommendation additional information is given. This allows not only finding relevant authors for the user himself but also finding relevant connections between different colleagues (addressing $R1 - 2$).

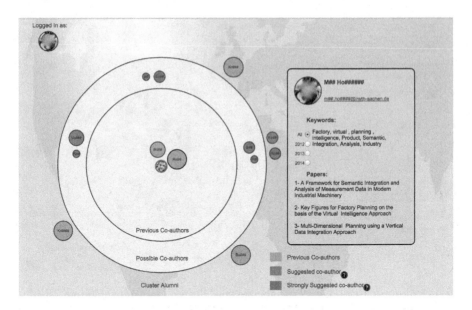

Fig. 2. Prototype 2 showing only recommended co-authors. The rings indicate the level of recommendation (inner ring = previous co-authors, outer ring = similar topics, common co-authors)

Thus fostering the creation of a mental model of the organizational structure and organizational knowledge. In both prototypes clicking on a bubble opens a panel that reveals the authors name, picture, and email-address. Additionally the list of keywords and publications are shown, which can be filtered according to their years (addressing R3).

Our second prototype focused on highlighting only the recommendations for the user by leaving out all non-suggested co-authors (see Fig. 2). This should reduce cognitive load and direct the users attention. Suggestions are placed in orbits according to their suggestion as a co-author. Previous co-authors that are not in the cluster are placed outside of the bubble, addressing the requirement of also showing but at the same time identifying external collaborators (addressing R4). Suggested co-authors are placed in the medium orbit. Placement of bubbles within orbits is done using a force-based layout. Authors from the same institute attract each other, while others repel.

Both prototypes can be seen in a short video online[1].

7   Prototype Evaluation – User Study

We tested the developed prototypes, which were based on our requirements analysis, with two participants from the interview study and eight additional

---

[1] A short video demonstration can be found at: https://vimeo.com/120483587.

users ($N = 10$, see also Table 1). We evaluated it using a scenario-based speak-aloud procedure. Both final visualizations were tested in all trials. We randomized the ordering of the visualization between subjects.

Participants were first asked to interpret the visualization without any interaction. In a second step participants were asked to interact with the visualization and speak about the changes in the visualization. In a third step, finding a possible co-author was given as a task and an evaluation of the suggestion was asked for. Lastly, the participants should freely comment on the visualizations and compare both for suitability. The visualizations were then assessed using the system usability scale (SUS) and the net promoter score (NPS). Both are scales that can be used to quickly judge a tool as a whole for usability and loyalty. They do not provide insights into details of usability problems.

7.1   User Study Results and Conclusions

As there are similarities and differences between the two visualizations, we decided to split our results into five sections, first describing both common and specific results separately. The evaluation then investigates the validity of our approach and possible applications. All findings relate to two prototypes from the last iteration of our participatory design process.

7.2   General Findings

As interviewees compared publication efforts of their colleagues to the size of the bubble, all immediately concluded that the size of the bubble is proportional to number of papers per person and that larger bubble represent more active and experienced researchers. Users tried to understand our suggestion system by analyzing and comparing their own work, keywords, and papers with previous coauthors to those of each suggested person from the visualization.

All users understood the meaning of colors by hovering over the legend, which explained the reasoning for the different colors. Users found a notification system that informed them about changes in their graph helpful and necessary for long term use. Overall, interviewees preferred to have both visualizations side by side to map necessary information more easily and quickly.

Quantitatively the SUS showed a mean of $M=82.5$ ($SD=24.4$) indicating a high acceptance of the prototype. The NPS analysis yields 4 Promoters, 6 Passives and 0 Detractors. The overall NPS is 40 indicating good usability and possible loyalty.

Reflections on Prototype 1. This prototype supports the process of decision making by locating key players, their publication effort and connections at institutional level.

Self-awareness, which is another key issue in large organizations, is now partly resolved by being able to consciously track who does what, when and where. By hovering over a group of people connections and topics that over-arch institutional collaboration become visible.

Table 2. Example transcripts from the interviews for the three result categories

Category	Transcripts
Confirmation	*"Oh, I have met this person at a conference recently and we have agreed to write a paper together."*
Discovery of new knowledge	*"I do not know the person but it seems like what he does really fits good to my work. I think I can work with him together."*
	"Now I know which person I could contact that has related work in this institute for an interdisciplinary publication."
Problem solving	User hovers over a suggested co-author: *"This visualization could help us having a publication from multiple disciplines."*

Our visualization also gives an opportunity for exploring possibilities of collaboration between researchers who already know each other. Some participants mentioned that the visualization contained more information about them than they previously knew. During the speak-aloud scenarios utterances like *"oh he works there?"* or *"I didn't know she is also interested in ... "* occured.

Over all, it became clear that users did not follow a specific pattern to rate or rank suggested collaborators. All preferred to use their own instinct and background knowledge to investigate and choose between suggestions.

Reflections on Prototype 2. This type of visualization enhanced information delivery by removing all unrelated researchers. Participants were much quicker in finding possible co-authors but lacked insights on organizational structure. The closeness of authors, caused by the force-layout, was understood by all users. The benefit of showing external collaborators was well received by the participants. This visualization caused most participants to state that both visualizations should be combined or presented next to each other.

7.3 Validity of the Approach

From our video transcription we extracted all statements that relate to the usefulness of our system. We grouped them into three categories: *Confirmation, discovery of new knowledge,* and *problem solving* (see Table 2). Each had 5, 6 and 3 distinct statements respectively. From these statements we derive that our approach successfully addresses RQ2 and RQ3. Our approach is a valid type of visualizing collaboration in a large research organization, which allows finding collaborators and provides a means of creating organization awareness.

7.4 Possible Applications

In addition to finding co-authors through our visualization, interviewees suggested that they could also apply the system to solve other challenges such as finding literature (n=2), discovering experts (n=3), locating people with access to particular facilities or hardware (n=1) and also simplify the process of developing proposals for research grants (n=1).

From our point of view similar visualizations could be used on an institutional level to visualize topics addressed by various institutions, revealing institutes that address similar topics. These could be used in competitor analyses or collaboration scenarios.

8   Limitations and Future Work

For our visualizations, we performed both a requirements analysis and a user study in an iterative participatory design process. As future work we would like to include some of the features that were suggested to optimize user fit in the next iteration. As an example, we want to give users the ability to accept or reject a suggested collaborator after evaluation of their relevance. This feedback should be integrated into the recommendation algorithm. Furthermore recommendations could be generated by using text-mining procedures instead of keyword analysis (although this design study did not focus on data generation).

Another example is to display the keyword similarities between the user and suggested co-authors or the capability of viewing co-authors of each particular paper. By extending the scope to suggesting particular papers instead of authors, we could allow the user to judge the relative importance of a certain keyword for the researcher in question.

Furthermore the approach should be extended to include collaborators that have not published yet. This would require new researchers to fill a profile indicating research interests using keywords. Also finding a way of visualizing a missing track record without breaking the natural mapping of size and track record should be considered.

A limitation is the specific sample from one research cluster. To generalize our approach we could map our visualization to other contexts. The bubbles could also reflect institutes from an entire department or school in order to understand collaboration in a university as a whole. Whether the visualization will effectively scale is yet to be answered. Whether the approach can be used in non-academic scenarios also warrants investigation. The choice of bubbles might be effective only because a research cluster is a loosely coupled organization. In more structred enterprises other forms of representation might be more accurate.

In our approach we assume a relative homogeneous user group. Since regional, organizational and disciplinary cultural differences can lead to a very heterogeneous user group, factors of user diversity must be considered when dealing with data of employees. In addition finding an expert still leaves the task of starting collaboration. Knowledge sharing is social process and requires more than simple tool assistance.

Only titles were used for the extraction of keywords. Using full texts or abstracts should reveal better keywords in the long run as would manual keyword selection by users. Furthermore, no disambiguation of keywords or synonym detection was applied. Particularly in interdisciplinary settings this is a strong requirement. Thus, in this regard our system does not help overcome disciplinary language barriers.

The sample for this study was relatively small (approx. 5 % of the research cluster). For a better quantitative evaluation more participants should be considered. Publication data was only selected from 2012 to early 2014, limiting the insights from senior researchers and very recent publications.

Acknowledgments. The authors thank the German Research Council DFG for the friendly support of the research in the excellence cluster "Integrative Production Technology in High Wage Countries". This work was funded in part by the German B-IT Foundation.

References

1. Jacobs, J.A., Frickel, S.: Interdisciplinarity: a critical assessment. Ann. Rev. Sociol. **35**, 43–65 (2009)
2. Repko, A.F.: Interdisciplinary Research: Process and Theory. SAGE Publications, Thousand Oaks (2011)
3. Marzano, M., Carss, D.N., Bell, S.: Working to make interdisciplinarity work: investing in communication and interpersonal relationships. J. Agr. Econ. **57**(2), 185–197 (2006)
4. Cummings, J.N., Kiesler, S.: Who collaborates successfully? prior experience reduces collaboration barriers in distributed interdisciplinary research. In: Proceedings of the 2008 ACM Conference on CSCW, pp. 437–446. ACM (2008)
5. Valdez, A.C., Schaar, A.K., Ziefle, M., Holzinger, A.: Enhancing interdisciplinary cooperation by social platforms. In: Yamamoto, S. (ed.) HCI 2014, Part I. LNCS, vol. 8521, pp. 298–309. Springer, Heidelberg (2014)
6. Valdez, A.C., Schaar, A.K., Ziefle, M., Holzinger, A., Jeschke, S., Brecher, C.: Using mixed node publication network graphs for analyzing success in interdisciplinary teams. In: Huang, R., Ghorbani, A.A., Pasi, G., Yamaguchi, T., Yen, N.Y., Jin, B. (eds.) AMT 2012. LNCS, vol. 7669, pp. 606–617. Springer, Heidelberg (2012)
7. Agasisti, T., Catalano, G., Landoni, P., Verganti, R.: Evaluating the performance of academic departments: an analysis of research-related output efficiency. Res. Eval. **21**(1), 2–14 (2012)
8. Liu, X., Bollen, J., Nelson, M.L., Van de Sompel, H.: Co-authorship networks in the digital library research community. Inf. Process. Manage. **41**(6), 1462–1480 (2005)
9. Morel, C.M., Serruya, S.J., Penna, G.O., Guimarães, R.: Co-authorship network analysis: a powerful tool for strategic planning of research, development and capacity building programs on neglected diseases. PLoS Neglected Trop. Dis. **3**(8), e501 (2009)
10. Liu, Y., Goncalves, J., Ferreira, D., Xiao, B., Hosio, S., Kostakos, V.: CHI 1994–2013: mapping two decades of intellectual progress through co-word analysis. In: Proceedings of the 32nd Annual ACM Conference on Human Factors in Computing Systems. ACM (2014)

11. Huang, T.H., Huang, M.L.: Analysis and visualization of co-authorship networks for understanding academic collaboration and knowledge domain of individual researchers. In: 2006 International Conference on Computer Graphics, Imaging and Visualisation, pp. 18–23. IEEE (2006)

12. Wu, M.Q.Y., Faris, R., Ma, K.L.: Visual exploration of academic career paths. In: Proceedings of the 2013 IEEE/ACM International Conference on Advances in Social Networks Analysis and Mining, pp. 779–786. ACM (2013)

13. Yu, W., Yesupriya, A., Wulf, A., Qu, J., Khoury, M.J., Gwinn, M.: An open source infrastructure for managing knowledge and finding potential collaborators in a domain-specific subset of pubmed, with an example from human genome epidemiology. BMC Bioinf. 8(1), 436 (2007)

14. Chaiwanarom, P., Ichise, R., Lursinsap, C.: Finding potential research collaborators in four degrees of separation. In: Cao, L., Zhong, J., Feng, Y. (eds.) ADMA 2010, Part II. LNCS, vol. 6441, pp. 399–410. Springer, Heidelberg (2010)

15. Ehrlich, K., Lin, C.Y., Griffiths-Fisher, V.: Searching for experts in the enterprise: combining text and social network analysis. In: Proceedings of the 2007 International ACM Conference on Supporting Group Work, pp. 117–126. ACM (2007)

16. Loepp, B., Hussein, T., Ziegler, J.: Choice-based preference elicitation for collaborative filtering recommender systems. In: Proceedings of the 32nd Annual ACM Conference on Human Factors in Computing Systems, pp. 3085–3094. ACM (2014)

17. Zhang, J., Ackerman, M.S., Adamic, L.: Expertise networks in online communities: structure and algorithms. In: Proceedings of the 16th International Conference on World Wide Web, pp. 221–230. ACM (2007)

18. Kretschmer, H.: A new model of scientific colloboration part 1. theoretical approach. Scientometrics 46(3), 501–518 (1999)

19. Settles, B., Dow, S.: Let's get together: the formation and success of online creative collaborations. In: Proceedings of the CHI 2013, pp. 2009–2018 (2013)

20. Wen, Z., Lin, C.Y.: On the quality of inferring interests from social neighbors. In: Proceedings of the 16th ACM SIGKDD, pp. 373–382. ACM (2010)

21. Schaar, A.K., Valdez, A.C., Ziefle, M.: Publication network visualization as an approach for interdisciplinary innovation management. In: 2013 IEEE International Professional Communication Conference (IPCC), pp. 1–8. IEEE (2013)

22. Mayring, P.: Qualitative inhaltsanalyse. In: Baur, N., Blasius, J. (eds.) Handbuch Methoden der empirischen Sozialforschung. Springer, Wiesbaden (2010)

23. Watanabe, N., Washida, M., Igarashi, T.: Bubble clusters: an interface for manipulating spatial aggregation of graphical objects. In: Proceedings of the 20th Annual ACM Symposium on User Interface Software and Technology, pp. 173–182. ACM (2007)

Branding, Marketing and Consumer Behaviour

The Influence of Trust Building User Interface Elements of Web Shops on e-Trust

Andreas Auinger[1]([⊠]), Werner Wetzlinger[1], and Liesmarie Schwarz[2]

[1] University of Applied Sciences Upper Austria, Campus Steyr,
Wehrgrabengasse 1-3, 4400 Steyr, Austria
{andreas.auinger,werner.wetzlinger}@fh-steyr.at
[2] Voglsam GmbH, Dorfplatz 5, 4492 Hofkirchen, Austria
l.schwarz@fitrabbit.com

Abstract. In this paper we examine how different trust building user interface elements in web shops affect trust in B2C Internet vendors (e-trust). We identified trust seals, consumer reviews and contact options as trust building elements and conducted an online experiment using multiple versions of a fictional web shop. Using a between-subjects design we presented participants with pages of the web shop containing these GUI elements. Afterwards subjects rated the e-trust. We found that only trust seals had a significant influence on e-trust. Since we expected a higher influence of the trust-building elements we additionally conducted an eye tracking study that showed that participants did not direct much attention to these elements, which we conclude is the reason for the weak influence of trust-building elements.

Keywords: e-Commerce · e-Trust · Eye-tracking · Conversion optimization

1 Introduction

The main goal of web shops is to convert shoppers' product navigation into purchases [1]. Many shoppers visit web shops, but globally only about 3 % actually convert [2].

One substantial influence on the purchase decision of a web shop visitor is the perceived risk of buying. Trust is an important factor in economic and social interactions. This is especially the case when there is uncertainty, because trust can reduce the perceived risk [3].

Research of the last 15 years shows (e.g. [4, 5]) that it is especially difficult for B2C e-commerce retailers (e-vendors) to convey trust through their online shops, caused by a lack of personal interaction and limited options to evaluate the quality of products and services, which could negatively influence their buying decision [6]. Consequently, consumers' trust and perceived risk have strong impacts on their purchasing decisions and are therefore key success factors in e-commerce [7]. Consumer trust is relevant on multiple engagement levels in e-commerce: Trust in (i) the *Internet technology* facilitating the transaction, (2) the *vendor* and (3) *third parties* to safeguard the exchange [8]. Within these categories numerous factors have strong effects on Internet consumers' trust in the website (e.g. consumers' trusting disposition, reputation of the vendor, privacy concerns, security concerns and the information quality) [7].

© Springer International Publishing Switzerland 2016
F.F.-H. Nah and C.-H. Tan (Eds.): HCIBGO 2016, Part I, LNCS 9751, pp. 365–376, 2016.
DOI: 10.1007/978-3-319-39396-4_33

Structure of the Paper. The remaining paper is structured as follows: In Sect. 2 we derive the trust building elements from literature. Section 3 describes the research methodology and the results of an online experiment. Section 4 presents the method and results of the subsequently conducted eye tracking study. Finally, Sect. 5 discusses the results and draws conclusions.

2 Trust Building User Interface Elements

Due to missing direct consumer contact, online vendors try to convey their qualities by the graphical user interface (GUI) and its trust building elements such as contact options [9], trust seals, or consumer reviews on products and shops [10].

Recent studies on trust seals lead to different findings in respect to their effect: Some find significant and positive impacts of Web assurance seals on consumer trust (e.g. [11–15]), yet others do not find significant impacts (e.g. [7, 11, 16–19]). Additionally, different kinds of seals (privacy assurance, security assurance, transaction-integrity assurance) seem to have different effects on trust [12]. Also their position on the website seems to have an important influence. Generally, trust assurances (third party trust seals) perform better when displayed in the information-searching stage, while vendor specific trust assurances (e.g., warranty and return policy, product quality guarantee, and delivery on time) lead to higher initial trust when displayed in the choice stage [11].

Consumer generated reviews are a second well researched topic. Generally, positive consumer reviews seem to increase sales whereas negative reviews normally decrease sales [20, 21], but negative reviews can also increase sales due to increased visibility [22, 23]. It has also been shown that consumer reviews on web shops are a strong predictor of trustworthiness judgments [16], but the literature review led to no results which investigated the impact of product reviews on the trustworthiness of the vendor.

Thus while trust building elements like consumer reviews are widely used on web shops there is still a lack of knowledge on their actual effect on consumer behavior and opinions [6]. Furthermore, consumer reviews have not been contrasted with the influence of other trust building elements such as trust seals or also contact options on Web shops.

Therefore, this research investigates the influence of selected trust building user interface elements on trust and how they affect the purchase intention of consumers. Different trust building elements can be categorized based on their purpose [24] and their origin [11]. Based on a comprehensive literature study[1], we chose trust seals (which convey trust in the shop and the company), contact options (which convey trust in the shop and the company itself) and consumer reviews (which convey trust in the product) as trust building elements for our research, because they reflect all categories

---

[1] *Databases*: ACM, IEEE, Business Source Premier, EconLit, PsycINFO, PSYNDEX, SocINDEX, Sciencedirect, Sprinter Link; *Search Terms:* Combinations and Variations of Trust and e-commerce; *Analysis:*The first 100 search results of every database search result were analyzed.

most replicable (see Table 1). The influenced trusting beliefs are based on the research of [25], which will be described in more detail below.

Table 1. The analyzed trust building graphical user interface elements

Trust Element	Purpose	Origin	Influenced Trusting Belief	Graphical Representation
Trust Seal	Recommendation of third parties - trust in the shop and the company	Endorsement by an independent third party	Integrity, benevolence and ability	
Contact Options	Emotional security - trust in the shop and the company	Endorsement by the e-vendor	Integrity	
Consumer Reviews and (positive and negative)	Credibility of the web content - trust in the product	Endorsement by other consumers	Integrity and ability	

The research is based on a 2-step empirical study including (i) a *quantitative trust experiment* asking for the effect of trust building elements on web shop pages and (ii) an *eye tracking study*, testing the cognition of these elements.

3 Online Trust Experiment

3.1 Research Model

The *main objective* of the experiment was to measure the impact of the selected trust elements (trust seal, contact options, positive consumer reviews, negative consumer reviews) on consumer trust in B2C Internet vendors, defined by the established research model on e-trust by Gefen and Straub [25]. It measures e-trust using the dimensions *integrity*, *predictability*, *ability* and *benevolence*. These dimensions are described as follows:

- **Integrity** is a characteristic of an e-vendor that convinces consumers that their expected outcomes from the interaction will be fulfilled and that the e-vendor is honest and reliable and will keep promises made.
- **Predictability** is a quality that conveys to consumers that they can be sure about actions an e-vendor will take and what outcomes to expect.
- **Ability** is a characteristic of an e-vendor that conveys competence, knowledge about products and the excellence of services offered.
- **Benevolence** is a characteristic of an e-vendor that conveys its well meaning, considers how its actions affect the consumer and puts consumers' interests before its own.

Using the model of Gefen/Straub to measure trust of consumers in e-vendors (e-Trust) we examine the effects of trust building elements. We aim to answer the following questions (c.f. Fig. 1):

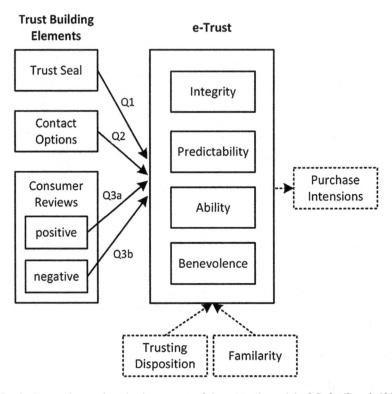

Fig. 1. Research questions in the context of the research model of Gefen/Straub [25]

- **Q1:** Does the presence of a trust seal influence the trust of a potential consumer in the e-vendor?
- **Q2:** Does the presence of contact options influence the trust of the potential consumer in the e-vendor?
- **Q3a:** Does the presence of positive consumer reviews influence the trust of the potential consumer in the e-vendor?
- **Q3b:** Does the presence of negative consumer reviews influence the trust of potential consumer in the e-vendor?

The results of Gefen/Straub show that an increase in e-trust leads to an effect on purchase intention [25]: The analysis shows that Purchase Intentions were affected by Familiarity (control variable) and by e-trust (R^2 = 37 %). Among the dimensions of e-Trust, only Integrity and Predictability affected Purchase Intentions. Most of the dimensions of e-Trust were affected, albeit not strongly, by Trusting Disposition and by Familiarity.

Hence, we assume that finding an influence of the trust building elements on e-trust would lead to an increase in purchase intentions, which subsequently should positively affect the conversion rate of an e-vendors online shop.

3.2 General Experimental Approach

Multiple aspects of an e-vendor's Web shop (e.g. functionality, design, search options, check-out process, etc.) can influence user perception of how trustworthy they are [26]. Consequently, a laboratory experiment seemed appropriate to assure internal validity [27]. Since we planned to only test the influence of graphical user interface elements, we chose not to use a fully functional Web shop, but to present screenshots of certain Web shop pages to participants.

Additionally, we wanted to avoid any brand effects of existing Web shops, since brands are strong trust builders [28]. Accordingly, we decided to incorporate the trust elements in a fictional web shop to prevent affectations.

The study was carried out using a between-subjects design. Multiple versions of web shop pages were designed containing the different trust elements in systematic combinations. Each participant saw only one of these different versions and had to fill out an online questionnaire afterwards. Consequently, measured values are independent of each other, as every participant was only measured once [29].

3.3 Tested Web Shop Content

We used two shop pages for testing: a *product overview page* and a *product detail page*. Subsequently, page one provided an overview of all products of a certain category showing product images, the product title and a short description. Page two showed detailed information about just one product. The web shop was built following the layouts of the three web shops with the highest revenues in Austria, which at the time of the study were www.amazon.at, www.universal.at and www.ottoversand.at. The trust elements were applied on the pages according to their nearby similar positions in the three web shops (see screens in Figs. 2 and 3).

To measure the impact of the trust building elements, five different versions of these pages were created: containing (i) no trust elements, (ii) positive rating, (iii) negative rating, (iv) trust seal and (v) contact options. Each of these five versions was assigned to one subject group (Table 2).

The types of presented products can also influence the effect of trust building elements. There is a direct correlation between this effect and the product price: The higher the product price, the stronger the influence of trust building arguments on consumers [30]. Additionally, consumer reviews are said to have a different effect on the uncertainty of consumers about the product performance regarding experience goods rather than search goods [31, 32]. Therefore, we decided to use an experience good with a price range that can also include more expensive products. Based on the results of a study examining the effects of multiple communication practices on consumer uncertainty about product performance by [32], we chose an MP3-player as the

Scanpath of the overview page

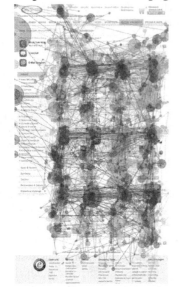

Heatmap of the overview page

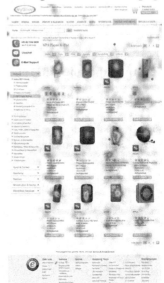

Fig. 2. Scanpath and heatmap of overview page

Scanpath product details page

Heatmap product details page

Fig. 3. Scanpath and heatmap of product details page (case 1 with negative rating)

Table 2. Experimental setting

	Trust seal	Positive consumer review	Negative consumer review	Contact options
Experimental group 1	X			
Experimental group 2		X		
Experimental group 3			X	
Experimental group 4				X
Control group				

experience good. Since this item may also have a high price, we considered it to be an appropriate product to measure the effects of trust building elements.

3.4   Procedure and Measurement

The link to the online experiment was sent out to students of Austrian universities via email. Participants were shown screenshots of the two selected shop pages (each on one page) and instructed to examine the two pages. There was no time limit and participants could switch between the pages as they liked. A third page contained multiple statements to measure the constructs of the research model (see Fig. 1). We selected the items shown in Table 3 from the research model of [25] corresponding to the constructs described above. An item asking about overall trust was added. All items were rated on a 7-point Likert scale.

Table 3. The measurement items

Construct	Item	Origin
Integrity	I do not doubt the honesty of MyShop.com	Gefen/Straub
	I expect MyShop.com will keep promises they make	Gefen/Straub
Benevolence	I expect that MyShop.com's intentions are benevolent	Gefen/Straub
Ability	MyShop.com is competent	Gefen/Straub
Predictability	I am quite certain what to expect from MyShop.com	Gefen/Straub
Overall trust	How trustful do you perceive MyShop to be?	Added

3.5   Results of the Online Trust Experiment

Characteristics of the Sample. The survey ran two weeks and had a response of 268 in total for the five experimental groups (more than 50 per group). The majority of participants were students (68 % female, 32 % male) with 89 % being younger than 30 years old (average age 25). 50 % of participants said they are fully familiar with purchasing electronic equipment online. Only 9.3 % claimed to be absolutely unfamiliar with purchasing electronic equipment online.

Analysis of Variance. Since data was collected using a Likert scale, it can be considered as interval scaled and parametric methods can be used [27]. To test the influence of the trust elements an analysis of variance (ANOVA) was conducted. It showed a significant variance (p-value 0.007). A post-hoc-test (Bonferroni correction) comparing the means revealed that only the group with trust seals showed significant differences to the control group, where no trust elements were displayed (Table 4). The trust seal was the only trust building element with a significant influence on e-trust (p-value 0.05). In this case the difference in means was 0.641 and effect size was 0.548, which corresponds to a medium to strong positive effect [33].

Table 4. Multiple comparison (Bonferroni).

Questionnaire version (I)	Questionnaire version (J)	Mean difference (I-J)	Std. error	Sig.
No trust element	Negative consumer review	.146	.231	1.00
	Positive consumer review	−.226	.230	1.00
	Trust seal	−.641*	.227	.05
	Contact options	−.349	.226	1.00
Negative reviews	No trust element	−.146	.231	1.00
	Positive consumer review	−.372	.233	1.00
	Trust seal	−.787*	.230	.01
	Contact options	−.495	.230	.32
Positive reviews	No trust element	.226	.230	1.00
	Negative consumer review	.372	.233	1.00
	Trust seal	−.415	.230	.71
	Contact options	−.123	.228	1.00
Trust seal	No trust element	.641*	.227	.05
	Negative consumer review	.787*	.230	.01
	Positive consumer review	.415	.229	.71
	Contact options	.292	.225	1.00
Contact options	No trust element	.349	.226	1.00
	Negative consumer review	.495	.229	.32
	Positive consumer review	.123	.228	1.00
	Trust seal	−.292	.225	1.00

* The mean difference is significant at the .05 level.

4 Eye Tracking Study

The experiment showed very weak influence of the trust building GUI elements on trust. Since we expected the influence to be much stronger, we supposed that perhaps participants did not notice the trust elements. We therefore resolved to conduct an eye tracking study [34] to find out whether users see the trust building elements and how much attention they pay to them.

The participants received two different sets of instructions for the tested web shop pages (product overview page, product details page):

- **Product Overview Page Task:** *You will see a web shop. Which of the 12 MP3-Players is most appealing to you? Click on the most interesting product.*
- **Product Details Page:** *You will see another screenshot of the web shop for 25 s now. Consider whether the displayed product is interesting for you.*

The three trust building elements were on both of these sites. The product details page showed positive ratings (5 stars and positive comments) for the first half of the participants and negative ratings (1 star and negative comments) for the second half.

4.1 Eye Tracking Results

Eye tracking was carried out about 3 weeks after the online experiment with 55 new business students between 20 and 30 years old. Results showed that the trust elements attracted hardly any attention. On the products overview page the elements received the following attention:

- **Trust Seal:** No participant fixated on the trust seal.
- **Contact Options:** 23.6 % fixated on the contact options, but the amount of dwell time was short (0.5 % of total dwell time).
- **Ratings:** All participants noticed at least one of the ratings, but aggregated total dwell time was again brief (2.4 % of total dwell time).

On the product details page the elements received the following attention:

- **Trust Seal:** Only 3 participants fixated on the trust seal.
- **Contact Options:** 54.5 % fixated on the contact options, but dwell time was short (400 ms, 1.6 % of total dwell time).
- **Ratings:** There is very little difference between 1-star ratings and 5-star ratings. About 60 % of participants fixate on the ratings and spend a similar dwell time (5 stars: 252 ms, 1 % of total dwell time; 1star: 279 ms, 1.1 % of total dwell time) on them.
- **Reviews:** 1-star reviews (case 1) and 5-star reviews (case 2) also have a similar hit ratio (1 star: 25 %; 5 stars: 29 %), but the dwell time average is slightly higher on 1-star reviews (1 star: 1290 ms; 5 stars: 1085 ms).

5   Interpretation and Conclusion

The results of the qualitative online experiment showed that for Web shop users trust in the e-vendor is an important influencing factor on purchase intentions. However, the result of the evaluation only identified trust seals as having a significant influence on e-trust. Reviews and contact options had no significant impact on the e-trust construct. To examine the reason, a subsequent eye tracking study was conducted revealing that only very few participants fixated on the trust seal. The other trust building elements were fixated on by a much higher proportion of participants. Based on this finding, especially the trust seal was of particular interest for our interpretation of these results. We derived the position of the trust seal from the layout of the most popular web shops in Austria. In retrospect, this was not the right decision for our experiment, because the trust building effect of this seal may be of minor importance for well-established e-vendors, as they are already trusted by a large portion of the population. A valid conclusion is that positioning the trust seal in the left bottom corner of a Web shop page may be ineffective if a shop relies on its trust building effect. These findings are in line with current research from [35] that shows that trust seals are more effective for small e-vendors and new shoppers, thus serving as partial substitutes for both shopper experience and a seller's sales volume.

References

1. Zhou, L., Dai, L., Zhang, D.: Online shopping acceptance model - a critical survey of consumer factors in online shopping. J. Electron. Commer. Res. **8**, 41–62 (2007)
2. Monetate: Ecommerce Quarterly Report Q3 (2015). http://www.monetate.com/resources/research/#ufh-i-34269668-ecommerce-quarterly-q3-2015
3. Pavlou, P.A.: Consumer acceptance of electronic commerce: integrating trust and risk with the technology acceptance model. Int. J. Electron. Commer. **7**, 101–134 (2003)
4. Papadopouou, P., Kanellis, P., Martakos, D.: Investigating trust in e-commerce: a literature review and a model for its formation in customer relationships. In: AMCIS 2001 Proceedings, pp. 791–798 (2001)
5. Habibi, R., Hajati, Z.: Trust in e-commerce. Int. J. Innov. Appl. Stud. **10**, 917–922 (2015)
6. Benlian, A., Titah, R., Hess, T.: Differential effects of provider recommendations and consumer reviews in e-commerce transactions: an experimental study. J. Manage. Inf. Syst. **29**, 237–272 (2012)
7. Kim, D.J., Ferrin, D.L., Rao, H.R.: A trust-based consumer decision-making model in electronic commerce: the role of trust, perceived risk, and their antecedents. Decis. Support Syst. **44**, 544–564 (2008)
8. Kim, D.J., Song, Y.I., Braynov, S.B., Rao, H.R.: A multidimensional trust formation model in B-to-C e-commerce: a conceptual framework and content analyses of academia/practitioner perspectives. Decis. Support Syst. **40**, 143–165 (2005)
9. Pavlou, P.A., Liang, H., Xue, Y.: Understanding and mitigating uncertainty in online exchange relationships: a principal-agent perspective. MIS Q. **31**, 103–136 (2007)
10. Ahrholdt, D.: Erfolgsfaktoren einer E-Commerce-Website: Empirische Identifikation vertrauensfördernder Signale im Internet-Einzelhandel. Gabler Verlag/GWV Fachverlage, Wiesbaden/Wiesbaden (2010)

11. Li, H., Jiang, J., Wu, M.: The effects of trust assurances on consumers' initial online trust: a two-stage decision-making process perspective. Int. J. Inf. Manage. **34**, 395–405 (2014)
12. Hu, X., Wu, G., Wu, Y., Zhang, H.: The effects of Web assurance seals on consumers' initial trust in an online vendor: a functional perspective. Decis. Support Syst. **48**, 407–418 (2010)
13. Rifon, N., LaRose, R., Choi, S.M.: Your privacy is sealed: effects of web privacy seals on trust and personal disclosures. J. Consum. Aff. **39**, 339–362 (2005)
14. Noteberg, A., Christiaanse, E., Wallage, P.: Consumer trust in electronic channels: the impact of electronic commerce assurance on consumers' purchasing likelihood and risk perceptions. e-Serv. J. **2**, 46–67 (2003)
15. Odom, M.D., Kumar, A., Saunders, L.: Web assurance seals: how and why they influence consumers' decisions. J. Inf. Syst. **16**, 231–250 (2002)
16. Utz, S., Kerkhof, P., van den, Bos, J.: Consumers rule: how consumer reviews influence perceived trustworthiness of online stores. Electron. Commer. Res. Appl. **11**, 49–58 (2012)
17. Hui, K.-L., Teo, H.H., Lee, S.-Y.T.: Privacy assurance, field experiment, privacy statement, privacy seal, monetary incentive, information request. MIS Q. **31**, 19–33 (2007)
18. Mcknight, D.H., Kacmar, C.J., Choudhury, V.: Shifting factors and the ineffectiveness of third party assurance seals: a two-stage model of initial trust in a web business. Electron. Mark. **14**, 252–266 (2004)
19. Wang, S., Beatty, S.E., Foxx, W.: Signaling the trustworthiness of small online retailers. J. Interact. Mark. **18**, 53–69 (2004)
20. Chevalier, J.A., Mayzlin, D.: The effect of word of mouth on sales: online book reviews. J. Mark. Res. **43**, 345–354 (2006)
21. Dellarocas, C., Zhang, X., Awad, N.F.: Exploring the value of online product reviews in forecasting sales: the case of motion pictures. J. Interact. Mark. **21**, 23–45 (2007)
22. Berger, J., Sorensen, A.T., Rasmussen, S.J.: Positive effects of negative publicity: when negative reviews increase sales. Mark. Sci. **29**, 815–827 (2010)
23. Vermeulen, I.E., Seegers, D.: Tried and tested: the impact of online hotel reviews on consumer consideration. Tour. Manag. **30**, 123–127 (2009)
24. Ibrahim, E.N.M., Md Noor, N.L., Mehad, S.: "Seeing Is Not Believing But Interpreting", inducing trust through institutional symbolism: a conceptual framework for online trust building in a web mediated information environment. In: Smith, M.J., Salvendy, G. (eds.) HCII 2007. LNCS, vol. 4558, pp. 64–73. Springer, Heidelberg (2007)
25. Gefen, D., Straub, D.W.: Consumer trust in B2C e-commerce and the importance of social presence: experiments in e-products and e-services. Omega **32**, 407–424 (2004)
26. Kim, E., Tadisina, S.: Factors impacting customers' initial trust in e-businesses: an empirical study. In: 38th Annual Hawaii International Conference on System Sciences, pp. 170–180
27. Bortz, J., Döring, N.: Forschungsmethoden und Evaluation. Springer, Heidelberg (2006)
28. Anwar, A., Gulzar, A., Sohail, F.B., Akram, S.N.: Impact of brand image, trust and affect on consumer brand extension attitude: the mediating role of brand loyalty. Int. J. Econ. Manage. Sci. **1**, 73–79 (2011)
29. Gravetter, F.J., Forzano, L.-A.B.: Research Methods for the Behavioral Sciences. Wadsworth Cengage Learning, Belmont (2012)
30. Kim, D., Benbasat, I.: Trust-assuring arguments in B2C e-commerce: impact of content, source, and price on trust. J. Manage. Inf. Syst. **26**, 175–206 (2009)
31. Park, C., Lee, T.M.: Information direction, website reputation and eWOM effect: a moderating role of product type. J. Bus. Res. **62**, 61–67 (2009)
32. Weathers, D., Sharma, S., Wood, S.L.: Effects of online communication practices on consumer perceptions of performance uncertainty for search and experience goods. J. Retail. **83**, 393–401 (2007)
33. Cohen, J.: A power primer. Psychol. Bull. **112**, 155–159 (1992)

34. Holmqvist, K., Nyström, M., Andersson, R., Dewhurst, R., Jarodzka, H., van de, Weijer, J.: Eye Tracking: A Comprehensive Guide to Methods and Measures. Oxford University Press, Oxford (2011)

35. Özpolat, K., Jank, W.: Getting the most out of third party trust seals: an empirical analysis. Decis. Support Syst. **73**, 47–56 (2015)

"Tell Me Who You Are, and I Will Show You What You Get" - the Use of Individuals' Identity for Information Technology Customization

Sonia Camacho[✉] and Andres Barrios

School of Management, Universidad de Los Andes, Bogotá, Colombia
{so-camac,andr-bar}@uniandes.edu.co

Abstract. Individuals are constantly demanding more customization of the products they use, and companies are using different customization strategies to fulfill individuals' demands. This study analyzes relevant literature on the relationship between technology and identity, and explores how identity theory can be used to customize a particular information system (IS). With this analysis, the study examines individuals' willingness to adopt such a tailored IS in the face of privacy concerns and the possibility of using such IS in different contexts of their life (e.g. at work, at home). The research model proposed in this study will be validated using an experiment.

Keywords: Identity · Customization · Privacy

1 Introduction

In a scene of the Hollywood movie "Her", Theodore, the main character, purchases an operating system (OS) with artificial intelligence that is designed to adapt and evolve. When Theodore runs the OS, a male voice asks three personal questions: (a) Are you social or anti-social? (b) Would you like a male or female voice? And (c) how would you describe your relationship with your mother? Theodore answers the questions and the OS restarts and it is now customized according to those answers. This scene of the movie exemplifies the aim of this paper, to explore how users' expressions of identity can be used for information systems' personalization.

Information technologies (IT) have affected the social structures where our individual and social lives are embedded [1]. For example, individuals' constant mobility and the lack of division between home and work are supported by technology developments [2]. Prior research analyzed the effects of the relation between IT and individuals' identity. In this regard, Carter and Grover [3] reviewed and classified those studies according to their focus on: (a) IT as a determinant of individuals' identity development, where for example Stein et al. [4] analyzed the role of IT artifacts in professionals' identity construction; (b) IT as a medium for individuals' self-expression, where for example Walther [5] analyzed how individuals utilize computer-mediated-communications to manage others' impressions of themselves; and (c) IT as a consequence of

F.F.-H. Nah and C.-H. Tan (Eds.): HCIBGO 2016, Part I, LNCS 9751, pp. 377–385, 2016.
DOI: 10.1007/978-3-319-39396-4_34

individuals' identities, where for example Lee et al. [6] suggested that work-related IT is easily adopted when aligned with the worker's self-perception.

Despite these results, and to the best of our knowledge, no study has analyzed the way in which an individual's identity can be used for IT customization. This concept, also known as personalization, refers to "the ability to provide content and services that are tailored to individuals based on knowledge about their preferences and behaviors" (p. 84) [7 as cited in 8]. The underlying assumption of customization is that harmonizing the IT attributes with users' attitudes and values will lead to greater users' satisfaction.

In order to address this gap, in this work-in-progress paper we explore (1) how a social psychology variable like identity can be used to customize a particular information system (IS), and (2) the extent to which individuals are willing to adopt such tailored IS in the face of privacy concerns and the possibility of using such IS in different contexts of their life (e.g. at work, at home).

2 Theoretical Background and Research Model

2.1 Social Identity Theory

One of the most important conceptualizations about the relation between individuals and society was developed by James in his book, 'Principles of Psychology' [9]. In the book, the author explains that the sense of self emerges in the interaction between how I see myself ('I' self), and how others see me ('me' self) in a particular social context. This conceptualization places an individual's sense of self as a constant cognitive process that emerges in her/his social interactions [10].

One of the theoretical perspectives that has analyzed the dynamics among the society, the individual, and the self is called Symbolic Interactionism [11]. From this perspective, in every social network individuals have different positions known as roles (e.g. parent), and these positions have different expectations about how they should be played (e.g. taking care of children) [12]. In individuals' recurring interactions with their social networks (e.g. family), they recognize themselves as occupants of these positions and choose to play them accordingly [13]. Through the role-playing, individuals identify and internalize these positions, developing different identities around them. Therefore, individuals have many identities as they play different societal roles, and identities are constantly constructed, revised, and changed across individuals' different social interactions [14].

From a Symbolic Interactionism perspective, these individuals' behaviors are associated with their social identifications. According to Stryker [15], the individual self is structured by different identities that are organized in a salience hierarchy. Identity salience is defined as "the probability that an identity will be invoked across a variety of situations" (p. 286) [12]. Hence, in a specific situation individuals' behaviour is the result of the salience of an identity associated with the role they perform in the social structure. For example, an individual might have a parent and worker identities. In the specific situation of buying a car, if the individual has her/his parent identity as first in the identity hierarchy salience, she/he will prefer the car's features associated with safety (e.g., air bags) to the car's features associated with his worker identity (e.g., power, speed).

In sum, from a Symbolic Interactionism perspective, social structures are made of interconnected positions referred to as roles. Each role is linked to activities (e.g., practices) and resources (e.g., products), which in turn become symbols that convey meanings through which individuals interact with their social network. In the individuals' interaction with society, their interpretation and enactment of these roles generate a self that is structured by different identities. With time, individuals' patterned social interaction maintains and facilitates the development of new social structures [12].

This theoretical framework is suitable for this study since the ubiquitous nature of IT allows individuals to perform different roles (e.g., co-worker, parent, friend) while interacting with technology [3]. In addition, the salience of a particular individual's identity may be utilized as a means to customize the IT with which that individual interacts. In this way, the customized IT would become one of the resources the individual utilizes to express her/his salient identity.

2.2   Research Model and Hypotheses

The proposed research model is shown in Fig. 1. The constructs and hypotheses included in the model are described below.

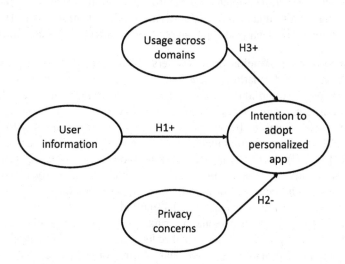

Fig. 1. Research model

User Information. Users' demographic information has been utilized for personalization, web search, and targeted advertising purposes [16, 17]. In particular, demographics-based recommendation systems have been used as a method for personalization in e-commerce interactions. In those situations, demographic information is explicitly obtained from users and the site may recommend products based on the preferences of users with similar demographics [18]. However, this approach requires that companies are able to collect complete and reliable demographic information and users may be reluctant to provide such information due to inconvenience or privacy concerns [17, 18]. Moreover, this approach assumes that in a particular moment in life, individuals have similar needs and wants [19] and this may not be the case. Therefore, and as suggested by the marketing segmentation literature, this approach might be supplemented by using psychographic and behavioral variables [20].

One such variable could be a user's identity. An individual's identity is known to be a motivator of behaviors [3, 21, 22]. In the marketing literature, it has been found that individuals use brands to express and validate their identity [23–25]. Consumers may pay more attention to identity-related stimuli (e.g., a product that appeals to a particular identity), react more positively to advertisement featuring individuals with a desired identity (e.g., a celebrity) or engage in behaviors that are linked to their identity [26]. Moreover, consumers can customize the products they acquire (e.g., selecting a particular ringtone in a mobile phone) to reflect their identity [3]. Considering these findings, it could be expected that users would be willing to adopt an app that is personalized by using their identity information. Users would engage in what is known as verification activities (i.e., behaviors that reinforce individuals' identities) [27] by using such an app [3]. Bearing in mind the limitations of using a demographic-based customization and the potential of creating a positive association between an individual's identity and a product (e.g., a personalized app) [26], we propose that users will be more willing to adopt a personalized app that has elicited their identity-related information than one that has elicited their demographic-related information. Therefore, we hypothesize that:

H1: Eliciting identity-related information as the user information will lead to a higher intention to adopt the personalized app than eliciting demographic-related information.

Privacy Concerns. Information privacy refers to individuals' ability to control the extent to which their information is acquired and used [28, 29]. Information privacy concerns (herein to be referred to as privacy concerns) refer to "an individual's subjective view of fairness within the context of information privacy" (p. 337) [30]. Privacy concerns have been found to be a detrimental factor for individual's willingness to provide personal information to companies and to conduct e-commerce transactions (see for example [31–33]). In the same vein, previous research has found that privacy concerns may negatively influence individuals' intention to use personalized services online (either through computers or mobile devices) (see for example [8, 34, 35]). In light of the previous results, it is expected that individuals will have privacy concerns related to the collection of their personal information (either demographic- or identity-related) and that those privacy concerns will reduce their intentions to adopt a personalized app that requires providing such personal information. Thus, we hypothesize that:

H2: Privacy concerns are negatively related to the intention to adopt the personalized app.

Usage Across Domains. As mentioned in the introduction, IT is ubiquitous in people's social and personal life and as such, it influences their identity development [1]. This has become more salient as IT has become more interconnected (i.e., usable across devices), and people are able to use it across different life situations [3]. At an individual level, people's enactment of certain roles and identities involves the use technology. For example, a person can use a particular budget application for both her/his work expenses using a desktop computer and her/his house expenses using her/his mobile phone. In addition, at a social level, IT also intertwines with individuals' social networks.

For example, in a single Facebook account, individuals might have work and family friends or groups of friends and may employ different mechanisms to manage their roles (e.g., worker and parent) separately (e.g., restricting content to some viewers) [36]. Considering that individuals receive several benefits from utilizing IT (e.g., mobile devices) in different spheres of their life, such as managing time more effectively, and having flexibility in the performance of tasks [37], it is expected that individuals will be more willing to adopt a personalized app from which they could obtain such benefits. Therefore, we hypothesize that:

H3: The usage across domains is positively related to the intention to adopt a personalized app.

3 Methodology

The hypotheses proposed in the research model will be validated through an experiment with a two-group, between-subject design. The two groups involve a different type of user information collected: identity-related versus demographics-related information used to customize the IS.

3.1 Experimental Procedure

Participants will be adults that (1) can have one of the proposed identities (e.g., worker, parent) as salient and (2) have downloaded and used mobile apps. They will be recruited using a market research firm, after obtaining ethical clearance from the authors' university. Those participants will be contacted via e-mail and will be provided with a URL, where they will find the experimental treatments and questions to answer.

After obtaining participants' consent, they will be randomly assigned to one of the two groups of the type of information collected. In the "demographic" group, participants will be asked questions related to their age, gender, occupation, income, and level of education. Those are traditional demographic variables used in marketing segmentation [38]. Participants in the "identity" group will be asked to rank five social identities (i.e., parent, worker, friend, member of a religious group, and student) according to their relative importance in their lives (as per Callero [39]). This ranking of identities is justified considering that identities that are central to an individual's self have the greatest potential to influence behaviors [3, 40]. Next, participants will be asked questions to make the top-ranked identity salient (see items in Table 1 below). Making an identity salient increases the possibilities of observing the effects of that identity on an individual's attitudes and behavior [26, 41].

The information elicited from participants will be utilized to personalize the screen that participants will see next. In that screen, participants will see the features the app has to offer. In addition, a sample screen of how the app would look will be shown to participants. Next, they will be asked questions related to their privacy concerns, the extent to which they would use the app in different contexts (e.g., at home, at work), and intentions to adopt the personalized app. Manipulation checks will also be performed after showing participants the app's screen. Other questions will be collected with the purpose of controlling for their influence on the endogenous construct of the model, such as familiarity with mobile apps, extent of usage of mobile apps, and whether participants have used an app with a similar purpose to that of the app shown during the experiment. Finally, an open-ended question will be asked to probe for reasons participants would decide or not to adopt such a personalized app.

3.2 Measurement Instrument

In order to measure the constructs proposed in the research model, previously validated scales will be adapted to the context of this study. Table 1 below summarizes the scales (with their sources) that will be used in this study.

Table 1. Summary of constructs and sources for their scales

Construct	Source	Items
Identity salience	Callero [39]	Being a _____ 1. is an important part of who I am 2. is something about which I have no clear feelings (R) 3. means more to me than _____ 4. is something I rarely think about (R) 5. I would feel a loss if I were forced to give up _____
Privacy concerns	Smith et al. [42] Collection dimension	Thinking about the questions you were asked to customize the app… 1. It usually bothers me when companies ask me for this kind of information. 2. When companies ask me for this kind of information, I sometimes think twice before providing it. 3. It bothers me to give this kind of information to be able to use an app. 4. I am concerned that companies are collecting too much personal information about me.
Intention to adopt the personalized app	Wang and Benbasat [43]	1. Assuming that I had access to this app, I intend to use it. 2. Assuming that I had access to this app, I predict that I would use it. 3. Assuming that I had access to this app, I plan to use it
Personalization (manipulation check)		This app offers personalized features based on my name-of-identity (demographic) characteristics
Possibility to use across domains	Hong and Tam [44]	The use I would give to this app would be: (entirely personal – entirely business) 1. I expect that I would be able to use this app at anytime, anywhere. 2. I would find this app to be easily used at work and at home. 3. I expect this app would be available to use whenever I need it

3.3 Pilot Study

A pilot study will be conducted to test the personalized screens that participants will see after the demographic- or identity-related information is elicited. In this study, graduate students from the authors' university will be involved and will be assigned to one of two groups: the "identity" group and the "demographics" group. In each group, participants will see first a non-personalized screen of the app (so they get familiar with it). Next, they will be asked identity- or demographic-related questions as per the experimental procedure described above. Then, participants will see the personalized screen of the app and will be asked to rate the extent to which the screen has been personalized according to the collected information, using a Likert scale. Finally, participants will be given the space (with an open-ended question) to provide their comments or suggestions on how the personalization can be improved.

3.4 Model Validation and Sample Size

The proposed research model will be validated using linear regression analysis. In the model, user's information will be specified as a dummy variable (i.e., "demographics" condition – 0, "identity" condition – (1). Post-hoc analyses will be run to determine the differences between groups in terms of privacy concerns and possibility to use the personalized app across domains. The required minimum sample size to validate the proposed model can be determined by following Faul et al. [45] requirements to detect a medium size effect, with a power of 0.80 and alpha of 0.05, in between-subjects designs with 2 groups. In this case, the minimum number of participants that would need to be recruited is 64 per group (128 in total). In order to account for potential spoiled responses, a total of 160 participants will be recruited.

4   Potential Contributions and Limitations

From a theoretical point of view, the results will contribute to the advancement of the IS literature in the area of customization by proposing social psychology variables as an input for the customization process. In addition, the study will evaluate the effect of this type of customization on the technology adoption process, as well as the barriers that need to be overcome to drive this adoption. From a practical perspective, the study will provide IS designers with a new variable (i.e., an individual's identity) to use in the customization of their systems.

This study has some limitations. First, individuals' identities may not necessarily be constant or coherent. They may change overtime (what has been known as identity projects) or may generate tensions within the individual (due to the pursuit of conflicting goals). Therefore, customization based on identity may need to adapt and evolve according to those changes. Future research may consider this possibility by conducting longitudinal studies and verifying that the customized features keep valid over time for users. Second, this study will test the effect of identity-based customization in one particular app. The antecedents explored here may need to be expanded to consider other types of apps or the use of customized computer software.

References

1. Ling, R.: From Ubicomp to Ubiex (Pectations). Telematics Inf. **31**(2), 173–183 (2014)
2. Bauman, Z.: Liquid Modernity. Polity Press, Cambridge (2000)
3. Carter, M., Grover, V.: Me, My Self, and I(T): conceptualizing information technology identity and its implications. MIS Quart. **39**(4), 931–957 (2015)
4. Stein, M.-K., Galliers, R.D., Markus, L.M.: Towards an understanding of identity and technology in the workplace. J. Inform. Technol. **28**(3), 167–182 (2013)
5. Walther, J.B.: Selective self-presentation in computer-mediated communication: hyper-personal dimensions of technology, language, and cognition. Comput. Hum. Behav. **23**(5), 2538–2557 (2007)
6. Lee, Y., Lee, J., Lee, Z.: Social influence on technology acceptance behavior: self-identity theory perspective. Data Base Adv. Inf. Syst. **37**(2–3), 60–75 (2006)
7. Adomavicius, G., Tuzhilin, A.: Personalization technologies: a process-oriented perspective. Commun. ACM **48**(10), 83–90 (2005)
8. Sheng, H., Nah, F.F.H., Siau, K.: An experimental study on ubiquitous commerce adoption: impact of personalization and privacy concerns. J. Assoc. Inf. Syst. **9**(6), 344–376 (2008)
9. James, W.: Principles of Psychology. Holt, New York (1890)
10. Mead, G.: Mind, Self and Society. University of Chicago Press, Chicago (1934)
11. Blumer, H.: Symbolic interactionism: perspective and method. Prentice Hall, Englewood Cliffs (1969)
12. Stryker, S., Burke, P.: Past, present, and future of an identity theory. Soc. Psychol. Q. **63**, 284–297 (2000)
13. Reed, A.: Social identity as a useful perspective for self-concept-based consumer research. Psychol. Market. **19**, 235–266 (2002)
14. Kaiser, S.: The Social Psychology of Clothing. Macmillan Publishing Company, New York (1990)
15. Stryker, S.: Symbolic Interactionism: A Social Structural Version. Benjamin/Cummings, Menlo Park (1980)
16. Kim, J.W., Lee, B.H., Shaw, M.J., Chang, H.L., Nelson, M.: Application of decision-tree induction techniques to personalized advertisements on internet storefronts. Int. J. Electron. Commun. **5**(3), 45–62 (2001)
17. Zhong, E., Tan, B., Mo, K., Yang, Q.: User demographics prediction based on mobile data. Pervasive Mob. Comput. **9**(6), 823–837 (2013)
18. Wei, C.P., Easley, R.F., Shaw, M.J.: Web-based recommendation systems for personalized e-commerce shopping. In: Shaw, M.J. (ed.) E-Business Management, pp. 249–276. Springer, Los Angeles (2002)
19. Wedel, M., Kamakura, W.A.: Market Segmentation. Methodological and Conceptual Foundations. Springer, Norwell (1999)
20. Kotler, P., Armstrong, G.: Principles of Marketing, 8th edn. Prentice-Hall International, Englewood Cliffs (1999)
21. Bhattacharjee, A., Berger, J., Menon, G.: When identity marketing backfires: consumer agency in identity expression. J. Consum. Res. **41**(2), 294–309 (2014)
22. Oyserman, D.: Identity-Based motivation: implications for action-readiness, procedural readiness, and consumer behavior. J. Consum. Psychol. **19**(3), 250–260 (2009)
23. Berger, J., Heath, C.: Where consumers diverge from others: identity signaling and product domains. J. Consum. Res. **34**(2), 121–134 (2007)
24. Escalas, J., Bettman, J.R.: Self-Construal, reference groups, and brand meaning. J. Consum. Res. **32**(3), 378–389 (2005)

25. Chernev, A., Hamilton, R., Gal, D.: Competing for consumer identity: limits to self-expression and the perils of lifestyle branding. J. Mark. **75**(3), 66–82 (2011)
26. Reed, A., Forehand, M.R., Puntoni, S., Warlop, L.: Identity-Based consumer behavior. IJRM **29**(4), 310–321 (2012)
27. Swann Jr., W.B., Rentfrow, P.J., Guinn, J.S.: Self-verification: the search for coherence. In: Leary, M.R., Tangney, J.P. (eds.) Handbook of Self and Identity, pp. 367–383. Guilford, New York (2005)
28. Westin, A.F.: Privacy and Freedom. Atheneum, New York (1967)
29. Xu, H., Luo, X.R., Carroll, J.M., Rosson, M.B.: The personalization privacy paradox: an exploratory study of decision making process for location-aware marketing. Decis. Support Syst. **51**(1), 42–52 (2011)
30. Malhotra, N.K., Kim, S.S., Agarwal, J.: Internet Users' Information Privacy Concerns (IUIPC): the construct, the scale, and a causal model. Inform. Syst. Res. **15**(4), 336–355 (2004)
31. Dinev, T., Hart, P.: An extended privacy calculus model for e-commerce transactions. Inform. Syst. Res. **17**(1), 61–80 (2006)
32. Korzaan, M.L., Boswell, K.T.: The influence of personality traits and information privacy concerns on behavioral intentions. J. Comput. Inform. Syst. **48**(4), 15–24 (2008)
33. Udo, G.J.: Privacy and security concerns as major barriers for e-commerce: a survey study. ICS **9**(4), 165–174 (2001)
34. Chellappa, R.K., Sin, R.G.: Personalization versus privacy: an empirical examination of the online consumer's dilemma. Inf. Technol. Manage. **6**(2–3), 181–202 (2005)
35. Ho, S.Y.: The attraction of internet personalization to web users. Electron. Mark. **16**(1), 41–50 (2006)
36. Skeels, M.M., Grudin, J.: When social networks cross boundaries. In: GROUP 2009 Proceedings of the ACM 2009 International Conference on Supporting Group Work. ACM, New York (2009)
37. Duxbury, L., Smart, R.: The "Myth of Separate Worlds:" an exploration of how mobile technology has redefined work-life balance. In: Kaiser, S., Ringlstetter, M.J., Eikhof, D.R., Cunha, M.P.E. (eds.) Creating Balance?, pp. 269–284. Springer, Berlin (2011)
38. Lin, C.F.: Segmenting customer brand preference: demographic or psychographic. JPBM **11**(4), 249–268 (2002)
39. Callero, P.L.: Role-Identity salience. Soc. Psychol. Q. **48**(3), 203–215 (1985)
40. Stets, J.E., Biga, C.F.: Bringing identity theory into environmental sociology. Sociol. Theory **21**(4), 398–423 (2003)
41. Puntoni, S., Sweldens, S., Tavassoli, N.: Gender identity salience and perceived vulnerability to breast cancer. J. Mark. Res. **48**, 413–424 (2011)
42. Smith, H.J., Milberg, S.J., Burke, S.J.: Information privacy: measuring individuals' concerns about organizational practices. MIS Quart. **20**(2), 167–196 (1996)
43. Wang, W., Benbasat, I.: Interactive decision aids for consumer decision making in e-commerce: the influence of perceived strategy restrictiveness. MIS Quart. **33**(2), 293–320 (2009)
44. Hong, S.J., Tam, K.Y.: Understanding the adoption of multipurpose information appliances: the case of mobile data services. Inform. Syst. Res. **17**(2), 162–179 (2006)
45. Faul, F., Erdfelder, E., Lang, A.-G., Buchner, A.: G* power 3: a flexible statistical power analysis program for the social, behavioral, and biomedical sciences. Behav. Res. Methods. **39**(2), 175–191 (2007)

Social Influence and Emotional State While Shopping

Jesus Garcia-Mancilla[1], Victor R. Martinez[2], Victor M. Gonzalez[1($\boxtimes$)], and Angel F. Fajardo[1]

[1] Department of Computer Science, ITAM, Mexico City, Mexico
{jgarc293,victor.gonzalez,angel.fajardo}@itam.mx
[2] Signal Analysis and Interpretation Lab,
University of Southern California, Los Angeles, USA
victorrm@usc.edu

Abstract. New technologies are opening novel ways to help people in their decision-making while shopping. From crowd-generated customer reviews to geo-based recommendations, the information to make the decision could come from different social circles with varied degrees of expertise and knowledge. Such differences affect how much influence the information has on the shopping decisions. In this work, we aim to identify how social influence when it is mediated by modern and ubiquitous communication (such as that provided by smartphones) can affect people's shopping experience and especially their emotions while shopping. Our results showed that large amount of information affects emotional state in costumers, which can be measured in their physiological response. Based on our results, we conclude that integrating smartphone technologies with biometric sensors can create new models of customer experience based on the emotional effects of social influence while shopping.

1 Introduction

The shopping experience at brick and mortar businesses is changing with the introduction of ubiquitous systems and technologies, which allow customers to query social networks and search engines whenever they are unsure with a purchase decision. This social question asking phenomenon, as described by Morris [1] in his survey of 2010, shows that about half of the people ask their friends from social networks their opinion about a product, restaurant, place, technology, or events, and around a third part had done it in several occasions. Since not all responses are weighted equally, social closeness is an important factor to take into consideration. The closer the social tie, the more influential the answer will be [2]. This is more visible when the costumer is asked to give an opinion: they usually refer to comments from friends, family, and colleagues rather than mass media reports or expert opinions [3]. Most of the time social influence in a decision only comes from closer ties, partly because the answers in social networks tend to be sparse [4]. That is the reason that recently e-commerce websites use a recommendation systems were users leave comments and rate the products, this reduces the search complexity, and improve decision quality [5].

© Springer International Publishing Switzerland 2016
F.F.-H. Nah and C.-H. Tan (Eds.): HCIBGO 2016, Part I, LNCS 9751, pp. 386–394, 2016.
DOI: 10.1007/978-3-319-39396-4_35

However, during a social question asking process, it is necessary to use additional mental resources to access, use and interpret information in order to make satisfying decisions [6,7]. Based on the theory that only a limited amount of information can be processed by a person [8], extra or unnecessary quantities of information can lead to mental fatigue and stress [9]. As to save time and avoid a heavy reasoning process, customers tend to rely on emotion and external opinions to help in their decision [10]. Hence, shopping decision-making is a process usually loaded with emotional biases, and highly sensitive to external influence [2,5,11,12]. To provide a good experience to the customers, retailers need to take special attention in minimizing cognitive load while keeping in mind that excessive information may be detrimental to the customers overall mood [13].

New developments in wearable technologies provide a great opportunity to help people in their decision-making during a regular shopping experience. Previous works have been capable of leveraging the use of biometric-signals sensors, such as Galvanic Skin Response (GSR), Hear Rate (HR), Skin Temperature (SKT), in order to establish a relationship between a user physical state and the emotions that he or she experiences [10,14]. For example, variation in GSR has been found to be related to the intensity (arousal) of specific emotions [15]. GSR has been widely used for emotion assessment, stress identification and cognitive load [16,17]. Solovey et al. [18] created a methodology to evaluate cognitive load on drivers, correlating the cognitive load with the GSR. This same variation, with the information provided by heart rate, can be used to identify when a person encounters a new challenge [19]. Moreover, feeling confident about a purchase can make a person to feel more relaxed. As a result of this relaxation, the skin temperature rises, as well as the heart rate, due to the parasympathetic activity of the nervous system [20]. This bodily response has been classified as an indicator of relaxation level along with a lower heart rate [21].

In this work, we argue that social influence modifies a person's mood, specifically in the context of shopping. Mood has been shown to have important effects on consumer behavior and decision-making processes [22], while also modifying the way a customer judge their shopping experience [13]. Therefore, our main hypothesis can be stated as follows: in retail context and under social influence, the emotions that a customer experiences are related to his/her shopping decision and shopping experience. That is to say that physiological variables such as GSR, HR or SKT are capable of capturing events where a purchase decision improves the shopping experience. Under this hypothesis we designed an experiment were participants could select a product from different categories, having support from different sources of information through the use of a smartphone with WhatsApp Messenger. A smart watch recorded all the biometric signals necessary for later analysis.

1.1 Limitations

The main limitation of this work is related to the use for this study of a smart band wrist wearable by commercial name Basis Peak(TM), which counts with GSR, HR, SKT sensors, and which takes a measurement every minute. We could not find any way around this. In contrast, the GSR wearable used by Hernandez [23] can take up to 60 measurements per minute.

2   Method

Experiments were done in the months of June and July 2015. At the end of each test, participants received a $5 cash-card for taking part in the study. We chose to use WhatsApp Messenger in order to have natural feedback from participants, since all participants had experience with this type of messenger and could use their own smartphone.

2.1   Participants Demographics

In this study, 34 participants (17 women) were recruited from a pool of under-graduate students, ranging in age from 18 to 27 years ($\mu = 21.24, \sigma = 2.23$). All of them were highly experienced with mobile messaging apps, rating themselves as highly proficient. Thirteen participants (38.23 %) reported having 10 to 20 different messenger conversations in an average week. Participants were familiar with the group functionality of the mobile messaging app, with ten belonging to 3 to 5 groups, twelve being part of 5 to 10 different groups, seven to 10 to 20, and four with 20 or more groups. Using a multiple option questionnaire, we could see that our participants usually go to retail shops to buy clothing (88 %), footwear (76 %), fragrances (62 %) and technology (59 %). Only 9 % of them buy wine in a departmental store. The majority of participant reported asking their friends or family for help with purchasing decisions, with 27 of them frequently appealing to their closest ones suggestions, 2 having done only once or twice, and 5 never having it done before.

2.2   Procedure

Once a participant was selected to do the experiment, he or she was randomly assigned to either the experimental or the control group. Then, a member of the team would ask the participant to put a Basis Peak(TM) smart band on and while the reading started, a member of the team explained the procedure to the participant and asked to sign the consent form, allowing to be videotaped and allowing us to use the data for academic proposes. In the case of the control group, immediately after the previous steps, the participants went to a mock-up department store. On the case of the experimental group, we ask them first to start a group on his/her phone with friends and family who could help them to take a decision and then add a contact named "participant-lumia" that was link to a 500 Nokia Lumia smartphone. This smartphone was then given to the participant with the contacts of six different experts (a man and a woman from each of the three product categories), and a group named "crowdsource" with several contacts added that the participant did not know before.

Fig. 1. Participant selecting products and asking to her friends via smartphone (chat)

Mock-Up Department Store. The mock-up department store designed for the experiment was a classroom adapted for this purpose. We disposed tables for each of the categories, one for Gourmet Food (wines), other for Technology (tablets), and two for Health and Beauty items (perfumes, one for men and other for women). The brands of all the products are detailed in the Table 1. To help the participants to play the role of a customer in a department store, decoration was placed on each table. On one of the walls, we projected video ads from a department store's YouTube channel, and posters lent us by the department store's management, were placed on above all product tables. To help on the later analysis, we put a camcorder to record all the room to see most of the reactions of the participants. On Fig. 1 we can see pictures of a participant asking on the phone.

Once the participant enters the mock-up store, he or she had a few seconds to familiarize with it while one of the researchers gave a brief introduction to the products that had to be chosen. The order of the tables was randomly counter-balanced and once the participant arrived to a table, a staff member presented the three options that had to be selected. In the control group, after the

Table 1. Options available for each category

Category	Options
Gourmet Food (wine)	Montesierra, Sangre de Toro, Rioja Cuné
Technology (tablets)	iPad, Samsung Galaxy 3, Ghia i7
Men's H &B (fragrances)	Benetton Sport, Cold, Perry Ellis America
Women's H &B (perfumes)	Nature, Forever Dreams, Tommy Girl

participant selected a product, they had to answer why he or she chose that option and if he had to ask someone about the products, whom he or she would choose. On the experimental group, the participant was introduced to the respective experts of the product category, and then they had to decide which one to ask about the products (the man or the woman). Finally, they had to message the crowdsource group and his/her friends and family. No additional instructions were given, each participant was free to contact each source as he or she liked (text, picture or audio). Once the decision was made or 10 min passed on the table, the participants continue to the next table and so on until the three decisions were made. At the end of the experiment, the participants of both groups had to answer an inventory to assess their emotions during the experiment called Positive and Negative Affect Schedule (PANAS) [23].

2.3   Information Sources

Participant's interactions were limited to text media messages using WhatsApp messenger, so, making phone calls or using SMS were not allowed during the test. Participants in the experimental setting had access to three distinct information resources:

Social Groups. Each participant created a group of friends and family using the mobile application. It was due at the beginning of each experiment in case they want to ask for a recommendation during the purchasing decision.

Product's Experts. For each product category (in our case, Health & Beauty, Gourmet Food and Technology), participants had to choose one expert to contact using WhatsApp, and ask for some product's reviews in order to take their decision. A total of six personas of different genders were created, with different name, age, occupation, face picture, motivations, goals and frustration, each one simulating a different expert in each the product categories. Using a Wizard of Oz method, we instructed a member of staff to converse with the participant answering from a pre-defined set of answers. All answers were the same regardless of the gender of the expert, thus, all participants received the same information from the experts.

Crowdsource **Group.** Friends and family of the staff members were invited to help during the experiment. They were added to a WhatsApp's group called "Crowdsource", with a total of 15 members (8 men and 7 women). We did not give any explicit instruction as to how to respond the participants inquires, however we did provide the group with the names and brands on display beforehand. All members information (e.g., their names) was anonymized on the phone the participants were using.

2.4   Processing Biometrics Signals

The activity-tracking wristband Basis Peak(TM) is set to capture the following body signals: HR, SKT, and GSR. A measurement is taken every minute, and stored in the clock's internal memory until it is synced with a mobile device and cloud server. We downloaded the records from the Basis Peak cloud server, and split the data by participant. In order to make a fair comparison between signals and statistics approach was used. For each measurement we obtained mean, variance, median, minimum and maximum. We also obtained these descriptive statistics for the first 5 and the last 5 min of the experiment, and for the signal without considering neither the first 5 nor the final 5 min. This resulted in a dataset consisting of 34 participant's signals by 73 descriptive statistics. These statistics were centered and scaled by taking the mean and dividing by one standard deviation. To have a better understanding on the signals and to give a stress evaluation, we calculate it with a formula that uses heart rate, skin temperature and galvanic skin response to give a stress level value, and a filter proposed to automatically detected stress [24]. We correlate this information with the PANAS results.

3   Results

When comparing the self-reported metrics between groups using a Fisher's exact test, we were unable to find any significant difference at the $p = 0.05$ level. However, there was a slight tendency, on the $p = 0.1$ level, for participants on the experimental setting to feel slightly more nervous ($p = 0.10$).

Furthermore, not only stress related emotions were seen in our results. Other negative emotions, like irritability and anger values on the PANAS were reported by the experimental group. We confirmed the latter, with biometric data collected in our experiment; the variance of the ST was lower on the control group ($t(14.179) = -2.3459$; $p < 0.05$), and as explained by Ekman [10], this could be due to the higher emotional charge on the experimental group, caused by anger (higher ST) or by stress (lower ST).

To calculate the participants' stress, the values of HT, ST and GSR were normalized and fed through a filtering algorithm. This algorithm highlighted that the participants from the experimental group had more stressful events, with most of them lasting longer, than their control counterparts do. A significant difference on the mean stress level was found between the groups ($t(6 : 0856) = 17 : 725$; $p < 0.01$).

The experimental group participants reported more negative emotions like stress, and according to the classification filter [24], 11 out of 16 presented stress episodes as shown in the Fig. 2, whereas in the control group (Fig. 3), only 4 users presented stress.

Our results point towards a relation between the external input, the shopping task and the self-reported emotions felt during the experiment. We then focused our efforts to find if such relations reflect on the participant's biometrics.

The HR is the main biometric variable that gave us a clear differentiation between groups. While the experimental group had the higher max value, the mean was higher in the control group; this could be due the great variation between subjects, while the values in the control group where more uniform,

Fig. 2. Experimental group

Fig. 3. Control group

in the experimental group, had more changes because not all the subjects had the same levels of stress. Based on the results from the correlations test on the results of the formulas applied to calculate stress level, we confirmed that the atypical data, like a stress episode, have to be analyzed separately. As Khazan [25] explains, in biofeedback therapy this type of data is used to characterize emotional states. Based on this, we considered appropriated to calculate the stress level after a filter detects the stress on the person. Finding a significant difference when it was used.

4 Conclusion

Social influence is an important factor to assess while evaluating the shopping experience at stores because this it is likely to emerge with the presence of smartphones, which facilitate interaction with friends and networks while evaluating products. Recent studies show that more than 89 % of smartphone owners use their phone in the store [26]. This could lead to a better experience, but not in all cases as shown in this work. We found that when too much information is given to the participant, he tends to experience more negative emotions as seen in the PANAS results. Capturing such emotions can now be done easier and in real time with new wearable technology that could give us even less subjective results; HR, GSR and ST have been proved to be good metrics to measure negative emotions like stress, and give a better insight of post-test instruments such as the PANAS. The use of wearable devices like the smart-watch Basis Peak(TM) could be an important addition to the studies that evaluate shopping experience in the context of understanding the requirements of technologies for shopping with smartphone interaction.

Acknowledgment. This work has been supported by Asociación Mexicana de Cultura A.C. and the Consejo Nacional of Ciencia and Tecnología of Mexicó (CONACyT)

References

1. Morris, M.R., Teevan, J., Panovich, K.: What do people ask their social networks, and why?: a survey study of status message Q&A behavior. In: Proceedings of the SIGCHI Conference on Human Factors in Computing Systems, pp. 1739–1748. ACM (2010)
2. Panovich, K., Miller, R., Karger, D.: Tie strength in question & answer on social network sites. In: Proceedings of the ACM 2012 Conference on Computer Supported Cooperative Work, pp. 1057–1066. ACM (2012)
3. Hsu, M.H., Yen, C.H., Chiu, C.M., Chang, C.M.: A longitudinal investigation of continued online shopping behavior: an extension of the theory of planned behavior. Int. J. Hum. Comput. Stud. **64**, 889–904 (2006)
4. Paul, S.A., Hong, L., Chi, E.H.: Is twitter a good place for asking questions? a characterization study. In: ICWSM (2011)
5. Kowatsch, T., Maass, W.: In-store consumer behavior: how mobile recommendation agents influence usage intentions, product purchases, and store preferences. Comput. Hum. Behav. **26**, 697–704 (2010)
6. Baddeley, A.: Working memory and language: an overview. J. Commun. Disord. **36**, 189–208 (2003)
7. Sterelny, K.: Cognitive load and human decision, or, three ways of rolling the rock up hill. Innate Mind **2**, 218–233 (2006)
8. Miyake, A., Shah, P.: Models of Working Memory: Mechanisms of Active Maintenance and Executive Control. Cambridge University Press, New York (1999)
9. Setz, C., Arnrich, B., Schumm, J., La Marca, R., Troster, G., Ehlert, U.: Discriminating stress from cognitive load using a wearable EDA device. IEEE Trans. Inf. Technol. Biomed. **14**, 410–417 (2010)
10. Ekman, P., Levenson, R.W., Friesen, W.V.: Autonomic nervous system activity distiguishes among emotions. Sci. **221**(4616), 1208–1210 (1983)
11. Hill, R.P., Gardner, M.P.: The buying process: effects of and on consumer mood states. Adv. Consum. Res. **14**, 408–410 (1987)
12. Nakayama, M., Sutcliffe, N., Wan, Y.: How dependent are consumers on others when making their shopping decisions? J. Electron. Commer. Organ. **9**, 1–21 (2011)
13. Swinyard, W.R.: The effects of mood, involvement, and quality of store experience on shopping intentions. J. Consum. Res. **20**, 271–280 (1993)
14. Schwartz, M.S., Andrasik, F. (eds.): Biofeedback A Practitioner's Guide, 3rd edn. The Guilford Press, New York (2003)
15. Liu, F., Liu, G., Lai, X.: Emotional intensity evaluation method based on Galvanic skin response signal, pp. 257–261. IEEE (2014)

16. Khawaji, A., Zhou, J., Chen, F., Marcus, N.: Using Galvanic Skin Response (GSR) to measure trust and cognitive load in the text-chat environment, pp. 1989–1994. ACM Press (2015)
17. Nourbakhsh, N., Wang, Y., Chen, F., Calvo, R.A.: Using Galvanic skin response for cognitive load measurement in arithmetic and reading tasks. In: Proceedings of the 24th Australian Computer-Human Interaction Conference, pp. 420–423. ACM (2012)
18. Solovey, E.T., Zec, M., Garcia Perez, E.A., Reimer, B., Mehler, B.: Classifying driver workload using physiological and driving performance data: two field studies, pp. 4057–4066. ACM Press (2014)
19. Saha, S., Nag, P., Ray, M.K.: A complete virtual instrument for measuring and analyzing human stress in real time. In: 2014 International Conference on Control, Instrumentation, Energy and Communication (CIEC), pp. 81–85. IEEE (2014)
20. Romeijn, N., Raymann, R.J.E.M., Møst, E., Te Lindert, B., Van Der Meijden, W.P., Fronczek, R., Gomez-Herrero, G., Van Someren, E.J.W.: Sleep, vigilance, and thermosensitivity. Pflügers Archiv Eur. J. Physiol. **463**, 169–176 (2012)
21. Regula, M., Socha, V., Kutilek, P., Socha, L., Hana, K., Hanakova, L., Szabo, S.: Study of heart rate as the main stress indicator in aircraft pilots. In: 16th International Conference on Mechatronics-Mechatronika (ME), pp. 639–643. IEEE (2014)
22. Armitage, C.J., Conner, M., Norman, P.: Differential effects of mood on information processing: evidence from the theories of reasoned action and planned behaviour. Eur. J. Soc. Psychol. **29**, 419–433 (1999)
23. Watson, D., Clark, L.A., Tellegen, A.: Development and validation of brief measures of positive and negative affect: the PANAS scales. J. Pers. Soc. Psychol. **54**, 1063 (1988)
24. Garcia-Mancilla, J., Gonzalez, V.M.: Stress quantification using a wearable device for daily feedback to improve stress management. In: Zheng, X., et al. (eds.) ICSH 2015. LNCS, vol. 9545, pp. 204–209. Springer, Heidelberg (2016). doi:10.1007/978-3-319-29175-8_19
25. Khazan, I.Z.: The Clinical Handbook of Biofeedback: A Step-by-Step Guide for Training and Practice with Mindfulness. Wiley, Chichester (2013)
26. Anderson, C., Egol, M., Froseth, H., Kaminkow, B.A., Kristofek, B., Madden, K., Manikas, T., Mcalenney, M., Paley, M.: Mobile in-store research how in-store shoppers are using mobile devices. Technical report. Google Shopper Marketing Agency Council (2013)

Sensing Distress – Towards a Blended Method for Detecting and Responding to Problematic Customer Experience Events

Sue Hessey[1](✉) and Will Venters[2]

[1] BT Plc Research and Innovation, Ipswich, UK
Sue.hessey@bt.com
[2] London School of Economics and Political Sciences, London, UK
W.Venters@lse.ac.uk

Abstract. Excellent Customer Experience (CE) is a strategic priority for many large service organisations in a competitive marketplace. CE should be seamless, and in most cases it is, with customers ordering, paying for and receiving services that align with their expectations. However, in rare cases, an exceptional process event leads to service delivery delay or failure, and both the customer and organisation end up in complex recovery situations as a result. Unless this recovery is handled effectively inefficiency, avoidable costs and brand damage can result. So how can organisations sense when these problems are occurring and how can they respond to avoid these negative consequences? Our paper proposes a blended methodology where process mining and qualitative user research combine to give a holistic picture of customer experience issues, derived from a particular customer case study. We propose a theoretical model for detecting and responding to customer issues, and discuss the challenges and opportunities of such a model when applied in practice in large service organisations.

Keywords: Customer experience · Process mining · HCI

1 Introduction –Why Is This Approach Different to Other Customer Experience Research?

Customer Experience (CE) research covers a wide variety of angles, all worthy but often not brought together for maximum impact. For example UI design testing on ecommerce sites is often concerned with optimising ordering sequences, but may not address the user journey when these orders go wrong. Similarly CE research in larger groups, via focus groups may give generic issues retrospectively – not reflecting "here and now" issues. The related field of Customer Relationship Management (CRM) research often involves processes and systems use in call centres [e.g. 1] – but how often is that tied into customer experience? At a macro level, text analysis of social media can provide hot issues in customer experience, and Net-Promoter Score surveys [2] provide quantitative clues to the same but lack specificity of findings. In the back- end, process mining and mapping gives information that describes what has gone wrong and how badly but doesn't say what the effect on the customer actually is.

© Springer International Publishing Switzerland 2016
F.F.-H. Nah and C.-H. Tan (Eds.): HCIBGO 2016, Part I, LNCS 9751, pp. 395–405, 2016.
DOI: 10.1007/978-3-319-39396-4_36

Given Duncan et al. (2013) argue that *"most companies perform fairly well on touchpoints, but performance on journeys can set a company apart."* [3], there seems a paucity of methods able to connect qualitative process perspectives with quantitative process mining data on customer experience to help improve such customer "journeys". Indeed Duncan et al. (2013) [3] sensibly recommend that *"a company should draw on customer and employee surveys along with operational data across functions at each touchpoint, to assess performance"*, though they acknowledge that this is a difficult endeavour as it requires the acquisition and integration of a large range of different types of empirical material, both qualitative and quantitative.

Our work seeks to achieve this by combining process mining with HCI, something discussed by Holziger [4], and Shneidermann [5] who underline the importance of integrating data mining with effective, usable data visualisation. In a business context, this would enable business managers and company strategists to control what data they are seeking so they can make decisions efficiently and adaptively.

Although a detailed analysis of the customer experience case study is detailed elsewhere (forthcoming) we here concentrate on documenting the adopted methodology as a novel way of enabling large service organisations to detect customer distress episodes and respond to them in a timely fashion, thereby minimising potential brand damage and maximising customer advocacy. Our contribution is thus methodological and practice, providing HCI researchers with a means of linking process mining and HCI, and providing practitioners with a means of detecting, addressing, and better understanding customer distress. We demonstrate our novel combination of process mining and qualitative research through the analysis of a case study of a problematic customer experience journey, and thus demonstrate the benefit of this combined approach. We first look at the approach to the case study which inspired our thinking.

2   Background

The authors of this paper were made aware of a particular customer's journey via family contacts. It involved the customer's problematic delivery of a super-fast broadband connection from a telecommunications provider. In the vast majority of these types of orders, such connections are provided with no problems whatsoever. However in this one exceptional case, a process event occurred in the organisation's back-end, effectively cancelling the customer's order – which the customer could not know about. When he was made aware of the situation, he struggled to get his service delivery back on track. Problems will always occur in large complex organisations but it is the customer's experience of how the recovery is dealt with which is a key issue. Due to the duration and number of different representatives of the organisation who were involved in dealing with this customer's journey it was clear that this case study was worthy of investigation, to understand how the interfaces between the customer and the company, the underlying delivery process, and the recovery process were sub-optimal and where they could be improved.[1]

---

[1] The customer case was finally resolved to the customer's satisfaction. The customer remains a customer of the organisation some 18 months after the case was closed.

The researchers had access to the company systems and the customer himself to accumulate a significant data corpus to analyse. The blended skills of the researchers (Information Systems and HCI/ethnography) were then fully deployed to analyse the

Table 1. The richness and detail of the data corpus for this one case study allowed the researchers to understand (a) the structured, process-driven recovery path (which was seen to fall onto a failure path on numerous occasions) against (b) how the process failures manifested themselves to the customer, and indeed how the various interfaces between the customer and organisation throughout the recovery process affected customer experience over time. It also informed the initial understanding of the data sources that would be needed in the model for detecting and responding to customer distress more generically. With the data sources in place we started to consider some preliminary questions before creating the model.

Data source	Analysis technique	Data Format
Customer	1. Semi-structured interview to discuss experiences of the customer's interactions with the organisation. 2. Full transcription of recorded interview, coding of key themes [8], core issues identified and prioritised.	Highest priority issues presented as text data (derived from transcription and coding sequence).
	1. Mapping of sequence and content of interactions *from the customer's perspective*. 2. Qualitative analysis of content of interactions.	Records of interactions with the company as recorded by the customer, i.e. prints of emails, detailed records of phone conversations, SMS messages, hard copy letters, social media posts etc.
Customer Care advisors (first line and High-Level case handlers) and their managers	1. "Sit-along", non-participant observations: observing advisors managing in-bound calls similar in context to our case study via a "splitter" from the advisor's headset. These were conducted in situ in the call centre to give contextual data (e.g. environmental, system use etc.). 2. 9 x Semi-structured interviews to explore the process and subjective experiences of handling calls of this nature. 3. Interviews recorded, transcribed, coded [8], with core issues identified and prioritised.	High-level themes presented as text data (derived from transcription of interviews and observation notes during calls, followed by coding sequence).
Company systems	1. Manual analysis of customer's journey from the organisations' perspective.	Customer records and advisor notes from CRM system, presented in Excel and Word Table format.
	1. Expert evaluation [9] and high-level user evaluation of UI of advisors' KM and CRM systems.	Text capture of issues, presented in PowerPoint format.
Process mining	1. Causal factor analysis of customer case. 2. Cross-check of process mining "map" against subjective customer experience and CRM notes. 3. Analysis of automated messaging sequence to the customer.	Process "map" generated to indicate location of significant causal factors and subsequent attempted recovery path through automatic and manual processes within the organisation.

case. Our theoretical approach reflected a process philosophy [6], and draws heavily upon Langley's [7] strategies for theorising process data. Langley argues that *"process research that incorporate narrative, interpretive and qualitative data are more imme-diately appealing for the richness of process detail they provide"*. We drew upon this argument to believe that linking the often hidden process-data within the company's data-warehouse with such narrative qualitative data would provide additional insight and address the arguably neglected process dimension of Customer Experience research.

3   Data Corpus for the Case Study

The data corpus for the case study comprised quantitative and qualitative sources and analysis techniques as outlined Table 1 below:

4   Using CRM Notes and Customer Feedback to Identify Distress Indicators

While creating the model, one of the questions we considered was: what indicates customer distress? To approach this we combined CRM system analysis with direct customer experiences (expressed through the customer interview and his own notes) to identify system and process-related issues which manifest themselves in customer distress. For example, drawing lessons from our case study, relevant Distress Indicators included:

- The length of time an order has been delayed exceeding an acceptable threshold (taking the original scheduled delivery date as a start-point).
- The number of times the customer has had to call the organisation beyond an accept-able range (e.g. between 0 and 1).
- The number of different reference numbers given for a customer case, (causing distress by provoking confusion) above an acceptable range (e.g. 1 is acceptable, 2 causes confusion etc.,)
- The number of different phone numbers given to a customer for different departments throughout a customer journey (again causing distress by provoking confusion) above an acceptable range.
- The subjective record of the emotional state of the customer, as recorded after an interaction with an advisor and sometimes (but not always) captured in the advisor notes.

The advantage of deriving Distress Indicators quantitatively from the CRM system notes alone, is that they are easily accessible for analysis. However, when they are combined with post-interaction survey results and advisor notes, they can give a more powerful indication – from the system, the advisor and the customer himself - that a distressful episode is taking place and a response is needed.

5   Using Process Mining to Understand Causal Factors for Distress

Again, while creating the model we asked: what can we analyse from the process records to help us locate what causes customer distress? For this, we looked at Process Mining, because, according to Aalst [10], it provides *"comprehensive sets of tools to provide fact-based insights and to support process improvements"*. It is used to reflect *actual* events, taken from log files – often across disparate systems - so that comparisons can be made with the process model (i.e. the model of the process in its ideal state) [11]. Our case study, which concerns the recovery of an order which has deviated from the "happy path" of a standard delivery process, gave us an example where process mining enabled the researchers to make this comparison, plus compare where subjective customer experience issues occurred in parallel.

We used a process mining tool developed in-house (called "Aperture" [12]) to generate a process "map" from a number of data sources (events from the CRM system, for example) for the case study (see Fig. 1). We referred to this when determining the process-related distress-inducing causal factors. From doing this, we found the process event which represented a "turning point" in the journey, resulting in the order falling from the happy path into a recovery path.

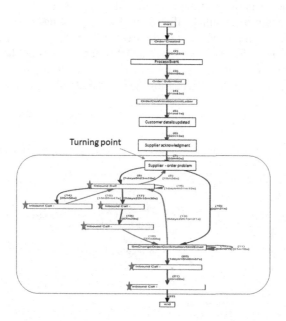

Fig. 1. Process map of customer journey to identify process events - excerpt

Figure 1 shows the results of the "turning point", as derived from the system logs at this early stage in the customer journey. Note the repeated inbound calls from the customer (indicated by stars in Fig. 1.) and re-work which follows. (This is only part of the entire process map, to give an example of the visualisation and usage of the tool).

In further analysis, the process map also showed us where some automated processes were still continuing (automated communications to the customer for example) despite delivery processes being halted or delayed in the back-end. And it was also possible to see on the map where the customer was responding to these communications. Drawing parallels between this map, the CRM system notes and the customer's subjective experiences of when these process events occurred gave a powerful and holistic picture of customer experience episodes which caused distress – from the customer's and the organisation's perspective. Finally, in collaboration with our engineering teams, we could compare this "actual" state with an ideal process state to see where assumptions in the process were incorrect and needed remedial action.

6   Introducing the Model for Detecting and Responding to Customer Distress

The proposed model above summarises the data sources and steps involved in the Detecting Phase and proposes the outline areas for categorising the resulting responses identified (i.e. the recommendations) in the Responding Phase. This categorisation of recommendations into "People", "Process" and "System" can assist the organisation in prioritising interventions and applying resources to deliver the improvements suggested (whilst being aware that in some scenarios these three areas may need to be addressed together) (Fig. 2).

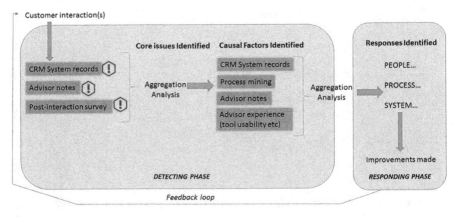

Fig. 2. Proposed model for detecting and responding to customer distress

Note also within the model the Feedback Loop, which can be used for cost-benefit modelling of any interventions. This is especially true if investment is needed to make the improvements suggested. The model could be used to project likely reductions in the incidence of Distress Indicators, e.g. improved automated communications (Response) can lead to a reduction in number of calls a customer makes to chase the order (Distress Indicator). Improvements can be tactical, or strategic, but all can and should be continually measured so that the Feedback Loop of improvement can be sustained.

Equally, post-intervention success measures can be gained by taking measures of individual elements, but aggregated to give an entire picture of improved customer service and reduced customer distress by quantitative and qualitative means, e.g.

1. From the *Customer's* perspective: customer satisfaction scores improve for individual customers and overall (using customer survey scores)
2. From the *Advisor's* perspective: subjective measures ("how easy is it to do your job?" etc.) and quantitative efficiency measures (throughput, productivity etc.).
3. From the *Process* perspective: Using process mining, quantifying the reduction in causal factors, and quantifying the number of repeated actions throughout the process.

7   Detecting and Responding to Customer Distress - the Case Study

In this section we demonstrate how the model contributed to a set of recommended improvements resulting from the detection of one particular core issue. (Incidentally, it was evident in this case study that causal factors often acted together to cause overall customer distress. Similarly, the responses identified were inter-related and interventions needed to be considered collectively).

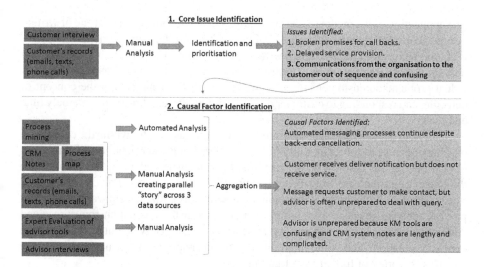

Fig. 3. Detecting phase - core issue and causal factor identification

Figures 3 and 4 demonstrate how the sequence of activities and data sources were used to identify a core issue, how the causal factors of the issue were identified and what responses (recommendations for improvements) were identified as a result:

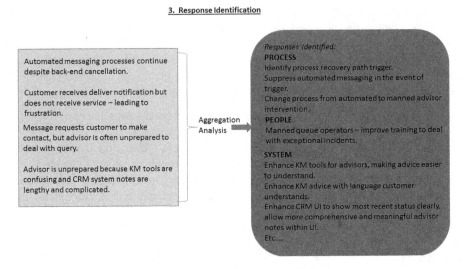

Fig. 4. Responding phase (Recommendations)

8   Next Steps

The application of the model to the case study is still in its infancy at the time of writing – some short-term tactical changes (e.g. html content and UI improvements on advisor KM tools) have been implemented, with longer-term interventions in the pipeline. The next immediate step therefore is to test the efficiency of the model against other individual problematic customer journeys. We also consider approaching the concept of detecting and responding to customer distress within different dimensions, namely time and scale.

Time. Our analysis revealed the significance of time as an actor within the case study, and suggests a need for temporality to be considered in greater detail (reflecting a call of [13, 14]): in this case study, the customer became distressed at various points, with the longevity of the case itself being a cause of distress. Further, polychronicity [15] (the doing of multiple things at the same time) within the CRM system was, through our process analysis, revealed as significant in creating distress as the customer received conflicting messages from different systems which were effectively out of sync with the evolving situation. The "time-map" of the customer journey to demonstrate distress episodes is worthy of further investigation.

Scale. In this case study we analysed one distressed customer's journey among a base of orders that are being case-managed or are going through the complaints procedure. Rather than seeking to capture a quantitative representation of these large numbers of orders, we adopted a single case study approach which allowed much richer analysis and revealed lessons for wider cases. Although this approach was valuable, there may be possibilities in increasing the scale, i.e. to make the model apply across a larger customer base. For this more automated approaches (such as text analytics) will need to be considered (see Discussion).

For our case study, we were fortunate to have a customer who was willing and able to share his experiences with us in great detail. For the current model, we propose the use of surveys and advisor notes where very detailed qualitative customer research is not practical due to the effort involved in collecting and analysing data. But a next step may be to supplement the surveys and notes data via qualitative in-depth interviews with a smaller number of specific customers after problematic cases. In addition, where Distress Indicators are flagged in particular journeys it may be possible (with privacy considerations) to identify customers with problems early on and engage researchers into the system with the same conditions/problems who must then follow the same journey, documenting it as they progress to provide insight into the customer's experience of that journey.

9   Discussion

Our model is intended to provide a framework for organisations with a means of linking process mining and HCI techniques, to enable better detection and response to customer distress episodes. We accept that this is not without its challenges, however. For instance, use of the model depends on the skills and availabilities of the practitioners to carry it out, leading to questions such as: Is it better to deploy one researcher with passable knowledge of process mining *and* qualitative interviewing (for example) to carry out as many steps as they can, or deploy many more researchers who are experts in their individual areas? Would time and resources allow for the latter? Would they be able to work together effectively to provide effective output? For the former, would the output be deep enough to produce valuable insight? But would this approach be cheaper and quicker?

Similarly, engagement with the development community, tasked with deploying recommendations from use of the model, should be done at an early stage, to provide governance and balance the recommendations with business objectives, especially if the recommendations are costly.

In the future, technology developments may be deployed to relieve the workload experienced by the researchers in carrying out the manual steps in this particular case study. Text analytics for example can used to summarise core issues from the vast quantities of free-text in customer communications, interview verbatims and advisor notes. Additionally, data visualisation techniques can be deployed such that business decision makers can decide how to respond to customer distress episodes via an intuitive interface which gives them what they need to respond in shorter time-frames. We hope that our model can evolve to incorporate these developments over time, and that other organisations can use it as a baseline for their own business needs.

Acknowledgements. Thanks to Florian Allwein of LSE for additional data from advisor interviews and observations. Thanks also to William Harmer of BT for his Process Mining expertise.

References

1. Richardson, H.J., Howcroft, D.: The contradictions of CRM – a critical lens on call centres. Inf. Organ. **16**(2), 143–168 (2006)
2. Reichheld, F.: The one number you need to grow. Harvard Bus. Rev. **81**(12), 46–55 (2003)
3. Duncan, E., Rawson, A., Jones, C.: The truth about customer experience. Harvard Bus. Rev. **91**(9), 90–98 (2013)
4. Holziger, A.: Human-Computer Interaction and Knowledge Discovery (HCI-KDD): What is the benefit of bringing those two fields to work together? (HCI-IR) In: IADIS Multiconference on Computer Science and Information Systems (MCCSIS), Interfaces and Human-Computer Interaction, pp. 13–17 (2011)
5. Shneiderman, B.: Inventing discovery tools: combining information visualization with data mining. In: Jantke, K.P., Shinohara, A. (eds.) DS 2001. LNCS (LNAI), vol. 2226, pp. 17–28. Springer, Heidelberg (2001)
6. Seibt, J.: Process Philosophy. The Stanford Encyclopedia of Philosophy (2013)
7. Langley, A.: Strategies for theorizing from process data. Academy of management. Acad. Manage. Rev. **24**(4), 691–710 (1999)
8. Corbin, J., Strauss, A.: Basics of Qualitative Research 3e, Chap. 8, pp. 163-164 (2008)
9. Nielsen, J., Molich, R.: Heuristics evaluation of user interfaces. In: Proceedings of the SIGCHI Conference on Human Factors in Computing Systems, p. 249 (1990)
10. Aalst, W.: Process Mining: Discovery, Conformance and Enhancement of Business Processes (preface). Springer, Heidelberg (2011)
11. Burattin, A.: Process mining. In: Burattin, A. (ed.) Process Mining Techniques in Business Environments. LNBIP, vol. 207, pp. 33–47. Springer, Heidelberg (2015)
12. Taylor, P., Leida, M., Majeed, B.: Case study in process mining in a multinational enterprise. In: Aberer, K., Damiani, E., Dillon, T. (eds.) SIMPDA 2011. LNBIP, vol. 116, pp. 134–153. Springer, Heidelberg (2012)
13. Reddy, M.C., Dourish, P., Pratt, W.: Temporality in medical work: time also matters. Comput. Support. Coop. Work (CSCW) **15**(1), 29–53 (2006)

14. Langley, A., et al.: Process studies of change in organization and management: unveiling temporality, activity, and flow. Acad. Manage. J. **56**(1), 1–13 (2013)
15. Lee, H.: Time and information technology: monochronicity, polychronicity and temporal symmetry. Eur. J. Inf. Syst. **8**, 16–26 (1999)

The Multisensory Effects of Atmospheric Cues on Online Shopping Satisfaction

So-Jeong Kim[1] and Dong-Hee Shin[2(✉)]

[1] Department of Interaction Science, Sungkyunkwan University,
25-2 Sungkyunkwan-ro, Jungro-gu, Seoul, South Korea
ai.gimso@gmail.com
[2] School of Media and Communication, Chung-Ang University,
Seoul, South Korea
dshin1030@cau.ac.kr

Abstract. This study investigates the way how consumers react to colors and scents as two independent atmospheric cues in stores, given that the two independent variables, were classified into two different levels of cool (blue or citrus-mint) and warm (red or citrus-vanilla) depending on the properties of those. In this study, a 2 (color: blue vs. red) × 3 (scent: no scent vs. cool vs. warm) factorial design was conducted. The results show that ambient cues have an impact on customer emotions such as pleasure and arousal, leading to better shopping satisfaction when they interact together. The results of these sensory interactions indicated that cool visual and olfactory cues received higher ratings than warm cues did.

Keywords: Online shopping · Atmospherics · Store environment · Color · Scent · Multisensory · Emotion · Satisfaction

1 Introduction

Consumers usually prefer e-commerce to brick and mortar retail stores because of the many benefits from online shipping such as delivery services, times savings, as well as better price for shopping [1]. As the number of online shoppers increases, Digital marketers have heavily focused on shopping mall site design to attract more customers' attentions among over other sites. Website design creates the store environment, which produces the atmosphere, and then it affects emotional states of shoppers [10, 11, 15]. These affective states increase customer satisfaction [16]. Therefore, a web-based environment plays a significant role in the context of online shopping.

By differently setting surrounding cues in a store atmospherics can take a different form. The environmental features consist of social, design (e.g., color and layout) and ambient factors (e.g., sound, smell, and lighting) [10]; thus, marketers manipulate these factors to improve the store environment by stimulating five senses [12]. On a website, we have mainly investigated whether color dominates an entire interface [25] as a

---

The original version of this chapter was revised: The affiliation of the second author was corrected.
The erratum to this chapter is available at 10.1007/978-3-319-39396-4_54

F.F.-H. Nah and C.-H. Tan (Eds.): HCIBGO 2016, Part I, LNCS 9751, pp. 406–416, 2016.
DOI: 10.1007/978-3-319-39396-4_37

visual cue or design factor. In other words, color causes a sight sensation when consumers face a website. The visual aspects such as colors, blue or red, induce pleasant and arousing feelings [2], and these emotional states modify shopping-related behaviors [3, 15, 36]. In this respect, we manipulated design factors strategically in order to produce an atmospherics within a website. Researchers, however, have rarely addressed ambient factors, compared with design factors; this study investigates ambient factors as non-visual cues in terms of diversity and then, we suggest a new interaction model by considering ambient factors.

Based on design factors, the sensory modalities using ambient factors such as audition and tactility have been generally used in order to improve overall experience and satisfaction. The interaction model for vision and olfaction has yet to be established in the context of web-based environment. However, TTA, IT association, suggested "olfaction and its applications will make next computing environments promote the related industries" as olfactory technology increases such as user interface for olfactory information presentation [34; p. 8] and thus, we anticipate the effects of olfactory cue by interacting visual cues in computer environment' context.

One of ambient factors, olfactory cues are likely to interact with visual information in the ambiguous state; for example, color can help enhance the ability to recognize olfactory information (e.g., yellow with lemon) [4]. In addition, the sense of smell induces pleasant or arousing emotions [32] and leads to changes of behavior [5], evaluation [32], and satisfaction [22]. Therefore, the interaction of visual and olfactory cues is not informative but situational and ambient cue that can provoke positive responses or behaviors from shoppers using the browser. To elicit a plenty of sensation, olfactory researches have studied in various industries such as gallery, movie, and advertisement. For instance, Dunkindonuts ads in the U.S. domestic market used olfactory stimulus by using automatic aroma spray. This Ad provides viewers with a scent related to a visual information, resulting in sales increase. In this light, a physical environmental feature, olfactory cue should reflect on web-based environment in order to enhance affective consumer behavior in online shopping. Technological approach such as olfactory display [17], which is not universally developed, can be provided to shoppers who face website; thereby the influences of olfactory cue in web-based environment are expected to result in effectiveness as much as an external environment. Therefore, this study examines the effects of color, scent, or both of those cues on satisfaction toward e-commerce by changing an emotional state and this study investigates which type (blue vs. red) of environmental background is preferred. Then, this research proposes a new interface to utilize olfactory cue.

2   Literature Review

2.1   S-O-R Framework

Robert and John provided the framework on the effects of environmental features in the context of store environment [26]. They examined the model with three levels of stimulus - organism - response (S-O-R) and their study showed that surrounding cues as the stimulus have significantly influence on customer's emotional state as the organism. Furthermore, these emotional states have subsequent effect on approach/

avoidance, which is positive/negative actions by evoked feelings, as responses [15]. To investigate store environment, previous researches have been applied this model [10, 15]. Therefore, we used an S-O-R framework in this study.

2.2   The Environmental Features

In a situation in which a website created and operated, a wide variety of determinants of changes in the store environment such as social (interactions between customers and employees), design (visual cue), and ambient (smell, lighting, and sound as non-visual cue) factors have been investigated in previous studies [10, 15, 39]. These factors can influence a mood within retail stores positively or negatively, because individual perception on stimuli and responses is relevant to one's senses [27]. Dijkstra [7] indicated that all environmental conditions come into operation among architectural features, design features and ambient features. Similarly, web environment features, such as color, scent, and lighting, affect consumers' emotions [12]. Color and scent as ambient cues play a key role in evoking a feeling focused on pleasure and arousal [10, 32]. With the application of these determinants, digital marketers configure websites to present a design the first time a shoppers logs on. The can easily update and redesign a website, which is not possible in the case of offline stores [6]. By allowing consumers to enjoy an emotional experience from a website visit, atmospheric cues can greatly improve overall customer satisfaction during online shopping.

As far as the most dominant design factors are concerned, color is an easy and convenient cue to change the atmospherics of the environment compared to other cues [36]. Although visual features can help consumers enjoy shopping by directly delivering a plenty of information, they are less likely to provided differentiated experience as diverse sensations in e-commerce as in brick-and-mortar stores. In other words, digital markers use ambient factors as a method to create a new atmospherics, and thus, shoppers can experience a wide range of sensations as soon as possible. In a study by Wang [38], olfactory cues are associated with an environment in the context of situation. That means, the sense of smell depends on surrounding cues. Thus, researches regard the application of olfactory cue as potentially important ones.

Olfactory display can enable user's nose to deliver olfactory cue [17]. In other words, a user can sense the diffused olfactory information through tube or air canon attached to the side of the screen. In this respect, in e-commerce, it is possible to improve the store environment not only with a typical application using design factors but also with a new application employing ambient factors.

2.3   Affective Emotions Depending on Types of Colors and Scents

Color. In store design, colors can attract customer attention and deliver a different mood in accordance with their properties; those have a wide range of meanings, such as excitement, energy, calmness, happiness, and so on [24]. The types of colors are divided into cool (short) and warm (long) by wavelength, which are concerned with eliciting feelings [2]. In a study, colors in the same category are likely to show a similar expression. Bellizzi and Hite [3] mentioned that cool colors (blue) make people feel relaxed, peaceful, calm, pleasant, tender, and comfortable. Colors such as red, in contrast, convey a sense of arousal, excitement, distraction, negation, tenseness, and stimulation [37]. In other words, emotions are opposite depending on the color attributions [3]. Red color has disadvantages such as tenseness and negation, and therefore, cool-colored backgrounds are perceived positively by shoppers [2, 12]. Despite the disadvantage, marketers use red-based environments in stores or on websites because a red design draws more attention than blue [3]; however, in previous studies, shoppers prefer blue-based environment, which induces pleasure and arousal, in shopping malls because they feel to be pleasant and peaceful. Therefore, it is necessary to explore what color is meaningful in a web-based environment and what color produces higher levels of positive affective states in online shopping.

Scent. Ambient scent may have influence on behavior, mood, and response, as well as memory [4], in comparison with other sensory cues [28]. A study by Spangenberg et al. [32] examined whether environmental scents affect consumers in store evaluations, which, in turn, lead to positive behaviors [4, 5]. In general, scents are categorized as floral, citrus, woods, spices, and mints [32]. Spangenberg et al. [32] evaluated citrus and mint as pleasant scents. Research by Doucé and Janssens [8] showed that citrus mixed with mint creates a pleasant environmental mood. The smells of citrus and mint belong to the cool category and they have fresh/light features [21] and high-arousing [12]. In the warm category, floral, woody, and oriental are affiliated, most of which form a warm, calm, smoothing, and relaxed atmosphere [18] and those are low-arousing [12]. To produce a pleasant and arousing web-based environment, citrus has mainly used in marketing. The smell of citrus elicits feelings of pleasure, happiness and serves as a powerful way of affecting product perception, resulting in sales [5]. In this light, there is no problem of blending citrus as the base-scent with different scents (cool or warm) to derive environmental atmospherics in dissimilar directions.

2.4   Multisensory Between Vision and Olfaction

Generally, the aim of marketing is to deliver an experience for a product by stimulating a great deal of senses. In the traditional method, vision or hearing as the dominant senses is available; however, the other senses (touch and smell) are now possible in e-commerce with the development of technology. In recent years, other methods have been applied to produce cross-modality as well as to present diverse senses [20, 28, 39]. In a wide range of multi-modality, there has been little research on the interacting application of visual and olfactory cues such as colors and scents in online shopping [20]. The combination of vision and olfaction has been studied in advertisements [29, 35] as well as marketing [10, 12], both of cues are similar in that they provide people with information via visual media. For example, a study by Seo et al. [29] showed that the sense of smell could help immerse viewers in visual content. Ellen and Bone [9] demonstrated that the effects of scent have impact on attitudes and product-related evaluation in the context of advertising. Kaye [13] showed that the possibility of delivering olfactory cues in combination with visual media (e.g., web sites, games, and films). In summary, the olfactory information helps drawing shoppers' attention, interacting with visual cue. In addition, color enhances a consumer's ability to identify the sense of smell [12, 30, 40] when surrounding cues are coherent [21] because it is difficult to recognize olfactory cue alone [4]. The combination of vision and olfaction has influence on experience [21] and satisfaction [16] by causing a pleasant and arousing emotion. By appealing to visual and olfactory cues, a web-based environment enables shoppers to change their emotional states, and then it leads to an improved shopping experience compared to other environment provided by only one sense.

2.5   Customer Satisfaction

By creating an emotional state by using website features, a store environment contributes to customer satisfaction [16, 33]. According to Szymanski and Hise [33], website design as an atmospheric cue (e.g., convenience, merchandising, site design, and financial security) affects satisfaction through a pleasurable shopping experience. Pleasure describes a sense of positive responses, and these reactions induce a hedonic experience in the Internet environment [20]. In other words, website design aims to form customer experience [31]. Thus, this study examined how visual and olfactory cues as components vary affective states and then it demonstrated the effects of the combination with surrounding cues on consumer satisfaction over the Internet.

3   Method

We designed a 2 (color: cool vs. warm) by 3 (scent: no-scent vs. cool vs. warm) factorial design in order to explore the effects of sensory cues, both independently and dependently, and identify the preference for different types of visual and olfactory cues on customer satisfaction as affective approach toward e-commerce. In this experiment, we manipulated the color and scent stimuli of environmental cues as independent variables and we measured satisfaction with the shopping experience as a dependent variable. Before the main experiment, we had conducted some pretests on visual and olfactory stimuli were. In addition, we have performed the experiment in the laboratory, maintaining the same environment as much as possible, because the olfactory technique could not be directly applied again repeatedly right after a specific scent was used. Besides, it would be difficult to use the olfactory technology that still is not universally developed.

3.1   Pretest: The Color Stimulus

To select relevant visual stimulus (color), thirty participants consisting of 13 males (43.3 %) and 17 females (56.7 %) performed a manipulated check on preferences for some specified websites involved in colors such as G-market and Enuri with a blue background and the other websites such as 11st, Interpark, and Auction with a red background. The mean age of the participants was 25.57 years ($SD = 2.909$) in the age category of 21–36 years. A scale consisting of 25 items on a 5-point Likert-type scale (e.g., web appearance (6 items), entertainment (6 items), information (4 items), transaction (4 items), response (3 items), and trust (2 items)) was used [14]. We have conducted a repeated measure ANOVA and analyzed the meaning of the results for each color conditions. For the blue environment, G-market was chosen as a cool type

($M_{\text{G-market}}$ = 2.89, M_{Enuri} = 2.81, F = 10.012, p < .01); Interpark as a warm type was selected as the red environment (M_{11st} = 2.63, $M_{\text{Interpark}}$ = 2.78, M_{Auction} = 2.61, F = 4.725, p < .05).

3.2 Pretest: The Scent Stimulus

We blended the smell of citrus with two different scents (citrus-mint and citrus-vanilla) so that shoppers might enjoy and improve their shopping experience. The smell of citrus conveys a sense of pleasure and arousal [32], and it acts as a powerful way of improving product perception and the increasing sales [5], Moreover, it has a substantial impact on satisfaction [20]. The smell of mint makes people pleased and aroused, as the same as citrus does [32]. Finally, the smell of vanilla has a positive effect on pleasant emotion [12]. In this light, the smell of mint as a cool category and the smell of vanilla as a warm category were selected, depending on previous studies [8, 18] and their properties [21].

3.3 Participants & Design & Measure

To measure overall satisfaction toward e-commerce in response to environmental stimuli, 90 South Korean undergraduate students who were not visually or olfactorily impaired participated in the experiment. The mean age of the participants was 24.32 years (SD = 2.731) in the age category of 17–36 years. Furthermore, they already have some experiences of online shopping on the G-market and Interpark websites. By the scheme of the experiment, we have randomly assigned the ninety participants to the six groups with different conditions. Each group was composed of 15 participants. The stimuli were composed of different types (cool vs. warm) of colors and scents. The satisfaction questionnaire was adapted from studies by Lin [16] and McKinney et al. [19]. In addition, a satisfaction measurement of the effects of pleasure and arousal were added [23]. All responses were evaluated with a 7-point Likert-type scale, ranging from 1 (totally disagree) to 7 (totally agree). The Table 1 shows the questionnaire's factor, items, and sources for independent and dependent variables.

Table 1. The questionnaire dependent variable

Category	Factor	Sources	Items
Satisfaction	Overall satisfaction	McKinney et al. [19]	2
	Customer satisfaction	Lin [16], Oliver and Swan [23]	9

3.4 Main Experimental Hypothesis & Procedure

This study provides an explication of the effects of environmental features such as visual cue only, olfactory cue only, and both visual and olfactory cue by evoking emotional states. In this light, this study proposes the following research hypotheses:

H1: Visual cues have an influence on the satisfaction.
H2: Olfactory cues have a positive effect on the satisfaction.
H3: The interaction between visual and olfactory cues has an influence on the satisfaction.

To explore how the effects of environmental cues contribute to improving satisfaction toward e-commerce, we have conducted the experiments in a laboratory room with five seats and no windows in four experimental stages. Table 2 shows the experimental procedure.

Table 2. The experimental procedure

Stage	Explanation
1: Preparation	All the necessary conditions (laptop, environmental conditions) and the visual and olfactory stimuli were prepared. The purpose of the study and expected outcomes of the environmental features such as visual and olfactory stimuli were told to the participants; then, they were asked to fill out confirmation on data collection.
2: Experimental task	The participants had to search and purchase a specific item by instructions (e.g., electronics devices and related accessories) within a controlled category on specific websites for approximately 20–30 min.
3: Questionnaire	Upon completion, participants filled out a digital questionnaire, as in Table 2, about shopping satisfaction.
4: Question & Answer	After participants had finished the overall experimental tasks, their answers were debriefed.

Prior to the experimental task, we randomly arranged online shopping malls such as G-market and Interpark depending on the number of participants on the laptop. In addition, the icon toward digital questionnaire was prepared to be getting started within the laptop computer. For olfactory conditions, a diffuser and a candle were placed, out of sight, in the room in order to spray into the air 2 h before the experiment started. We controlled the olfactory stimulus in the room in which the experiment took place by means of an automatic injection that operated whenever a new participant comes in the laboratory. To change the olfactory cues, we suspended the experiment for two days, and we ran the air conditioner to get rid of the previous olfactory cues in the room. We also maintained the other conditions the same as for the other olfactory stimuli. The experiment proceeded in an orderly way (no scent, citrus-mint, and citrus-vanilla). The total time spent by an individual was approximately 30–40 min. We conducted the other conditional experiments were conducted in the same way as designed.

4   Results

The effects of visual and olfactory cues such as colors and scents in e-commerce for the six different conditions. The main data were statistically analyzed with two-way analysis of variance (ANOVA; $F(5, 84) = 3.210$, $p < .05$). We observed a statistically significant difference between groups in accordance with the scent condition (Table 4). Table 3 shows that the interaction effect was significant ($F = 5.044$, $p < .01$); thus, satisfaction differed depending on the interactions of cues. We conducted a post-hoc comparison with the Duncan test and the test results indicated that the effect of ambient scent was larger than that of the no-scent (Table 4).

The effects of both independent variables are illustrated in Fig. 1. The results suggested that satisfaction was enhanced if two independent variables were congruent (Table 4 and Fig. 1); Under the cool-type conditions, the participants were significantly likely to feel satisfaction compared with the warm-type conditions ($M_{\text{Cool-Blue}}$ = 5.28, $M_{\text{Warm-Red}}$ = 5.09). Therefore, this study found a significant main effect and interaction. In several conditions, the subject and variables with cool properties had more impact on satisfaction in e-commerce than warm ones.

Table 3. The results of analysis of variance of the mean catch by color and scent

Source of variation	df	MS	F	P	Partial Eta Squared
Color	1	1.484	1.779	.186	.021
Scent	2	7.653	9.177	.000***	.179
Color × Scent	2	4.207	5.044	.009**	.107
Error	84	.834			
Total	90				

$*p < .05, **p < .01, ***p < .001$

Table 4. Mean and standard deviation values for each experimental condition

Source	M	SD	N	Source	M	SD	N	F	P	Ducan
No-scent (a)				*Warm (c)*						
Blue	4.23	1.013	15	Blue	4.50	1.141	15			
Red	3.69	.900	15	Red	5.09	.697	15	3.210	.011*	a <
Cool (b)				*Total*						
Blue	5.28	.483	15	Blue	4.67	1.009	45			b,c
Red	4.46	1.069	15	Red	4.41	1.054	45			
				Total	4.54	1.034	90			

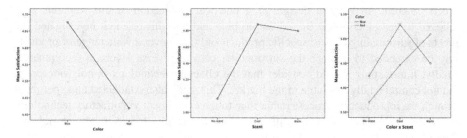

Fig. 1. Effects of color, scent, and color × scent satisfaction (Color figure online)

5   Discussion and Conclusions

The aim of our research is to analyze the interactions between visual and olfactory cues in e-commerce and then to determine whether surrounding features are appropriate for a web-based environment. Environmental cues, which in turn contribute to better emotional states, lead to the satisfaction toward e-commerce.

Our findings demonstrate the effect of ambient scent to enhance satisfaction and support visual cues. The results also suggest higher levels of satisfaction when scent and color are matched. As indicated in studies by Milotic [21] and Shankar et al. [30], vision and olfaction increase their sensory effect when they mutually depend the other. The effects of color, however, could not be demonstrated. Although the results do not support the color's influence, the blue-based environment's rating is higher than red-based environment based upon the research. Furthermore, the participants generally preferred cool olfactory cues (citrus-mint) which evoke pleasant and arousing emotions to the warm olfactory cues (citrus-vanilla), although the presence of scent tends to be favorable compared with the absence of scent in common with Bellizzi and Hite [3] 's research. Therefore, the cool-related environment increased customer satisfaction likewise the results from the previous researches [2, 12]. In other words, sensory cue with cool properties can act as a trigger to induce a pleasure and arousal in environments. By taking advantage of these effects, digital marketers can make individual shoppers improve a satisfaction in their own environment.

The sensory cues have a significant influence on affective response in the context of online shopping; thereby we can expect that to the sensory cues substantially change affective behaviors such as intention. In this respect, the application of olfactory may broaden the scope of the interaction such as auditory and haptic cues. Besides, it is meaningful to use the combination of olfactory and visual cues, except for color, to improve behavior or response evoked by emotional state. These environmental cues carry a shade of meanings depending on their properties. The interaction between visual and olfactory cues increased satisfaction levels for shoppers. This study provides empirical support to retailers how to construct a web-based environment that influences customer satisfaction. Despite these findings, this research has limitation; for example, it does not reflect on a wide variety of properties.

Even though we reached some meaningful conclusions, we could not prove the effects of color. So, future research are recommended to expand the types of colors not limited to red and blue which interact with ambient scents in order to examine the effects of color. In website design, as a practical application of this research, it is believed to test other colors in addition to blue and red; this research investigated the effects of surrounding cues to specific products only, however a wide range of products may be extended to explore the surrounding cues at diverse levels in e-commerce. Finally, future study should consider that the olfactory technology is not widespread and not commercially available in the market. This study also conducted an experiment through the reproduction process rather than to the experiment via olfactory technology directly; thereby there may be differences on the results between laboratorial and commercial environments. In this respect, future study needs to consider approaching this point in a different way.

With these suggestions, knowing that environment features have relevance to atmospherics and satisfaction based on conditions, digital marketers have opportunity to propose a new interface that can be applied to a variety of visual contents such as ads and website in that design is required for content.

Acknowledgments. The National Research Foundation of Korea Grant funded by the Korean Government (NRF-2014S1A5B1014964) supported this work.

References

1. Ahn, T., Ryu, S., Han, I.: The impact of the online and offline features on the user acceptance of Internet shopping malls. Electron. Commer. Res. Appl. **3**(4), 405–420 (2005)
2. Babin, B.J., Hardesty, D.M., Suter, T.A.: Color and shopping intentions: the intervening effect of price fairness and perceived affect. J. Bus. Res. **56**(7), 541–551 (2003)
3. Bellizzi, J.A., Hite, R.E.: Environmental color, consumer feelings, and purchase likelihood. Psychol. Mark. **9**(5), 347–363 (1992)
4. Bone, P.F., Ellen, P.S.: Scents in the marketplace: explaining a fraction of olfaction. J. Retail. **75**(2), 243–262 (1999)
5. Chebat, J.C., Michon, R.: Impact of ambient odors on mall shoppers' emotions, cognition, and spending: a test of competitive causal theories. J. Bus. Res. **56**(7), 529–539 (2003)
6. Childers, T.L., Carr, C.L., Peck, J., Carson, S.: Hedonic and utilitarian motivations for online retail shopping behavior. J. Retail. **77**(4), 511–535 (2002)
7. Dijkstra, K.: Understanding healing environments: Effects of physical environmental stimuli on patients' health and well-being. University of Twente (2009)
8. Doucé, L., Janssens, W.: The presence of a pleasant ambient scent in a fashion store: the moderating role of shopping motivation and affect intensity. Environ. Behav. (2011). doi:10. 1177/0013916511410421
9. Ellen, P.S., Bone, P.F.: Does it matter if it smells? Olfactory stimuli as advertising executional cues. J. Advertising **27**(4), 29–39 (1998)
10. Eroglu, S.A., Machleit, K.A., Davis, L.M.: Empirical testing of a model of online store atmospherics and shopper responses. Psychol. Mark. **20**(2), 139–150 (2003)
11. Fiore, A.M., Jin, H., Kim, J.: For fun and profit: hedonic value from image interactivity and responses toward an online store. Psychol. Mark. **22**(8), 669 (2005)
12. Hulshof, B.: The influence of colour and scent on people's mood and cognitive performance in meeting rooms. M.A. thesis, University of Twente (2013)
13. Kaye, J.J.: Making scents: aromatic output for HCI. Interactions **11**(1), 48–61 (2004)
14. Kim, S., Stoel, L.: Apparel retailers: website quality dimensions and satisfaction. J. Retail. Consum. Serv. **11**(2), 109–117 (2004)
15. Koo, D.M., Ju, S.H.: The interactional effects of atmospherics and perceptual curiosity on emotions and online shopping intention. Comput. Hum. Behav. **26**(3), 377–388 (2010)
16. Lin, H.F.: The impact of website quality dimensions on customer satisfaction in the B2C e-commerce context. Total Qual. Manag. Bus. Excellence **18**(4), 363–378 (2007)
17. Matsukura, H., Yoneda, T., Ishida, H: Smelling screen: technique to present a virtual odor source at an arbitrary position on a screen. In: Proceedings of the 2012 IEEE of Virtual Reality Short Papers and Posters (VRW), pp. 127–128. IEEE, March 2012
18. Mattila, A.S., Wirtz, J.: Congruency of scent and music as a driver of in-store evaluations and behavior. J. Retail. **77**(2), 273–289 (2001)

19. McKinney, V., Yoon, K., Zahedi, F.M.: The measurement of web-customer satisfaction: an expectation and disconfirmation approach. Inf. Syst. Res. **13**(3), 296–315 (2002)
20. Menon, S., Kahn, B.: Cross-category effects of induced arousal and pleasure on the Internet shopping experience. J. Retail. **78**(1), 31–40 (2002)
21. Milotic, D.: The impact of fragrance on consumer choice. J. Consum. Behav. **3**(2), 179–191 (2003)
22. Morrison, M., Gan, S., Dubelaar, C., Oppewal, H.: In-store music and aroma influences on shopper behavior and satisfaction. J. Bus. Res. **64**, 558–564 (2011)
23. Oliver, R.L., Swan, J.E.: Consumer perceptions of interpersonal equity and satisfaction in transactions: a field survey approach. J. Mark. 21–35 (1989)
24. Ou, L.C., Luo, M.R., Woodcock, A., Wright, A.: A study of colour emotion and colour preference. Part I: colour emotions for single colours. Color Res. Appl. **29**(3), 232–240 (2004)
25. Pelet, J.É.: Effects of colours on the attitude towards an e-commerce website: a multicultural approach. Zeszyty Naukowe Małopolskiej Wyższej Szkoły Ekonomicznej w Tarnowie **2**, 163–170 (2013)
26. Robert, D., John, R.: Store atmosphere: an environmental psychology approach. J. Retail. **58**, 34–57 (1982)
27. Richard, M.O.: Modeling the impact of internet atmospherics on surfer behavior. J. Bus. Res. **58**(12), 1632–1642 (2005)
28. Schifferstein, H.N., Cleiren, M.P.: Capturing product experiences: a split-modality approach. Acta Psychol. **118**(3), 293–318 (2005)
29. Seo, H.S., Roidl, E., Müller, F., Negoias, S.: Odors enhance visual attention to congruent objects. Appetite **54**(3), 544–549 (2010)
30. Shankar, M.U., Levitan, C.A., Prescott, J., Spence, C.: The influence of color and label information on flavor perception. Chemosens. Percept. **2**(2), 53–58 (2009)
31. Song, J., Zahedi, F.M.: A theoretical approach to web design in e-commerce: a belief reinforcement model. Manag. Sci. **51**(8), 1219–1235 (2005)
32. Spangenberg, E.R., Crowley, A.E., Henderson, P.W.: Improving the store environment: do olfactory cues affect evaluations and behaviors? J. Mark. **60**, 67–80 (1996)
33. Szymanski, D.M., Hise, R.T.: E-satisfaction: an initial examination. J. Retail. **76**(3), 309–322 (2000)
34. TTA: Reference Model Interaction between contents and olfaction recognition system, TTA standard report, Telecommunications Technology Association (2015)
35. Toncar, M., Fetscherin, M.: A study of visual puffery in fragrance advertising: is the message sent stronger than the actual scent? Eur. J. Mark. **46**(1/2), 52–72 (2012)
36. Turley, L.W., Milliman, R.E.: Atmospheric effects on shopping behavior: a review of the experimental evidence. J. Bus. Res. **49**(2), 193–211 (2000)
37. Valdez, P., Mehrabian, A.: Effects of color on emotions. J. Exp. Psychol. Gen. **123**(4), 394 (1994)
38. Wang, C.Y.V.: The scent of creativity. M.A. thesis, University of Gothenburg (2009)
39. Wu, C.S., Cheng, F.F., Yen, D.C.: The atmospheric factors of online storefront environment design: an empirical experiment in Taiwan. Inf. Manag. **45**(7), 493–498 (2008)
40. Zellner, D.A., Kautz, M.A.: Color affects perceived odor intensity. J. Exp. Psychol. Hum. Percept. Perform. **16**(2), 391 (1990)

A Short-Term Twofold Impact on Banner Ads

Harald Kindermann[✉]

University of Applied Sciences Upper Austria, Wehrgrabengasse 1-3, 4400 Steyr, Austria
harald.kindermann@fh-steyr.at

Abstract. In light of the situation that banner ads are normally ignored by the target group, the question arises of whether the placement of such ads is reasonable. Referring to the mere exposure effect and priming mechanism, some impact can be derived, however, not always as desired. Depending on existing positive or negative predispositions toward a specific brand, the effect of such a banner can be either positive or negative. It seems that a banner from a negatively perceived brand triggers negative predisposition, hence leading to decreased brand choice.

Keywords: Mere exposure effect · Banner blindness · Priming · Implicit memory · Inattentional blindness

1 Introduction

Banner advertisements are familiar to everyone and are usually placed at the top or right lateral of diverse websites with the aim of attracting visitors' attention so that they click on the banner. Such a click increases the so-called click-through rate (CTR), a metric which is often used as an indicator for the success of banner ads [1–3]. Nevertheless, a discussion about the meaningfulness of the CTR as an indicator for success has been started in recent years [3, 4].

Within the scientific community, a common assumption is that when people visit websites, they usually have specific goals in mind – they behave in a goal-oriented way [5]. An example could be a person that is looking for daily news on a website of a newspaper. Since people automatically filter out all information that is not relevant for the achievement of a specific goal, banners will mostly be ignored and thus not consciously perceived. This effect is known as inattentional blindness, which leads to banner blindness [6–8].

Nevertheless, considering the approach of business practice, the CTR is often the sole indicator for capturing the efficiency of banner ads. Consequently, in order to optimize this CTR, the primary focus must be placed on drawing the banner's attention to the target group. It therefore seems obvious that animated instead of static banners are more capable of capturing the target group's attentiveness. Unfortunately, more or less the opposite holds true. Despite common arguments referring to motion effect theory, experimental studies reveal the contrary effects [4]. At this point, the question arises of what additional measures can be helpful to increase the efficiency of banner ads. Should banners become increasingly larger or more animated, even with the risk of producing

F.F.-H. Nah and C.-H. Tan (Eds.): HCIBGO 2016, Part I, LNCS 9751, pp. 417–426, 2016.
DOI: 10.1007/978-3-319-39396-4_38

irritated consumers? It is argued here that these options may be wrong. This conjecture is strongly backed by Heath and Heath et al. [9, 10].

To understand the theoretical background, it is of utmost importance to appreciate all the psychological coherences on how banners affect visitors of a website. To gain a more holistic view on this matter, it is necessary to not only measure metrics like CTR. Instead, marketing experts should consider the fact that unconsciously perceived information and advertising play an important role when considering advertising efficiency. Although this impact is widely known in the scientific community and already well-documented [3, 4, 11–14], it must be emphasized that this aspect is mostly disregarded in business practice.

One explanation for such implicit advertising effects is the so-called *mere exposure effect* [15, 16], which refers to a psychological phenomenon by which people tend to develop a preference for things merely because they have become familiar with them and therefore, these things are perceived as less threatening [17]. It is important to note that this effect does not depend on any conscious awareness of the initial exposure [18–20]. Concisely, it can be assumed that familiarity may decrease the perceived risk associated with a brand, which is likely to lead to preference formation and thus affects brand choice positively [21].

Taken together, the following hypotheses can be proposed:

Hypothesis 1a: A banner ad on a website will not be taken into account when visitors behave in a goal-oriented way. As a result, the existing banner will be neglected.
Hypothesis 1b: In the event that a brand is initially unknown, even unconsciously perceived banners positively affect a spontaneous brand choice.

However, the assumption in hypothesis 1b is just one side of the coin. What happens if the advertised brand is already familiar and people have a certain attitude toward this known brand? In such a case, a banner activates all the accessible representations and associations, which have already been memorized due to past exposure and experiences. This effect is called priming [22–24]. At this point, it needs to be emphasized that such an activation of previously stored information does not always have to be positive. Normally, the target group should be influenced in such a way that the sales volume of a product is increased in the near future. Considering, however, that priming activates the entire existing associative network of the advertised product or brand, including all positive and negative representations, it must be assumed that the effect of a banner can be both positive and negative – predominately depending on how easily accessible certain aspects of the product or brand are. In the event of a person with mainly negative representations towards a product or brand, a banner activates this negative mental model [25]. In cases of neutral representations, again the mere exposure effect comes into play. These assumptions lead to the second hypotheses:

*Hypothesis 2a: If a target group already has a **positive** representation of a product or a brand, a banner **positively** affects a spontaneous brand choice.*
*Hypothesis 2b: If a target group already has a **negative** representation of a product or a brand, a banner **negatively** affects a spontaneous brand choice.*
*Hypothesis 2c: If a target group has a **neutral** representation of a product or a brand, a banner **positively** affects a spontaneous brand choice.*

2 Empirical Studies

2.1 Pilot Study

In order to see to what extent the proposed banner blindness occurs, an experimental pilot study was carried out with eye-tracking techniques. For the purposes of this study, first simple banners of three different soft drink brands (Pfanner, Bravo, Happy Day) were designed and included on the right lower corner of an existing web page of a German newspaper (see Fig. 1). For the pilot study, we recruited n = 80 participants from the University of Applied Sciences Upper Austria who were randomly assigned to three experimental groups and one control group (n = 20 each). Depending on the group affiliation (experimental group 1, 2, 3 or control group), the subjects were confronted with the screenshot of the web page including one of the aforementioned banners or with the version without such a banner (group 1 = "Pfanner", group 2 = "Bravo", group 3 = "Happy Day", group 4 = "no banner") - see arrows in Fig. 1. At the beginning of the experiment, each subject received the following instructions:

> "For the purposes of evaluating the structure of a website of a newspaper, you will see a screenshot of this site. Please search for the word "Solidaritätszuschlag". For this task, you do not have any time pressure. After finding the word, please click on it with the mouse cursor. Afterwards, your task is finished."

This task was set for distraction purposes in order to trigger real goal-oriented behavior. While the participants were searching for the specific word, eye gazes were recorded with eye tracking equipment (SMI Red 250).

Fig. 1. Control group and experimental group of the pilot study

Immediately after fulfilling the task, the subjects received further instructions. They were asked to declare their preferences of three fruit juice brands. For this purpose, they were subsequently confronted with all three possible pairs of the previously mentioned three brands. The different brand pairs were presented in random order ("Bravo vs. Pfanner"|"Bravo vs. Happy Day"|"Pfanner vs. Happy Day" – see Fig. 2). Separately for each pair, they had to spontaneously select their preferred brand.

Fig. 2. All brand pairs for the selection task

2.2   Results of the Pilot Study

Firstly and foremostly, the pilot study's purpose was to reveal if the banner attracted any visual attention. The results of the eye tracking largely confirmed hypothesis 1a. More than 85 % of the subjects did not fixate on the banner one single time. The remaining subjects did so, but only once. On a critical note, none of them could mention the brand name of the banner ad, when asked afterwards. These results clearly support hypothesis 1a.

Secondly, it appears that for those subjects who did not know (or were only slightly familiar with) the depicted brands, banner placement leads to a higher brand preference compared to the control group. These results are in line with the aforementioned mere exposure effect and are initial indicators for the confirmation of hypothesis 1b.

In addition, those subjects who are well familiar with the brands seem to perceive the banner in line with their existing positive or negative representations of the respective brand. This tendency supports the aforementioned assumption that the priming effect reinforces both positive and negative brand choices.

Due to the small sample size of this pilot study, these results reveal just a tendency, which should be interpreted with care. In order to underpin the results of this pilot study, subsequent research has been undertaken.

2.3   Main Study: Results and Discussion

For the sake of proving the aforementioned hypotheses, we developed an online experiment. The setup largely resembled the one used in the pilot study, yet with different brands and other websites. As can be seen in Fig. 3, the main study consisted of four experimental groups and two control groups. The six screenshots and complete instructions for the distraction task were included in six online questionnaires. The only difference between these questionnaires was that the screenshots included a different banner.

In this online experiment, 905 students of the University of Applied Sciences Upper Austria participated. First these students were randomly divided into six groups. Each group was asked to answer one of the six questionnaires. All questionnaires started with a question about existing predispositions towards a random choice of brands. The four banner brands were included in this choice. Afterwards, they received the same instructions as previously given in the pilot study. Subsequently, one screenshot per questionnaire was presented (see Fig. 3) where the specific word of the distraction task had to be sought. When finished, they had to answer some demographic questions and these two questions concerning banner blindness:

Do you remember if there was a banner on the screenshot?
If yes, what brand was it?

At the end, the students had to select their preferred brand out of two (see Fig. 4), again in line with the previously conducted pilot study.

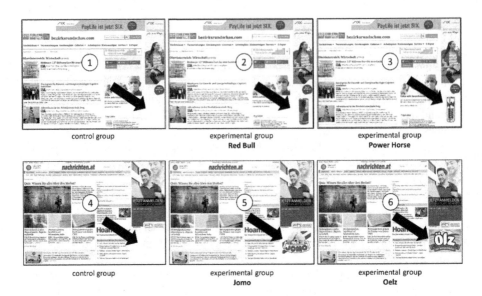

Fig. 3. The different control groups and experimental groups of the research

Fig. 4. Brand choice possibilities

The mean age of the participants was M = 24.99 years (range: 16–29, SD = 7.32) and consisted of 418 females (46.2 %) and 487 males (53.8 %).

At first, answers given to the two questions concerning banner blindness were analyzed. More than 75 % of the students reported that they were unaware of any banner.

The remaining 25 % stated that they had seen a banner, yet the majority of them could not name the correct brand. Just a few of them (n = 7) gave the correct answer. These results again support hypothesis 1a.

For the confirmation of hypotheses 2a–c, and to control possible interdependencies between existing predispositions toward the brands used, we divided the existing six samples into four subsamples per banner brand.

- First subsample: students with a positive predisposition toward the banner brand.
- Second subsample: students with a negative predisposition toward the banner brand.
- Third subsample: students with no/neutral predisposition toward the banner brand.
- Fourth subsample: students who did not know the respective banner brand.

This division is necessary in view of the existing set of preferences with regard to the brand choice which had to be made by the respondents. The fact is that when someone needs to make a decision between two brands, the respective decision highly depends on the existing predisposition towards both brands. Against this background, this relevant differentiation into four groups had to be taken.

The respective selected brand of two brands offered was the dependent variable of our experiment. In order to analyze and evaluate the brand choice of the subjects, a predisposition-dependent analysis in the form of a contingent table was carried out. A chi-square test was calculated to identify significant coherences.

Table 1 depicts all the calculated results and it becomes obvious that many subsamples contained too few subjects, as indicated with "n.a." (not analyzed). Consequently, an evaluation of such samples does not make any sense. In view of this limitation, a further point needs to be taken into account. As can also be seen in Table 1, the available sample sizes are rather small and the calculated results have to be interpreted with care just as in the pilot study. In a similar vein, the chi-square test gives slightly non-significant results (chi-square value > 0.05 but < 0.1). Taking all these factors into account, it is impossible to confirm the formulated hypotheses 1b and 2a, 2b and 2c.

Nevertheless, the existing data show a distinct trend, which supports all the hypotheses but of course, does not confirm them. As such, it appears reasonable to have a closer look at the results in Table 1.

Let us begin with **hypotheses 1b and 2c.** If a person did not know the banner brand (here "Jomo"), and she or he had a negative or neutral predisposition towards its competing brand (here "Oelz"), then the banner of the unknown brand (="Jomo-banner") increased the choice probability in favor of the banner brand (="Jomo"). For the actual results please see cells 8c & 8d 8e (+33.3 %; "Jomo"), 11c & 11d & 11e (+16.7 %; "Jomo"), 20h & 20i & 20j (+14.2 %; "Power Horse").

Hypothesis 2a corresponds with cells 1c & 1d & 1e (+30 %; "Jomo"), 21c & 21d & 21e (+7.1 % "Power Horse"). As can be seen from these results, an initial **positive** representation of a brand affects a spontaneous brand choice **positively.**

Table 1. Results of the spontaneous brand choice

column	a	b	c	d	e		f	g	h	i	j
		average predisposition towards ...		decision for "Jomo"				average predisposition towards ...		decision for "Oelz"	
line	n	Jomo	Oelz	control group (no banner)	exp. group ("Jomo"-banner)	difference	n	Oelz	Jomo	control group (no banner)	exp. group ("Oelz"-banner)	difference
1	14	1	1	20.0%	50.0%	30.0%	7	1	1	n.a.	n.a.	n.a.
2	9	2	1	n.a.	n.a.	n.a.	0	2	1	n.a.	n.a.	n.a.
3	17	3	1	0.0%	0.0%	0.0%	2	3	1	n.a.	n.a.	n.a.
4	77	4	1	2.8%	2.4%	-0.4%	0	4	1	n.a.	n.a.	n.a.
5	9	1	2	n.a.	n.a.	n.a.	16	1	2	100.0%	100.0%	0.0%
6	11	2	2	20.0%	0.0%	-20.0%	11	2	2	80.0%	63.6%	-16.4%
7	7	3	2	n.a.	n.a.	n.a.	6	3	2	n.a.	n.a.	n.a.
8	16	4	2	16.7%	50.0%	33.3%	0	4	2	n.a.	n.a.	n.a.
9	0	1	3	n.a.	n.a.	n.a.	22	1	3	100.0%	91.7%	-8.3%
10	10	2	3	0.0%	0.0%	0.0%	5	2	3	n.a.	n.a.	n.a.
11	20	3	3	0.0%	16.7%	16.7%	19	3	3	100.0%	90.9%	-9.1%
12	51	4	3	0.0%	2.9%	2.9%	0	4	3	n.a.	n.a.	n.a.

	n	average predisposition towards ...		decision for "Red Bull"			n	average predisposition towards ...		decision for "Power Horse"	
		Red Bull	Power Horse	control group (no banner)	exp. group ("Red Bull"-banner)	difference		Power Horse	Red Bull	control group (no banner)	exp.group ("Power Horse"-banner)	difference
13	9	1	1	n.a.	n.a.	n.a.	6	1	1	n.a	n.a.	n.a.
14	1	2	1	n.a.	n.a.	n.a.	65	2	1	2.9%	3.2%	0.3%
15	0	3	1	n.a.	n.a.	n.a.	31	3	1	7.1%	5.9%	-1.2%
16	0	4	1	n.a.	n.a.	n.a.	32	4	1	0.0%	0.0%	0.0%
17	73	1	2	97.1%	100.0%	2.9%	0	1	2	n.a	n.a.	n.a.
18	39	2	2	77.8%	81.0%	3.2%	41	2	2	22.2%	17.4%	-4.8%
19	34	3	2	94.1%	94.1%	0.0%	10	n.a.	n.a.	n.a	n.a.	n.a.
20	0	4	2	n.a.	n.a.	n.a.	20	4	2	22.2%	36.4%	14.2%
21	27	1	3	92.9%	100.0%	7.1%	0	1	3	n.a	n.a.	n.a.
22	8	2	3	n.a.	n.a.	n.a.	37	2	3	5.9%	0.0%	-5.9%
23	8	3	3	n.a.	n.a.	n.a.	18	3	3	0.0%	9.1%	9.1%
24	0	4	3	n.a.	n.a.	n.a.	13	4	3	0.0%	0.0%	0.0%

Legend:
1=subjects have a **positive** predisposition towards this brand
2=subjects have a **negative** predisposition towards this brand
3=subjects have a **neutral** predisposition towards this brand
4=subjects don't know this brand
n= number of subjects
n.a.=not analyzed (because of a too small sample size)

Hypothesis 2b corresponds with cells 6c & 6e & 6e (−20.0 %; "Jomo"), 11h & 11i & 11j (−16.4 %; "Oelz"), and 41h & 41i & 41j (−4.8 %; "Power Horse"). These results reveal that an initial **negative** representation of a brand affects a spontaneous brand choice **negatively**.

3 Conclusion

This contribution sheds some light on how banner ads influence brand choices. In the event of a more or less unknown brand, banner ads may have a positive impact on shaping attitudes, leading to a positive predisposition towards the brand. These coherences are based on the mere exposure effect, which is widely accepted.

Particular caution has to be taken if the brand is already known, and if stored representations of a brand are available in the associative network of the consumers' brains. In such a case, the banner activates all of the existing positive or negative information. Thus, a banner is only supportive if somebody has memorized mainly positive representations. In all other cases, the opposite holds true, and the possibility is high that such a banner deteriorates future purchasing behavior.

In planning a marketing campaign, specific attention needs to be called to these aspects, especially in view of the fact that is in no one's interest to reduce the sales of the advertised product.

Due to the outlined limitations, a follow-up study is recommended. In order to reach sufficient samples sizes in all necessary subsamples, we recommend that the overall sample go beyond n = 1000. In addition, it would be advisable to integrate just two brands instead of four. Moreover, a selection of highly polarizing brands would increase the probability of attaining well-distributed samples, which is especially relevant in view of the consumers' predisposition towards the selected brands. A further factor that may come into play is the gender of the participants and should hence be taken into account.

References

1. Robinson, H., Wysocka, A., Hand, C.: Internet advertising effectiveness: the effect of design on click-through rates for banner ads. Int. J. Advertising **26**, 527–541 (2007)
2. Lohtia, R., Donthu, N., Hershberger, E.K.: The impact of content and design elements on banner advertising click-through rates. J. Advertising Res. **43**, 410–418 (2003)
3. Yoo, C.Y.: Unconscious processing of web advertising: effects on implicit memory, attitude toward the brand, and consideration set. J. Interact. Mark. **22**, 2–18 (2008)
4. Lee, J., Ahn, J.-H.: Attention to banner ads and their effectiveness: an eye-tracking approach. Int. J. Electron. Commer. **17**, 119–137 (2012)
5. Cho, C.-H.: Why do people avoid advertising on the internet? J. Advertising **33**, 89–97 (2004)
6. Mack, A., Rock, I.: Inattentional Blindness. MIT Press, Cambridge (1998)
7. Benway, J.P.: Banner blindness: the irony of attention grabbing on the World Wide Web. In: Proceedings of the Human Factors and Ergonomics Society Annual Meeting, vol. 42, pp. 463–467 (1998)
8. Pagendarm, M., Schaumburg, H.: Why are users banner-blind? The impact of navigation style on the perception of web banners. J. Digital Inf. **2** (2006)
9. Heath, R.: Low involvement processing—a new model of brands and advertising. Int. J. Advertising **19**, 287–298 (2000)
10. Heath, R., Brandt, D., Nairn, A.: Brand relationships: strengthened by emotion, weakened by attention. J. Advertising Res. **46**, 410–419 (2006)
11. Lee, A.Y.: Effects of implicit memory on memory-based versus stimulus-based brand choice. J. Mark. Res. (JMR) **39**, 440–454 (2002)

12. Meyers-Levy, J., Malaviya, P.: Consumers' processing of persuasive advertisements: an integrative framework of persuasion theories. J. Mark. **63**, 45–60 (1999)
13. Courbet, D., Fourquet-Courbet, M.-P., Kazan, R., Intartaglia, J.: The long-term effects of e-advertising: the influence of internet pop-ups viewed at a low level of attention in implicit memory. J. Comput. Mediated Commun. **19**, 274–293 (2014)
14. Kindermann, H.: Priming effect and inattentional blindness: an experimental study on decision making (Poster). In: Sixth European Conference on Sensory and Consumer Research, Copenhagen (2014)
15. Moreland, R.L., Zajonc, R.B.: Exposure effects in person perception: familiarity, similarity, and attraction. J. Exp. Soc. Psychol. **18**, 395–415 (1982)
16. Lee, A.Y.: The mere exposure effect: an uncertainty reduction explanation revisited. Pers. Soc. Psychol. Bull. **27**, 1255–1266 (2001)
17. Grimes, A., Kitchen, P.J.: Researching mere exposure effects to advertising. Int. J. Mark. Res. **49**, 191–219 (2007)
18. Mandler, G., Nakamura, Y., Van Zandt, B.J.: Nonspecific effects of exposure on stimuli that cannot be recognized. J. Exp. Psychol. Learn. Mem. Cognit. **13**, 646 (1987)
19. Janiszewski, C.: The influence of nonattended material on the processing of advertising claims. J. Mark. Res. **27**, 263–278 (1990)
20. Janiszewski, C.: Preconscious processing effects: the independence of attitude formation and conscious thought. J. Consum. Res. **15**, 199–209 (1988)
21. Baker, W.E.: When can affective conditioning and mere exposure directly influence brand choice? J. Advertising **28**, 31–46 (1999)
22. Meyer, D.E., Schvaneveldt, R.W.: Facilitation in recognizing pairs of words: evidence of a dependence between retrieval operations. J. Exp. Psychol. **90**, 227 (1971)
23. Meyer, D.E., Schvaneveldt, R.W.: Retrieval and Comparison Processes in Semantic Memory Attention and Performance IV. Academic Press, New York (1973)
24. Tulving, E., Schacter, D.L.: Priming and human memory systems. Science **247**, 301–306 (1990)
25. Johnson-Laird, P.N.: Mental Models: Towards a Cognitive Science of Language, Inference, and Consciousness. Harvard University Press, Cambridge (1983)

Improving Online Customer Shopping Experience with Computer Vision and Machine Learning Methods

Zequn Li, Honglei Li[✉], and Ling Shao

Department of Computer and Information Sciences,
Northumbria University, Newcastle upon Tyne, UK
{zequn.li,honglei.li,ling.shao}@northumbria.ac.uk

Abstract. Computer vision and pattern recognition has achieved great developments in last decade, especially the feature categorizing and detection. How to exploit the new techniques in this research area has rarely discussed in the information systems field. This paper aims at exploring the opportunities from the most recent development from computer vision area from the online shopping experience perspective. We discussed the possibility of extracting meaningful information from images and apply this to the online recommendation system to improve online customer shopping experience. Implications to both researchers and practitioners are discussed. The contribution of these papers are twofold, firstly, we have summarized the state-of-the-art of the computer vision development in the online shopping recommendation system, especially in the fashion industry; secondly, we have provided some potential research gaps for on how computer vision method could be used in the information systems field.

Keywords: Online recommendation system · Machine learning · Shopping experience · Image processing · Fashion recommendation

1 Introduction

In recent years, with the development of online shopping, the shopping experience of online customer has been investigated by many researchers [4, 26, 28, 36] from different perspectives. Among these studies an important issue of online shopping experiences lies in the difference between online and offline shopping experience [10, 18]. These researches showed that the socioeconomic variables which traditionally considered being import have changed to be insignificant as before but security aspect tends to be more related. Based on those findings, on-line shopping websites are built to improve the shopping experience from several perspectives including quality control of website [26], interface design for elderly people [27], service quality experience [4] etc. Previous studies have identified that product uncertainty and low retailer visibility will have negative impact on customer satisfaction and thus poor online shopping experiences [33]. Researchers have endeavored to capture more information about products and other features to enhance customers' online shopping experience including utilizing big data, computer vision, and machine learning techniques recently developed.

© Springer International Publishing Switzerland 2016
F.F.-H. Nah and C.-H. Tan (Eds.): HCIBGO 2016, Part I, LNCS 9751, pp. 427–436, 2016.
DOI: 10.1007/978-3-319-39396-4_39

The online recommendation systems for improved customer online shopping experience have gained popularity because the past transaction data could be used to predict customers purchasing choices [45]. At the same time, there are many successful solutions for online customer recommendation systems [2, 39]. For example, Amazon had increased nearly 30 % of its sales by developing the online recommendation system from customer browsing history. At the same time, the online recommendation system also helps Amazon to control the security and price of the selling item by analyzing the big data provided by customers and products [31, 38]. However, most existing online recommendation systems are developed from readable text [3, 21, 40], leaving many new types of data such as image and multimedia data unused. Multimedia data and image data provides much rich information than readable texts. How to extract meaningful information from multimedia resources like images and apply the extracted information into the online shopping recommendation systems has rarely been considered mainly due to the relevantly new development of computer vision technologies. This study aims at exploring the new techniques from Computer Vision and Machine Learning perspective and proposing a framework of integrating these new techniques with the existing online shopping recommendation systems. The fashion and clothing industry are used in this study as an example to explore such possibility.

We firstly reviewed past research from online shopping experience perspective, mainly on the design of online shopping website or online customer satisfaction, followed by a search for the Computer Vision methods which may be applied to improve online shopping experience. We reviewed most top conferences on Computer Vision such as Computer Vision and Pattern Recognition and ACM Multimedia Conference, especially targeting at the fashion and clothing area. The review results demonstrated that attribute learning method could be used to improve online shopping experience. We illustrated this by demonstrating how fashion item recommendation system could be developed with attribute learning method in computer vision. The implications to both researchers and practitioners are then discussed.

2   Computer Vision Methods and Online Recommendation Systems

The previous research of online shopping behavior [30] shows the dimensions of web site design, reliability, responsiveness, and trust affect overall service quality and customer satisfaction. This paper mainly explore how online shopping experience could be improved from the web site design perspective and explores what new type of technologies from Computer Vision could be used to improve the website design. Meanwhile, we also try to discuss the implications of machine learning and computer vision on information systems theories. We firstly discussed the recent developments in the Computer Vision area and then explore how these new techniques could be applied into the online shopping recommendation system.

2.1 Extract Semantic Attributes from Images

Early studies on online recommendation system rarely consider image as an important factor but only to display the pictures clearly to achieve the optimal product effects [16]. The information in the picture is not fully explored mainly because the image processing techniques haven't been fully developed in early days. Alongside the development of the Image Interactivity technology which enables the creating and manipulation of product images, the potential to exploit more feature from images increase. In the beginning, researchers started focusing on sketching and modelling fashion items [7]. Recently, due to the techniques from machine learning, Computer Vision is witnessed some big breakthroughs. One of the major breakthroughs in Computer Vision is the recognition of image categories [14, 29, 42]. The first improvement comes with feature representation of images, for example, at the feature level, there are kinds of features that could be extracted by different methods including SIFT [24], GIFT [35], Histograms of Oriented Gradient (HOG) [11], Local Binary Pattern (LBP) [1], Maximum Response Filters [43]). Based on these features, a well-trained model could be developed to classify different objects, such as shirts, shoes or hats into categories. The semantic attributes provided by researcher can be used to further assist object classification. Some business solutions had already used this method to preform image mining and achieved satisfactory results [5]. An example of semantic Attribute on Clothes is shown in Table 1.

Table 1. Example of semantic attribute on clothes [5]

Colors	Patterns	Materials	Structures	Looks	Persons	Sleeves	Styles
Beige	Animal print	Cotton	Frilly	Black/ white	Child	Long	Nerd
Black	Zebra	Denim	Knitted	Colored	Boy	Short	Outdoor
Blue	Leopard	Fur	Ruffled	Pastel	Girl	None	Preppy
Brown	Argyle	Lace	Wrinkled	Gaudy	Female		Punk
Gray	Check-ered	Leather			Male		Rock
Green	Clotted	Silk					Romantic

However, the problem with this kind of recognition mechanism is that it usually ignores certain type appearance of objects such as the color and texture. In order to solve this problem, some new models were introduced to learn visual attributes [15]. By using this method, human understandable properties could be extracted from images. If we put those properties as labels attached to images, then we can group images by a combination of labels [13, 25]. For example, we can describe a shirt in a specific style with black and white stripes or a white shirt with red round on it and classify clothes with these properties. By using those methods, we could extract some high level semantic features from images such as clothing style, patterns and textures. But these methods only work well with clear and simple image data. As a result, in the realistic online shopping environment, those methods can hardly handle the complex and noisy image resources.

In order to solve this problem, some object detection models have been developed [9, 46]. These models use human pose estimation or simple object detection method to locate the interesting item in an image so that attribute learning method can be applied only to those located item. With this kind of preprocessing method, we could extract semantic attributes from images in a real online shopping environment. There is already some success research in this area. Actually, there is already some success research on this. For example, through collection of a well labelled dataset, Chen et al. [8] extracted complex semantic features from clothing in Fig. 1. Moreover, Liu et al. [32] collected both top and bottom clothes and identified the semantic feature relations between them, which enable them to make further suggestion on item combinations of clothes.

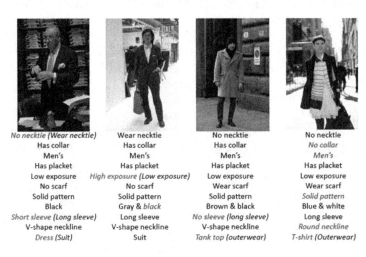

No necktie (Wear necktie)	Wear necktie	No necktie	No necktie
Has collar	Has collar	Has collar	No collar
Men's	Men's	Men's	Men's
Has placket	Has placket	Has placket	Has placket
Low exposure	High exposure (Low exposure)	Low exposure	Low exposure
No scarf	No scarf	Wear scarf	Wear scarf
Solid pattern	Solid pattern	Solid pattern	Solid pattern
Black	Gray & black	Brown & black	Blue & white
Short sleeve (Long sleeve)	Long sleeve	No sleeve (long sleeve)	Long sleeve
V-shape neckline	V-shape neckline	V-shape neckline	Round neckline
Dress (Suit)	Suit	Tank top (outerwear)	T-shirt (Outerwear)

Fig. 1. Extract clothing attribute

As shown above, applying those information collected from Computer vision method could help to improve the design of website and improve not only the description of products but also the shopping experience. However, based on the research of the complexity of website, Park and Kim [36] separated the whole web site into six aspects and find the importance of each part is not equal, and the design of website should not be too complex [17]. So when applying these new technologies into online shopping environment, we need to consider the complexity of new feathers. To apply the huge amount of information provided by Computer Vision methods, certain work is required to be done in information system area to measure the effects of those semantic features. Currently there is no research in the information systems area trying to explore the usage of computer vision methods to improve customer experience. This paper aims at exploring the new perspective and new theories that might arise from the interaction between computer vision and information systems research areas.

2.2 Enrich Recommendation System with Image Features

Analyzing the customers' behavior from their shopping history and using these information to make recommendations to customers so that customers shopping experience could be enhanced has become a trend in most e-commerce websites [10, 36]. Currently, most online shopping websites such as Amazon and eBay make suggestions to their customer by analyzing customers searching or shopping history. This method is successful because related items or products similar to those from their browsed history could be pushed to customers. The limitation is that all the predictions are only based on the item-to-item or user-to-item combinations [31, 37]. The algorithm of these models only considers the relations between item and user or item and item, but ignores the features of the products themselves.

The most salient features extracted from images in e-commerce websites would be used to enhance online recommendation systems and thus shopping experience. Extracted feathers could be those descriptive feathers perceived by human beings such as color and style etc. For example, clothes on Amazon web-site usually contains 5 labels: color, style of sleeve, material and brand, but from the pictures provided by website we can extract more than 10 additional labels such as length, cut, pocket, collar, and material etc. [8, 12]. Moreover, new algorithm could be built based on some public training datasets [5, 23], and well trained model can automatically extract the clothing part and analyzing possible labels from each clothes. These labels could be implemented from human perspectives and some cognitive factors could also be used to extract useful information from clothes pictures. For instance, personality type could be used to classify clothes style based on attributes extracted from images. There is thus a possibility to provide more accurate description of products from higher cognitive and conceptual level so that customers could be provided more enriched products information at higher conceptual and cognitive level.

The overall trend for online fashion recommendation system enables the online shopping systems to be more personalized. There are some successful examples for the fashion recommendation systems through mining the combination of both text and image features. Jagadeesh et al. [22] proposed a fashion recommender by analyzing the color model from street images for item recommendation. Iwata et al. [20] collected text and image data from fashion magazines to build a topic based recommendation system. These two works are item based which only consider the relationship between items and the item-user relationship is not considered here. With the development of social networks, personalized recommendation systems with image features are gaining popularity in recent research. Sigurbjornsson et al. [41] proposed a personalized tag recommendation system based on a Flickr dataset. In this work, they analyzed the frequently used tags of customers to automatically recommend personalized tags for newly added photos. And another research from Yue et al. [47] provided a similar personalize recommendation system by collecting customers' feedbacks. This type of research mostly concentrates on the customer side, and provides recommendations by finding similar customers. Meanwhile, there is also some research considering both user-to-item and item-to-item relationship at the same time. In Hu et al.'s [19] research, they built a model

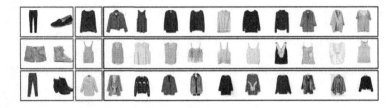

Fig. 2. Finding tops to match with given bottom and shoes with image features [19]

with each customer's preferred fashion items and then combined these items to make a personalized recommendation for a set of fashion item as shown in Fig. 2.

As shown in Fig. 2, researchers build various recommendation systems through mining the large set of data collected from computer vision methods. However, the current contribution of these new papers is mostly on the new mathematical methods or algorithms that could handle different types of datasets. These works only focus on the recommendation algorithm from the technology perspective. How customers will response to this new type of data hasn't been investigated from the information systems perspective. What type of features shall be extracted? Which features are more salient in improve online customers shopping experience haven't been explored as well.

2.3   Image Analysis with Humans in the Loop

Most Computer Vision problems are solved by machine learning algorithms and there is no need to build a huge image dataset to be learned by that algorithm. Rather researchers need to collect a well labelled fashion dataset for training purpose. The quality of that dataset determined the accuracy of the computer vision model in a certain degree. However, the collection of that dataset is normally expensive and time consuming. Specifically, in fashion and clothing industry, the product and style are changing ever year and fashion companies update their dataset frequently. To solve this issue, the humans in the loop method is proposed [6, 34]. In this method, humans answers are collected for some specifically designed questions, and these questions are formed as human knowledge to enrich the model. Compared with the previous algorithm, the Humans in the loop method use less dataset and get more intelligent results in a dynamic way.

The current progress for humans in the loop methods only have been widely used in animal datasets [6] or unfamiliar classes [44]. There are not any works on fashion items mainly because the feedbacks on fashion items are different among different customer groups, which is not like those structured feedbacks on animals. To improve the humans in the loop methods for the fashion items, more feedbacks from different customer groups could be adopted in the algorithm. The past marketing research findings on customer segmentation could be considered to apply into the humans in the loop methods. The integration of previous marketing theories and information systems theories is expected to contribute to the humans in the loop methods.

3   Conclusion

The purpose of this research aims at exploring the potential to combine the computer vision method with information system method to improve the online shopping experience. We have reviewed and visited a series of computer vision methods and machine learning skills, especially from the fashion area, followed by the current development of online shopping recommendation systems. We found that most online shopping recommendation systems only used the text information from the products and a large amount of information from pictures are not considered in the current online recommendation systems.

We proposed that more fine and enriched information extracted form product pictures with computer vision methods could improve the online shopping experience, and illustrated with the current progress in this area. Although, the potential for the online recommendation system through computer vision methods is very promising there are still many issues to be tackled. We have proposed two important perspectives to be considered to better apply computer vision methods into online recommendation systems. Firstly, what type of semantics features shall be used to build the conceptual models to extract attributes from products pictures? We may have fantastic computer vision techniques but customers may not like any information extracted from product pictures. The conceptual models and even past marketing theories could be used to make the conceptual features more meaningful for computer vision methods. Secondly, with the humans in the loop methods, what type of customer knowledge shall be used to build the algorithm for fashion items?

To apply the computer vision methods into online recommendation system, it's thus essential to gain insights and knowledge from customers' perspective. More research shall focus on testing and investigating customer feedbacks on the current online recommendation systems through computer vision methods. There are also some issues to be solved before applying extracted information from images to the online recommendation system from the technology perspective. Those new algorithms mentioned above all concentrate on the technology side, and most of them only work well with detailed labelled training data. In realistic situation, it might difficult to build the well labelled training data and the images to be analyzed also contain lots of noise data. In this case, the performance of current Computer Vision algorithms should be carefully tested before putting in use.

References

1. Ahonen, T., Hadid, A., Pietikainen, M.: Face description with local binary patterns: application to face recognition. IEEE Trans. Pattern Anal. Mach. Intell. **28**(12), 2037–2041 (2006)
2. Andersen, R., Borgs, C., Chayes, J., Feige, U., Flaxman, A., Kalai, A., Mirrokni, V., Tennenholtz, M.: Trust-based recommendation systems: an axiomatic approach. In: Proceedings of the 17th International Conference on World Wide Web, pp. 199–208. ACM (2008)

3. Banko, M., Cafarella, M.J., Soderland, S., Broadhead, M., Etzioni, O.: Open information extraction for the web. In: IJCAI, vol. 7, pp. 2670–2676 (2007)
4. Bauer, H.H., Falk, T., Hammerschmidt, M.: eTransQual: a transaction process-based approach for capturing service quality in online shopping. J. Bus. Res. **59**(7), 866–875 (2006)
5. Bossard, L., Dantone, M., Leistner, C., Wengert, C., Quack, T., Van Gool, L.: Apparel classification with style. In: Lee, K.M., Matsushita, Y., Rehg, J.M., Hu, Z. (eds.) ACCV 2012, Part IV. LNCS, vol. 7727, pp. 321–335. Springer, Heidelberg (2013)
6. Branson, S., Wah, C., Schroff, F., Babenko, B., Welinder, P., Perona, P., Belongie, S.: Visual recognition with humans in the loop. In: Daniilidis, K., Maragos, P., Paragios, N. (eds.) ECCV 2010, Part IV. LNCS, vol. 6314, pp. 438–451. Springer, Heidelberg (2010)
7. Chen, H., Xu, Z.J., Liu, Z.Q., Zhu, S.C.: Composite templates for cloth modeling and sketching. In: Proceedings of the IEEE Computer Society Conference on Computer Vision and Pattern Recognition, vol. 1, pp. 943–950 (2006)
8. Chen, H., Gallagher, A., Girod, B.: Describing clothing by semantic attributes. In: Fitzgibbon, A., Lazebnik, S., Perona, P., Sato, Y., Schmid, C. (eds.) ECCV 2012, Part III. LNCS, vol. 7574, pp. 609–623. Springer, Heidelberg (2012)
9. Chen, X., Mottaghi, R., Liu, X., Fidler, S., Urtasun, R., Yuille, A.: Detect what you can: detecting and representing objects using holistic models and body parts. In: Proceedings of the IEEE Conference on Computer Vision and Pattern Recognition, pp. 1971–1978 (2014)
10. Childers, T.L., Carr, C.L., Peck, J., Carson, S.: Hedonic and utilitarian motivations for online retail shopping behavior. J. Retail. **77**(4), 511–535 (2002)
11. Dalal, N., Triggs, B.: Histograms of oriented gradients for human detection. In: IEEE Computer Society Conference on Computer Vision and Pattern Recognition, CVPR 2005, vol. 1, pp. 886–893. IEEE (2005)
12. Di, W., Wah, C., Bhardwaj, A., Piramuthu, R., Sundaresan, N.: Style finder: fine-grained clothing style detection and retrieval. In: 2013 IEEE Conference on Computer Vision and Pattern Recognition Workshops (CVPRW), pp. 8–13. IEEE (2013)
13. Farhadi, A., Endres, I., Hoiem, D., Forsyth, D.: Describing objects by their attributes. In: IEEE Conference on Computer Vision and Pattern Recognition, CVPR 2009, pp. 1778–1785. IEEE (2009)
14. Fei-Fei, L., Perona, P.: A Bayesian hierarchical model for learning natural scene categories. In: IEEE Computer Society Conference on Computer Vision and Pattern Recognition, CVPR 2005, vol. 2, pp. 524–531. IEEE (2005)
15. Ferrari, V., Zisserman, A.: Learning visual attributes (2008)
16. Fiore, A.M., Kim, J., Lee, H.H.: Effect of image interactivity technology on consumer responses toward the online retailer. J. Interact. Mark. **19**(3), 38–53 (2005)
17. Guo, Y.M., Poole, M.S.: Antecedents of flow in online shopping: a test of alternative models. Inf. Syst. J. **19**(4), 369–390 (2009)
18. Hernández, B., Jiménez, J., Martín, M.J.: Age, gender and income: do they really moderate online shopping behaviour? Online Inf. Rev. **35**(1), 113–133 (2011)
19. Hu, Y., Yi, X., Davis, L.S.: Collaborative fashion recommendation: a functional tensor factorization approach. In: Proceedings of the 23rd Annual ACM Conference on Multimedia Conference, pp. 129–138. ACM (2015)
20. Iwata, T., Wanatabe, S., Sawada, H.: Fashion coordinates recommender system using photographs from fashion magazines. In: IJCAI Proceedings of International Joint Conference on Artificial Intelligence, vol. 22, p. 2262. Citeseer (2011)
21. Jacobs, P.S.: Text-Based Intelligent Systems: Current Research and Practice in Information Extraction and Retrieval. Psychology Press, New York (2014)

22. Jagadeesh, V., Piramuthu, R., Bhardwaj, A., Di, W., Sundaresan, N.: Large scale visual recommendations from street fashion images. In: Proceedings of the 20th ACM SIGKDD International Conference on Knowledge Discovery and Data Mining, pp. 1925–1934. ACM (2014)

23. Kalantidis, Y., Kennedy, L., Li, L.J.: Getting the look: clothing recognition and segmentation for automatic product suggestions in everyday photos, pp. 105–112 (2013)

24. Ke, Y., Sukthankar, R.: PCA-SIFT: a more distinctive representation for local image descriptors. In: Proceedings of the 2004 IEEE Computer Society Conference on Computer Vision and Pattern Recognition, CVPR 2004, vol. 2, p. II-506. IEEE (2004)

25. Kovashka, A., Grauman, K.: Attribute adaptation for personalized image search. In: 2013 IEEE International Conference on Computer Vision (ICCV), pp. 3432–3439. IEEE (2013)

26. Kuo, H.M., Chen, C.W.: Application of quality function deployment to improve the quality of internet shopping website interface design. Int. J. Innov. Comput. Inf. Control 7(1), 253–268 (2011)

27. Kuo, H.M., Chen, C.W., Hsu, C.H.: A study of a B2C supporting interface design system for the elderly. Hum. Factors Ergon. Manuf. Serv. Ind. 22(6), 528–540 (2012)

28. Lai, C.Y., Shih, D.H., Chiang, H.S., Chen, C.C.: The key factors of influence consumer online shopping behavior: using the IQA approach. In: Proceedings of the 8th WSEAS International Conference on E-Activities and Information Security and Privacy, pp. 286–291. World Scientific and Engineering Academy and Society (WSEAS) (2009)

29. Lazebnik, S., Schmid, C., Ponce, J.: Beyond bags of features: spatial pyramid matching for recognizing natural scene categories. In: 2006 IEEE Computer Society Conference on Computer Vision and Pattern Recognition, vol. 2, pp. 2169–2178. IEEE (2006)

30. Lee, G.G., Lin, H.F.: Customer perceptions of e-service quality in online shopping. Int. J. Retail Distrib. Manag. 33(2), 161–176 (2005)

31. Linden, G., Smith, B., York, J.: Amazon.com recommendations: item-to-item collaborative filtering. IEEE Internet Comput. 7(1), 76–80 (2003)

32. Liu, S., Feng, J., Song, Z., Zhang, T., Lu, H., Xu, C., Yan, S.: Hi, magic closet, tell me what to wear! In: Proceedings of the ACM Multimedia, pp. 619–628 (2012)

33. Luo, J., Ba, S., Zhang, H.: The effectiveness of online shopping characteristics and well-designed websites on satisfaction. MIS Q. 36(4), 1131–1144 (2012)

34. Mensink, T., Verbeek, J., Csurka, G.: Learning structured prediction models for interactive image labeling. In: 2011 IEEE Conference on Computer Vision and Pattern Recognition (CVPR), pp. 833–840. IEEE (2011)

35. Oliva, A., Torralba, A.: Modeling the shape of the scene: a holistic representation of the spatial envelope. Int. J. Comput. Vision 42(3), 145–175 (2001)

36. Park, C.H., Kim, Y.G.: Identifying key factors affecting consumer purchase behavior in an online shopping context. Int. J. Retail Distrib. Manag. 31(1), 16–29 (2003)

37. Poon, A., Maltzman, R., Taylor, J.: Method and system to recommend further items to a user of a network-based transaction facility upon unsuccessful transacting with respect to an item, US Patent 8,275,673, 25 Sep 2012

38. Rijmenam, M.: How amazon is leveraging big data (2016). https://datafloq.com/read/amazon-leveraging-big-data/517

39. Robillard, M.P., Walker, R.J., Zimmermann, T.: Recommendation systems for software engineering. IEEE Softw. 27(4), 80–86 (2010)

40. Schmitz, M., Bart, R., Soderland, S., Etzioni, O., et al.: Open language learning for information extraction. In: Proceedings of the 2012 Joint Conference on Empirical Methods in Natural Language Processing and Computational Natural Language Learning, pp. 523–534. Association for Computational Linguistics (2012)

41. Sigurbjörnsson, B., Van Zwol, R.: Flickr tag recommendation based on collective knowledge. In: Proceedings of the 17th International Conference on World Wide Web, pp. 327–336. ACM (2008)

42. Torralba, A., Oliva, A.: Statistics of natural image categories. Netw. Computat. Neural Syst. **14**(3), 391–412 (2003)

43. Varma, M., Zisserman, A.: A statistical approach to texture classification from single images. Int. J. Comput. Vision **62**(1–2), 61–81 (2005)

44. Wah, C., Belongie, S.: Attribute-based detection of unfamiliar classes with humans in the loop. In: Proceedings of the IEEE Conference on Computer Vision and Pattern Recognition, pp. 779–786 (2013)

45. Witten, I.H., Frank, E.: Data Mining: Practical Machine Learning Tools and Techniques. Morgan Kaufmann, San Francisco (2005)

46. Yamaguchi, K., Kiapour, M.H., Ortiz, L.E., Berg, T.L.: Parsing clothing in fashion photographs. In: 2012 IEEE Conference on Computer Vision and Pattern Recognition (CVPR), pp. 3570–3577. IEEE (2012)

47. Yue, Y., Wang, C., El-Arini, K., Guestrin, C.: Personalized collaborative clustering. In: Proceedings of the 23rd International Conference on World Wide Web, pp. 75–84. ACM (2014)

Why People Resist to Internet Finance

From the Perspective of Process Virtualization Theory

Zhengzheng Lin[1], Yulin Fang[2], Liang Liang[1], and Jun Li[1(✉)]

[1] University of Science and Technology of China, Hefei, China
{hana33,lliang,lijun23}@mail.ustc.edu.cn
[2] City University of Hong Kong, Kowloon Tong, Hong Kong
ylfang@cityu.edu.hk

Abstract. With the advancements of information technology, internet finance as a IT-enabled virtualization of business process has gain a fast-growing marketplace. However, little is known about why there is still a widely reluctance to use internet finance. Based on process virtualization theory and user resistance literature, we postulate a research model of user's resistance to internet finance by integrating the process characteristic factors, external influence and internal influence of user. Finally, we discuss the potential contributions and limitations of the study, as well as ideas about related future research. Throughout the study, we use the process virtualization theory as a means of integrating discussion and survey approach is chosen to collect data and empirically test the model in future research. The potential theoretical contributions are mainly made to user resistance literature and internet finance implementation. Meanwhile this study provides explanations of why certain users tend to resist to internet fiancé while others not.

Keywords: User resistance · Internet finance · IT-enabled virtualization

1 Introduction

In this new era of information technology, more and more processes, previously performed through physical channels, are migrated virtually via information technology in the last decade [1, 2]. For example, financial banking processes are performed increasingly through internet channels, rather than through bank branches [2]. However, in spite of a fast-growing marketplace, internet finance as an IT-enabled virtualization of business process has encountered a reluctance to use from user community.

User resistance, which is identified by various IS research as the primary reason for IS failure [3, 4], becomes a salient problem for researchers to investigate. Although the drivers and manifestations of user resistance have been extensively studied in previous literature [5–7], those studies mainly rest on the conceptual level. Besides, while most of those studies focus on user resistance in mandatory organizational settings, few research probe into the user resistance in the context of discretionary use such as internet finance. Moreover, there is paucity of empirical study in the field of user resistance [7]. Hence this empirical study is set out to investigate our central research question:

© Springer International Publishing Switzerland 2016
F.F.-H. Nah and C.-H. Tan (Eds.): HCIBGO 2016, Part I, LNCS 9751, pp. 437–445, 2016.
DOI: 10.1007/978-3-319-39396-4_40

- What factors affect user's resistance to internet finance?

In order to address the research question, we build our research on process virtualization theory (PVT) and user resistance literature. By integrating the factors identified in PVT and user resistance literature, we posit that (a) process characteristics—sensory requirement, relationship requirement, synchronism requirement, identification and control requirement, and perceived risk, (b) external influence—perceived critical mass, and (c) internal influence—self-efficacy, will jointly influence user's resistance to internet finance.

The remainder of the paper is organized as follows. First, we review the existing literature on user resistance and PVT to discuss the theoretical foundation of this study. Our research model and hypotheses are then developed in the subsequent section, followed by a brief description of methodology. Finally, we discuss the potential theoretical and managerial implications of this study, as well as its limitations and directions for future research.

2   Theoretical Background

2.1   User Resistance

User resistance has received relatively little attention in literature when compared to user acceptance. In psychology research, user resistance is defined as an individual's tendency to avoid making changes [8] while in management research it has commonly been conceptualized as conduct that seeks to maintain the status quo or persistent avoidance of change [9].

In IS domain, resistance has been conceptualized as behaviors of users that intended to prevent the implementation and use of a new IS [10] or an adverse reaction to the changes associated with a new IS [3, 11]. However, as shown in Table 1, there is no consensus in the literature on how user resistance should be defined.

Recently user resistance has been conceptualized as a multidimensional construct, which contains five basic elements (i.e. manifestations of resistance, subjects of resistance, object of resistance, perceived threats, and initial conditions) [7, 17]. Generally, user resistance can be defined as behaviors occur following perceptions of changes associated with the interaction between user and IT. In this study, user resistance refers to the opposition of a user to perform a specific process virtually.

Although there has been more attention in IS domain paid to user resistance, existing studies on user resistance tend to be more conceptual. There is a dominance of case studies which only enumerate the manifestations and drivers of user resistance [7] in this area. However, the little empirical studies on user resistance [11, 18] usually investigate resistance only in mandatory organizational settings [19]. Therefore, this study is set our to explore and empirically the antecedents of user resistance of IT-enabled virtualization.

Table 1. Definition of user resistance

Conceptualization	Definition	Citation
A behavior	Behaviors intended to prevent the implementation or use of a system or to prevent system designers from achieving their objectives	[10]
	An adverse reaction to a proposed change, which may manifest itself in a visible, overt, fashion or may be less obvious and covert	[3]
	IS Avoidance: The individual has the opportunity and even the need, but consciously circumvents using the system	[12]
Cognition	A cognitive force precluding potential behavior	[13]
A psychological state	A normal psychological reaction when a person perceives the consequences of an IT implementation as negative	[14]
An organizational disruption	A signal from a system in equilibrium that the costs of change are perceived as greater than the likely benefits	[15]
A process	A two-phase process: an initial phase that is cognitive or emotional and a second one consisting of the decision to resist	[16]

2.2 Process Virtualization Theory

We adopt the process virtualization theory (PVT) to build the theoretical foundation for investigating the causes of user resistance. PVT was proposed by Overby to explain and predict whether a process is amenable or resistant to being conducted virtually [20]. PVT analyzes the "virtualizability" of a process from the user's perspective while "virtualizability" here describes whether and to what extent a process can be carried out virtually after the traditional physical interaction between people or between people and objects has been removed" [20].

Here the process is widely defined as a set of steps to achieve certain objective [20] and transitions of processes via physical channels to virtual channels through the media of information technology are referred as IT enabled process virtualization. For example, the migration of shopping to the online shopping, the migration of education to e-learning, and the migration of financial banking to Internet finance are various forms of IT-enabled virtualization.

According to PVT, there are four main factors that will negatively influence the virtualizability of a process: (a) sensory requirement—"the need for process participants to be able to enjoy a full sensory experience of the process, other participants, and objects", (b) relationship requirement—"the need for process participants to interact with one another in a social or professional context", (c) synchronism requirement—"the degree to which the activities that make up a process need to occur quickly with

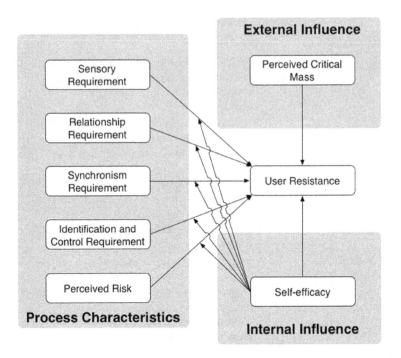

Fig. 1. Research model

minimal delay", and (d) identification and control requirement—"the degree to which the process requires unique identification of process participants and the ability to exert control over/influence their behavior" [20]. In other words, if any of these requirements increases, the process will become less amenable and more resistant to being conducted virtually.

Although PVT provides great insights for understanding the phenomenon of IT-enabled virtualization, there is paucity of empirically research following this stream. Only Overby and Konsynski [1], and Balci [2] provide quantitative evidence of PVT. Hence we will bring fresh insights for PVT by adopting and empirically validating it in the context of IT-enabled virtualization.

3   Research Model

Based on PVT and literature on user resistance, we propose the research model of user resistance to internet finance as depicted in Fig. 1.

3.1   Sensory Requirement

In this study, sensory requirement is defined as the degree to which users need to enjoy a full sensory experience of internet finance. Sensory experiences not only include tasting, seeing, hearing, smelling, and touching other process participants or objects, it also includes the overall sensation that participants feel when engaging in a process (e.g., excitement, vulnerability) [20]. In IT-enabled virtualization, sensory requirement become salient as the lack of physical interaction usually makes it hard for users to establish a sensory connection to other people, objects, and the process. Although the advancements of IT have facilitated the sensory virtualizations of internet finance to some extent, there are still some virtualizations cannot meet user's requirement of sensory connections. For example, users will gain the sense of accomplishment when they complete their financial business in traditional physical setting, e.g. bank branch. Such sensation associated with conducting the act in person is difficult to replicate in the IT-enabled virtualization. Thus, if users need to enjoy a high level of sensory experience that internet finance may fail to provide, they will tent to resist to internet finance. Therefore we propose:

- H1. Sensory requirement will positively influence user's resistance to internet finance.

3.2 Relationship Requirement

Relationship requirement here is defined as the degree to which users need to interact with one another in a social or professional context when conducting business through internet finance. Interaction in a social or professional context is suggested to trigger knowledge acquisition, trust, and friendship development [20]. Previous literature indicated that the communication cues, such as gestures and posture, in physical interaction will help express the interpersonal attentiveness and thus facilitate the relationship development [21]. Accordingly, the lack of those communication cues in internet finance will make it difficult for users to fulfill their relationship requirement. For example, due to the complexity of internet finance, users will be more reassured to confirm the details of financial product through interaction with bank clerks rather than peruse the terms and conditions of the product by themselves. Besides, if users want to build a long-term relationship with financial providers, they will find it harder to build it virtually in internet finance. Similar to users with high sensory requirement, users with high requirement of relationship will tend to resist internet finance. Hence, we propose:

- H2. Relationship requirement will positively influence user's resistance to internet finance.

3.3 Synchronism Requirement

In this study, synchronism requirement refers to the degree to which users need internet finance to occur quickly with minimum delay. While synchronism is naturally associated with financial business in physical settings, there is usually some extent of delay in internet finance. For example, users are often asked to submit their transaction request first and wait for the review process and final approval when they conduct financial businesses through internet finance. If user needs certain process to be conducted in a synchronous manner as in traditional physical settings, internet finance will likely be resisted. Hence we propose:

- H3. Synchronism requirement will positively influence user's resistance to internet finance.

3.4 Identification and Control Requirement

In this study, identification and control requirement is defined as the degree to which internet finance requires unique identification of participants and the ability to exert control/influence over their behavior. Previous literature argued that it is important to know the identity of the other party when developing a relationship [20]. However, since users cannot physically inspect others to confirm their identity in IT-enabled virtualization, many virtualized processes failed to satisfy the identification and control requirement [20]. In internet finance, it is difficult to detect who is engaging in the process and even possible for other people to hide their identity. For example, users that prefer purchasing financial products from experienced professionals cannot identify who is actually handling their business when using internet finance. For this reason, users with high requirement of identification and control tend to resist to the virtualization. Therefore, we propose:

- H4. Identification and control requirement will positively influence user's resistance to internet finance.

3.5 Perceived Risk

Perceived risk refers to the degree of risk associated with the IT-enabled virtualization perceived by users. It has long been established that perceived risk is a prominent barrier to the acceptance and diffusion of new IS. Gerrard and colleagues [22] found that the most frequently mentioned reason of why certain users resist internet finance is the risk associated with the service. Compared to physical processes, users may even perceive that they will face more uncertainties if they conduct financial businesses virtually through internet finance [23]. Specifically, users often perceive high level of risk associated with the performance of adopting new IS [24] and expect a negative outcome of using it [25], which eventually lead to resistance. Hence we consider perceived risk as a prominent factor that will positively affect user resistance to internet finance and propose:

- H5. Perceived risk will positively influence user's resistance to internet finance.

3.6 Perceived Critical Mass

As the external influence of user, perceived critical mass in this study is defined as the degree to which a user believes that most of his or her peers/friends/relatives are using internet finance. Unlike subjective norm. perceived critical mass indicate the observed aggregate behaviors in user's personal network, rather than only focus on the expectation from user's important others [26]. It is proposed that the larger the proportion of individuals in one's personal network that are engaged in certain innovation behavior, the more likely the individual will act the same behavior [27]. In other word, under social pressure associated by perceived critical mass, users will tend to alleviate their resistance towards IT-enabled virtualization. Therefore, we propose:

- H6. Perceived critical mass will negatively influence user's resistance to internet finance.

3.7 Self-efficacy

As an internal influence, self-efficacy here is defined as an individual's confidence in his or her own ability to adapt to internet finance (i.e., ways of perform tasks with internet finance). User's self-efficacy is considered as a crucial internal factor that can enhance feelings of control [11] since whether difficulties of internet finance will be viewed as challenges to be mastered or threats to be avoided depending highly on it [28]. Users with a high level of self-efficacy are likely to have stronger capability to deal with the problems and difficulties of internet finance despite their various requirements. However, users with a low level of self-efficacy feel discouraged and may be more inclined to resist the virtualization because of their requirements of internet finance. Moreover, perceived risks will also be more manageable for users with high self-efficacy. Thus we propose both direct and indirect influence of self-efficacy on user resistance to internet finance:

- H7a. Self-efficacy will negatively influence user's resistance to internet finance.
- H7b. Self-efficacy will weaken the influence of sensory requirement on user's resistance to internet finance.
- H7c. Self-efficacy will weaken the influence of relationship requirement on user's resistance to internet finance.
- H7d. Self-efficacy will weaken the influence of synchronism requirement on user's resistance to internet finance.
- H7e. Self-efficacy will weaken the influence of identification and control requirement on user's resistance to internet finance.
- H7f. Self-efficacy will weaken the influence of perceived risk on user's resistance to internet finance.

4 Methodology

4.1 Research Design

To analyze the above research model, survey approach is chosen to collect data and empirically test the model. We will gather our data by asking informants who are familiar with conduct financial businesses, either through physical channels or internet finance, to complete the questionnaires. Measurement of all the constructs in our research model will be adopted and adapted from existing validated scales [1, 2, 26, 29].

4.2 Data Analysis

Partial least squares (PLS) is selected to evaluate the proposed model and hypotheses. It is suitable for assessing theories in the early development stages [30] and is appropriate for small to medium sample sizes [31].

5   Potential Contribution and Future Work

Based on process virtualization theory and user resistance literature, this study serves as an initial attempt to investigate the factors that influence user resistance to internet finance. The potential theoretical contributions of this study are mainly made to user resistance literature. As seldom studies investigate user resistance at individual level in discretionary settings, we apply process virtualization theory framework to an internet finance setting and introduce perceived risk as additional process characteristic, perceived critical mass as external influence and self-efficacy as internal influence of user.

This study has potential practical implications as well. It provides explanations of why users resist to internet finance in spite of all the advantages it provides. It could be used to derive recommendations for overcoming some implement problems of internet finance services.

However, this study has some limitations. It presents a relatively simplified picture of the complex phenomenon of user resistance. In future research, we can take the service quality into account to develop further understanding. Moreover, we can go beyond internet finance and probe into the influences of those factors on other IT-enabled virtualization.

References

1. Overby, E.M., Konsynski, B.: Task-technology fit and process virtualization theory: an integrated model and empirical test. Emory Public Law Research Paper, pp. 10–96 (2010)
2. Balci, B.: Why people reject or use virtual processes: understanding the variance of users' resistance (2015)
3. Hirschheim, R., Newman, M.: Information systems and user resistance: theory and practice. Comput. J. **31**(5), 398–408 (1988)
4. Laumer, S., Eckhardt, A.: Why do people reject technologies: a review of user resistance theories, in Information systems theory. In: Dwivedi, Y.K., Wade, M.R., Schneberger, S.L. (eds.) Information Systems Theory, pp. 63–86. Springer, New York (2012)
5. Jiang, J.J., Muhanna, W.A., Klein, G.: User resistance and strategies for promoting acceptance across system types. Inf. Manage. **37**(1), 25–36 (2000)
6. Joshi, K.: A model of users' perspective on change: the case of information systems technology implementation. MIS Q. **15**(2), 229–242 (1991)
7. Lapointe, L., Rivard, S.: A multilevel model of resistance to information technology implementation. MIS Q. **29**(3), 461–491 (2005)
8. Oreg, S.: Resistance to change: developing an individual differences measuer. J. Appl. Psychol. **88**(4), 680–693 (2003)

9. Bovey, W.H., Hede, A.: Resistance to organisational change: the role of defence mechanisms. J. Manag. Psychol. **16**(7), 534–548 (2001)
10. Markus, M.L.: Power, politics, and MIS implementation. Commun. ACM **26**(6), 430–444 (1983)
11. Kim, H.-W., Kankanhalli, A.: Investigating user resistance to information systems implementation: a status quo bias perspective. MIS Q. **33**(3), 567–582 (2009)
12. Kane, G.C., Labianca, G.: IS avoidance in health-care groups: a multilevel investigation. Inf. Syst. Res. **22**(3), 504–522 (2011)
13. Bhattacherjee, A., Hikmet, N.: Physicians' resistance toward healthcare information technology: a theoretical model and empirical test. Eur. J. Inf. Syst. **16**(6), 725–737 (2007)
14. Ang, J., Pavri, F.: A survey and critique of the impacts of information technology. Int. J. Inf. Manage. **14**(2), 122–133 (1994)
15. Keen, P.G.W.: Information systems and organizational change. Commun. ACM **24**(1), 24–33 (1981)
16. Ferneley, E.H., Sobreperez, P.: Resist, comply or workaround? an examination of different facets of user engagement with information systems. Eur. J. Inf. Syst. **15**(4), 345–356 (2006)
17. Rivard, S., Lapointe, L.: Information technology implementers' responses to user resistance: nature and effects. MIS Q. **36**(3), 897–A5 (2012)
18. Kim, H.-W.: The effects of switching costs on user resistance to enterprise systems implementation. IEEE Trans. Eng. Manage. **58**(3), 471–482 (2011)
19. Barth, M., Veit, D.: Electronic service delivery in the public sector: understanding the variance of citizens' resistance. In: 2011 44th Hawaii International Conference on System Sciences (HICSS). IEEE (2011)
20. Overby, E.: Process virtualization theory and the impact of information technology. Organ. Sci. **19**(2), 277–291 (2008)
21. Jarvenpaa, S.L., Leidner, D.E.: Communication and trust in global virtual teams. Organ. Sci. **10**(6), 791–815 (1999)
22. Gerrard, P., BartonCunningham, J., Devlin, J.F.: Why consumers are not using internet banking: a qualitative study. J. Serv. Mark. **20**(3), 160–168 (2006)
23. Akinci, S., Aksoy, S., Atilgan, E.: Adoption of internet banking among sophisticated consumer segments in an advanced developing country. Int. J. Bank Mark. **22**(3), 212–232 (2004)
24. Garcia, R., Bardhi, F., Friedrich, C.: Overcoming consumer resistance to innovation. MIT Sloan Manage. Rev. **48**(4), 82 (2007)
25. Martinko, M.J., Zmud, R.W., Henry, J.W.: An attributional explanation of individual resistance to the introduction of information technologies in the workplace. Behav. Inf. Technol. **15**(5), 313–330 (1996)
26. Lou, H., Luo, W., Strong, D.: Perceived critical mass effect on groupware acceptance. Eur. J. Inf. Syst. **9**(2), 91–103 (2000)
27. Valente, T.W.: Network models of the diffusion of innovations. Comput. Math. Organ. Theor. **2**, 163–164 (1995)
28. Bandura, A.: Self-efficacy in Changing Societies. Cambridge University Press, New York (1995)
29. Balci, B., Grgecic, D., Rosenkranz, C.: Why people reject or use virtual processes: a test of process virtualization theory (2013)
30. Fornell, C., Bookstein, F.L.: Two structural equation models: LISREL and PLS applied to consumer exit-voice theory. J. Mark. Res. **19**, 440–452 (1982)
31. Chin, W.W.: The partial least squares approach to structural equation modeling. Mod. Methods Bus. Res. **295**(2), 295–336 (1998)

How Does the Device Change Your Choice: A Goal-Activation Perspective

Yang Liu[1]($\boxtimes$) and Deliang Wang[2]

[1] National University of Singapore, 15 Computing Drive, Singapore 117418, Singapore
yangliu@comp.nus.edu.sg
[2] Institute of High Performance Computing,
1 Fusionopolis Way, #16-16 Connexis, Singapore 138632, Singapore
wangdl@ihpc.a-star.edu.sg

Abstract. Mobile channel has contributed more and more traffic and sales in the online market. Despite considerable empirical investigations on sales across multiple devices, questions remain as to whether and how devices would influence consumer judgment and choice. Drawing on the Goal-Activation Theory and Decision System Theory, we posit that tablets trigger experiential goals and thus lead to preference for hedonic products; however, PCs and laptops trigger instrumental goals and thus lead to preference for utilitarian products. The effect is mediated by the decision system (relying on feelings vs. relying on logic). Data collected from an online experiment supported our hypotheses. Overall, this paper explains and demonstrates why the device would change consumer decision system and preference and the findings would benefit both researchers and practitioners.

Keywords: Mobile commerce · Consumer decision · Affective computing

1 Introduction

With the development of mobile technology, people could shop on various devices, e.g., tablet, PC, laptop, and smart phone. According to IBM, during 2015 Valentine's week, the mobile devices (tablets and smart phones) contribute to 46.5 % of online traffic and the conversion rate of tablets is catching up with PCs [1]. Despite the popularity of mobile commerce, it is found that consumers tend to behave differently when shopping on different devices. For example, Han et al. [2] found that consumers bought more distinct products after adopting iPad. It was also found that the types of products people bought online also varied by devices. Approximately 50 % of PC and tablet owners purchased clothing and accessories on their devices, compared to just 28 % of mobile phone users; 49 % of PC owners purchased electronics on their PC, compared to 41 % of tablet owners, and just 21 % of mobile phone users. It motives us to investigate whether and why consumer's preference and decision might be influenced by the device they are using.

Why do people purchase different products with different devices? Prior literature indicates that many factors could contribute to this phenomenon, e.g., information

© Springer International Publishing Switzerland 2016
F.F.-H. Nah and C.-H. Tan (Eds.): HCIBGO 2016, Part I, LNCS 9751, pp. 446–456, 2016.
DOI: 10.1007/978-3-319-39396-4_41

accessibility, device portability, device use context and trust in the platform [3]. Despite these factors, one potentially underestimated factor is the nature of the device and the concepts the device represents. A series of empirical studies have demonstrated that abstract concepts activated by unrelated tasks would play an important role in human judgment and decision making. For example, using words such as "support" and "share" to construct sentences can activate the concept of "cooperation", leading people to sacrifice personal benefits for the public good subsequently [4]. Similarly, consumers are more likely to choose a high-priced option after being exposed to words invoking prestige goals in an irrelevant sentence correction task [5]. Although people could shop on both tablets and PCs and sometimes use the devices interchangeably, they use the two devices quite differently in their daily life. Tablets are mainly for entertainment purpose while PCs are more for work purpose. Therefore, a device might convey specific information, which may activate different goals and thus influence consumer judgment and decision making.

Hence, this article seeks to enhance the understanding of how the device affects consumer decision system (reliance on feelings vs. reliance on logic during decision making tasks) and product choice (hedonic products vs. utilitarian products) from a goal-activation perspective. In particular, we predict that as people typically use tablets for entertainment, tablets may activate experiential goals; in contrast, as people typically use PCs for in-depth thinking and rigorous work, PCs may activate instrumental goals. Prior literature suggests that these goals will influence which system (feelings vs. logic) would dominate in the decision making process [6]. Therefore, we further predict that on tablets, consumers are more likely to rely on feelings than those using PCs. Consequently, they are more likely to choose a hedonic option.

The remaining paper is organized as follows. First, we review literature on consumer purchasing behavior across devices, goal-activation and consumer decision system theories. Drawing on these theories, we develop our hypotheses, followed by the description of methodology and the report of data analysis results. Lastly, contributions and limitations of this study are discussed.

2   Literature Review

2.1   Consumer Behavior with Different Devices

As smartphones and tablets are increasingly growing in popularity, it becomes imperative for firms and researchers to understand how consumers browse and make decisions on various devices. In particular, tablets provide a balance between portability and navigational convenience. They become an importance channel for e-commerce. Prior literature indicates that at the macro level tablet channel acts as a substitute for the PC channel but a complement for the smartphone channel [7]. At the micro level, mobile-device consumers are found to be more likely to undertake simple decision-making tasks [8]. Moreover, they tend to browse products casually, which leads to the purchase of more impulse and diverse products [7]. However, it is unknown that whether people would make different decisions on different devices when facing the same choice set.

Many factors might contribute to difference in browsing patterns and purchasing behavior on different devices. For example, Bang et al. [9] identified usability and ubiquity as core features that distinguished the mobile channel from traditional channel. Other differences between tablets and PCs include platform safety, interaction modes (touchscreen vs. mouse), use context [3, 10, 11]. Tablets are believed to be less safe but provide better sensory experience than PCs. Despite these features, a tablet is usually regarded as a hedonic product while a PC is usually regarded as a utilitarian product. Thus, they may activate different shopping goals and mindset when consumer shop with them. As prior literature suggests that consumer decision and choice are driven by goals, in this study, we try to understand the effects of the device (tablets vs. PCs) from a goal-activation perspective. We aim to investigate whether tablets and PCs could trigger different shopping goals and subsequently influence consumer decision process and final choice.

2.2 Goal-Activation Theory

Goals are an increasingly important concept in consumer behavior. Goals can influence what information we attend to, what attribute we use to make a decision and what product category is considered [12]. The Goal-Activation Theory views goals as knowledge structures in long-term memory [4, 13]. As goals are not purely independent but interconnected with concepts in mind, exposure to any of these concepts can spontaneously trigger the goal, which in turn guides subsequent behavior [14]. For example, Zhou and Pham [15] found that evaluating financial products such as individual stocks in trading accounts would trigger a promotion focus, whereas evaluating financial products such as mutual funds in retirement accounts would trigger a prevention focus. Similarly, using words such as "memory" and "impression" to construct sentence could activate different information processing goals (memorization vs. impression formation), thus leading to different information processing pattern [16]. These and similar findings all provide support for the underlying notion that goals are cognitive structures that can be activated on exposure to associated concepts stored in memory, thus influencing subsequent behavior.

In particular, experiential goals and instrumental goals are two types of goals consumers hold when making purchase decisions [17]. Driven by experiential goals, consumers seek for experiential satisfaction, which leads to preference for luxuries, hedonic products and affect-rich products. On the contrary, driven by functional goals, consumers seek for utility, which leads to necessities, utilitarian products and affect-poor products [18]. As people usually use tablets for entertainment and use PCs or laptops for work, the stereotype of tablet is hedonic and the stereotype of PC or laptop is utilitarian. Hence, the device may unconsciously trigger different shopping goals, which would guide consumer decision process and influence their preference and choice.

2.3 Consumer Decision System

How do consumers choose whether to have a rich, creamy Häagen Dazs ice cream as a dessert or a healthy but perhaps less tasty bowl of fresh juice? It is decided either in a cognitive, logic-based way or in an affective, feeling-based way [6, 19, 20]. When people make decisions relying on cognition and logic, they tend to assess, weigh, and combine attribute information into an overall evaluative judgment. In contrast, when people make decisions relying on feelings, they tend to inspect their momentary feelings. The dominant decision system (feelings or logic) will determine consumer choice. Whether people rely on feelings or rely on logic is dependent on several factors, which could be grouped into five categories, i.e., the salience of the feelings, the representativeness of the feelings for the target, the relevance of the feelings to the judgment, the evaluative malleability of the judgment, and the level of processing intensity [21]. In particular, it has been found that consumers are more likely to rely on their feelings in making a decision when their processing resources are limited or when they have an experiential consumption goal. In contrast, consumers are more likely to engage in cognitive, logic-based decision making when they have an instrumental consumption goal [6, 22]. Therefore, as the device might trigger different goals, it would lead to different level of reliance on feelings when consumers are making decisions.

Decision system has several impacts on consumer judgement and preference. For example, prior literature suggests that compared to judgments based on the logic-based system, judgments based on the affective system tend to be rendered faster, more polarized, more holistic, more context dependent and less sensitive to numerical quantities [23, 24]. Moreover, reliance on feelings will lead consumers to an affectively-superior product and luxurious option [17]. Therefore, decision system is a helpful way to explain consumer judgment and decision.

3 Hypothesis Development

Drawing on goal-activation theory and consumer decision system theory, we propose our research model as below (Fig. 1).

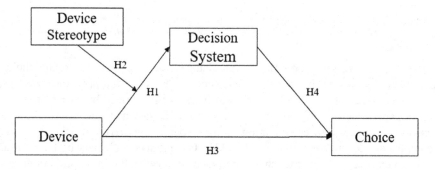

Fig. 1. Research model

Because of the marketing positioning of PC and tablet as well as individual device usage, people may think a tablet is more experiential and a PC is more instrumental. Flurry [25] reported that people spent more than 70 % of their time on games (32 %), social networking (more than 25 %) and other entertainment tasks (e.g., photo, watch video) (more than 15 %) when using mobile devices. Time spent on utility and productivity only took around 12 %. As our initial perceptions of objects, both conscious and unconscious, are stored in memory and are simulated or played back on subsequent encounters, we may naturally activate experiential goals when exposed to tablets. Similarly, as PCs and laptops are utility tools, people may naturally link them with work, in-depth thinking and responsibility, which further activate instrumental goals. Prior study indicates that these goals would influence consumer decision system, i.e., among consumers that have experiential motive (compared to consumers with instrumental motive), feelings will play a more important role in consumer decision making [6]. Therefore, people making decisions on tablets, who have stronger experiential motive, will be more likely to rely on feelings. When holding the experiential tablet, consumers might naturally step into a "relax" mode, which constrains their deliberate thinking. Therefore, we propose that

H1: Compared with consumers who make decisions on PCs, consumers making decisions on tablets are more likely to rely on feelings.

Furthermore, as with other cognitive structures, the extent to which object exposure evokes a goal and guides subsequent behavior appears to differ across people as a function of the strength of the goal–object association [26]. For example, Sengupta and Zhou [27] found that hedonically tempting food, such as chocolate could activate a promotion focus and influence subsequent food choice in a completely unrelated choice task. However, this effect only existed among people who are impulsive eaters. They argued that this was because only for impulsive eaters, there was an automatic link between hedonically tempting food and promotion focus. Similarly, people may hold different perception towards the digital devices. For users who also work on tablets and have fun on PCs or laptops, their perception of device stereotype is much weaker. Hence, the automatic link between the device and experiential goals is weaker. As a consequence, the device would not have much impact on their decision system. Therefore, we propose that

H2: The effect of the device on the decision system is moderated by perception of device stereotype. That is, for consumers who have stronger device stereotype beliefs, the effect would be stronger.

We further investigate how the device changes consumer preference and choice. Recent years saw a surge of interest in consumer hedonic vs. utilitarian choice. Hedonic products are ones whose consumption is primarily characterized by an affective and sensory experience of aesthetic or sensual pleasure, fantasy and fun; while utilitarian products are ones whose consumption is more cognitively driven, instrumental, and accomplishes a functional or practical task [31]. One product could have both utilitarian benefits, i.e., functional, instrumental, and practical benefits of consumption offerings, as well as hedonic benefits, i.e., aesthetic, experiential, and enjoyment-related benefits [17, 28, 29]. As we posit that tablets could activate experiential consumption goals while PCs could activate functional consumption goals, it is conceivable that consumers using tablets might have a higher chance to select a hedonic option than consumers using PCs or laptops. Therefore, we propose that

H3: Consumers making decisions on tablets are more likely to choose a hedonic option than consumers making decisions on PCs.

Despite the direct goal-activation effect, we also investigate the role of the decision system, which has always been recognized as an important antecedent in consumer decision making. Prior literature suggests that even when experiential goals are activated, consumers might not choose to indulge. For example, Kivetz and Simonson [30] found that consumers attached greater weight to the utilitarian (versus hedonic) dimension unless they believed that they had "earned" the right to indulge. Similarly, Okada [31] found that choice of hedonic option typically required much effort for justification when the "logic" system dominated. As the decision system theory suggests that relying on feelings leads to more holistic and impulsive decisions and the device would influence the dominance of the two systems (feelings vs. logic), we propose that

H4: The effect of the device on consumer preference for hedonic (vs. utilitarian) products is mediated by the decision system.

4 Methodology

4.1 Experimental Design

An experiment was conducted to test the hypotheses. To investigate the effects of the device on consumer decision system and choice, two responsive webpages were developed to present the hedonic product (Hotel A) and utilitarian product (Hotel B). Responsive web design is an approach aimed at crafting sites to provide an optimal viewing experience—easy reading and navigation with a minimum of resizing, panning, and scrolling—across a wide range of devices (from desktop computer monitors to mobile phones). Subjects were asked to browse information about the two hotels either on a PC or on a tablet and make a choice between the two.

On each page, we provided a short description about the hotel, eight images (four of them presented hotel facilities and four of them presented room facilities), textual location, facility and service information, as well as scores on general services, location, room facilities, food and drinks, activities, hotel facilities. Prior literature suggests that consumers judge the utility of a hotel based on location characteristics (e.g., near places of interest, near public transportation, near downtown) and service characteristics (e.g., hotel class, number of internal amenities) [32]. Therefore, Hotel A, which represented the hedonically-superior option, was featured as newly-built, uniquely-decorated, but far from downtown and providing limited services and room space; Hotel B, which represented the utility-superior option, was featured as less modern and aesthetic, but with good location and services and large room space.

4.2 Sample and Experimental Procedures

We recruited 80 participants from Amazon Mechanical Turk in total. Prior literature suggests that Amazon Mechanical Turk is a reliable way for data collection [33]. 40 participants were asked to complete the task on a PC or a laptop and 40 participants were asked to complete the task on a tablet. We added verification code on our experiment website, i.e., if the participants were not using the device as required to complete the task, they could not access the webpages and subsequent survey link.

The participants were instructed to browse two hotel webpages and make a choice between the two in the scenario that they would be travelling to Singapore. After they made their decision, they would be redirected to an online questionnaire. In the questionnaire, we first measured their hotel choice and how they made the decision, i.e., relying on feelings or relying on logic, adapted from Chang and Pham [34]. This was followed by a four-item scale measuring arousal [35] and a three-item scale measuring task involvement [36], captured as control variables. Lastly, we asked participants how they perceived the two hotels (utilitarian or hedonic) and how they perceived the device stereotype, i.e., to what extent they categorized PC as a utilitarian product and tablet as a hedonic product.

5 Data Analysis

We first checked whether the two hotels differ in terms of hedonic/utilitarian characteristics. Before asking the participants to evaluate the hotels, we gave definitions on hedonic product and utilitarian product. On a seven-point scale, participants indicated the extent to which they categorized Hotel A as hedonic (1 = "utilitarian," and 7 = "hedonic"). We repeated the same question for Hotel B. The t-test showed that Hotel A was a more hedonic option compared with Hotel B (5.18 vs. 4.19, $t(79) = 3.891$, $p < 0.05$). Self-reported task involvement, arousal, device stereotype did not differ between the tablet group and PC/laptop group (all $p > 0.05$).

We first analyzed whether the device had an impact on the decision system. The decision system was measured on two 7-point agree-disagree items [34]: (1) I made my decision of which hotel to stay based on overall feelings towards the hotel; (2) I made my decision of which hotel to stay based on the logical balance of pros and cons of living in the hotel. Responses to these two items were combined into a composite scale in which lower scores indicated greater reliance on logic assessment and higher scores indicated greater reliance on feelings. ANOVA result shows that on tablets (mean = 4.28), participants were more likely to rely on feelings than participants who completed the task on PCs (mean = 3.73, $F(1,78) = 9.354$, $p < 0.05$). As consumer decision system is also contingent on situational emotional state, we did ANCOVA with arousal ($\alpha = 0.75$) and task involvement ($\alpha = 0.847$) as control variables. Result showed that after controlling for these factors, the device still had an impact on decision system ($F(1,76) = 8.125$, $p = 0.012 < 0.05$). Therefore, H1 was supported.

To further investigate whether the impact of the device on the decision system was dependent on device stereotype, we conducted regression analysis. Device stereotype was measured on two 7-point items: (1) To what extent do you think laptop/PC is Utilitarian/Hedonic? (1-utilitarian, 7-hedonic) (2) To what extent do you think tablet is Utilitarian/Hedonic? (1-utilitarian, 7-hedonic). A composite scale was calculated in which lower scores indicated stronger device stereotype perception. Results of regression showed a significant main effect of device ($b = -1.49$, $t(76) = -3.68$, $p < 0.05$)

and interaction effect of the device and device stereotype on the decision system ($b = 1.23$, $t(76) = 2.98$, $p < 0.05$). No significant result of device stereotype on the decision system was detected. A median-split regression showed that when people had stronger stereotype perception, the effect of the device on the decision system would be stronger, which supported H2.

A logistic regression was performed to ascertain the effect of the device on preference for hedonic (vs. utilitarian) products. The result showed that consumers who made decisions on tablets were more likely to choose the hedonic option ($p < 0.05$). Therefore, H3 was also supported.

Lastly, we tested the mediation effect of the decision system. We performed 5000 bootstrap resamples using Preacher and Hayes's [37] SPSS macro, as recommended by Zhao et al. [38], to test the indirect path (i.e., the path from the device to choice via decision system). The results showed that the device influenced the decision system ($b = -0.55$, $p < 0.05$) and the choice ($b = -0.99$, $p = 0.03 < 0.05$) and the decision system influenced the choice ($b = 0.80$, $p < 0.05$). Given that the bias-corrected 95 % confidence interval did not include zero (-1.18 to -0.06) and that the significance of the effect of the device was reduced ($b = *-0.99$ to $b = -0.67$) after including the decision system, we concluded that the decision system mediates the effect of the device on the choice.

6 Discussion

6.1 Contributions

This study offers several theoretical contributions. First, it shows the device has an impact on consumer preference. Though industry data and prior research indicate that product categories purchased from tablets and PCs are quite different, it is largely due to value of the products, trust in mobile payment, product accessibility on both channels, etc. We provide a new perspective to understand this phenomenon, i.e., a goal-activation perspective. In particular, we show that even when the above factors are kept constant, the device still has an impact on consumer choice. Second, we explain this effect with decision system theory. Our study shows that tablets activate experiential goals, which further lead to feeling-based thinking and hedonic choice; in contrast, PCs activate instrumental goals, which further lead to logic-based thinking and utilitarian choice. It enriches the literature on decision system theory by showing that decision system could not only be influenced by salience of feelings and information processing intensity, but also by contextual factors, such as the device.

Our findings are also important for practitioners. As we found that consumers concerned more about hedonic dimensions on tablets, retailer should highlight the hedonic aspects of their products or present more hedonic products on mobile channels. Our findings indicate that mobile platforms might be a better channel for hedonic product marketing. In addition, when designing for different portals, a more entertaining portal might benefit mobile users more while a more functional portal might benefit PC users more. That is, affective design would benefit the mobile channel more. For consumers, they may need to be cautious that tablets may lead to hedonic seeking, impulsivity and self-regulation failure, especially for those who often play games and use entertainment apps on tablets.

6.2   Limitations and Future Directions

There are some limitations of this study. First, we recruited our subjects from Amazon Mechanical Turk. Since we required subjects to complete the task on tablet in one condition and participants could choose whether to complete the task voluntarily, there might be a selection bias although our result showed that there was not much difference in the two groups in terms of device usage. Second, we propose that the device influences the decision system and the choice because different devices (i.e., tablets and PCs) activate different concepts represented in mind. In this study we use device stereotype to capture "device-consumption goal" link strength. However, a more rigorous way is to use IAT test [39]. In addition, this study did not consider cross-device browsing and purchasing behavior although nowadays people typically own more than one digital devices and use them interchangeably for online shopping.

As our experiment provides initial evidence that the device affects the consumer decision system, we could further investigate whether more affective interface design would benefit the mobile channel more. For example, we could investigate whether providing the same product information with different webpage designs would change consumer judgment. We expect to see that the device would moderate the effect of webpage aesthetics on product evaluation. In particular, the positive effect of webpage aesthetics on product evaluation would be more salient on tablets. In addition, as feeling-based processing and logic-based processing differ in terms of speed, consistency and regulation focus, we consider collecting objective data to investigate whether the effect of the device on the choice could be explained by these factors. We could also investigate whether on mobile channels, consumers are more novelty-seeking, risk-tolerant, and impulsive.

Acknowledgement.   The work is supported by A*STAR Joint Council Office Development Programme "Social Technologies + Programme".

References

1. IBM: Love is in the air for online retailers. http://www-01.ibm.com/software/marketing-solutions/benchmark-hub/valentines-2015.html
2. Han, S.P., Ghose, A., Xu, K.: Mobile commerce in the new tablet economy. In: The 34th International Conference on Information Systems, Milan, Italy (2013)
3. Kourouthanassis, P.E., Giaglis, G.M.: Introduction to the special issue mobile commerce: the past, present, and future of mobile commerce research. Int. J. Electron. Comm. **16**(4), 5–18 (2012)
4. Bargh, J.A., Gollwitzer, P.M., Lee-Chai, A., Barndollar, K., Trötschel, R.: The automated will: nonconscious activation and pursuit of behavioral goals. J. Pers. Soc. Psychol. **81**(6), 1014–1027 (2001)

5. Chartrand, T.L., Huber, J., Shiv, B., Tanner, R.J.: Nonconscious goals and consumer choice. J. Consum. Res. **35**(2), 189–201 (2008)
6. Pham, M.T.: Representativeness, relevance, and the use of feelings in decision making. J. Consum. Res. **25**(2), 144–159 (1998)
7. Xu, K., Chan, J., Ghose, A., Han, S.: Battle of the channels: the impact of tablets on digital commerce. Manag. Sci. (2015, forthcoming)
8. Maity, M., Dass, M.: Consumer decision-making across modern and traditional channels: e-commerce, m-commerce, in-store. Decis. Support Syst. **61**, 34–46 (2014)
9. Bang, Y., Lee, D.-J., Han, K., Hwang, M., Ahn, J.-H.: Channel capabilities, product characteristics, and the impacts of mobile channel introduction. J. Manag. Inf. Syst. **30**(2), 101–126 (2013)
10. Brasel, S.A., Gips, J.: Tablets, touchscreens, and touchpads: how varying touch interfaces trigger psychological ownership and endowment. J. Consum. Psychol. **24**(2), 226–233 (2014)
11. Chong, A.Y.-L., Chan, F.T., Ooi, K.-B.: Predicting consumer decisions to adopt mobile commerce: cross country empirical examination between China and Malaysia. Decis. Support Syst. **53**(1), 34–43 (2012)
12. Garbarino, E., Johnson, M.S.: Effects of consumer goals on attribute weighting, overall satisfaction, and product usage. Psychol. Mark. **18**(9), 929–949 (2001)
13. Kruglanski, A.W., Shah, J.Y., Fishbach, A., Friedman, R., Chun, W.Y., Sleeth-Keppler, D.: A theory of goal systems. Adv. Exp. Soc. Psychol. **34**, 331–378 (2002)
14. Shah, J.Y., Kruglanski, A.W.: When opportunity knocks: bottom-up priming of goals by means and its effects on self-regulation. J. Pers. Soc. Psychol. **84**(6), 1109–1122 (2003)
15. Zhou, R., Pham, M.T.: Promotion and prevention across mental accounts: when financial products dictate consumers' investment goals. J. Consum. Res. **31**(1), 125–135 (2004)
16. Chartrand, T.L., Bargh, J.A.: Automatic activation of impression formation and memorization goals: nonconscious goal priming reproduces effects of explicit task instructions. J. Pers. Soc. Psychol. **71**(3), 464–478 (1996)
17. Dhar, R., Wertenbroch, K.: Consumer choice between hedonic and utilitarian goods. J. Mark. Res. **37**(1), 60–71 (2000)
18. Khan, U., Dhar, R., Wertenbroch, K.: A behavioral decision theory perspective on hedonic and utilitarian choice. In: Ratneshwar, S., Mick, D.G. (eds.) Inside Consumption: Frontiers of Research on Consumer Motives, Goals, and Desires, pp. 144–165 (2005)
19. Pacini, R., Epstein, S.: The relation of rational and experiential information processing styles to personality, basic beliefs, and the ratio-bias phenomenon. J. Pers. Soc. Psychol. **76**(6), 972–987 (1999)
20. Schwarz, N., Clore, G.L.: Feelings and phenomenal experiences. In: Social Psychology: Handbook of Basic Principles, vol. 2, pp. 385–407 (1996)
21. Greifeneder, R., Bless, H., Pham, M.T.: When do people rely on affective and cognitive feelings in judgment? A review. Pers. Soc. Psychol. Rev. **15**(2), 107–141 (2011)
22. Shiv, B., Fedorikhin, A.: Heart and mind in conflict: the interplay of affect and cognition in consumer decision making. J. Consum. Res. **26**(3), 278–292 (1999)
23. Lee, L., Amir, O., Ariely, D.: In search of homo economicus: cognitive noise and the role of emotion in preference consistency. J. Consum. Res. **36**(2), 173–187 (2009)
24. Hsee, C.K., Rottenstreich, Y.: Music, pandas, and muggers: on the affective psychology of value. J. Exp. Psychol. Gen. **133**(1), 23–30 (2004)
25. Flurry: Apps Solidify Leadership Six Years into the Mobile Revolution. http://flurrymobile.tumblr.com/post/115191864580/apps-solidify-leadership-six-years-into-the-mobile
26. Shah, J.: The motivational looking glass: how significant others implicitly affect goal appraisals. J. Pers. Soc. Psychol. **85**(3), 424–439 (2003)

27. Sengupta, J., Zhou, R.: Understanding impulsive eaters' choice behaviors: the motivational influences of regulatory focus. J. Mark. Res. **44**(2), 297–308 (2007)

28. Chitturi, R., Raghunathan, R., Mahajan, V.: Form versus function: how the intensities of specific emotions evoked in functional versus hedonic trade-offs mediate product preferences. J. Mark. Res. **44**(4), 702–714 (2007)

29. Voss, K.E., Spangenberg, E.R., Grohmann, B.: Measuring the hedonic and utilitarian dimensions of consumer attitude. J. Mark. Res. **40**(3), 310–320 (2003)

30. Kivetz, R., Simonson, I.: Self-control for the righteous: toward a theory of precommitment to indulgence. J. Consum. Res. **29**(2), 199–217 (2002)

31. Okada, E.M.: Justification effects on consumer choice of hedonic and utilitarian goods. J. Mark. Res. **42**(1), 43–53 (2005)

32. Ghose, A., Ipeirotis, P.G., Li, B.: Designing ranking systems for hotels on travel search engines by mining user-generated and crowdsourced content. Mark. Sci. **31**(3), 493–520 (2012)

33. Mason, W., Suri, S.: Conducting behavioral research on amazon's mechanical turk. Behav. Res. Meth. **44**(1), 1–23 (2012)

34. Chang, H.H., Pham, M.T.: Affect as a decision-making system of the present. J. Consum. Res. **40**(1), 42–63 (2013)

35. Mehrabian, A., Russell, J.A.: A measure of arousal seeking tendency. Environ. Behav. **5**(3), 315–333 (1973)

36. Mittal, B.: A comparative analysis of four scales of consumer involvement. Psychol. Mark. **12**(7), 663–682 (1995)

37. Preacher, K.J., Hayes, A.F.: Assessing mediation in communication research. In: The Sage Sourcebook of Advanced Data Analysis Methods for Communication Research, pp. 13–54 (2008)

38. Zhao, X., Lynch, J.G., Chen, Q.: Reconsidering Baron and Kenny: myths and truths about mediation analysis. J. Consum. Res. **37**(2), 197–206 (2010)

39. Greenwald, A.G., McGhee, D.E., Schwartz, J.L.: Measuring individual differences in implicit cognition: the implicit association test. J. Pers. Soc. Psychol. **74**(6), 1464–1480 (1998)

Interactive e-Branding in e-Commerce Interfaces: Survey Results and Implications

Dimitrios Rigas[✉] and Hammad Akhtar Hussain

University of West London, London W5 5RF, UK
{Dimitrios.Rigas,Hammad.Hussain}@uwl.ac.uk

Abstract. This paper explores user views on the way in which interactive e-branding techniques are perceived. A survey consisting of 100 respondents was contacted to address the questions relating to the topic. It was found that current techniques may improve the effectiveness, efficiency and user satisfaction. The paper discusses the findings and concludes with recommendations for further work to improve the overall user experience through interactivity. Virtual shopping assistance was also identified as a factor that can aid users further to resolve problems during their online engagement.

Keywords: Interactivity · e-Branding · e-Commerce interfaces · Effectiveness · Efficiency · User satisfaction · e-Loyalty · Virtual shopping assistants

1 Introduction

According to the Office of the National Statistics, £716.0 million was spent weekly in June 2014. This represents a rise of 11.2 % as compared to June 2013 [1]. Additionally, spending was increased in e-departmental stores by 16.0 % year on year. With the trend of online shopping increasing, organisations are seeking to brand online (e-branding) effectively and interact with online customers strategically.

There has been a significant increase in interactive websites that allows the customers to view their products of interest in a greater depth. For example, 3d illustrations of products and live online chat systems which are integrated into websites so that customers may interact with other users who may have experienced the product.

2 e-Branding, Multimodality and Online User Experience

Online branding or e-branding has become a topic of significant research interest [2]. Traditionally branding is known as the creation of a value through different means, leading to repeat purchase [3–6]. Therefore, it has become essential for organisations to have an online presence and a strong online brand identity. Because a strong brand identity assures consumers of unseen products and assures quality [7–10]. Branding is the process of creating value through the provision of a consistent offer and customer experience that satisfies customers. As customers develop trust in the brand through satisfaction of use and experience, companies have the opportunity to start building

F.F.-H. Nah and C.-H. Tan (Eds.): HCIBGO 2016, Part I, LNCS 9751, pp. 457–467, 2016.
DOI: 10.1007/978-3-319-39396-4_42

relationships. When a brand satisfies customers, potential competitors cannot easily enter their market due to the brand leadership. Branding therefore enables a company to grow identity and increase the opportunity of repeat business through brand loyalty. According to Simmons [33] *"companies with a history of strong brands are likely to maintain greater control over the balance of power between them and customers, and command higher market share and premium price against generic, unbranded, equiv-alents"* [34]. A strong and successful brand helps organisations to maintain a leading market position. Branding helps an organisation to achieve economies of scale which helps to introduce new products and/or services [35]. Branding has acquired a lot of research attention but its role and contribution to business performance has remained questionable. The same applies to the area of e-branding.

Regardless of the vast sums of money being invested in online advertising, the return on advertisement on the e-commerce is not well defined. E-commerce companies spend several times of their annual sales revenue in order to have an online presence [36]. Online success can be achieved through online branding [29, 37] and it is vital in the highly competitive online market.

Previous research [9] suggests that e-brands may increase customers' trust in an environment where physical products or services are unseen. However, the large number of websites has caused confusion and frustration for Internet users [32]. However, customer re-purchasing is likely to be a familiar brand. Ibeh et al. [34] suggests that consumers establish online relationships with brands that are remembered when re-purchasing. These relationships and trust on a brand can be enhanced through interac-tivity and interactive avatars. Having limited time and cognitive resources and over-whelmed by the information online consumers tend to minimize information overload through mental shortcuts, one of which is e-branding.

A research by Cheskin Research [38] showed that brand is first fundamental aspect of building and maintaining trust on the internet followed by navigability, fulfilment, presentation and technology. Similar results have been found in a research by Rigas and Hussain [11] that one of the major factors to shop online are online brands, convenience and prices.

Several factors of interactions are missing from the e-commerce as compared to face to face interactions [12]. Therefore according to many authors, an effective website design is critical to the success of electronic commerce, and the functionality, usability, ease-of-navigation and interfaces of the websites themselves are vital building blocks for sustainable success [13–16]. Furthermore, researchers [17] demonstrate that website interactivity helps to meet customer expectations by providing a number of fundamental elements. But some authors [18] argue that businesses do not understand the 'user-website interaction' aspect.

It has been agreed by Senger et al. and Rigas and Almutairi [19, 20] that interactions need to be managed and aided throughout the buying cycle most importantly in the web-environments. Interaction are of two types, face to face and e-dialogue, both have their own distinctions but e-dialogue involves the transfer of both tactic and explicit knowl-edge [21].

Interactive e-commerce websites must have three antecedents according to Yen [22] to have a positive purchase effect on the customer: Information richness, retailer brand

and extended offers. These three dimensions of e-commerce are considered to have the strongest impact on the purchase decision online [23–26].

Loyalty has always been important for organisations whether it be online or offline. But according to Senger et al. [19], the use of IT with the aid of multimedia improves the perception of trust. However when price differences are minimal consumers tend to buy from online stores which they trust [27]. Furthermore when trust develops for a website the customers proactively look for new content on it [28].

There have been no researches carried out about a relation between multimodality and loyalty when shopping online. Although the issue and the benefits of multimodality in e-branding remains unclear there are authors who have concluded that e-branding will come to an end [29, 30] but others [31, 32] argue that an organisation cannot be successful on the internet without e-branding. Therefore, after looking at the current and previous literature in concern with the interactive e-branding it is clear that this area needs research about successful practises, their weaknesses and developments on them. And whether the development of interactive multimodal branding will lead to brand loyalty through satisfaction, trust, and ease of use? The literature also shows a gap in the area of Artificial Intelligence (AI) where online assistants would interact and would have the ability to deal with customer queries.

Existing literature draws out the importance of multimodals to acquire loyalty and create e-branding environment on the internet but the existing literature does not dwell on the use of 'interactive' multimodals, which is a significant area and still under-researched.

3   Methodology, Survey and Sample

A survey was contacted using a questionnaire that gathered an overall user viewpoint on topics relating to online shopping, virtual assistants, e-branding and multimodal e-branding. The questionnaire consisted of 45 questions of which 7 questions required a Likert-style answer and 33 questions required a user selection from a menu of different options. All the questions were compulsory with the exception of two questions that were open ended and have not formed a part of this survey. The response rate was 100 %. The questionnaire could be completed by respondents either on paper or on-line. The results were analysed using SPSS. The sample was opportunistic. The population which would be useful for this research would be the consumers who shop online and are critical would help to identify the weaknesses in the current interfaces.

A total of 100 respondents were asked to carry out the questionnaire. Of which 100 (100 %) valid responses were received back. There were two cases which selected not to identify their gender and they have been deemed as invalid responses and that accounted to 2 % of invalid responses. The number of males who participated in the research were 48 (50 %) and the number of females were 48 (50 %).

4   Findings and Analysis

From the questionnaire various factors were selected to compare and contrast their effect on the effectiveness, efficiency and the user-satisfaction of the users. The findings are discussed according to:

1. *Internet Usage:* To find out about the user-satisfaction it was important to find out the amount of time spent on the internet and what devices were used to access it.
2. *Factors to shop and not to shop online:* Various consumers have various needs and therefore it was important to explore the factors to shop online and factors which refrain from shopping online.
3. *Social Media influence:* These days social media influences quite a lot of purchases therefore it was important to find out how and which social media influences the purchase decision.
4. *Knowledge about e-branding and multimodals:* most of the consumers know about e-commerce and e-branding however multimodals are not very known to consumers therefore for consumers to understand multimodal e-branding it is important to know whether there is an understanding of multimodality.
5. *Information seeking and Artificial Intelligence (AI):* consumers seek information online through FAQ's, forums and etc. However, this information seeking and the whole interactivity can be improved through the integration of Artificial Intelligence in the form of Virtual Shopping Assistants for e-retailers.
6. *Effectiveness, Efficiency and User-Satisfaction:* the current effectiveness, efficiency and the user-satisfaction from the current e-commerce interfaces will be explored to see the areas of and for improvement.

Figure 1 below shows the respondent profile of the sample. 45 % of the respondents had a degree and 18.30 % had a postgraduate degree. In terms of internet proficiency, 62.70 % of the male respondents described themselves as advanced users of internet compared to 37 % of female respondents. 48.10 % of the females described themselves as having an intermediate or Practical Application knowledge of using the internet.

Figure 2 shows the data relating to the internet usage of the sample. 58.30 % of the respondents were internet users for more than 8 years and only 1.3 % of the respondents had internet experience between 1 to 3 years. When respondents were asked about the frequency of accessing the internet, results showed that 65 % of the respondents accessed the internet 6–10 times daily. Approximately, 33.3 % of the respondents spent more than 20 h weekly on the internet. The results also showed that at least 30 % of the respondents spent 6–10 h weekly on the internet. Only 10 % of the respondents spent 0–5 h weekly on the internet. This shows that most of the sample used were familiar with the internet and spent almost one day in the whole week on the internet.

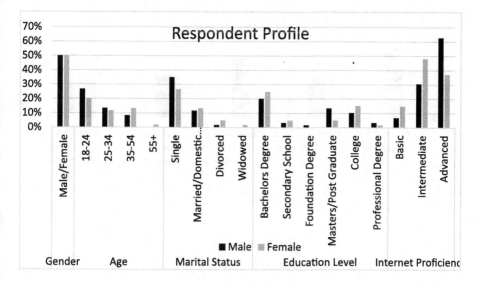

Fig. 1. Respondent profile

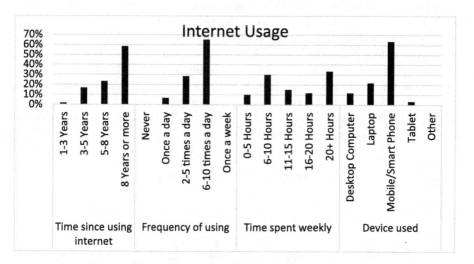

Fig. 2. Internet usage statistics

Customers were asked about buying online behaviours to know the viewpoint and the influence which social media has on the buying behaviour. Figure 3 shows that 91.70 % of the sample were online purchasers and 55 % of the respondents were influenced by social media.

Approximately 75 % of the respondents had shopped from e-retailers (e.g. Amazon or eBay). 55 % of the respondents agreed that current e-commerce websites were usable.

Moreover, 48.30 % of the respondents thought that they will benefit by a "*virtual shopping assistant*", this highlights the willingness to accept new interface technologies.

Fig. 3. Buying online

It also points towards an area that is underdeveloped. Figure 4 shows the frequency of use of social media platforms. 20.40 % of the respondents thought that they fully influenced from Facebook and 46.20 % thought that were never influenced by Twitter. The second most influential platform was YouTube with 18.20 %. This was attributed to the ability of users to watch reviews of products prior to purchasing. This highlights that e-commerce platforms are likely to benefit by providing relevant links of videos relating to the products on social platforms. 25.90 % and 24.50 % of the respondents thought that they usually influenced by Facebook and Instagram respectively. This may be due to the integration between the apps that allows users to share their posts simultaneously with one being a platform for sharing images only.

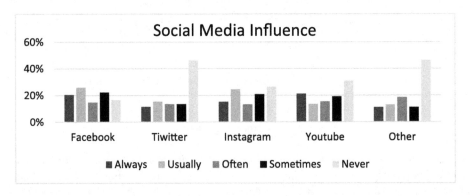

Fig. 4. Influence from social media

4.1 Influencing Factors to Purchase Activity

This part of the survey investigated the factors that motivates or demotivates people to online purchasing. The results are depicted in Figs. 5 and 6. The results showed that *time saving* (55.20 %), *convenience* (53.40 %) and *price* (50.90 %) were the top three reasons that motivated people to shop online. These results are in agreement with previous findings by Rigas and Hussain (2015). In addition, it appears from the findings in this survey that brands/e-brands (and associated attributes) were not thought by respondents to be the most important factors. 29.10 % of the respondents followed a recommendation by a peer.

Fig. 5. Factors to shop online

Figure 6 shows the factors which refrain the shoppers from online activity. These were delivery times (76.70 %), risk of credit card frauds (48.30 %), ordering the wrong item (46.70 %) and subsequently returning those items (43.40 %).

The survey also obtained an overall viewpoint of the respondents regarding their knowledge about multimodal and e-branding. The results in Fig. 7 show that 61.70 % of the respondents are aware of e-branding, and 73.40 % were not familiar of multimodality. Interestingly, 65 % of the respondents thought that they had never experienced multimodal e-branding. When respondents were asked about the possibility of associating an e-brand with an interactive character, 81.70 % of the respondents thought that such an association will aid them to remember an e-brand. 61.70 % of the respondents had never came across an interactive character on an e-commerce interface or platform. 70 % thought that an interactive characters will motivate users to repeat purchase.

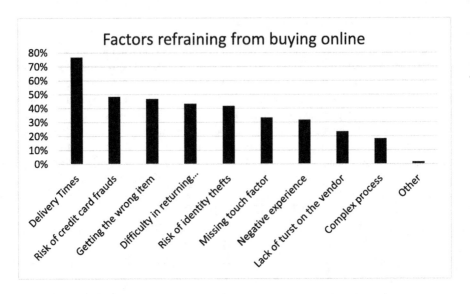

Fig. 6. Factors refraining from buying online

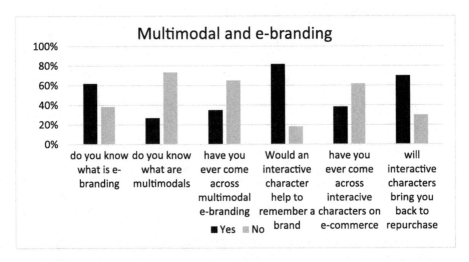

Fig. 7. Multimodals and e-branding

Respondents were also asked whether current interfaces could be improved through virtual shopping assistants. 58.30 % agreed that such facility would be desirable. 66.70 % of the respondents had never experienced a virtual assistant. This indicates some scope for further development in this direction (see Fig. 8). 60 % of the respondents reference the *frequently asked questions section*. A virtual assistant could be utilised in that section of the interface and may lead to a better efficiency and user-satisfaction.

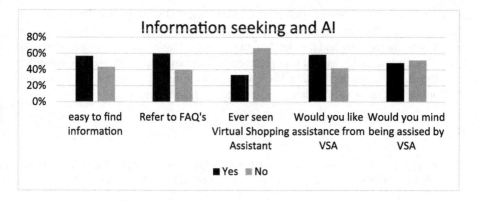

Fig. 8. Information seeking and AI

To know more about the effectiveness, efficiency and user-satisfaction of the current e-commerce interfaces respondents were asked about presentation, checkout times and the user-satisfaction during their online transactions. Figure 9 shows that 54 % of the respondents felt that the current presentation created an urge to purchase. 60 % of the respondents indicated that their transactions were cancelled before completion due to an error. 61.70 % respondents said that the current checkout times were fast. 44.15 % of the respondents were generally not satisfied with their overall online experience.

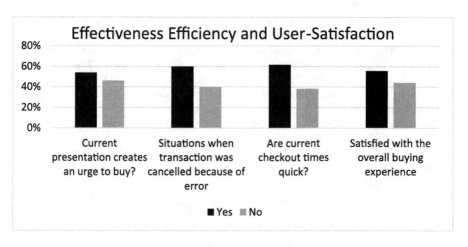

Fig. 9. Effectiveness, efficiency and user-satisfaction

5   Conclusion: Implications for Interactive e-Branding

It is difficult to generalise with convenience sample. However, this survey shows that there is at least a prima facie case that multimodality in the form of a virtual assistant will benefit not only the consumers but also the e-retailers. Furthermore, online product reviews in popular social media platforms also play a role in consumer purchase decision. The users of e-commerce platforms can benefit by using these interfaces in a more effective, efficient and satisfied manner. The e-retailers can benefit by increasing multimodal interactivity and thus leading to repeat purchases. There is a need to investigate these prima facie cases of user preference in e-commerce user interfaces in order to establish a better understanding of the ways that multimodal features can be used in this context and the way in which users can accept these techniques.

References

1. Office for National Statistics: Consumer Trends of United Kingdom for 2014 (2014). http://www.ons.gov.uk/ons/rel/consumer-trends/consumer-trends/q2-2014/index.html. Accessed 30 Jan 2015
2. Rowley, J.: Online branding. Online Inf. Rev. **28**(2), 131–138 (2009)
3. Aaker, D.: Managing Brand Equity: Capitalising on the Value of a Brand Name. Free Press, New York (1991)
4. de Chernatony, L., McDonald, M.: Creating Powerful Brands: The Strategic Route to Success in Consumer, Industrial, and Service Markets. Butterworth-Heinemann, Oxford (1992)
5. Kapferer, J.: Strategic Brand Management. Free Press, New York (1992)
6. Hankinson, G., Cowking, P.: Branding in Action: Cases and Strategies for Profitable Brand Management. McGraw-Hill, New York (1993)
7. Ries, A., Ries, L.: 11 Immutable Laws of Internet Branding. Harper Collins, London (2000)
8. Bergstrom, A.: Cyber branding: leveraging your brand on the internet. Strateg. Leadersh. **28**(4), 10–15 (2000)
9. Berry, L.: Cultivating service brand equity. J. Acad. Mark. Sci. **28**(1), 128–137 (2000)
10. Mitchell, L.: Branding equals smart e-business. Infoworld **22**, 47–48 (2000)
11. Rigas, D., Hussain, H.A.: The role of brand loyalty and social media in e-commerce interfaces: survey results and implications for user interfaces. In: Fui-Hoon Nah, F., Tan, C.-H. (eds.) HCIB 2015. LNCS, vol. 9191, pp. 347–357. Springer, Heidelberg (2015)
12. Chadwick, S.A.: Communicating trust in e-commerce interactions. Manage. Commun. Q. **14**(4), 653–658 (2001)
13. Constantinides, E.: Influencing the online consumer's behaviour: the web experience. Internet Res. **14**(2), 111–126 (2004)
14. Yen, B., Hu, P.J.-H., Wang, M.: Toward an analytical approach to effective web site design: a framework for modelling, evaluation and enhancement. Electron. Commer. Res. Appl. **6**, 159–170 (2007)
15. Lim, H., Widdows, R., Hooker, N.H.: Web content analysis of e-grocery retailers: a longitudinal study. Int. J. Retail Distrib. Manage. **37**(10), 839–851 (2009)
16. Colla, E., Lapoule, P.: Les facteurs clés du succés des cybermarchés: les enseignements du cas Tesco. Décis. Mark. **61**, 35–45 (2011)
17. Dholakia, R.R., Zhao, M.: Retail web site interactivity. Int. J. Retail Distrib. Manage. **37**(10), 821–838 (2009)
18. Hasley, J., Gregg, D.G.: The outcomes of user interactions with retail websites: semantics and nomenclature. J. Technol. Res. **5**, 1–53 (2014)
19. Senger, E., Gronover, S., Riempp, G.: Customer web interaction: fundamentals and decision tree. In: AMCIS 2002 Proceedings, Paper 270 (2002)
20. Rigas, D., Almutairi, B.: An empirical investigation into the role of avatars in multimodal e-government interfaces. Int. J. Sociotechnol. Knowl. Dev. (IJSKD) **5**(1), 14–22 (2013)

21. Gurgul, G., Rumyantseva, M., Enkel, E.: Customer integration–establish a constant bilateral knowledge flow. Diskussionspapier des Research Centers Knowledge Source der Universität St. Gallen (2002)
22. Yen, Y.-S.: The interaction effect on customer purchase intention in e-commerce: a comparison between substitute and complement. Asia Pac. J. Mark. Logist. **26**(3), 472–493 (2014)
23. Burt, S., Davies, K.: From the retail brand to the retailer as a brand: themes and issues in retail branding research. Int. J. Retail Distrib. Manage. **38**(11/12), 865–878 (2010)
24. Kim, E.Y., Kim, Y.-K.: Predicting online purchase intentions for clothing products. Eur. J. Mark. **38**(7), 883–897 (2004)
25. Chu, W., Choi, B., Song, M.R.: The role of on-line brand awareness and infomediary reputation in increasing consumer purchase intention. Int. J. Electron. Commer. **9**(3), 115–127 (2005)
26. Hume, M.: Understanding core and peripheral service quality in customer repurchase of the performing arts. Manag. Serv. Qual. **18**(4), 349–369 (2008)
27. Strader, T.J., Shaw, M.J.: Consumer difference for traditional and Internet markets. Internet Res. Electron. Netw. Appl. Policy **9**(2), 82–92 (1999)
28. Rhea, D.: Trust me. Critique **14**, 74–149 (2000)
29. Sinha, I.: Cost transparency: the net's real threat to prices and brands. Harv. Bus. Rev. **78**, 43–51 (2000)
30. Chevron, J.: Is the internet really killing brands? (2000). www.jrcanda.com/art-netkillsbrands.html. Accessed 2001
31. McGovern, G.: The Caring Economy (2000). www.thecaringeconomy.com. Accessed July 2001
32. Carpenter, P.: e-Brands-Building on Internet Business at Breakneck Speed. Harvard Business School Press, Boston (2000)
33. Simmons, G.J.: "i-Branding": developing the internet as a branding tool. Mark. Intell. Plan. **25**(6), 544–562 (2007)
34. Ibeh, K.I.N., Luo, Y., Dinnie, K.: e-Branding strategies of internet companies: some preliminary insights from the UK. J. Brand Manage. **12**(5), 355 (2005)
35. Steven, C.: Issues in Branding. Reuters Report, Datamonitor Plc., London (1999)
36. Epstein, M.J.: Implementing successful e-commerce initiatives. Strateg. Finance **86**(9), 22–29 (2005)
37. Chevron, J.: Is the internet really killing brands? (2000)
38. Cheskin Research: Ecommerce trust study (1999). www.cheskin.com. Accessed January 2016

The Social Dimension of Mobile Commerce – Engaging Customers Through Group Purchase

Wee-Kek Tan[(✉)], Hock-Hai Teo, Chuan-Hoo Tan, and Yang Yang

Department of Information Systems, National University of Singapore,
Computing 1, 13 Computing Drive, Singapore, 117417, Singapore
{tanwk,teohh,tancho,yangy119}@comp.nus.edu.sg

Abstract. Social commerce and mobile commerce have become increasingly popular in recent years because they enhance customer's shopping process and increase businesses' revenue. However, the extant literature does not prescribe sufficient design guidelines for implementing social commerce in a mobile commerce context. This research draws on the idea of group purchase to inject an element of social commerce into mobile commerce. A set of mobile commerce design features is carefully contrived to support group purchase in a process that maximizes social interaction among customers and their shopping partners. This could potentially increase user engagement with the mobile commerce application and encourage customer loyalty and repeated purchase.

Keywords: Mobile commerce · Social commerce · Group buying · Engagement · Design science

1 Introduction

Shopping in the brick-and-mortar sense is typically a social process [1]. Indeed, researchers have found that shoppers who are accompanied by friends or family members tend to spend more time shopping and purchase more products as compared to individual shoppers [2]. Oddly, traditional e-commerce typically provides a relatively lonely shopping experience where customers receive product information from sellers in a one-way fashion and do not have the ability to communicate with friends or family members. Customers find such traditional e-commerce business model to be insufficient and the shopping process to be unsatisfying [3]. Nowadays, there is an increasing desire among customers for more social and interactive ways of online shopping. [4]. Driven by this prominent trend, a new e-commerce model called social commerce that is more shoppers-centric has emerged in recent years [5].

Both businesses and customers can benefit from the adoption of social commerce. Compared to traditional e-commerce, social commerce offers multiple interactive approaches like online chatting, postings and comments [3]. With these social features, customers can better express themselves and share their information with other customers [6], and also consult trusted individuals for shopping advice. Such shared information and experiences contributes to the formation of social knowledge, which other customers can use to make more informed purchase decisions [7]. Businesses also

© Springer International Publishing Switzerland 2016
F.F.-H. Nah and C.-H. Tan (Eds.): HCIBGO 2016, Part I, LNCS 9751, pp. 468–479, 2016.
DOI: 10.1007/978-3-319-39396-4_43

benefit from the shared social knowledge as they are able to gain more accurate insights into the shopping expectations of customers and develop successful business strategies. With appropriate business strategies that are adapted for social commerce, it is possible for businesses to increase sales and stimulate user engagement [8]. Despite its increasing popularity, researchers have given scant attention to concepts, applications and design features of social commerce. Most studies focuses on analyzing social commerce based on current implementations like Groupon and Facebook Starbucks, but limited studies have been conducted to develop a prototype that implements all the desirable and essential features identified to make a successful social commerce application [9]. Current generation of social commerce applications merely feature interactive tools such as online chatting, postings and comments [3] without a coherent business-technology strategy for inducing customers to make purchases over the shopping social process.

Parallel to the development of social commerce, mobile commerce, which is the conduct of e-commerce over mobile devices, has also gained prominence with the rapid development of mobile wireless communication technology [10]. Mobile commerce possesses several advantages over traditional e-commerce such as ubiquity, personalization, flexibility and dissemination that promises businesses unprecedented market opportunities [11]. These qualities make mobile commerce especially suitable for the adaptation of social commerce. The ubiquity nature of mobile commerce allows businesses to link customers with their shopping partners anywhere at any time. The flexibility associated by mobile devices enables customers to multi-task with their mobile devices, i.e., to shop on the go while performing other tasks. The dissemination attribute of mobile commerce allows businesses to broadcast marketing messages simultaneously to multiple customers within a specific geographical area.

Unfortunately, the extant literature has given even lesser attention to social commerce over mobile devices compared to traditional e-commerce. The present research aims to conceptualize a viable business-technology strategy for conducting social commerce over mobile devices from a design science perspective. Specifically, we draw on the idea of group purchase, which has been implemented as a standalone business model by a number of traditional e-commerce websites [12] but has not yet been implemented in social commerce. A set of mobile commerce features is carefully contrived to support group purchase in a process that maximizes social interaction among customers and their shopping partners. Using the seven-stage engagement cycle [13] as theoretical lens, we also explain how incorporating this social element could possibly increase user engagement level with the mobile commerce application and consequently encourage customer loyalty and repeated purchase [8].

2 Theoretical Background

2.1 Social Commerce

Social commerce generally refers to commerce activities that are mediated by social media [14] or by word-of-mouth in online marketplaces [15]. Compared to e-commerce, social commerce is more customer-centric [16] and focuses on facilitating purchase decisions arising out of social interaction. Social commerce is presently implemented using two major approaches each with different emphasis on either e-commerce or social media [9].

The first approach focuses more on e-commerce and brings social media platform into e-commerce websites. In this approach, the primary goal is to enable purchases and sales conversion. The support for interaction among customers is kept at a minimal level. For instance, an e-commerce website that adopts this approach might share a customer's purchased product on a social media platform in the form of a news feed or post thus leading the interaction away from the e-commerce website to that social media platform. This technique merely provides a topic for the customer's new postings on Facebook, for example. Hence, this implementation approach does not fully support the needs of social commerce in the sense that such use of social media does not facilitate actual sales transactions from taking place. More specifically, customers might have a difficult time finding friends who have purchased the same products that they wish to buy in order to seek advice since the social media platform does not capture the transaction history of customers.

The second approach focuses more on social media and brings e-commerce into social media platforms. The e-commerce elements in social media platforms usually manifest in the form of advertisings and promotions. Using the "like" feature provided by social media platforms, customers could locate friends who are interested in similar promoted products or services. Customers could also comment on the postings or chat privately with their friends. The "tag" function allows other users to alert their friends to newly posted promotions. Hence, this function encourages viral marketing. Despite the rich social interactivity, one limitation of this approach is that social media platforms do not support the actual purchase of products and customers are forced to return back to traditional e-commerce websites to make the purchase.

In a similar fashion, social commerce may also be implemented in the mobile commerce context using either approach. In the first approach, a mobile commerce application could feature plugins provided by different social media platforms. In the second approach, the mobile applications of social media platforms could implement various advertisings initiatives, in particular those that leverage on location-based services. Each implementation approach has its pros and cons. A successful social commerce application should include best practices from both approaches. However, in this research, we will focus more on the first approach since the objective is to delineate effective design feature for mobile social commerce applications.

2.2 Design Features of Social Commerce

Various studies in the extant literature have suggested and summarized a list of features that e-commerce websites should adopt in order to transform themselves into effective social-commerce websites. For instances, Najjar [17] identified social media connections, storefronts, product recommendations, product customization, product contextual simulation, flash sales and mobile commerce as viable features that aspiring social commerce merchants should consider. A more in-depth and systematic study conducted by Huang and Benyoucef [3] classified social media tools into five categories that include social connection, social communities, social media marketing, social shopping and social applications. Unfortunately, these studies tended to focus on individual features and do not prescribe a holistic framework to guide traditional e-commerce merchants in the adoption of social commerce.

To mediate this problem, Huang and Benyoucef [9] proposed a conceptual model for social commerce design that summarized both the design features of e-commerce websites and social media platforms. The conceptual model extends and improves on Fisher's three layer of social design [18] by adding in a commerce layer. Collectively, these four layers of social commerce features include individual, community, conversation and commerce. The authors validated the effectiveness of the model via an empirical study that examined the designing of both social commerce implementation approaches, i.e., e-commerce focus and social media focus.

According to Huang and Benyoucef [9], there are three design features that are currently not found in both e-commerce focus and social media focus implementation approaches. They are community support, relationship maintenance and group purchase. Out of these three features, group purchase is the most viable feature for engendering purchases over the shopping social process. This research focuses on delineating design features geared towards supporting group purchase that are suitable for implementation in a mobile commerce application. At the same time, relevant design features from all four layers will be synthesized into a coherent social commerce design strategy for the mobile commerce context.

2.3   Group Purchase

The basic and core concept of group purchase is to provide volume discounts [12]. On the one hand, customers are encouraged to bargain together to reach certain aggregated purchasing quantity in order to obtain a lower price [20]. On the other hand, sellers can use this demand aggregation to sell in bulk so as to achieve higher efficiency in term of inventory turnover rate [21]. Consequently, both customers and sellers benefit from the group purchasing process [12]. There are two pricing mechanisms that are commonly used for group buying – namely dynamic pricing [12] and fixed pricing [20] – and these can be implemented using collaborative online shopping technology.

In dynamic pricing, the price of product changes according to customers' activities and customers have the power to negotiate the price with sellers in an active manner [12]. However, dynamic pricing mechanism suffers from two pitfalls [22]. First, dynamic pricing models are often difficult for general consumers to understand and merchants must spend time, effort and financial resources to educate their customers. Second, dynamic pricing models could involve a lengthy waiting period that prevents impulsive buying and discourage customers with urgent demand.

Fixed pricing mechanisms can address the problems that are associated with dynamic pricing. Sellers set a fixed price lower than the retails price and a required group size to make the purchase. Fixed pricing delivers a clear and easily understood message to customers on the discount that they could get for a certain number of participants. Moreover, shorter time limit motivates potential customers to act fast on purchasing and monitor the websites on a daily basis to learn about new deals.

Synthesizing the pros and cons of both dynamic and fixed pricing mechanisms, a successful group buying model should feature a simple and readily understandable pricing model in conjunction with a short waiting time period. We further propose that in order to leverage on the ubiquity and personalization nature of mobile commerce, additional enhancements could be made such as providing an even shorter time frame for customers to complete all group buying related activities and additional reward for bringing additional customers to participate in the group purchase.

2.4 Collaborative Online Shopping

Besides featuring an attractive pricing model, another critical success factor for group purchase is an efficient communication tool for customers to propagate the deal information to their social network. This enables a deal to be closed rapidly such that everyone can enjoy the group discount [20]. Various approaches has been suggested by researchers with collaborative online shopping featuring co-browsing and shared navigation concept being cited as one of the most popular ones.

Co-browsing enables two or more users to share the same view in their browser in real-time [23]. By allowing one user to view the movements and activities of others, co-browsing provides a new way of communication between users in remote locations. It has been applied to the e-commerce context to facilitate interactive shopping activities among users in distant locations, i.e., collaborative online shopping. Co-browsing increases users' perception of the psychological presence of their shopping companions. This in turn leads to greater engagement level in the online shopping task [24]. Compared to a chat-only approach, this psychological presence also gives users a more satisfying shopping experience.

Shared navigation support is defined as the way that collaborative shopping companions use to navigate to products of common interests. For instance, it enables remote users to view a same web page through their browsers. Shared navigation is superior to separate navigation in reducing the occurrence of uncoupling and facilitating the resolution of uncoupling [23]. Uncoupling is a state in which collaborative shoppers lose coordination with their shopping companions. With fewer uncoupling incidents, a group of customers can communicate more efficiently to identify potential customers who are interested in purchasing the same products. Moreover, visible browsing behavior of the other parties and the awareness of the shared context enhance shoppers' perceptions that their shopping companions are socially close to them [25]. In this research, co-browsing and shared navigation will be purposefully adapted to a mobile commerce app context that relies on a touch-screen interface.

2.5 Engagement

The notion of engagement has been well studied by scholars from a wide variety of disciplines, including marketing, management, social psychology and information systems [26]. O'Brien and Toms [27] suggest that engagement provides a holistic framework for understanding the integration between users and the system. Through the use of this framework, users' experience with the system can be improved from purely functional to pleasurable and memorable. In the context of e-commerce, engagement refers to a multi-stage process of gaining customers' interest and sustaining such interest sufficiently in order to gain their attention on product or brand [23]. Through this process, customers create deep connection with the seller, brand or product and are more driven to make purchases and interact with the seller or other customers overtime [28]. Similarly, Bowden [26] defined engagement as a psychological process that contributes to the creation of loyal and returning customers who are likely to make repeated purchases. For most businesses, customer engagement is an important sales driver and is widely regarded as a predictor to business success [29]. Thus, social commerce applications should be designed for engaging customers in order to be successfully. A possible approach to achieve customer engagement is the seven-stage engagement cycle for making IT applications more engaging [13].

The engagement cycle consists of seven stages including connection, interaction, satisfaction, retention, commitment, advocacy and eventually engagement. A social commerce application is considered to have successfully engaged customers when they form a stable social network and make repeated purchases in the future thus generating a sustainable stream of revenue. Moreover, engaged customers would continue to recruit new customers through word-of-mouth or referral and thus creating a new iteration of the customer engagement cycle in an iterative and incremental manner. We adapted the definition of each stage to fit our present context of social commerce. In the next section, we will discuss at length how various design features could be incorporated into a mobile application for enabling social commerce in a manner that engages customers effectively.

3   Requirements Analysis and Design

3.1   Feature Set of Social Commerce Mobile Application

Using the engagement cycle as the theoretical lens, we will (1) delineate a set of features for a social commerce mobile application that is primarily based on group purchase, (2) highlight the relationships between these features and the social commerce design conceptual model [9]; and (3) explain how these features collectively lead to effective customer engagement. These features are grouped into eight modules altogether including five modules of features that are related to social commerce, two modules that are specifically related to group purchase and one basic features module that supports the other seven modules. They are listed in Table 1.

3.2   Basic Features

The basic features are designed according to the corresponding individual design principle of Huang and Benyoucef's [9] conceptual model for social commerce design. They provide users with personal profile, content profile and activity profile. In terms of supporting engagement, the basic features provide a basis for a customer to connect with other customers and therefore serve as a preparation for establishing connections using the friend list features [13]. Most of the basic features are supported by both implementations of social commerce applications.

Table 1. Proposed features of social commerce mobile application

Feature group	Brief description	Conceptual design feature	Engagement Stage
Basic features	Personal profile Update buyer profile Provide product infor-mation profile Perform order and trans-actions Provide transaction histories	Personal Profile, Content Profile, Activity Profile, Ordering, Payment Mechanism	Connection
Friend List	Add new friend through friend request by user-name Approve friend requests Add follow request by username Chat with a single user	Connection	Connection, Interaction
Group Chat	Create a chat group from friends in the friend list Chat within a group Add new members to group	Community support	Connection, Interaction
Referral	Refer friends from friend list to other friends Refer purchased prod-ucts to friends	Information sharing	Connection, Advocacy
Rating and Comment	View ratings and comments from follower Bookmark ratings and comments Like ratings and comments View number of followers who liked and bookmarked certain rating and comment	Social Content Presenta-tion, Topic Focus, Content Creation, Information Sharing, Social Proof	Connection, Interaction, Retention, Commit-ment
Notification	Notify unviewed friend referral Notify product referrals from friends Show liked rating and comments Show unfinished group purchase transac-tions	Notification, Relation-ship Maintenance	Connection
Co-shopping	Co-browsing among group members via scrolling and tapping on screen Chat among group members via text messages Request to lead the co-browsing activity	Topic Focus, Community Support, Connection, Group Purchase, Reci-procity, Participation	Connection, Interaction
Group Purchase	Basic group purchase deal Time limited group purchase deal Increasing discount group sales deal	Topic Focus, Relation-ship Maintenance, Group Purchase	Satisfaction, Commit-ment

3.3   Social Commerce Related Features

The friend list features proposed are based on the connection design features in the community layer of the conceptual model. The friend list establishes connections between users by creating, storing and displaying the contacts of users. Users can chat via text messages with their friends in a one-to-one manner or in a group format. The friend list features collectively fulfill the engagement stage of connection as it maintains all the user's contacts. Moreover interaction is improved through the perform e-commerce, e.g., Facebook, it is not supported in e-commerce websites that utilize social media platforms.

The group chat features allow users to create chat groups freely and users can group their friends into a community to achieve their own shared objectives. The referral features support two types of referral, which are friend referrals and product referrals. For creating friend referrals, users can refer friends from their friend list to other friends via the chat box. Users receiving the friend referral can use it to create friend requests. When requests are approved, new friends will be added to the friend list. Users can also create product referrals from the products that they have purchased to their existing friends. The rating and comment features support four out of the five design features proposed in the conversation layer of the conceptual model. Users can give ratings and write comments on products and the corresponding sellers after making purchase. The ratings and comments are considered as social contents created by users and therefore satisfy the requirement of the content creation feature. Users who are followers can easily view the ratings and comments on products purchased by the users whom they are following. Moreover, ratings and comments from other users that an individual is following provide social proof under the commerce layer in terms of recommendations and advice to help potential buyers to make purchase decisions. There are four types of notifications including friend referral, product referral, liked rating and comments and unfinished group purchase transactions.

3.4   Group Purchase Related Features

Co-shopping adopts the concept of shared navigation and co-browsing. It allows users to form co-shopping groups with respect to a specific group purchase deal. After a co-shopping group has been created, members of the group can start to co-browse the product information. To enable members to communication with each other besides co-browsing, co-shopping also enables members to perform group chatting in the chat box beneath the group purchase deal. After all members have reached a consensus, they can proceed to make the purchase.

The basic idea of co-browsing as explained in the earlier discussion on collaborative online shopping is to enable multiple users to view each other's activities on a browser, which in our context has been replaced with mobile screen. User activities that are synchronized among co-shopping group members are scrolling and tapping gestures. A combination of both actions performed by a particular user is sufficient for other users to locate the position s/he is currently focusing on. In this way, coordination and inter-action are improved. However, when multiple users try to scroll or tap the screen simultaneously, the mobile application's screen might become confusing. To avoid this problem, every co-shopping group has an owner who is also the default leader. The owner can appoint other members to be the leader temporarily and the new leader would have the power to synchronize the movement and actions with the rest of the group members.

Besides co-browsing, text chatting is also included in co-shopping to facilitate communications among members. The chat feature that is supported in co-shopping is similar to that supported in group chat. The only difference is that the customers can swipe the chat box down to hide it at the bottom of the screen when they want to browse the product information. This design element is added after considering the screen size limitation of the mobile device by hiding unused user interface elements outside the view of users and bringing them back when they are needed.

Group purchase features collectively provide three different deal mechanisms, namely basic sales, time-limited sales and increasing discount sales. Our design features address the long duration and high complexity limitations of the original pricing mechanisms. Moreover, to leverage on impulsive buying, the features are also designed to motivate and facilitate customers to close the deal as soon as possible. Each basic sales deal has an expiry date in duration of days and can be defined by the seller based on the product nature or promotion objectives. All basic sales transactions must be completed before the expiry date. Unsuccessful customers cannot purchase the same deal again. This provides customers with incentives to complete the group purchase within the specific deadline. The basic sales mechanism also requires a minimum number of customers to participate. Customers in a particular group can purchase the deal whenever it has met the quorum. This approach shortens customers waiting time and encourages them to communicate among themselves to complete to deal as early as possible. Time-limited sales mechanism has an important distinction from the basic sales mechanism, i.e., a fixed time frame to complete the deal. When the first member in a group chooses to purchase the deal, the timer will start and every member must complete the deal before a certain short period of time to successfully purchase the deal. Otherwise, the deal will be cancelled and the members in the co-shopping group cannot participate in the same time-limited sales again. This approach is to induce impulsive purchase behavior in customers and reduce the sale time for sellers. An increasing discount sales deal offers a lower price when more customers participate, i.e., the concept of dynamic pricing. To avoid a long waiting period, users can make the purchase as long as they meet the minimum group size.

4   Design Science Artifact

Design science research emphasizes the creation of artifacts in the form of a construct, a model, a method or an instantiation. This research focuses on methods of the group purchase social process and instantiation of the mobile commerce application.

Methods are a set of steps used to perform a task. We have defined several methods that lead to the successful conclusion of a group purchase transaction. These include adding a friend by the customer, creating a group chat, co-shopping and co-browsing

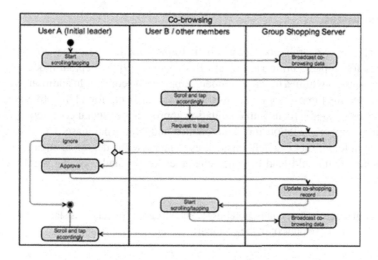

Fig. 1. The co-browsing method

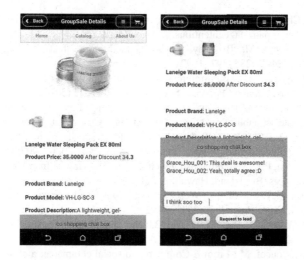

Fig. 2. Screenshots of the mobile commerce application showing co-shopping and co-browsing

with existing chat groups, making group purchases and receiving notification on unfinished group purchases. An important recurrent theme among these methods is the emphasis on the social interaction between a customer and his/her shopping partners. A process diagram of the co-browsing method is shown in Fig. 1. Instantiations are realized information systems built according to the specification of the three preceding artifacts. A fully functional prototype of a mobile commerce application that incorporates all the group purchase social design features delineated in Table 1 was developed together with a supporting server-side backend. Screenshots showing the co-shopping and co-browsing methods are shown in Fig. 2.

5   Conclusion

In summary, this research proposes a holistic framework that prescribes concrete design guidelines for implementing Huang and Benyoucef's [9] conceptual model for social commerce design within a mobile commerce application context. In addition, we explicitly addressed the three design features that are currently not found in both e-commerce focus and social media focus implementation approaches of social commerce. They are community support, relationship maintenance and group purchase. Collectively, the entire design feature set can help businesses to increase the degree of engagement with its customers that could lead to better customer loyalty and repeated purchase in the long-term.

Acknowledgements. The authors gratefully acknowledge the research assistance of Yifeng Hou and Yisi Fu in the development of the prototype.

References

1. Evans, K.R., Christiansen, T., Gill, J.D.: The impact of social influence and role expectations on shopping center patronage intentions. J. Acad. Mark. Sci. **24**(3), 208–218 (1996)
2. Sommer, R., Wynes, M., Brinkley, G.: Social facilitation effects in shopping behavior. Environ. Behav. **24**(3), 285–297 (1992)
3. Huang, Z., Benyoucef, M.: User preferences of social features on social commerce websites: an empirical study. Technol. Forecast. Soc. Chang. **95**, 57–72 (2015)
4. Gutzman, A.: Real-time Chat: What are You Waiting For?, 16 March 2000. https://www.researchgate.net/publication/247341900_Real-time_Chat_What_are_you_waiting_for
5. Liang, T.P., Ho, Y.P., Li, Y.W., Turban, E.: What drives social commerce: the role of social support and relationship quality. Int. J. Electron. Commer. **16**(2), 69–90 (2011)
6. Parise, S., Guinan, P.J.: Marketing using web 2.0. In: 41st Hawaii International Conference on System Sciences, Big Island, Hawaii, p. 281 (2008)
7. Constantinides, E., Fountain, S.J.: Web 2.0: conceptual foundations and marketing issues. J. Dir. Data Digit. Mark. Pract. **9**(3), 231–244 (2008)
8. Lee, S.H., DeWester, D., Park, S.R.: Web 2.0 and opportunities for small businesses. Serv. Bus. **2**(4), 335–345 (2008)
9. Huang, Z., Benyoucef, M.: From E-Commerce to social commerce: a close look at design features. Electron. Commer. Res. Appl. **12**(4), 246–259 (2013)
10. Wu, J.H., Wang, S.C.: What drives mobile commerce? an empirical evaluation of the revised technology acceptance model. Inf. Manage. **42**, 719–729 (2005)
11. Siau, K., Lim, E.P., Shen, Z.: Mobile commerce: promises, and research agenda. J. Database Manage. **12**(3), 4–13 (2001)
12. Kauffman, R.J., Wang, B.: Bid together, buy together: on the efficacy of group-buying business models in internet-based selling. In: Lowry, P.B., Cherrington, J.O., Watson, R.R. (eds.) The E-Business Handbook, pp. 99–137. CRC Press, Boca Raton (2002)
13. Sashi, C.M.: Customer engagement, buyer-seller relationships, and social media. Manage. Decis. **50**(2), 253–272 (2012)
14. Curty, R.G., Zhang, P.: Social commerce: looking back and forward. Proc. Am. Soc. Inf. Sci. Technol. **48**(1), 1–10 (2011)

15. Dennison, G., Bourdage-Braun, S., Chetuparambil, M.: Social Commerce Defined. White Paper No. 23747, IBM Corporation, Research Triangle Park, NC (2009)
16. Wigand, R.T., Benjamin, R.I., Birkland, J.L.: Web 2.0 and beyond: implications for electronic commerce. In: 10th International Conference on Electronic Commerce, Innsbruck, Austria, p. 7. ACM Press, New York (2008)
17. Najjar, L.J.: advances in E-Commerce user interface design. In: 1st International Conference on Human Interface and the Management of Information, Part II, Orlando, FL, USA, pp. 292–300 (2011)
18. Fisher, E.: Social Design, Facebook Developers (2010). https://developers.facebook.com/socialdesign
19. Rayport, J.F., Jaworski, B.J.: Introduction to E-Commerce. McGraw-Hill/Irwin, Boston (2002)
20. Ni, G., Luo, L., Xu, Y., Xu, J., Dong, Y.: optimal decisions on group buying option with a posted retail price and heterogeneous demand. Electron. Commer. Res. Appl. **14**(1), 23–33 (2014)
21. Li, C., Sycara, K.: Algorithm for combinatorial coalition formation and payoff division in an electronic marketplace. In: 1st International Joint Conference on Autonomous Agents and Multiagent Systems, Part 1, pp. 120–127. ACM, New York (2002)
22. Cook, J.: Venture Capital: Where Mercata Led, Consumers were Unwilling to Follow, Seattle Post – Intelligencer, 12 January 2001. https://seattlep-i.nwsource.com/business/vc122.shtml
23. Zhu, L., Benbasat, I., Jiang, Z.: Let's shop online together: an empirical investigation of collaborative online shopping support. Inf. Syst. Res. **21**(4), 872–891 (2010)
24. Seedorf, S., Thum, C., Schulze, T., Pfrogner, L.: Social co-browsing in online shopping: the impact of real-time collaboration on user engagement. In: 22nd European Conference on Information Systems, Tel Aviv, Israel (2014)
25. Kraut, R.E., Fussell, S.R., Siegel, J.: Visual information as a conversational resource in collaborative physical tasks. Hum.-Comput. Interact. **18**(1), 13–49 (2003)
26. Bowden, J.L.H.: The process of customer engagement: a conceptual framework. J. Mark. Theor. Pract. **17**(1), 63–74 (2009)
27. O'Brien, H.L., Toms, E.G.: What is user engagement? a conceptual framework for defining user engagement with technology. J. Am. Soc. Inf. Sci. Technol. **59**(6), 938–955 (2008)
28. Forrester Consulting: How Engaged are Your Customers?, 9 March 2011. http://www.adobe.com/engagement/pdfs/Forrester_TLP_How_Engaged_Are_Your_Customers.pdf
29. Neff, J.: OMD proves the power of engagement. Advertising Age **78**(27), 3–4 (2007)

Digital Innovation

Diffusion of Innovations: The Case Study of Oman's e-Payment Gateway

Badar H. Al-Lawati and Xiaowen Fang[✉]

School of Computing, College of Computing and Digital Media,
DePaul University, Chicago, IL 60604, USA
badar.allawati@gmail.com, xfang@cdm.depaul.edu

Abstract. In 2006 the Government of Oman has embarked on a strategy called 'Digital Oman' which, aims to make government services available electronically throughout the country, and to facilitate e-Commerce in all of its forms. Part of the e-Government initiative was to develop an e-Payments gateway to facilitate the online payments for users of different departments and services. The Information Technology Authority (ITA) of the Sultanate of Oman has taken up the strategic initiative to drive the development of e-Payments in Oman. The ePayment gateway is one of a kind in the region, and it was implemented in partnership with MasterCard's "MiGS" platform. The project has been live for over 8 years, yet neither the number of customers nor the value of transactions is close the initial projections. The project is about to reach a dead end and get replaced with another solution. In this paper we apply the Diffusion of Innovations Model [12] in a case study to identify the issues and propose a solution for future initiatives.

Keywords: ePayment gateway · Electronic payment systems · Diffusion of innovations

1 Introduction

Oman "The Sultanate of Oman" is an Arab state on the southwest coast of the Arab peninsula, with a total area of 119,498 Sq./Mi. and a total population of around 4,000,000. 75 % of the population is between the ages of 14–60, almost 90 % of them have completed at least their Secondary Level Schooling [14].

Under the directions of the Omani Royal Decree 52/2005 the Government of Oman has embarked on a strategy called 'Digital Oman' which, aims to make government services available electronically throughout the country, and to facilitate e-Commerce in all of its forms. Part of the e-Government initiative was to establish a transaction processing mechanism to facilitate the electronic government enabled services. In 2006 the government of Oman decided to develop an e-Payments gateway to facilitate the online payments for users of different departments and services through the government's Information Technology arm, The Information Technology Authority (ITA).

The ITA approached the Central Bank of Oman (CBO) to get the necessary permits to establish an electronic payments processing house under the umbrella of the ITA. However, due to the laws and regulations of the Central Bank of Oman, only licensed

© Springer International Publishing Switzerland 2016
F.F.-H. Nah and C.-H. Tan (Eds.): HCIBGO 2016, Part I, LNCS 9751, pp. 483–490, 2016.
DOI: 10.1007/978-3-319-39396-4_44

financial institutions are permitted to collect and process payments within the country. So the ITA had to tie-up with a Local Bank to host the solution and run the operations while complying with the CBO's regulations. After months of evaluating different scenarios, the ITA signed an agreement with Bank Muscat S.A.O.C (34.25 % Owned by the Government) along with MasterCard's online payments platform (MiGS). Based on this agreement, Bank Muscat will host MasterCard's solution and will offer the technical & financial systems support, while the ITA will conduct country-wide marketing, awareness, & promotion campaigns. With all these efforts to digitize the government services and transactions, the concept of charging a commission per transaction is against the Laws of government income as per the regulations of the Ministry of Finance. So while the ITA was pushing for their strategy into revolutionizing the government services, some parts of the government weren't fully on board. On another hand the CBO also considered it as a breach of their monitory role as governing body of the financial sector within the country. While facing these major obstacles before the project even started, the ITA decided to take the lead and work with Bank Muscat into launching this project at the earliest time. The project needed a communications provider and so they allied with Oman Telecommunications Company S.A.O.G (a 51 % government owned company) to provide all the necessary communication channels between different portions of the end-to-end solution. In 2008, the ITA along with Bank Muscat officially launched Oman's first ePayment Gateway in cooperation with the Royal Police of Oman (ROP) as the pilot partner. The project was a success at the beginning. ROP stopped accepting cash completely, and customers had to pay using cards on the spot or use the online services and pay online at their convenience. Many other government and private organizations decided to jump onboard and integrate their online services with the ePayment Gateway within the first few months of its launch. Within the first two years there were many successful fraud cases against the ePayment Gateway. The Omani law didn't even have a definition of a cybercrime, nor did the gateway have a fraud prevention/detection tool. By early 2011 the Omani Cyber Law was declared through the Royal Decree 12/2011. The ePayment Gateway received a patch update to include a new fraud detection module that will monitor every transaction carefully.

Early 2015, the ITA revised its MasterCard's' based platform, and decided to implement a new platform: Cyber Source, Visa's state-of-the-art solution that comes with enhanced interface, improved security & fraud prevention module, and a cheaper commission per transaction. Starting from May 2015 all new merchants were integrated with the new platform.

The government of Oman represented in the ITA has spent a tremendous number of man hours implementing this gateway and spent a big amount to get this service to its current status. Today after 8 years since the commercial launch of the gateway, the total number of transaction just hit 1,000,000 transactions with a total value of just over $100,000,000, with less than 200 merchants (including both government and private entities). This project has not been successful so far. Recently the Central Bank of Oman has announced that they are implementing a totally new national ePayment Gateway in-house, mandating all national banks to route the domestic online transactions (90 % of the current transactions of ITA ePayment Gateway) through this gateway which will put ITA's ePayment Gateway to an end.

The research objective is to study the resistance and the non-technical implementation challenges faced by the ITA in rolling out the e-Payments Gateway using a case study approach. The findings will likely shed lights on adoptions of other IT technologies in the same region.

2 Literature Review

Information and Communication Technology (ICT) has moved very quickly into organizations and become one of the main tools of the organizational success. This rapid movement of ICT has changed almost every aspect of the organizational processes and the way they do the work. Part of this change is the payments and the financial portion. Organizations are moving towards accepting online payments, and transferring their Business-2-Business into an online-based automated payments and transactions system. This change raised concerns about accepting technology and adapting to using computers as part of the daily routine job. Change within social systems is usually resisted by some members of the society [16] especially changing the way we do things. People tend to resist changes to their habits or routines naturally. "Norms in social systems correspond to habits in individuals. They are customary and expected ways of behaving, members of the organization demand of themselves and of other members conformity to the institutional norms" [17]. Change has become a standard in Management and Organizations textbooks. Kreitner [6] looks at change as a "stone tossed into a still pond" it creates waves in all directions without the ability to predict the impact and in which direction is it heading.

Many researchers have touched the area of change resistance within the information technology field. In his paper about the MIS implementation and what causes resistance in the MIS field, Markus [8] roots the problem to being one or a combination of the following three factors: (1) People's related resistance factors: resisting due to internal "personal" factors. (2) System's related resistance factors: resisting due to factors inherent in the system or application being implemented. (3) Interaction between people and the system: characteristics of system conflicting with characteristics of the people. Markus [8] used the interaction theory to explain how people within the same group would have different responses to different settings. Resistance to change causes failure in projects, especially when it comes to technology related projects. One of the commonly used models to explore adoption/diffusion of technology related products is the Technology Acceptance Model (TAM) developed by Davis [4] to assess the user adaptation to technology. Davis & Venkatesh extended this model in 2000 [15] to examine the user acceptance of Information technology, "The goal of TAM is to provide an explanation of the determinants of computer acceptance that is general, capable of explaining user behavior across a broad range of end-user computing technologies and user populations, while at the same time being parsimonious and theoretical" [3, 15]. The TAM Model is based on 2 main components: "Perceived Usefulness" & "Perceived Ease of Use". Another well-established model is the Diffusion of Innovations model introduced by Rogers [11], Rogers defines the diffusion as "the process in which an innovation is communicated through certain channels over time among the members of a social system" [9]. In his framework, Rogers [10] defines five main attributes of any innovation that make for the major part of the adoption rate of any innovation:

- Relative Advantage - The degree to which an innovation is seen as better than the idea, program, or product it replaces.
- Compatibility - How consistent the innovation is with the values, experiences, and needs of the potential adopters.
- Complexity - How difficult the innovation is to understand and/or use.
- Triability - The extent to which the innovation can be tested or experimented with before a commitment to adopt is made.
- Observability - The extent to which the innovation provides tangible results.

In the 5th edition of his book, Rogers [12] encourages researchers in the field of diffusion to consider additional attributes that could be important in a specific situation of a specific innovation. Rogers' [10] framework was built on 5 main variables that determine the rate of adoption for any innovation (in general): Perceived Attributes of Innovation (Relative Advantage, Compatibility, etc.), Type of Innovation-Decision (Optional, Collective, & Authority), Nature of the Social System, & Extent of Change agents' promotion efforts.

Rogers defines 5 major stages that a decision regarding an innovation usually goes through before it is accepted or rejected:

- The Knowledge Stage: when the individual learns about the existence of innovation and searches for information about the innovation.
- The Persuasion Stage: when an individual forms a favorable or unfavorable attitude towards an innovation without directly making a decision about adopting or rejecting the innovation.
- The Decision Stage: when the individual chooses to adopt or reject a specific innovation, however the user would try the innovation before adopting or rejecting it.
- The Implementation Stage: would the innovation be applicable to put in practice? During this stage the innovation could lose some of its features to meet the user's requirements during the implementation.
- The Confirmation Stage: when the individual seeks support for his decision, either by accepting or rejecting the innovation.

An innovation, no matter how well designed, would be perceived as useless if it is not adapted [2]. Decision makers of any new innovation should always keep in mind that maximizing the adoption rate is a key element in the success of the product or service. In order to maximize the adoption of new innovations, stakeholders need to understand the factors that contribute in adoption or diffusion of that innovation. Electronic Payment Systems have led to different results. Some have succeeded like PayPal & M-Paisa, while others have failed like CyberCash, Digicash, eCharge, & many others [7]. There has been very limited research on the failure cases, as most of the research in electronic payment systems have focused on the successful cases [5, 13]. One of the reasons behind the lack of research within the failure cases is due to the difficulty in getting access into those unsuccessful cases. Currently Electronic Payment systems in the Middle East region are facing a lack of users and a low value of total transactions [1]. The Oman's ePayment

Gateway is a very unique case, due to the vision it had at the beginning and the challenges it went through, and the changes it is currently going though that might be putting it to an end. In a study of an Electronic Payment System failure, Lim et al. [7] identify several factors as the reasons behind the un-successful adoption of different electronic payment systems: Cooperation with exiting entities, Trust, Security, Simplicity, Mutuality of Stakeholder Benefits, Proper Marketing Initiatives, Visibility & Clear Direction, & Missing to attend to customer's problems.

3   Conceptual Framework

In this study, we have chosen the Diffusions of Innovations theory [12] as the theoretical framework to guide our study. Most of the observations made in the initial interviews match with the components and attributes of Diffusion of Innovations framework:

- Relative advantage: many major stakeholders of the project didn't see any relative advantage of taking part in this project.
- Compatibility: this project is still being looked at as un-safe and un-stable by some organizations and individuals.
- Complexity: many organizations are still facing difficulties in integrating this project within their systems because the process is too complex.
- Trialability: the end users don't have the option to test or try the product before the commitment to using it.
- Observability: big proportion of the population is not aware of the existence of this project.

4   Methodology

For this study of a low adopted innovation, we plan to conduct a case study. In this case study we are trying to answer those questions of why Oman's ePayment Gateway didn't succeed in reaching its potential goal in offering a full fledge payment processing house within Oman, and how can other eGovernment transformation projects can do to avoid falling in the same mistakes.

4.1   Preliminary Observations

To prepare for the case study, we have had initial meetings with top-management of the stakeholders of this project, we have created a high level set of observations from those meetings, and the meetings included the following (Table 1):

The notes taken during these meetings were analyzed and coded by one of the authors. A few major problems were identified in the scope of the project, which matches with the innovation's attributed defined by Rogers [12]. Some of the problems identified through coding the initial observations are:

- Lack of unified electronic transformation vision between different stakeholders involved in the project. This is what Rogers defines as Relative Advantage.

- Some of the government organizations involved in the project didn't seem to understand the value and the vision of the project, and hence decided not to be involved in it.
- The scope of this project is part of the e-Government transformation initiative. However the Ministry of Finance doesn't accept paying a commission per transaction, which means that the scope had a major flaw. This is what Rogers defines as compatibility in his model, where this project didn't seem to be compatible with the accepted trends and values of the community it is serving.

Table 1. Preliminary Observations with top-management

Job Title	Division/Department	Organization
Team Leader	e-Payment Department	Information Technology Authority
Assistant General Manager	Cards & eBanking Division	Bank Muscat S.A.O.C
Department Head	Business Operations Department	Central Bank of Oman

Based on the preliminary observations, we have devised a 5-stage case study to continue our inquiry.

4.2   Stage 1: Preparation for Data Collection

Through our initial round of observations we have identified 3 stakeholders of Oman's ePayment Gateway project:

- The Information Technology Authority: The Project Owner.
- The Central Bank of Oman: The Regulator.
- Bank Muscat: The Service Provider.

We will be conducting comprehensive interviews with 2 employees from the technical teams, marketing teams, and operations teams from each of those 3 stakeholders respectively. We are currently devising a structured survey to measure the five main factors impacting adoption of innovations: relative advantage, compatibility, complexity, trialability, and observability. We will also request access to any internal documents related to the project from those 3 stakeholders, those documents could by anything from internal reports, to internal memos, to incident and transaction reports. Those reports will be evaluated and analyzed without disclosing any confidential or sensitive information. Through accessing those documents, we will be able to identify the customer database, and from this database we will be able to categorize them based on the nature of business (government services, private services, banks, non-profit organizations, etc.). After that we are going to approach at least two from each category to be surveyed. We are still working on the instruments creation of the survey and interviews.

4.3   Stage 2: Initial Data Collection

Interviews will be conducted with key stakeholders. Relevant documents or other sources of information will be collected for further analysis. A survey will be administered in the field to key stakeholders and current & potential users of the e-Payments Gateway.

4.4   Stage 3: Initial Data Analysis

Surveys, interviews, and documents will be analyzed. Multiple sources of information will be used to triangulate and to identify key findings. New hypotheses will be proposed.

4.5   Stage 4: Hypothesis Testing

A follow-up survey will be developed and conducted in the field to test hypotheses proposed in Stage 3.

4.6   Stage 5: Final Data Analysis and Conclusions

The follow-up surveys will be analyzed and findings will be summarized. Conclusions will be drawn.

5   Current Progress & Future Work

We are currently in Stage 1, as we are preparing for data collection. At this point we are identifying the interviewees from each of the 3 stakeholders of the project as well as preparing survey instruments and interview guides. Future work for this study is to create the proper measures and conduct the interviews and surveys, as well as analyze them.

References

1. Abrazhevich, D.: Electronic payment systems: issues of user acceptance. In: Stanford-Smith, B., Chiozza, E. (eds.), E-work and E-commerce. Citeseer (2001)
2. Chigona, W., Licker, P.: Using diffusion of innovations framework to explain communal computing facilities adoption among the urban poor. Inf. Technol. Int. Dev. 4(3), 57 (2008)
3. Davis, F.D.: Perceived usefulness, perceived ease of use, and user acceptance of information technology. MIS Q. 13, 319–340 (1989)
4. Davis Jr., F.D.: A technology acceptance model for empirically testing new end-user information systems: theory and results. Ph.D. thesis, Massachusetts Institute of Technology (1986)
5. Kniberg, H.: What makes a micropayment solution succeed. Institution for Applied Information Technology, Kungliga Tekniska Högskolan, Kista (2002)
6. Kreitner, R.: Management, 5th edn. Houghton Mifflin, Boston (1992)
7. Lim, B., Lee, H., Kurnia, S.: Exploring the reasons for a failure of electronic payment systems: a case study of an australian company. J. Res. Pract. Inf. Technol. 39(4), 231–244 (2007)

8. Markus, M.L.: Power, politics, and MIS implementation. Commun. ACM **26**(6), 430–444 (1983)
9. Rogers, E.M.: Diffusion of Innovations, vol. 18, no. 20, p. 271. Free Press, New York (1983)
10. Rogers, E.M.: Diffusion of Innovations, p. 12. Free Press, New York (1995)
11. Rogers, E.M.: Diffusion of Innovations, vol. 1, pp. 79–134. Free Press of Glencoe, New York (1971)
12. Rogers, E.M.: Elements of diffusion. Diffus. Innov. **5**, 1–38 (2003)
13. Truman, G.E., Sandoe, K., Rifkin, T.: An empirical study of smart card technology. Inf. Manag. **40**(6), 591–606 (2003)
14. UN Data: Country Profile. http://data.un.org/CountryProfile.aspx?crName=OMAN
15. Venkatesh, V., Davis, F.D.: A theoretical extension of the technology acceptance model: Four longitudinal field studies. Manage. Sci. **46**(2), 186–204 (2000)
16. Watson, G.: Resistance to change. Am. Behav. Sci. **14**(5), 745 (1971)
17. Whyte, W.H.: The Organization Man. University of Pennsylvania Press, Philadelphia (2013)

Improving the Front End of Innovation: The Case of Mobile Commerce Services

Karen Carey[✉] and Markus Helfert

School of Computing, Dublin City University, Dublin 9, Ireland
Karen.carey6@mail.dcu.ie, Markus.helfert@computing.dcu.ie

Abstract. This paper builds on an earlier publication [1] where an Interactive Assessment, namely 'The Mobile (M) Concept Assessment Instrument' was proposed to assist with defining and evaluating m-Commerce (mobile) services in the early stages of creation (i.e. the innovative stages). The paper begins by proving a background to the research problem along with a brief overview of the M-Concept Assessment Instrument. This is followed by a description of the instruments implementation within two real-world m-Commerce organizations. This includes a description of the participant's interaction with and use of the instrument. The paper then concludes with the results of the instruments implementation and its overall impact on the process for creating m-Commerce services.

Keywords: Innovation process · Front end of innovation · Mobile commerce services

1 Introduction

This research focuses on the process for creating mobile (m) commerce services. The early stages of innovation also referred to as the 'front end of innovation' (FEI) [23], is critical to the creation of m-Commerce services. This is as choices made at the front end will ultimately determine which m-service 'concept' will be considered for development and consequently commercialization. The FEI poses several challenges for the creation of m-Commerce services. For example, this process is characterized as ambiguous, uncertain and ill-defined, [2–4]. As a result, it is difficult to define or evaluate the m-service 'concept'. A poorly defined 'concept' can lead to a poorly designed 'service' and consequently a poor consumer/user experience. This research concentrates on improving the FEI activities in the context of m-Commerce services.

In particular, the paper details the implementation of an Interactive Assessment instrument, namely: The Mobile (M) Concept Assessment Instrument - to assist with defining and evaluating m-Commerce services [1] - within the innovation process of two m-Commerce organizations. A brief overview of the M-Concept Assessment Instrument [1] is provided along with a detailed description of its implementation within the m-Commerce organizations. This includes the use of the instrument by the participants (i.e. m-Commerce development teams) when defining their m-service concepts.

© Springer International Publishing Switzerland 2016
F.F.-H. Nah and C.-H. Tan (Eds.): HCIBGO 2016, Part I, LNCS 9751, pp. 491–501, 2016.
DOI: 10.1007/978-3-319-39396-4_45

Using empirical data gathered within these organizations, the paper then demonstrates an improvement to the front end of the organizations innovation process, as a result of the instruments implementation. In particular, the questions outlined in Table 1 and discussed in Sect. 3 are addressed.

Table 1. Case study questions

Case study questions	
I	How has structure and transparency been altered?
II	How has the exchange of key information been altered?
III	How has understanding been altered?

2 Background: Challenges with M-Commerce Innovation and the M-Concept Assessment Instrument

In recent years it has been argued that too many mobile service innovations fail, or do not achieve their creator's expectations, [5–7]. A possible reason for this is due to poor decision making at the early innovation stages. For example, research suggests high failure rates in the new product/service development are due to the deficiencies in effectively and efficiently managing the front end activities in the innovation process, [8–13]. Effectively managing the activities in the FEI can contribute to the overall success of a new product/service, [14, 15]. This is difficult to achieve as:

- The front end is characterized by its ambiguous nature, high uncertainty or by ill-defined processes [2–4]. As a result decisions are typically made on an ad–hoc basis and ignore key information, [16, 17].
- Key information is often ignored, if it is not exchanged effectively, [18]. This is difficult as information regarding service innovation is tacit and hardly formalized [19].
- This tacit and hardly formalized information can impact the decision makers understanding and consequently decision making in the innovation process, [16].

To address these challenges an Interactive Assessment, namely 'The Mobile (M) Concept Assessment Instrument' was introduced in an earlier publication [1]. A screenshot of this instrument is illustrated in Fig. 1. This paper builds on this earlier publication by describing the instruments impact on the process for creating m-Commerce services. Firstly a brief overview of the instrument is summarized in Sect. 2.1.

2.1 The M-Concept Assessment Instrument

The M-Concept Assessment Instrument aims to assist with defining and evaluating mobile services (e.g. m-Commerce services) in the front end of innovation. To do so m-Commerce innovators and development teams must use the instrument as a 'questionnaire tool'. The overall use of the instrument is divided into three parts, Fig. 1.

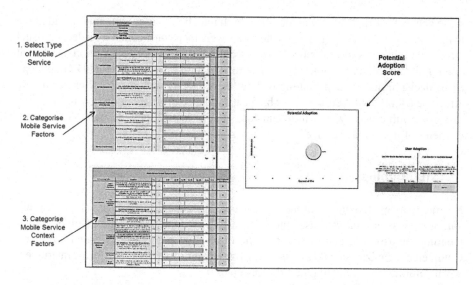

Fig. 1. M-Concept Assessment Instrument for defining and evaluating m-service concepts [1] (Color figure online)

- Firstly, it is necessary to select the particular type of mobile service you are creating from the dropdown list, e.g. transaction service, information service etc. This is illustrated as activity one in Fig. 1. This will filter the aggregated data in the background, so the data field from the relevant data table will be presented in the 3D-Graph.
- The second activity involves defining the particular mobile service characteristics which the mobile concept is likely to comprise of. This includes answering questions in relation to the characteristics of the mobile service and allocating scores to the categories which best describe their concept. For example, the development teams will consider factors such as service complexity and intuitiveness etc. This is illustrated as activity two in Fig. 1.
- The third activity in Fig. 1, defines the particular characteristics of the context within which the mobile concept is likely to be used. This involves answering questions in relation to the context of use and allocating scores to the categories which best describe their concept. Here the development team will consider factors such as the intended use situations etc.

Based on the scores that have been allocated to each of the questions, the mobile service concept is now classified in terms of the assessment instrument. For example, the type of service, its characteristics and the intended context of use, are categorized. The team will now get a 'potential' adoption score, which is represented in a three 3D-Graph. This is illustrated in Fig. 1. This adoption outcome is based on existing mobile service adoption data, which has been classified, aggregated and stored in the background of the assessment instrument [1]. The potential adoption score is divided into three parts; low, moderate and high adoption. Adoption is based on 'intention to use' [20]. Low intention to use is captured as any score under the threshold of 40 %. Any score above 41 % represents a moderate to high intention to use. Moderate would move to high once past 60 % Fig. 1. These categories were then color-coded for a deeper visual effect. Red indicates low adoption, dark green indicates moderate adoption and bright green indicates high adoption, Fig. 1. The information provided by the 3D Graph, can assist decision makers understating of how these factors will positively or negatively affect the adoption of their service. This visual aid also provides necessary information in a perceptible way, which they can later use to justify their decisions for certain elements of the mobile service.

3   Methodology

In order to assess the impact of the M-Concept Assessment Instrument [1] on the innovation process, a multiple case study approach [21] is applied. This involves implementing the assessment instrument in the innovation process of two real world m-Commerce organizations and assessing the participant's experiences with the instrument when defining and evaluating mobile concepts.

Firstly, case study questions are specified to frame what specifically is to be investigated, these questions are outlined, Table 1. These are formed based on the challenges in the innovation process reported in Sect. 2.

- The first challenge states the innovation process lacks structure and transparency and as a result decisions are made on an ad hoc basis and ignore key information [2–4, 16, 17]. To understand if the instrument addresses this issue, the first question asks: How has structure and transparency been altered? Transparency in terms of this research this is the concept of facilitating any course of action with relevant and necessary information, in an organised and structured way, [17, 24].
- The second challenge suggests key information is often ignored as it is not exchanged effectively [18]. As a result the second question asks: How has the exchange of key information been altered? In terms of this research information exchange refers to the interpersonal exchange of information among the participants, [25].
- Finally, it was recognized that this key information is tacit and hardly formalized which therefore impacts decision makers understanding and consequently their decisions in the innovation process [16, 19]. Therefore the final question asks: How has understanding been altered? Understanding in terms of this research refers to the team member's comprehension of key decision elements, [24, 26–28].

Consequently, these questions highlight the main focus of this paper. These are addressed in Sect. 5 where the data analysis and findings are reported.

Secondly, profiles of the participating organisations are created, these are provided in Table 2. This table includes an overview of the following: the organisation (i.e. sector and size), the organisations innovation process, the participants and the m-Commerce concept to be defined and assessed using the M-Concept Assessment Instrument.

Table 2. Case profiles

Case	Case Study One (CS1)	Case Study Two (CS2)
Organisational Sector	Private	Private
Organisational Size	Small; <50 employees	Small; <50 employees
Innovation Process Activities	Semi-structured, formal but flexible Innovation Process	Semi-structured, formal but flexible Innovation Process
Participants	Project Manager, Design Engineer, Marketing, 2 Software Engineers, Business Analyst	Project Manager, Design Engineer, Service Administration and Support
Mobile Concept	Mobile Payment Transaction Service	Mobile Historic Information Service

Thirdly, the instrument is implemented in the innovation process of these m-Commerce organisations and used by the participants. At this stage data is collected. Firstly, observation data including field notes, template data and print out data is collected by the researcher on-site during the study. These document observations of the participant's interaction with the instrument during the study. Secondly, semi-structured interviews are conducted with each of the participants to capture their experiences with the instrument following its use. Each interview lasts for approximately 30–35 min and is recorded and transcribed.

Lastly, the observation and interview data is analysed following the hybrid inductive/deductive thematic analysis approach [22] in order to answer the case study questions outlined in Table 1. This involves allocating codes to the data (i.e. assigning labels) which are then inspected and connected to identify patterns and themes.

4   Case Studies: Implementation of the M-Concept Assessment Instrument and Data Collection

This section details the case studies conducted with two m-Commerce organisations to investigate the impact of the M-Concept Assessment Instrument on their innovation process.

4.1   Case Study One (CS1) – Mobile Transaction Service

Organisation: The first study is conducted in a private m-Commerce organisation, based in Galway, Ireland. Using the categorisation of company size proposed by the European Commission, the organisation is categorised as a small organisation with less than fifty employees. Six members of their mobile service development team participated in the study. This included a project manager, a design engineer, a business analyst, two software engineers and one member from marketing.

Innovation Process: Their innovation process is categorized as semi-structured. They have formal activities in practice such as formal client meetings, yet the process still remains flexible. The activities in the process will adjust depending on their clients' needs. For example, some activities may be necessary for one client but not for the next. Taken as a whole, there is no formal definition of the activities which take place within their innovation process.

Mobile Concept: The concept assessed using the M-Concept Assessment Instrument was a 'Mobile Payment Transaction Service'. The aim of this service is to allow one to process small payment transactions in retail/mobile shops (e.g. food at a grocery store or fruit and vegetables at a market stall) on your smartphone, anytime any-where. The end users need to create a profile and purchase online tokens, which they can use as credit for their products. The supplier can approve payment of the products by selecting an option 'approve' when the customer notifies them of the products they wish to purchase.

Instrument Implementation and Use: The study was carried out on-site at the organization. A presentation demonstrating the console of the assessment instrument was given to the participants. After this, the assessment was conducted by the participants, which involved using the M-Concept Assessment Instrument to further define and evaluate their *'Mobile Payment Transaction Service'*. During the study the participants read the instrument questions together as a group exercise. The exercise began with one member suggesting their opinion, this continued until each member in the group had voiced their opinion. The team then debated which score to allocate to each question. This continued until all questions were answered. Based on the scores allocated to each question, the instrument calculated the potential adoption score automatically. The potential adoption score received in this case was 90 %. This means CS1'S *'Mobile Payment Transaction Service'* fitted into the category *'high intention to adopt'*. This indicates that the service is likely to be adopted by its potential customers (users).

Data Collection: The observation and interview data was collected using the techniques outlined in Sect. 3. This resulted in a total of 78 pages of qualitative data which was stored in 'NVivo' a qualitative data analysis software tool. The analysis of this data and the main study findings are reported in Sect. 5.

4.2 Case Study Two (CS2) – Mobile Information Service

Organization: The second study was conducted in a private m-Commerce organization, based in *Dublin*, Ireland. Using the categorization of company size proposed by the European Commission, the organization is categorized as a small organization with less than fifty employees. Three members of their mobile service development team participated in this study. These participants included; a project manager who is also a senior software engineer, a designer who specializes in UX design and a member from service administration and support.

Innovation Process: Similar to CS1, their innovation process is categorized as semi-structured. They have formal activities in practice such as such as, Special Interest Group (SIG) meetings yet the process still remains flexible. The activities in the process will adjust depending on their clients' needs. For example, some activities may be necessary for one client but not for the next. Taken as a whole, there is no formal definition of the activities which take place within their innovation process.

Mobile Concept: The concept assessed using the M-Concept Assessment Instrument was a *'Historic-Information Mobile Service'*. The service aims to make historical information more accessible to the average person, i.e. in the tourism industry. The service will include a map with 'time capsules' throughout various locations on the map. These time capsules will include information of historical events, which took place at those locations.

Instrument Implementation and Use: Similarly to CS1 the study was carried out on-site at the organization. The participants used the M-Concept Assessment Instrument to further define and evaluate their *'Historic-Information Mobile Service'*. During the study the participants read the instrument questions together as a group exercise. The exercise began with one member suggesting their opinion, this continued until each member in the group had voiced their opinion. The team then debated which score to allocate to each question. This continued until all questions were answered. Based on the scores allocated to each question, the instrument calculated the potential adoption score automatically. The potential adoption score received in this case was 60.43 %. This means CS1'S *'Historic-Information Mobile Service'* fitted into the category *'high intention to adopt'*. This indicates that the service is likely to be adopted by its potential customers (users). Once the assessment was complete, the team reviewed their adoption score. As their score was just slightly above the 60 % they agreed certain factors such as 'use situation' may need to be redefined.

Data Collection: Similarly to CS1 the observation and interview data was collected using the techniques outlined in Sect. 3. This resulted in a total of 60 pages of qualitative data which was also stored in the NVivo database for analysis. The analysis of this data and the main study findings are reported in Sect. 5.

5   Data Analysis and Findings

The data from the two cases was analyzed using the thematic analysis technique described in Sect. 3. References made by the participants to a specific change in the innovation process was recorded, inspected and coded. There were a total of 514 references to a change in the innovation process captured in the data, Table 3. The rigorous analysis of these 514 references resulted in 4 major themes and 22 subordinate themes to explain the data and consequently the impact of the instrument on the innovation process. These themes and the number of references they received from each case are summarized in Table 3. The four major themes are now corresponded with the questions from Table 1 to understand the impact of the m-Concept Assessment Instrument.

Table 3. Themes traced in the data as a result of M-Concept Assessment Instrument

Themes traced as a result of assessment instrument	No. of References	
	CS1	CS2
I. TRANSPARENCY	9	16
Thoroughness	16	9
Structure	20	14
Structure of the Assessment Instrument	10	4
Structure of Activities	17	6
Control	3	0
II. COMMUNICATION	22	11
Quality of Information Exchanged	6	5
Relevant Information	7	10
Consistent Information	0	5
Complete Information	5	3
Information Exchange	17	6
Integrated Exchange	14	8
Engaged Exchange	14	7
III. UNDERSTANDING	16	20
Simplification	15	9
Understanding of the Mobile Concept	23	18
Consistency	6	6
Understanding of Roles	14	5
Guidance	9	10
IV. USER EXPERIENCE	8	6
Value	12	11
Usefulness	6	9
Appropriateness	8	12
Efficiency	7	7
Ease of Use	10	3
TOTAL REFERENCES	**294**	**220**

- **I. TRANSPARENCY:** In relation to the first question in Table 1: *How has structure and transparency been altered?* The data suggests the activities in the innovation process were clearer and conducted in a more thorough manner. In addition, the activities were described as well structured, and therefore easier to manage or control. One participant suggested: "*…using the instrument you can determine whether to move forward to the design stages, or back to the last activity*". This resulted in the activities and roles becoming more 'transparent'. Consequently these changes were recorded under the overarching theme '*Transparency*'. This theme therefore suggests: m-Commerce organizations can clearly and thoroughly define and evaluate mobile concepts in a more structured and controlled manner via the assessment instrument.

- **II. COMMUNICATION:** In relation to the second question in Table 1: *How has the exchange of key information been altered?* The data suggests the exchange of information was more integrated as the opinions of all participants were taken on board. Additionally, the participants were more engaged when exchanging information in the innovation process. Furthermore, the information exchanged, was described as relevant, complete and consistent. This resulted in improved communication during the innovation process. Consequently these changes were recorded under the overarching theme *'Communication'*. This theme therefore suggests: by using the instrument, m-Commerce organizations can exchange relevant and complete information necessary to define and evaluate mobile concepts in a more integrated and engaged manner.
- **III. UNDERSTANDING:** In relation to the third question in Table 1: *How has understanding been altered?* The data suggests it is easier to define the concept as the instrument illustrates the alternative characteristics which describe the mobile concept and its context of use. In addition, the instrument simplified the act of evaluating mobile concepts in the innovation process. For example, based on the categories selected to define the concept a potential adoption score is presented in a 3D-Graph. As a result, the understanding of the key decision elements was improved. Consequently these changes were recorded under the overarching theme *'Understanding'*. This theme therefore suggests the simplification and guidance of the innovation activities by the instrument can enable m-Commerce organizations to comprehend key decision elements in the innovation process.
- **IV. USER EXPERIENCE:** The theme 'User Experience' also emerged from the data, Table 3. This refers to the participant's perceptions and experience with the assessment instrument, [29]. A positive user reaction with the assessment instrument was traced in both cases. For example, the data suggests the assessment instrument is valuable as it can prevent problems arising in the later testing stages. This is as using the instrument can highlight issues prior to development. The instrument also resulted in each participant being more informed and up-to date with the mobile concept, reducing the number of informal discussions. The data also suggests that little effort was required to use the instrument and therefore it is easy to use. For example, one of the participants suggested: "...*the assessment is laid out like a spreadsheet exercise; you simply has to assign scores to the categories*".

The major themes and almost all of the subordinate themes referenced in case study one, have also been referenced in case study two, Table 3. Analytical generalization suggests if two or more cases are shown to support the same outcomes replication can be claimed [21]. Thus, replication is claimed. This is an important conclusion for the creators of m-Commerce services as organizations that fit the profiles of the organizations in this study should expect similar outcomes to emerge following implementation of the M-Concept Assessment Instrument [1].

6 Conclusion

This paper built on an earlier publication [1], where an Interactive Assessment, namely 'The Mobile (M) Concept Assessment Instrument' was proposed to assist with defining and evaluating m-Commerce (mobile) services. In particular, the paper demonstrated an improvement to the process for creating m-Commerce services as a result of implementing the instrument in two real world m-Commerce organizations. Evidence of changes to (i) the structure of the innovation activities were found. This resulted in the activities and roles becoming more *transparent*. In addition, changes to (ii) the exchange of key information was recognized, which resulted in improved *communication* during the innovation process. Finally, evidence that (iii) the innovation activities were 'simplified' was also presented. This resulted in improved *understanding* of key decision elements in the process for creating m-Commerce services. Along with these changes to the innovation process a positive user experience with the assessment instrument was traced across both cases. These findings hold important implications for creators of m-Commerce services, as organizations which fit similar profiles to those within this study should expect similar outcomes to emerge following implementation of the M-Concept Assessment Instrument. Consequently they can also benefit from an improvement to their innovation process. Further case study investigations are currently being undertaken to extend the generalization of the findings.

Acknowledgments. This research is funded by the Irish Research Council (IRC). The authors would like to acknowledge their support. Additionally, the authors would like to extend their appreciation to the participating organizations for their commitment to this research.

References

1. Carey, K., Helfert, M.: An interactive assessment instrument to improve the process for mobile service application innovation. In: Fui-Hoon Nah, F., Tan, C.-H. (eds.) HCIB 2015. LNCS, vol. 9191, pp. 244–255. Springer, Heidelberg (2015)
2. Akbar, H., Tzokas, N.: An exploration of new product development's front-end knowledge conceptualization process in discontinuous innovations. Br. J. Manag. **24**(2), 245–263 (2013)
3. Aagaard, A., Gertsen, F.: Supporting radical front end innovation: perceived key factors of pharmaceutical innovation. Creativity Innov. Manag. **20**(4), 330–346 (2011)
4. Jörgensen, J.H., Bergenholtz, C., Goduscheit, R.C., Rasmussen, E.S.: Managing inter-firm collaboration in the fuzzy front-end: structure as a two-edged sword. Int. J. Innov. Manag. **15**(01), 145–163 (2011)
5. Carlsson, C., Rossi, M., Tuunainen, V.K., Walden, P., Hampe, J.F., Scornavacca, E., Tuunanen, T.: Introduction to mobile value services, mobile business and mobile cloud minitrack. In: 46th Hawaii International Conference on System Sciences, pp. 1323–1323. IEEE (2013)
6. Nikou, S., Mezei, J.: Evaluation of mobile services and substantial adoption factors with analytic hierarchy process (AHP). Telecommun. Policy **37**(10), 915–929 (2013)
7. Gao, S., Krogstie, J., Siau, K.: Developing an instrument to measure the adoption of mobile services. Mob. Inf. Syst. **7**(1), 45–67 (2011)

8. Postma, T.J., Broekhuizen, T.L., Van den Bosch, F.: The contribution of scenario analysis to the front-end of new product development. Futures **44**(6), 642–654 (2012)

9. Poskela, J., Martinsuo, M.: Management control and strategic renewal in the front end of innovation. J. Prod. Innov. Manag. **26**(6), 671–684 (2009)

10. Sætre, A.S., Brun, E.: Strategic management of innovation: managing exploration-exploitation by balancing creativity and constraint. Int. J. Innov. Technol. Manag. **9**(04), 1250025 (2012)

11. Cooper, R.G.: Winning at New Products: Creating Value Through Innovation. Basic Books, New York (2011)

12. Ho, Y., Tsai, C.: Front end of innovation of high technology industries: the moderating effect of front-end fuzziness. J. High Technol. Manag. Res. **22**(1), 47–58 (2011)

13. Verworn, B., Herstatt, C., Nagahira, A.: The fuzzy front end of Japanese new product development projects: impact on success and differences between incremental and radical projects. R&D Manag. **38**(1), 1–19 (2008)

14. Alam, I.: Removing the fuzziness from the fuzzy front-end of service innovations through customer interactions. Ind. Mark. Manag. **35**(4), 468–480 (2006)

15. Kim, J., Wilemon, D.: Strategic issues in managing innovation's fuzzy front-end. Eur. J. Innov. Manag. **5**(1), 27–39 (2002)

16. Hannola, L., Ovaska, P.: Challenging front-end-of-innovation in information systems. J. Comput. Inf. Syst. **52**(1), 66 (2011)

17. Gregory, R., Failing, L., Harstone, M., Long, G., McDaniels, T., Ohlson, D.: Structured Decision Making: A Practical Guide to Environmental Management Choices. Wiley, Chichester (2012)

18. Garvey, W.D.: Communication: The Essence of Science: Facilitating Information Exchange Among Librarians, Scientists, Engineers and Students. Elsevier, Burlington (2014)

19. Bouwman, H., De Vos, H., Haaker, T.: Mobile Service Innovation and Business Models. Springer, Heidelberg (2008)

20. Davis, F.D.: Perceived usefulness, perceived ease of use, and user acceptance of information technology. MIS Q. **13**, 319–340 (1989)

21. Yin, R.K.: Case Study Research: Design and Methods. Sage Publications, Thousand Oaks (2013)

22. Fereday, J., Muir-Cochrane, E.: Demonstrating rigor using thematic analysis: a hybrid approach of inductive and deductive coding and theme development. Int. J. Qual. Meth. **5**(1), 80–92 (2008)

23. Koen, P., Ajamian, G., Burkart, R., Clamen, A., Davidson, J., D'Amore, R., Elkins, C., Herald, K., Incorvia, M., Johnson, A.: Providing clarity and a common language to the. Res. Technol. Manag. **44**(2), 46–55 (2001)

24. Cabantous, L., Gond, J., Johnson-Cramer, M.: Decision theory as practice: crafting rationality in organizations. Organ. Stud. **31**(11), 1531–1566 (2010)

25. Desanctis, G., Gallupe, R.B.: A foundation for the study of group decision support systems. Manag. Sci. **33**(5), 589–609 (1987)

26. Schwenk, C.R.: Cognitive simplification processes in strategic decision-making. Strateg. Manag. J. **5**(2), 111–128 (1984)

27. Marques, G., Gourc, D., Lauras, M.: Multi-criteria performance analysis for decision making in project management. Int. J. Proj. Manag. **29**(8), 1057–1069 (2011)

28. MacKenzie, D.: Is economics performative? Option theory and the construction of derivatives markets. J. Hist. Econ. Thought **28**(1), 29–55 (2006)

29. Morville, P.: Facets of the User Experience. Semantic Studios (2004). http://semanticstudios.com/user_experience_design/

Information Technology Adoption: Do Performance Objectives and Incentive Structures Make a Difference?

Brenda Eschenbrenner[✉]

University of Nebraska at Kearney, Kearney, NE, USA
eschenbrenbl@unk.edu

Abstract. User adoption of information technology (IT) is important to organizations to maximize their return on investment. However, if appropriate support is not structured to encourage this endeavor, subsequent IT usage may be problematic. Of the various types of organizational support, performance objectives may be structured to influence user IT learning and adoption efforts. Although previous research has addressed adopting IT and deciding when to learn IT, research has not looked at the impact that performance objectives, along with the appropriate incentives, can have on this endeavor. This research study proposes to explore this issue to lend insights into the influence that performance objectives and incentive structures can have on a user's decision to learn and adopt IT, as well as subsequent performance outcomes. The potential contribution includes suggestions for appropriate support structures to establish that contribute to IT adoption and proficient IT usage.

Keywords: Information technology · Performance objectives · Incentive structures · IT learning · IT adoption

1 Introduction

Organizations invest in new information technology (IT) on a continuous basis with the expectation that IT users will deploy these technologies to their fullest extent so return on investment will be maximized. Therefore, it's important for IT users to learn and adopt newly implemented IT. However, if organizations do not provide the appropriate support structures to invigorate this behavior, proficient IT usage may be lacking. Supporting structures can also be inconsistent or insufficient in explicitly developing proficient IT usage.

The general expectation is that IT users are to become proficient with a newly implemented IT, even when the appropriate support or incentive structures that would encourage them to deploy a new IT is not devised. The belief may be that such usage is implied. However, providing incentives that focus on task completion without encouraging users to explore better ways of accomplishing it may discourage users from applying the most appropriate IT to complete a task. Hence, technology may not be used to the greatest extent that it could, and the resources that are being invested in new technologies may be wasted.

© Springer International Publishing Switzerland 2016
F.F.-H. Nah and C.-H. Tan (Eds.): HCIBGO 2016, Part I, LNCS 9751, pp. 502–510, 2016.
DOI: 10.1007/978-3-319-39396-4_46

Although many are concerned with individual IT usage, they are equally concerned with or even more concerned with accomplishing overarching, short-term performance objectives such as meeting quarterly reporting deadlines or financial targets. Hence, many performance objectives are written as such to focus users' efforts and attention on achievement of these overarching, short-term performance objectives. Although technology may be utilized by an individual to accomplish these performance objectives, its explicit use may not be required. Also, IT users may be encouraged to use a new technology or inspired to use the new technology through training. However, the actual objectives that are established for IT users do not incorporate these learning aspects and utilization of new technology (or the means) but focus on completing the final objective (the ends).

Therefore, the research question posed is: Do performance objectives and incentive structures that explicitly focus on learning and adopting new technologies as well as achieving accurate outcomes, respectively, result in greater utilization of the technology and higher quality performance outcomes?

To answer this question, an experiment will be conducted to assess the effectiveness of performance objectives and incentive structures which vary in terms of incorporating (1) learning and adopting technology objectives and (2) task completion only or accurate task completion incentives. The findings will provide insight into an individual's propensity to learn and adopt technology (specifically, software applications) and apply it to a task when it is explicitly indicated rather than implicitly stated. Also, the results will provide insights into the quality of outcomes that are realized when incentive structures are focused on achieving accuracy versus task completion, and what influence this may have on the overall selection of technology to be applied.

2   Literature Review

IT users are faced with a challenging decision – should they: (1) invest the time and effort to learn and adopt novel technology that may accomplish a task better, or (2) utilize other familiar technology or means to complete the task so no added learning investment is needed and there is greater certainty regarding the outcome. This dilemma is consistent with the cognitive cost/benefit framework which proposes "individuals weigh benefits (impact on correctness, speed, and justifiability) and costs (mental effort of information acquisition and computation) before choosing a strategy for processing information in decision-making." [1, p. 1830]. Previous research results suggest that organizations need to consider the relationship between compensation structures and IT adoption which can have an important influence on final task performance [2]. Previous studies have combined and expanded upon previous models and research of technology adoption by developing the coping model of user adaptation (CMUA) [3]. The model proposes that adapting or modifying technology can bring about a disruption to the work environment, and users can cope with the change with a variety of strategies, from benefit maximization to self-preservation. Therefore, upon the introduction of a new technology, individuals can respond in a variety of manners – with some leading to full utilization of the new technology and others avoiding it and finding alternative means to complete existing tasks.

Previous research suggests that performance measures that are nonfinancial are more likely to foster innovation and risk taking [4]. Therefore, if performance objectives are focused on activities such as learning a technology (versus simply completing a task or getting the job done), they may encourage users to innovate and explore the technology and find new, better, and more creative ways to accomplish tasks with it. Previous research has also had some focus on learning and applying technology. For example, research has focused on the impact of various incentive contracts on learning and performance outcomes [5]. The study found that individuals with incentive-based contracts (versus flat-wage contracts) were more likely to learn (revise their beliefs), increase effort (longer task duration), and improve performance. As another example, research has examined the influence that perceived usefulness, time pressures, and subjective norms have on an individual's decision to learn novel technology functions [6]. The findings indicated that supportive structures can directly influence whether or not one elects to pursue learning and incorporating technology into work routines.

However, previous studies have not explicitly focused on the impact of incorporating performance objectives and incentive structures for IT users, and their subsequent impact on successful technology adoption and performance outcomes. In other words, what has not been evaluated is the impact of performance objectives supporting learning and applying a technology and the resulting choice of whether or not to learn a new technology that may assist one to accomplish tasks better. Also, when incentive structures are established that explicitly determine how an individual may be compensated, different choices in actions may occur. If the individual is to produce a high-quality outcome, they may be more inclined to select the technology that has a better fit with the task even if it requires an investment to learn. However, if the individual is not given incentives to produce a high-quality outcome, then they may be more inclined to select a more familiar technology that doesn't require the learning investment even if the quality of the outcome suffers. Hence, the research objective for this study is to evaluate the impact of performance objectives that explicitly incorporate learning and adoption (i.e., specify learning and adopting the technology) and incentive structures that focus on producing quality outcomes (i.e., accurate task completion).

3   Theoretical Foundation and Hypotheses Development

In conducting this research, transaction cost economics, attribution theory, technology-to-performance chain, and task-technology fit model provide the theoretical basis for the hypotheses.

3.1   Transaction Cost Economics

Transaction cost economics has been applied in organizational contexts in which the task or transaction costs are examined under various governance structures [7–10]. These transactions can vary by degree of asset specificity (change in value that may occur if an investment made in a particular transaction is reallocated), unknowns/uncertainties, and frequency [8, 10]. Although transaction cost economics has been studied from an organizational perspective, individual-level application is relevant as well. Contract theory has been proposed to be applicable to a variety of transactions [10]. In the context of contracts, the substance of performance objectives can be viewed as a contract because employees are eligible for rewards if the performance objectives are accomplished according to pre-determined criteria. Transaction cost economics can be applied to employment contracts because of the unique nature of job tasks and processes.

Employment contracts have been proposed to be deficient and give employees volition regarding task completion [10]. Therefore, employment contracts can introduce variability in performance outcomes because of the discretion provided in methods or manners utilized to accomplish tasks. Transaction cost economics' assumptions include bounded rationality and opportunism [8]. Bounded rationality implies individuals have cognitive limitations regardless of their intentions, and opportunism suggests that individuals may prioritize their own interests above other interests.

In applying transaction cost economics to the decision an employee makes in deciding whether or not to learn and apply a new technology to a particular job task, transaction costs exist for the employee in terms of the time and effort required to learn the technology and apply it to the task (versus performing the task using existing, familiar methods). Because of bounded rationality, the employee may intend to perform the task in the most effective and efficient manner possible, but cannot predict whether learning and utilizing the new technology will yield those results. Hence, a level of uncertainty arises. Also, considering the assumptions of opportunism, an employee would be more likely to pursue the option that provides him/her with greater rewards or least costs or effort, even if at the expense of the organization.

When learning and adopting technology performance objectives are not included and incentive structures are based on task completion only, the employee may focus on completing the task with known methods (i.e., not learn and adopt the new technology) because it reduces the level of uncertainty in achieving the incentives which provides opportunities for monetary rewards. Therefore, the following hypothesis is proposed.

H1: Individuals will have a greater propensity to use a familiar technology to complete a task if the incentive specifies task completion only and there is no learning and adopting technology performance objective than when a learning and adopting technology performance objective is provided.

3.2   Attribution Theory

Attribution Theory proposes that individuals make causal attributions to explain behavioral phenomena, or explain why people behave the way they do [11]. These causal attributions have been demonstrated to be the stimulus for subsequent actions or the response that one has [12]. For example, previous research found that when individuals were subject to a binding contract, their cooperative efforts were attributed to the constraints of the contract [13]. However, when a nonbinding contract was utilized, cooperative efforts were attributed to trustworthiness. Karsten [12] found similarities between the casual attributions of IS professionals and IS users when successful performance outcomes were achieved by IS users. However, when unsuccessful outcomes were realized, causal attributions deviated.

Therefore, research has shown, through the application of Attribution Theory, that when specific intentions are not made explicit, individuals may attribute the behaviors of another with their own explanations. Individuals may interpret the particular event with their own meanings and derive their own implications of another's actions or inactions. Hence, when incentive structures do not specify that the quality of the outcome from IT use is more important than obtaining any outcome, IT users may attribute getting the task completed to be of greater importance than getting the task completed accurately. IT users may attribute incentive structures that provide no impetus for achieving a certain level of quality results to an organization's lack of concern for quality and a greater concern for just "getting it done." In conjunction with transaction cost economics, IT users may act opportunistically and complete the task with a more familiar technology even if it may result in less accurate outcomes. Therefore, incentive structures that specifically incorporate accomplishing a task with greatest accuracy may be more likely to result in individuals selecting the technology that will produce the most accurate results. Hence, individuals will be more likely to learn and adopt a new technology that is a better fit with the task and can provide more accurate outcomes than utilize a familiar technology even if no learning and adopting technology performance objectives are given.

Based on the above, the following hypotheses are proposed:

H2: Individuals will have a greater propensity to learn and adopt a new technology to complete a task if the incentive specifies task completion accuracy and there is no learning and adopting technology performance objective than when the incentive specifies task completion only.

H3: Individuals will have a greater propensity to learn and adopt a new technology to complete a task if the incentive specifies task completion accuracy and there is a learning and adopting technology performance objective than when the incentive specifies task completion only.

3.3 Technology-to-Performance Chain and Task-Technology Fit

According to the technology-to-performance chain, technology that is appropriate to complete the task and utilized by an individual can produce positive performance outcomes [14]. Task-technology fit (TTF) has been "defined as the extent that technology functionality matches task requirements and individual abilities. Task-technology fit is presumed to lead to higher performance" [1, p. 1829]. Specifically, "TTF is the correspondence between task requirements, individual abilities, and the functionality of the technology." [14, p. 218]. To the extent that technologies have greater TTF, improved performance outcomes are more likely to occur.

Greater utilization of a technology alone will not necessarily produce positive outcomes. If the technology used to accomplish the task is not the most effective or appropriate (i.e., it is less likely to produce the most accurate results), then performance may suffer. Therefore, individuals who continue to utilize existing technologies that are less likely to produce accurate outcomes may not improve performance. If individuals adopt a new technology that is more likely to produce accurate outcomes (i.e., has a more appropriate fit to the task), then individual performance can be positively impacted. Hence, the incentive structures and performance objectives given to an employee can influence his/her choice of technology to accomplish the task and the quality of the outcome.

Based on the above, the following hypothesis is proposed:

H4: Individuals will have a greater propensity to learn and adopt a new technology to complete a task if a learning and adopting technology performance objective is provided and the incentive specifies task completion accuracy than when a learning and adopting technology performance objective is not provided.

4   Research Method

4.1   Overview

To test the research hypotheses for this study, a 2×2 design is proposed (see Fig. 1) in which performance objectives and incentive structures are manipulated. Subjects will carry out tasks to analyze accounting information using either Microsoft Excel or Access. The research subjects will receive the same training and complete the same exercises, but will receive variations in their performance objectives (learning and adopting technology performance objective versus no performance objective) and incentives (task completion only versus task completion accuracy). Subjects will be randomly assigned to one of the four experimental conditions and will be asked to not disclose the specifics of their performance objectives and incentives to other subjects. The subjects will receive training along with their performance objectives and incentives (performance objectives and incentives will be given before the training commences). In the following week, subjects will complete the associated exercises with either Microsoft Excel or Access. A pre-study questionnaire will be administered before the initial training, and a post-study questionnaire will be administered after the exercises are completed. The time allowed for training and exercise completion will be held constant for each condition.

Learning & Adopting Objective	Y	Learn & Adopt New Technology Objective and Task Completion Incentive	Learn & Adopt New Technology Objective and Task Completion Accuracy Incentive
	N	No Learn & Adopt New Technology Objective and Task Completion Incentive	No Learn & Adopt New Technology Objective and Task Completion Accuracy Incentive
		Task Completion	Task Completion Accuracy
		Incentive Structure	

Fig. 1. Research Design

Course credit for the task will be based on the assigned incentive structure. Analysis of the effects of the different performance objectives and incentive structures will be assessed by comparing the method used to complete the task (Microsoft Excel or Access), and number of exercises completed correctly.

4.2 Subjects

Undergraduate students who are experienced Microsoft Excel users but are not experienced with Microsoft Access will be recruited. Students will receive the same training, and will receive their grade (final course credit earned) upon completion of the experiment.

Table 1. Research Conditions

Condition	Condition description
1	Incentives specify task completion and no performance objectives given. Course credit earned based on number of tasks completed, regardless of accuracy (2 points per task, total of 3 tasks per session possible or total of 6 points per session to be earned).
2	Incentives specify accuracy of task completion and no performance objectives given. Course credit earned based on number of tasks accurately completed (2 points per correct answer, total of 3 answers per session possible or total of 6 points per session to be earned).
3	Incentives specify task completion and performance objectives specify learning and adopting new technology. Course credit earned based on how well they have learned Microsoft Access (2 points per task, total of 3 tasks per session possible or total of 6 points per session to be earned).
4	Incentives specify accuracy of task completion and performance objectives specify learning and adopting new technology. Course credit earned based on how well they have learned Microsoft Access AND completed tasks accurately (2 points per correct answer, total of 3 answers per session possible or total of 6 points per session to be earned).

4.3 Procedure and Measures

In the initial session, subjects will be trained on Microsoft Excel (a refresher course) and Microsoft Access. During the initial training, they will also be asked to complete a demographic questionnaire in which they rate their need for cognition and need for achievement on a scale of 1 to 7 (with 1 being completely unmotivated and 7 being extremely motivated). Also, measures of computer self-efficacy, previous technology/ software experience, level of familiarity with Excel, and level of familiarity with Access will be gathered. The training session will entail reviewing (for Excel) and learning (for Access) those skills needed to complete the required exercises for the following week. The exercises will be tailored so that they can be completed with either Microsoft Excel or Access, but utilizing Excel will be more complicated and cumbersome and, hence, more prone to errors. The performance objectives and incentives structures for each condition are summarized in Table 1.

After completion of the exercises, they will receive their course credit earned. They will also be asked which technology they chose to use (Excel or Access) to complete the exercises and asked "Why they chose to use that particular technology". The latter part of this question will ask them to first rate on a scale of 1 to 7 (1 being completely unimportant to 7 being extremely important) if factors such as "Familiarity with the technology", "Instructor concern with using the Technology", "Ability to meet Learning Objectives", "Ability to achieve Course Credit", "Greater efficiency", "Greater effectiveness", etc. were weighed in their decision. They will also have the opportunity to provide any open-ended feedback after these ratings. Measures of number of exercises completed correctly will be taken and assessed by the researcher and one other individual who is familiar with Microsoft Excel and Access.

5   Results and Discussion

A 2 × 2 between-group factorial ANOVA will be used for data analysis. For hypothesis 1, analyses will be made of the use of technology (Excel versus Access) and accuracy of outcomes between the performance objective conditions (learning and adopting technology performance objective versus none). For hypothesis 2, analyses will be made of the technology selection and accuracy of the outcomes made for each group between the incentive structures conditions (task completion only incentive versus task completion accuracy incentive).

For hypothesis 3, analyses will be made of the use of technology (Excel versus Access) and the accuracy of the outcomes when the incentive structure indicates that accuracy of task completion is to be rewarded and learning and adopting technology performance objectives are provided. For hypothesis 4, analyses will be made of the use of technology (Excel versus Access) and the accuracy of the outcomes between the performance objective conditions (learning and adopting technology performance objective versus none) when incentives for task completion accuracy are given.

6   Implications and Conclusion

If the hypotheses are supported, this will indicate that given the choice of the means to complete a task, an IT user is more likely to select a familiar means and focus on completing a task regardless of being trained on a new technology that could provide a more efficient means and accurate task completion. Therefore, those who are concerned with the adoption of a new technology should align performance objectives with these concerns in order to derive the behavior that is desired from their IT users. Also, the results will imply that establishing incentive structures that are based on the quality of outcomes achieved can lead to individuals selecting a technology that is more appropriate for the task, which can result in more successful task outcomes. The results from this study would also imply that the application of a new technology will not just happen automatically, even after training has occurred, and assumptions should not be made that IT users know the importance of learning and adopting a new technology.

In conclusion, this research proposes to look at the influence that variations in performance objectives and incentive structures can have on the learning/adoption of a new technology and task performance outcomes. If IT users are being evaluated on other criteria that do not necessarily require new technology's use, then IT users may be confused as to the appropriate actions to take – use a familiar means to complete the task so the objective has more certainty to be met or take a risk and invest the time to learn the technology and use it to complete the task. Overall, this research will contribute to the knowledge of performance objectives' and incentive structures' influences (as well as their variations) on IT users' decisions to learn and adopt a technology to achieve higher quality outcomes versus just getting the job done.

References

1. Goodhue, D.L.: Understanding user evaluations of information systems. Manag. Sci. **41**(12), 1827–1844 (1995)
2. Mauldin, E.: An experimental examination of information technology and compensation structure complementarities in an expert system context. J. Inf. Syst. **17**(1), 19–42 (2003)
3. Beaudry, A., Pinsonneault, A.: Understanding user responses to information technology: A coping model of user adaptation. MIS Q. **29**(3), 493–524 (2005)
4. Chow, C.W., Van der Stede, W.A.: The use and usefulness of nonfinancial performance measures. Manag. Account. Q. **7**(3), 1–8 (2006)
5. Sprinkle, G.B.: The effect of incentive contracts on learning and performance. Account. Rev. **75**(3), 299–326 (2000)
6. Loraas, T., Wolfe, C.J.: Why wait? Modeling factors that influence the decision of when to learn a new use of technology. J. Inf. Syst. **20**(2), 1–23 (2006)
7. Covaleski, M.A., Dirsmith, M.W., Samuel, S.: Changes in the institutional environment and the institutions of governance: extending the contributions of transaction cost economics within the management control literature. Account. Organ. Soc. **28**(5), 417–442 (2003)
8. Spekle, R.: Explaining management control structure variety: A transaction cost economics perspective. Account. Organ. Soc. **26**(4/5), 419–442 (2001)
9. Widener, S.K.: An empirical investigation of the relation between the use of strategic human capital and the design of the management control system. Account. Organ. Soc. **29**(3/4), 377–401 (2004)
10. Williamson, O.E.: The economic institutions of capitalism. Free Press, New York (1985)
11. Coletti, A.L., Sedatole, K.L., Towry, K.L.: The effect of control systems on trust and cooperation in collaborative environments. Account. Rev. **80**(2), 477–500 (2005)
12. Karsten, R.: An analysis of IS professional and end user causal attributions for user-system outcomes. J. End-User Comput. **14**(4), 51–73 (2002)
13. Malhotra, D., Murnighan, J.K.: The effects of contracts on interpersonal trust. Adm. Sci. Q. **47**(3), 534–559 (2002)
14. Goodhue, D.L., Thompson, R.L.: Task-technology fit and individual performance. MIS Q. **19**(2), 213–236 (1995)

The Outcome-Based Collaborative Brainstorming of Strategic Service Design

Rich C. Lee[✉]

National Sun Yat-sen University, Kaohsiung, Taiwan
richchihlee@gmail.com

Abstract. During the phases of an innovation lifecycle, from the value proposition to realization, is about brainstorming especially in its early phases. The success of the brainstorming process depends on many factors, the diversity of the team members, the boundary spanning capability, the ability of foreseeing the insight of risks in the future, etc. On the other hand, the innovation is also a collaborating process of exploring the differentiating value propositions from the target competitors or the benchmark artifacts in the market; the outcomes must be clear to kickoff the next step of the initiative. How to encourage the team members to make their best efforts to contribute their thoughts and ideas and come out with a rational decision about the resolution with consensus is the key to the successful brainstorming process. This paper presents a novel brainstorming process, including the roles, the responsibilities, the facilitating, the workflow, and the theories behind, for service design and got satisfied results from the empirical cases that were government-funded service projects.

Keywords: Open Innovation Model · Service design · Brainstorming · Group decision

1 Introduction

Nowadays the most effective approach of differentiating against the business rivals is through innovation (Aghion et al. 2014). The challenges of innovation are from various perspectives: (1) how to create a culture that encourages creativity and innovation (Alamsyah and Yerki 2015); (2) how to develop the winning ideas that are customer-centered; (3) how to create a feasible action plan to boost the breakthrough of products and services; (4) how to manage these under developing ideas to be an asset for further inspiration; (5) how to let the top management support these ideas through involvement and understanding; and (6) how to effectively communicate the ideas with the functional departments (Baker 2015). Apparently, the innovation is the synergy of those outcomes that generated by the brainstorming process, thus the quality of the brainstorming will determine the impact of the innovation.

The essence of innovation is to identify the competitive services against rivals based on the firm's resources which are not easy to mimic and to replicate. But the firms are always short of some resources for their initiatives, apply the Open Innovation Model—collaborating with the complementary partners to mature a new

© Springer International Publishing Switzerland 2016
F.F.-H. Nah and C.-H. Tan (Eds.): HCIBGO 2016, Part I, LNCS 9751, pp. 511–518, 2016.
DOI: 10.1007/978-3-319-39396-4_47

product or service–seems to be the answer of expediting the time-to-market. The competitive services have three supporting pillars (Qiu 2014): (1) **science**—giving the support from the theory or the facts to the innovation; (2) **management**—effectively and efficiently using the resources to develop and realize the innovation; and (3) **engineering**—realizing the innovative service products or business model. The innovation is a holistic thinking model mixed with the perspectives of (Ho 2014): (1) **social**—how customers can be benefited and how our society will be influenced from the innovative services; (2) **technology**—how technologies will be applied, integrated, and derived to substantiate the innovation; (3) **economic**—how the innovative services will improve the firm's financial status and lead the whole value chain to grow; and (4) **policy**—the tactics of the firm to promote the innovative services or the principles of sustaining them. The competitive services are also the *target*—such as building the ecosystem, creating a new business model, designing a new product or service, and enhancing the firm's core competence—of the strategy of the innovation, it must begin with the scanning against the current situation as the *baseline*—such as the capability of the firm, the SWOT of products and services in the market, and set a series of *sequencing plans or initiatives*—such as marketing the value propositions, designing the excellent services and selling them—to mitigate the gap to success (Simon et al. 2014) (Fig. 1).

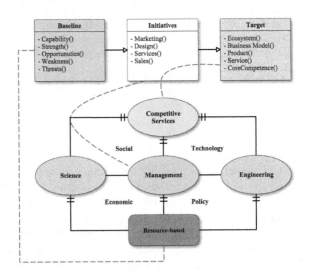

Fig. 1. The service science approach of innovation

This paper aims to answer that how to make people contribute their best knowledge, experiences, and ideas to stimulate the innovation effectively. The common brainstorming of thinking may include: (1) **time frames**—such as waiting for another technology or market to be more mature to accept the innovation, different ones might change the essence of the issue; (2) **locations**—such as deployed the innovation in the city or the rural, different ones would bring broader views about the issue; (3) **attributes**—such as consumed the services by genders or ages, different ones could be more thoughtful to the solution; (4) **roles**—such as from the service buyer or the user's perspective, different ones could change the way of design; and (5) **context**—such as applying the same innovation on various contexts, different ones might appreciate the innovation more and shorten the time-to-market. Therefore, the diversity of the brainstorming team will help the innovation cover more aforementioned perspectives. The competitive services, the target, are the outcome of the brainstorming; without the outcome which should meet the expectation of the executives will be a kind of resource waste, a dead-weight loss of organizational activities, certainly cannot expect it will lead to any innovation.

2 The Outcome-Based Brainstorming Process

The major issue of brainstorming is the cost of communication, especially when its outcome does not meet the expectation of the executive. The reasons why the outcome is not effective and satisfied are: (1) the executive did not disclose the expected outcome specifically; (2) the executive did not play any part of the brainstorming; (3) the team members did not have the equal opportunity of sharing the idea; (4) there was no one leading the discussion effectively; (5) the arguments either were not based on the solid ground nor had a balanced perspective; (6) the discussion did not reach the consensus; (7) the discussion ended up with a list of tangled view points but no tangible outcome; (8) the discussion was conducted under a unequal influence or imbalanced power atmosphere; (9) some details of the discussion including possible value points were trimmed off due to lacking of sufficient notes; and (10) others such as incompetent team members who just could not deliver the outcome.

To improve the brainstorming, this paper presents a novel approach to encourage the team members to contribute their thoughts more efficiently by using the similar form of workshop (Simons et al. 2015). First, to lower down the insufficient communication, a big team needs to break into smaller groups, and reorganizes each group based on the roles and their responsibilities during the brainstorming as illustrated in the Table 1. There are two categories of roles; each role is associated with a nickname to emphasize its characteristics. The first category includes the **Executive**—its nickname is the *Emperor* making the final judgment calls on the direction of the further brainstorming, explicitly expresses the expectations and the goals from the brainstorming—and the **Facilitator**—its nickname is the *Judge Dredd* (borrowed from a famous comic and movie character) mastering the theme, guides the brainstorming process and inspires the groups' creativeness, while the other one contains the roles: (1) **Presenter**—its nickname is the *Silverback*, leads the discussion and manages the direction of value propositions; (2) **Informant**—its nickname is the *Eagle* overseeing the big picture, giving the supporting information to the proposition; (3) **Secretary**—its nickname is the *Lioness* hunting the prey, keeps records of the details of threads; (4) **Writer**—its nickname is the *Peacock* showing off the value points, distils the threads into valuable points; and (5) **Challenger**—its nickname is the *Wild Duck* always thinking out of the box, works as a critique role to maintain the quality of the discussion, in a group.

Table 1. The roles and their responsibilities

Role	Nickname	Description
Executive	Emperor	Giving the specific expectation about the outcome from the brainstorming process
Facilitator	Judge Dredd	Facilitating the brainstorming process and leading the discussion toward the expected outcome
Presenter	Silverback	Representing the team, elaborating the ideas to the public, managing the internal resources to reach the objective
Informant	Eagle	Giving the empirical or scientific evidence to support the argument
Secretary	Lioness	Keeping the discussion threads and organizing these notes for further referencing
Writer	Peacock	Gathering the information, discussion threads and drafting the bulletins of the argument for latter presentation
Challenger	Wild Dock	Observing the discussion process to see if there is any obstacle, raising questions to test the validity against the argument

For better result from the brainstorming, the Fig. 2 illustrates the ideal layout of the discussion room (Pavelin et al. 2014); there are long-bench tables for the groups named as *Tn*, *n* is the identification of the group; each table equips with a big screen or a projector for easy communication; the notation of *RnA* represents the *Silverback*, the alpha male of the herd of gorillas, the rest are the other roles in the group. In the center of the layout is the table where the *Emperor* and the *Judge Dredd* work at. The round table is also acted as the commanding office during the brainstorming.

As Fig. 3 illustrated, in the beginning, the *Emperor* gives the goals and the expectations from the coming brainstorming to all participants. The *Judge Dredd* explains how the brainstorming will be conducted to all, asks group members to introduce themselves about their expertise and the background respectively, finally gives a well-known case to save time in understanding the issues, as an exercise to let the participants be familiar with the brainstorming process. This simulation is essential to the success of the latter brainstorming in the real theme; therefore, if time permits, let the group members play as many roles as possible. In many occasions, the *Judge Dredd* also usually plays the domain expert on that problem theme to disclose the potential issues, the background understanding about the issues, and the possible directions about the solution of the issues.

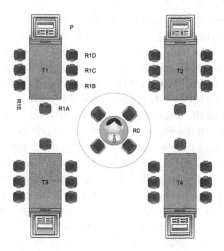

Fig. 2. The ideal layout for brainstorming

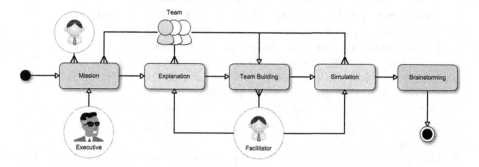

Fig. 3. The preparation for brainstorming

3   The Empirical Cases of Brainstorming

There were three selected empirical cases presented in this paper, applying the afore-mentioned brainstorming method for service design: (A) **service innovation**—the hybrid team members came from various research centers who intended to initiate a joint-project by leveraging their core competencies; (B) **business model exploration**—a large number of executives came from the selected small and medium business were looking for the possibility of using the Big Data to explore their new business opportunities and to improve the existing business efficiency; and (C) **extending knowledge**—the graduate management school students from different nations learned what the Smart Factory is and discussed the issues about it from various perspectives.

From the empirical cases, the proposed brainstorming method reached a promising result especially in the big diverse team by breaking them into smaller groups. This is a critical task to the success of the brainstorming; the grouping criteria should be based on the members who are complementary in: (1) business (2) competence and

(3) personality. For better result, interviewing all attendees and categorizing their characteristics is a good practice. Usually it is not easy to identify who are appropriate to play the *Silverback* and the *Wild Duck* roles. However, the proposed brainstorming method can also be a leadership and critique training; the group members can take turns to play all the roles for different topics if the brainstorming time is long enough.

The *Judge Dredd* must have adequate domain knowledge and experiences so that he/she can guide and lead the discussion toward the goal set by the *Emperor* and make his/her best efforts to reach the expected outcome with consensus. The *Eagle* requires to have a strong knowledge network in which can be effectively used in backing up the propositions. The *Lioness* uses a mind-map like tool to keep discussion threads efficiently in details; when a discussion is warm, the group might need to slow down the discussion to give more time in keeping these threads if there is no handy tool in place. The *Peacock* consolidates and re-organizes these discussion threads into concise bulletins and drafts them on the whitepaper to let the *Silverback* elaborate the value points easily. How to assign proper tasks as a CEO and to lead the discussion smoothly as the stimulus are the major challenges to the *Silverback*.

The *Silverbacks* can learn the skills from each other during the brainstorming. The *Wild Duck* does not join the discussion, but observes the discussion where it goes wrong and reminds the team to keep the track on the issues. If all groups have the same goal of outcome, then the *Wild Duck* requires to switch over to other groups for a small period of time and brings back the valuable points to the belonging group. The *Silverback* takes into account these points to lead addition rounds of discussion to see if there is anything can be used in improving the group value proposition.

The time management for the whole brainstorming process is another critical task; if the discussion time is too short, the propositions may be too shallow to conclude a solid outcome; otherwise the brainstorming will exhaust the enthusiasm and the energy of the members; the effect will be deflated for a marathon brain-melting discussion. The *Judge Dredd* needs to have a draft plan in mind about how many issues or phases can be discussed within the brainstorming period and how long it takes for each issue or phase.

Finally, the *Judge Dredd* asks all groups' *Silverbacks* to articulate their ideas, why they think this way about the issues, and taking the challenges from other group members respectively. The challenged group works as a team to keep the questions and the discussion threads, finding the evidences that can back up the proposed view points, and eventually refine them based on the new coming comments from others. Each participant has two votes to elect the best ideas among the other groups (voting for the belonging group was not permitted). If two groups have the same number of votes, re-vote against these two ideas until the best idea is elected.

The *Judge Dredd* gives a deep brief to the *Emperor* before he/she reviews all value propositions from the groups. The proper attitude of the *Emperor* should be to encourage the efforts that the groups had made instead of criticizing about the rough works after the brainstorming. Because the brainstorming is a continuous spiral-convergent process; identifying the feasible objectives from each brainstorming process will accumulate the synergy of outcomes. It is a good practice that incorporates with existing knowledge management system to solicit, capture, organize, disseminate, and reuse these outcomes as knowledge. This will expand the soliciting circle to other tacit contributors; such a knowledge-network eventually evolves into a value chain, a knowledge ecosystem (Table 2).

Table 2. Three empirical cases of the brainstorming

Facilitation	Brainstorming
A 	
A big hybrid team from various organizations wished to identify the potential collaborative service product that would amplify their existing competence, to elaborate the value propositions and the associated implementation through the three-day brainstorming process.	
B 	
A government funded one-day training for the selected small-medium enterprises who wished to explore the potential business opportunity or differentiating approach by adopting the Big Data to extend and expand their existing business.	
C 	
A three-hour seminar and workshop for the graduate business school students from different nations, its purpose was to let the students understand how Smart Factory works and disclose the complexibility about the issue.	

4 Conclusion

To make the innovation more effectively, it is not just about the talent of the members, but also about the cultural and atmospheric environment. Creative thinking is no longer an attribute that's nice to have, but a critical competency for any organization seeking the excellency in business. If the brainstorming is not conducted properly, the whole session may become chaotic, divergent, results in nothing, and thus certainly viewed by the participants as a waste of time. Measuring the outcomes from the brainstorming is the necessary evil to ensure that all participants will reach the goal and meet the expectations with the consensus, that were set by the executives. This paper presents a practical framework for effective brainstorming; not just shooting for the feasible outcomes, but also improving the abilities—leadership (Herrmann and Felfe 2014), teamwork, dealing with conflicts, making fact-based arguments, learning from the peers—of staffs through the process. Such a framework will improve the quality of organizational culture, and most importantly, to transform the organization as the incubator of creativeness.

References

Aghion, P., Bechtold, S., Cassar, L., Herz, H.: The Causal Effects of Competition on Innovation: Experimental Evidence. National Bureau of Economic Research (2014)

Alamsyah, F., Yerki, B.T.: Does an innovation culture improve company performance? links to dynamic capabilities and leadership capability. Adv. Sci. Lett. **21**(6), 1676–1680 (2015)

Baker, C.A.: Catalytic Conversations: Organizational Communication and Innovation. Routledge, Abingdon (2015)

Herrmann, D., Felfe, J.: Effects of leadership style, creativity technique and personal initiative on employee creativity. Br. J. Manage. **25**(2), 209–227 (2014)

Ho, K.K.J.: Formulation of a systemic PEST analysis for strategic analysis. Eur. Acad. Res. **2**(5), 6478–6492 (2014)

Pavelin, K., Pundir, S., Cham, J.A.: Ten simple rules for running interactive workshops. PLoS Comput. Biol. **10**(2), e1003485 (2014)

Qiu, G.R.: Service Science: The Foundations of Service Engineering and Management. Wiley, New York (2014)

Simon, D., Fischbach, K., Schoder, D.: Enterprise architecture management and its role in corporate strategic management. Inf. Syst. e-Bus. Manage. **12**(1), 5–42 (2014)

Simons, A.P., Benders, J., Marneffe, W., Pijls-Johannesma, M., Vandijck, D.: Workshops as a useful tool to better understand care professionals' views of a lean change program. Int. J. Health Care Qual. Assur. **28**(1), 64–74 (2015)

The Role of HCI in Cross-Sector Research on Grand Challenges

Roger Lew[1(✉)], Nathan Lau[2], Ronald L. Boring[3], and John Anderson[1]

[1] University of Idaho, Moscow, ID, USA
{rogerlew,jwa}@uidaho.edu
[2] Virginia Polytechnic Institute, Blacksburg, VA, USA
nathan.lau@vt.edu
[3] Idaho National Laboratory, Idaho Falls, ID, USA
ronald.boring@inl.gov

Abstract. Cross-sector or collaborative research between government, academia, industry, and public stakeholders is essential to find innovative solutions to 21st century grand challenges. The proliferation of cyberinfrastructure and cyber physical systems will play critical roles in managing information and large scale human machine systems. While available data, processing power, and model complexities grow at an accelerating rate, the information processing capacity of human cognition does not. Human computer interaction research is needed to bridge this gap and enable the development, operation, and analytics of emerging, integrated, large-scale, multi-user, realtime systems.

Keywords: Grand challenges · Cyberinfrastructure · Cyber physical systems · Coupled natural human systems · Critical infrastructure · Decision support tools

1 Introduction

Grand challenges describe problems with socio-political as well as technical complexities. As we approach 2050 and a future with 9.5 billion human inhabitants providing energy, food, water, health-care, and other necessities in a sustainable manner will be grand challenges. The Global Footprint Network [1] estimates that our current demand for renewable ecological resources and services is more than what could be sustainable if provided by 1.5 Earths. An additional concern is that critical infrastructure and ecological services are becoming increasingly vulnerable to both anthropocentric and natural threats. Simultaneously, technological development is occurring at an accelerating pace [2]. One has only to look at the progression of computational power, internet path, and tool use, among other trends for evidence of this acceleration. Grand challenge innovations are often looking for technologically innovative "silver bullets" or what Silicon Valley would term "disruptions."

Disruptions describe technological innovations capable of providing industry level paradigm shifts [3]. For example, consider the shift from private vehicle ownership to autonomous vehicles summoned on-demand with ridesharing (Google Car + Uber + car2go). Personal vehicles spend on average 95 % of their time parked. Such a

© Springer International Publishing Switzerland 2016
F.F.-H. Nah and C.-H. Tan (Eds.): HCIBGO 2016, Part I, LNCS 9751, pp. 519–530, 2016.
DOI: 10.1007/978-3-319-39396-4_48

paradigm shift could reduce the number of vehicles by a factor of ten, reclaim much of the one-third of city land dedicated to vehicle storage, while reducing per capita transportation expenses and increasing transportation safety [4]. However, solving grand challenges requires more than just technological innovation.

Problems are often multi-faceted with regulatory, cultural, and economic considerations in addition to the ecological and utilitarian ones. For example a shared vehicle model could have unintended negative consequences: economic efficiency gains from autonomous vehicles would likely result in increased consumption and/or a willingness to commute farther distances due to the ability to do productive work while commuting. Cost efficiencies would be nullified if automotive travel per capita saw a net increase. We also observe economic and social disruption for the displaced taxi or limousine drivers that may elevate the economic inequality without effective workforce development and welfare support. The complexities surrounding grand challenges translate to complex solution spaces. The problems cannot be solved by finding a way to optimize a single variable or even a set of variables. Many of the 21st century problems we are facing require understanding that systems are adaptive and exhibit high order interactions with one another and that must be taken into consideration in order to manage tradeoffs. Finding innovative solutions to tradeoffs requires interdisciplinary as well as cross-sector research teams from stakeholders, private sector, government, and academia. Building a shared understanding of the problem from technical, social, economic, and ecological perspectives is an essential first step to working out solutions that stand a chance in the real-world.

Here we begin by examining some of the technological visions of the future that provide the framework for building innovative solutions.

1.1   Cyberinfrastructure Vision

Cross-sector collaboration has many challenges. Here, we begin by examining the technical. Increasing the interoperability of cyberinfrastructure (CI) is a key component to conquering grand challenges. Briefly, cyber infrastructure is the hardware and software that enables the storage and retrieval of data. Current CI is often segmented and specialized to specific domains [5]. For example, a hydrologist might have a set of databases that are compatible with their tools, but those tools and databases may not be compatible with those used by a waste water engineer. In contrast, future CI is "heralded as a transformative force, enabling new forms of investigation and cross-disciplinary collaboration" [6]. The vision would be enabled by CI that is end-to-end from the collection of data to the analysis, storage and dissemination [5, 6]. End-to-end CI would provide guided or automated acquisition and processing of data, run model simulations/forecasts, analyze the results, provide statistical reports, and visualize the results. For this to occur cross-sector/interdisciplinary collaboration is necessary. Academics may be well suited to resolve unknown relationships between variables but are less inclined to know how to deploy those results or models inside of a resilient CI framework and need the assistance of computer information specialists. Industry and public stakeholders need decision support tools to form decisions based on the best available data and models.

Ideally, decision support tools can encapsulate expert knowledge for use by industry and public stakeholders.

Future CI will not only streamline human computer interaction (HCI) between domain experts and their tools but increase the accessibility of tools to non-domain experts. In the National Science Foundation [7] CI vision stipulates that open access built upon an open technological framework is essential. This will increase the accessibility of scientific information to the public and enable stakeholders and government agencies to participate in a *virtual community* alongside researchers. CI needs to be built to simultaneously serve both basic and applied research in academic, governmental, and industrial sectors. Researchers benefit by gaining exposure to real-world needs which can serve as a catalyst to theoretical research. An open-framework also provides educational opportunities for K-12 as well as workforce development for the next generation of technical professionals. Education can be difficult to be privatize for the entire public, but an educated workforce can improve every sector. Additional benefits of the openly available resources are increases in the capacity of the academic and industrial sectors; reducing unnecessary redundancy leads to more sustainable research and stakeholders better served by industry. The community as a whole benefits through better access to data, tools, and computational resources. This is a paradigm shift from the translational research mode, by which basic research may eventually find its way to industry through a unidirectional process. In contrast, the cross-sector/interdisciplinary model features problems posed by government agencies or stakeholders; the community then engages in problem-solving through developing shared understanding of the problem.

Achieving this vision will require robust, complex, multi-layered technologies for monitoring environments in real-time, assessing their state, providing decision support to human supervisors, and implementing control actions. A heterogeneous group of users will need to interact with CI at every layer for a variety of purposes. For this reason human computer interaction becomes a critical consideration in the design and implementation of cyberinfrastructure. The end goal is to produce technology that results in better integration of policy, strategic (management) and operations decision making. However, HCI applies not only to the interfaces used by policy makers, managers, and stakeholders. HCI is important at every layer of the CI stack. CI when combined with highly distributed sensors and data streams could form large scale cyber physical systems (to be discussed). Systems will expose web APIs for other services (machines) to interact with them. However, they will also expose user interfaces for human computer interaction. Some web-services might allow sensor readings to be placed into a database, others provide a means of retrieving data, running a model simulation, or visualizing the model forecasts or predictions.

Trends suggest that implementing solutions to grand challenges will require distributed cyber infrastructure built on the defacto standard TCP/IP protocol. Care needs to be taken in the design of the web APIs as well as the user interfaces for each of these web-services. Web-services will provide the coupling between sectors. In some scenarios it will be technologically feasible for systems to communicate independent of human users. In other scenarios human users will be needed to monitor, operate, maintain, and administer on-line systems. Longer time scale problems with interacting factors might be suited for decision support tools capitalizing on the analytics provided by new cyber infrastructure. Analytics will be able to aggregate the vast amounts of sensor and simulation data as well as social trends from online social networks. While the information processing and storage capabilities are likely to increase exponentially, the cognitive capacities of human users are unlikely to keep pace. HCI will become essential to verification and validation of interfaces to ensure that they meet task requirements. The proliferation of data and processing power provides opportunities and arguably necessity for advanced visualization of data and virtualization of physical systems.

Coupled Natural and Human Systems Research. Coupled natural and human systems consider how both biophysical and human factors interact with one another. Ecological systems provide valuable ecological services to communities that must be managed to maintain the health of ecosystems and the sustainability of ecological services. Ecological services are becoming increasingly strained by human population growth and climate change. Considering human influences is essential to understand the coupled natural and human systems as a whole. In the United States, federal, academic, and industry, and NGO are actively collaborating to develop ecosystem service concepts to further national environmental and economic objectives [8].

Properly implemented cyberinfrastructure could greatly enhance cross-sector research. Currently academic researchers might use and develop highly sophisticated biophysical models for basic research that go unused or under-utilized by governmental regulatory agencies and stakeholders. These models may still require manually acquiring and processing input datasets despite the enormous growth in data and increased availability of data via web-services. Instead, it remains common place for domain experts to spend their careers learning how to use highly specialized models. The codebases of these models are often the result of decades of research and several "person decades" worth of effort. The problem is that for many of these models, collecting/acquiring and processing the input datasets is still a manual process. The inputs as well as the outputs are in non-standard formats. Domain experts spend a large amount of their time learning technical details of file formats and software systems that are irrelevant to the science they are actually interested in.

Embracing modular, test-driven, scalable, open cyber-infrastructure frameworks could offer productivity gains, leverage citizen science, provide tools and analytics for regulatory agencies, and provide decision support for stakeholders. Web services should be developed that allow for data intensive analysis of geographic regions of interest without needing to know specifics about where to acquire the data or how the data is formatted. Future technology could provide:

- Ability to assess physical systems at multiple time resolutions and temporal scales
- Ability to understand the complex adaptive interactions of human, technological, and ecological systems
- Mitigation of climate change impacts, increased sustainability, managed ecological services
- Regulations that allow trade of "nature as capital" to pursue environmental goals [8].

1.2   Cyber-Physical Systems (CPS) Vision

The proliferation of cyberinfrastructure combined with increased sensor availability and lower costs will enable the monitoring and control of physical systems. Rajkumar et al. [9] describe CPS as "physical and engineered systems whose operations are monitored, coordinated, controlled and integrated by a computing and communication core." CPS will improve the efficiency of existing systems and provide new capabilities. CPS is in many ways aligned with the cyberinfrastructure vision discussed earlier although it is not synonymous. Cyberinfrastructure is built to address information management needs. CPS arise from engineering domains and operate in real-time employing both sensors monitoring and actuators affecting the physical world. CPS exist at a variety of scales and many technologies can be classified as falling under its umbrella: personal medical devices such as prostheses, adaptive automation in vehicles, drones, smart-buildings, smart-cities, power distribution networks, and even planetary scale risk monitoring of critical infrastructure from empirical data and models of natural resource use and climate change [10]. Traditional embedded systems focus more on the cyber components, whereas CPS takes a holistic approach integrating the cyber and physical components [11].

Cyber physical systems can replace analog and mechanical control systems while offering increased reliability and efficiency. Advanced adaptive control systems are being developed that can change strategy based on the stability of the system. When the system is more stable the controller can optimize efficiency, whereas when the system is close to the operating envelope the controls can act more aggressively to stabilize the system [12].

Strides are being made at the small scale, but at the large scale challenges remain. According to Sztipanovits et al. [13] the largest obstacle to CPS is system integration. Systems can be designed and modelled digitally. The components can be specified and manufactured, but building the physical system is still less than a science. A second challenge to large scale CPS is economic deployment of sensors and actuators at a planetary scale to measure and forecast critical indicators [9].

Critical Infrastructure Research. Critical infrastructure represents another grand challenge that commonly involves government, industry and academia. For example, phaser measurement units (PMU) enabling smart grids involves substantial collaborative research. However, HCI research targets effective HCI and human factors engineering except for heavily regulated sectors such as nuclear power and commercial aviation. In heavily regulated and safety critical sectors, collaborative HCI research commonly focuses on improving user interfaces and measuring human performance, a conventional application of the discipline for critical infrastructures. However, critical infrastructure can also engage in recent HCI research approaches such as social informatics more common in the private sectors. For instance, UBER is increasing the availability and efficiency of the transportation infrastructure (i.e., roads and cars). HCI research can potentially introduce novel concept of operations for the government to maximize availability, security and efficiency of critical infrastructure but such 'revolutionary' changes require additional research opportunities.

Smart-grid communication networks are typically described as connecting power generation plants, power distribution networks, and consumers. However, necessity exists for cross-sector communication. Academics might need access to real-time and historic data for research purposes. National laboratories have high performance computing resources that can aid operations and research. Renewable energy generation and energy consumption is highly dependent on meteorological conditions. Smart-grids will need high-resolution, localized forecasts to schedule power ramp-ups. Regulatory and standards organizations will also need real-time communication to ensure compliance as well as develop and manage existing standards [14]. Lastly, consumers might wish to modify consumption based on dynamic pricing per market demands.

1.3 Participatory Culture Vision

To the dismay of skeptics, the small contributions of millions of users have accumulated in high value resources as well as advancements in science and technology. Wikipedia has over 35 million articles in 288 languages. Foldit is an online protein folding game with a community of 240,000 players. Among several notable contributions to science, these players improved the activity of an enzyme by 18 fold in a matter of weeks [15]. These accomplishments were possible despite the fact that the vast majority of internet users have little or no technological or programming prowess. Good interfaces make it possible for smart individuals with limited technical skills to contribute to crowdsourcing efforts like Wikipedia and Foldit [16]. Crowdsourcing local expertise and cognitive processing power is perhaps an underutilized resource for managing 21st grand challenges.

Citizen science refers to scientific research conducted by nonprofessional scientists. In the modern context it usually refers to citizens collaborating with professional scientists in the collection and processing of data [17]. Ecological data collection is expensive and it is unlikely that remote sensing will be able to fully capture measurements of biodiversity with the granularity needed for decision making and regulation anytime in the near future [18]. Citizen science can be enhanced through HCI research that can reduce the variability of novices engaging in scientific research tasks. HCI is also needed in validating data collected by citizens.

Providing public stakeholders with tools that can convey scientific knowledge in a manner that is more accessible to non-domain expertise and allowing them to examine how particular actions will affect the future state of their environments and communities could provide positive democratizing effects on public decision making. Without such tools public stakeholders must rely on the authority to gain insight into the inter-workings of their environments. By being able to interactively manipulate policies, environmental factors, or decisions under a variety of scenarios ordinary citizens can gain understanding into the non-linearly dynamics of their system and potential risks that they might want to avoid.

2   Cross-Sector Collaboration

Having already discussed technical challenges of cross-sector/interdisciplinary research we turn our attention to non-technical challenges facing collaborators. The merits and incentives for interdisciplinary research are evident but cross-sector and interdisciplinary research can be challenging. Bryson et al. [19] remark that organizations *fail* into collaborations. Collaborations take place when organizations cannot get what they want without collaborating. Here we examine the perspectives and goals of government, academic, industry, and stakeholder sectors. Together these sectors comprise the social infrastructure that maintains the availability of critical infrastructure and ecological services through a shared power structure.

2.1   Government (Funding Agencies, National Labs, Regulatory Agencies)

Government is a multidimensional construct, ranging from legislative bodies, to funding agencies, to defense agencies, to research laboratories, and to regulatory agencies. Each one views the role of research and development differently. In the United States, for example, the federal legislature must strike a balance between reducing public spending and ensuring the economic competitiveness and national security through public expenditures. Legislative bodies must therefore navigate short-term electability and long-term vision for government.

A consistent push for national security has ensured some stability of defense research and development, including more recently the advent of cybersecurity. Technology development has helped provide competitive advantage to U.S. defense tools, and HCI has been deployed as a tool to help improve performance of technologies deployed in defense contexts, from better avionics for pilots, to augmented reality headsets for ground soldiers, to better intruder detection systems for cyber applications. Defense agencies like the Defense Advanced Research Projects Agency (DARPA) ensure that emerging HCI technologies are realized and implemented. DARPA regularly hosts grand challenges that feature an HCI component.

Beyond defense applications, there remain many government agencies that champion basic research and development. The National Science Foundation (NSF) and National Institutes of Health (NIH) underwrite foundational research, primarily in academia, to further scientific goals. These goals can include HCI opportunities, such as improved medical device interfaces.

Federal research laboratories, including those operated on behalf of NASA or the U.S. Department of Energy (DOE), serve as a resource to explore research that the private sector cannot or should not perform. As industries become viable, such as commercial space travel, federal funding subsides in these research facilities. Yet, they remain an important capability to meet government research needs and develop technologies that may provide advantage to U.S. interests. Additionally, during periods of economic downturn, private sector funding in research and development may decline; federal research facilities are a key component to maintaining a vibrant national research culture that spans economic ebbs and flows. An important part of the national laboratory framework entails partnering with academia and the private sector. Increasingly, Small

Business Innovation Research (SBIR) has become a vessel toward commercialization of technologies developed in federal research facilities. In terms of HCI, these laboratories often house human factors departments and work to apply human factors including HCI to technologies that are under development.

Finally, there are regulatory bodies - agencies serving to protect and promote public safety. Historically, these agencies are at the forefront of HCI because they regulate the safety of technologies used by humans. From consumer safety, to automobile safety, to highway safety, to aviation safety, to nuclear safety, these agencies are large consumers of research to determine safety solutions. While some research is done in-house certain agencies may contract with outside sources to conduct safety research. A grand challenge arises in the face of technological disaster, such as the Deepwater Horizon Incident. The regulatory agencies must quickly mobilize research to address high profile public safety concerns, and HCI is one technology that ensures the operational safety of technologies under scrutiny.

2.2   Academia

Traditional academic positions, namely tenure-track professors, are driven to produce knowledge for publications and train students for their graduate degrees. Though compatible with goals established in government and industry, these two key drivers lead to some characteristics that are shared with other sectors but others that are unique to academia. First, academic research tends to be theory-driven (loosely defined) while laboratory research is tightly-controlled such that findings are both generalizable and repeatable. For repeatability, the rigor on scientific method is also a major focus. The research products are meant to be publishable or public, rather than strictly commercial interests. This contrasts to the applied or problem driven research most typical in the focus of the government and industry, which emphasizes on what works in a practical setting (rather than what is optimal in an ideal setting). For some parts of the government and commonly for industry, the work is often kept proprietary rather than public. On occasions, academic researchers do have "field work" opportunities that facilitate testing of theory-driven findings and formulation of new theories.

Second, academic research tends to produce work in accordance with academic cycles or "academic time scale" as much of the work is carried out by graduate students. The academic time scale means that (i) students can only be recruited at specific times of the year for at least two years, and (ii) some training time is required to prepare the students to carry out the work. The academic time scale is thus different from both government and industry operating per fiscal year cycles and expecting immediate progress on projects. On occasion, academic researchers are able to align their schedule to work with government and industry, typically involving some lead time for synchronizing time cycles across the parties.

Within academic institutions incentives may not exist for cross-sector collaboration. Work that does not result in publications demotivate academics if other incentives are not in place. Interdisciplinary work has more unknowns, more collaborators and consequently more channels of communication. Those factors make collaborative work less productive. If the only metric considered is time per publication it becomes difficult for researchers to justify time spent on collaborative efforts. Collaborative research becomes effective when the key drivers, such as student graduation and time constraints, are aligned across the three sectors. Thus, fostering research across sectors to make progress on grand challenges depends partly on our efforts in creating the setting conducive to the participation. We believe there are three feasible ways to significantly improve the setting for cross-sector collaboration, especially with respect to working with academia.

First, synchronization between "academic" and "fiscal" time is essential for collaborative engagement. One potential method is that the government should strive to provide constant access as a "field" for academic research. In other words, the government may treat itself as a "field" where graduate students can go observe and collect data, regardless of direct project sponsorships. This can lead to formulation basic and applied HCI research to pursue either across or within sectors. Further, graduate students are constantly being trained in the field, and thus can be productive at the beginning of any sponsored project that often has a much tighter fiscal deadline. The government needs to prescribe controls on accessibility and support as appropriate. This method of engaging academics for supporting the government is feasible because academic institutions have some flexibility in conducting unfunded research activities that private sectors generally cannot provide.

Second, long-term or predictable funding could also enhance collaborative research. However, long term planning is often challenging. One potential method is extending the collaboration nature of existing internship opportunities in the government or potentially industry. Internships can be dependent on research participation for the government, improving the expertise and integration of graduate students in the government settings. This method coincides with the proposal to increase government access to academic research.

Third, academic institutions need to develop students not only with competencies within multiple disciplines given the complex nature of grand challenges, but also with the skill of switching between the operating modes of research and practice/industry work. One potential solution is that academic institutions need to provide formal incentives for training students and researchers in translating research into application/technology. Otherwise, collaboration between government and industry with academia can remain "rocky" or only effective for specific research groups.

2.3 Industry

Industry is driven to fill market demands and is generally more application-centric and productivity driven. Industry provides services, engineering and design, construction, equipment to clients in both private and public sectors. Success requires finding economically viable means for delivering goods and services. Technological industry giants such as Google and Apple have sufficient capital to make significant investments in research development and have made significant contributions in advancing and deploying cyber infrastructure [17], although the trend does not hold across industry. Corporations and utilities can be successful without having to develop innovative intellectual property by licensing technology and focusing on business fundamentals.

Open architecture and data access will reduce barriers of entry for startups developing applications that have the ability to connect users to information for both entertainment and decision making. The small scale of startups can actually be advantageous in new markets as it can make them more adaptable and nimble compared to larger counterparts. Funding startups can be problematic and open access to data resources can ease those requirements by not only eliminating direct costs of data but indirect costs for tools to access data.

2.4 Public Stakeholders

Here we refer to public stakeholders as citizens and communities/organizations organized and united around a common cause. They share a concern or an interest in a particular issue or set of issues. Communities can be geographically segregated or segregated in cyberspace. Communities can vary in their level of political organization, resources, authority. Public stakeholders are beholden to only themselves and in this context are problem-centric. They know what they value (e.g. clean water, cheap gas, etc.) and take actions to maximize those values. Freeman [20] describes stakeholders as "any group or individual who is affected by or can affect the achievement of an organization's objectives." Their power is derived from influence others in the public sphere to affect the market and politics.

The most challenging aspects of cross-sector collaborations are likely to be non-technical with communication at the forefront. Individuals spend significant portions of their lives in the same discipline and become "united by customs, tradition, and adherence to a largely common worldview(s)" [21]. Cross-sector and interdisciplinary research can become burdened because participants view the world in fundamentally different ways [22]. Collaborators do not need to develop a common philosophical basis for how they view the world, but it can be beneficial for collaborators to gain insight into mindsets of collaborators because they influence how they see the value of their effort and their collaborations [23]. Workforce development of individuals who can span disciplines and sectors are likely going to be highly valuable for cross-sector research endeavors. In particular, there is a need for individuals who are trained to "understand and address the human factors dimensions of working across disciplines, cultures, and institutions using technology-mediated collaborative tools" [5].

3   Conclusions

Despite the harsh reality of climate change and dwindling natural resources, technology provides reasons to be optimistic about the future. Human and natural systems are becoming increasingly interdependent as new technologies pervade. Technology offers a double-edge sword of enabling us to manage our environments through intervention while producing systems that are technologically dependent. Care must be taken to avoid unintended consequences and ensure future generations have access to currently available critical infrastructure and ecological services. Additionally, care requires both qualitative and quantitative analysis of the systems as well as blunt discussion regarding values, concerns, and tradeoffs when it comes to forming decisions. HCI forms the bridge from our holistic understanding of the world – the nexus of information, models, and analysis represented across the web of cyberinfrastructure – and our collective mindfulness.

4 Disclaimer

This work of authorship was prepared as an account of work sponsored by an agency of the United States Government. Neither the United States Government, nor any agency thereof, nor any of their employees makes any warranty, express or implied, or assumes any legal liability or responsibility for the accuracy, completeness, or usefulness of any information, apparatus, product, or process disclosed, or represents that its use would not infringe privately-owned rights. Idaho National Laboratory is a multi-program laboratory operated by Battelle Energy Alliance LLC, for the United States Department of Energy.

Acknowledgement. This work was partially supported by NSF award number IIA-1301792 from the NSF Idaho EPSCoR Program and by the National Science Foundation.

References

1. Global Footprint Network: Earth Overshoot Day, 8 August 2015. http://www.footprintnetwork.org/en/index.php/GFN/page/earth_overshoot_day/
2. Kurzweil, R.: The Singularity is Near. Penguin Group, New York (2005)
3. Brooks, S., Leach, M., Lucas, H., Millstone, E.: Silver bullets, grand challenges and the new philanthropy, (STEPS Working Paper 24) (2009)
4. Schonberger, B., Gutmann, S.: A Self-driving future: At the intersection of driverless cars and car sharing. Signline Institute (2013)
5. Atkins, D.E., Droegemeier, K.K., Feldman, S.I., Garcia-Molina, H., Klein, M.L., Messerschmitt, D.G., Messina, P., Ostriker, J.P., Wright, M.H.: Revolutionizing science and engineering through cyberinfrastructure. In: Report of the National Science Foundation Blue-Ribbon Advisory Panel on Cyberinfrastructure (2003)
6. Ribes, D., Lee, C.P.: Sociotechnical studies of cyberinfrastructure and e-Research: current themes and future trajectories. Comput. Support. Coop. Work **19**, 231–244 (2010)
7. National Science Foundation: Cyberinfrastructure vision for 21st century discovery, March 2007
8. Schaefer, M., Goldman, E., Bartuska, A.M., Sutton-Grier, A., Lubchenco, J.: Nature as capital: Advancing and incorporating ecosystem services in United States federal policies and programs (2015)
9. Rajkumar, R., Lee, I., Sha, L., Stankovic, J.: Cyber-Physical systems: the next computing revolution. In: Design Automation Conference, Anaheim, California, USA (2010)
10. Lee, E.A.: Cyber physical systems: design challenges. In: 11th IEEE Symposium on Object Oriented Real-Time Distributed Computing (ISORC) (2008)
11. Zhang, Y., Xie, F., Dong, Y., Yang, G., Zhou, X.: High fidelity virtualization of cyber-physical systems. Int. J. Model. Simul. Sci. Comput. **4**(2), 1340005 (2013)
12. Wolf, W.: Cyber-physical systems. Embed. Comput. **42**(3), 88–89 (2009)

13. Sztipanovits, J., Koutsoukos, X., Karsai, G., Kottenstette, N., Antsaklis, P., Gupta, V., Goodwine, B., Baras, J., Wang, S.: Toward a science of cyber-physical system integration. Proc. IEEE **100**(1), 29–44 (2012)
14. National Institute of Standards and Technology: Technology, measurement, and standards challenges for the smart grid, March 2013
15. Marshall, J.: Online Gamers Achieve First Crowd-Sourced Redesign of Protein. Scientific America, 22 January 2012. http://www.scientificamerican.com/article/victory-forcrowdsourced-biomolecule2/
16. Executive Office of the President President's Council of Advisors on Science and Technology: Report to the president and congress. Designing a digital future: Federally funded research and development in networking and information technology, December 2010
17. Silvertown, J.: A new dawn for citizen science. Trends Ecol. Evol. **24**(9), 461–471 (2009)
18. Dickinson, J.L., Zuckerberg, B., Bonter, D.N.: Citizen science as an ecological research tool: challenges and benefits. Ann. Rev. Ecol. Evol. Syst. **41**, 149–172 (2010)
19. Bryson, J.M., Crosby, B.C., Stone, M.M.: The design and implementation of cross-sector collaborations: propositions from the literature. Public Adm. Rev. **66**(s1), 44–55 (2006)
20. Freeman, R.E.: Strategic Management: A Stakeholder Approach. Cambridge University Press, Cambridge (2010)
21. Sternberg, R.: Academic tribalism, 27 February 2015. http://chronicle.com/blogs/conversation/2014/02/26/academic-tribalism/. Accessed 26 Feb 2014
22. O'Rourke, M., Crowley, S., Gonnerman, C.: On the nature of cross-disciplinary integration: a philosophy framework. Stud. Hist. Philos. Sci. Part C Stud. Hist. Philos. Biol. Biomed. Sci. **56**, 62–70 (2015)
23. Robinson, B., Vasko, S.E., Gonnerman, C., Christen, M., O'Rourke, M.: Human values and the value of humanities in interdisciplinary research. Cogent. Arts Humanit. **3**(1), 1123080 (2016)

Building IT Capabilities to Deploy Large-Scale Synchronous Online Technology in Teaching and Learning

Stephen Low[✉], Jenson Goh, Yeung Sze Kiu, and Ivy Chia

SIM University, Singapore, Singapore
{stephenlowwk, jensongohcl, skyeung,
ivychiasm}@unisim.edu.sg

Abstract. Through the use of a case study methodology, this paper presents a case of a large scale implementation of a synchronous teaching technology called Blackboard Collaborate by the School of Science and Technology (SST) in SIM University, Singapore. The technology Blackboard Collaborate is being used in SST to replace the typical "face-to-face" tutorial class experience of its students across 10 undergraduate degree programmes in 131 courses (or modules). This study aims to answer two research questions: (1) What are the IT capabilities that are needed to ensure the effective use of the synchronous online technology in a University's teaching and learning environment? and (2) How can these IT capabilities be developed within a University? It will present a theoretical model of what key IT capabilities a University needs in order to support the large scale deployment of a synchronous online technology like Black-board Collaborate.

Keywords: IT capabilities · IS solutions · Asynchronous online technology

1 Introduction

According to de Freitas and Neumann (2009), a synchronous system that collectively provides participants with the basic tools for synchronous communication has the following three core functions: (a) live audio and video; (b) shared visuals and/or whiteboards; and (c) text chat. In practice, enabling and ensuring the effectiveness of the use of this synchronous online technology in a classroom is not a trivial feat. It is a constant challenge especially in a University context where discussion that promotes critical and analytical thinking among students and professor/lecturer is crucial to a student's learning.

While IT capabilities have been discussed widely in a variety of contexts especially in the organization research literature, they have not been applied in the context of University's teaching and learning. Given the dynamic change in the education landscape especially with the introduction of Massive Open Online Courses (MOOCs), many universities have been struggling to incorporate new synchronous online technology into its teaching and learning practices. However, given the large amount of changes and resources involved in the deployment of these technologies, many professors are reluctant to leverage upon these technologies for teaching and learning.

F.F.-H. Nah and C.-H. Tan (Eds.): HCIBGO 2016, Part I, LNCS 9751, pp. 531–544, 2016.
DOI: 10.1007/978-3-319-39396-4_49

Often, they fear the changes will affect their teaching rating and impart their promotion. These have limited the adoption of these technologies for teaching and learning. Students may also face difficulties in adapting to these new technologies as compared to the familiar face-to-face lecturing. IT department often is confronted by the daunting task to convince and prove to both the professors and students that adopting these technologies would be beneficial.

Developing ways to overcome these challenges to assure the good adoption of these technologies by students and professors is one of the key drivers behind our study. Specifically, we are interested to answer two research questions: (1) What are the IT capabilities that are needed to ensure the effective use of the synchronous online technology in a University's teaching and learning environment? and (2) How can these IT capabilities be developed within a University?

Using a case study methodology, this paper presents a case of a large-scale implementation of a synchronous teaching technology called Blackboard Collaborate by the School of Science and Technology (SST) in SIM University, Singapore. The technology Blackboard Collaborate is being used in SST to replace the typical "face-to-face" tutorial class experience of its students across 10 undergraduate degree programmes in 131 courses (or modules). A minimum of three Virtual Synchronous On-Line Learning (VSOLL) sessions using the software system from BlackBoard Collaborate were conducted per course to cover the course content in each semester.

Each session is recordable and everyone would use a headset for audio communication. For non-verbal communication, students would interact with their peers and the instructor using the text-chat function. In order to ensure that audio is communicated in an orderly manner, a hand-raise button is available for each student to "raise" his/her hand before asking a question. This mode of teaching and learning mirrors closely to a face-to-face session in the classroom but they are taking place in a real-time, distributed-online environment, as demonstrated in the recording of an actual synchronous seminar conducted in Athabasca University's doctoral programme (Bainbridge 2015).

This paper describes how Blackboard Collaborate is used for not only teaching, but discussed what are key IT capabilities that are essential to assure the success of such large-scale deployment within a University context. Using interview and secondary data collected from the case organization, this study will present what are key IT capabilities that a University needs in order to support the large-scale deployment of a synchronous online technology like Blackboard Collaborate. By doing so, this study becomes one of the rare studies in the literature that looks into how IT capabilities can enhance and enable the Human-Computer interactions among students and professors to assure the successful deployment of a large-scale synchronous online technology for teaching and learning.

2   Literature Review

Large-scale implementation of Blackboard Collaborate is rare. Of the studies found, only Canada's Athabasca University is found to practice large-scale implementation of synchronous technology at its doctoral and master programmes in distance education which are taught fully online using Adobe Connect with "no face-to-face requirements for completion of the degree" (de Freitas and Neumann 2009). Elsewhere the deployment of synchronous technologies is implemented at individual courses level. The University of Southern Queensland (Reushle and Loch 2008), the Southern Cross University (Rowe and Ellis 2010), and the Hong Kong University of Science and Technology (HKUST 2012) are some universities using Collaborate at a small-scale level. Hence, as far as we know, the teaching and learning literature lacks study that looks comprehensively into the ways in which large-scale deployment of synchronous online technology for teaching and learning can be achieved. With the growing emphasis on driving eLearning in a University context, this gap within the literature is an important area that our study seeks to fill.

Reviewing the existing literature on online learning, we noted that three theoretical framework stands out and they include the Blended Online Learning Design (BOLD) (Power and Vaughan 2010), the Community of Inquiry (Garrison et al. 2000) and Multi-access Learning (Irvine et al. 2013). Each framework provided ideas to inform us on the important elements that must be put in place in order for online learning to happen among students. For instance, Power and Vaughan (2010) argued that for online learning to be effective, we need a combination of synchronous online learning activities and asynchronous learning management system-based learning activities. Garrison et al. (2000) offered three key 'presences' for online learning to be effective and they are: (1) cognitive presence; (2) social presence; and (3) teaching presence. They asserted that when the professors and students experienced all three of these presences, a community of inquiry is formed and this is when online learning would take place effectively. Finally, Irvine et al. (2013) argued the importance of providing students with different course delivery modes (e.g. face-to-face or online) to personalize their learning experiences while taking a course. They reaffirmed that by providing such multi-access to various course delivery modes to students, learning experiences in an online context of students would be enhanced. Notwithstanding the various teaching and learning theories presented in the literature, there is little discussion on how to create such effective learning environment within a University context. Specifically, what are the key IT capabilities that are essential in creating such an environment remains unknown. This is one of the key motivations behind this study.

For the purpose of this study, IT capability is defined as "the ability to use effectively and deploy IT-based resources in combination or co present with other resources and capabilities" (Bharadwaj 2000, p. 171). We would like to argue that IT capability is essential as the development of that capability enables the organization to continuously leverage educational value from the system. One of the functions of IT capability is to enable the organization to develop, add, integrate, and release key resources over time (Wade and Hulland 2004). The challenge for any practitioner is to understand what contributes towards the development of IT capability within the educational context.

This paper views capabilities as sets of competences required by an organisation to successfully implement and use information systems; this done in line with the organizational strategic goals. To us, the extent of IT system success depends largely on the organization's ability to carry out and manage change processes. Removing current problems and hurdles to progress towards more integrated processes and systems is a necessary means to achieving a leaner and more effective IT system. We will examine this further in a later section.

Reviewing the literature on IT capabilities, we found that there are different fundamental components or characteristics of organizational IS capability. They largely centre around infrastructure, networking, management capability human resources, technology assets or even IT enabled-intangibles and processes (Bharadwaj 2000; Ross et al. 1996). Not all IT capability frameworks could be used in the educational context. For example, Feeny and Wilcocks (1998) suggested a classification of nine IS capabilities consisting of Leadership, Business Systems Thinking, Relationship Building, Architecture Planning, Making Technology Work, Informed Buying, Contract Facilitation, Monitoring and Vendor Development. While comprehensive, the framework (at this level of granularity) serves little use for anchoring the development of IT capabilities in delivering synchronous learning. Indeed, writings on IS capability tend to be viewed within the dimension of business rather than educational processes (e.g. Kim et al. 2011; Agarwal et al. 2014; Raymond et al. 2014). Hence, the paper seeks to discover the effective key IT capabilities which results in the success of large-scale deployment for synchronous learning at Universities as in the case of ours. To do this, we need to deploy a research design to capture the processes taking place during implementation. We will discuss this further in the next section.

3 Methodology

The School of Science and Technology (SST) at SIM University (UniSIM) was selected as the case organization for this study. The school was selected for the following reasons. First, the senior management of the school decided to implement a school-wide use of a virtual classroom tool called Blackboard 'Collaborate' to conduct online synchronous classes for more than 3,000 students distributed across ten different degree programmes. As far as we are aware of, this is one of the largest online synchronous technology implementation in Singapore. Second, the success of such implementation inevitably requires strong IT capabilities to be nurtured and developed within the school. Third, data collected from the post-implementation review shown that the implementation was a successful one with almost no difference between student's grades before and after implementation. Fourth, due to the success of this implementation, the University is now considering extending the use of Blackboard 'Collaborate' to all the schools within the University which would involve an addition of more than 10,000 students. Overall, our findings revealed that the School had demonstrated its ability to develop strong IT capabilities to ensure the continued success of this implementation within the University.

The use of case method is ideal for our study because of two reasons. First, the large-scale implementation of this synchronous teaching tool across the school inevitably involves very complex interactions among business and IT staff, processes, hardware, software, and IT infrastructure that cannot be separately examined out of its organizational context (Pentland 1999). Hence, case method is considered one of the most effective research methods to uncover these complex relationships and its shared understanding among all the key stakeholders involved in this project (Klein and Myers

1999). Second, given the IT capabilities have not been examined in the teaching and learning context in the literature, an exploratory case study focusing on developing a theory to explained this phenomenon through the collection of rich data in a real world context is highly recommended (Eisenhardt and Graebner 2007; Pan and Tan 2011).

Data were collected over a three year, six-semester period from January 2012 to December 2015. The entire process can be broken down into three phases namely, preliminary, onsite interviews and post-hoc. In the preliminary phase, a comprehensively archival analysis of secondary sources (e.g. project documents, articles, videos and images) was conducted to identify key themes on IS capabilities that can be analyzed. This allowed us to fine tune the research design and interviewees for the subsequent onsite interview phase. In the onsite interview phase, interviews of all the key stakeholders were collected by a team of researchers. Each interview was digitally recorded in video/audio. This generates rich and thick descriptions on the implementation from interviewees that are critical to our study objective. An iterative data analysis process was adopted during these interviews which required the researchers to systematically and iteratively combed through the primary and secondary data sources mentioned above and validated it with our theoretical observations onsite and/or the existing literature (Eisenhardt and Graebner 2007; Locke 2001) to ensure close data-theory alignment. A preliminary research model was derived in this process with the potential constructs on IT capabilities identified and we have used this model as a "sensitizing device" (Klein and Myers 1999, p. 75) to guide our subsequent onsite interviews. This process is repeated until a state of theoretical saturation was reached i.e. significant overlaps in constructs start to occur in the subsequent data collected and the additional data did not provide new insights to corroborate, extend or refute the propositions of our emergent model (Eisenhardt 1989; Eisenhardt and Graebner 2007). In the post-hoc phase, a final round of confirmatory data analysis was conducted to ensure the reliability and validity of our model. When we uncovered inconsistencies during this phase, we would cross-check it with the researchers' field notes, discussions with colleagues, (Walsham 2006) and in some cases, clarifications with informants.

4 Project Background

The drive for the introduction of synchronous technology in SST stemmed from an operational key performance indicator (KPI) required by UniSIM for all schools to offer 50 % of her courses in a UniSIM defined "e-learning mode" of delivery. Ordinarily, a typical 5-credit (or 150 study hour) course would comprise of six, 3 h face-to-face seminars/tutorials delivered over a 6-week or 12-week duration, depending on whether the course had a laboratory element or otherwise. Should a course contain a laboratory element, the 6 face to face sessions will be delivered alternately with the laboratory sessions, making the course 12 weeks' long. The policy of converting a course to the "e-mode" entailed the removal of three, face-to-face classroom based seminars/tutorials and replace these with "e-mode" type learning. The senior management at SST after weighing and deliberating on various teaching delivery strategies as reported under "Introduction" and "Methodology" decided to adopt the delivery of the "e-mode" sessions for all converted courses using a form of synchronous on-line technology over asynchronous methods. The selected teaching deployment resulted in the running of synchronous on-line seminars/tutorials for 131 courses converted to the "e-mode" in gradual phases on a semester basis over a period of three years. Table 1 describes the management's perceived value of deploying synchronous on-line technology over an alternative asynchronous delivery method, such as those deployed by MOOCs. The scale of successful deployment of virtual synchronous on-line learning (VSOLL) sessions at SST is not trivial requiring a total of 360, 3-hour, or 1080 h of VSOLL per annum. This would require a massive increase in IT capabilities required for SST to successfully sustain and deliver the 1080 h of VSOLL sessions with a consistently high quality of service to the 3000 students serviced (see Table 2 on implementation scale). Figure 1 illustrates the operational structure that was set up to support the mass implementation of VSOLL in SST. This is termed "Large Scale Synchronous Teaching Technology" (LSSTT).

Table 1. Benefits of a LSSTT environment

- Ability to design a unique course content presentation to fit local part-study environment that fits the student profile governed by locality and culture of learning
- Teaching of Science and Technology to fit local student profile/study environment must be media rich enabled by interactivity and collaboration
- Choice of session to attend in multi-group courses
- Conduct frequency not tied in to fixed schedule (ease on logistics)
- Self-paced learning with private "chat" channel to instructor
- Lesson delivery and attendance not confined to campus/classroom allocated – economical savings of flying in overseas guest lecturers as well as ability of faculty to conduct virtual lessons for students based overseas
- Playback review through archiving/recording (aligned with local learning styles of students at SIM University)
- Easing logistical requirements to hold face-to-face administrative meetings with teaching staff and students through the use of VSOLL for administrative meetings

5   Discussion

This section commences with a discussion of what we had uncovered in our study for the Large Scale Synchronous Teaching Technology (LSSTT) implementation in the School. Figure 2 illustrates the detailed steps adopted by SST to ensure the successful implementation of the mass VSOLL delivery over the measured period from January 2012 to December 2015.

Based on the iterative analysis of our data, we have uncovered the following IT capabilities that played a critical role in ensuring a successful and sustainable LSSTT system and they are identified as following: (1) IS Infrastructure Capability; (2) Content Delivery IS Capability; (3) Network Capability; and (4) Management Capability. The IS capabilities were identified through our iterative analysis of our collected data. Table 3 shows the list of interviews conducted within SST.

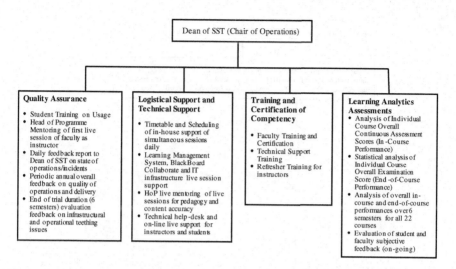

Fig. 1. Operational structure to support virtual synchronous on-line learning (VSOLL) on a large scale (LSSTT)

Table 2. Extent of scale of implementation of LSSTT in SST

• System supports the teaching and learning needs of 3000+ students in SST
• A total of 131 courses spread over 10 undergraduate degree programmes are currently running the "e-mode" of VSOLL delivery
• SST has a daily capacity peak of 22 VSOLL parallel sessions delivered simultaneously
• Over the period January 2012 to December 2015 (6 semesters) SST conducted a total of 2200 + h of VSOLL and conducted regular mass student and teaching staff briefings (up to a maximum capacity for 1000 simultaneous users)
• Currently running a microsite for 300 students selectively enroll to attend VSOLL sessions alongside SST students. The participants can choose any course from the list of available courses presented and join in discussion groups with the local students
• Use VSOLL to deliver an overseas guest lecturer from North Eastern University, United States on the History of Media. Local students gathered with their lecturer within SST premises whilst the overseas speaker delivered the lesson from his home in the United States in year 2015
• A faculty member conducted a class for about 100 postgraduate students from UNTAR University, Indonesia on Scientific Research methods. The lecturer was based in SST whilst the students attended the lessons synchronously on-line in Jakarta

When attempting to identify the nature of the IS capabilities within this LSSTT implementation, we attempted to distinguish IT capabilities into resources and processes. This approach is advocated in recent studies in IS capabilities (e.g. Agarwal et al. 2014) as extant literature in IT capabilities is often unclear about this distinction which often leads to conflicting and confusing results. Table 4 summarizes these IT capabilities required to support sustainable and high quality LSSTT in SST and the representative quotes extracted from our data collected.

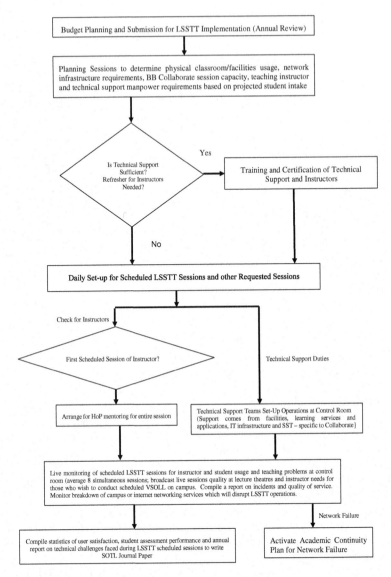

Fig. 2. Implementation of VSOLL at SST

6 IS Infrastructure Capability

As the professor/lecture delivering a VSOLL session no longer works alone but within the larger framework of other fellow professors/lecturers simultaneously (up to 22 courses to date) delivering content in a single evening to the part-time students in SST, the IS Infrastructure Capability must include the IT resources provided by UniSIM's Learning Applications and Services (LSA) as well as manpower from SST in the form of two full-time managers and a group of part-time IT specialists to provide operational

Table 3. Data sources to extract IT capabilities to support LSSTT through semi-structured interviews

Designation of Interviewees	No. of Interviewees	No. of Interviews
Technical Manager	2	4
Head of Programme	1	1
Experienced Teaching Staff	1	1
School IT Infrastructure and Laboratory Manager	1	1
Research Fellow	1	1
Senior Management	1	1
Total number of Interviews		9

on-line support to students and teaching staff for VSOLL content delivery. LSA, being a part of the university's Learning Services Cluster, provides manpower to support operations daily to users such as individual technical troubleshooting via the telephone and liaising with BB Collaborate the software service provider of the VSOLL system to handle issues such as academic continuity and dynamic service bandwidth provides to support the simultaneous VSOLL sessions every evening. Without the synergistic interactions and working collaborations between LSA and SST IT technical specialists/managers LSSTT technology cannot be successfully realized over the trial period of Jan 2012 to December 2015.

7   Content Delivery IS Capability

Prior to the introduction of VSOLL in January 2012, all professors/lecturers in SST have been training by the university's Teaching and Learning Centre (TLC) to deliver lecture content face-to-face. Introducing VSOLL introduced the new challenges of (1) the ability to effectively use the BB Collaborate VSOLL tool to teach synchronously on-line, (2) accepting on-line delivery from overseas academics at the same time possess the ability to deliver synchronous on-line content overseas and (3) reduce maximally the number of face-to-face meetings with students and teaching staff by providing the full-time academic administrators in SST with the ability to conduct synchronous on-line briefings to large groups of students and/or teaching staff, bearing in mind that SST provides only part-time degree programmes. The immediate availability of such manpower to delivery content and managed the delivery was not available in January 2012, but capability was gradually built up as the number of "e-mode" courses increased over the study period of six semesters.

8   Network Capability

Reviewing the work flow for network capability to recover to normal LSSTT operations as well as the provisions for academic continuity of LSSTT due to sudden network disruptions, SST relies on (1) its IT Managers to provide operational guidance/liaison with LSA/BB Collaborate as well as to students/staff, (2) the IT

Table 4. IT capability to support LLSTT in SST

IT Capability	Processes	Resources	Representative quotes
IS Infrastructure Capability	Resource Planning	• Learning Services and Applications Centre, UniSIM • Budget to purchase supporting hardware and maintenance of hardware	*"Preparations for LSSTT must commence way ahead of start of semester to ensure that IT Network and Learning Application Resources are fully available to support LSSTT. Additionally, all required operational and teaching spaces must be pre-booked to before the start of the semester so that both support and teaching staff can have avail to these resources immediately"*
	Manpower for Daily Management of LSSTT Sessions	• Full-time technical managers • Part-time IT specialists	
Content Delivery IS Capability	Ability to teach synchronously on-line	• Experienced and trained lecturers in VSOLL • Training Rooms with networked PCs	*"Every teaching staff new to VSOLL must be accompanied by a HoP [Head of Programme] sitting aside him/her when delivering the first VSOLL lesson and this should be carried out on campus"* *"One must accept and embrace the new VSOLL technology and methodology in order to teach well synchronously on-line. This also entails conducting rehearsals before actual lessons take place so that one is totally comfortable during delivery"*
	Delivering Contents Overseas	• Establishments of MOUs • Technical Management from SST • Experienced and trained lecturers in VSOLL • LSA second level support	
	Ability to conduct mass briefings to students and teaching staff (part-time)	• Technical Management from SST • Experienced and trained full-time lecturers in VSOLL	

(Continued)

Table 4. (*Continued*)

IT Capability	Processes	Resources	Representative quotes
		• LSA second level support	
Network Capability	Ensured academic continuity under all operating conditions	• Technical Managers	*"Network integrity and adequate capacity is absolutely vital to ensure academic continuity in a LSSTT implementation"*
		• IT Communication System with students and teaching staff	
		• IT Logistics for alternative presentations (ITS)	
		• Network Dongles	
Management Capability	Consistent Quality of Teaching and Operations during a VSOLL session	• Quality Check for new teaching staff on BB Collaborate Competency	*"It is extremely important that every teaching staff is fully conversant with the usage of the BB Collaborate VSOLL Tool prior to the start of the first lesson"*
		• Quality check at end of each evening on all simultaneous sessions	*"From a strategic viewpoint, the synchronous on-line mode of lesson delivery offers features closest to that of*
		• Head of programme individual guidance at VSOLL sessions	*the face-to-face mode. Besides it offers a platform for overseas guest lectures to be delivered on-line, local teaching staff delivering on-line lessons to overseas students as well as a reduction of logistics by cutting down mass student and staff face-to-face meetings"*
		• Dean of School – organization of community of practice activities	
		• Faculty training in use of BB Collaborate as a VSOLL tool with competency test	

business continuity (BCM) expertise from the university's Infocomm Technology and Support Group (ITS) and (3) the rapid deployment of network dongle devices in the event of campus network failure.

9   Management Capability

Management Capability to co-ordinate and effect changes in a dynamic way is central to the maintenance of a high quality of service as well as sustain LSSTT in SST in the long term. As such, this essential function is led by the Dean of School who provides the strategic guidance and planning for the whole LSSTT delivery plan. He is assisted at the academic programme level, by the school's ten Head of Programmes (HoP), who are trained to manage the delivery of courses by teaching staff in their respective programmes. Each HoP ensures that a teaching staff delivering a VSOLL session for the first time is guided in a face-to-face manner. For this first delivery session, every first-time delivery of a VSOLL session must be carried out in a seminar room in the presence of both HoP and teaching staff for the full duration of the lesson. Teaching staff are then at liberty to deliver the remaining planned VSOLL sessions either in SST or outside the campus. A school Research Fellow (RF) specializing in the teaching pedagogy of VSOLL alongside an IT Technical Manager (TM) will jointly provide a series of training sessions to every teaching staff assigned to deliver VSOLL sessions. At the end of every training session, each teaching staff must pass a practical competency test to ensure that he/she is sufficiently competent to handle the technical requirements of delivering a VSOLL session. Although this appears superficially trivial, experience gathered through the running of such VSOLL sessions show that technical competency of the teaching staff delivering the lesson could "make or break" the morale/attention span of the students. After a presentation of VSOLL of four semesters, the school formed a Community of Practice (CoP) to promote VSOLL technology through the organization of a Collaborate Day, where experienced practitioners shared effective teaching strategies for VSOLL delivery in diversely different courses such as Mathematics and Biomedical Engineering, together with the "bells and whistles" of how to improve student participation/feedback on assessment of learning. In conclusion, the most important element of Management Capability involves the change management of mindsets in the technical support teams, the teaching staff, the HoP as well as students. This is additionally monitored through regular quality of service checks and audits.

10   Conclusion

This study started to answer two key research questions namely: (1) what are the key IT capabilities a University needs in order to support the large-scale deployment of a synchronous online technology like Blackboard Collaborate; and (2) how are these IT capabilities can be systematically developed.

Based on the case of UniSIM, we had identified the four key IT capabilities namely (1) IS Infrastructure Capability; (2) Content Delivery IS Capability; (3) Network Capability; and (4) Management Capability that are required to assure the effective large-scale deployment of synchronous online technology in the teaching and learning context. We had also provided a process on how these IT capabilities are systematically developed within UniSIM.

By addressing our research questions, this study has contributed to the literature and practice in the following ways. First, our study is one of the few attempts to examine IT capabilities in the teaching and learning context. We had also presented a viable IT capability development roadmap for other universities to mimic that we believed would be helpful in increasing the chances of driving such implementation. Second, our study contributes to the literature on IT capabilities and teaching and learning by extending this theory of IT capabilities into the field of teaching and learning. We believe this will enrich the discussion of IT capabilities going forward.

There are two limitations with our study. First, our inductively derived theory applied only to one case organization. To ensure its statistical generalizability, our theory can be tested by statistical means in future studies. Second, our study unfortunately only shed lights on how to implement a successful large-scale online synchronous teaching tool implementation. It does not shed light on how the success of this initiative can be sustained over time and on how to scale its success to include more students. Future research can consider adopting a longitudinal approach to provide more insights in these areas.

References

Agarwal, N., Soh, C., Sia, S.K.: IT capabilities in global enterprises. Paper presented at the Pacific Asia Conference on Information Systems (2014). http://aisel.aisnet.org/pacis2014/311

Bainbridge, S.: EDDE806 Research Seminar II Recording (Dr. Tony Bates - Teaching in a Digital Age) (2015). https://connect.athabascau.ca/p3ae5iggugd/

Bharadwaj, A.: A resource-based perspective on information technology capability and firm performance: an empirical investigation. MIS Q. 24(1), 169–196 (2000)

de Freitas, S., Neumann, T.: Pedagogic strategies supporting the use of synchronous audiographic conferencing: a review of the literature. Br. J. Educ. Technol. 40(6), 980–998 (2009)

Eisenhardt, K.M.: Building theories from case study research. Acad. Manag. Rev. 14(4), 532–550 (1989)

Eisenhardt, K.M., Graebner, M.E.: Theory building from cases: opportunities and challenges. Acad. Manag. J. 50(1), 25–32 (2007)

Feeny, D.F., Wilcocks, L.P.: Core IS capabilities for exploiting information technology. Sloan Manag. Rev. 39(3), 9–21 (1998)

Garrison, D.R., Anderson, T., Archer, W.: Critical inquiry in a text-based environment: computer conferencing in higher education. Internet High. Educ. 2(2–3), 87–108 (2000)

HKUST: Teaching over virtual classroom (2012). http://celt.ust.hk/event/teaching-over-virtual-classroom. Accessed 12 Feb 2016

Irvine, V., Code, J., Richards, L.: Realigning higher education for 21st century learning through multi-access learning. MERLOT J. Online Learn. Teach. 9(2), 172–186 (2013)

Kim, G., Shin, B., Kim, K.K., Lee, H.G.: IT capabilities, process-oriented dynamic capabilities, and firm financial performance. J. Assoc. Inf. Syst. 12(7), 487–517 (2011)

Klein, H.K., Myers, M.D.: A set of principles for conducting and evaluating interpretive field studies in information systems. MIS Q. 23(1), 67–93 (1999)

Locke, K.: Grounded Theory in Management Research. Sage, Thousand Oaks (2001)

Pan, S.L., Tan, B.C.C.: Demystifying case research: a structured-pragmatic-situational (SPS) approach to conducting case studies. Inf. Organ. 21(3), 161–176 (2011)

Pentland, B.T.: Building process theory with narrative: from description to explanation. Acad. Manag. Rev. **24**(4), 711–724 (1999)

Power, M., Vaughan, N.: Redesigning online learning for international graduate seminar delivery. J. Distance Educ. **24**(2), 19–38 (2010)

Raymond, L., Uwizeyemungu, S., Fabi, B., St-Pierre, J.: IT capability configurations for innovation: an empirical study of industrial SMEs. In: Conference Proceedings of the 2014 47th Hawaii International Conference on System Sciences (2014)

Reushle, S., Loch, B.: Conducting a trial of web conferencing software: why, how and perceptions from the coalface. Turk. Online J. Distance Educ. **9**(3), 19–28 (2008)

Ross, J.W., Beath, C.M., Goodhue, D.L.: Develop long-term competitiveness through it assets. Sloan Manag. Rev. **38**(1), 31–45 (1996)

Rowe, S., Ellis, A.: Moving beyond four walls: a fully online delivery model. Paper presented at the Proceedings of the World Conference on Educational Multimedia, Hypermedia and Telecommunications, ED-MEDIA, Toronto, Canada (2010)

Wade, M., Hulland, J.: The resource-based view and information systems research: review, extension and suggestions for future research. MIS Q. **28**(1), 107–138 (2004)

Walsham, G.: Doing interpretive research. Eur. J. Inf. Syst. **15**(3), 320–330 (2006)

The Five Forces of Technology Adoption

Dan McAran[✉] and Sharm Manwani

Henley Business School, University of Reading, Reading, UK
danmca@hotmail.com, sharm.manwani@henley.ac.uk

Abstract. The Technology Acceptance Model (TAM), and the models derived from TAM, dominate user acceptance of technology theory. This research uses a web-based questionnaire directed towards legal professionals solicited using the social media site LinkedIn. The research included open-ended questions, within a quantitative survey instrument and received 154 usable responses. In TAM3, Venkatesh and Bala organize the theoretical framework of preceding factors of Perceived Usefulness and Perceived Ease of Use into four categories. The findings reinforced the existence of the Venkatesh and Bala factors that affect technology adoption but reveal additional multi-dimensional factors related to the context of legal technology. It is proposed that analyzing the Five Forces of Technology Adoption: (1) Individual, (2) Social, (3) System, (4) Facilitating Conditions, and (5) Context, could extend our understanding of technology acceptance. In summary, the paper offers a novel interpretation, characterizing five forces of technology adoption - an analogy to Porter's model.

Keywords: Technology acceptance · Technology adoption · Context

1 Introduction

The increased pervasiveness of computer (and mobile) technology in all spheres of human life is all encompassing. There is concern, most profoundly expressed by several authors in the 2007 special issue of the Journal of the Association of Information Systems entitled Quo Vadis TAM – Issues and Reflections on Technology Acceptance Research [1] that despite the extent of the research performed on user acceptance of technology few design specifications or interventions have emerged to enhance or promote user acceptance of technology.

This research is focused on technology used by legal professionals to do legal work (henceforth: 'legal technology') and uses a web-based questionnaire directed towards legal professionals asking them to complete the survey instrument based on their personal experiences with a self-selected legal technology product.

Venkatesh and Bala [2] identify four factors as important in understanding a technology adoption situation: (1) Individual Differences, (2) System Characteristics, (3) Social Influence, and (4) Facilitating Conditions. Open-ended questions related to these factors in the survey instrument provide insights on the importance of context in technology adoption. The results of this research reveal additional multi-dimensional factors closely related to the particular context of legal technology that affect technology acceptance, most notably the legal profession practice context.

© Springer International Publishing Switzerland 2016
F.F.-H. Nah and C.-H. Tan (Eds.): HCIBGO 2016, Part I, LNCS 9751, pp. 545–555, 2016.
DOI: 10.1007/978-3-319-39396-4_50

While the four factors identified by Venkatesh and Bala [2] are, at face value, quite robust, the relative effect of these factors will likely vary based on the nature of the technology and the industry to which it relates. An analogy can be made to the application of Porter's Five Forces [3] to an industry analysis where for one industry a particular factor may be of high importance and in a second distinct industry may be insignificant. This analysis is also supported in the work of Chau and Hu [4]. One objective of this research is to explore how these specific contextual factors can be identified for a given context/technology, in this case legal technology.

Chau and Hu [4] applied the Technology Acceptance by Individual Professionals (TAIP) model to a professional group - physicians - which may have similar technology acceptance characteristics as members of the legal profession. Brown et al. [5] combined a model of collaboration technology and the UTUAT model to develop a model that explains adoption of collaboration technology. In doing so they elaborated the antecedents of Perceived Usefulness (PU) and Perceived Ease of Use (PEOU) specific to collaboration technology. Venkatesh et al. [6] extended the Unified Theory of Use and Acceptance of Technology (UTUAT) theory to consumer markets with the creation of UTUAT2 to include constructs for hedonic motivation, price value and habit. In a similar manner the proposed research seeks evidence of the contextual nature of antecedent factors particular to user acceptance of legal technology.

This paper is organized as follows: Sect. 2 is the literature review; Sect. 3, the research methodology; Sect. 4, the results and discussion. Section 5 is the conclusion.

2 Literature

Porter [3] postulated five forces which determine the state of competition in an industry. These are: (1) Threat of new entrants, (2) Bargaining power of customers, (3) Bargaining power of suppliers, (4) Threat of substitute products or services, and (5) Intensity of competition.

These Five Forces can be viewed as contextual forces that affect the state of competition in an industry. Porter [3] elaborates that a firm's strategy can be based on the analysis of these forces. This leads to the conjecture that it may be possible to develop a strategy in regards to the acceptance of a technology product by performing an analysis of the contextual forces for a specific technology and context.

A search was conducted to locate literature in which Porter's Five Forces had been used as an analogy or template to characterize a set of 'forces' characterizing another domain: only four relevant papers were identified.

In an outline of a study of the adoption of cloud computing by IT outsourcing services, Fung [7] used a model combing Porter's Five Forces [3] as antecedents to two constructs with general similarity to the PU and PEOU in the Technology Acceptance Model (TAM) of Davis [8]. These corresponding factors are Perceived Benefits of Cloud Computing – corresponding to PU – and Perceived Ease of Adoption of Cloud Computing – corresponding to PEOU. The dependent variable was IT Outsourcing Service Provider's Intention to Adopt Cloud Computing which has correspondence to the Behavioral Intention variable also found in TAM. As the research has yet to be conducted, Fung [7], in his paper, presented only the literature review, research problem, methodology, and research design.

Rice [9] used an analogy to Porter's Five Forces in regards to risk management. Rice [9] identifies the following 'forces' specific to a model designed to understand risk management: (1) Internal Organization, (2) Industry, (3) Information, (4) Infrastructure, and (5) Influences and uses this framework to assess risk in a military helicopter acquisition project. The Information component is composed of "software availability and functionality, information systems backups, and network security" (p. 379).

In a study of technology adoption in manufacturing firms Kristianto et al. [10] discuss leadership as a technology adoption 'force'. Blandford and Adams [11] analyze 'forces' and barriers to technology adoption in healthcare.

Kroenung and Eckhardt [12] also illustrate the constructs appropriate for a particular technology adoption model depend on context. Notably, in one of the limited number of mixed method research projects in IS, Brown et al. [13] compared seven models of technology adoption in the household and comment.

> Our findings suggest that context-specific models do indeed offer richer insights, compared to more general models, which calls into question the conventional wisdom about generalizability being the most critical criterion for theory development; rather, it suggests...a focus on the context can be more fruitful (p. 1942).

In this research, the existing Porter's Five Forces are not used as antecedent constructs in the TAM model, but used as an analogy to describe specific forces that affect technology acceptance. We conclude that research into a professional context analysis of legal technology acceptance is worthwhile from both an academic and a practitioner perspective.

3   Research Methodology

The existence of significant prior research combined with the exploratory nature of a different context supports a mixed methods approach to investigating factors affecting technology acceptance. The research used a triangulation design combining a quantitative survey with open-ended questions. Ågerfalk [14] notes the close connection between mixed methods research, critical realism, and the emergent design science research which are significant components of this research.

The research methodology found in user acceptance of technology has been almost exclusively focused on surveys (questionnaires) and case studies [15]. A notable exception to the pattern of quantitative research is Venkatesh and Brown [16] in which adoption of personal computers at home was explored. Venkatesh and Brown [16] found additional insights through the use of qualitative methodology:

> ...the breakdown into more detailed dimensions was possible due to the use of open-ended questions. In fact, the data coding process helped identify dimensions that had not been accounted for in prior research, providing further support that the use of open-ended items helped to overcome a priori expectations, resulting in a more complete understanding of the phenomena. (p. 83)

This research similarly uses open-ended questions in the survey instrument based on the factors outlined by Venkatesh and Bala [2]: (1) Individual differences, (2) System characteristics, (3) Social influence, and (4) Facilitating conditions. The research respondents were solicited using the social media site LinkedIn [17]. The population solicited was legal professionals (lawyers, paralegals, law clerks, and legal assistants). Posts were made to LinkedIn legal related groups. The LinkedIn message system (InMails) and a legal technology email news service were also used to solicit respondents.

The questionnaire requested respondents to complete the questionnaire based on their perceptions of products they were currently using. The following legal technology products were listed by default: (1) Westlaw, (2) PC Law, (3) LexisNexis – Quicklaw, (4) Fastcase, (5) AccessData – Summation, and (6) Sage – Timeslips. The respondents were also permitted to enter a legal technology product of their own choice.

The following open-ended questions were included in the questionnaire:

1. Are there factors specific to you personally that influence your decision on whether to use or not to use a legal technology product?
2. Are there factors specific to the people you work with or the social situation where you work that influence your decision on whether to use or not to use a legal technology product?
3. Are there factors specific to the information system or other technology you use at work that influence your decision on whether to use or not to use a legal technology product?
4. Are there factors specific to the work environment, technical support available, other help available, or other related factors at work that influence your decision on whether to use or not to use a legal technology product?

This research used a web-based questionnaire directed towards legal professionals solicited using the social media site LinkedIn [17]. The research included open-ended questions, within a quantitative survey instrument. The questionnaire received 154 usable responses.

The analysis of the responses to these questions was facilitated by the assignment of double codes to sections of text. Miles and Huberman [18] state "…multiple coding is actually useful in exploratory studies" (p. 65). As an example, a respondent who self-identified as a small business owner and who indicated the importance of cost related to profitability of the small business was assigned a code of 'Cost' and assigned to the Personal factor because 'Cost' is a personal motivator for a small business owner. This text was also assigned to the separate Cost factor analysis. Using this approach a more holistic array of factors affecting technology acceptance was constructed. As will be discussed, a separate analysis was created to highlight unique contextual subthemes related to legal technology.

4   Results and Discussion

4.1   Introduction

The results of this research show that contextual factors add significant insight in line with the findings of Chau and Hu [4] over and above the 4 factor model developed by Venkatesh and Bala [2]. The interpretation of the Personal factor was expanded beyond narrow demographic factors to include any sub-theme which emerged that had an aspect that could be characterized as a personal experience. The interpretations of Social, System, and Facilitating Conditions have been similarly expanded.

Most of the textual responses were assigned two codes, and consequently appear in more than one specific analysis. This has resulted in a set of analyses that are inter-related and overlap. This process does allow, however, for the identification of the inter-relationships between themes, such as the inter-relationship between the Usefulness sub-theme of Quality and the Professional Practice sub-theme of Professional Usefulness – there is considerable overlap between these two themes, but not complete overlap. As an example, 'Simplification of Work' would be a general aspect of Quality, but not specifically identified with Professional Practice.

4.2   Personal Factors

The responses characterized under Personal Factors were classified into the following 9 sub-themes: (1) Personal Experience, (2) Cost as a Personal Factor, (3) Personal Perception/Trust of Legal Tech Supplier, (4) Personal Age, (5) Personal Computer Skills, (6) Personal Preference, (7) Personal Skills, (8) Personal Work Preferences, and (9) Personal Innovativeness.

4.3   Social Factors

Social factors were identified as important in the adoption and use of technology to do legal work. There are three summary points identifiable in the Social Factor analysis:

1. The highly contextual nature of social factors in technology adoption. This is particularly evident in the factors mentioned of 'taught at law school', and 'peer acceptance of the technology'. The reference to the use of technology taught in law schools is an interesting reflection of macro contextual social factors which influence technology acceptance. This would have similarity to an 'industry force' [3].
2. For some legal professionals, the law firm management (often the senior lawyers) determines if other lawyers or legal staff use legal technology.
3. A significant proportion of the practitioners stated they are not influenced by 'people/social' factors in the adoption of legal technology.

4.4   System Factors

There were seven sub-themes identified related to System. Among the responses that were categorized as related to System, there was considerable overlap with other contextually related themes.

1. Ability to collaborate overlaps with Collaboration identified under Social Factors.
2. Fit with Workflow overlaps with Personal Work Practices, identified under the Personal Factors.
3. The System factor sub-themes of Technology Integration and Technical Compatibility form a significant part of the Compatibility Factor analysis.

4.5   Facilitating Conditions

The comments of respondents classified under Facilitating Conditions highlight the evolving nature of the modern law office where complete integration of all applications and technology platforms is emerging as the standard. Many of the responses appearing in the analysis above are also represented in other contextual analyses presented in this paper. The most interesting result was in regards to the comments respondents made in regards to technical support. Consequently, the analysis of technical support is broken out into a separate analysis.

4.6   Contextual Factors

Contextual factors distinct from the four Venkatesh and Bala [2] factors discussed above emerged in the research and are discussed in this section.

Professional Practice. The many comments and high focus on aspects of professional usefulness of legal technology correspond to the findings of Chau and Hu [4] in regards to the introduction of telemedicine technology in Hong Kong: "Physicians, as a group, appear to be fairly pragmatic in their technology evaluation and selection by focusing on practical utility rather than on technological novelty" (p. 212). The same statement appears to be true for members of the legal profession as well. There are six areas of particular interest in the results that are categorized as the following Professional Practice sub-themes: (1) Case Specifics, (2) Practice Area Considerations, (3) Professional Utility, (4) Legal Profession Culture, (5) Client Factors, and (6) Professional Standard.

Quality Factors. The responses characterized under Quality were classified into the following 14 sub-themes: (1) Degree User Friendly, (2) Uniqueness of Legal Technology, (3) Degree Technology Integrated, (4) Degree of Usefulness, (5) Quality of Design, (6) Degree of Ease of Use/Intuitive, (7) Degree Adaptable, (8) Degree of Technical Quality, (9) Degree of Flexibility, (10) Degree of Data Quality, (11) Degree Familiar, (12) Degree of Compatibility, (13) Availability of Enhancements, and (14) Degree of Trialability.

Again there is significant overlap with the sub-themes of Quality with other analyses. Most notably the sub-themes of Degree Technology Integrated and Degree of

Compatibility are included in the separate Compatibility analysis. Many of the specific items mentioned in the Usefulness and Data Quality sub-themes also appear in the Professional Practice section.

Cost Factors. Comments coded as 'Cost' frequently were mentioned by respondents. Multiple responses were received in regards to 'Cost/Benefit', 'Price', and 'Switching Costs'. The results indicate a broad concern with cost in the adoption of legal technology, with 11 different aspects identified. This highlights the importance of cost as a factor in technology acceptance and use.

Management Factors. Comments related to Management also appear under the Facilitating Conditions analysis. Many respondents indicated that use of a particular legal technology was required as part of the job. Most of the respondents who indicated that use of a particular legal technology was mandatory were non-lawyer legal staff, such as paralegals, law clerks, legal assistants. However, a number of lawyers working for other lawyers indicated that use of a particular legal technology was mandated. Several comments indicated internal firm power relationships determined what legal technology could be utilized. Management control of overhead costs and management's decision making ability on what technology to provide were also mentioned.

Compatibility Factors. There were 15 responses coded as 'Compatibility'. The main focus was on compatibility with cellphones and the cloud; compatibility with Microsoft products; and the ability to integrate and synchronize with other technologies. Data synchronization, data sharing, and database integration were also mentioned. One respondent mentioned integration with iPad and another user mentioned compatibility with technology for the visually impaired. The theme of Compatibility can be seen as a sub-theme of System related considerations, but it is useful to highlight the growing importance of integration with emerging technologies.

Technical Support. Technical support had numerous comments from respondents in the research. Consequently, the analysis of the responses made in regards to technical support was performed separately. The responses indicate the high importance the respondents attached to technical support, and moreover, the high standards the respondents require for technical support. This can be seen in the numerous and detailed commentary on technical support requirements identified by the respondents. The comments also indicate a level of frustration with the quality of technical support.

Training Factors. The small number of comments in regard to training was quite unexpected: there were only nine comments in the research that explicitly referred to training. One lawyer commented that finding time to train staff was an issue.

4.7 Unique Contextual Subthemes Related to Legal Technology

This analysis does not provide new information, but provides an overall summary of the more interesting subthemes identified using the open-ended questions. The specific factors identified here are the sub-themes identified for both the four factors identified by Venkatesh and Bala [2] and the contextual themes that emerged. In this research the following factors were identified as salient and specific to the legal technology:

1. Legal Usefulness.
2. Client Focus.
3. Usefulness to the Case-at-Hand.
4. Use by Business Partners.
5. The Availability of In-House Support.
6. The Influence of Professional Legal Culture.
7. The Essential Nature of the Product to Practice.
8. The Importance of Fit with Work Flow.
9. The Integration of the Legal Technology into Practice.
10. Organization Factors.
11. Cost of Substitutes.

Additional analyses could be prepared for other technologies and contexts allowing for an appreciation of similarities or differences to legal technology.

4.8 Discussion

The factors identified by Venkatesh and Bala [2] – (1) Personal, (2) People, (3) Social, and (4) Facilitating Conditions have been maintained but the following additional contextual factors have emerged for legal technology: (1) Professional Practice, (2) Quality, (3) Cost, (4) Management, (5) Compatibility, (6) Technical Support, and (7) Training.

In addition, a separate analysis has been prepared to highlight unique contextual subthemes related to legal technology. This additional contextual analysis could be compared to other similarly prepared contextual analyses for other technologies and contexts; such as technology used by medical, engineering, or academic professions.

Further analysis could also be prepared for differing technologies based on the relative strength of the four factors identified by Venkatesh and Bala [2] (Personal, People, Social, and Facilitating Conditions) using a rating system in regards to importance of each factor. A simple rating system might use the following four classifications: (1) No Importance, (2) Low Importance, (3) Moderate Importance, and (4) High Importance; allowing for further comparative analysis.

The above analysis supports the general results of TAM research over the last 30 years. However, the results indicate the definite limitations of a number of the constructs comprising TAM3 in relation to legal technology. Notably in this research the TAM3 constructs of Computer Playfulness, Perceived Enjoyment, Image, and Result Demonstrability appear to have low or reduced importance to the acceptance of legal technology. The constructs appearing in TAM3 could also be used as the basis for comparative analyses of varying technologies used in specific contexts. Yet another basis of preparing a comparative analysis would be the Shih and Venkatesh [19] determinants of the Use-Diffusion model. The general correspondence of this research to the research of Lewis [20] and Manker [21] supports the validity of this research and the generalizability of this research.

The results support the high importance of context in the adoption of technology in professional practice. Chau and Hu [4] identify three contexts influencing technology adoption: the implementation context, the technological context, and the individual context (p. 216). For Chau and Hu [4] the relevant context was the adoption of telemedicine technology in Hong Kong. In this research the relevant context is the adoption of legal technology by professionals mainly based in North America, but the insights developed by Chau and Hu [4] concerning these contexts remain important.

These observations suggest that to understand technology acceptance for any specific technology, it would be necessary to consider the contextual factors specific to the technology under consideration. It also indicates that the value of simple models of technology acceptance may be of decreasing value because of the increased specialization of IT and the increasing importance of context in their acceptance and use. Novel approaches, new models, and more innovative ways of exploring technology acceptance may be required.

In this research we postulate the existence of Five Forces of Technology Adoption: (1) Personal, (2) Social, (3) System, (4) Facilitating Conditions, and (5) Context: these could potentially be factors determining the different models of technology acceptance that appear in the literature including those already mentioned of Brown et al. [5] for collaboration technology and Venkatesh et al. [6] for consumer markets with UTUAT2.

The results also show the benefit of using mixed methods in technology acceptance research – in this case open-ended questions. The use of such data when creating a technology acceptance model for a specific technology within a particular configuration of the Five Forces of Technology Adoption would provide additional insight to the particular case at hand; facilitating the design of a model.

With this focus on designing a technology acceptance model for a specific technology and context we build the 'IT Artifact' [22, p. iii]. We also bring IS academic research closer to design. As Simon [23] notes:

> Everyone designs who devises courses of action aimed at changing existing situations into preferred ones. ...Design, so construed, is the core of all professional training... Schools of engineering, as well as schools architecture, business, education, law, and medicine, are all centrally concerned with the process of design (p. 111).

This comment of Simon concerning design supports the increasing interpretation of IS research as a design science [24].

4.9 Limitations, Future Research, Management Implications, and Contribution

There are two general limitations to this research (1) this research is cross-sectional, and (2) this research accessed a segment of the target population who had sufficiently good skills to use internet social media; they may not be representative of the total target population. It would be particularly interesting to explore the differences in factors that influence user acceptance of technology among professions. As an example 'cost' and 'technical support' were found to be significant factors in this research, it would be of interest to determine if these two factors were also important among law, medicine, engineering, academic, and accounting practitioners.

5   Conclusion

This research has identified 'Context' as an additional important factor to technology acceptance in addition to the factors identified by Venkatesh and Bala [2]. The four factors identified by Venkatesh and Bala [2] plus Context can be viewed as analogous to Porter's Five Forces [3]. Using this analogy to understand the factors that affect technology adoption can be seen as corresponding to the understanding the individual forces identified by Porter [3] as a pre-requisite to understanding a specific industry. This research suggests the addition of a fifth force 'Context' as key to technology adoption. This research is intended to lead to the development of new approaches to understanding and researching technology adoption. As an illustration, we recommend developing a strategy for a new technology product's acceptance through an analysis of the individual and interacting forces affecting technology acceptance.

In addition, a significant finding in that cost is a barrier to using legal technology. Further, technical support has been found to be highly important in regards to legal technology. The research introduces the concept of Five Forces of Technology Acceptance. As far as the author is aware this is the first research study related to technology acceptance that has used social media (LinkedIn) to solicit respondents.

References

1. Hirschheim, R.: Introduction to the special issue on Quo Vadis TAM – issues and reflections on technology acceptance research. J. Assoc. Inf. Syst. **8**(4), 211–218 (2007)
2. Venkatesh, V., Bala, H.: Technology acceptance model 3 and a research agenda on interventions. Decis. Sci. **39**(2), 273–315 (2008)
3. Porter, M.E.: How competitive forces shape strategy. Harvard Bus. Rev. **57**(2), 137–145 (1979)
4. Chau, P.Y.K., Hu, P.J.: Examining a model of technology acceptance by individual professionals: an exploratory study. J. Manag. Inf. Syst. **18**(4), 191–229 (2002)
5. Brown, S.A., Dennis, A.R., Venkatesh, V.: Predicting collaboration technology use: integrating technology adoption and collaboration research. J. Manag. Inf. Syst. **27**(2), 9–53 (2010)
6. Venkatesh, V., Thong, J.Y.L., Xu, X.: Consumer acceptance and use of information technology: extending the unified theory of acceptance and use of technology. MIS Q. **36**(1), 157–178 (2012)
7. Fung, H.P.: Using porter five forces and technology acceptance model to predict cloud computing adoption among IT outsourcing service providers. Internet Technol. Appl. Res. **1**(2), 18–24 (2014)
8. Davis, F.D.: A technology acceptance model for empirically testing new end-user new information systems: theory and results. Unpublished doctoral dissertation. MIT Sloan School of Management. Cambridge, MA (1986)
9. Rice, J.: Adaptation of Porter's Five Forces Model to Risk Management. Defense Acquisition University (2010)
10. Kristianto, Y., Ajmal, M., Tenkorang, A.R., Hussain, M.: A study of technology adoption in manufacturing firms. J. Manuf. Technol. Manag. **23**(2), 198–211 (2012)

11. Blandford, A., Adams, A.: Adoption, adaptation, surface compliance and obstruction: responses to new technologies in healthcare. In: Proceedings of HCI4Med Workshop at HCI 2008 (2008)

12. Kroenung, J., Eckhardt, A.: The attitude cube - a three-dimensional model of situational factors in IS adoption and their impact on the attitude–behavior relationship. Inf. Manag. **52**(60), 611–627 (2015)

13. Brown, S.A., Venkatesh, V., Hoehle, H.: Technology adoption decisions in the household: a seven-model comparison. J. Assoc. Inf. Sci. Technol. **66**(9), 1933–1949 (2015)

14. Ågerfalk, P.J.: Embracing diversity through mixed methods research. Eur. J. Inf. Syst. **22**(3), 251–256 (2013)

15. Choudrie, J., Dwivedi, Y.K.: Investigating the research approaches for examining technology adoption issues. J. Res. Pract. **1**(1), Article D1 (2005). http://jrp.icaap.org/index.php/jrp/article/view/4/7. Accessed 8 May 2010

16. Venkatesh, V., Brown, S.A.: Longitudinal investigation of personal computers at home: adoption determinants and emerging challenges. MIS Q. **25**(1), 71–102 (2001)

17. LinkedIn Social Media Site (2015). https://www.linkedin.com/. Accessed 28 May 2015

18. Miles, M.B., Huberman, A.M.: Qualitative Data Analysis, 2nd edn. Sage Publications, Thousand Oaks (1994)

19. Shih, C.-F., Venkatesh, A.: Beyond adoption: development and application of a use-diffusion model. J. Mark. **68**(1), 59–72 (2004)

20. Lewis, G.: The factors that influence a lawyer's use of and ability to develop effective electronic information seeking behaviour. Master's thesis, School of Information Management. Victoria University of Wellington, New Zealand (2014)

21. Manker, C.: Factors Contributing to the Limited Use of Technology in State Courtrooms. Unpublished Ph.D. dissertation. Walden University, Wisconsin, USA (2015)

22. Weber, R.: Editor's comments: still desperately seeking the IT artifact. MIS Q. **27**(2), iii–xi (2003)

23. Simon, H.A.: The Sciences of the Artificial, 3rd edn. The MIT Press, Cambridge (1996)

24. Hevner, A.R., March, S.T., Park, J.: Design science in information systems research. MIS Q. **28**(3), 75–105 (2004)

Digital Innovation and the Becoming
of an Organizational Identity

Nikolaus Obwegeser[1(✉)] and Stefan Bauer[2]

[1] School of Business and Social Sciences, Aarhus University, Aarhus, Denmark
nikolaus@mgmt.au.dk
[2] Institute for Information Management and Control,
Vienna University of Economics and Business, Vienna, Austria
stefan.bauer@wu.ac.at

Abstract. Today, companies often face rapid and substantial change of their business environment. To stay competitive, firms are forced to engage in continuous innovation of their products and services. Moreover, the digitization of society and organizations has led to an increase in radical and disruptive innovations across all industries and trades. As a result, companies often find it difficult to develop an organizational identity – a shared understanding of "who are we" and "what makes us different from others". In this article, we combine extant theory on both digital innovation and identity formation processes to develop a conceptual model of identity formation, highlighting the dynamics between innovation and identity formation. We use our model to discuss symptoms that organizations might experience when engaging in digital innovation, shaping the process of identity development. Finally, we suggest future research topics to investigate the relationship between innovation and identity formation processes.

Keywords: Digital innovation · Organizational identity · Growth

1 Introduction

In this article, we look at the effect of digital innovations on the process of organizational identity formation in growing companies. Today, companies often face rapid and substantial change of their business environment and are therefore forced to engage in continuous innovation of their products and services [9]. Moreover, the digitization of society and organizations has led to an increase in radical and disruptive innovations across all industries and trades [31]. As a result, these companies often find it difficult to develop an organizational identity – a shared understanding of "who are we" and "what makes us different from others" within members of the same organization [1]. We argue that this situation is especially challenging for growing small and medium enterprises (SMEs), as they (i) have not yet developed a strong identity and (ii) experience additional stress, both external and internal, due to their growth processes.

To investigate the dynamic interplay of incremental versus radical innovation with relation to the process of organizational identity formation, we combine extant theory on both digital innovation and identity formation processes to develop a conceptual

© Springer International Publishing Switzerland 2016
F.F.-H. Nah and C.-H. Tan (Eds.): HCIBGO 2016, Part I, LNCS 9751, pp. 556–564, 2016.
DOI: 10.1007/978-3-319-39396-4_51

model of identity formation. While theory on identity formation has produced a number of valuable findings, deep insights into the sources, antecedents and mechanics of identity (re-)configuration, especially with regard to inception of identities in newly formed entities, remain scarce [18]. Our research focuses particularly on the role of changing innovation patterns due to the ongoing digitization of our society. Change due to digitization or new technologies often has implications beyond the technology itself. As [28] points out, digital innovation can impact firms in a way that they "may ultimately need to develop an entirely new organizational identity whereby both organizational members and external constituents must alter deeply held assumptions and beliefs about what the firm represents".

To explore this complex phenomenon, which is difficult to observe directly, we construct a conceptual model to illustrate the interaction between the processes and support discussion. We use our model to elaborate on symptoms that organizations might experience when engaging in digital innovation, shaping the process of identity development. Moreover, we discuss the practical implications of our model and suggest future research topics to investigate the relationship between innovation and identity formation processes.

The remainder of this article is structured as follows. First, we introduce the state-of-the-art in research on organizational identity as a process as well as on digital innovation. Second, we present and discuss our proposed conceptual model. We conclude our paper with a discussion of implications, limitations and pointers for promising future research.

2 Theoretical Background

2.1 Organizational Identity as a Process

Organizational identity has traditionally often been seen as a rather static attribute, an entity or characteristic of an organization, focusing on the "who are we?" question [1]. [17] refer to the aspects of endurance, distinctiveness and centrality that are widely used to describe an organizational identity. Only recently, building on social psychology, researchers have started to argue for a view of organizational identity as a process of development and change over time. [24] points to three process dimensions of organizational identity: relational, behavioral and symbolic. As an analogy, [15] remark that the process view on organizational identity can be compared to viewing a full motion picture about an organization, while the characteristic based view provides only a single snapshot or picture of the organization. Following that line of argument, we argue that the process-oriented perspective on organizational identity is particularly useful when investigating young and growing companies in competitive environments. Thereby, the influence of digital innovation activities on the development of an organizational identity can be observed in detail and the specific effects can be analyzed. The process view purposefully challenges the original notion of endurance of an identity, building on the fact that this aspect has remained understudied. According to [4] "identity endurance is rarely seen as a puzzle to be explained; it is assumed as relatively unproblematic and remains empirically neglected".

In a review of literature on identity processes, [24] finds that identity processes are often associated with other processes, such as sense-making, learning, changing, among others. [5] suggests that there does not exist such a thing as an "identity process", but that identity itself is rhetorical and thus the result or "content" of other "basic" processes. To investigate identity from a process perspective, [24] proposes three potential avenues for researchers: processes about identity, process unique to identity, and the interplay of processes in identity dynamics. Pertaining to the first, he argues that researchers could address the role of identity as "an outcome, antecedent, or content" of another process. Pertaining to the second, researchers could investigate processes that are unique to identity creation and maintenance. Thirdly, he posits that investigating the role and interplay of multiple processes in identity dynamics will likely yield interesting results. [18] identify three common themes that can be found in research on organizational identity formation: informal organization, human agency and environmental adaptation.

We find that the process view provides a highly useful perspective for the purpose of our study, as it allows us to understand how the interplay of different forces influence and shape the becoming of an organizational identity.

2.2 Digital Innovation

As an emerging area of research in information systems, the concept of digital innovation refers to "a product, process, or business model that is perceived as new, requires some significant changes on the part of adopters, and is embodied in or enabled by IT" [12]. Traditional industries and their practices are becoming more and more entangled in today's digital infrastructures and are therefore required to rethink and adopt their innovation strategies [16, 31]. Digital innovation spans across the disciplines of technology management on the one side, and IT innovation on the other side [26]. In contrast to purely technical innovation, digital innovations always include a business perspective, which can be categorized in process, product or business model innovation [12]. Digital process innovations, or new ways of doing old work, were among the first drivers of new technologies in the workplace [27]. Digital product innovation refers to the integration of technological novelty as part of the product offerings of a firm [32]. Business model innovation by means of digital technologies is becoming more and more crucial in various markets, e.g. newspapers and publishing houses [3].

Technological change does not take place in a vacuum, but rather influences all other elements of information systems, such as people, tasks and processes, and knowledge. A change in the IS strategy of an organization needs to be reflected in both business strategy and organizational strategy, to ensure goal congruence and alignment throughout the organization [23]. Some IS scholars go as far as to conceptualize the social and the material as inseparable, or sociomaterial [20, 26]. Thus, digital innovation is found to be more disruptive to an organizations working culture or identity as traditional, incremental innovations.

3   Model Development

This chapter is used to develop and present our conceptual model on innovation and the identity process. In the following, we will first present the dimensions of our model (identities over time & growth) and then introduce and discuss the two figures that together constitute our model (see Figs. 1 and 2).

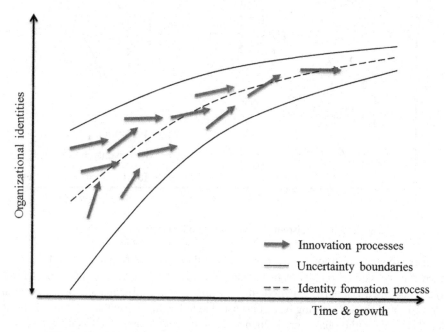

Fig. 1. Traditional (incremental) innovation and the formation of identity

3.1   Identity Inception, Uncertainty and Formation over Time and Growth

While research on identity processes, formation and (re-)construction related to mature organizations has provided a great amount of insights [7, 25], research on the inception of identity in newly formed organizations (such as startups) has only recently gained the attention of academics [6]. [14] were among the first to follow the creation of a new entity (a college within a university) to reveal and understand the dynamics in the inception process of a new identity. [18] investigate Dutch microbreweries to introduce a new theoretical model of how different sources can act as antecedents to organizational identity and then become imprinted into the identity of nascent organizations. They state that research on identity inception is still in an early stage, and no uniform theory has yet been established to guide future investigations [18].

However, what unites most models and theories focusing on the early identity creation process is the notion that identity becomes more stable over time, theorized for example as a form of continuous and repeated imprinting of external and internal expectations [24]. Nascent organizations, such as startups or newly founded divisions

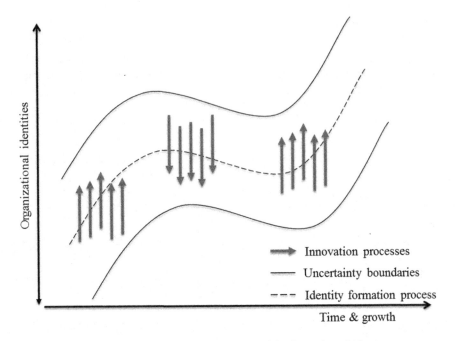

Fig. 2. Digital (disruptive) innovation and the formation of identity

of an existing organization are not certain about their organizational identity. [14] identified four sequential phases of the organizational identity inception process, namely (i) articulating a vison, (ii) experiencing a meanings void, (iii) engaging in experiential contrasts, and (iv) converging on a consensual identity. In addition, the authors theorize that those sequential phases are influenced by recurring themes such as the attainment of distinctiveness or the negotiation of identity claims that shape the process of identity formation [14].

Our model does not focus on the micro-level mechanisms that constitute identity creation but conceptualizes the identity process as a background process to an organization's lifecycle. Thus, while being aware of the complex and non-linear internal formation processes of organization, we simplify the external view on the identity process from an abstract perspective as a linear process. Within our model (see Fig. 1) we include so called "uncertainty boundaries" to demonstrate the convergence of a shared organizational identity over time, thus reducing the uncertainty of the identity.

3.2 Traditional Innovation and Identity

From the perspective of the resource-based view (RBV) of the firm and its extensions, it has been shown that organizational identity can serve as a pivotal organizational resource [10, 29]. Product and process innovation contributes to renewal processes in firms, as it demands firms to acquire new or reconfigure existing competences and capabilities [9]. [9] builds upon [13] 's definition and describes organizational renewal as "the building and expansion of organizational competences over time, often involving a change in the organization's product domain". Similarly to [9], who states that product innovation is not only influenced by an organizations resources and competences but that this relationship also exists vice-versa, we argue that the relationship between firm identity and firm innovative behavior is reciprocal and interdependent. Thus, a change in a firm's innovative behavior is likely to have a direct or indirect effect on its organizational identity. In our model (Fig. 1), the traditional (incremental) innovation processes are shown as arrows. Our model shows that these innovation patterns are indifferent or supportive to the formation of an organizational identity, as they can act as one of many potential sources to the iterative process of identity creation, yet they do not challenge or disrupt already imprinted identity beliefs.

3.3 Digital Innovation and Identity

The quest for sustainable competitive advantage has long been the driving force of both academics and practitioners when investigating firms in the market. The ubiquitous availability of information technology and the widespread digitalization of our society has led to an increase in market balancing speed and created a hyper reactive, highly competitive business environment. Some scholars argue, though not undisputed [21], that sustained competitive advantage may no longer achievable in more and more markets and should therefore not be driving organizational strategies, but organizations should rather strive to be agile to compete better in such times of hypercompetition [8, 22, 30]. The technological advancement of society has thus not only led to an increase in innovation opportunities but at the same requires firms to continuously engage in such radical, disruptive changes in order to survive on the market.

Organizational strategists have long known and underlined the importance of continuous innovation for the success and competitiveness of firms [11, 19]. However, the way organizations innovate has to be adopted to fit these turbulent environments, requiring a shift from traditional, incremental innovation patterns to more radical approaches [9]. Research on digital innovations has demonstrated the possibilities of disruptive innovations, building on newly developed technologies or new business cases for existing technologies [32]. Thus, companies engage in recurring patterns of radical, technology-driven innovation [31].

The role of technological innovation, and how it affects the process of identity formation internal and external to the organization has been investigated in multiple contexts [2, 28]. [2] focuses on the role of enterprise systems implementation on identities and shows that the change in power and roles triggered by the implementation of an ERP system challenges professional identities. [28] proposes the label of identity-challenging technologies to describe technologies that "deviate from the expectations associated with an organization's identity". He finds that such technologies are hard to capitalize on, since organizations cannot fully recognize and realize the benefits of technology when blurred by the filter of a challenged identity and because of the difficulty of changing organizational routines that are embedded in or defining for the challenged identity [28].

To account for these dynamics between radical innovation patterns and their influence to organizational identity formation, our model depicts the change in the identity process as triggered by recurring disruptive innovation patterns over time (see Fig. 2). Unlike in situations of traditional (incremental) innovation processes, digital (radical) innovation processes are not indifferent or supportive but disruptive and challenging to the process of identity convergence. Researchers argue that "even seemingly minor shifts from a technological standpoint may challenge the existing organizational identity if, by pursuing the new technology, the organization violates the core features associated with its existing identity" [28]. Moreover, we posit that such recurring disruptions to identity formation hinder the (i) the convergence towards a shared identity and thus (ii) keep the organization from reducing the uncertainty about its identity, as depicted in Fig. 2.

4   Implications, Limitations and Further Research

In this article we synthesize two research streams within the IS and organization science literature that have recently gained much attention and are likely to be of great interest for scholars in the future, namely organizational identity from a process perspective and the effects of shifting innovation patterns in organizations due to the digitization of society. We propose a conceptual model that demonstrates the disruptive tensions of digital innovations to the process of identity formation in an organization. Our model shows that digital innovation increases the difficulty of companies to convergence towards an organizational identity.

From a process management perspective, unclear organizational identities can lead to issues related to the identification of core and supporting processes. Moreover, digital innovation could force firms to shift IS/IT-processes from the periphery towards the core of a company's value chain.

Research has found that agile organizations are better prepared to react to changing market demands, especially in hypercompetitive markets, and are therefore more likely to survive and succeed in such markets. Management of digital innovations on process-, product- and business model level is supportive to the agility of an organizations [26]. It has yet to be investigated what role a strong versus weak, broad versus narrow organizational identity plays, in relation to agility. While a broad identity might support the need for flexibility required by some innovations, it can be hypothesized that a lack of a clear identity may lead to a rather unguided trial and error pattern in product and service offerings.

The paper is limited in several ways. First, we build on the rapidly growing literature base of two adjacent fields that have not yet converged towards mature theories. Thus, future research might invalidate the current knowledge base and our model. Second, and related to the first point, we lack empirical evidence to test and validate our model and the underlying principles.

We conclude therefore with a call for more empirical research into the relationships between identity and digital innovation, particularly from a process research perspective, to allow for insights into the interplay of the different forces that shape growing organizations.

References

1. Albert, S., Whetten, D.A.: Organizational identity. Res. Organ. Behav. **7**, 263–295 (1985)
2. Alvarez, R.: Examining technology, structure and identity during an Enterprise System implementation. Inf. Syst. J. **18**(2), 203–224 (2008)
3. Amit, R., Zott, C.: Creating value through business model innovation. MIT Sloan Manag. Rev. **53**(3), 41–49 (2012)
4. Anteby, M., Molnár, V.: Collective memory meets organizational identity: remembering to forget in a firm's rhetorical history. Acad. Manag. J. **55**(3), 515–540 (2012)
5. Cheney, G.: On the various and changing meanings of organizational membership: a field study of organizational identification. Commun. Monogr. **50**(4), 342–362 (1983)
6. Clegg, S.R., et al.: Desperately seeking legitimacy: organizational identity and emerging industries. Organ. Stud. **28**(4), 495–513 (2007)
7. Corley, K.G., Gioia, D.A.: Identity ambiguity and change in the wake of a corporate spin-off. Adm. Sci. Q. **49**(2), 173–208 (2004)
8. D'Aveni, R.A.: Waking up to the new era of hypercompetition. Wash. Q. **21**(1), 183–195 (1998)
9. Danneels, E.: The dynamics of product innovation and firm competences. Strateg. Manag. J. **23**(12), 1095–1121 (2002)
10. Eisenhardt, K.M., Santos, F.M.: Knowledge-based view: a new theory of strategy. In: Handbook of Strategy and Management, vol. 1, pp. 139–164 (2002)
11. Englund, R.: Wellsprings of knowledge: building and sustaining the sources of innovation (book). J. Prod. Innov. Manag. **13**(3), 270–272 (1996)
12. Fichman, R.G., et al.: Digital innovation as a fundamental and powerful concept in the information systems curriculum. MIS Q. **38**(2), 329–343 (2014). A15
13. Floyd, S.W., Lane, P.J.: Strategizing throughout the organization: managing role conflict in strategic renewal. Acad. Manag. Rev. **25**(1), 154–177 (2000)
14. Gioia, D.A., et al.: Forging an identity: an insider-outsider study of processes involved in the formation of organizational identity. Adm. Sci. Q. **55**(1), 1–46 (2010)
15. Gioia, D.A., Patvardhan, S.: Identity as process and flow. In: Constructing Identity In and Around Organizations, vol. 2, pp. 50–62 (2012)
16. Henfridsson, O., Lind, M.: Information systems strategizing, organizational sub-communities, and the emergence of a sustainability strategy. J. Strateg. Inf. Syst. **23**(1), 11–28 (2014)
17. Kreiner, G., et al.: Elasticity and the dialectic tensions of organizational identity: how can we hold together while we're pulling apart? Acad. Manag. J. **58**, 981–1011 (2014)
18. Kroezen, J.J., Pursey, H.P.M.A.R.: Organizational identity formation: processes of identity imprinting and enactment in the Dutch microbrewing landscape. In: Constructing Identity In and Around Organizations, pp. 89–127 (2012)
19. Lengnick-Hall, C.A.: Innovation and competitive advantage: what we know and what we need to learn. J. Manag. **18**(2), 399–429 (1992)
20. Leonardi, P.: Materiality, sociomateriality, and socio-technical systems: what do these terms mean? How are they different? Do we need them? In: Leonardi, P.M., et al. (eds.) Materiality and Organizing: Social Interaction in a Technological World, pp. 25–48. Oxford University Press, Oxford (2012)
21. McNamara, G., et al.: Same as it ever was: the search for evidence of increasing hypercompetition. Strateg. Manag. J. **24**(3), 261–278 (2003)
22. O'Shannassy, T.: Sustainable competitive advantage or temporary competitive advantage: improving understanding of an important strategy construct. J. Strateg. Manag. **1**(2), 168–180 (2008)

23. Pearlson, K.E., Saunders, C.S.: Managing and Using Information Systems: A Strategic Approach, 4th edn. Wiley, New York (2009)
24. Pratt, M.: Rethinking identity construction processes in organizations: three questions to consider. In: Constructing Identity In and Around Organizations, pp. 21–49 (2012)
25. Ravasi, D., Schultz, M.: Responding to organizational identity threats: exploring the role of organizational culture. Acad. Manag. J. **49**(3), 433–458 (2006)
26. Svahn, F. et al.: A threesome dance of agency: mangling the sociomateriality of technological regimes in digital innovation. In: International Conference on Information Systems, pp. 1–18 (2009)
27. Swanson, E.B.: Information systems innovation among organizations. Manag. Sci. **40**(9), 1069–1092 (1994)
28. Tripsas, M.: Technology, identity, and inertia through the lens of "The Digital Photography Company". Organ. Sci. **20**(2), 441–460 (2009)
29. Whetten, D.A., Mackey, A.: A social actor conception of organizational identity and its implications for the study of organizational reputation. Bus. Soc. **41**(4), 393–414 (2002)
30. Wiggins, R.R., Ruefli, T.W.: Schumpeter's ghost: is hypercompetition making the best of times shorter? Strateg. Manag. J. **26**(10), 887–911 (2005)
31. Yoo, Y., et al.: Organizing for innovation in the digitized world. Organ. Sci. **23**(5), 1398–1408 (2012)
32. Yoo, Y., et al.: The new organizing logic of digital innovation: an agenda for information systems research. Inf. Syst. Res. **21**(4), 724–735 (2010)

Leadership and Innovation Growth: A Strategic Planning and Organizational Culture Perspective

Dimitrios Rigas[✉] and Yehia Sabri Nawar

University of West London, London W5 5RF, UK
{Dimitrios.Rigas,Yehia.Nawar}@uwl.ac.uk

Abstract. It is imperative to better understand the influence of strategic planning and organisational culture on the leadership-performance relationship within SMEs in emerging and established economies. This research contributes to a better understanding of the direct and indirect relationship that exists between leadership styles and SMEs performance within developing countries. Furthermore, this research provides managers and SME operators, within the Egyptian context, a more detailed level of understanding of the mediator influence of strategic planning. In addition, the moderating impact of organisational culture on enhancing and increasing SMEs performance is also examined. The paper investigates the role of leadership styles in SME's overall performance by examining the relationship between strategic planning, organisational structure and leadership styles. How leadership styles affect SME's Performance through the moderating effect of organisational culture and the mediating influence of strategic planning? Moreover, the paper examines the direct and indirect relationship between leadership styles, organisational culture, strategic planning and SME's performance in one integrated model in the context of an emerging economy. A cross-sectional design was chosen to critically evaluate different Egyptian SMEs. An opportunistic manufacturing SME sample (n = 50) was used. The results indicated significant positive relationships amongst the variables as demonstrated statistically using correlation sand multiple regressions. For example, positive correlations were observed between leadership, organisational culture, strategic planning and performance. Regression tests demonstrated that transformational and transactional leadership styles have a positive influence on organisational performance.

Keywords: Leadership styles · Strategic planning · Organisational culture · Organisational performance · SMEs · Emerging economy · MENA region · Egypt

1 Introduction

Recently, leadership styles, strategic planning, organisational culture and performance concepts have been a subject of growing interest for both academics and professionals [1]. Several studies attempted to investigate the associations between leadership, organisational culture types, strategic planning formulation and implementation and

© Her Majesty the Queen in Right of the United Kingdom 2016
F.F.-H. Nah and C.-H. Tan (Eds.): HCIBGO 2016, Part I, LNCS 9751, pp. 565–575, 2016.
DOI: 10.1007/978-3-319-39396-4_52

organisational performance in both developed and developing countries at different situations from different perspectives during the 20th century in the field of organisational studies and social science [4].

Consequently, many researchers as well as professionals considered those concepts together as the key success factor for many organisations in both developed and developing countries [6]. Moreover, leadership, organisational culture and strategic planning enable the improvement of SMEs performance and growth [4, 22].

Despite the growing number of studies between those constructs, there has been limited empirical work done on the relationship of these factors in one fully integrated model [9]. There is a lack of empirical work on the indirect relationship amongst these variables. For instance, there is limited work on the mediating or moderating impact of different factors on leadership-performance relationship within SME's context [7, 11]. Moreover, there are very few studies that investigate potential mediators that have an impact on leadership-performance within developing countries and especially in the Middle East and North Africa (MENA) region. Therefore, this study aims to understand this relationship further within this context by taking into consideration the mediating influence of strategic planning and the moderating impact of organisational culture on Egyptian SME's.

2   Performance, Leadership and Strategic Planning

2.1   SMEs Performance

There is a significant impact of small and medium enterprises (SMEs) economic growth rate for both developed and developing economies [6]. SMEs help to sustainably develop [5, 15] technologically advance innovative solutions to both private and public sectors [1]. They can also provide opportunities for investment and entrepreneurship [26]. Currently, there is a renewed interest to further understand leadership, organisational culture and strategic planning [3] given the need for sustainability and growth [11].

Leadership has a direct influence on group process and outcomes (Bass 1990) and affects growth and development [25, 27]. It has been extensively researched under many different approaches and methods [20]. According to Stogdill [21] organisational performance is defined as a *"set of financial and non-financial indicators, which offer information on the degree of achievement of objectives and results"*. Van den Berg and Wilderson [23] model firm performance on the basis of the Balance Scorecard, differentiated between *financial* and *non-financial* measurement of performance (Table 1).

2.2   Leadership Styles

Leadership styles have been a subject of growing interest for both academics and professionals in the fields of Management, organisational behaviour as well as organisational studies [11]. The leadership concept has been the focus of studies for the past twenty years and gradually became a topic of intense interest. This interest stems

Table 1. Financial and non-financial components of Balance Scorecard [23]

Financial indicators	Non-financial indicators
(a) Return on Assets (ROA)	(a) Financial perspective
(b) Working capital	(b) Customer orientation perspective
(c) Return on Investment (ROI)	(c) Organisational effectiveness
(d) Return on Equity (ROE)	(d) Learning and growth perspective

out from the fact that leaders provide guidelines and they have to motivate their followers to accomplish tasks [2]. According to Robbins and Judge's study [17], leadership has been defined as a process of interaction between one or more members of a group working towards the same interest. In this context, a leader is considered as being the main driving force for any collaborative teamwork. Stogdill [21] justified the significant role of a leader in restructuring problems, establishes priorities and initiates developmental operations. Furthermore, a leader is seen as a person with popular traits of personality, character and charisma [10].

The Full-range leadership model was proposed by Tosi et al. [22]. It has been continuously tested by various researchers and remains the most widely accepted and researched. The Full range leadership theory was the catalyst that moved the leadership field forward from the trait approaches of the 1930s, the behavioural approaches of the 1950s and 1960s, and the contingency theories of the 1960s and 1970s. The Full-range leadership model is arguably the most validated leadership model in use today [18]. It consists of three distinct leadership styles; *transformational*, *transactional* and *laissez-faire* leadership. These three styles are represented by nine distinct factors of leadership using the survey instrument called *Multifactor Leadership Questionnaire*. Until now, the full range theory of leadership comprises of five transformational leadership factors, three transactional and one non-transactional laissez-faire. Albloshi and Nawar [2] concluded that despite some of the shortcomings in the theoretical background and measurement, the Multifactor Leadership Questionnaire form 5X, which is used in this study, is a valid and reliable instrument that can adequately measure the nine components including the Full-range theory of leadership.

2.3   Organisational Culture

Organisational culture has attracted significant research attention from the last decade of the 20th century [20]. Researchers have attempted to provide a universal acceptable definition of organisational culture. However, there is no single definition of organisational culture [20]. Robbins and Judge [17] provided a comprehension definition that could be applied to almost all types of organisations:

"For any given group or organisation that has a substantial history, organisational culture is

(a)   *A pattern of basic assumptions,*
(b)   *Invented, discovered, or developed by a given group,*

(c) *As it learns to cope with its problems of external adaptation and internal integration.*

(d) *That has worked well enough to be considered valid and, therefore,*

(e) *Is to be taught to new members as the*

(f) *Correct way to perceive, think, and feel in relation to those problems"* [17].

The competing values framework for organisational analysis was developed by Antonakis and House [3], Moorman [14], and Bass [7]. The focus has been on organisational effectiveness. It is based on two dimensions that emphasise the competing values of (a) *focus* (external versus internal) and (b) *structure* (control versus flexibility). These two dimensions are the basis of a matrix of four quadrants with each of which representing a different type of culture. These are (1) *clan*, (2) *adhocracy*, (3) *hierarchy*, and (4) *market* [7].

2.4 Strategic Planning

Strategic planning roots back to the mid of the 20th century between 1950s and 1960s. Initially, it was, strategic management that gained its reputation primarily within military contexts. Progressively, the term was widely introduced in business activities and governmental agencies. According to Robbins and Judge's [17], strategic management is considered to be a management tool. It includes different components that enable organisations to establish their goals and objectives. Currently, strategic planning is considered as an effective tool to produce and evaluate organisational strategy [19]. Nawar and Dagam [15] defined strategic planning as an organisational process in which decisions are made by different departments concerning specific goals and activities. Robson [27] defined strategic planning as *"the process of developing and maintaining consistency between the organization's objectives and resources and its changing opportunities"* [27].

3 Conceptual Model and Hypothesis Development

3.1 Leadership and SMEs Performance

Leaders are considered as the major catalyst factor for the success, improvement performance and growth of an organisation for both developed and developing countries. The significant impact of leadership styles on an organisation's performance is well document in the literature. This relationship is well documented with a strong association between the two concepts [26]. Most research findings argue that the leadership style has a significant impact on the performance output. Leaders can significantly increase the motivation of employees in order to achieve the desirable and required objectives as well as boosting and sustaining firm performance [26]. The impact of leadership on SME's is well documented in the literature review. Robbins and Judge [17] studied the effect of leadership styles on the business performance of SMEs within a Malaysian context. They concluded that there is a significant positive association between both transactional transformational leadership style and business performance within small to medium enterprise SME's. Furthermore, they suggest that there is a negative association between passive avoidant leadership style and firm performance. In Fact, this paper aims to re-examine the relationship between leadership styles and SMEs performance with focusing on moderating and mediating impact of organisational culture and strategic planning. More specifically, the paper investigates the direct and indirect relationship between different research constructs.

3.2   Strategic Planning as *Mediator* on Leadership and Performance

Several studies have addressed the relationship between the leadership styles and strategic planning, the impact of leadership styles on organisational performance, and the influence of strategic planning on a firm's performance. However, most of those studies are limited to assessing associations between those variables in large enterprises. They focus on investigating the direct relationship between leadership styles, strategic planning on SME's performance considering each concept separately [16]. They have also been carried out in the developed western context. Limited research has focused on investigating the relationship between leadership styles and strategic planning in relation to SME's performance within developing or emerging economies. Also, there is a limited research to the indirect relationship between these variables. A gap in the existing literature can be identified on whether organisational culture mediates the relationship between leadership styles and organisational effectiveness. The paper describes some results that aim to understand better this gap.

3.3   Organisational Culture as *Moderator* on Leadership and Performance

Few empirical studies investigated the moderation impact of organisational culture on the relationship between leadership and performance. Albloshi and Nawar [2] examined the moderating effect of organisational culture type on the relationship between leadership and knowledge management process in the context of small-to-medium sized enterprises operating in Austria. They found that the effectiveness of leadership behaviour depends upon the type of organisational culture. They also suggest that leaders should use this mechanism effectively in order to establish the forms of thinking and the levels of motivation and behaviours that are important for the organisation (Fig. 1).

4   Hypotheses and Methodology

4.1   Proposed Hypothesis

Based on the existing literature review, this paper proposes the following research hypotheses:

H1:   There is a significant relationship between leadership styles and SMEs performance.

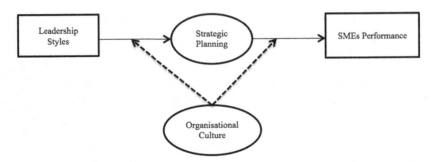

Fig. 1. Conceptual framework of the mediation impact of strategic planning and the moderation effect of organisational culture on leadership performance within Egyptian SMEs.

H2: The relationship between leadership style and organisational performance is moderated by organisational culture.

H3: Strategic planning mediates the effect of leadership styles on organisational performance.

In order to achieve the main objectives of this study and to evaluate the research propositions, a positivistic research philosophy was followed by a deductive research design. A quantitative research method was applied in which the data collection was implemented using a self-administrated questionnaire. The questionnaires were distributed as "hard copies" to target participants. This approach was considered to be the most appropriate way to collect the data within the Egyptian context for several reasons. Firstly, official reports and data on the SME's are limited due to poor reporting practices in the manufacturing sector in Egypt. Secondly, telephone interviews and postal surveys are not widely used in Egypt due to its high cost and low response rate. Lastly, as this is a national study, it is vital that a wide geographical spread of respondents is obtained. A convenient sample technique was used in order to collect data from 50 SMEs operating in Egypt. In fact, 50 out of 75 organisations agreed to participate in this study. The data collected was analysed using the Statistical Package for Social Sciences Version 22 (SPSS 22).

4.2   Research Instruments

The Multifactor Leadership Questionnaire (MLQ form 5X) developed by Bass et al. [6] was used to measure the full range leadership styles (independent variables) from Iranian private organisations. The full range leadership styles developed by Bass and Avolio were derived from Burns study [5] on the transformational and transactional leadership. The transformational leadership style was measured based on 5 different dimensions. These were (a) idealised attributes, (b) idealised behaviours, (c) inspirational motivation, (d) intellectual stimulation, and (e) individual consideration. Consequently, transactional leadership style was measured using two dimensions: (a) contingent reward and (b) management by expectation active. In addition, passive/avoidant leadership style was measured using two dimensions: (a) management by expectation passive and (b) Laissez-Faire. A 5-point Likert scale ranging from *not at all* to *frequently, if not always* (5) was used to assess leadership styles in this specific study.

On the other hand, the moderator variable organisational culture in this study was measured using the *Competing Values Framework* (CVF). It is widely accepted as the most appropriate measurement instrument for this measurement [21]. The CVF was developed by Bass and Nawar and Dagam [7, 15] and consists of four main types. These are (a) clan culture, (b) adhocracy culture, (c) market culture, and (d) hierarchy culture. Again, the 5-point Likert scale was used to assess this parameter.

The third section of the questionnaire measures the strategic planning (as a mediator variable) using a multidimensional approach adapted for this study. The characteristic of the strategic planning measurement scale was taken from a valid test in the literature introduced by Yukl and Van Fleet [26]. The SME's performance (as a dependent variable) was measured using the concept of a Balanced Score Card developed by Robbins and Judge [17, 24]. The final section of the questionnaire gathered demographic data of the sample.

4.3   Procedure

Four different stages of data analysis were followed with the aid of SPSS (version 22 [5, 15]). The first stage checked the reliability analysis of all variables under investigation through the Cronbach Alpha method. The second stage analysed the demographic part of the questionnaire of the sample using descriptive statistics. The third stage evaluated the direct relationship between the independent variables (leadership styles), dependent variable (SMEs performance), the mediator variable (strategic planning) and moderator variable (organisational culture) using correlation coefficients and regression analysis. This determined the degree of associations between pairs of variables. Finally, the last stage evaluated the indirect relationship between research variables and gathered an overall viewpoint of the role organisational culture as moderator and strategic planning as mediator of the relationship between leadership styles and organisational performance within Egyptian SMEs. A multiple regression analysis was used in order to test the proposed hypothesis.

5   Results and Discussions

Figure 2 shows the demographic analysis of the sample. 80 % of the respondents were aged between 25 and 34 with a gender distribution of 40 % males and 60 % females. 50 % of the sample was educated at a postgraduate level. Approximately 50 % of the sample had prior working experience ranging between 6 and 10 years and 45 % of the sample was operating in the construction sector.

Table 2 shows the results from Cronbach alpha that measured the internal consistency of the variables corroborated other findings in the literature relating to the acceptable level of reliability analysis [8, 12].

Egypt

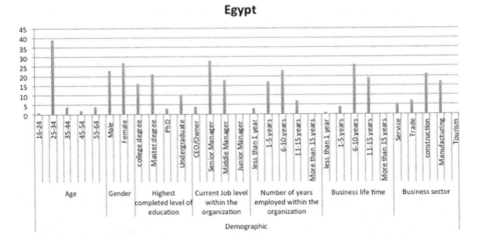

Fig. 2. Demographic profile of the Egyptian sample

Table 2. Indicates that all variables investigated were reliable

Variable/Factor	Reliability Analysis	Mean	SD
Leadership Style	0.780	3.75	0.549
Transformational	0.483	3.66	0.673
Transactional	0.594	3.56	0.254
Passive/Avoidance	0.644	3.23	0.66
Organisational Culture	0.677	2.88	0.82
Strategic Planning	0.786	3.66	0.657
Organisational Performance	0.662	3.21	0.67

Table 3 is divided into two parts, the first part shows the direct relationship between the variables, and the second part shows the indirect. For the direct relationship between the variables, there are five positive and one negative relationships:

(a) A positive between leadership styles and organisational performance.
(b) A negative between strategic planning and organisational performance.
(c) A positive between organisational culture and performance.
(d) A positive between leadership styles and organisational culture.
(e) A positive between leadership and strategic planning.
(f) A positive between strategic planning and organisational culture.

These findings are in support of this study's hypotheses. As for the indirect relationship, three outcome relationship results were found. There is a positive indirect

Table 3. Testing research hypotheses using correlations and regression.

Relationships	R^2	F	T	β	Supported
Direct relationships					
LS and OP	.322	99.918**	9.996**	.471**	Supported
LS and OC	.240	57.146**	7.560**	.374**	Supported
LS and SP	.279	95.627**	10.754**	.523**	Supported
OC and OP	.303	152.289**	12.341**	.510	Supported
SP and OC	.267	80.455**	9.251**	.707**	Supported
SP and OP	.166	55.394**	7.241**	.442**	Supported
Indirect relationship					
LS to OC to OP	.382	108.060**	9.522**	.961**	Supported
LS to OP to OE	.326	84.828**	9.756**	.483**	Supported

** High significant level, showing the strength of the relationships.

relationship between transactional leadership and organisational performance. Therefore, organisational culture moderates the relationship between leadership and organisational performance. There is also a positive indirect relationship between leadership and organisational performance. This relationship is mediating by the existence of strategic planning.

6 Conclusion and Future Work

The results suggest that organisational culture is considered as a moderator on the relationship between different leadership style and organisational performance. Strategic planning is considered as mediator on the relationship between leadership-performance relationships within Egyptian's SMEs. These findings are significant as they provide an overall viewpoint of the existence of direct and indirect relationships between the parameters of leadership and organisational performance in emerging economies. This study is a part of wider study that aims not only to identify these relationships in emerging economies but also to compare those results with developed economies. The identification of similarities and difference between the two contexts is important to help us understand the way in which framework conceptual models can be adapted for particular geographical locations and contexts.

References

1. Abd-El-Salam, E.M., Shawky, A.Y., El-Nahas, T., Nawar, Y.S.: The relationship among job satisfaction, motivation, leadership, communication, and psychological empowerment: an egyptian case study. SAM Adv. Manage. J. **78**(2), 33–50, Spring 2013
2. Albloshi, F.A., Nawar, Y.S.: Assessing the impact of leadership styles on organisational performance: the case of Saudi Private SME's. J. Organ. Stud. Innov. **2**(2), 66–77 (2015)

3. Antonakis, J., House, R.: Instrumental leadership: measurement and extension of transformational–transactional leadership theory. Leadersh. Q. **25**(4), 746–771 (2014)
4. Arham, A.: Leadership and performance: the case of Malaysian SMEs in the services sector. Int. J. Asian Soc. Sci. **4**(3), 343–355 (2014)
5. Avolio, B.J., Bass, B.M.: Multifactor Leadership Questionnaire: Manual and Sampler Set, 3rd edn. Mindgarden, Redwood City (2004)
6. Bass, B.M., Avolio, B.J., Jung, D.I., Berson, Y.: Predicting unit performance by assessing transformational and transactional leadership. J. Appl. Psychol. **88**(2), 207–218 (2003)
7. Bass, B.M.: From transactional to transformational leadership: learning to share the vision. Organ. Dyn. Winter **18**(3), 19–31 (1990)
8. Bryman, A.: Social Research Methods. Oxford University Press, Oxford (2012)
9. Bryman, A., Bell, E.: Business Research Methods, 3rd edn. Oxford University Press, Cambridge (2012)
10. Kaplan, R.S., Norton, D.P.: The Strategy-focused organization: how balanced scorecard companies thrive in the new business environment. Harvard Business School Press, Boston (2001)
11. Kaplan, R.S., Norton, D.P.: Using the balanced scorecard as a strategic management system. Harv. Bus. Rev. **74**(1), 75–85 (1996)
12. Metwally, A.H., El-bishbishy, N., Nawar, Y.S.: The impact of transformational leadership styles on employee satisfaction. Bus. Manage. Rev. **3**(5), 32–42 (2014)
13. Nawar, Y.S.: Organisational commitment: as a mediator on the relationships between leadership styles and job satisfaction in new emerging economy. Retail Bus. Manage. J. **2**(7), 432–466 (2015)
14. Nawar, Y.S.: Leadership practices in non-western country: a case study of one of the biggest Egyptian's FMCG. Int. J. High. Educ. Manage. **4**(1), 22–38 (2015)
15. Nawar, Y.S., Dagam, O.V.: The practice of ethical work climate within public sector: an organisational culture perspective. J. Organ. Stud. Innov. **2**(4), 34–41 (2016)
16. Nawar,Y.S., Nazarian, A., Hafeez, K.: The influence of strategic Planning and Organizational Culture on Leadership-Perfromance Relationship. The Case of Egypt Private SME'S. British Academy of Management Conference (2015)
17. Robbins, S.P., Judge, T.A.: Organizational Behavior, 15th edn. Pearson Education, Upper Saddle River (2013)
18. Robson, W.: Strategic Management and Information Systems: An Integrated Approach. Prentice Hall, Englewood Cliffs (1994)
19. Smircich, L.: Concepts of culture and organisational analysis. Adm. Sci. Q. **6**(28), 339–359 (1983)
20. Stanislavov, I., Ivanov, S.: The role of leadership for shaping organizational culture and building employee engagement in the Bulgarian gaming industry. Turizam: znanstveno-stručni časopis **62**(1) (2014)
21. Stogdill, R.: Handbook of Leadership, 1st edn. Free Press, New York (1974)
22. Tosi, H.L., Rizzo, J.R., Carroll, S.J.: Managing Organizational Behavior, 3rd edn. Blackwell, Oxford (1994)
23. Van den Berg, P.T., Wilderson, C.P.M.: Defining measuring and comparing organisational cultures. Appl. Psychol. Int. Rev. **53**(4), 570–582 (2004)
24. Yücel, C., Karataş, E., Aydın, Y.: The relationship between the level of principals' leadership roles and organizational culture. Procedia Soc. Behav. Sci. **93**, 415–419 (2013)
25. Yukl, G.: Leadership in Organizations, 8th edn. Pearson Education, Upper Saddle River (2012)

26. Yukl, G., Van Fleet, D.D.: Theory and research on leadership in organizations. In: Dunnette, M.D., Hough, L.M. (eds.) Handbook on Industrial and Organization Psychology, pp. 147–197. Consulting Psychologist, Palo Alto (1992)
27. Zaridis, A., Mousiolis, D.: Entrepreneurship and SME's organizational structure. elements of a successful business. Procedia Soc. Behav. Sci. **148**, 463–467 (2014)

Comparative Study on China-Italy Design Driven Innovation Strategy Furniture Firms

Zhang Zhang, Jianxin Cheng$^{(\boxtimes)}$, Chaoxiang Yang, and Yongyan Guo

East China University of Science and Technology,
Shanghai, People's Republic of China
ziziedelweiss@gmail.com, 13901633292@163.com,
darcy_yang@foxmail.com, 22434310@qq.com

Abstract. Three types of knowledge are essential for design driven innovation mode: user's needs, technological opportunities and product language. Among them, product language plays a crucial role. In this work, eighteen representative Italy design driven innovation furniture firms based on Milan design week field study and twelve Chinese firms according to field study on Shanghai international furniture exhibition in recent two years have been selected as research cases. Workshop has been launched to draw the business model canvas to analyze the product language, product design and socio-cultural context for each case. Subsequently, difference between Chinese and Italian design driven innovation strategy furniture firms was discussed.

Keywords: Design driven · Furniture firm · Innovation strategy · China-Italy

1 Introduction

Italy modern furniture is famous all over the world for its high quality and extraordinary design. The distinctive development pattern also becomes to be the template for small and medium-sized furniture enterprises [1]. Meanwhile the product capacity of Chinese furniture industry grows rapidly over the past forty years [2]. Especially, referring to World Furniture Outlook Seminar in 2015, in the last five years, the product capacity of Chinese furniture industry grows steadily and always occupies the first place in the whole world. After five stages development of fill the blank of the market, improve product quality, expanding product scale, packaging design and regional competition, design driven mode has been introduced in Chinese furniture industry in 2004. The furniture market and product have been further subdivided, which directly results in the emergence of large numbers of designer furniture brands. This phenomenon can also be confirmed in the three domestic furniture exhibitions in recent years. All these facts reveal that design driven mode has formed in Chinese furniture industry currently. However, the gap existed between China and Italy furniture industry has to be faced. In order to shrink this gap, comparative study on China-Italy design driven innovation strategy furniture firms have been carried out in this work. The purpose of this paper is to explore the development law of China and Italy furniture firms, respectively, and further to provide comprehension of the culture pattern for each firm to adapt.

© Springer International Publishing Switzerland 2016
F.F.-H. Nah and C.-H. Tan (Eds.): HCIBGO 2016, Part I, LNCS 9751, pp. 576–583, 2016.
DOI: 10.1007/978-3-319-39396-4_53

2 Design Driven Innovation Strategy

The introduction of design driven innovation strategy into the traditional business industries is at an early stage. Most of the investigations and applications of business strategy have focused on technology push innovation strategy and market-pull innovation strategy. The two strategies are proposed by the Italian professor Giovanni Dosi in 1982 [3]. The principle of technology driven innovation strategy is to increase high technology continuously for the firm, therefore it can possess competitive advantages. The market-pull innovation strategy is a classical one which has bearing on product communication. In 2003, based on the study of Italian firms, professor R Verganti brought forward the third innovation approach: design driven innovation strategy, where the innovative driving source of this strategy is design [4]. It is profitable for traditional industries, but it also serves on a deeper purpose in enhancing the lives of individuals. As a scheme, it expands and elaborates on the concept of form, in order to better capture the communicative and semantic dimension of a product. At its best, the design movement seeks to bring radical innovations to product language that has to adapt to new circumstances of economic competition, patent user requirements, social expectation and deeper cultural understanding [5]. For this reason, this strategy can lead to competitive advantage for manufacturers and currently more and more traditional furniture firms in China as in any other country adopted this strategy to upgrading.

Design driven innovation strategy is based on the idea that each product has a particular language and meaning. As shown in Fig. 1, this strategy includes three types of knowledge of user's needs, technological opportunities and product language. Among them, the objective of product language as developed in the 1980s at HfG Offenbach is to enable a special crossover of theory and practice in design [6]. Therefore, it plays a crucial role in the three types of knowledge [3]. Differ from the traditional methodologies in product development process, a reverse procedure was adopted in design driven innovation strategy. That is, customer's needs are collected to extract the product language in the former approach. To the latter one, product

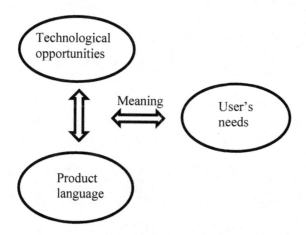

Fig. 1. Design driven innovation strategy

language is obtained based on the research on socio-cultural context. Further, the chosen product language is used to create specific information and symbols to guide customer's needs.

As most designers know, proposing new product language (a set of signs, symbols, and icons) implies an understanding of the inner dynamics of socio-cultural context. It goes beyond what is currently visible and must be researched and developed through a continuous process. To support this perspective, let's consider the example of the Italy lamps industry. In the 1950s, the concept of "light design" (buying light instead of lamps) was proposed. As an innovation of meaning, the designers underline this innovation through the choice of product language. However, this concept is too obscure to be found in books or in sociological scenarios of the future. Under this circumstance, the corresponding socio-cultural context related to this concept was investigated to form the specific product language, and the product with new characteristics was then designed. Many similar success cases can be found in present Italy furniture firms [6].

3   Research Procedure

Figure 2 shows the research flow of design driven innovation strategy. A firm wants to deploy an innovation strategy based on design driven innovation needs to access knowledge of socio-cultural context to extract product language (convergence process). It may have several channels within which it may access this tacit and distributed knowledge, developing interactions with users, suppliers, other firms, training institutes, and so on. Subsequently, following the extracted product language, product design can then be performed (divergence process).

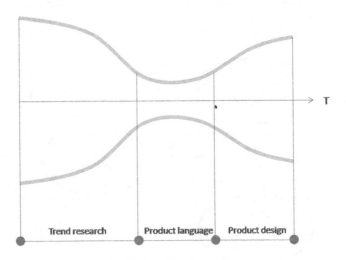

Fig. 2. Design driven research flow

Table 1 lists research procedure, content and method applied in this paper. Case study was firstly performed to analyze product language, product design and socio-cultural context. Subsequently, difference between Chinese and Italian design driven innovation strategy furniture firms was discussed.

Table 1. Research procedure, content and method

Procedure	Contents	Method
Case study	Product language	Value proposition
	Product design	Testing board
	Socio-cultural context	Deduction
Comparative study	Comparative study on design innovation strategy	Inductive discussion

4   Case Study

As the premise and foundation of comparative study, case study was performed in this paper. Representative design driven innovation furniture firms in both countries were selected as cases firstly. Workshop was then launched to draw the business model canvas for each case. Modules of value proposition and testing board in obtained business model canvas were used to analyze product language, product design. Socio-cultural context was deduced based on the results obtained above.

4.1   Case Selection

A total of 30 representative Italy-China design driven innovation furniture firms were selected as case in this paper. Among them, eighteen Italian furniture firms were selected based on Milan design week field study. Twelve Chinese firms were chosen according to field study on Shanghai international furniture exhibition in recent two years. All cases are listed in Table 2.

Table 2. Research cases

Italian cases (18)				Chinese cases (12)		
Alessi	B&B Italia	Edra	LAGO	Madebamboo	Ziinlife	Pingze
Alias	Calligaris	Fendi casa	Moroso	Sozen	Banmoo	Wanwu
Arflex	Cappellini	FLEXFORM	Poliform	Moreless	Morning	
Arper	Dedon	Flou		Smartwood	Shanliang	
Baxter	Driade	KARTELL		Fnji	U+	

4.2   Product Language and Product Design

4.2.1   Business Model Canvas

The business model canvas [7], which was proposed by Alexander Osterwalderis a strategic management and entrepreneurial tool, and composes of nine modules.

It allows you to describe, design, challenge, invent, and pivot your business model. In this paper, workshop has been launched to draw the business model canvases for each case. Fifty seven senior students from East China University of Science and Technology were participated in this workshop. Among them, 30 students are major in industrial design, and the others are major in product design. During this workshop, contents and function of the nine modules have been illustrated to all the participators, and then blank business model canvas downloaded and printed from the official website of strategyzer. All the participators are required to finish the allocated work including information collection, canvas posting and keywords extraction in time.

4.2.2 Product Language Analysis

Within the nine modules in business model canvas, value proposition module is closely linked with product language. Then, production language analysis for each case can be realized by acquirement of value proposition module [8]. In this paper, value proposition questionnaire was used to extract value keywords and portray testing board based on business model canvas obtained above. Figures 3 and 4 show the value proposition questionnaire sample and value proposition questionnaire example, respectively.

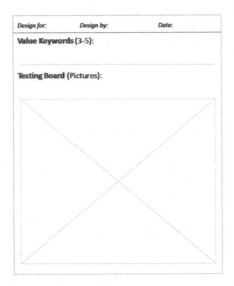

Fig. 3. Sample questionnaire of value proposition

4.3 Socio-cultural Context Research

Italian furniture firms construct their socio-cultural context in a wide range. However, most Chinese firms are mainly focus on classical furniture, architecture and nature domain [9, 10].

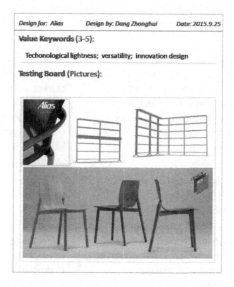

Fig. 4. Example of value proposition questionnaire

5   Comparative Discussion

All the firms selected in this paper can be divided into five categories according to market hierarchies: art, luxury, high-end, middle-end and low-end market. On this basis, comparative discussion on China-Italy furniture firms was performed. The results are listed in Table 3.

Table 3. Comparative discussion on China-Italy furniture firms

	Italy	China
Art market	Sample number: 2;	Sample number: 0;
	High-frequency product language words: Avant-grade, freedom, diversity, collection;	High-frequency product language words: None;
	Product design characteristics: Designers are not design products, they design the process. The routine design procedure has been broken. Every product has uniqueness	Product design characteristics: In the Chinese furniture art market, mainstream products are in Chinese classical style using rare and expensive materials. However, modern design furniture is hard to pile into this market
Luxury market	Sample number: 3;	Sample number: 1;
	High-frequency product language words: Handcrafted, eternity, royal;	High-frequency product language words: Zen style, handcrafted;

(*Continued*)

Table 3. (*Continued*)

	Italy	China
	Product design characteristics: The furniture design quality for luxury market is almost equal to the high-end market products design. But product quality is superior and elaborated, handcraft is close to perfect	Product design characteristics: The furniture design quality for luxury market is higher than the high-end market products. Products are in intensive Zen style. Product quality is superior and elaborated, handcraft is close to perfect
High-end market	Sample number: 11;	Sample number: 10;
	High-frequency product language words: Fun, modular, fashion, changeable fun, multi-function, customization;	High-frequency product language words: Traditional culture;
	Product design characteristics: Many firms are oriented into this market. So the product language is plentiful and concrete	Product design characteristics: Product language of Chinese traditional culture has been used by most firms. Description words for product are too abstract to be understood
Middle-end market	Sample number: 2;	Sample number: 4;
	High-frequency product language words: Modular, lifestyle;	High-frequency product language words: Fun, colorful, solid wood, eco-friendly;
	Product design characteristics: Designers were preferred to use straight lines. Modular design is applied to product system. One component could be used in several products. Those components are also easily for an industrial production. Those Italian brands designed several lifestyles and created different interior atmosphere to match levels of customers' needs	Product design characteristics: The construction of those four firms system is unfinished. For instants, two of them didn't build the network platform. Products are designed for young consumers. Products have the characteristics of fun and miniaturization. Components and parts are difficult to industrial production, so the production efficiency is low and firms scale is small
Low-end market	Sample number: 0;	Sample number: 0;
	High-frequency product language words: None;	High-frequency product language words: None;
	Product design characteristics: None	Product design characteristics: None

6   Conclusion and Prospects

Comparing to the Italy furniture industry, the introduction of design driven innovation strategy into China is at an early stage. Under the background of coexistence of opportunities and challenges, comparative investigation on China-Italy design driven innovation strategy furniture firms is necessary. In this paper, case study was used to analyze the three types of knowledge of design driven innovation strategy. Inductive discussion was subsequently performed. The results show that, differing from Italy furniture firms, the local firms made great efforts to extract design elements from traditional culture, which were then applied to modernized design. The differences between China-Italy design-driven innovation furniture firms can be summed up into the following 4 aspects:

- Italian furniture firms are more concerned about systematic design. Once the product language was determined, the whole product-service-system was then built to follow this product language;
- Italian manufacturer has an obvious advantage in technology and equipment;
- Design driven innovation strategy is not suitable for low-end market firms;
- Serious homogenization phenomenon for selection of production language in high-end market Chinese furniture firms need to be noticed.

Acknowledgments. We thank the financial support by "the Fundamental Research Funds for the Central Universities" (No. 2222014010), the "Chen Guang" Project supported by Shanghai Municipal Education Commission and Shanghai Education Development Foundation (No. 13CG67).

References

1. Florio, M., Peracchi, F., Sckokai, P.: Market organization and propagation of shocks: the furniture industry in Germany and Italy. Small Bus. Econ. **11**(2), 169–182 (1998)
2. Tracogna, A.: China furniture outlook. Centre for Industrial Studies (CSIL) (2013)
3. Dosi, G.: Technological paradigms and technological trajectories: a suggested interpretation of the determinants and directions of technical change. Res. Policy **11**(3), 147–162 (1982)
4. Verganti, R.: Design as brokering of languages: innovation strategies in Italian firms. Des. Manage. J. (Former Ser.) **14**(3), 34–42 (2003)
5. Verganti, R.: Design, meanings, and radical innovation: a metamodel and a research agenda. J. Prod. Innov. Manage **25**(5), 436–456 (2008)
6. Battistella, C., Biotto, G., Toni, A.F.D.: From design driven innovation to meaning strategy. Manage. Decis. **50**(4), 718–743 (2012)
7. Osterwalder, A., Pigneur, Y.: Business Model Generation: A Handbook for Visionaries, Game Changers, and Challengers. Wiley, New York (2013)
8. Osterwalder, A., Pigneur, Y., Bernarda, G., et al.: Value Proposition Design: How to Create Products and Services Customers Want. Wiley, New York (2015)
9. Robb, D.J., Xie, B., Arthanari, T.: Supply chain and operations practice and performance in Chinese furniture manufacturing. Int. J. Prod. Econ. **112**(2), 683–699 (2008)
10. Tong, L.I.: Analysis of original furniture design based on traditional Chinese culture. Packag. Eng. **16**, 003 (2015)

Erratum to: The Multisensory Effects of Atmospheric Cues on Online Shopping Satisfaction

So-Jeong Kim[1] and Dong-Hee Shin[2](✉)

[1] Department of Interaction Science, Sungkyunkwan University, 25-2
Sungkyunkwan-ro, Jungro-gu, Seoul, South Korea
ai.gimso@gmail.com
[2] School of Media and Communication, Chung-Ang University,
Seoul, South Korea
dshin1030@cau.ac.kr

Erratum to:
Chapter 37 in: F.F.-H. Nah and C.-H. Tan (Eds.)
HCI in Business, Government, and Organizations:
eCommerce and Innovation
DOI: 10.1007/978-3-319-39396-4_37

The initially published affiliation of the author Shin, D., was incorrect. The correct affiliation is as follows:
School of Media and Communication, Chung-Ang University.

The updated original online version for this chapter can be found at 10.1007/978-3-319-39396-4_37

© Springer International Publishing Switzerland 2016
F.F.-H. Nah and C.-H. Tan (Eds.): HCIBGO 2016, Part I, LNCS 9751, p. E1, 2016.
DOI: 10.1007/978-3-319-39396-4_54

Author Index

Ahangama, Sapumal I-165
Ahmed Shaikh, Zubair II-259
Al-Lawati, Badar H. I-483
Allwein, Florian I-283
Anderson, John I-519
Aquino Junior, Plinio Thomaz II-140
Archer, Norm II-3
Ariaeinejad, Maryam II-3
Auinger, Andreas I-365
Aviña, Glory Emmanuel II-131

Bajko, Robert II-273
Baker, Michael II-151
Balu, Alan I-26
Barrios, Andres I-377
Bastarache-Roberge, Marie-Christine II-91
Bates, Corrie II-424
Bauer, Stefan I-556
Birska, Sylwia II-403
Boblan, Ivo II-369
Borchers, Jan I-350
Boring, Ronald L. I-519
Boudreaux, David II-209
Brauner, Philipp II-16
Bretschneider, Richard A. II-395
Bretschneider-Hagemes, Michael II-403
Brown, David I-26

Calero Valdez, André I-350, II-16
Camacho, Sonia I-377
Carey, Karen I-491
Chao, William S. II-117
Chen, Guoqing I-341
Chen, Liang-Chu I-294
Cheng, Jianxin I-576
Cheng, Wei-Chung II-28
Chia, Ivy I-531
Chiu, Ming-Hsin II-28
Choi, Ben C.F. I-141, I-177
Chu, Mei-Tai II-302
Chu, Tsai-Hsin I-3
Claybaugh, Craig C. II-39
Compagna, Diego II-369
Cornelio, Chester II-380

Coursaris, Constantinos K. I-16
Courtemanche, François II-91
Cyr, Dianne II-99

Dattatri, Adithya I-26
Deaton, Phillip J. II-47
Détienne, Françoise II-151
Du, Rong I-248

Elias, Fadi II-3
Ellegast, Rolf II-281
Eschenbrenner, Brenda I-502

Fajardo, Angel F. I-386
Fang, Xiaowen I-483
Fang, Yulin I-437
Fels, Deborah I. II-273
Fernandes, Fernando Timoteo II-140
Fickes, Benjamin I-26
Förster, Tim I-306
Friemert, Daniel II-281
Garcia-Mancilla, Jesus I-386

Gauthier, John II-241
Ghandour, Rajab I-82
Gianfortune, Marisa II-380
Goh, Jenson I-531
Gonzalez, Victor M. I-386
Govaere, Virginie II-290
Groff, Jonathan II-151
Gross, Benno II-403
Gu, Qican I-189
Gulden, Jens I-198
Günthner, Willibald A. II-358
Guo, Xunhua I-341
Guo, Yongyan I-576

Hall, Richard H. I-37
Hartmann, Ulrich II-281
Hassan, Raheel II-412
He, Daqing I-61
Helfert, Markus I-491, II-79
Hessey, Sue I-283, I-395

Hodson, Jaigris   I-106
Hoffman, Matthew   II-241
Hsieh, Chia-Jung   I-294
Huang, Hsieh-Hong   I-228
Huang, Zhao   I-46
Huelke, Michael   II-313
Hussain, Hammad Akhtar   I-457

Ismirle, Jennifer   II-159
Izard, John   II-183

Jackson, James E.   II-159
Jiang, Hansi   I-270
Jiang, Qiqi   I-189

Kang, Lele   I-153
Karlinger, Michael   I-330
Kerluku, Endri   II-403
Khosla, Rajiv   II-302
Kim, So-Jeong   I-406
Kindermann, Harald   I-417
King, John   I-319
Kirshner, Samuel N.   I-177
Kittinger, Robert   II-241
Kiu, Yeung Sze   I-531
Kluge, Johanna   II-171
Kong, Jonas   I-210
Koppenborg, Markus   II-313
Ku, Yi-Cheng   I-258
Kuijper, Arjan   I-306
Kuo, Shu-Fang   I-3

Laskowitz, Adam   I-218
Lau, Nathan   I-519
Lawton, Craig   II-241
Lee, Rich C.   I-511, II-110
Lee, Yen-Hsien   I-3
Léger, Pierre-Majorique   II-91
Lew, Roger   I-519
Li, Honglei   I-427
Li, Jun   I-437
Li, Lei   I-61
Li, Xuan   I-153
Li, Zequn   I-427
Liang, Liang   I-437
Lichtschlag, Leonhard   I-350
Lien, Yen-Hsuan   I-294
Lin, Yi-Ling   II-117
Lin, Zhengzheng   I-437

Liu, Chi-Lun   I-228
Liu, Su   I-270
Liu, Yang   I-446
Low, Stephen   I-531
Lundell, Jay   II-424
Lungfiel, Andy   II-313
Lynch, Kevin   I-319

Maguire, Martin   II-56
Manwani, Sharm   I-545
Mapes, Kristen   I-72
Marquardt, Manuela   II-369
Martens, Mirco   II-369
Martinez, Victor R.   I-386
Matsumoto, Masumi   I-238
Mayerhofer, Stefan   II-434
Mayrhauser, Christian   I-330
McAran, Dan   I-545
McCallum, Ryan   II-348
McCreary, Faith   II-67
McKay, Elspeth   II-183
Medaglia, Carlo Maria   II-231
Miao, Yumeng   I-248

Naber, Birgit   II-313
Nah, Fiona Fui-Hoon   II-110, II-412
Naji, Faysal   II-3
Narzt, Wolfgang   II-434
Nawar, Yehia Sabri   I-565
Nguyen, Khanh   II-302
Nickel, Peter   II-313, II-325

O'Bara, Ian   II-159
Obwegeser, Nikolaus   I-556
Opromolla, Antonio   II-231

Patterson, Heather   II-67
Pei, Lei   II-196
Peng, Chih-Hung   I-258
Philipsen, Ralf   II-16
Pomberger, Gustav   II-434
Poo, Danny Chiang Choon   I-165
Potts, Liza   I-72
Pourzolfaghar, Zohreh   II-79

Rapanos, Ted   II-3
Resseguier, Beverly   II-91
Riaz, Nazish   I-94
Rigas, Dimitrios   I-82, I-94, I-457, I-565

Robelski, Swantje II-337
Romanyk, Christopher II-348

Salehi, Pejman II-348
Salomon, Kathryn A. II-209
Schumann, Martin II-434
Schwarz, Liesmarie I-365
Sénécal, Sylvain II-91
Sergueeva, Ksenia II-446
Shao, Ling I-427
Shaw, Norman II-446, II-457
Shih, I-Chiang I-294
Shin, Dong-Hee I-406
Sia, Choon Ling I-258
Siau, Keng II-412
Silic, Mario II-99
Silva, Austin II-110
Sirendi, Regina II-221
Sonderer, Kathy I-319
Speed, Ann II-241
Stabauer, Martin I-330
Stacey, Michael II-3
Sun, Baowen I-270
Swierenga, Sarah J. II-159

Tam, Alexander I-26
Tan, Chuan-Hoo I-468, II-110
Tan, Wee-Kek I-468
Tang, Allen I-26
Tarkus, Astrid II-434
Taveter, Kuldar II-221
Teo, Hock-Hai I-468
Terrenghi, Lucia I-238
Thum, Simon I-306
Tong, Yu I-258
Traynor, Brian I-106
Tseng, Jen-Tsung I-294
Twyman, Nathan W. II-412

ur Rehman, Aqeel II-259

van der Land, Sarah F. I-118
Van Osch, Wietske I-16
Venters, Will I-395

Volpi, Valentina II-231
vom Stein, Antti Matthias II-358

Wachtel, Amanda II-241
Wang, Deliang I-446
Wang, Hongwei I-189
Wang, Jiaqi I-341
Wang, Kanliang II-110
Wang, Qian I-258
Wang, Tianmei I-270
Wang, Yun-Feng II-251
Waseem, Ashraf Ali II-259
Wei, Qiang I-341
Weichselbaum, Otto II-434
Weidemann, Alexandra II-369
Wetzlinger, Werner I-365
Wild, Gian I-129
Wilkes, Gil I-106
Willemsen, Lotte M. I-118
Wilton, Barbara G.E. I-118
Wioland, Liên II-290
Wischniewski, Sascha II-337
Wu, Manli I-153
Wu, Yi I-141, I-177

Xu, Shuang II-380

Yan, Zhijun I-270
Yang, Chaoxiang I-576
Yang, Hangzhou I-270
Yang, Yang I-468
Yang, Yu-Chen II-117
Yazdi, Mohammad Amin I-350
Yu, Jie I-141
Yu, Wang Yang I-46

Zafiroglu, Alexandra II-67
Zhang, Chengzhi I-61
Zhang, Qiping II-196
Zhang, Zhang I-576
Zhao, J. Leon I-153
Ziefle, Martina I-350, II-16, II-171

Printed in the United States
By Bookmasters